INTERNATIONAL ENERGY AGENCY

ENERGY TECHNOLOGY PERSPECTIVES 2008

In support of the G8 Plan of Action

Scenarios & Strategies to 2050

INTERNATIONAL ENERGY AGENCY

The International Energy Agency (IEA) is an autonomous body which was established in November 1974 within the framework of the Organisation for Economic Co-operation and Development (OECD) to implement an international energy programme.

It carries out a comprehensive programme of energy co-operation among twenty-seven of the OECD thirty member countries. The basic aims of the IEA are:

- To maintain and improve systems for coping with oil supply disruptions.
- To promote rational energy policies in a global context through co-operative relations with non-member countries, industry and international organisations.
- To operate a permanent information system on the international oil market.
- To improve the world's energy supply and demand structure by developing alternative energy sources and increasing the efficiency of energy use.
- To promote international collaboration on energy technology.
- To assist in the integration of environmental and energy policies.

The IEA member countries are: Australia, Austria, Belgium, Canada, Czech Republic, Denmark, Finland, France, Germany, Greece, Hungary, Ireland, Italy, Japan, Republic of Korea, Luxembourg, Netherlands, New Zealand, Norway, Portugal, Slovak Republic, Spain, Sweden, Switzerland, Turkey, United Kingdom and United States. Poland is expected to become a member in 2008. The European Commission also participates in the work of the IEA.

ORGANISATION FOR ECONOMIC CO-OPERATION AND DEVELOPMENT

The OECD is a unique forum where the governments of thirty democracies work together to address the economic, social and environmental challenges of globalisation. The OECD is also at the forefront of efforts to understand and to help governments respond to new developments and concerns, such as corporate governance, the information economy and the challenges of an ageing population. The Organisation provides a setting where governments can compare policy experiences, seek answers to common problems, identify good practice and work to co-ordinate domestic and international policies.

The OECD member countries are: Australia, Austria, Belgium, Canada, Czech Republic, Denmark, Finland, France, Germany, Greece, Hungary, Iceland, Ireland, Italy, Japan, Republic of Korea, Luxembourg, Mexico, Netherlands, New Zealand, Norway, Poland, Portugal, Slovak Republic, Spain, Sweden, Switzerland, Turkey, United Kingdom and United States.
The European Commission takes part in the work of the OECD.

International Energy Agency (IEA),
Head of Communication and Information Office,
9 rue de la Fédération, 75739 Paris Cedex 15, France.

FOREWORD

Towards an energy technology revolution

The world's current energy prospects are – put simply – unsustainable. Despite all the talk about climate change, in recent years energy demand has continued to increase and global CO_2 emissions along with it. At the same time importing countries are increasingly concerned about energy security even as oil, gas and coal prices reach record highs.

The G8 and IEA energy ministers asked the IEA to identify and advise on scenarios for a clean, clever and competitive energy future. In response, the IEA has delivered a number of publications. This year's edition of *Energy Technology Perspectives 2008* builds on the *Energy Technology Perspectives 2006* and the *World Energy Outlook 2007*.

This new study revises our estimates of what would need to be done to return CO_2 emissions to current levels by 2050 and, for the first time, details what could be done to reduce them by 50% in that same timeframe. These objectives cannot be reached without unprecedented technological change and deployment, in all aspects of energy production and use. This study identifies the technology challenges that must be met to make the transition. And it evaluates the scale of the practical change needed to achieve that outcome.

The change needed to achieve the aims of either long-term scenario is daunting, amounting to nothing less than an energy revolution. Yet even the most stringent goal can be realised, with sufficient worldwide commitment. But do the commitment and will genuinely exist?

Attaining either outcome would require a radical and fundamental change in our current energy systems over a period of only forty years. To halve today's emission levels would require additional investments of the order of USD 45 trillion. Although this is a large number in absolute terms, it is small relative to the expected growth in global economic activity over the next forty years - and small relative to the cost of not taking action.

It is reassuring to know that human ingenuity can rise to this challenge. Existing technology – primarily energy efficiency – is an obvious first step, but it is ultimately new technologies that hold promise of economic opportunity and benefit for all the world's countries – and a strong basis for common action toward common objectives.

The International Energy Agency plays a key role in promoting technology development and uptake though its network of Implementing Agreements. We hope this analysis will stimulate even more international technology collaboration both within the IEA framework and outside it. Extensive RD&D, deployment and market development will be needed. Policy levers must be better understood to put in place the long-term incentives that will encourage industry to take decisions to reach the outcomes we seek. And the market needs to ensure the framework conditions to stimulate innovation and maximise the impact we can achieve with scarce global resources.

We look forward to working with governments and industry in realising the vision presented in this document.

Nobuo Tanaka

Executive Director

ACKNOWLEDGEMENTS

This publication was prepared by the International Energy Agency's Office of Energy Technology and R&D (ETO), in close association with the Economic Analysis Division (EAD) and the Office of Long-term Co-operation and Policy Analysis (LTO). Neil Hirst, Director of the ETO, provided invaluable leadership and inspiration throughout the project. Robert Dixon, Head of the Energy Technology Policy Division until October 2007 and Peter Taylor, Acting Head of the Energy Technology Policy Division from November 2007, offered important guidance and input.

Dolf Gielen was the project leader and had overall responsibility for the design and development of the study. The other main authors were Kamel Bennaceur, Jeppe Bjerg, Pierpaolo Cazzola, Hugo Chandler, Roger Dargaville, Paolo Frankl, Lew Fulton, Debra Justus, Tom Kerr, Steven Lee, Emi Mizuno, Cédric Philibert, Jacek Podkanski, Ralph Sims, Cecilia Tam, Michael Taylor and Peter Taylor. Stan Gordelier and Pal Kovacs of the OECD Nuclear Energy Agency wrote the chapter on nuclear power generation.

A number of consultants have contributed to different parts of the publication:

Niclas Mattsson (Chalmers University of Technology, Sweden) and Uwe Remme (IER University Stuttgart, Germany) helped in the Energy Technology Perspectives model analysis. John Newman (France) contributed to the sector analysis and the industry chapter.

Gillian Balitrand and Simone Brinkmann helped to prepare the manuscript. The manuscript was edited by Rob Wright and Samantha Wauchope.

Many other IEA colleagues have provided important contributions, in particular, Sankar Bhattacharya, Fatih Birol, Laura Cozzi, Mark Ellis, Mary Harries-White, Nobuyuki Hara, Jens Laustsen, Takehiko Matsuo, Samantha Olz, Takao Onoda, Antonio Pflüger, Carrie Pottinger, Brian Ricketts, Jonathan Sinton, Ulrik Stridbaek and Ming Yang.

Production and distribution assistance was provided by the IEA Communication and Information Office: Rebecca Gaghen, Muriel Custodio, Corinne Hayworth, Bertrand Sadin, Sophie Schlondorff and Sylvie Stephan added significantly to the material presented.

Special thanks go to Robert Dixon, (Council on Environmental Quality, United States), Claude Mandil (former IEA Executive Director, France), and Toshiyuki Shirai (Ministry of Economy, Trade and Industry, Japan) for their encouragement, support and suggestions.

This work was guided by the IEA Committee on Energy Research and Technology (CERT). Its members and the IEA Energy Advisors provided important guidance that helped to improve substantially the policy relevance of this document. The Standing-Group on Long-Term Co-operation, the Working Party on Energy End-Use Technologies, the Working Party on Renewable Energy Technologies, the Working Party on Fossil Fuels and the Buildings Co-ordination Group all provided valuable comments and suggestions.

The global energy technology model used for this study has been developed in close collaboration with the IEA ETSAP Implementing Agreement. Various national modelling teams have contributed to the refinement of the ETP model. GianCarlo Tosato (ETSAP, Italy) has co-ordinated this effort.

Risø National Laboratory: Technical University of Denmark (wind energy), VTT-Finland (bioenergy) and Utrecht University – the Netherlands (industry) provided additional technology data support.

IEA Implementing Agreements

The technology analysis in this book draws extensively upon the IEAs unique international network for collaboration on energy technology. Numerous experts from IEAs Committee on Energy Research and Technology (CERT), its Working Parties and from many of its 40 Implementing Agreements (IA) have contributed with data and other input. Some of these experts are listed below:

Advanced Fuel Cells IA
Heather Haydock

Bioenergy IA
Göran Berndes
Adam Brown
Kees Kwant
Bjorn Telenius

Demand Side Management Programme IA
Hans Nilsson

Energy Conservation in Buildings and Community Systems Programme IA
Hermann Halozan
Clare Hanmer
Debbie Myers

Geothermal IA
Chris Bromley
Mike Mongillo
Ladislaus Rybach

Heat Pumping Technologies IA, Heat Pump Centre
Roger Nordman

Hybrid and Electric Vehicles Technologies and Programmes IA
Sigrid Muntwyler
Martijn van Walwijk

Hydrogen IA
Mary-Rose de Valladares

IEA Clean Coal Centre
Colin Henderson, London

IEA Greenhouse Gas R&D Programme IA
John Davison

Industrial Energy-Related Technology Systems IA
Thore Berntsson

Ocean Energy Systems IA
Gouri Bhuyan

Photovoltaic Power Systems Programme PVPS IA
Stefan Nowak

Renewable Energy Technology Deployment IA
Daniel Argyropoulos
Annette Schou

Solar Heating and Cooling IA
Pamela Murphy
Ron Judkoff

Wind Energy Systems IA
Ana Estanqueiro
Jaapt Hooft
Patricia Weiss Taylor

Expert reviewers

A large number of reviewers provided valuable feedback and input to the analysis presented in this book:

Rune Aarlien, SINTEF Energy Research, Norway; Edi Assoumou, Ecole National Superieure de Paris, France ; Giuseppe Astarita, Federchimica, Italy ; Monica Axell, SP Technical Research Institute of Sweden; Chris Bayliss, International Aluminium Institute, United Kingdom; Morgan Bazilian, Energy and Natural Resources, Ireland; André B. Bemba, Ministry of Economy, Slovak Republic; Markus Blesl, IER, University of Stuttgart, Germany; Janne Breyer, Vattenfall, Sweden; Peter Brun, Vestas Wind Systems A/S, Denmark; Isabel Cabrita, INETI, Portugal; Yasmine Calisesi, Swiss Federal Office of Energy, Switzerland; Terry Carrington, Department for Business, Enterprise & Regulatory Reform, United Kingdom; Christa Clapp, United States Environmental Protection Agency, United States; Francesco de la Chesnaye, United States Environmental Protection Agency, United States; Norela Constantinescu, Euroheat & Power, Belgium; Carmen Difiglio, United States Department of Energy; Richard Doornbosch, OECD, France; George Eads, CRA International, United States; Sandra Eager, BP, United Kingdom; Wolfgang Eichhammer, Fraunhofer – ISI, Germany; Nick Eyre, Environmental Change Institute, United Kingdom; Gaute Erichsen, Ministry of Foreign Affairs, Norway; Monika Frieling, BMU, Germany; Sabine Froning, Euroheat & Power, Belgium; Helmut Geipel, Germany; Michel Gioria, ADEME, France; Francesco Gracceva, ENEA, Italy; Paul Gunning, United States Environmental

Protection Agency, United States; Arne Höll, BMWi, Germany; Jake Handelsmann, American Forest & Paper Association, United States; Claire Hanmer, Carbon Trust Co, United Kingdom; Sophie Hartfield, Office of Climate Change, United Kingdom; Herman Halozan, Graz University, Austria; Andreas Hardeman, International Air Transport Association (IATA), Belgium; Fuminori Horiya, Heat Pump and Thermal Storage Technology Centre of Japan; Sophie Hosatte, NRCAN, Canada; Frans Van Hulle, European Wind Energy Association, Brussels; Rune Ingels, Yara, Norway; Craig Jones, Department for Business, Enterprise & Regulatory Reform, United Kingdom; Antonio Joyce, INETI, Portugal; Martin Junginger, Copernicus Institute / Utrecht University, the Netherlands; Ryan Katofsky, Navigant Consulting, Inc., United States; Ron Knapp, Australian Aluminium Council, Australia; Christian Kornevall, WBCSD, Switzerland; Paul Lako, ECN, the Netherlands; Theo de Lange, ECN, the Netherlands; Joergen Lemming, National Laboratory for Sustainable Energy, Risoe/ DTU, Denmark; Tono Makoto, Heat Pump and Thermal Storage Technology Centre of Japan; George Marsh, Department for Business, Enterprise & Regulatory Reform, UK; Thomas Martinsen, Institute for Energy Technology, Norway; Terry McCallion, EBRD, United Kingdom; Marijke Menkveld, ECN, the Netherlands; Marco Mensink, CEPI, Belgium; Arnaud Mercier, European Commission, the Netherlands; Nicholas W Miller, GE Infra, Energy, United States; Nobuaki Mita, Japan Petrochemical Industry Association, Japan; Jan Corfee-Morlot, OECD, France; Aksel Mortensgaard, Danish Energy Agency, Denmark; Greg Nemet, La Follette School of Public Affairs and Nelson Institute for Environmental Studies, University of Wisconsin, United States; Steffen Nielsen, Danish Energy Authority, Denmark; Roger Nordman, SP Technical Research Institute, Sweden; Malcolm S Orme, Fabermaunsell, Switzerland; Martin Patel, Utrecht University, the Netherlands; Angel Perez-Sainz, European Commission, Belgium; Jeffrey Petrusa, Research Triangle Institute, United States; Steve Plotkin, Argonne National Laboratory, United States; Mary Preville, NRCAN, Canada; Angelika Pullen, Global Wind Energy Council, Belgium; Shaun Ragnauth, United States Environmental Protection Agency, United States; Ashish Rana, Reliance Industries, India; Stine Leth Rasmussen, Permanent Delegation of Denmark to the OECD; Fiona Riddoch, Cogen Europe, Brussels; Claes Rytoft, ABB, Switzerland; Jayant Sathaye, Lawrence Berkeley Laboratory, United States; Steve Sawyer, Global Wind Energy Council; Rainer Schneider, PT Julich, Germany; Vianney Schyns, Utility Support Group, the Netherlands; Ad Seebregts, ECN, the Netherlands; Norman Shilling, GE Energy; Jim Skea, Research Director, United Kingdom Energy Research Centre; Andrew Smith, Technical Advisor, Energy Efficiency and Conservation Authority, New Zealand; Kim Smith, NRCAN, Canada; Merrill Smith, United States Department of Energy; Peter Snowdon, Shell, the Netherlands; Yasunobu Suzuki, Japan Gas Association; Bert Stuij, SenterNovem, the Netherlands; Shogo Tokura, The Kansai Electric Power Co., Japan; Ferenç Toth, International Atomic Energy Agency, Austria; Richard Taylor, International Hydropower Association, London; Robert Tromop, Monitoring and Technical, EECA, New Zealand; Fridtjof Unander, ENOVA, Norway; Martine Uyterlinde, ECN, the Netherlands; Roberto Vigotti, ENEL, Italy; Florin Vladu, UNFCCC, Germany; Ian Waitz, Massachusetts Institute of Technology, United States; Clas-Otto Wene, Wenergy, Sweden; Martin Weiss, Utrecht University, the Netherlands; Chen Wenying, Tsinghua University, China; Robert Williams , Princeton Environmental Institute, United States; Ernst Worrell, Ecofys, the Netherlands; Remco Ybema, ECN, the Netherlands.

Workshops

A number of workshops and meetings were held in the framework of this study. The workshop participants have contributed valuable new insights, data and feedback for this analysis:

- Using Long-Term Scenarios for R&D Priority Setting, IEA Expert Group on RD&D Priority Setting and Evaluation, 15-16 February 2007, Paris;
- ETP 2008 - Towards Country Level Granularity, 4-5 June 2007, Paris;
- International Workshop on Technology Learning and Deployment, 11-12 June 2007;
- Trends in RD&D Priorities and Funding, IEA Expert Group on RD&D Priority Setting and Evaluation, 3-5 September 2007, Utrecht;
- Industry Scenarios and Indicators: Expert Review Workshop, 1-2 October 2007, Paris;
- Deploying Demand-Side Energy Technologies, 8-9 October 2007, Paris;
- Renewables in ETP2008, 7 November 2007, Paris;
- Chief Technology Officer Roundtable, 16 January 2008, Paris;
- Tracking Industrial Energy Efficiency and CO_2 Emissions: The Way Forward, 11-12 February 2008, Paris.

This study has been supported by voluntary contributions and in-kind support of many IEA governments, including, Canada, Denmark, Finland, France, Germany, Italy, Japan, the Netherlands, Norway, Sweden and the United Kingdom. Also the secondment of Kamel Bennaceur by Schlumberger and the secondment of Steven Lee by the United States Department of Energy are gratefully acknowledged.

The individuals and organisations that contributed to this study are not responsible for any opinions or judgements contained in this study. Any errors and omissions are solely the responsibility of the IEA.

Comments and questions are welcome and should be addressed to:

Dolf Gielen
Office of Energy Technology and R&D
International Energy Agency
9, Rue de la Fédération
75739 Paris Cedex 15
France

Email: Dolf.Gielen@iea.org

TABLE OF CONTENTS

PART 2

The Transition from Present to 2050

PART 3

Energy Technology: Status and Outlook

Chapter 7 Fossil fuel-fired power plants and CO_2 capture and storage 251

Chapter 8 Nuclear 283

Chapter 9 Biomass and bioenergy 307

LIST OF FIGURES

Chapter 1 Introduction

Chapter 2 Scenarios

Chapter 6 Investment issues

Chapter 7 Fossil fuel-fired power plants and CO_2 capture and storage

Chapter 12 Hydro, geothermal and ocean energy

Chapter 13 Electricity systems

Chapter 14 Methane mitigation

Chapter 15 Transport

Chapter 16 Industry

Chapter 17 Buildings and appliances

LIST OF TABLES

Chapter 16 Industry

Chapter 17 Buildings and appliances

Annex A IEA Energy Technology Collaboration Programme

Annex B Framework assumptions

Annex C Technology development needs

EXECUTIVE SUMMARY

Introduction

We are facing serious challenges in the energy sector. The global economy is set to grow four-fold between now and 2050 and growth could approach ten-fold in developing countries like China and India. This promises economic benefits and huge improvements in people's standards of living, but also involves much more use of energy. Unsustainable pressure on natural resources and on the environment is inevitable if energy demand is not de-coupled from economic growth and fossil fuel demand reduced.

The situation is getting worse. Since the 2006 edition of *Energy Technology Perspectives* (ETP), global CO_2 emissions and oil demand have increased steadily. At 7% above our previous outlook, today's best estimates under our "business-as-usual" Baseline scenario foreshadow a 70% increase in oil demand by 2050 and a 130% rise in CO_2 emissions. That is, in the absence of policy change and major supply constraints. According to the Intergovernmental Panel on Climate Change (IPCC), a rise in CO_2 emissions of such magnitude could raise global average temperatures by 6°C (eventual stabilisation level), perhaps more. The consequences would be significant change in all aspects of life and irreversible change in the natural environment.

A global revolution is needed in ways that energy is supplied and used. Far greater energy efficiency is a core requirement. Renewables, nuclear power, and CO_2 capture and storage (CCS) must be deployed on a massive scale, and  carbon-free transport developed. **A dramatic shift is needed in government policies,** notably creating a higher level of long-term policy certainty over future demand for low carbon technologies, upon which industry's decision makers can rely. **Unprecedented levels of co-operation among all major economies** will also be crucial, bearing in mind that less than one-third of "business-as-usual" global emissions in 2050 are expected to stem from OECD countries.

In short, the **global energy economy will need to be transformed** over the coming decades. The aim of this book is to explain how. It presents an in-depth review of the status and outlook for existing and advanced clean energy technologies, offering **scenario analysis** of how a mix of these technologies can make the difference. This edition of *Energy Tcchnology Perspectives* also offers **global roadmaps of the 17 technologies** that we believe can make the largest contributions, showing what action is needed to realise their full potential, and when.

Our scenario analysis deals solely with energy-related CO_2 emissions, which account for most of anthropogenic greenhouse gas emissions. However, the ultimate climate change effect of reductions in energy-related emissions will depend, to some degree, on whether other emissions can be reduced similarly. Therefore a chapter on methane, another important greenhouse gas, is included.

The analysis presented here draws on modelling work within the IEA Secretariat and expertise from the IEA international energy technology collaboration network. *Energy Technology Perspectives* is a companion to the IEA *World Energy Outlook 2007*, taking the same Baseline scenario to 2030 and extending it to 2050. The present study carries forward the analysis contained in the 2006 edition of ETP, in the light of the IPCC 4th Assessment Report released in November 2007.

Several different scenarios are presented. The set of ETP 2008 "ACT Scenarios" shows how global CO_2 emissions could be brought back to current levels by 2050. The set of ETP 2008 "BLUE Scenarios" targets a 50% reduction in CO_2 emissions by 2050. This summary focuses on just one scenario from each set, the ACT Map and the BLUE Map.

ACT scenarios

Technologies that already exist, or are in an advanced state of development, can bring global CO_2 emission back to current levels by 2050. Emissions need to peak between 2020 and 2030. The ACT Map scenario implies adoption of a wide range of technologies with marginal costs up to USD 50[1] per tonne of CO_2 saved when fully commercialised. This level of effort affects certain energy related activities profoundly. It would approximately double the generating costs of a coal power station not equipped with CO_2 capture and storage. The marginal cost figure is twice that estimated two years ago in ETP 2006, mainly reflecting accelerating trends in CO_2 emissions and an approximate doubling of some engineering costs, in part due to the declining value of the dollar.

The task is difficult and costly. Additional investment needs in the energy sector are estimated at USD 17 trillion between now and 2050. This is on average around USD 400 billion per year, roughly equivalent to the gross domestic product (GDP) of the Netherlands, or 0.4% of global GDP each year between now and 2050.

BLUE scenarios

But returning emissions to 2005 levels may not be enough. The IPCC has concluded that emissions must be reduced by 50% to 85% by 2050 if global warming is to be confined to between 2°C and 2.4°C. G8 leaders agreed at the Heiligendamm Summit in 2007 to seriously consider a global 50% CO_2 reduction target.

Reducing CO_2 emissions by 50% (from current levels) by 2050 represents a tough challenge. This scenario implies a very rapid change of direction. Costs are not only substantially higher, but also much more uncertain, because the BLUE scenarios demand deployment of technologies still under development, whose progress and ultimate success are hard to predict. **While the ACT scenarios are demanding, the BLUE scenarios require urgent implementation of unprecedented and far-reaching new policies in the energy sector.**

1 All costs are in real 2005 US dollars.

Based on optimistic assumptions about the progress of key technologies, the BLUE Map scenario requires deployment of all technologies involving costs of up to USD 200 per tonne of CO_2 saved when fully commercialised. If the progress of these technologies fails to reach expectations, costs may rise to as much as USD 500 per tonne. At the margin, therefore, the BLUE Map scenario requires technologies at least four times as costly as the most expensive technology options needed for ACT Map. However, the *average* cost of the technologies needed for BLUE Map is much lower than the marginal, in the range of USD 38 to USD 117 per tonne of CO_2 saved. Figure ES.1 shows how the marginal costs of CO_2 abatement in 2050 increase as the targeted CO_2 savings increase beyond those in ACT Map to reach the higher levels needed for BLUE Map.

Figure ES.1 ▶ Marginal emission reduction costs for the global energy system, 2050

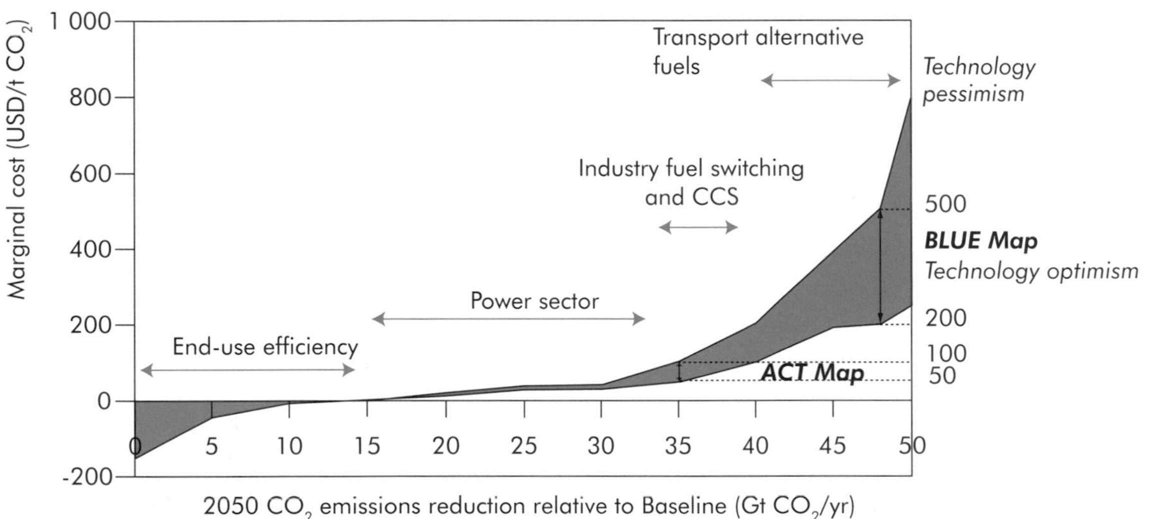

Additional investment needs in the BLUE Map scenario are USD 45 trillion over the period up to 2050. They cover additional R&D, larger deployment investment in technologies not yet market-competitive (even with CO_2 reduction incentives), and commercial investment in low-carbon options (stimulated by CO_2 reduction incentives). The total is about USD 1.1 trillion per year. This is roughly equivalent to the current GDP of Italy. It represents an average of some 1.1% of global GDP each year from now until 2050. This expenditure reflects a re-direction of economic activity and employment, and not necessarily a reduction of GDP. While there will be impacts on global GDP, these are hard to predict and beyond the scope of this analysis.

Benefits from investment

While the additional investments required for both ACT and BLUE scenarios are a measure of the task ahead, they do not represent net costs. This is because technology investments in energy efficiency, in many renewables and in nuclear power all reduce fuel requirements. **In both ACT and BLUE scenarios, the estimated total undiscounted fuel cost savings for coal, oil and gas over the period to 2050 are greater than the additional investment required** (valuing these fuels at Baseline prices). If we discount at 3%, fuel savings exceed additional investment needs in the ACT Map scenario, but not in the BLUE scenarios. Discounting at 10%, results in the additional investment needs exceeding fuel savings in both the ACT and BLUE scenarios.

Some investments, of course, are very cost-effective, particularly in energy efficiency. By contrast, at the high-cost end of the range required for the BLUE scenarios, some investments are only economic with a high CO_2 reduction incentive. Not all the necessary investments reduce fuel costs, however. Investment in CCS will *increase* the amount of coal needed for a given electrical output, because of the reduction in power station efficiency.

A more balanced oil market

In addition to their environmental benefits, the ACT and BLUE scenarios also show a more balanced outlook for oil markets. In the ACT Map scenario, demand for oil continues to grow. It rises by 12% between now and 2050, which is much less than in the baseline. The BLUE Map scenario shows a much more marked difference, with oil demand actually 27% *less* than today in 2050. However, in all scenarios massive investments in fossil fuel supply will be needed in the coming decades.

The technology revolution

In both ACT and BLUE scenarios, **energy efficiency improvements in buildings, appliances, transport, industry and power generation represent the largest and least costly savings**. Next in the hierarchy of importance come measures to substantially **decarbonise power generation.** This can be achieved through a combination of renewables, nuclear power, and use of CCS at fossil fuel plants. Whichever the final target, action in all these areas is urgent and necessary. It is particularly important to avoid lock-in of inefficient technologies for decades to come. In the BLUE Map scenario, higher-cost options **such as CCS in industry and alternative transport fuels need to be deployed.** Figure ES.2 shows the sources of CO_2 savings in the BLUE Map scenario compared to the Baseline scenario. Policy makers should remember that long lead times are frequently required to implement changes and that priorities in each country will vary according to national circumstances. Reducing energy sector methane emissions, moreover, is also an important part of an overall climate change strategy, as these emissions offer significant near-term and cost-effective greenhouse gas reduction opportunities.

Figure ES.2 ▶ Comparison of the *World Energy Outlook 2007* 450 ppm case and the BLUE Map scenario, 2005-2050

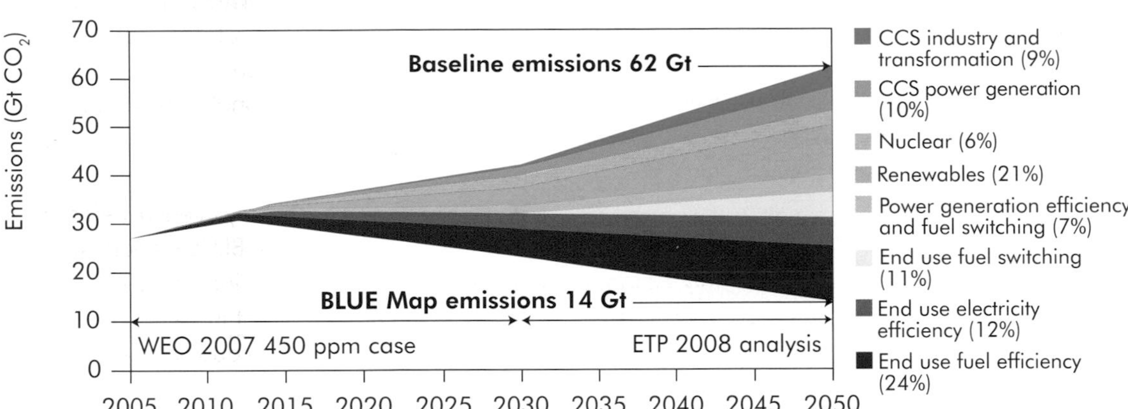

Buildings and appliances

The ACT scenarios can become reality using technologies for buildings and appliances widely available today and economically viable on a life-cycle cost basis. But the BLUE scenarios call for new and emerging technologies; in some cases technologies will be required that are only economic at relatively high CO_2 reduction costs, at least when initially deployed. Widespread conversion of buildings to very low energy consumption, and even "zero" energy buildings, are part of the scenario. **The policy implications for efficiency standards for buildings and appliances are huge.** A combination of building-shell measures, heat pumps, solar heating and highly efficient appliances and lighting reduces energy needs in buildings as well as shifting fuel use to renewables and low-carbon electricity. USD 7.4 trillion of additional investment in residential and service sector buildings is needed for the BLUE Map, against USD 2.6 trillion for the ACT Map scenario.

The power sector

CO_2 capture and storage for power generation and industry is the most important single new technology for CO_2 savings in both ACT Map and BLUE Map scenarios, in which it accounts for 14% and 19% of total CO_2 savings respectively. BLUE Map includes higher-cost applications of CCS for industry and gas power stations. **There is a massive switch to renewables for power generation, especially to wind, photovoltaics, concentrating solar power and biomass.** By 2050, 46% of global power in the BLUE Map scenario comes from renewables. Application of all renewable technologies combined, across all sectors, accounts for 21% of CO_2 savings in the BLUE Map scenario against the Baseline scenario. A substantial switch to nuclear contributes 6% of CO_2 savings, based on the construction of 32 GW of capacity each year between now and 2050. Nuclear accounts for nearly one-quarter of power generation in BLUE Map and hydro for half as much, building on the important role both technologies already play in the Baseline scenario. Figure ES.3 illustrates the annual rates at which new power generation capacity would need to be added in each scenario.

Figure ES.3 ▶ **Additional investment in the electricity sector in the ACT Map and BLUE Map scenarios (compared to the Baseline, 2005-2050)**

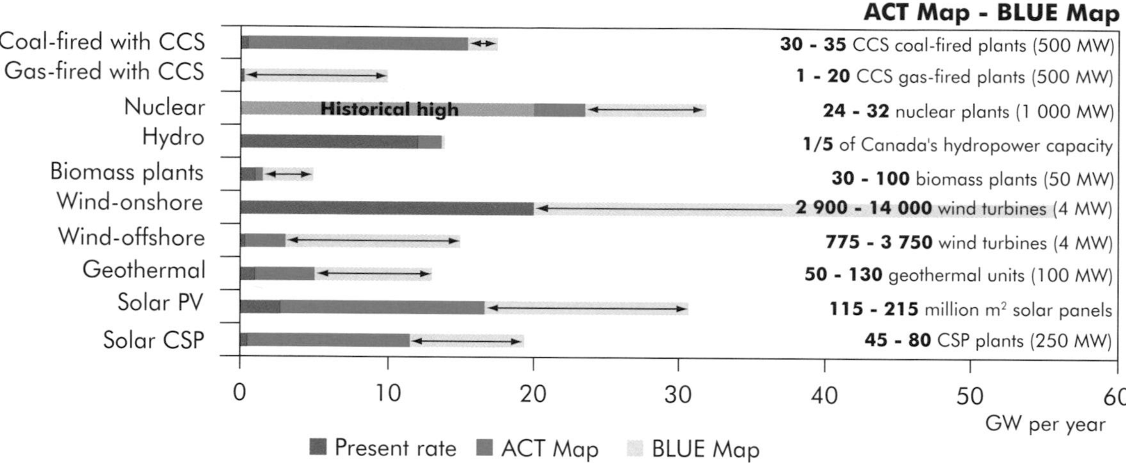

A broad range of scenarios for power generation are considered, from which it can be seen that **considerable flexibility exists for individual countries to chose which precise mix of CCS, renewables and nuclear technology they will use to decarbonise the power sector.** Total additional investment in the power sector (excluding transmission and distribution) amounts to USD 0.7 trillion in the ACT Map scenario and USD 3.6 trillion in the BLUE Map scenario. These investment figures are the net result from combining higher capital costs per unit of capacity with a one-fifth reduction in electricity production due to end-use electricity savings. **Substantial early retirement of capital stock occurs in the BLUE scenarios.** For example, one-third of all coal-fired power plants not suitable for CCS will need to close before the end of their technical life. It is recognised that this will be a large step for countries heavily reliant on coal, but a necessary step requiring careful management.

Transport

In the ACT Map scenario, energy and emissions in the transport sector are saved largely through major **improvements in the efficiency of conventional vehicles** and through the increased penetration of hybrids. Low-carbon footprint biofuels play a part, principally as a replacement for gasoline to fuel cars. It is essential to curb the current trend towards larger, heavier vehicles.

The BLUE Map scenario is very challenging for the transport sector and **requires significant decarbonisation of transport,** which is likely to be **costly** in a sector dominated by oil products and the internal combustion engine. Low-carbon biofuels are expected to play a significant role in the BLUE Map scenario, within the limits of sustainable production and cropping. Trucks, shipping, and air transport are the chief users of biofuels, since other non-hydrocarbon options are likely to be very expensive to apply to these transport modes. While electric batteries and hydrogen fuel cells are the main alternatives for cars, it is difficult to judge at this stage which of these technologies – or which combination of them – will be the most competitive. Based on fairly optimistic assumptions about technology progress and cost reductions, electric and fuel cell vehicles are expected to cost around USD 6 500 more in 2050 than conventional vehicles. In the BLUE Map scenario, nearly one billion electric and fuel cell vehicles need to be on the roads by 2050. Transport represents the largest single area of investment in the scenarios. Additional investment needs in transport are USD 33 trillion in BLUE Map and USD 17 trillion in ACT Map.

Industry

Directly or indirectly, manufacturing industry accounts for more than one-third of global energy use and CO_2 emissions. The iron and steel, and cement industries represent roughly half of industry's emissions; chemicals and petrochemicals are the other very large sources. Heavy industry has a good record of energy efficiency gains in recent years, driven by the need to manage energy costs. But substantial potential exists for further efficiency gains, especially in less energy-intensive industries, notably through more efficient motor drive systems and combined heat and power. Potential also exists for technology advances that are specific to each industry and for application of CCS.

Very large reductions in CO_2 emissions from industry are hard to achieve. In the ACT Map scenario, energy-related CO_2 emissions from industry are 63% higher in 2050 than in 2005. In the BLUE Map scenario they are 22% below today's level, largely reflecting the widespread application of CCS at large, energy intensive plants. Direct and indirect CO_2 savings in the BLUE Map scenario are substantial, at nearly 10 Gt of CO_2 per year. The BLUE Map scenario requires additional investment over the Baseline of USD 2.5 trillion in the upgrading of industrial plant – mainly in the steel, cement, and pulp sectors – and for increased deployment of CCS.

Energy efficiency trends

Big improvements are needed compared to recent energy efficiency trends. Energy efficiency in OECD countries has been improving at just below 1% per year in recent times. A sharp decline from the rate achieved in the years immediately following the oil price shocks of the early 1970s. The ACT Map scenario requires sustained global energy efficiency improvements of 1.4% per year and the BLUE Map scenario calls for 1.7%. While these percentage differences may seem small, the difference of 0.3 percentage points between ACT Map and BLUE Map results in 1 544 Mtoe of additional final energy savings in 2050, 20% of total world final energy use today.

Research, development and demonstration

Some of the technologies needed for the BLUE scenarios are not yet available. Many others require further refinement and cost reductions. A huge effort of research, development, and demonstration (RD&D) will therefore be needed. Yet public- and private-sector spending on energy RD&D has been declining compared to the levels of the 1970s and 1980s and has now stabilised at a relatively low level. Many OECD countries spend less than 0.03% of GDP. The exception is Japan, which spends 0.08%. Private-sector energy RD&D spending now far exceeds public-sector outlay. While details are difficult to establish, independent studies have suggested that public-sector RD&D needs to increase by between two and ten times its current level. We do not set a specific target, but it is clear that **a major acceleration in RD&D effort is needed** both to bring forward new technologies and to reduce costs of those already available. **Further advances and lower cost solutions are needed for critical technologies such as solar PV, advanced coal plant, advanced biofuels, CO_2 capture, electric batteries, fuel cells and hydrogen production**. Even with large increases, the cost of R&D is relatively modest – typically one order of magnitude lower – than that of full scale demonstration and deployment programmes. **Well directed energy R&D represents excellent value for money.**

Government support is also needed for the larger-scale demonstration of new technology, reducing the risks of the first stage of commercialisation. **There is an urgent need for the full-scale demonstration of coal plants with CCS.**

Basic science in areas such as geology, physics, chemistry, materials, biochemistry, nanotechnology and applied mathematics can trigger breakthroughs in critical areas. **It is essential to enhance the science base and its links with technology.**

Deployment and technology learning

Most new technologies have higher costs than the incumbents. It is only through *technology learning* as a result of marketplace deployment that these costs are reduced and the product adapted to the market. **Governments must enhance their deployment programmes.** Second-generation renewables, for example solar and biofuels, are amongst the technologies with the greatest potential. In the ACT Map scenario, we estimate that USD 2.8 trillion needs to be spent between now and 2050 on the additional costs (above market value) of deploying new technology. For the BLUE Map scenario, the figure is USD 7 trillion.

Regulation

The barriers to new technology deployment are not always economic. To overcome these barriers, carefully designed regulations and standards are often the most effective policy measures. **Tough efficiency regulations for buildings, appliances and vehicles will be essential** in all scenarios. In both developed and developing countries, enhancing efficiency regulations, and strengthening their enforcement often represent attractive, cost-effective policy options for immediate action. A critical element for the success of the BLUE scenarios will be public acceptance of standards necessary to achieve very low-energy and zero-energy buildings and a four-fold reduction in the CO_2 intensity of vehicles.

Incentives

Private-sector investment is – and will remain – the primary facilitator of technology deployment and diffusion. The IEA has discussed the implications of the BLUE and ACT scenarios with chief technology officers from 30 leading international energy companies. They stressed **the urgent need to design and implement a range of policy measures that will create clear, predictable, long-term economic incentives for CO_2 reduction in the market.** Only on this basis will business be empowered to undertake the huge investment programmes required.

This analysis does not attempt to specify the mechanisms that will be needed, recognising that this is to some extent the subject of negotiations in the context of the United Nations Framework Convention on Climate Change. For the ACT scenarios, we have estimated that these mechanisms will need to be sufficient to incentivise technologies which, when fully commercialised, have a marginal cost of USD 50 per tonne of CO_2 saved. For BLUE, the figure is at least USD 200 per tonne of CO_2 saved, and could be as high as USD 500 if the progress of key technologies is disappointing. The incentives need to be applied globally, within all major economies, through a variety of policy measures.

These do not necessarily have to be uniform incentives with the same value for all technologies. Especially in the BLUE scenarios, **it may be appropriate to have targeted schemes for the most expensive technologies.** Packages of measures, which could take a variety of forms, need to be in place for OECD countries by 2020 and for other major countries by 2030. The BLUE scenario assumes significant further tightening beyond these dates. To achieve full impact, and for a smooth transition, it is essential that the expectation of the targets and incentives is clearly established well in advance.

Public opinion

Governments will need to give a lead to public opinion, making the connection between the urgent need to address climate change, which is widely recognised, and specific projects required, which often face public opposition. Neither the ACT nor the BLUE scenarios can be achieved without a major shift in priorities, and in the BLUE scenarios, **this needs to be radical and urgent.**

Taking forward international collaboration

International collaboration is essential to accelerate the development and global deployment of sustainable energy technologies in the most efficient way. A network for this already exists. The IEA itself has by far the most comprehensive network, in which thousands of technology experts from around the world co-ordinate their energy technology programmes. The EU energy technology programmes, Asia Pacific Partnership, Carbon Sequestration Leadership Forum, the Biofuels Partnership, and the International Partnership for a Hydrogen Economy, the Generation IV International Forum and the Global Nuclear Energy Partnership are other important examples. **These networks need strong international leadership from policy makers at senior level.**

This book offers first attempts at global roadmaps for key energy technologies. We have identified 17 key technologies for energy efficiency, power generation and transport. They are at the heart of the energy technology revolution. We describe the actions required to deliver their potential. They are specific to each technology and depend, in part, on their current state of development. Such roadmaps can be particularly useful in providing guidance on how much abatement should be sought from each sector and technology, as well as on whether this process is on track. **Further development of these roadmaps under international guidance, drawing together the energy technology programmes of all major economies, and in close consultation with industry, can provide the focus for the much closer international collaboration needed to achieve a global energy technology revolution.** The IEA is ready to support this effort to achieve a more sustainable energy future.

Table ES.1 ▶ **Key roadmaps in this study**

Supply side	Demand side
■ CCS fossil-fuel power generation	■ Energy efficiency in buildings and appliances
■ Nuclear power plants	■ Heat pumps
■ Onshore and offshore wind	■ Solar space and water heating
■ Biomass integrated-gastification combined-cycle and co-combustion	■ Energy efficiency in transport
■ Photovoltaic systems	■ Electric and plug-in vehicles
■ Concentrating solar power	■ H_2 fuel cell vehicles
■ Coal: integrated-gastification combined-cycle	■ CCS in industry, H_2 and fuel transformation
■ Coal: ultra-supercritical	■ Industrial motor systems
■ Second-generation biofuels	

Chapter 1 INTRODUCTION

Secure, reliable and affordable energy supplies are fundamental to economic stability and development. The erosion of energy security, the threat of disruptive climate change and the growing energy needs of the developing world all pose major challenges to energy decision-makers.

This book deals with those challenges. Innovation in energy technologies and a better use of existing technologies will be fundamental to this. The book provides an analysis of the status and future prospects of key energy technologies. It outlines the barriers to the implementation of change and the measures that may be needed to overcome those barriers. It explores how technology can change our energy future.

In recent years, fossil fuel prices have risen considerably. IEA long-term projections for fossil fuel prices have also been revised upward over the past few years. So far, the impact of fuel price increases on global economic growth has been mitigated by a combination of factors such as the decline of the United States dollar compared to other main currencies, sustained energy subsidies in large parts of the world and the decline of energy costs relative to world GDP in the past decades. At the same time, the remaining oil and gas resources are concentrated in a smaller number of countries. This raises concerns about energy security and the prospect that sustained high prices may harm economic growth. Reduced fossil fuel dependency is in many countries a key energy policy target.

These energy security concerns are compounded by the increasingly urgent need to mitigate greenhouse gas emissions, including those relating to energy production and consumption. About 69% of all CO_2 emissions are energy related, and about 60% of all greenhouse emissions can be attributed to energy supply and energy use (IPCC, 2007). The IEA's *World Energy Outlook 2007* projects that unless current policies change, global energy-related CO_2 emissions will grow 57% by 2030 from 2005 levels. Oil demand will increase by 40%. By 2030, fossil fuels remain dominant, meeting 84% of the world's incremental energy needs. The bulk of the new CO_2 emissions and increased demand for energy will come from developing countries. Even when analysing the impact of policies and measures already under consideration, global CO_2 emissions rise 27% over current levels.

The United Nations Intergovernmental Panel on Climate Change (IPCC) has concluded that only scenarios resulting in a 50% to 80% reduction of global CO_2 emissions by 2050 compared to 2000 levels can limit the long-term global mean temperature rise to 2.0 to 2.4 degrees Celsius (IPCC, 2007; *see* Table 1.1). Higher emission levels will result in more significant climate change. The Stern review has concluded that the benefits of limiting temperature rises to two degrees would outweigh the costs of doing so, although other analyses result in varying conclusions depending on the assumptions on which they base their calculations (Stern, 2007; Nordhaus, 2007).

The goal of the analysis in this book is to provide an IEA technology perspective on the cost of deep emission reductions. The analysis does not deal with the political feasibility of such targets.

However, it is obvious from the start that such a target cannot be met if only OECD countries comply. Non-OECD countries must also take action to adopt clean energy technologies. All countries must take action immediately if the goal of a halving of energy related CO_2 emissions in 2050 compared to the 2005 level is to remain technically feasible.

Table 1.1 ▶ **The relation between emissions and climate change according to Climate Change 2007, IPCC**

Temperature increase (°C)	All GHGs (ppm CO_2 eq.)	CO_2 (ppm CO_2)	CO_2 emissions 2050 (% of 2000 emissions) (%)
2.0-2.4	445-490	350-400	–85 to –50
2.4-2.8	490-535	400-440	–60 to –30
2.8-3.2	535-590	440-485	–30 to +5
3.2-4.0	590-710	485-570	+10 to +60

Source: IPCC, 2007.

The political context

At the IEA Ministerial Meeting in May 2007, ministers concluded: "We need to respond to the twin energy-related challenges we confront: ensuring secure, affordable energy for more of the world's population, and managing in a sustainable manner the environmental consequences of producing, transforming and using that energy" (IEA, 2007). They committed themselves to reinforcing their efforts to "accelerate the development and deployment of new technologies", and called on the IEA "to continue to work towards identifying truly sustainable scenarios and on identifying least-cost policy solutions for combating energy-related climate change".

Leaders of the Group of Eight (G8) countries have agreed on the need to "act with resolve and urgency now to meet our shared and multiple objectives of reducing greenhouse gas emissions, improving the global environment, enhancing energy security and cutting air pollution in conjunction with our vigorous efforts to reduce poverty" (FCO, 2005). This was reinforced at the June 2007 summit in

Heiligendamm, Germany: "In setting a global goal for emissions reductions in the process we have agreed today involving all major emitters, we will consider seriously the decisions made by the European Union, Canada and Japan which include at least a halving of global emissions by 2050" (Federal Press Office, 2007).

The ongoing United Nations Framework Convention on Climate Change (UNFCCC) process and the United States-led 17 Major Economies (ME) Energy Security and Climate Change Initiative are seeking to secure the terms and conditions of a new global agreement that addresses climate change without damaging economic development or diminishing energy security. The ME process will culminate in a Leaders Summit in mid-2008. The goal of the ME process is to complete a framework for a new global agreement on climate change, particularly through reinforcing and accelerating progress in the United Nations. Special attention is focused on long-term targets, technology and sectoral approaches.

The purpose and scope of this study

Reducing the impact of climate change requires an integrated and global response. Energy systems must play a central role in this response, which has to address environmental stewardship, economic growth and energy supply and security. The development and deployment of new clean energy technologies will be fundamental.

This book addresses many of the challenges identified at the IEA Ministerial Meeting in May 2007. It is also part of the IEA response to the request made by G8 leaders to "advise on alternative energy scenarios and strategies aimed at a clean, clever and competitive energy future" (FCO, 2005). It is intended to be a key reference for policy-makers and others interested both in existing and emerging clean energy technologies, policies and practices. It provides roadmaps for technology policy and international technology cooperation that are essential to meet shared energy policy goals.

The analysis builds on the study underpinning the IEA's *Energy Technology Perspectives 2006: Scenarios and Strategies to 2050*. It explores, among other alternatives, a scenario for reducing emissions by 50% by 2050. Drawing from *World Energy Outlook 2007*, it extends the analysis by two decades. The scenarios are consistent with our need for economic growth. Focusing on technology and technology pathways, it explains the scenarios along with their cost ceilings. The choice of policy instruments is not detailed. The 2008 *World Energy Outlook* will include an in-depth assessment of post-2012 climate change framework architecture, including the merits of cap-and-trade systems, sectoral approaches and hybrid options, and will examine the use of scenarios as an input to climate negotiations.

The study draws heavily on the extensive IEA store of data and analysis, and is a result of close co-operation between all IEA offices. It has profited greatly from the unique international IEA network for collaboration on energy technology, described in Annex A. More than five thousand experts from 39 countries participate in the IEA Committee on Energy Research and Technology (CERT), its Working Parties and in 42 Implementing Agreements. The analysis in this book has benefited from numerous contributions from network members.

The objectives of this book are to:

- Review and assess the status and prospects for key energy technologies in electricity generation, road transport, buildings and appliances, and industry.
- Examine through least-cost scenario analysis the potential contributions that these energy technologies can make to improve energy security and to reduce the environmental impacts of energy provision and use.
- Discuss strategies on how to help these technologies make this contribution.

It has three major components:

Part I: *Technology and the Global Energy Economy to 2050* presents in Chapter 2 a set of scenarios to 2050. These scenarios include energy technologies and best practices aimed at reducing energy demand and emissions and diversifying energy sources. This is the first time such results have been detailed for the G8+5 countries. It is also the first time an IEA scenario (BLUE) has explored a 50% emissions reduction. The chapter also addresses the post-2050 outlook and its consequences for the 2025-2050 timeframe.

Part II: *The Transition from the Present to 2050* suggests short- and medium-term strategies that can use energy technologies to help the world to move towards a more sustainable energy future, and sets out technology roadmaps that can achieve this objective. It explores the roles of RD&D (research, development and demonstration), deployment and investment (the three steps in the technology lifecycle) in supporting policy outcomes.

Part III: *Energy Technology: Status and Outlook* provides a detailed review of the status and prospects of key energy technologies in power and heat generation, in road transport, in industry, and in buildings and appliances. It highlights the potential for technologies in these sectors and their costs, and discusses the barriers that each technology must overcome before its full potential can be harvested.

Implications of the scenarios for climate change

The review focuses on three key scenarios – a Baseline scenario, an ACT Map scenario and a BLUE Map scenario. These are described in more detail in Chapter 2. As shown in Figure 1.1, each has different implications for CO_2 emissions:

- In the Baseline scenario, CO_2 emissions would rise from 27 Gt in 2005 to 62 Gt in 2050. CO_2 concentrations would rise from 385 ppm today to 550 ppm in 2050.

- In the ACT Map scenario, CO_2 emissions would peak at around 34 Gt in 2030 and drop to today's level by 2050. This would result in a CO_2 concentration of 485 ppm in 2050. Provided emissions continue to fall, reaching 14 Gt by 2100, this would result in stabilisation at 520 ppm in the long term.

- The BLUE Map scenario explores the energy implications of a reduction of global Greenhouse Gas (GHG) emissions to 50% of current levels by 2050. In this scenario, CO_2 emissions would peak in the next decade, fall to 14 Gt in 2050, and stabilise afterwards. This most ambitious scenario could result in a stabilisation of CO_2 concentrations at 450 ppm. It should be noted that other emission scenario pathways could meet this target as well, and that the timing of the peak could also be somewhat later. This issue is not further elaborated in this study.

- Between 2050 and 2100, the energy economy would be virtually decarbonised in both the ACT Map and BLUE Map scenarios.

- Provided non-CO_2 emissions are also significantly reduced (Box 1.1), the BLUE Map scenario could be consistent with a world average temperature change of two to three degrees Celsius above pre-industrial levels.

Figure 1.1 ▶ **Energy-related CO_2 emission and CO_2 concentration profiles for the Baseline, ACT Map and BLUE Map scenarios**

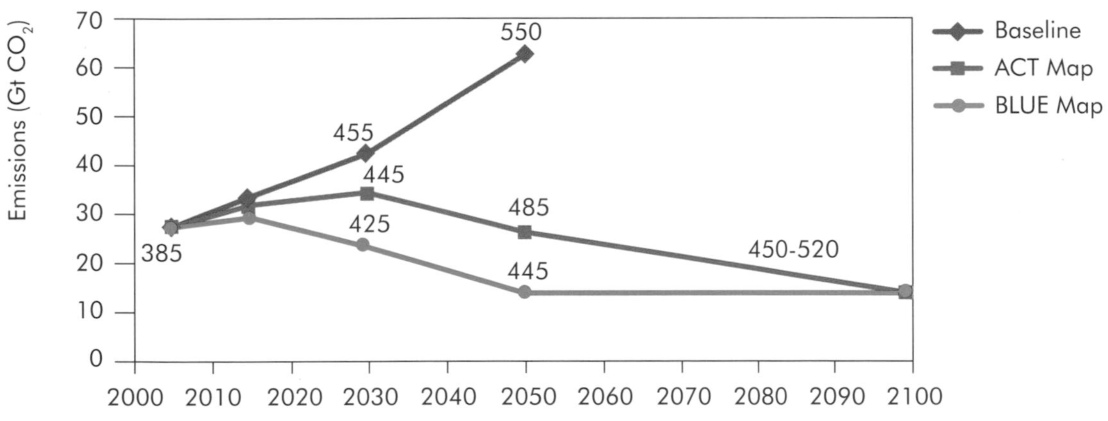

Note: Figures refer to CO_2 concentrations by volume (ppm CO_2).

Key point

Only the BLUE Map scenario is consistent with a long-term stabilisation at 450 ppm CO_2.

These scenarios merely serves to reinforce the scale of the challenge we face in transforming energy systems and the importance of our taking steps to do so as soon as possible. This book above all aims to support that effort.

Box 1.1 ▶ Reduction of greenhouse gas emissions that are not related to energy use

The CO_2 concentration in the atmosphere is 385 ppm, and is rising by about 2 ppm per year. Approximately 58% of all emitted CO_2 stays in the atmosphere. Based on these facts, it is possible to estimate future CO_2 emissions and concentration levels. However, the relation between anthropogenic emissions and climate change is far more complex than just this.

In 2004, 49 Gt of CO_2 equivalent emissions were released, of which 77% was CO_2 (IPCC, 2007). CO_2 emissions from fossil fuel combustion accounted for only slightly over half of the total emissions of the six groups of greenhouse gases covered by the Kyoto protocol. In reality, the situation is even more complicated – as other factors also have global warming or cooling effects.

Stabilisation of climate change at two to three degrees Celsius will require substantial cuts in emissions of non-CO_2 greenhouse gases and in non-energy related CO_2 emissions. There is no choice of doing either one or the other: both energy-related and other emissions need to be reduced significantly. Reducing methane emissions related to energy use is discussed in Chapter 14, and reducing CO_2 emissions from industrial processes in Chapter 16. But it is beyond the scope of this study to discuss the reduction of other gases in greater detail.

Apart from reducing emissions, it is also possible to enhance sinks that remove CO_2 from the atmosphere. Underground storage of CO_2 from combustion processes is discussed in detail in this study. But natural CO_2 capture and storage processes can also be enhanced, such as CO_2 uptake by oceans and through land use and forestry activities. These options are beyond the scope of this analysis. Non-CO_2 greenhouse gases will be discussed in more detail in the IEA World Energy Outlook 2008.

PART 1 TECHNOLOGY AND THE GLOBAL ENERGY ECONOMY TO 2050

Chapter 2 SCENARIOS

2

Key Findings

In the absence of new policies, global energy demand and CO_2 emissions will more than double by 2050

- *In the Baseline scenario, global CO_2 emissions grow rapidly, oil and gas prices are high, and energy security concerns increase as imports rise. In this scenario, energy CO_2 emissions in 2050 are 130% above the level of 2005. Oil demand is 70% above the 2005 level. These developments are not sustainable. Most of the growth in energy demand, and hence emissions, comes from developing countries.*

- *Despite CO_2 policies in many countries, the Baseline outlook has deteriorated considerably since publishing the last edition of Energy Technology Perspectives (IEA, 2006). Baseline CO_2 emission projections for 2050 have risen by 7%, primarily due to projections of higher economic growth, higher oil and gas prices, greater reliance on coal for power generation and an increased use of coal in the production of liquid transport fuels. We can not delay any further taking decisive action.*

Energy technologies can make the world's energy sector more sustainable

- *Emissions can be brought back to today's level by 2050 if measures with a cost of up to USD 50/t CO_2 are applied globally (as in the ACT scenarios). This can be achieved using existing technologies or those under development. Energy efficiency and emission reductions in power generation play a key role in meeting this target.*

- *A halving of worldwide emissions by 2050 (as in the BLUE scenarios) would be an extremely challenging target. This would require measures with a cost of up to USD 200/tCO_2. With less-optimistic technology assumptions, notably in transportation, marginal costs could be USD 500/t CO_2. The transition costs will be considerable. The average emission reduction costs in this scenario are about a fifth of the marginal cost, and range from USD 38/t CO_2 to USD 117/t CO_2.*

- *The outcomes envisaged in the BLUE scenarios are not possible with the technologies available today. All end-use sectors need to apply fuel-switching and carbon capture and storage (CCS), where appropriate, in combination with energy-efficiency measures. The transport sector especially will require new solutions, the cost of which will be very high. In all sectors, new technologies are needed to bring these costs down further.*

- *CO_2 emission reduction policies can help to avoid very significant supply challenges. This is especially the case in transportation. In both the ACT and BLUE scenarios, oil and gas demand are significantly below the Baseline level in 2050. In the BLUE Map scenario, oil demand is 27% below the 2005 level. However, fossil fuels remain a key element of the world's energy supply in 2050 in all scenarios.*

- *There is an urgent need for action in the next decade. Investments made in this period, due to the long life-span of capital equipment such as buildings, industrial installations and power plants, may need to be the subject of economically wasteful early replacement or refurbishment if emission reduction targets are to be met. The BLUE scenarios already envisage 350 GW of coal-fired power being replaced before the end of its life-span.*

- *The OECD countries account for less than one-third of global CO_2 emissions in 2050 in the Baseline scenario. Global emissions can only be halved if developing countries and transition economies contribute substantially.*

- *Deep emission cuts will require substantial application of CO_2 capture and storage, nuclear and renewable energy technologies. Emissions can only be cut significantly if all CO_2-free options play a role.*

- *Policies that raise the CO_2 target incrementally risk a lock-in of options and strategies that are unsuited for deep emission cuts. For example, the role of natural gas in power generation increases in the ACT scenarios for moderate targets but declines in the BLUE scenarios, where deeper emission cuts are needed.*

- *Financial incentives to achieve CO_2 reductions could take many forms and need to be supplemented by a range of other policy instruments.*

Key technology options in the ACT and BLUE scenarios

- *End-use energy efficiency accounts for 36% to 44% of the emissions reductions in the ACT and BLUE scenarios, compared to the baseline. CCS represents 14% to 19% of reductions, nuclear 6%, and renewables 21%. In addition to the flexibility individual countries have based on resource availability, some uncertainty about these shares exists, which is explored through the five scenarios for the power sector and four for transport. Improving energy efficiency should be a priority. Many efficiency measures can be implemented with relatively short lead times, and full life-cycle costs are often negative.*

- *In the ACT Map scenario, the rate of energy efficiency improvement increases to 1.4% per year from the 0.9% per year of the Baseline scenario, driving down final energy intensity by 2.2% per year on average. In the BLUE Map scenario even faster rates of energy efficiency improvement are seen (1.7% per year) and consequently final energy intensity falls by 2.5% per year.*

- *These improvements in energy efficiency result in substantial additional energy savings in 2050 in the ACT and BLUE scenarios compared to the Baseline scenario. In the ACT Map scenario the savings total 23% of baseline energy consumption in 2050. In the BLUE Map scenario, savings rise to 33% by 2050.*

- *Electricity will play an increasing role as a CO_2-free energy carrier. The near elimination of CO_2 emissions in the power sector is the cornerstone of achieving deep CO_2 emission reductions worldwide. Advances in new technologies are key to accomplishing this. Fossil fuels used with CCS, nuclear and renewables all have an important part to play. Each faces challenges to wider use at reasonable cost. A decarbonised power supply opens the prospect of increasing demand-side electrification as a zero-emission solution for the long term.*

- *To cope with increasing amounts of variable renewables, electricity grids will need to be improved and electricity storage technologies will need to be deployed on a larger scale. While the use of electricity as a substitute for fossil fuels plays an important role in the BLUE scenarios in 2050, this development will need to be accelerated beyond 2050.*
- *Decarbonising the transport sector is a major challenge. Demand for automobile travel is projected to increase more than threefold, while freight will grow at an even faster rate. Efficiency gains of 30% to 50%, available with conventional technology, will be insufficient to outweigh demand growth. Biofuels, electricity from the grid and clean hydrogen are the three CO_2-free energy carriers that can be used in this sector. All three need further development. The most challenging part is the emissions reduction for trucks, ships and air transportation. Second-generation biodiesel and jet biofuels look like the most viable alternatives for these transportation modes. As biofuel availability is limited, development of other alternatives for automobiles becomes imperative if deep emission cuts are to be achieved.*
- *Energy efficient appliances and lighting and better building shells play a key role in the ACT Map scenario. In the BLUE Map scenario, heat pumps and solar heating increase the emissions reduction in the buildings sector further. In the BLUE Map scenario, buildings must be retrofitted or replaced at an earlier stage.*
- *In the industry sector, a combination of energy efficiency (e.g. efficient motor systems), biomass use, CCS and optimisation of materials life-cycles can result in substantial reductions, but most of this potential has a relatively high cost.*
- *Sustainable and affordable CO_2-free power generation should be a priority. While CCS plays a key role in the ACT Map and BLUE Map scenarios in 2050, regional storage potentials may limit sustained reliance on CCS beyond 2050.*
- *A number of CO_2-free energy sources have huge potential. Solar, geothermal and nuclear fusion deserve special RD&D attention for the longer term, given their large resource potential and applicability in many parts of the world.*

Scenario characteristics

The scenarios in the *Energy Technology Perspectives 2008* study build on and are consistent with earlier IEA scenario analysis work, notably the ACT and TechPlus scenarios presented in *Energy Technology Perspectives 2006* (IEA, 2006) and the Reference scenario and the 450 ppm case published in *World Energy Outlook 2007* (IEA, 2007a).

The Baseline scenario reflects developments that will occur with the energy and climate policies that have been implemented to date. It is consistent with the *World Energy Outlook 2007* Reference scenario for the period 2005 to 2030. *World Energy Outlook* trends have been extended for the period 2030 to 2050, based on the new *Energy Technology Perspectives* model analysis. The pattern of economic growth changes after 2030, as population growth slows and the economies of developing countries begin to mature.

The implications of two policy objectives have been analysed. The ACT scenarios envisage bringing global energy CO_2 emissions in 2050 back to 2005 levels. The BLUE scenarios envisage halving those emissions. The BLUE scenarios are consistent with a global rise in temperatures of two to three degrees Celsius, but only if the reduction in energy-related CO_2 emissions is combined with deep cuts of other greenhouse gas emissions. Both scenarios also aim for reduced dependence on oil and gas. The ACT and BLUE scenarios are based on the same macro-economic assumptions as the Baseline scenario developed for this study. In all scenarios, world economic growth is a robust 3.3% per year between 2005 and 2050. In all scenarios too, the underlying demand for energy services is the same, *i.e.* the analysis does not consider scenarios for reducing the demand for energy services (such as by reducing indoor room temperatures or restricting personal travel activity). The framework assumptions are described in more detail in Annex B.

The ACT and BLUE scenarios explore what needs to be done if we are to meet their ambitious objectives. The analysis does not reflect on the likelihood of these things happening, or on the climate policy instruments that might best help achieve these objectives. The scenarios assume an optimistic view of technology development. It is clear that these objectives can only be met if the whole world participates (Box 2.1). How to get all countries on board is beyond the scope of this analysis.

Box 2.1 ▶ A global effort is needed

The OECD countries will account for less than one-third of global CO_2 emissions in 2050. Serious emission reductions will therefore be heavily dependent on developing countries and transition economies.

Expected economic growth in developing countries and their sheer population size make any meaningful global emissions reduction dependent upon their involvement. By 2050, out of a total world population of 9 billion people, only 1 billion will live in OECD countries. The Energy Technology Perspectives *analysis shows that, even with an incentive of USD 200/t CO_2, emissions cannot be stabilised without the participation of non-OECD countries. If OECD countries alone were to implement an incentive even at this level, global CO_2 emissions in 2050 would be 42 Gt,* i.e. *56% higher than in 2005.*

The ACT Map and BLUE Map scenarios contain relatively optimistic assumptions for all key technology areas. The BLUE Map scenario is more speculative than the ACT Map scenario insofar as it assumes technology that is not available today. It also requires the rapid development and widespread uptake of such technologies. Without affordable new energy technologies, the objectives of the BLUE Map scenario will be unachievable.

In total, five variants have been analysed for the power sector for both ACT and for BLUE. These are:

- MAP: relatively optimistic for all technologies.
- High nuclear (hi NUC): 2000 GW instead of 1 250 GW maximum nuclear capacity.
- No carbon capture and storage (no CCS).
- Low renewables (lo REN): assuming less cost reductions for renewable power generation technologies.
- Low end-use efficiency gains (lo EFF): assuming a 0.3% lower annual energy efficiency improvement, compared to MAP.

The second set of variants applies to the transport sector, where four variants for BLUE have been analysed:

- BLUE Map (a combination of high efficiency, biofuels, electric vehicles and hydrogen fuel cell vehicles).
- BLUE EV success: a variant that is optimistic with regard to the development of electric vehicles.
- BLUE FCV success: a variant that is optimistic with regard to the development of H_2 fuel-cell vehicles.
- BLUE conservative: a variant where neither EVs nor FCVs are assumed to achieve cost reductions sufficient for them to begin deployment. As a result, this scenario has higher transport CO_2 emissions than the other BLUE variant scenarios.

These four variants apply only to the BLUE scenarios, because in the ACT Map scenario only efficiency and biofuels are assumed to play an important role in the transport sector.

The reduction of energy related methane emissions is an intrinsic component of all of these scenarios. Methane emissions and their reduction in the ACT and BLUE scenarios are discussed in more detail in Chapter 14. Similarly, the scenarios assume a significant reduction in industrial-process CO_2 emissions in cement-making, as discussed in Chapter 16.

These scenarios are not predictions. They are internally consistent analyses of the least-cost pathways that may be available to meet energy policy objectives, given a certain set of optimistic technology assumptions. This work can help policy makers identify technology portfolios and flexible strategies that may help deliver the outcomes they are seeking. The scenarios are the basis for roadmaps that can help to establish appropriate mechanisms and plans for further international technology co-operation.

The results of the ACT and BLUE scenarios assume a wide range of policies and measures to overcome barriers to the adoption of the appropriate technologies. Both the public and the private sectors have major roles to play in creating and disseminating new energy technologies.

The increased uptake of cleaner and more efficient energy technologies envisaged in the ACT and BLUE scenarios will need to be driven by:

- *Increased support for the research and development (R&D)* of energy technologies that face technical challenges and need to reduce costs before they become commercially viable.
- *Demonstration programmes* for energy technologies that need to prove they can work on a commercial scale under relevant operating conditions.
- *Deployment programmes* for energy technologies that are not yet cost-competitive, but whose costs could be reduced through learning-by-doing. These programmes would be phased out when the technology becomes cost-competitive.
- *CO_2 reduction incentives* to encourage the adoption of low-carbon technologies. Such incentives could take a number of forms – such as regulation, pricing, tax breaks, voluntary programmes, subsidies or trading schemes. In the ACT scenarios, policies and measures are assumed to be put in place that would lead to the adoption of low-carbon technologies with a cost of up to USD 50 per tonne of CO_2 saved. The ACT scenarios are based on the incentives being in place from 2030 in all countries, including developing countries. In the BLUE scenarios the level of incentive continues to rise and reaches a level of USD 200 per tonne of CO_2 saved ten years later.
- *Policy instruments to overcome other commercialisation barriers* that are not primarily economic. These include enabling standards and other regulations, labelling schemes, information campaigns and energy auditing. These measures can play an important role in increasing the uptake of energy-efficient technologies in the buildings and transport sectors, as well as in non-energy intensive industry sectors where energy costs are low compared to other production costs.

Energy prices in each of the ACT and BLUE scenarios respond to changes in demand and supply. In the Baseline scenario, oil prices increase from USD 62 per barrel in 2030 to USD 65 per barrel in 2050 (in real present dollar terms). This price trajectory is consistent with the *World Energy Outlook 2007* Reference scenario (IEA, 2007a). At these prices, substitutes for conventional oil (such as tar sands) as well as transport fuels produced from gas and coal will begin to play a larger role. If the necessary investments in conventional oil and gas production do not materialize, the prices will be considerably higher (IEA, 2007a). The interaction between availability of energy resources, the energy technology used, the demand for energy services and energy prices is captured in the energy system model used for this analysis (see Annex B). While lower oil and gas demand in the ACT and BLUE scenarios will result in a price reduction, the precise impact on prices is uncertain.

The ACT scenarios were already presented in *Energy Technology Perspectives 2006* (IEA, 2006). A number of important changes have been made to the 2006 scenarios, however:

- Economic growth projections have been revised upward.
- Equipment costs have been revised upwards, due to a combination of rising material costs, strong demand growth in Asia, resource scarcity and a growing

lack of skilled labour. Typically, costs have risen by a factor of two. Long-term cost projections for certain key technologies have also been revised upwards.

It remains to be seen if these factors will be sustained over the coming decades, or if they will change. However, one significant consequence of this analysis is that the CO_2 incentive level for emissions stabilisation in the ACT scenarios has been raised from USD 25/t CO_2 to USD 50/t CO_2. It is a fact that, in the short and medium term, deployment costs have risen significantly for most technologies. This development has increased the challenge faced to achieve an energy transition compared to the situation two years ago.

Box 2.2 ▶ The alternative policy scenario

The Alternative Policy Scenario (APS) presented in IEA World Energy Outlook 2007 *describes outcomes that would result from the implementation of policies that are under consideration today. This scenario shows that such policies can reduce global CO_2 emissions from 41.9 Gt (the Reference scenario) to 33.9 Gt in 2030. This represents an increase over 2005 emission levels of 27%. Many aspects of APS are comparable with the ACT scenarios, but APS has no generic CO_2 incentive level, and it does not generate least-cost outcomes. Another important difference is that APS does not include CO_2 capture and storage, while CCS plays an important role in the ACT scenarios. As a result, CO_2 emissions in 2030 are lower in the ACT scenarios than in APS.*

CO_2 emission trends

In the *World Energy Outlook 2007* Reference scenario, CO_2 emissions increase from 27 Gt in 2005 to 42 Gt by 2030. Growth in CO_2 emissions continues in the *Energy Technology Perspectives* Baseline scenario, reaching 62 Gt of CO_2 in 2050, an unsustainable 130% increase from 2005. The average annual growth of CO_2 for the period 2005 to 2030 is 1.8%, compared to 2% for the period 2030-2050.

From 1990 to 2000, the average annual increase in emissions was 1.1% per year. Between 2000 and 2005, growth accelerated to 2.9% per year, despite the increased focus on climate change. High economic growth, notably in coal-based economies, and higher oil and gas prices (which have lead to an increase in coal-fired power generation) are the main reasons for the increase. Emissions from coal use increased by 1% per year between 1990 and 2000, but they rose by 4.4% per year between 2000 and 2005.

These recent trends also have an impact on the projections. The baseline outlook for 2030 and 2050 has considerably deteriorated since *Energy Technology Perspectives 2006*. Baseline CO_2 emission projections for 2050 have risen by 7%, due to higher economic growth forecasts, notably for China and India (both major coal-consuming economies) and because of higher oil and gas price projections, which result in a switch to more coal in the Baseline scenario (IEA, 2007a). This fuel-switching effect more than outweighs any additional efficiency gains caused by higher fuel prices.

Worldwide economic activity in 2050 is estimated in all three scenarios to be approximately four times that of 2005. Studies suggest that the impact of CO_2 policies on economic growth is probably small and unlikely to affect the conclusions of this study significantly (see Box 2.3).

In the Baseline scenario, primary energy use rises by 110%, and the carbon intensity of primary energy increases by 11%. Strong decoupling of economic activity and energy use – a consequence of technical energy efficiency gains and structural change – is overshadowed by rapid economic growth and the increasing carbon intensity of energy use. Although emissions from the power sector represent the largest absolute increase, emissions are forecast to rise relatively faster in the fuel transformation, transportation and industry sectors.

A shift towards more coal in the power sector energy mix, at the expense of oil and gas, contributes a significant proportion of the emissions growth in the Baseline scenario. Coal accounts for 52% of power generation in 2050. Although coal generation requires higher initial investment, investors will weigh this up against the risk of oil and gas prices continuing to increase in the next two decades. The investments undertaken during this period risk locking the world into a highly carbon-intensive energy future.

Oil and gas demand will also continue to rise. IEA analysis suggests it is unlikely that this demand will be constrained by a shortage of available reserves, although it is less clear that the necessary investment will occur in time to exploit those reserves. If investment in the OPEC countries and Russia does not materialise in the coming decades, oil and gas prices will rise further, thus increasing the demand for alternatives, whether high- or low-carbon. The BLUE scenarios show that deep emission reductions result in a significant reduction of oil demand by 2050 compared to today. Even so, all of the scenarios in this study assume technology will be developed to secure unconventional resources such as deep oil, arctic oil and ultra-heavy oil and to find new low-cost methods to develop small size oil and gas fields.

Even if the Baseline scenario is feasible from a resource perspective, it will result in unacceptable climate change. It will also make oil and gas importers increasingly reliant on energy imports from a relatively small number of supplier countries. This will create further supply security risks for importing countries and may undermine sustained economic growth.

The Baseline scenario is not a given, nor is it desirable from a sustainability standpoint. The ACT scenarios illustrate that, with the right decisions taken early enough, it is possible to move the energy system onto a more sustainable basis over the next half century, using technologies that are available today or that could become commercially available in the next decade or two. Achieving the objectives of the BLUE scenarios would be more costly and less certain and would require aggressive changes to the energy infrastructure.

In the ACT Map scenario, emissions are 35 Gt lower in 2050 than in the Baseline scenario (-56%). In the four ACT variants – high nuclear, no CCS, low renewables and low end-use efficiency gains – CO_2 emissions range between 5% below and

16% above 2005 levels. Emissions in power generation are reduced particularly significantly, through a combination of end-use electricity savings that lower demand and a reduction in CO_2 emissions per unit of electricity generated.

2

Figure 2.1 ▶ **Global CO_2 emissions in the Baseline, ACT Map and BLUE Map scenarios**

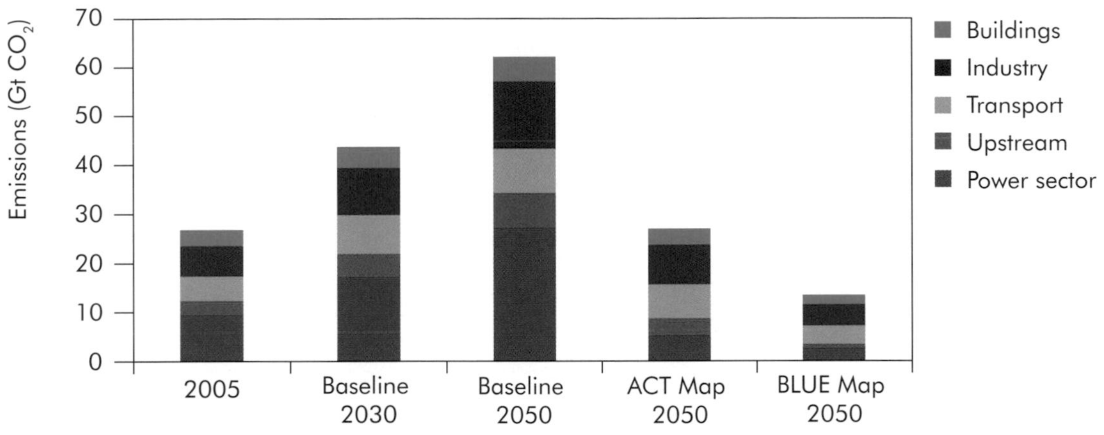

Key point

ACT Map implies deep emission cuts in power generation and the fuel transformation sector; BLUE Map implies deep emission cuts across all sectors.

In the BLUE Map scenario, emissions are 48 Gt lower in 2050 than in the Baseline scenario. In the BLUE variants (in which the five power sector variants are combined with four transport variants) CO_2 emissions are between 24% and 51% lower than in 2005.

Reductions in CO_2 emissions by contributing factor

Figure 2.2 shows the reduction of global energy-related CO_2 emissions over the period 2005 to 2050 for the BLUE Map scenario and for the *World Energy Outlook 2007* 450 ppm case (to 2030). The graph shows the consistency of the two IEA scenarios. End-use efficiency (for fuels and for electricity) and power sector measures dominate the short- and medium-term emission reductions. However, because of the deeper emission cuts needed by 2050, end-use efficiency and power sector options are supplemented by more CCS and end-use fuel switching between 2030 and 2050. This is the only way that the transportation sector and industry can achieve deep emission cuts.

Figure 2.2 suggests a peak in emissions around 2012. The later the peak and the higher it is, the more difficult it will be to achieve deep emission cuts by 2050. Achieving the outcomes implicit in the BLUE Map scenario will require the peak to be reached at moderate levels in the next one to two decades. If this does not happen, the target will be unachievable. Given the long lead times before new policies are put in place and will have effect, there is an urgent need for meaningful global action very soon.

Figure 2.2 ▶ **Contribution of emission reduction options, 2005-2050**

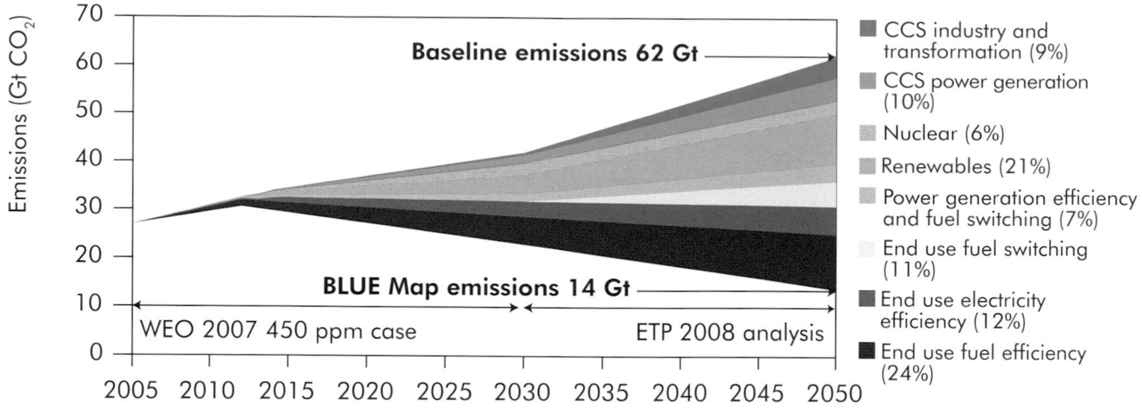

Emissions (Gt CO_2)
70
60
50
40
30
20
10
0
Baseline emissions 62 Gt
BLUE Map emissions 14 Gt
WEO 2007 450 ppm case
ETP 2008 analysis
2005 2010 2015 2020 2025 2030 2035 2040 2045 2050
CCS industry and transformation (9%)
CCS power generation (10%)
Nuclear (6%)
Renewables (21%)
Power generation efficiency and fuel switching (7%)
End use fuel switching (11%)
End use electricity efficiency (12%)
End use fuel efficiency (24%)

Key point

The BLUE Map scenario is consistent with the World Energy Outlook 2007 *450 ppm case.*

Figure 2.3 shows the emission reductions by sector for the period 2005 to 2050. The CO_2 reductions from electricity savings have been allocated to end-use sectors. This breakdown shows that in the next two decades, the power sector and all end-use sectors together play an equal part in the emission reduction effort. However beyond 2030, the end-use sectors have an increasingly important role to play in reducing emissions. Within the end-use sectors, energy efficiency measures in the buildings sector needs to play the biggest role in the next two decades, while the importance of industry and transport increases in the later decades. To meet the BLUE scenario emissions objectives, deep emission reductions are needed even in the transport sector beyond 2030.

Figure 2.3 ▶ **Reduction of energy-related CO_2 emissions from the Baseline scenario in the BLUE Map scenario by sector, 2005-2050**

Emissions (Gt CO_2)
70
60
50
40
30
20
10
0
Baseline emissions 62 Gt
BLUE Map emissions 14 Gt
WEO 2007 450 ppm case
ETP 2008 analysis
2005 2010 2015 2020 2025 2030 2035 2040 2045 2050
Power sector (38%)
Industry (19%)
Buildings (17%)
Transport (26%)

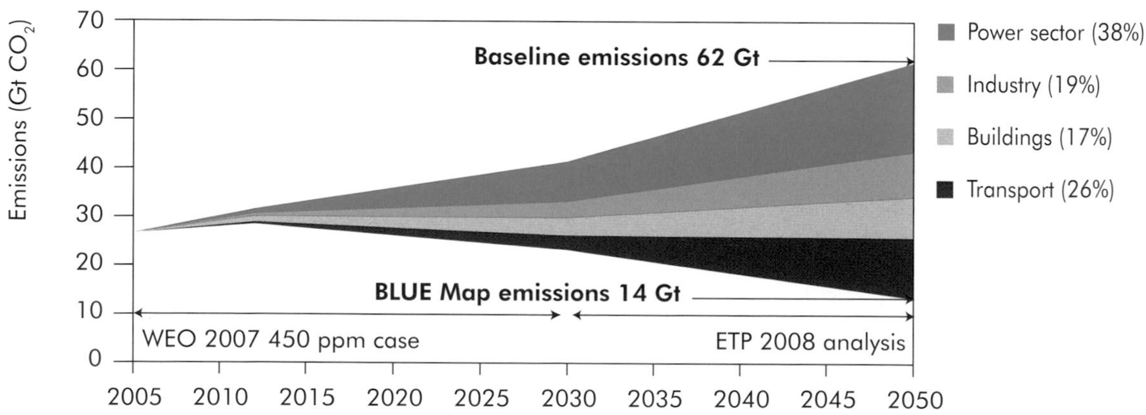

Key point

The share of end-use sectors in emission reduction increases between 2030 and 2050.

In the ACT Map and BLUE Map scenarios, OECD countries account for 30% of the total global emissions reduction compared to the Baseline scenario. In BLUE Map where a least-cost approach is aimed for, OECD countries reduce their emissions by more than half compared to 2005 levels, while non-OECD countries reduce their emissions by less than half. The difference reflects much higher economic growth in developing countries than in the OECD countries in coming decades, and it implies a significant effort in non-OECD countries. The sharing of the financial burden for such change is beyond the scope of this study.

In the ACT Map scenario, end-use efficiency provides the most emission reductions (44%) (Figure 2.4). Power generation accounts for 43% of the emissions reduction. This order of importance changes in the BLUE Map scenario: end-use efficiency accounts for 36% and changes in power generation account for 38%. CCS in power generation, fuel transformation and industry accounts for 14% to 19% of the total emissions reduction (Figure 2.4). Renewables account for 16% to 21% of the total emissions reduction. About a quarter of the renewables contribution in the BLUE Map scenario comes from biofuels, with most of the remainder from the use of renewables in the power sector. It should be noted that this underestimates the importance of nuclear and hydropower, as both options play already an important role in Baseline.

Figure 2.4 ▶ Reduction in CO_2 emissions from the Baseline scenario in the ACT Map and BLUE Map scenarios by technology area, 2050

ACT Map 35 Gt CO_2 reduction

Power fossil fuel switching and efficiency 17%
End-use fuel switching 1%
End-use fuel efficiency 28%
Electricity end-use efficiency 16%
Electrification 2%
Total renewables 16%
CCS power 8%
CCS industry and transformation 6%
Nuclear 6%

BLUE Map 48 Gt CO_2 reduction

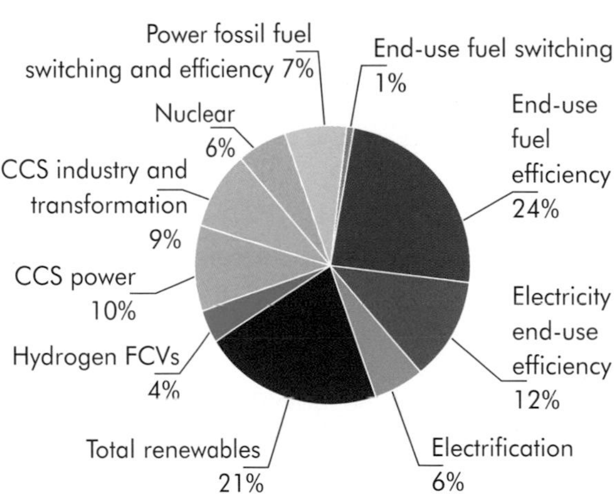

Note: CCS share accounts for the loss in energy efficiency.

Key point

End-use efficiency and power-generation options account for the bulk of emissions reduction.

Box 2.3 ▶ Costs and economic impacts

In this analysis:

- *Fuel prices ignore excise taxes and subsidies. Average current gasoline excise taxes in Europe equal about USD 400/t CO_2. A CO_2 incentive of USD 200/t CO_2 is equivalent to additional oil cost of around USD 80 per barrel (bbl).*

- *Transaction costs have not been specifically considered. This may underestimate costs in cases where millions of small-scale investment decisions are involved.*

- *Policy costs have been split into research, development and demonstration, deployment and technology learning, and investment. The cost of each of these components has been assessed separately (Chapters 4-6).*

- *All options are evaluated based on discounted costs. The discount rate varies by sector and by country. Regional and sector-specific discount rates have been applied that reflect a combination of capital availability and risk aversion.*

A switch from fossil fuels to other forms of energy will have supply security benefits. With the reduced levels of demand envisaged in the ACT and BLUE scenarios, oil and gas prices may fall, although this would be offset by the assumed carbon incentive which, at USD 200/t (the equivalent of USD 80/bbl) would represent a significant increase of oil and gas prices for end-users. For example, the oil price the consumers would "see" in the BLUE scenarios if the incentives were taxes based on the carbon content of the oil products would be the USD 120/bbl to USD 130/bbl price, despite lower global market prices. The actual level of oil and gas world market price reductions due to CO_2 policies is uncertain.

The study is based on a partial equilibrium model. While this approach provides important insights into the cost of policies for consumers and for the whole economy, the analysis does not assess the full GDP impacts. The re-distribution of production factors will affect the growth potential of the economy. Other studies have looked into the impact of climate policies on the global economic structure and economic growth. A recent OECD study has assessed the economic impacts of a 450 ppm scenario, which would equal a 45% reduction in global emissions by 2050 relative to 2005 levels – i.e. approximately the level aimed for in the BLUE scenarios. World GDP would be reduced by 2.4% in 2050 relative to the Baseline scenario. This would be equivalent to slowing annual world GDP growth rates by about one-tenth of one percent (0.1%) over 2005 to 2050. However, it should be noted that emission growth in the Reference Scenario of the OECD study is considerably lower than that of the Energy Technology Perspectives Baseline scenario, which helps to keep the cost down.

IPCC estimates also suggest that GDP impacts are of secondary importance, estimating that stabilisation around 550 ppm CO_2-eq would cost less than 1% of gross world product. For stabilisation between 445 and 535 ppm CO_2 eq, costs are less than 3% of GDP (IPCC 2007, pages 79-80). However, there may be important wealth-distribution consequences.

The IEA World Energy Outlook 2008 will model new frameworks for different stabilisation levels and their impacts on prices, investment levels and economic growth.

Sources: OECD, 2008; IPCC, 2007.

Table 2.1 provides a breakdown of emission reductions by technology option within each sector. The table shows the important contribution of the power sector in the ACT Map scenario and the importance of deep emission cuts in all end-use sectors in the BLUE Map scenario. A range of technologies is needed to meet the policy targets. Roadmaps for the most important technologies are elaborated in more detail in Chapter 3.

Table 2.1 ▶ **Emission reductions by sector and technology option in the ACT Map and BLUE Map scenarios in 2050**

	CO_2 Reduction ACT Map (Gt CO_2/yr)	**CO_2 Reduction BLUE Map** (Gt CO_2/yr)
Total	**35**	**48**
Power generation	**13.9**	**18.3**
CCS power generation	2.9	4.8
Wind	1.3	2.1
Solar – PV	0.7	1.3
Solar – CSP	0.6	1.2
Nuclear	2.0	2.8
IGCC	0.7	0.7
Ultra/Supercritical coal	0.7	0.7
BIGCC and biomass co-combustion	0.2	1.5
Gas efficiency	0.8	0.4
Fuel switching coal to gas	3.8	1.8
Hydro	0.3	0.4
Geothermal	0.1	0.6
Buildings	**7.0**	**8.2**
Fuel savings	2.0	2.5
Electricity efficiency	4.5	4.5
Solar heating	0.2	0.5
Heat pumps	0.3	0.8
Transport	**8.2**	**12.5**
Fuel efficiency	6.0	6.6
2nd generation biofuels	1.8	2.2
Plug-ins and electric vehicles	0.5	2.0
Hydrogen fuel-cell vehicles (FCVs)	0.0	1.8
Industry (incl. BF + coke ovens)	**5.7**	**9.2**
CCS industry and fuel transformation	2.0	4.3
Electric efficiency	1.0	1.4
Fuel efficiency	1.9	2.3
Fuel and feedstock switching	0.8	1.2

Note: Industry excludes process CO_2 emission reductions for cement. Blast furnaces and coke ovens have been allocated to industry. Transportation accounts for well-to-wheel effects (including fuel transformation). Emission reductions in power generation due to electricity savings in end-use sectors have been allocated to the end-use sectors. CCS is corrected for efficiency losses. CCS for CHP is allocated to the power sector and to industry following IEA energy accounting guidelines. BF=blast furnaces; BIGCC=biomass integrated gasifier combined cycle; CSP=concentrating solar power; FCV=fuel-cell vehicle; IGCC=integrated gasifier combined cycle.

The contribution of most technology options increases in the BLUE Map scenario compared to the ACT Map scenario. Exceptionally, the contribution of fuel switching from coal to gas in power generation and the efficiency improvement of gas-fired power plants decreases between the ACT Map and BLUE Map scenarios, as the share of fossil-fuelled – especially gas-fired – power generation in total power generation decreases. While a switch to gas can help to reduce emissions substantially compared to coal-fired power generation, it is not a CO_2-free power generation option. CCS is relatively expensive when applied to gas-fired power plants, so gas becomes a less attractive option in the BLUE scenarios. This case shows that more stringent policy goals can result in a very different energy system structure. Policies that raise the CO_2 target incrementally risk a lock-in of options and strategies that are unsuited for deep emission cuts. Clear and credible long-term targets can avoid such lock-in.

Power generation

The power generation sector is significantly influenced by CO_2 reduction incentives. Emissions are reduced considerably in the ACT and BLUE scenarios, partly due to reduced demand for electricity as a result of end-use efficiency gains. Electricity demand in the ACT Map scenario is 21% lower than in the Baseline scenario. Further efficiency gains in the BLUE Map scenario are dwarfed by the additional demand for CO_2-free electrification in buildings and in the transport sector (notably for heat pumps and plug-in hybrids). Electricity demand in the BLUE Map scenario is therefore only 15% below the Baseline scenario level and 17% above the demand in the ACT Map scenario.

Coal's share of power generation declines from 52% in the Baseline scenario to 17% in the ACT Map scenario. At the same time, gas increases from 21% to 29%. This represents a significant reduction in the average carbon intensity of electricity from fossil-fuelled power plants. In the BLUE Map scenario, the share of coal is slightly lower than in the ACT Map scenario (13%). The share of gas declines significantly (to 17%), reflecting the fact that CCS – applied to virtually all coal-fired power stations in BLUE Map – is significantly more expensive per tonne of CO_2 saved for gas than for coal. About 70% of gas-fired power is generated from plants equipped with CCS. In capacity terms, however, the share of plants with CCS is much lower, as gas peaking plants play an important role in the scenario. They act as backup for variable renewables, with a low number of operating hours.

Nuclear power generation already plays an important role in the Baseline scenario, with capacity increasing from 368 GW to 570 GW in 2050, and output increasing by 41%. As most of the standing capacity must be replaced in the next 45 years, the Baseline scenario implies on average more than 10 new reactors per year. Without this capacity replacement, more CO_2-emitting capacity would need to be built and emissions would be even higher. The nuclear share rises further in the ACT Map and BLUE Map scenarios. Nuclear power is constrained in the model at 1 250 GW, in order to reflect growth limitations based on past experience of maximum annual reactor construction rates (about 30 GW per year). Modelling of an increase to 2 000 GW (the HiNuclear scenario) shows that further nuclear expansion would be cost-effective in both scenarios, largely at the expense of fossil-fuelled plants with CCS. However it remains unclear whether such an increase would be acceptable or feasible, as it would imply fuel reprocessing on a massive scale, which poses a challenge for non-proliferation and the economics of nuclear power. The main insight from this scenario is that an even greater expansion of nuclear does not result in a further substantial reduction of emissions. The nuclear growth is largely at the expense of fossil-fuelled power plants with CCS.

The total share of renewables in power generation increases to 35% in the ACT Map scenario and to 46% in the BLUE Map scenario. In comparison, the current share of renewables is 18%. As total electricity production also more than doubles in the BLUE Map scenario between 2005 and 2050, it implies a more than four-fold increase of power production from renewables. Most of the growth is in emerging renewable technologies: wind, solar, biomass, and to a lesser extent geothermal. The use of hydropower also doubles from today's level.

CO_2 capture and storage (CCS)

The use of CCS in the industrial, fuel transformation and power-generation sectors accounts for 14% of the emissions reduction in the ACT Map scenario and 19% in the BLUE Map scenario. The total amount of CO_2 captured is 5.1 Gt to 10.4 Gt.

The growth of CCS between the ACT Map and BLUE Map scenarios accounts for 32% of the additional emissions reduction in the latter. The CO_2 reduction – using future advanced technologies – is approximately 10% to 20% lower than the total amount of CO_2 captured because CCS itself entails significant additional energy use. Fifty-four percent of this capture takes place in the power sector in the BLUE Map scenario (Figure 2.5). The remainder takes place in the fuel-transformation sector (refineries, synfuel production, blast furnaces) and in manufacturing industry such as cement kilns, ammonia plants and industrial CHP units.

In the power sector, the retrofit of power plants with CO_2 capture plays an important role in the ACT Map scenario. It plays a smaller part in the BLUE Map scenario, where CCS is adopted earlier into new build capacity. In the ACT Map scenario, 239 GW of coal-fired capacity is retrofitted with CCS by 2050, while 379 GW of new capacity is equipped with CCS. The new plants are largely IGCC based. In the BLUE Map scenario, only 157 GW of coal-fired capacity is retrofitted with CCS, while 543 GW of new capacity with CCS is installed. In the ACT Map scenario, 280 GW of new gas-fired capacity is equipped with CCS; this increases to 817 GW in the BLUE Map scenario. This includes industrial large-scale combined heat and power generation units (CHP). In addition, black liquor gasifiers are equipped with CCS in both scenarios and CCS is increasingly applied to industrial processes (e.g. cement kilns and iron production processes) and in the fuel-transformation sector (e.g. hydrogen production for refineries). CCS is especially important for industry because it is the only way to achieve deep emission cuts in the production of key commodities such as steel and cement.

Figure 2.5 ▶ **Use of CO_2 capture and storage in the ACT Map and BLUE Map scenarios**

BLUE Map 10.4 Gt CO_2 captured

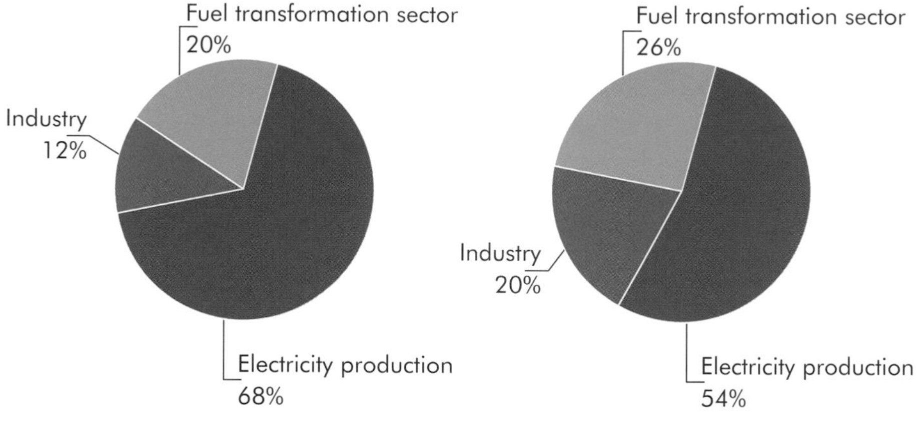

Key point

CO_2 capture and storage can play a key role outside the power sector.

Fuel switching in end-use sectors

Fuel switching in end-use sectors plays an important role in reducing emissions. Fuel switching to less carbon-intensive fuels in buildings, industry and transportation contributes between 9% and 16% of the CO_2 emissions reduction depending on the scenario.

In the Baseline scenario, electricity use triples and electricity increases its share of total final consumption from 17% in 2005 to 26% in 2050, despite significant energy efficiency gains. This is due to the rapid growth in electric end-uses such as appliances. There is also an impact from the increased use of electricity as a substitute for fossil fuels; particularly for heat pumps, and especially in countries where the CO_2 intensity of power generation is low. The share of electricity stays at 26% of total final consumption in the ACT Map scenario, but rises to 30% in the BLUE Map scenario in 2050, as low-carbon electricity increasingly substitutes for fossil-fuel uses.

In the ACT Map scenario, coal and oil lose market share in favour of gas and renewables. End-use fuel-switching accounts for 8% of the total CO_2 reduction, which equals approximately 2.9 Gt CO_2. The share of renewables in final energy use increases from 9% in the Baseline scenario to 16% in the ACT Map scenario.

The BLUE Map scenario assumes significant electrification in the buildings and transport sectors. In the buildings sector, heat pumps play an increasing role. In the transport sector, the scenarios assume an important role for plug-in hybrid and electric vehicles. These changes result in a rise in electricity demand of the order of 4 000 TWh. The CO_2 impact depends on the CO_2 intensity of electricity generation. In the BLUE Map scenario, the electricity sector is virtually decarbonised.

In 2050, the share of renewables in end-use increases to 23% in the BLUE Map scenario. Biomass plays a key role in the both the ACT Map and BLUE scenarios. In the BLUE scenario its use quadruples compared to baseline. At the same time, the efficiency of biomass use rises considerably as traditional biomass is phased out and modern biomass technologies gain significant market shares.

In the buildings sector, the use of biomass is constant in the Baseline scenario. Its use declines in the ACT Map and BLUE Map scenarios but, as it is used much more efficiently, the share of biomass in delivered energy services increases. Solar water heating and space heating systems increase more than threefold in the ACT Map scenario and six-fold between the Baseline and BLUE Map scenarios.

In 2050, the share of biomass and waste in industry increases from 6% in 2005 to 12% in the ACT Map scenario, and to 18% in the BLUE Map scenario. Part of this is biomass for steam and process heat. Biomass feedstocks also play an increasing role.

The ACT Map and BLUE Map scenarios assume a significant use of biofuels. In the transport sector, biofuels play an important role in emissions reduction. Their use increases from 19 Mtoe in 2005 to 570 Mtoe in the ACT Map scenario and 693 Mtoe in the BLUE Map scenario (Mtoe – million tonnes oil equivalent). Biomass is used differently in the BLUE scenario, to reach the modes of transport that lack other options (especially trucks, ships and aircraft). This results in an emphasis on second-generation biodiesel instead of bioethanol production. Cars and light trucks appear more likely to be amenable to switching to electricity and hydrogen fuel, especially after 2030, and may not need substantial biofuels to achieve large cuts in CO_2. However, the use of biofuels for all modes will depend on development of viable, sustainable, second-generation technologies that are not available today at acceptable cost. A major change in the world's effective management of agricultural and natural lands will also be needed.

Achieving deep emission reductions in the transport sector will be challenging. In both Map scenarios, modal shifts drive a reduction of about 15% in car, truck and air travel by 2050 relative to the baseline as more people use efficient public transportation. Far deeper reductions may be needed and strong policies to moderate travel growth may be required. But the prospects for new propulsion systems and fuel switching in transport depend on technology breakthroughs that cannot be reliably forecast at this stage. Electric vehicles (EVs) and hydrogen fuel cell vehicles will compete in the light-duty vehicle market, with plug-in electric hybrid vehicles a likely interim option. The "BLUE FCV Success" and "BLUE EV Success" variants assume over 90% sales share of fuel cell vehicles and electric vehicles respectively in all OECD countries by 2040, with non-OECD countries following about five to ten years later.

End-use energy efficiency improvements

In total, energy efficiency improvements constitute the single largest contributor to CO_2 emission reductions in both the ACT Map and BLUE Map scenarios. This is on top of significant efficiency gains in the Baseline scenario.

Final energy demand in 2050 is 3 311 Mtoe to 5 155 Mtoe (23% to 33%) lower in the ACT Map and BLUE Map scenarios than in the Baseline scenario. In the BLUE Map scenario, around 18% of this reduction occurs in industry, 40% in the transport sector and 37% in the buildings sector. These figures include the full benefits of electrification on final energy savings (electric technologies often have much higher end-use efficiencies than those using gas or oil products, but this excludes the losses in power generation).

Since 1973, global energy intensity (final energy use per unit of GDP) has declined at an average rate of 1.5% per year. This historical decoupling of energy consumption and economic growth has been the main factor restraining the growth of CO_2 emissions; the carbon intensity of energy use (CO_2 emissions per unit of energy) changed very little between 1973 and 2005. There are important differences in the rate of decline between regions. OECD countries achieved a rapid decline in energy intensity following the oil price shocks of the 1970s. However, since then the rate of reduction has slowed considerably and averaged at only 1.1% per year between 1990 and 2005, which is half the rate seen between 1973 and 1990. But as a result of particularly strong decoupling of energy use from economic growth in developing countries and transition economies, the overall rate of energy intensity reduction since 1990 has been slightly higher than in earlier decades.

Developments in final energy intensity result from a combination of changes in energy efficiency and changes in economic structure. Structural changes, such as a shift from the production of raw materials to less energy-intensive manufactured products, can play a significant role in some countries.

Since 1973, final energy intensity in a group of 11 OECD (OECD-11) countries has fallen by an average of 1.6% per year, with improvements in energy efficiency (corrected for structural changes) accounting for around three-quarters of this decline (IEA, 2004, 2007b). However, very different rates of energy intensity reduction and energy efficiency improvements were seen over time. In the years immediately following the oil price shocks of the early 1970s, final energy intensity decreased rapidly, largely as a result of energy efficiency improvements running at around 2.5% per year. Since then, lower rates of energy efficiency improvement have been the major reason for the slowdown in final energy intensity reductions. Since 1990, improvements in energy efficiency have averaged just less than 1% per year.

Differences in the rates of final energy intensity reduction and energy efficiency improvement are also seen among these countries. For instance, between 1973 and 2004, the rate of energy efficiency improvement in the United States and Germany averaged around 1.5% per year, whereas the rate of improvement in Japan (which already had low final energy intensity in 1973) was around half this level.

The impact of these energy efficiency improvements in OECD countries has been to significantly restrain the growth in final energy consumption. Without the energy efficiency improvements achieved since 1973, final 2004 energy use in the OECD-11 would have been 56% higher in 2004 than it actually was (Figure 2.7).

Figure 2.6 ▶ **Energy efficiency gains and structural change in major OECD countries, 1973-2004**

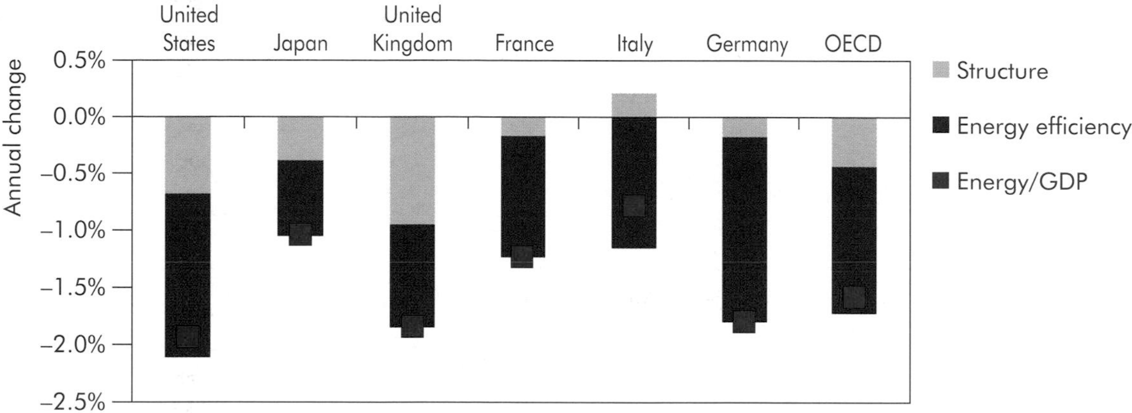

Note: "OECD" includes the following 11 countries: Australia, Denmark, Finland, France, Germany, Italy, Japan, Norway, Sweden, the United Kingdom and the United States, which together account for more than 75% of current total final energy use in OECD countries.

Sources: IEA, 2004 and IEA, 2007b.

Key point

In OECD countries, improvements in energy efficiency have been the most important factor driving reductions in final energy intensity.

Figure 2.7 ▶ **Long-term energy savings from improvements in energy efficiency, OECD-11, 1973-2004**

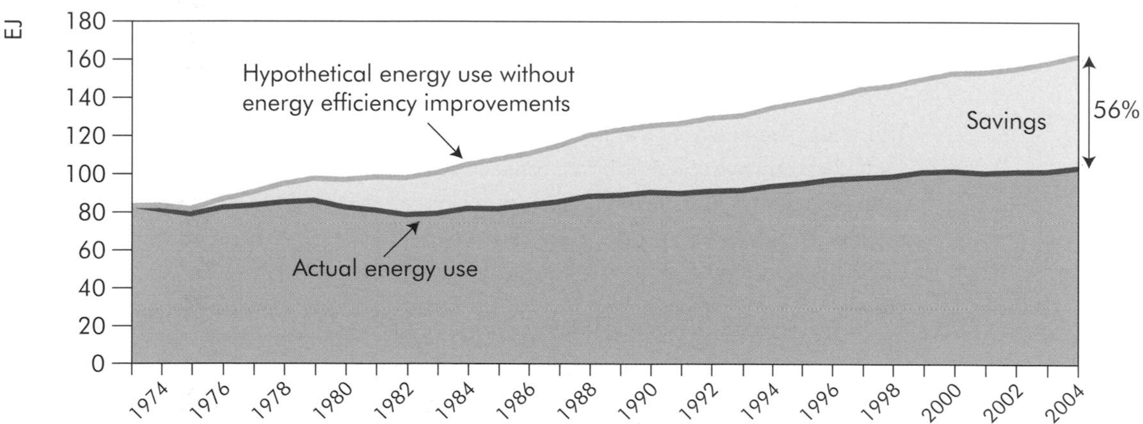

Source: IEA, 2007b.

Key point

Without 30 years of energy savings from improved energy efficiency, energy consumption in OECD countries would be more than 50% higher today.

The further decoupling of energy use and economic growth continues under all of the scenarios (Figure 2.8). Under the Baseline scenario, global final energy intensity falls at a rate similar to that seen over the past 30 years. This means that, by 2050, the amount of energy used on average to produce one unit of GDP will be less than half that needed today. In the ACT Map scenario, the global decline in energy intensity increases to an average rate of 2.2% per year between 2005 and 2050. This reduction in final energy intensity accelerates in the BLUE Map scenario to 2.5% per year, meaning that in this scenario, energy use per unit of GDP in 2050 is only about 30% of its level in 2005.

Figure 2.8 ▶ Historical and projected future changes in final energy consumption per unit of GDP, by region

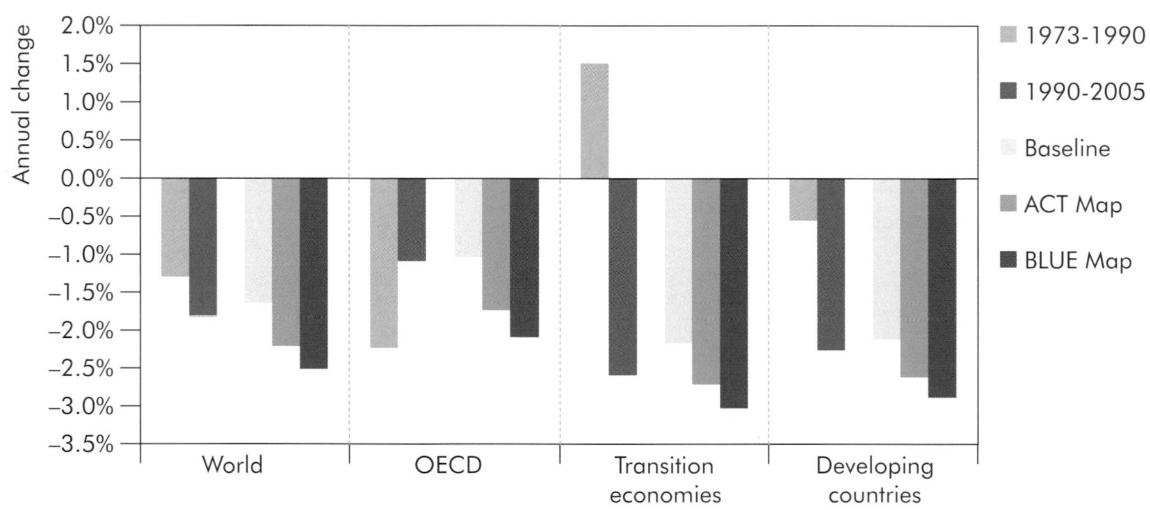

Key point

Under the ACT Map and BLUE Map scenarios, very strong reductions in final energy intensity occur across all regions.

The energy intensity of the transition economies declines by more than that of the OECD countries in all scenarios, reflecting the significant energy efficiency potential in these countries. Many developing countries have experienced rapid economic growth in recent years and have also seen their energy consumption relative to GDP decline rapidly with the modernisation of their economies. In the Baseline scenario, the strong decline in energy intensity continues, but at a slower rate than between 1990 and 2005. The introduction of more energy efficient end-use technologies in the ACT Map scenario increases the decline in energy intensity in developing countries to a rate slightly higher than in recent years. In the BLUE Map scenario this decline in the final energy intensity of developing countries increases to 2.9% per year.

Global economic growth in the Baseline scenario averages 3.3% per year between 2005 and 2050, whereas the average annual increase in final energy consumption is only 1.6% (Figure 2.9). This means that whereas global GDP more than quadruples over the period to 2050, final energy demand doubles. As in the past, the decoupling of energy consumption from economic growth results both from a structural and an energy efficiency effect. Changes in the structure of the economy lead to the underlying demand for energy services growing at 2.4% per year, a substantially lower rate than that of GDP. On average this structural effect therefore reduces final energy intensity by 0.8% per year. A somewhat larger impact on final energy intensity is due to the rate of energy efficiency improvements, which average 0.9% per year. This rate of improvement is in line with what has been achieved by OECD countries since 1990. In the Baseline scenario, the combined impacts of both structural and efficiency effects leads to a reduction in final energy intensity of 1.7% per year.

Over the period from 2005 to 2050, the cumulative energy savings from these improvements in energy efficiency play a significant role in limiting the increase in final energy demand under the Baseline scenario. In the absence of these savings, final energy demand would be 45% higher in 2050 (*i.e.* final energy demand would almost triple, rather than double).

Figure 2.9 ► Global trends in factors affecting final energy use under the Baseline scenario

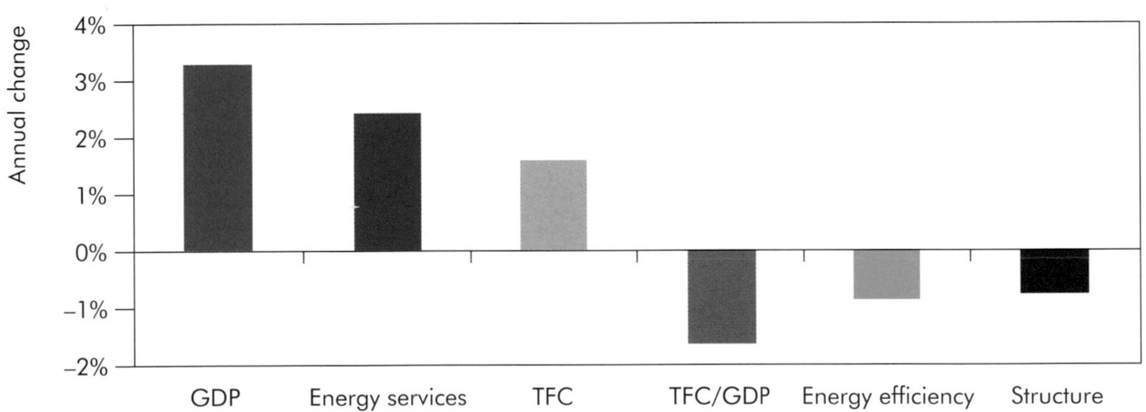

Note: The negative value for energy efficiency represents an improvement.

Key point

A combination of energy efficiency improvements and structural changes are responsible for reducing final energy intensity under the Baseline scenario.

In the ACT Map and BLUE Map scenarios there are substantial energy savings in the final demand sectors compared to the Baseline scenario, due to improvements in energy efficiency. In the ACT Map scenario, the rate of energy efficiency improvement increases to 1.4% per year from 0.9% in the Baseline scenario. This drives a reduction in final energy intensity of from 1.6% to 2.2% per year.

In the BLUE Map scenario, the increased deployment of new technologies further increases improvements in energy efficiency to 1.7% per year, with final energy intensity decreasing in line with these improvements to 2.5% per year (Figure 2.10). Structural effects are assumed to be the same under all three scenarios.

Figure 2.10 ▶ Contribution of energy efficiency and structural changes to reductions in final energy intensity under the scenarios

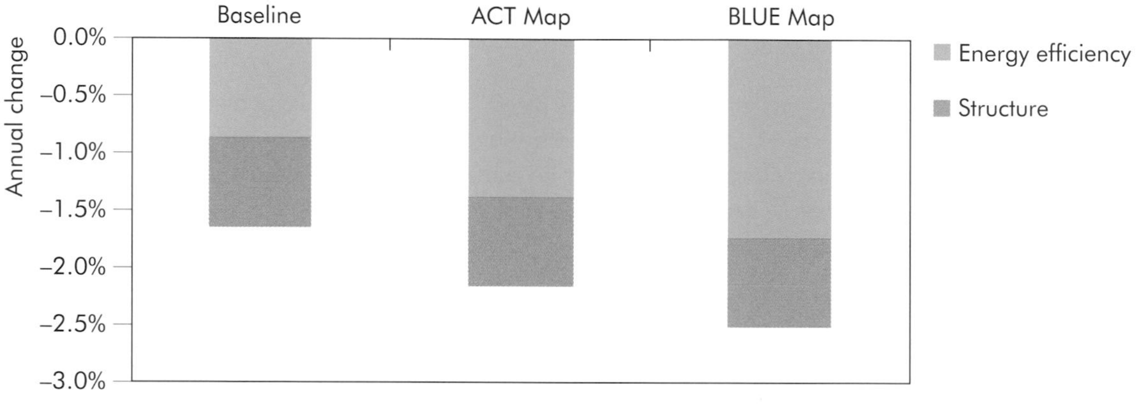

Key point

Increases in the rate of energy efficiency improvement are responsible for the faster reductions in final energy intensity under the ACT Map and BLUE Map scenarios.

Box 2.4 ▶ Final energy intensity trends in China: the role of energy efficiency and structural change

Between 1980 and 2000, China achieved a quadrupling of its GDP with only a doubling of energy consumption, showing a significant decoupling of the relationship between economic growth and energy consumption. This was a significant achievement, as increases in energy use typically tend to be faster than economic growth in the early stage of industrialisation.

The significant reductions in energy intensity were driven largely by improvements in energy efficiency. In 1980, the Chinese government began two major reforms. These involved allocating capital investment to energy efficiency and creating a network of energy conservation service centres throughout China. The institutions implementing energy efficiency continued to exert substantial influence through the mid-1990s.

Further analysis of the effect of efficiency changes and structural shift in nine industrial sub-sectors shows that from 1996 to 2003 there was steady efficiency improvement in China. However, the rate of efficiency improvement has slowed down somewhat since 2000 (see Figure 2.11). In the meantime, structural shifts within industrial sub-sectors, including a rapid growth in cement and steel production, have since 2001 more than offset the effect of efficiency improvements. In 2003, efficiency improvements in energy use in the industry sector was only about 30% of the increase in efficiency intensity due to structural shifts among industrial sub-sectors. As a result, the overall energy intensity of industry is higher today than its recent low point in 2001.

Figure 2.11 ▶ Contribution of energy efficiency and structure to changes in industrial energy consumption in China

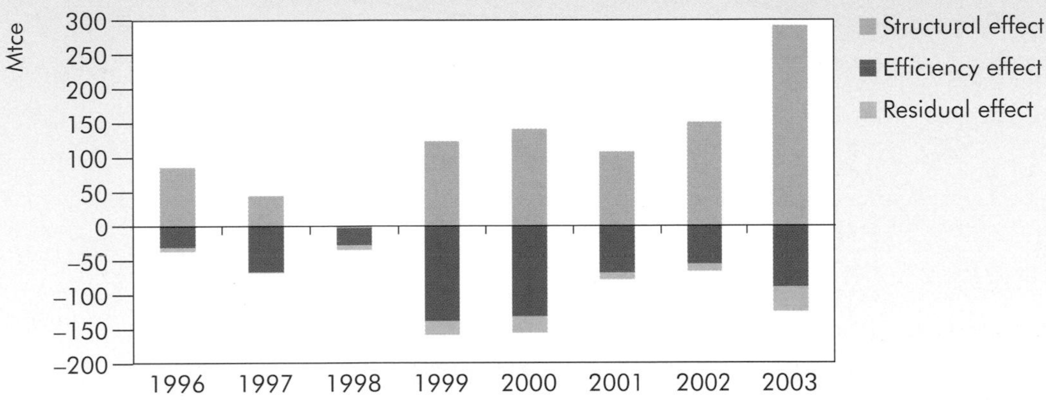

Source: Lin, *et al.*, 2006.

Key point

Recent increases in final energy intensity of China are due to the rapid expansion of energy intensive industrial sectors such as cement and steel.

Energy demand and CO_2 emissions by sector

Energy use increases in all sectors in the Baseline scenario. Energy use roughly doubles in power generation, industry, transportation and buildings. The timing of the growth differs, with an early rapid rise in industry as developing countries industrialise. The energy used for fuel transformation accelerates from an average annual growth rate of 2% between 2005 and 2030 to 4% per year between 2030 and 2050. This is due to the increased production of synfuels from coal and gas. The switch to coal for production of liquid transportation fuels is the main reason for the increasing rate of CO_2 emissions growth in the Baseline scenario after 2030.

Energy consumption in the transport, buildings and industry sectors increases on average by 1.5% per year between 2005 and 2050 in the Baseline scenario, *i.e.* slightly less than the 1.7% per year between 1971 and 2005. Driven by continued strong population and income growth in developing countries, transportation demand increases on average by 1.8% per year between 2005 and 2050. Energy consumption in the industrial sector grows at an average of 1.6% per year. About 64% of the growth in industrial energy consumption occurs in developing countries. Energy use in the buildings sector grows slightly more slowly, however, at on average 1.3% per year, with around 70% of this growth coming from developing countries.

Figure 2.12 ▶ Energy use by sector in the Baseline scenario

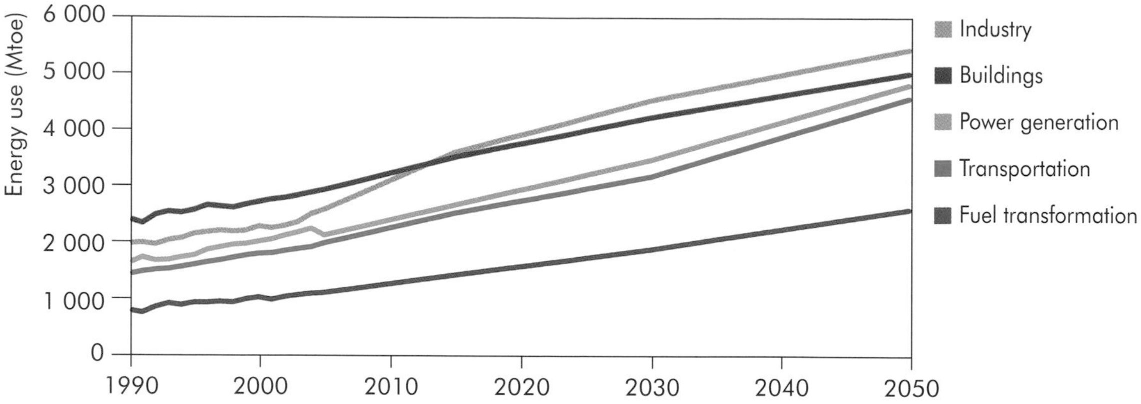

Note: Final energy use for end-use sectors, net consumption of power and fuel for the transformation sectors. The power-generation sector includes heat plants.

Key point

Baseline energy demand continues to grow rapidly in all sectors.

Emission reductions by sector for ACT Map and BLUE Map are shown in Table 2.2. Two indicators are used, one for the emissions reduction compared to the base year 2005, and the other for the emissions reduction compared to the Baseline scenario in 2050. The first is a measure for the emission reduction in absolute terms, the second is a measure for the reduction in CO_2 intensity (CO_2/energy). Table 2.2 shows that the effort in terms of intensity improvement is comparable across all end-use sectors. However, because the growth rate of the activity differs, the emissions reduction is quite different in absolute terms and emissions increase in some sectors in the ACT Map scenario, compared to the 2005 level.

Table 2.2 ▶ Percentage emission reductions by sector in ACT Map and BLUE Map, 2050

	Absolute reduction		Intensity reduction	
	ACT Map (%)	BLUE Map (%)	ACT Map (%)	BLUE Map (%)
Reference	**2005**	**2005**	**Baseline 2050**	**Baseline 2050**
Power sector	–43	–71	–81	–90
Other transformation	16	–62	–51	–84
Transport	31	–30	–42	–69
Industry	65	–21	–18	–60
Buildings	–2	–41	–36	–61
Total	2	–48	–57	–78

Note: Industry includes blast furnaces and coke ovens, as well as emissions from non-energy use of petrochemical feedstocks. Industrial process emissions are excluded.

In the ACT Map scenario, the net energy consumption of the electricity generation and heat sector grows by 15% between 2005 and 2050. Energy consumption in the fuel transformation sectors doubles. Synfuels from coal are largely replaced by increased biofuels production.

In the BLUE Map scenario, the net energy consumption for power generation increases by 21% compared to 2005. The increase in the BLUE Map scenario compared to the ACT Map scenario is due to increased demand for electricity and a switch to less-efficient but carbon-free forms of power generation. The energy consumed in the fuel-transformation sector – which includes refineries, coal-to-liquid, gas-to-liquid, blast furnaces and coke ovens – is about 10% less than in the Baseline scenario. The lower demand can be explained by end-use fuel demand reductions and changes in the iron and steel industry.

Energy savings compared to Baseline are achieved across all end-use sectors in all of the ACT and BLUE scenarios, although to differing degrees (Table 2.3). The largest reductions in energy use in the ACT Map scenario occur in the buildings sector, reflecting the significant technical potential to reduce space heating and cooling needs in both existing and new buildings, as well as to improve the energy efficiency of lighting, electric appliances and equipment.

Table 2.3 ▶ End-use energy savings in 2050 under ACT Map and BLUE Map, relative to the Baseline scenario

	Demand 2005 (Mtoe/yr)	Demand Baseline 2050 (Mtoe/yr)	Baseline Annual change 2005-2050 (%/yr)	ACT Map Annual change 2005-2050 (%/yr)	BLUE Map Annual change 2005-2050 (%/yr)	ACT Map Change compared to Baseline 2050 (%)	BLUE Map Change compared to Baseline 2050 (%)
Industry	2 564	5 415	1.7	1.5	1.3	–8.8	–16.9
Transportation	2 141	4 729	1.8	1.0	0.5	–30.8	–43.8
Buildings	2 913	5 234	1.3	0.4	0.2	–32.0	–39.8
Non-energy use	129	306	1.9	1.9	1.4	0.0	–20.2
Total end-use	7 748	15 683	1.6	1.0	0.7	–23.0	–32.9

Note: Non-energy use of petrochemical feedstocks is included in industry.

Energy savings in transport are also very significant in the BLUE Map scenario, reflecting innovations in both engine technologies and vehicle design. Industry makes somewhat smaller savings, reflecting the high efficiencies already achieved in a number of energy-intensive sectors and the need for energy that is intrinsic in most industrial processes.

In all sectors, energy demand continues to grow between 2005 and 2050. The highest growth rate is attained in industry, followed by transportation and buildings.

Final energy consumption in the industry, buildings and transport sectors grows on average 1.0% per year in the ACT Map scenario and 0.7% per year in the BLUE Map scenario (Table 2.3).

Total final energy demand is 23% lower in the ACT Map scenario in 2050 and 33% lower in the BLUE Map scenario compared to the Baseline scenario (Figure 2.13). Absolute savings in the industry sector in the BLUE Map scenario total about 900 Mtoe, around one-third of this is in OECD countries and two-thirds is in non-OECD countries. In the Buildings sector, savings total 2 083 Mtoe, with slightly less coming from OECD countries than from non-OECD countries. The buildings sector alone accounts for about 70% of the savings in electricity in the BLUE Map scenario. In the transport sector, total savings amount to around 1 954 Mtoe, with slightly larger savings coming from developing countries than from OECD countries.

Figure 2.13 ▶ Final energy use by sector in the Baseline, ACT Map and BLUE Map scenarios

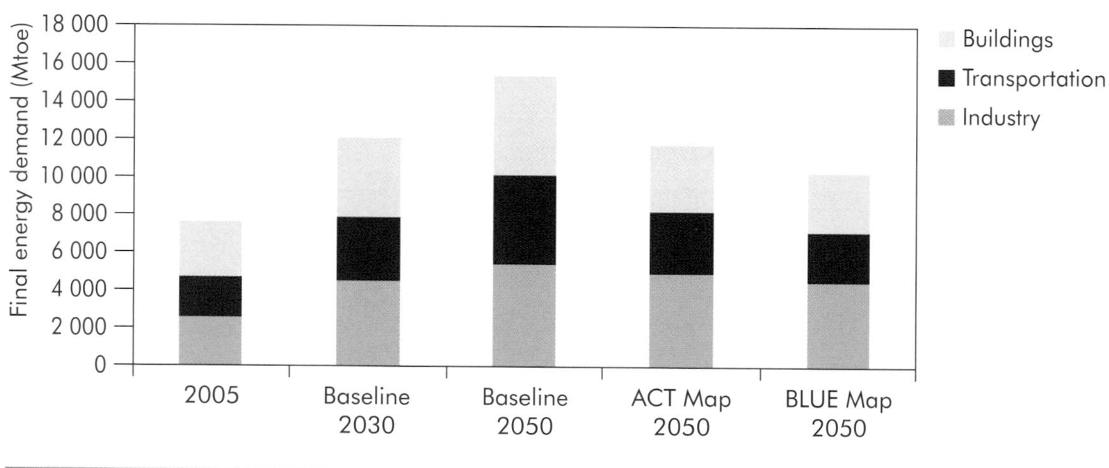

Key point

Final energy demand in ACT Map and BLUE Map is significantly less than in Baseline in 2050.

Figure 2.14 shows the marginal emission abatement curve against the Baseline for progressively more expensive technologies in terms of cost per tonne of CO_2 reduced. The y-axis shows the cost of the most expensive option that is applied to meet different levels of emissions reduction (on the x-axis). The cost bands reflect the difference between an optimistic view and a pessimistic view of specific technology developments.

The approximate position of categories of options is indicated by the arrows. While the objectives implicit in the ACT Map scenario can be achieved with end-use efficiency and changes in power generation, achievement of the BLUE Map scenario objectives will also require more costly measures in other end-use sectors.

Figure 2.14 ▶ Marginal emission reduction costs for the global energy system, 2050

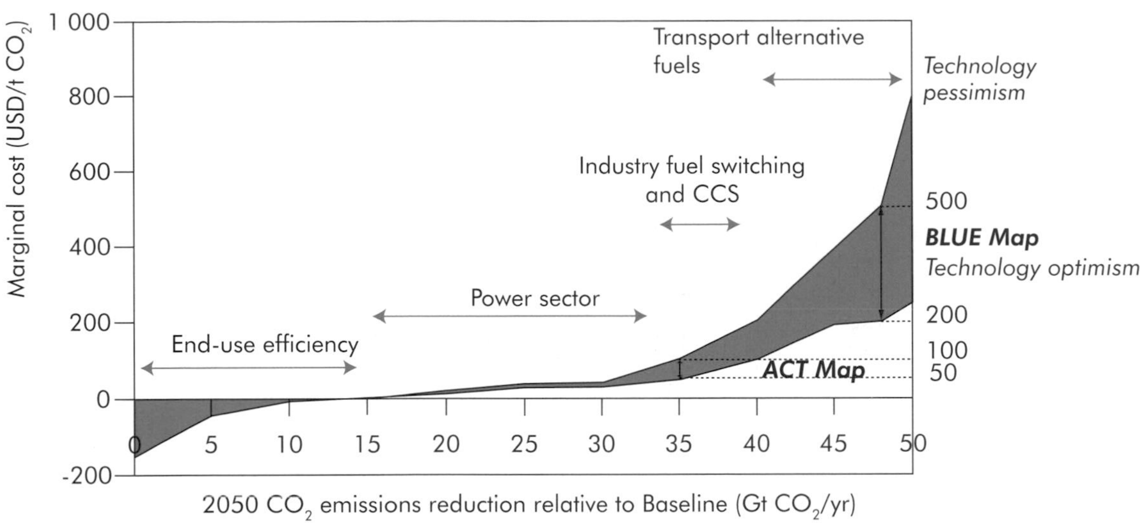

Key point

Marginal costs increase significantly between ACT Map and BLUE Map, and the cost uncertainty increases.

Figure 2.14 is a schematic, greatly simplified, representation. The curve consists of hundreds of options. It conveys, however, some important messages:

First, costs are relatively flat up to the ACT Map scenario objective of stabilising emissions at 2005 levels in 2050. But they rise quickly as the additional emissions reduction technologies implicit in the BLUE Map scenario are required.

Second, although there is a high degree of uncertainty about the cost of the cheapest reduction measures, they are clearly negative. There is less uncertainty about the cost of technologies needed to achieve the ACT Map target. But costs become more uncertain again as the measures needed to achieve the BLUE Map scenario emission reduction objectives come into play.

The uncertainty surrounding the efficiency options and the transport sector options is of a different kind. For efficiency, the main issue is accounting for transaction costs and for the cost of addressing some important non-economic barriers that prevent the uptake of economic energy efficient technologies. In the transport sector, the uncertainty hinges around the possibility of delivering technologies that are not available today at anything near an acceptable cost.

This analysis suggests that, given the distinct sector emission reduction pricing ranges and option characteristics, a single generic price or cap across the whole energy system may not be the best approach to incentivising CO_2 reductions, at least in the BLUE case. In such circumstances, cheaper options could benefit from large windfall profits, which would raise the pressure to change the basis of the approach.

The lower-end estimate of the incentive needed to achieve the objectives of the BLUE Map scenario is USD 200/t of CO_2 saved. More pessimistic assumptions about the cost of achieving savings, particularly in transport, suggest that a marginal cost of around USD 500 per tonne of CO_2 may be needed to bring about the necessary change. This curve assumes global action. If developing countries do not implement all options up to a cost level of USD 200/t, its shape would change significantly.

The analysis has not focused on "backstop" options at a price of several hundred USD/t, because most of these options have not yet been studied in great detail. However, these backstops would be cheaper than the upper end of the cost range of the transportation sector options. One example is the use of biomass for production of electricity with CCS. Therefore, while the cost of the marginal technology options in transportation shows a range of USD 200/t to USD 500/t, the lower end of the range is much more likely than the upper end.

Average costs are considerably lower than marginal costs. The total area under the curve in Figure 2.14 is a measure of the total additional annual cost in 2050. These costs range from USD 1.8 trillion to USD 5.6 trillion per year. Given the targeted reduction of 48 Gt, the average cost ranges from USD 38/t CO_2 to USD 117/t CO_2 in the BLUE Map scenario in 2050, making average costs only one-fifth the level of marginal costs.

Box 2.5 ▶ The importance of early action

While certain options are well suited for the ACT Map scenario, they may not represent the best way of achieving more substantial emissions reductions. This underlines the need for a long-term vision.

Capital stock built in the next decade may still be in use by 2050. There is an urgent need to clarify and agree on a set of long-term objectives to minimise the risk of needing to replace capital stock prematurely – and possibly at substantial additional cost. This is especially the case for power plants, buildings and industrial installations. In addition, long-term policy aims need to be settled quickly so as to reduce the policy risks faced by investors.

City and infrastructure planning processes also take significant time to change, sometimes on a time scale of decades. In the BLUE Map scenario it is assumed that the transition starts soon. Much more ambitious building efficiency standards are put in place and enforced in this scenario, and the building envelope of existing buildings is improved significantly as they are renovated. This way the number of buildings that need to be replaced before the end of their technical life span can be limited to a small percentage of the global building stock.

In the BLUE scenarios in the power sector a significant proportion of coal-fired power plants are closed down before they reach the end of their technical life span. This peaks around 2030, when around 350 GW of coal-fired capacity without CCS is mothballed or closed down.

Uncertainty about long-term targets also significantly increases policy cost. Modelling shows that constraining the decision-making time horizon to only 15 years, rather than extending it to 2050 as assumed in the scenarios, results in a significant increase in the CO_2 incentives needed to meet the target. The most significant cost increases occur in the 2015-2020 transition period. By 2050, the marginal costs for 14 out of 15 regions increases by 7% to 47% compared to the BLUE Map scenario, reflecting a CO_2 incentive level of between USD 214 and USD 293 per tonne. Only in one region were costs 10% lower than in the BLUE Map scenario. The message for policy makers is that credible long-term targets are needed to reduce very costly late adjustments to the energy system.

Electricity generation

In the Baseline scenario, global electricity production increases by 179% between 2005 and 2050 (Figure 2.15). In 2050, coal-based generation is forecast to be 252% higher than in 2005. It accounts for 52% of all power generation. Gas-fired power generation increases from 20% today to 23% in 2050. Nuclear decreases to 8%, hydro decreases to 10%, and wind increases to account for 2.5% of all power generation.

Electricity production is responsible for 32% of total global fossil fuel use and 41% of energy-related CO_2 emissions today. Improving the efficiency of electricity production therefore offers a significant opportunity to reduce the world's dependence on fossil fuels, and in so doing helps to combat climate change and improve energy security (Table 2.4).

Table 2.4 ▶ Technical fuel savings and CO_2 reduction potentials from improving the efficiency of electricity production

	Coal (Mtoe/yr)	Oil (Mtoe/yr)	Gas (Mtoe/yr)	All fossil fuels (Mtoe/yr)
OECD	134-213	12-24	60-81	205-320
G8	112-177	10-17	93-115	213-311
Plus Five*	189-244	7-12	7-10	20-27
World	356-504	36-64	105-134	494-702
	(Gt CO_2/yr)	(Gt CO_2/yr)	(Gt CO_2/yr)	(Gt CO_2/yr)
OECD	0.53-0.85	0.04-0.08	0.14-0.19	0.71-1.12
G8	0.44-0.71	0.03-0.06	0.22-0.27	0.69-1.03
Plus Five*	0.73-0.95	0.03-0.04	0.02-0.02	0.77-1.01
World	1.40-1.98	0.11-0.20	0.25-0.31	1.75-2.50

Note: Compared to the reference year 2005.

* Plus five is Brazil, China, India, Mexico and South Africa.

In the ACT Map scenario, significant savings in electricity demand in the buildings and industry sectors reduce the need for growth in generation capacity. Nonetheless, electricity demand more than doubles by 2050 in the ACT Map scenario. Demand in the BLUE Map scenario is 10% higher than in the ACT Map scenario, largely because of an increased demand for electricity for heat pumps and plug-in vehicles.

Figure 2.15 ▶ Global electricity production by fuel in the Baseline, ACT Map and BLUE Map scenarios, 2005, 2030 and 2050

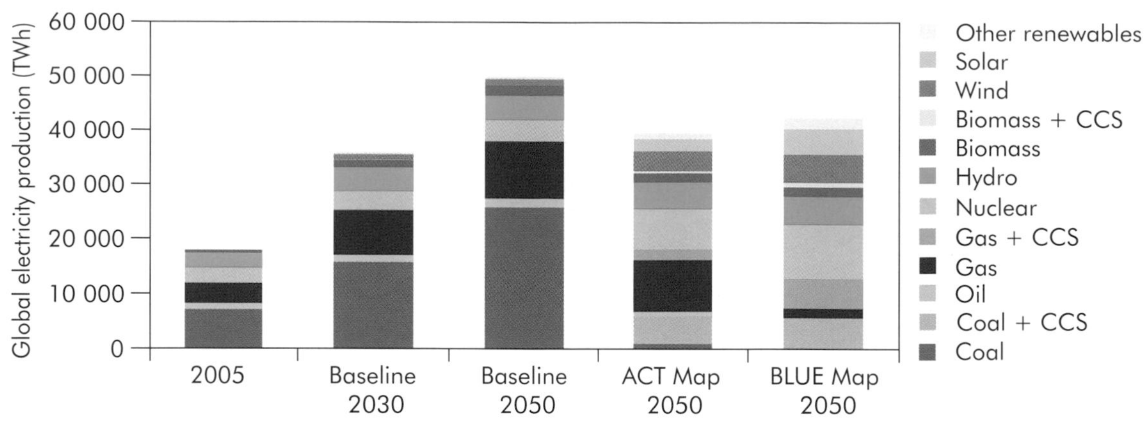

Key point

There is a major shift from fossil fuels to carbon-free alternatives in the ACT Map and BLUE Map scenarios.

The CO_2 emission reduction incentives and other measures introduced in the ACT Map scenario significantly change the electricity generation mix relative to the Baseline scenario (Table 2.5). These generally result in nuclear and renewables becoming more attractive compared to fossil-fuelled power. The share of gas-based power generation increases by 8% in the ACT Map scenario, but decreases to 17% in the BLUE scenario, in which virtually all coal-fired production and 76% of all gas-fired production is from plants equipped with CCS.

The power sector is the most important potential contributor to global emission reductions in both low-carbon scenarios. The power sector is virtually decarbonised in the BLUE Map scenario.

In the ACT Map scenario, power demand is reduced by 21% due to end-use efficiency measures and reductions in transmission and distribution losses. This results in reductions of more than 6 Gt of CO_2 by 2050 compared to the Baseline scenario. This savings increases to almost 7 Gt in the BLUE Map scenario. However, electricity demand is higher in this scenario because of switching from fossil fuels to electricity. Compared to the Baseline scenario, demand is 15% lower.

About 14 Gt of CO_2 emissions reduction is achieved in the ACT Map scenario as a result of changes on the supply side. This increases further to 18 Gt in the BLUE Map scenario. Figure 2.16 provides a breakdown of the relative importance of the supply-side measures.

Table 2.5 ▶ **Global electricity production by type for Baseline, ACT Map and BLUE Map scenarios and sensitivity analyses, 2050**

	2005	Baseline 2050	ACT Map	ACT noCCS	ACT hiNUC	ACT loREN	ACT loEFF	BLUE Map	BLUE noCCS	BLUE hiNUC	BLUE loREN	BLUE loEFF	BLUE hiOil&Gas	BLUE OECD	BLUE disc4%
Production (TWh/yr)															
Nuclear	2 771	3 884	7 336	7 336	15 865	7 336	7 336	9 857	9 857	15 877	9 857	9 857	9 857	6 809	9 857
Oil	1 186	1 572	882	832	864	885	875	133	123	150	210	332	113	905	29
Coal	7 334	25 825	949	2 531	566	1 277	1 206	0	353	0	0	0	0	14 666	326
Coal + CCS	0	3	4 872	0	2 732	5 915	5 367	5 468	0	4 208	7 392	7 461	6 509	1 006	3 139
Gas	3 585	10 557	9 480	12 696	7 619	10 953	10 935	1 751	4 260	1 570	1 747	2 073	1 358	5 974	338
Gas + CCS	0	83	1 962	0	1 850	2 024	2 108	5 458	0	4 926	6 711	6 820	3 765	3 062	4 491
Hydro	2 922	4 590	5 037	5 020	4 985	4 663	5 042	5 260	5 504	5 203	5 114	5 385	5 505	4 929	6 617
Bio/waste	231	1 682	1 578	2 124	1 609	1 487	1 606	1 617	3 918	1 606	1 448	1 689	1 842	1 540	1 474
Bio + CCS	0	0	402	0	401	406	400	835	0	678	1 103	1 077	864	363	1 567
Geothermal	52	348	934	937	731	909	934	1 059	1 059	1 059	1 059	1 059	1 059	746	1 059
Wind	111	1 208	3 607	4 654	2 680	2 735	3 908	5 174	6 743	4 402	3 988	5 951	6 395	2 811	8 786
Tidal	1	10	111	111	111	35	111	413	2 389	419	165	806	755	110	4 452
Solar	3	167	2 319	2 565	1 487	648	2 770	4 754	5 297	4 220	2 314	4 987	5 278	1 858	6 842
Hydrogen	0	4	1	0	0	1	1	559	517	472	664	649	720	239	1 240
TOTAL	**18 196**	**49 934**	**39 471**	**38 807**	**41 501**	**39 274**	**42 599**	**42 340**	**40 021**	**44 791**	**41 773**	**48 146**	**44 021**	**45 018**	**50 218**
Share (%)															
Nuclear	15	8	19	19	38	19	17	23	25	35	24	20	22	15	20
Oil	7	3	2	2	2	2	2	0	0	0	1	1	0	2	0
Coal	40	52	2	7	1	3	3	0	1	0	0	0	0	33	1
Coal + CCS	0	0	12	0	7	15	13	13	0	9	18	15	15	2	6
Gas	20	21	24	33	18	28	26	4	11	4	4	4	3	13	1
Gas + CCS	0	0	5	0	4	5	5	13	0	11	16	14	9	7	9
Hydro	16	9	13	13	12	12	12	12	14	12	12	11	13	11	13
Bio/waste	1	3	4	5	4	4	4	4	10	4	3	4	4	3	3
Bio + CCS	0	0	1	0	1	1	1	2	0	2	3	2	2	1	3
Geothermal	0	1	2	2	2	2	2	3	3	2	3	2	2	2	2
Wind	1	2	9	12	6	7	9	12	17	10	10	12	15	6	17
Tidal	0	0	0	0	0	0	0	1	6	1	0	2	2	0	9
Solar	0	0	6	7	4	2	7	11	13	9	6	10	12	4	14
Hydrogen	0	0	0	0	0	0	0	1	1	1	2	1	2	1	2
TOTAL	**100**	**100**	**100**	**100**	**100**	**100**	**100**	**100**	**100**	**100**	**100**	**100**	**100**	**100**	**100**
CO_2 emissions in 2050 (Gt CO_2/yr)	27 (2005)	62	27	31.3	25.6	27.6	29.3	14	20.4	13.4	14.2	15.0	13.3	41.6	7.7
Incremental cost in 2050 (trln. USD/yr)			NA	0.22	-0.07	0.03	0.12	NA	1.28	-0.12	0.04	0.20	-0.14	NA	NA
Marginal cost to meet target (USD/t CO_2)			50	76	41	54	64	200	394	182	206	230	179	NA	NA

Figure 2.16 ▶ Reduction in CO_2 emissions from the Baseline scenario in the power sector in the ACT Map and BLUE Map scenarios in 2050, by technology area

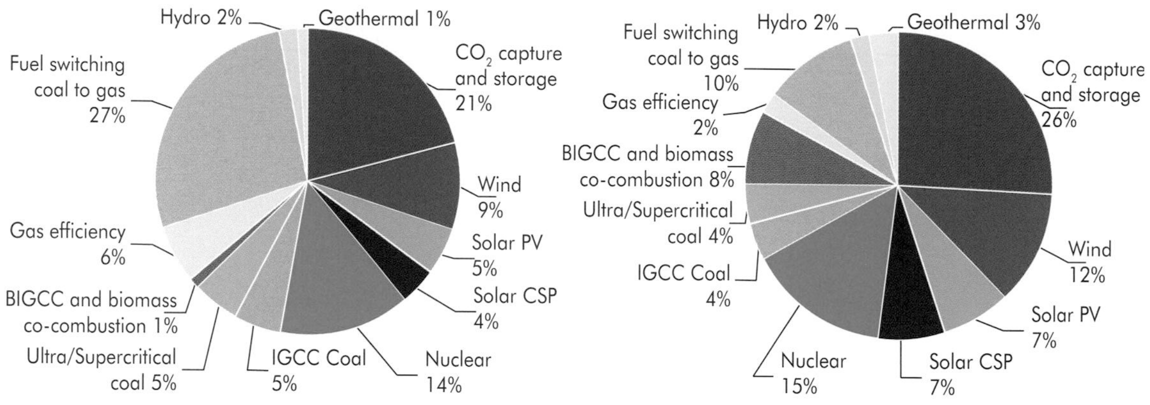

Note: Excludes the impact of end-use efficiency and electrification.

Key point

A mix of nuclear, renewables and CCS plays a key role in reducing emissions in the power sector.

The efficiencies of fossil-fuel power plants increase substantially in both the ACT Map and BLUE Map scenarios, to the extent that coal-fired plants with CCS in these scenarios are on average more efficient than coal-fired plants without CCS in the Baseline scenario (Figure 2.17). Integrated-gasifiers combined-cycles (IGCC) and ultra-supercritical steam cycles (USCSC) can both play a role in this scenario.

The use of combined heat and power (CHP) triples in the Baseline scenario in absolute terms between 2005 and 2050. Its share in power generation rises from 9% to 10%. In the ACT Map and BLUE Map scenarios, its share is even higher, rising to 17% in the ACT Map scenario and 14% in the BLUE scenario. In the IEA energy accounting system, the benefits of CHP show up as an efficiency gain for electricity generation.

Most electricity generated by coal-fired power plants in the ACT Map and BLUE Map scenarios, and half the gas-fired power generation in the BLUE Map scenario, comes from plants equipped with CCS. Retrofitting of coal plants with CCS plays a very significant role in the ACT Map scenario. But at the price of USD 200/t CO_2 envisaged in the BLUE scenario, there is sufficient economic incentive to accelerate the replacement of inefficient power plants before they reach the end of their life span. In the BLUE scenario, 350 GW of coal-fired power-plant capacity is closed down early. The remaining 700 GW consists of 80% new capacity that is equipped with CCS, and 20% retrofits with CCS.

The growth of CCS in the BLUE Map scenario compared to the ACT Map scenario is largely attributable to gas and biomass generation being fitted with CCS. As biomass contains carbon captured from the atmosphere, the capture and storage of that carbon results in a net CO_2 removal from the atmosphere. This can offset emissions elsewhere. However this option is costly: biomass transportation costs limit plant size and CCS benefits from economies of scale.

2

Figure 2.17 ▶ Net efficiencies of fossil-fuelled power plants

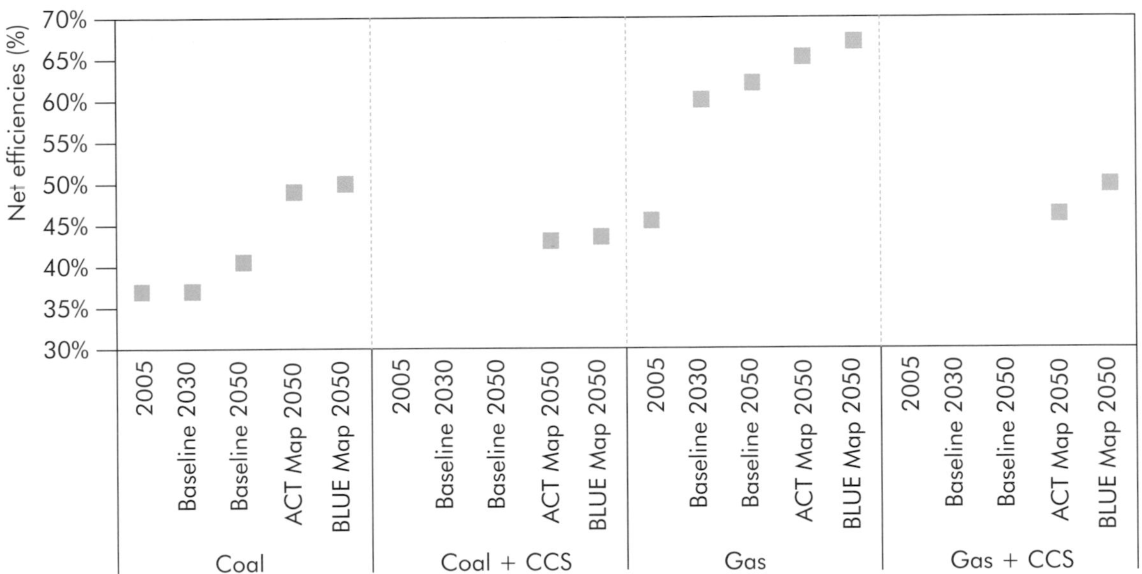

Notes: Data refer to average stock efficiency. Gas includes CHP credits following IEA accounting rules (which implies about 85% efficiency for large NGCC CHP plants).

Key point

Efficiencies of power plants increase in the ACT Map and BLUE Map scenarios, but the switch to CCS reduces the gains significantly.

The share of all electricity generation from renewables increases from 18% in 2005 to 35% in 2050 in the ACT Map scenario, and to 46% in the BLUE Map scenario (Figure 2.18). In the BLUE Map scenario, variable renewable generation (wind, photovoltaics and marine) produces around 20.6% of electricity worldwide in 2050 (about 3 500 GW).

Biomass and wind constitute the bulk of new renewables capacity up to 2020. After 2020, solar starts to make a more significant contribution. Hydro grows continuously over the whole period, but this growth levels off in 2030 to 2050 as the availability of suitable sites poses constraints. Hydro, wind and solar make an equally important contribution in the BLUE Map scenario in 2050.

Figure 2.18 ▶ Growth of renewable power generation in the BLUE Map scenario, 2000-2050

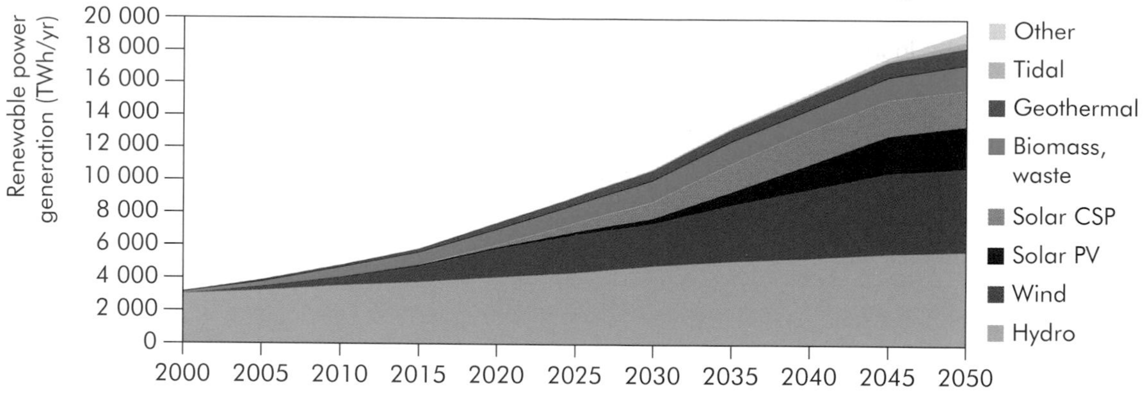

Key point

There is a very strong growth of different renewables options in BLUE Map.

About two-thirds of the anticipated solar capacity is based on photovoltaics (PV), with the balance coming from Concentrating Solar Power (CSP). The capacity factor for CSP is higher than for PV. It therefore generates about 40% of total solar power generation.

The integration of a large volume of variable capacity in grids will need careful management. But variability is not always a problem. For instance, the PV production profile matches well with the need for air conditioning. Variability can also be compensated for by additional electricity storage capacity. In the BLUE Map scenario, this increases from 100 GW today to 500 GW in 2050. This storage consists of a combination of pumped hydro storage, underground compressed air energy storage systems, and other storage options to a lesser extent. About 1 000 GW of gas-fired capacity also operates as reserve for these variable renewables.

Table 2.5 provides an overview of power sector results for all five ACT and BLUE scenarios. These variants show that total power generation, and the power generation mix, depends on the assumptions that are made in the different scenarios. This suggests that there is some room to choose among different CO_2-free power-generation options.

Among the BLUE variants, the one without CCS has the highest emissions. In this variant the share of coal-fired generation drops by 10%. The share of gas also declines. Total electricity demand is 7% lower and the share of renewables increases. CO_2 emissions increase not only in electricity generation, but also in industry and the fuel-transformation sector. As a consequence, it is not possible to achieve the target of halving CO_2 emissions implicit in the BLUE scenarios. This indicates the importance of CCS for climate policies.

In the high-nuclear variant, where nuclear generation is doubled to 2 000 GW in 2050, almost all of the nuclear capacity is used. This is largely at the expense of coal with CCS, but the share of renewables also declines by 3%. Total global emissions in this variant are 0.5 Gt lower in 2050 than in the BLUE Map scenario.

However this variant would require the construction of 50 GW of nuclear power, on average, every year between now and 2050. This is twice the highest recorded construction rate in the past.

In the low-renewables variant, the share of renewables is reduced by 5%, which is compensated by more CCS and, to a lesser extent, reduced electricity use.

Another way to look at these scenario variants is to assume a constant level of CO_2 reduction and to compare the impact on the marginal and total annual incremental policy costs. In this analysis, the impact on incremental cost is based on the difference in emissions between the Map case and the variant, multiplied by the marginal abatement cost (USD 50 and USD 200 for the ACT and BLUE scenarios respectively).

Box 2.6 ▶ Electricity prices in the scenario variants

The five power-sector variants result in important variations in the electricity prices. Table 2.6 provides an overview of how average prices across the 15 regions for the period 2030 to 2050 compare with the Baseline scenario prices for the same period. The price range is also indicated for the 15 regions.

Table 2.6 ▶ Annual average electricity price increases for the ACT Map and BLUE Map scenarios for the period 2030-2050, relative to the Baseline scenario

	Average increase 2030-2050 (%)	Increase range for world regions (%)	Change compared to MAP (% points)
ACT Map	58	26-116	
ACT noCCS	58	19-122	0
ACT hiNUC	47	10-119	–5
ACT loREN	61	21-119	+3
ACT loEFF	64	23-124	+6
BLUE Map	90	65-163	
BLUE noCCS	106	55-211	+16
BLUE hiNUC	81	37-162	–9
BLUE loREN	94	46-180	+4
BLUE loEFF	108	52-186	+18

Note: Electricity production costs excluding transmission and distribution.

The results show that the price increase compared to the Baseline scenario is higher in the BLUE scenarios than in the ACT scenarios. From 2030 to 2050, prices approximately double in the BLUE scenarios. Also, variations among the scenarios are more significant in the BLUE than in the ACT scenarios. The availability of CCS technologies and high end-use efficiency gains in the BLUE Map scenario results in prices that are lower by 16% to 18%. The availability of the full range of options is of great importance to achieve deep emission reduction targets. The range of price increases varies widely across the different regions, which can be attributed to differences in emission mitigation potentials and needs.

The highest additional cost occurs in the BLUE no CCS variant, where the annual cost in 2050 is USD 1.28 trillion higher than in the BLUE Map scenario (Table 2.5). This is an increase of about 71%. This shows again the critical importance of CCS for deep emission reductions. The impact on marginal costs, as calculated by the *Energy Technology Perspectives* model, is also highest in this case, where they nearly double to USD 394 per tonne of CO_2. Making more nuclear power available results in a USD 9/t CO_2 reduction in marginal costs in the ACT Map scenario (-18%) and a USD 18/t CO_2 reduction in the BLUE Map scenario (-9%).

Table 2.5 also shows the sensitivity of the BLUE Map scenario to high oil and gas prices. This variant (BLUE hiOil&Gas) is the only one in which OECD countries reduce emissions. Higher oil and gas prices (USD 65 to 70 per barrel, or bbl) have only a very limited (although positive) effect on emissions and costs. Marginal costs are reduced by 10%. This can be explained by the dominance of the CO_2 incentives on end-use fuel prices. Lowering the discount rate from the range of 3% to 28% across all regions and all sectors to 4% with the same incentive levels results in a much higher substitution of fossil fuels by electricity in the end-use sectors and in a much larger reduction in emissions.

Despite the increasing shares of coal and gas in the Baseline scenario, the CO_2 intensity of electricity generation declines marginally between 2005 and 2050 (Figure 2.19). This is a result of improvements in generation efficiency that more than outweigh the impact of the fuel mix becoming more CO_2 intensive. In the ACT Map scenario, CO_2 emissions per kWh are 76% lower than in the Baseline scenario. Electricity generation becomes largely decarbonised in the BLUE Map scenario, with CO_2 emissions per kWh being reduced by as much as 86%. The difference in the carbon intensity of electricity production between OECD and non-OECD countries narrows in both the ACT Map and the BLUE Map scenarios.

Figure 2.19 ▶ CO_2 intensity of electricity production by scenario

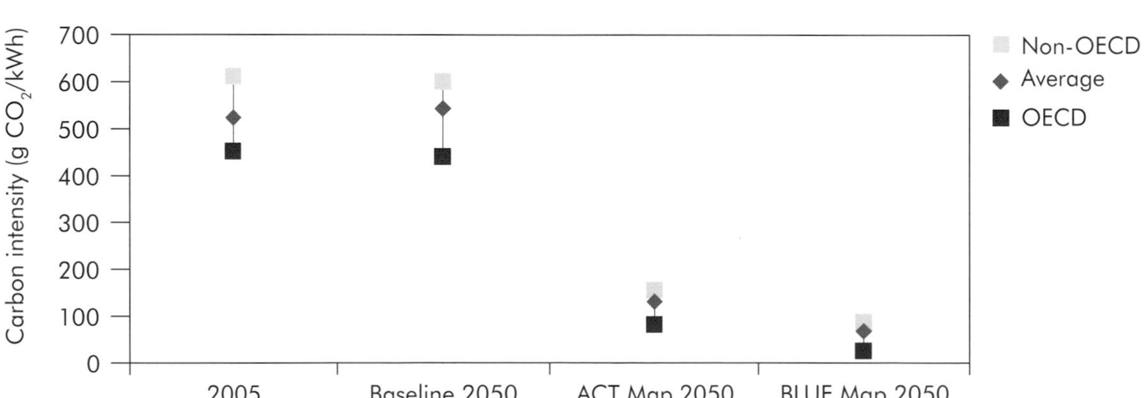

Key point

In the ACT scenarios, global CO_2 intensity of power production is less than half the baseline level in 2050, while the power sector is virtually decarbonised in the BLUE scenarios.

Figure 2.20 shows the marginal abatement curve for the power sector in the BLUE Map scenario. The cheapest emission reductions are achieved through end-use electricity savings. This represents about 7 Gt of emissions reduction, nearly one-third of the total potential. On the supply side, the cheapest reductions come from replacing baseload coal plants. However, costs increase substantially as emissions from gas baseload plants, shoulder load and even peaking plants are addressed to achieve a virtually carbon-free electricity sector.

The shape of the curve is influenced by RD&D and technology learning. As there is a greater technology development effort in the BLUE Map scenario than in the Baseline and ACT Map scenarios, the marginal cost for a given level of emissions reduction is lower in the BLUE Map scenario.

Emission reductions can exceed baseline emissions if biomass with CCS is widely applied for power generation. However, IEA analysis suggests this option would be costly, because of the relatively small scale of stand-alone biomass power plants due to logistical supply constraints.

Figure 2.20 ▶ Electricity sector marginal emission reduction costs for the BLUE Map scenario in 2050

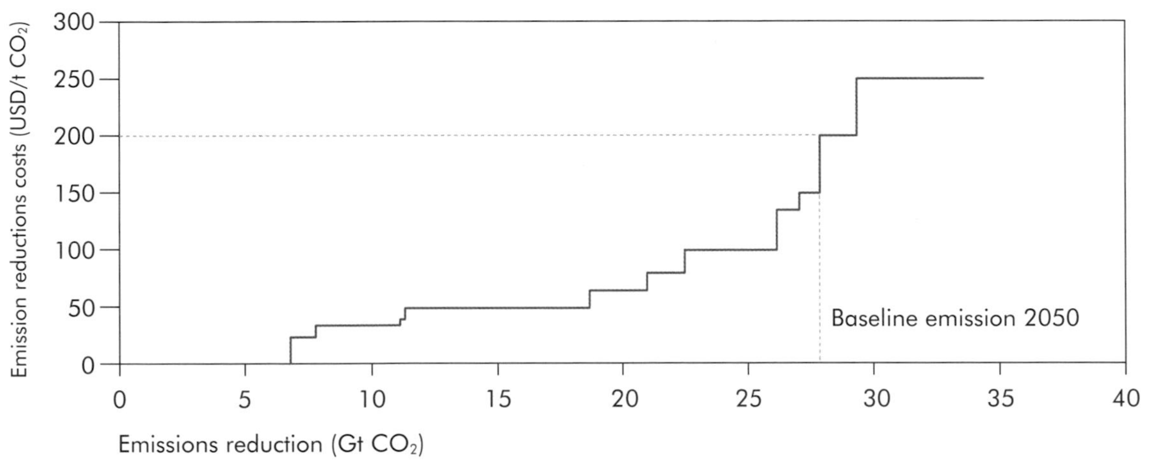

Key point

The costs of emission reductions in the power sector vary widely. Biomass with CCS at more than USD 200 per tonne CO_2 allows for negative sector emissions.

Transport

In the Baseline scenario, energy demand in the transport sector increases by 120% between 2005 and 2050 (Figure 2.21). Global transport energy demand in 2050 exceeds 4 700 Mtoe. Oil products provide 75% of this, and liquid synfuels produced from gas and coal account for about 22%. Biofuels, both biodiesel and ethanol, only contribute 3%.

Figure 2.21 ▶ Transport energy use in the Baseline, ACT Map and BLUE Map scenarios, 2005-2050

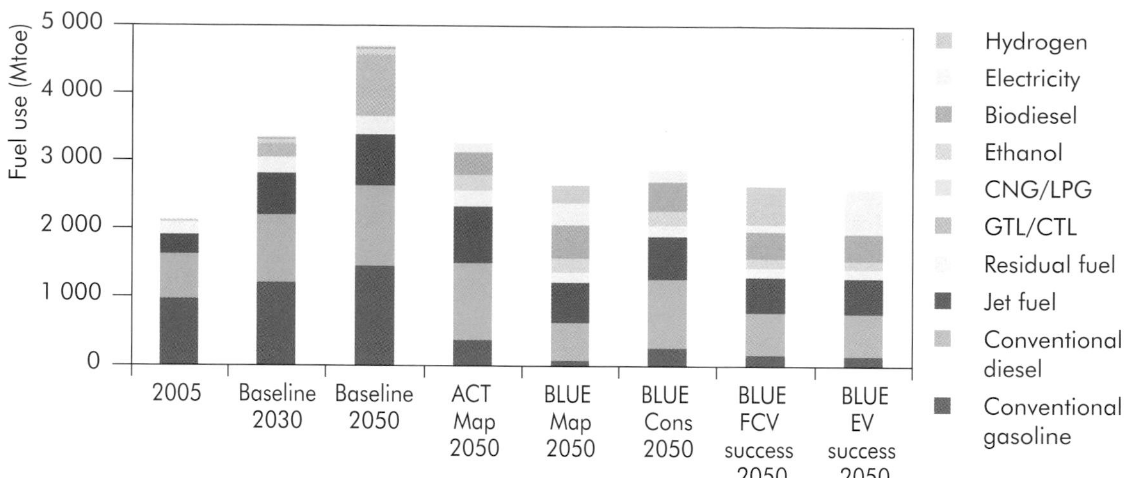

Key point

Demand for oil products in 2050 is 37% above the 2005 level in the ACT Map scenario, and 5% above to 38% below the 2005 level in the BLUE cases.

A number of scenarios were created for the transport sector, with variants of the BLUE Map scenario examined. The key assumptions for each of these scenarios are shown in Table 2.7. These assumptions help explain the results of the different scenarios.

The fuel efficiency of cars, trucks and other modes of transport is considerably higher in the ACT Map scenario than in the Baseline scenario, resulting in a 30% reduction in transportation fuel demand (1 464 Mtoe) compared to the Baseline scenario in 2050. Demand for conventional oil products in the ACT Map scenario in 2050 is 23% higher than in 2005. All synfuels are eliminated and oil product use is reduced by over one thousand Mtoe. This is equivalent to a reduction of 37 mbd (million barrels per day). These reductions, especially for synfuels, have important CO_2 benefits. Biofuels increase to 17% of total transportation fuel demand, with roughly equal shares of ethanol and biodiesel. Second-generation biofuels dominate, with sugar cane as the only first-generation biofuel feedstock that continues to provide significant fuel production after 2030.

Further fuel savings and emission reductions are possible, but they are more costly and depend on more speculative technology. The four BLUE scenario variants explore this. The BLUE Map scenario combines biofuels, electric vehicles and hydrogen fuel-cell vehicles, and assumes success in several key technologies, as described in the transport chapter. One BLUE scenario assumes earlier and greater success for electric vehicles (BLUE-EV), while another assumes earlier and greater success for hydrogen fuel cell vehicles (BLUE-FC). The BLUE conservative scenario assumes that neither hydrogen FCVs nor EVs are successful enough to play a significant role before 2050.

Table 2.7 ▶ **Transport scenario overview and key assumptions**

	Baseline	ACT Map	BLUE Map	BLUE conservative	BLUE FCV success	BLUE EV success
Scenario definition	Baseline projection	Based on *Energy Technology Perspectives* 2006, strong but cost-effective measures	Greater use of biofuels, deployment of EVs, FCVs	Stronger efficiency gains than ACT Map, more biofuels, no pure EVs or FCVs	Dominant FCVs for cars and trucks	Dominant EVs for cars and trucks
Light-duty vehicles	Total vehicle travel triples by 2050; fuel economy up to 20% better than 2005	Slight reductions in travel growth; 50% improvement in fuel economy; hybrids dominate; significant plug-ins by 2050	EVs, FCVs each reach 30%+ market share in 2050	Same as ACT Map except plug-in hybrids reach 40% share in 2050	FCVs reach 90% market share in 2050	EVs reach 90% market share in 2050
Trucks	Strong growth through 2050; 25% on-road efficiency improvement	Average 35% efficiency improvement including 50% hybridisation by 2050	Fuel cells and EVs each reach up to 25% of stock by 2050	Average 45% improvement; hybrids reach 80% of stock by 2050	Fuel cells reach 60% of medium truck stock by 2050, 30% of heavy	EVs reach 50% of medium truck stock by 2050, 25% of heavy
Other modes	Aircraft 30% more efficient in 2050; other modes 5-10% more efficient; strong growth in air, shipping	Aircraft 40% more efficient; shipping 20%; travel reductions via mode shift up to 15% in 2050	Slightly more efficiency improvement than ACT Map	Similar to BLUE Map	Similar to BLUE Map	Similar to BLUE Map
Biofuels	Stays below 70 Mtoe, mostly 1st generation	About 550 Mtoe in 2050, mostly 2nd generation	Slightly more than ACT Map, mostly biomass to liquids to replace petroleum diesel	Similar to ACT Map	Similar to ACT Map	Similar to ACT Map
Low GHG hydrogen	No H_2	No H_2	310 Mtoe in 2050	No H_2	790 Mtoe in 2050	No H_2
Low GHG electricity	25 Mtoe (mainly for rail)	70 Mtoe mostly for plug-in hybrids	285 Mtoe in 2050 for plug-ins and EVs	190 Mtoe in 2050 for plug-ins	95 Mtoe used in plug-in hybrids	740 Mtoe in 2050

Figure 2.22 ▶ Emission reductions in transportation compared to Baseline for the ACT Map and BLUE Map scenarios, 2050

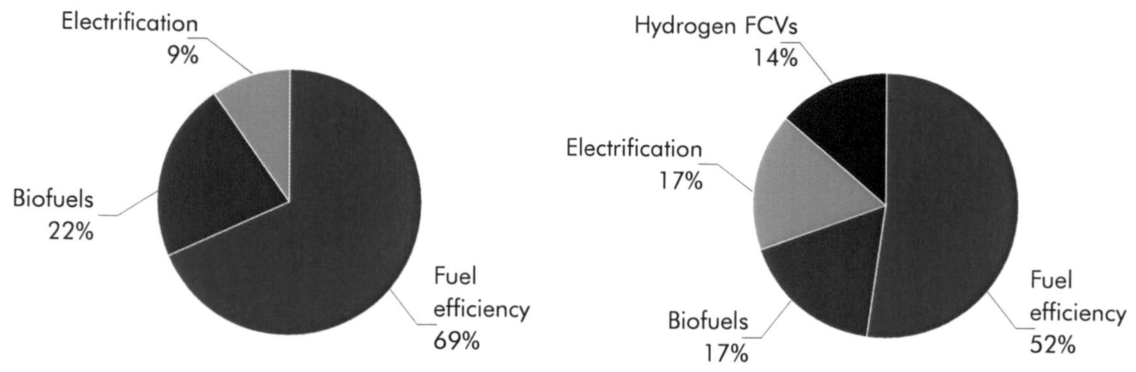

Key point

Fuel efficiency options dominate transport sector CO_2 reductions in the ACT Map scenario; alternative fuels play a larger role in BLUE Map.

In the BLUE scenario variants, fuel use in 2050 is up to 47% lower than in the Baseline. BLUE Map uses the most biofuels, about 700 Mtoe, representing 26% of total transport fuel demand. Biofuel demand in the other variants is between 500 Mtoe and 700 Mtoe. The use of conventional oil products is 35% below the 2005 level in the BLUE Map scenario. This constitutes a significant supply security benefit.

The contribution from hydrogen is near zero in the ACT Map scenario, where it remains a niche fuel. In the BLUE Map scenario, though, hydrogen plays a more important role. Fuel cell vehicle sales and the construction of a hydrogen infrastructure begin in earnest after 2020 and grow steadily over time. In "BLUE FC", fuel cell vehicles are assumed to reach a commercial scale by 2030 and to come to dominate vehicle sales in OECD countries by 2050. Electricity gains ground in all variants through plug-in hybrids, but reaches a much more prominent position in the EV variant – in which pure-electric vehicles are assumed to become fully commercial by 2030 and dominate vehicle sales by 2050.

On a life-cycle "well-to-wheels" basis, CO_2 emissions from transportation in the Baseline scenario, at 18 Gt in 2050, are 150% higher than in 2005 (Figure 2.24). Emissions increase faster on this basis than tailpipe emissions, due to the significant introduction of natural gas and coal-based synfuels in the Baseline scenario. The production of these fuels more than doubles emissions (relative to petroleum fuels) on a well-to-wheel basis. Tailpipe CO_2 emissions are about 13.8 Gt by 2050.

Figure 2.23 ▶ Use of biofuels, electricity and hydrogen in the transportation sector in the Baseline, ACT Map and BLUE scenarios, 2005-2050

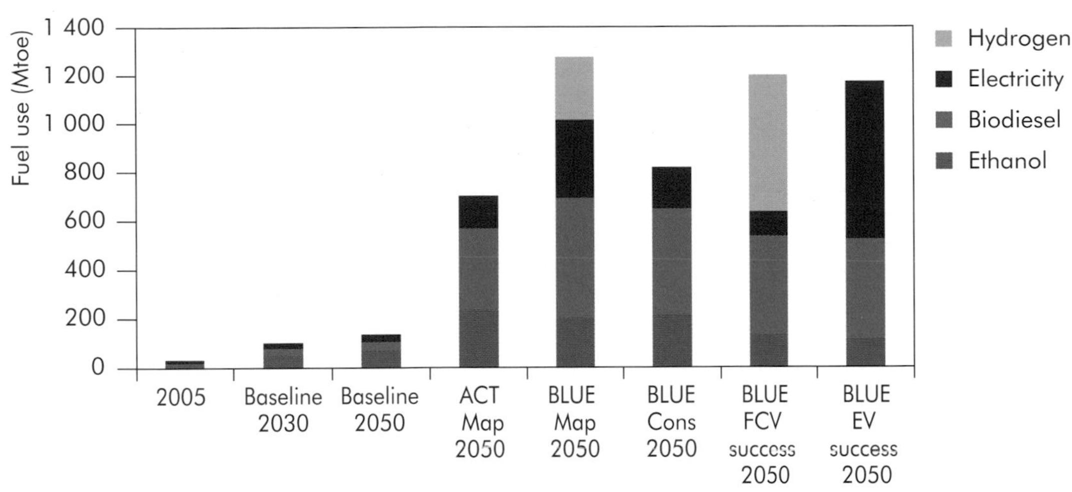

Key point

The use of alternative transportation fuels grows rapidly in the ACT Map and BLUE scenarios.

Growth in CO_2 emissions, like growth in energy demand, varies by region. Developing countries show much steeper increases than do developed countries. In the Baseline scenario, CO_2 emissions from transport in non-OECD countries increase by more than 300% by 2050, while OECD countries see an increase of about 50%. This is mainly due to differing rates of growth in vehicle sales and transport activity, but also to the faster deployment of clean and efficient transport technologies in OECD countries.

In the ACT Map scenario, well-to-wheel CO_2 emissions are 45% (8 Gt CO_2) lower by 2050 than in the Baseline scenario. Nearly half of this reduction is related to the elimination of synfuels, the other half coming from efficiency gains and from the use of biofuels. All biofuels in this scenario are second-generation or cane-to-ethanol after 2030, which averages about an 80% reduction in CO_2eq emissions on a well-to-wheel basis.

Further increases in efficiency and in the use of low-CO_2 fuels reduce emissions even further in the BLUE scenarios. By 2050, transport CO_2 emissions are about 20% below the level of 2005 in all of the BLUE variants except in BLUE conservative – where they are about 10% above 2005 levels (and about 2.5 Gt above the level of the other BLUE variant scenarios). The difference between the BLUE conservative variant and the other BLUE variants shows that emission reductions to below today's levels can only be achieved if transport technologies that are not available at an acceptable cost today come through to commercialisation.

In the BLUE Map scenario, efficiency gains for all transportation modes provide about half the CO_2 reduction. The other half comes from the use of biofuels and the introduction of electric and fuel cell vehicles.

Figure 2.24 ▶ Well-to-wheel CO_2 emissions in the transport sector in the Baseline, ACT Map and BLUE scenarios, 2005-2050

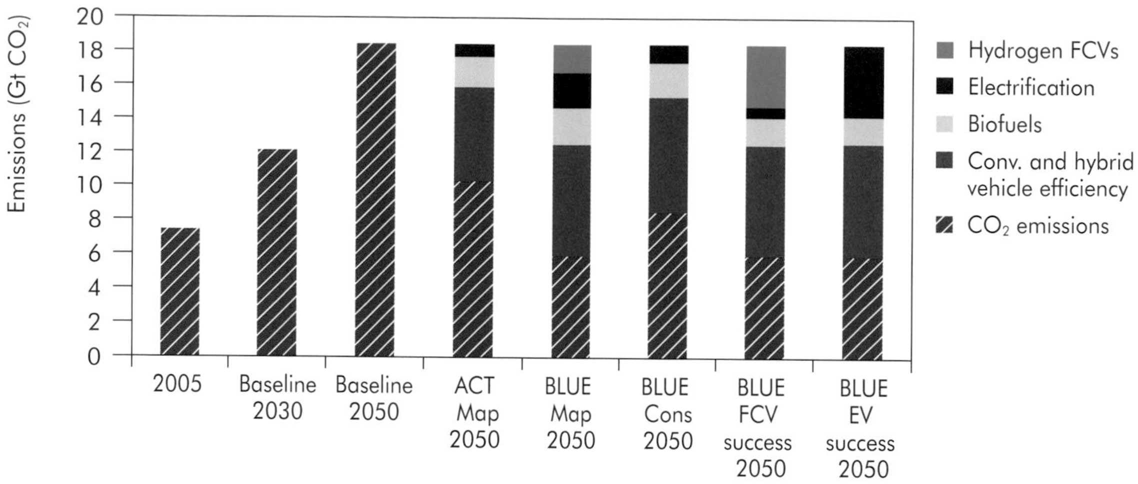

Key point

Improved fuel efficiency accounts for half of the CO_2 emissions reduction in the BLUE Map scenario: the combination of biofuels, electric and fuel cell vehicles accounts for the other half.

Despite the strong growth in fuel use to 2050 in the Baseline scenario, there are significant reductions in the fuel intensity of cars, vans, SUVs and small delivery trucks (light-duty vehicles, or LDVs) in this scenario (Figure 2.25). The fuel-intensity of new LDVs in 2050 averages some 17% less than it did in 2005. Among other things, this trend reflects policy-driven improvements to 2020 in OECD countries and China, and an expected rapid growth in sales of small and very small cars in countries such as India.

Additional improvements in the fuel economy of LDVs (and other modes) provide most of the CO_2 emissions reductions in the ACT Map scenario relative to the Baseline scenario. In this scenario, the average fuel intensity of new LDVs in 2050 is about 50% lower than the 2005 level. This reflects a combination of the maximum use of fuel-efficiency technologies in gasoline and diesel vehicles, increased dieselisation, and (by 2050) the dominance of hybrid-electric vehicles. It also assumes that the share of light trucks (including SUVs and vans) grows much more slowly than in the reference case. We also assume that by 2050 about 25% of hybrids are plug-in hybrids running about half the time on grid electricity. In comparison, in the Baseline scenario, hybrid-electric vehicles reach only about 10% of new vehicle sales worldwide by 2050, and none are plug-in capable.

In addition, in the ACT Map scenario just over one-third (35%) of medium-freight trucks and two-thirds of buses have hybrid systems by 2050. Efficiency improvements derived from the hybridisation of the powertrain (*i.e.* from regenerative braking, smaller engine size and increasing the time spent in the internal combustion engine's optimal operating range) leads to about a 30% improvement in energy efficiency in urban driving situations – where most delivery trucks and buses operate.

Figure 2.25 ▶ New LDV fuel economy in the Baseline, ACT Map and BLUE Map scenarios

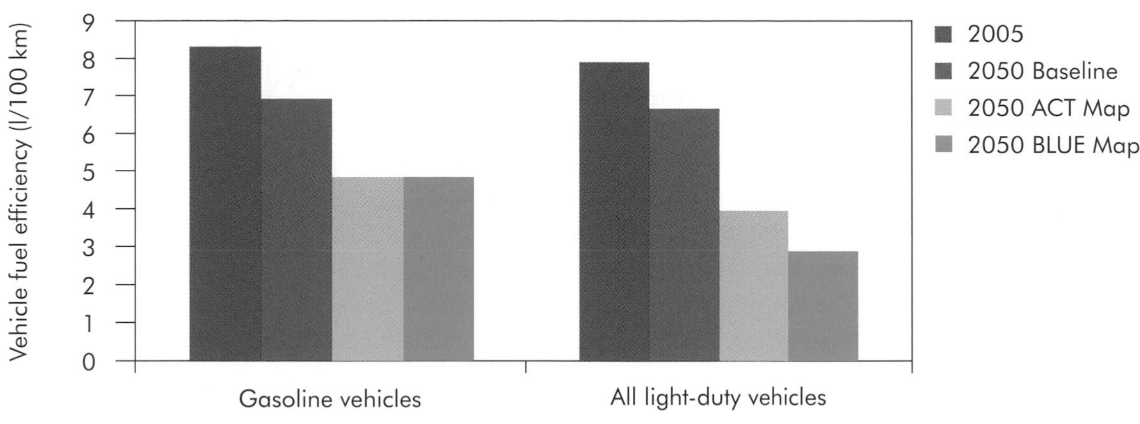

Key point

In 2050, average fuel intensity of new light-duty vehicles is 51% lower than the 2005 level in the ACT Map scenario and 63% lower in the BLUE Map scenario.

In the BLUE Map scenario, the fuel intensity of LDVs in 2050 is reduced to less than half the 2005 level in nearly every region. The additional improvements over the ACT Map scenario come mostly from the introduction of more plug-in hybrid-electric vehicles and pure EVs, and from the introduction of hydrogen FCVs. Pure EVs and FCVs are more energy-efficient than hybrids, and both reach 25% of sales, on average, around the world by 2050 in the BLUE Map scenario (although their shares are lower in non-OECD countries than in OECD countries). If either technology fully dominates (as in the EV and FCV BLUE variants), they are assumed to reach nearly 90% of sales by 2050 and to bring the average fuel consumption of new cars even lower than in the BLUE Map scenario. If neither option is successful, efficiency gains would be considerably lower, as reflected in the BLUE conservative scenario. The use of these different scenarios reflects the fact that, based on the data available today, it is not possible to identify a winning option for LDVs.

An important challenge in the achievement of the BLUE Map scenario outcomes is that non-LDV modes must also be decarbonised. Trucks, shipping and airplanes currently account for about half of the total energy used and CO_2 emitted in transportation, and their share is projected to grow to 60% in 2050 in the Baseline scenario. The efficiency potentials for these modes may be substantial, but it is more uncertain than for LDVs. The ACT and BLUE scenarios assume 10% to 30% additional technical efficiency gains beyond the baseline for long-haul trucks, rail, aircraft and ships. If 30% improvements in efficiency can be achieved for these modes, they will make an important contribution to overall emission reductions. But the role of electrification and fuel cells appears likely to be very limited in some of these modes, particularly in ships and aircraft. This may make the use of biofuels especially important in achieving deep reductions in these modes. Even the wide availability of low-carbon biofuels is uncertain, however. They are assumed to reach a maximum of only 30% fuel demand for these modes, helping to keep the total biofuels demand to 700 Mtoe or less in all scenarios. Overall, the CO_2 emissions in long-haul (heavy duty) trucking, aviation, and shipping sectors in 2050 are cut by about half in the BLUE variant scenarios compared to Baseline.

The transport sector has the highest emission reduction costs and sets the marginal emission abatement cost in the BLUE variant scenarios. The marginal abatement costs for LDVs are shown in Figure 2.26. Gasoline and diesel efficiency improvements are of negative net cost through 2030. By 2050, most advanced technology costs have come down substantially. The cost for new FCVs drops between 2030 and 2050 and is below USD 200/t in the optimistic case. For EVs, the costs are already slightly below USD 200/t in 2030.The optimistic case assumes successful RD&D, good rates of technology learning and robust sales. In the pessimistic case, the marginal abatement cost for FCVs and EVs is around USD 500/t, taking into account vehicle plus life-cycle fuel costs.

Plug-in hybrids have a lower abatement cost, but do not yield the same level of emissions reduction unless biofuels are used. In the BLUE Map scenario these biofuels are needed for other transportation modes.

Figure 2.26 ▶ Marginal abatement cost for light-duty vehicle options, 2015-2050

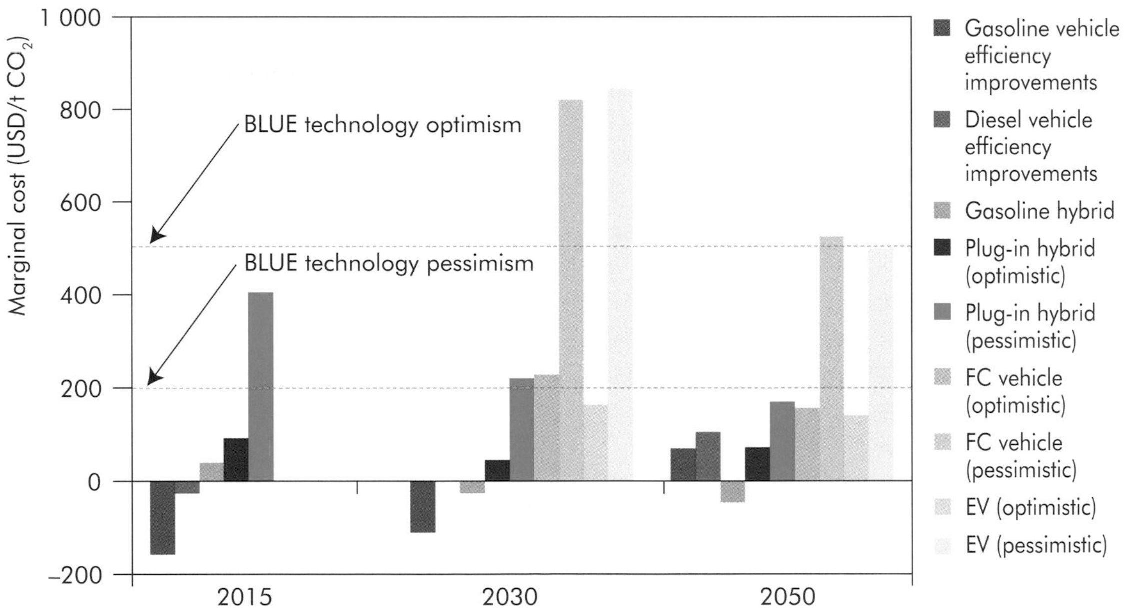

Key point

The abatement cost for light-duty vehicles determines the marginal abatement cost for the BLUE Map scenarios.

Given the high cost of emissions mitigation, the lack of readily available fuel substitutes and the fact that millions of small emission sources are involved, transport can be considered the most challenging sector for deep emission reductions.

Buildings

Total energy use in the buildings sector was around 2 900 Mtoe or 38% of global final energy consumption in 2005. The buildings sector consumed 57% of all electricity.[1] In 2005, 28% of the building sector's global energy needs were met by renewables, mainly traditional biomass in developing countries. Electricity accounted for 25%, with natural gas and oil together accounting for a further 37%. Overall, energy consumption in the residential sector is more than three times as high as in the service (commercial) sector. In OECD countries, the difference is less pronounced, with the service sector consuming around 459 Mtoe (39%) and the residential sector 721 Mtoe (61%).

The consumption of coal, oil and natural gas in the buildings sector produced only 38% of the sector's total direct and indirect CO_2 emissions in 2005. Allocating the upstream CO_2 emissions from electricity and heat generation to buildings results in 62% of the total direct and indirect emissions attributable to electricity and heat consumption. Total direct and indirect CO_2 emissions were 8.8 Gt CO_2 in 2005 (33% of total emissions).

In the Baseline scenario, energy demand in the buildings sector increases to 5 257 Mtoe in 2050, or 1.3% per year. The residential sector accounts for around 58% of this growth and the service sector for around 31%. The remainder is attributable to the agriculture and fishing sectors, and to other non-specified sectors. Continued economic growth leads to more demand for commercial floor space, and the number of households continues to expand. Electricity demand grows rapidly – at 2.4% per year – and accounts for most of the demand growth. Non-biomass renewables grow at 5.9% per year, but from a low base, while gas grows at 1.3%, heat at 1.5% and oil at 1%. Biomass growth is zero, while coal demand declines at 1% per year. CO_2 emissions attributable to the building sector increase by 129% between 2005 and 2050.[2]

The relatively modest growth in residential energy consumption, 1.2% per year, reflects unexceptional growth in the number of households through to 2050 and the saturation of demand for heat and hot water in most of the OECD and transition economies. Global energy consumption per household grows on average at only 0.1% per year. However, electricity gains a significant share, as electricity consumption in the residential sector more than triples to 1 200 Mtoe in 2050. Electricity use per household doubles on average, while non-electric fuel use per household declines by 19%. In developing countries, the reduced share of low end-use efficiency biomass in the household energy mix helps to offset to some extent the growth in electricity demand and in demand for other commercial fuels. The absolute level of energy consumption per household not only depends on the efficiency of energy use, but also varies significantly by region depending on climate, with cold-climate countries having much higher energy consumption needs than warm-climate countries.

1. The buildings sector is dominated by the residential and service sectors (accounting for around 88% of energy consumption), but also includes agriculture, fishing and "other non-specified" sectors.

2. Upstream CO_2 emissions for electricity and heat in 2030 and 2050 are calculated using the 2005 intensity of electricity and heat, so that the changes in the CO_2 emissions intensity of electricity generation are attributed to the power-generation sector.

Energy consumption in the service sector grows more strongly in the Baseline scenario, at 1.7% per year. This increase is driven by strong growth in commercial floor space, particularly in developing regions, as well as by increases in the level of energy services provided in commercial buildings, notably for air-conditioning. Electricity demand increases from 294 Mtoe to 744 Mtoe in 2050. The use of heat and renewables in the services sector grows strongly, but from low levels.

The use of renewables in the buildings sector increases by only 67 Mtoe between 2005 and 2050. This is the net result of a slight decline in biomass use, which is offset by rapid growth in solar and geothermal heating, albeit starting from a low level. The renewables share of consumption drops from 28% to 17%. Non-biomass renewables grow the most rapidly, at 5.9% per year between 2005 and 2050. However, they still represent only 2% of the sector's energy consumption in 2050. Electricity demand grows at 2.4% per year, becoming the largest energy source in the buildings sector by 2015 and accounting for 41% of the sector's energy consumption in 2050. This reflects the growing demand from electric appliances and other electrical uses. By 2050, 55% of final electricity use is accounted for by the buildings sector.

In the ACT Map scenario, buildings sector energy demand is around one-third less than in the Baseline scenario in 2050. In the BLUE Map scenario, demand is reduced by 41% against the baseline in 2050 (Figure 2.27). In the ACT Map scenario, fuel use reduces by between 31% and 41% by fuel, with the exception of non-biomass renewables, which increase by 144% over their Baseline level in 2050. In the BLUE Map scenario, fuel use reduces by between 35% and 63%, except for non-biomass renewables which increase by 285% compared to Baseline.

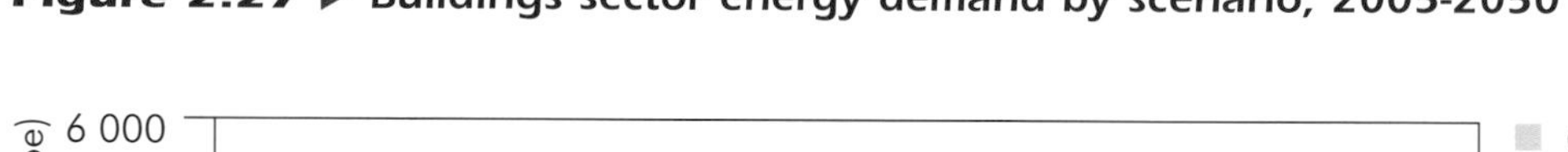
Figure 2.27 ▶ Buildings sector energy demand by scenario, 2005-2050

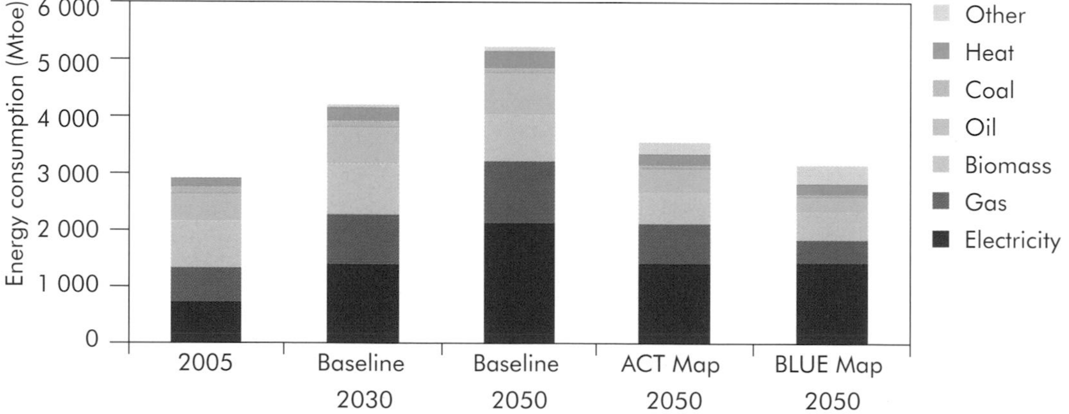

Key point

Major efficiency gains in ACT Map, only limited additional gains in BLUE Map.

Figure 2.28 shows the energy savings in each sub-sector by end use. In the ACT Map scenario, savings in the residential sector below the Baseline scenario in 2050 are 1 007 Mtoe or around 1.8 times those in the service sector (550 Mtoe). This ratio is little changed in the BLUE Map scenario as savings increase to 1 267 Mtoe in the residential sector and 682 Mtoe in the services sector. Savings in space and water heating account for around 60% of the savings in each scenario in the residential sector, while the same end uses account for around half of the savings in the service sector due to the relatively greater importance of the savings from lighting and other electrical uses in the service sector. In the ACT Map scenario, savings in the residential sector range from a low of 17% below the Baseline scenario for cooking to a high of 41% below the Baseline scenario for lighting. In the BLUE Map scenario this range is from around a 27% reduction in cooking to a reduction of around half in lighting and cooling. In the service sector, savings below the Baseline scenario range from a reduction of 28% in water heating to a high of 48% in cooling and ventilation. In the Blue Map scenario, this range of reduction below the Baseline scenario is from 38% to 58%.

Figure 2.28 ▶ Buildings sector energy savings in the ACT Map and BLUE Map scenarios by end-use

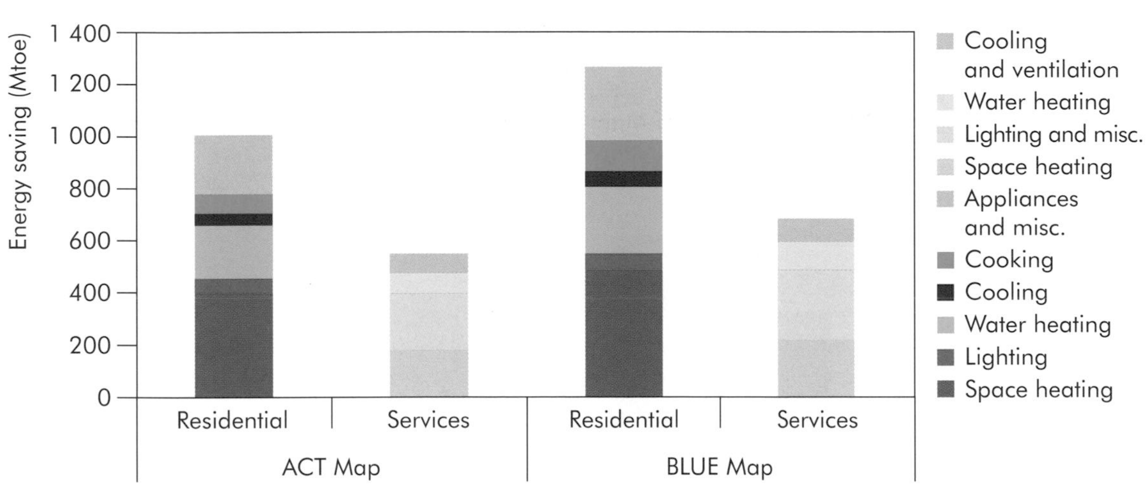

Key point

Space and water heating account for over half of total final energy savings.

In the ACT Map scenario, appliances are shifted to least life-cycle cost levels, whereas in the BLUE Map scenario they are shifted towards best-available technology. Lighting efficiency is improved by two-thirds to three-quarters in the BLUE Map scenario, reducing energy consumption to around half the baseline level. This could be reduced even further quite economically, depending on the success of commercialising LED lighting. Cooling demand is set to grow rapidly in the residential sector in the Baseline scenario, but from a very low level. Much of this growth will come from developing countries. In the BLUE Map scenario, this demand is reduced significantly, but it contributes only around 5% to the savings, due to its still low share.

In the BLUE Map scenario, efforts are needed to reduce all sources of emissions, including those from cooking. Substantial savings are achieved in developing countries by switching from the use of traditional biomass to modern biomass, particularly dimethyl ether (DME) produced from bioenergy sources. Marginal savings also occur in OECD countries, with the switch from gas or oil to electricity, as the near-complete decarbonisation of the electricity generation sector makes electricity an effective abatement option.

In the Baseline scenario, CO_2 emissions from the buildings sector increase by 129% between 2005 and 2050.[3] This is reduced significantly in the ACT Map scenario to 72% below the Baseline scenario level in 2050 (using the ACT Map 2050 emissions factor for electricity and heat). The reduction in coal consumption accounts for 1% of the CO_2 savings in the ACT Map scenario, with oil accounting for 7% and gas 6%. Direct fossil-fuel CO_2 emissions in the buildings sector are reduced by 6% from their 2005 level. In the ACT Map scenario, 86% of the savings are attributable to electricity savings (including upstream). Taking into account the reduction in the upstream CO_2 emissions intensity as a result of electricity decarbonisation, by 2050, direct and indirect CO_2 emissions from the buildings sector are reduced by 35% below 2005 levels (Figure 2.29).

Figure 2.29 ▶ Buildings sector CO_2 emissions by scenario, 2005-2050

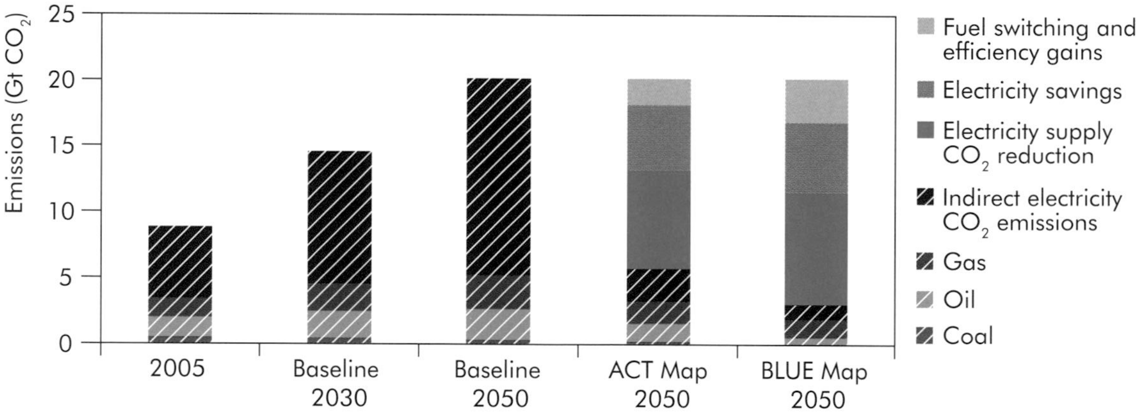

Note: Emission reductions due to increased use of heat pumps are considered part of fuel-switching and efficiency gains.

Key point

Electricity savings dominate CO_2 reductions.

3. These calculations use the 2005 electricity sector CO_2 emissions factor to allocate upstream power generation CO_2 emissions to the electricity consumed in the residential and services sectors. Any reduction or increase in the CO_2 intensity of power generation is then attributable to the power generation sector.

In the BLUE Map scenario, total CO_2 emissions are reduced by 85% below the Baseline scenario in 2050, allocating upstream emissions with the BLUE Map 2050 emissions factor. Direct emissions from coal, oil and gas are 64% lower than the baseline. The need to decarbonise the buildings sector in the BLUE Map scenario leads to an increased share of the savings coming from fossil fuels, with reductions in oil and gas consumption accounting for 11% and 7% of the emission reductions respectively.

The near complete decarbonisation of the electricity system in the BLUE Map scenario means that electrification, particularly for space and water heating, but also for cooking, becomes an important abatement option. Taking the reduction in the upstream emissions intensity of electricity and heat into account sees CO_2 emissions reduced by 85% from the baseline in 2050, equivalent to a 66% reduction on 2005 levels.

Figure 2.30 ▶ Buildings sector direct emissions marginal abatement cost curve for the BLUE Map scenario in 2050

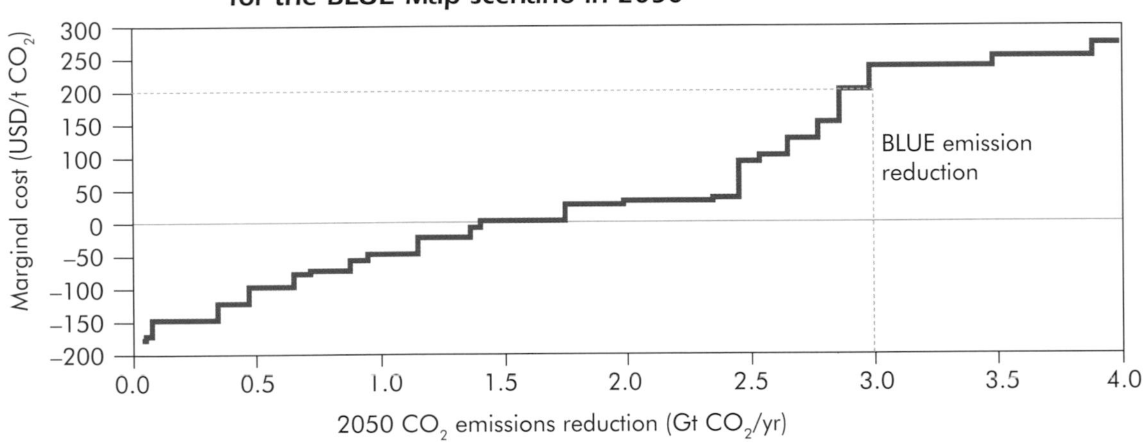

Note: Emission reductions due to increased use of heat pumps are considered part of fuel-switching and efficiency gains.

Key point

Direct emissions can be reduced by around 3 Gt for costs up to USD 200/t CO_2.

The buildings sector offers some of the lowest cost abatement options and is critical to achieving the ACT Map and Blue Map scenarios at reasonable cost. Measures with negative costs include tightening of new building standards for residential and commercial buildings, shifting to condensing gas boilers, district heating and small-scale CHP (in some circumstances), switching to heat pumps (in some circumstances), replacing single glazing with double-glazing (at time of refurbishment), solar hot water systems in developing countries, energy-efficiency improvements to the building shell at the time of refurbishment, and additional insulation of hot-water systems. However, these measures maybe more costly; much depends on individual country circumstances.

The BLUE Map scenario, however, requires a shift towards a substantially decarbonised buildings sector and this will require applying policies to market segments within the building sector where the costs begin to rise significantly. Options with positive costs include using heat pumps where insulation levels are already high for instance (USD 100-400/t CO_2), switching from gas-fired water heating to heat pumps, solar hot water systems in cold-climate countries, refurbishing buildings to passive house standards, replacement/reconstruction of part of the building stock. Significant uncertainty surrounds the right-hand side of the abatement cost curve as relatively few studies have looked at deep emissions cuts in the buildings sector (Figure 2.30).

In the ACT Map scenario, energy consumption in the buildings sector in 2050 is 1 684 Mtoe lower than in the Baseline scenario. The residential sector accounts for 60% of these savings. The adoption of more efficient technologies results in per-household energy consumption declining by between 0.2% and 0.9% on average per year between 2005 and 2050, depending on the region. This represents a reduction below the Baseline scenario level in 2050 of between 16% and 40%, depending on the region. District heating is 37% lower in the ACT Map scenario than in the Baseline scenario, reflecting the big potential for energy savings in buildings heated with district heat in transition economies (Table 2.8). Electricity demand is 30% lower than in the Baseline scenario and savings in electricity account for 35% of all savings in the residential sector. The reduction in biomass below the Baseline scenario in 2050 is 253 Mtoe, or 34%. This is largely a result of reduced biomass demand from the increased penetration of improved cooking stoves in developing countries, and from fuel-switching to modern energy sources.

Around 40% of all energy savings in the ACT Map scenario in the residential sector come from space heating. This reflects the impact of more energy-efficient regulations for new buildings and energy-efficient retrofits of existing buildings, as well as improvements in heating systems and their operation. Appliances account for 23% of the savings. Significant savings come from reduced standby power losses and from reductions in the consumption of a wide variety of small electric appliances. Water heating accounts for about 20% of total energy savings in the ACT Map scenario. Lighting and air conditioning show significant percentage reductions in consumption below the Baseline scenario (41% for lighting). Together they account for 10% of the total energy savings in households. Cooking contributes 7% of total global energy savings in the residential sector, all from non-OECD countries.

In the service sector, energy demand is reduced by 41% below the Baseline level in 2050. Fuel-switching and energy-efficiency result in significant reductions in fossil-fuel use. By 2050, the demand for fossil-fuels from the service sector is 36% of the sector's total energy demand in the Baseline scenario, 29% in the ACT Map scenario, and just 17% in the BLUE Map scenario. The largest percentage reductions occur for fossil-fuel use, while non-biomass renewables increase – from a very low base – by 538% over the Baseline level in 2050.

In the BLUE Map scenario, energy demand from the residential and services sector is reduced by 38% and 50% respectively below the Baseline scenario in

2050. Energy demand by fuel is reduced by between 17% and 90%, while non-biomass renewables increase by between 270% and 538% from their 2050 Baseline level.

Table 2.8 ▶ Energy demand reductions below the Baseline scenario by scenario in 2050

	Residential		Services		Buildings (total)	
	ACT Map	BLUE Map	ACT Map	BLUE Map	ACT Map	BLUE Map
Coal	–58%	–90%	–56%	–68%	–41%	–62%
Oil	–46%	–74%	–61%	–82%	–41%	–62%
Gas	–31%	–61%	–48%	–75%	–36%	–63%
Electricity	–30%	–27%	–39%	–45%	–34%	–35%
Heat	–37%	–45%	–31%	–17%	–31%	–35%
Biomass	–34%	–42%	–28%	–27%	–33%	–40%
Other/Solar	128%	270%	328%	538%	144%	285%
Total	**–31%**	**–38%**	**–41%**	**–50%**	**–32%**	**–41%**

Note: Buildings (total) includes reductions from the agriculture, fishing and "other non–specified" sectors.

Energy demand in the residential sector in the BLUE Map scenario is reduced by 38%. Fossil fuels' share of energy demand in the residential sector falls from 34% in 2050 in the Baseline scenario to 31% in the ACT Map scenario and just 19% in the BLUE Map scenario. The reduction in fossil-fuel demand for space heating is due to significant tightening of building standards, so that all new residential buildings in OECD countries meet the equivalent of the passive house standard from 2015 onwards. Cold-climate non-OECD countries will take a parallel path. The scenario assumes that policies are introduced to ensure that existing buildings are refurbished to passive house standards. This is a key component of the BLUE Map scenario, given the low capital stock turnover of the residential sector in OECD countries. Some 200 million houses and apartments will require energy efficiency refurbishment by 2050.

In the residential sector, water heating accounts for 20% of the savings in BLUE Map, as system efficiency is improved through the use of solar hot water, gas condensing boilers and heat pumps. Reductions in demand for lighting and appliances account for around 22% of the total savings in the BLUE scenario. Cooling demand is set to grow rapidly in the residential sector, but from a low starting level, with much of the growth coming from developing countries. In the BLUE scenario, this demand is reduced significantly, but only contributes around 5% to savings given its still-low share.

The service sector achieves significant savings from improved lighting efficiency, due to its generally higher levels of lighting and lighting hours compared to the residential sector. Water heating accounts for around 16% of service-sector savings in BLUE Map, and the share of hot water provided by heat pumps and solar hot water systems increases significantly. Solar hot water systems provide between 14% and 42% of hot water needs in the service sector in 2050, depending on the region. Tightened building standards are essential to reduce space heating intensity in the OECD countries and to reduce cooling loads in developing countries. Space heating and cooling account for 32% and 13% respectively of the savings in the BLUE Map scenario.

Energy consumption per household grows only very modestly in the Baseline scenario between 2005 and 2050. However, this masks significant growth in the demand for energy services, as policy-driven improvements in building shells and improving appliance efficiency in the OECD countries help to mute growth in energy demand. In developing countries, a switch to commercial energy and the more efficient use of biomass mean that even larger increases in energy services are met by relatively modest increases in per household energy consumption.

In the ACT Map and BLUE Map scenarios, global average energy consumption per household falls by 31% and 38% respectively by 2050 compared to Baseline (Figure 2.31). The relatively modest drop between ACT Map and BLUE Map represents the importance of fuel-switching to de-carbonise the buildings sector. Developing countries experience the smallest reduction below the Baseline scenario in both scenarios, in part reflecting their lower share of space and water heating.

Figure 2.31 ▶ Energy use per household by scenario

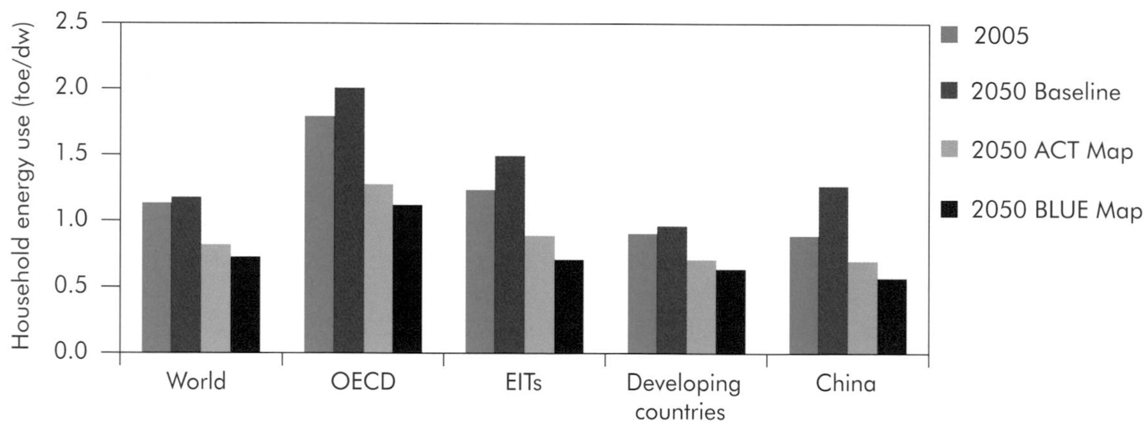

Key point

The ACT and BLUE scenarios result in significantly reduced energy use per household in all regions.

Industry

In the Baseline scenario, energy consumption in industry grows from 2 564 Mtoe in 2005 to 5 415 Mtoe in 2050. The changes in the fuel mix are relatively small. Final energy use in 2050 is 9% lower in the ACT Map scenario and 17% lower in the BLUE Map scenario compared to the baseline. While changes in the energy mix are relatively small in the ACT Map scenario, coal and oil use are significantly lower in the BLUE Map scenario, which is partly compensated for by increased use of biomass.

2

Figure 2.32 ▶ Industrial energy use in the Baseline, ACT Map and BLUE Map scenarios

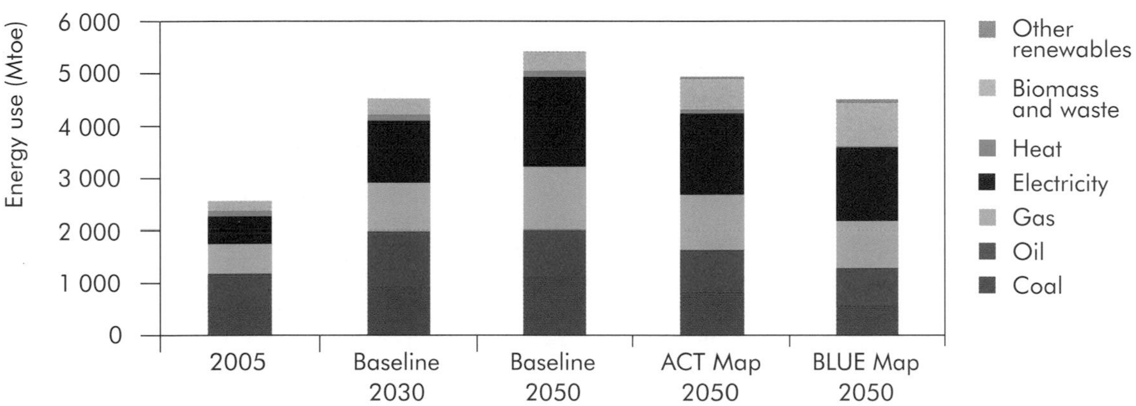

Note: In the IEA energy statistics, blast furnaces and coke ovens are accounted for in the "other transformation" sector. This figure excludes the transformation-sector component of industry activities. As these are typically industrial operations, they have been included with industry in the following analysis. The same applies for non-energy use (oil and gas feedstocks) for the chemical industry.

Key point

Industrial energy use more than doubles in the Baseline scenario between 2005 and 2050.

In the ACT Map scenario, the highest percentage reduction by 2050 is for coal use (24%), followed by gas (13%) and oil (11%). Electricity use declines by 9% and the use of biomass grows by 68%. The highest percentage reductions in the BLUE Map scenario, compared to the Baseline, are also for coal (-49%), gas (-25%) and oil (-22%). Electricity demand is reduced by 18%. Use of biomass increases by 128%.

The reduction in coal use can be attributed to fuel substitution and improvements in the efficiency of both iron- and steel-making and steam generation and use. The reduced oil use can be attributed to increased plastic recycling and a switch to biomass feedstocks. In general, the fuel substitution is from coal to natural gas and renewables. The reduction in electricity use can largely be attributed to the higher efficiency of motor systems. In addition, aluminium smelters, chlorine plants and electric-arc furnaces achieve a higher efficiency than in the Baseline scenario, due to the introduction of new technologies.

The percentage reduction is highest in the transition economies, followed by OECD countries and developing countries. The significant savings in transition economies can be explained by the currently low energy-efficiency of their industries.

In the iron and steel industry, existing energy-efficiency measures such as residual-heat recovery technologies in blast furnaces, coke ovens, basic oxygen furnaces, sintering plants and hot stoves are more widely applied. Larger furnaces, pre-reduction of iron ore during sintering, more reactive coke and top-gas recycling all reduce coal and coke use. The injection of waste plastic and its use in coke ovens increases. Direct reduced iron (DRI) will increasingly be produced at locations with cheap, stranded gas reserves, reducing the coal-based production of pig iron in large integrated plants. New technologies such as coal-based integrated smelt reduction and DRI production processes will reduce the coal and coke demand per tonne of iron and steel produced.

The remainder of the reduced coal demand is to a large extent accounted for by less coal use in boilers, notably in China and India. More-efficient boilers, better coal quality as a result of washing and improved operation of boilers all play an important role. More natural gas is substituted for coal, notably in small-scale boilers in urban environments. This development is driven by local air pollution concerns.

Apart from energy efficiency measures based on existing technologies, a large number of potential options for mitigating CO_2 emissions from industry have been considered in the ACT Map and BLUE Map scenarios. These include efficiency measures based on new technologies, including materials and product efficiency as well as process innovation, energy and feedstock substitution, and CO_2 capture and storage.

Figure 2.33 ▶ Industrial CO_2 emissions in the Baseline, ACT Map and BLUE Map scenarios, 2005 and 2050[4]

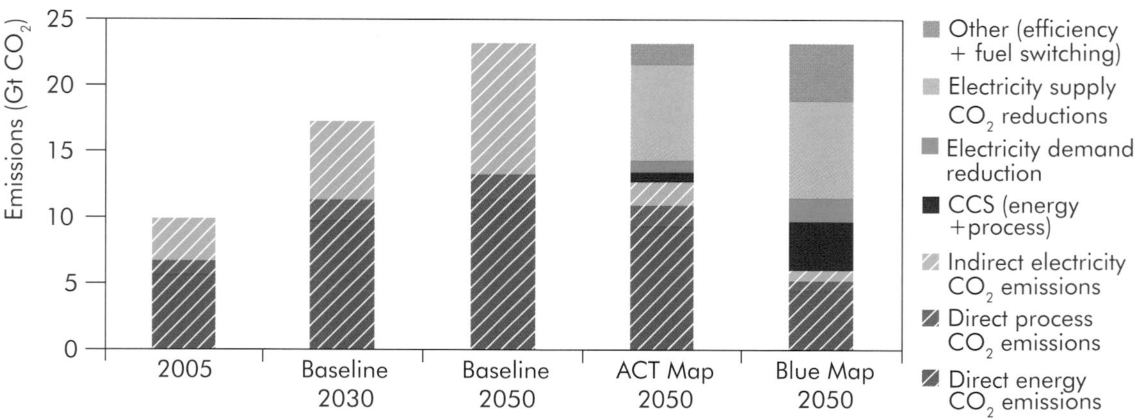

Key point

In 2050, industrial direct and indirect emissions in the ACT Map scenario are above the 2005 Baseline level, but drop below today's level in the BLUE Map scenario.

4. This figure includes upstream electricity emissions. These are allocated using the global average CO_2 emissions intensity for the electricity-generation sector in the specific year and scenario. The change in CO_2 emissions from upstream electricity generation over time in this figure is indicated separately. The coal use in coke ovens and blast furnaces is presented separately as well, as this is accounted for in the fuel-transformation sector. Process emissions that are related to industrial activity (mainly cement-making) but which are not related to energy use are also shown separately.

In the Baseline scenario, industrial CO_2 emissions, including the upstream emissions from electricity and heat generation and coal use in coke ovens and blast furnaces, and including process emissions, increase by 134% between 2005 and 2050, reaching 23.2 Gt CO_2 in 2050 (Figure 2.33). More than half are direct emissions, the remainder are indirect emissions in power generation. In the ACT Map scenario, direct emissions are reduced to 10.9 Gt CO_2 and in the BLUE Map scenario they are reduced to 5.2 Gt CO_2, a drop of 8 Gt CO_2, resulting in emissions that are 61% below the Baseline level in 2050 and 22% below the 2005 level. Total fuel and electricity savings account for 41% of the emissions reduction in the BLUE Map scenario (Figure 2.34). The main difference between ACT Map and BLUE Map scenarios in terms of emissions reduction is the growth in CCS use. In the BLUE Map scenario, CCS plays a key role and accounts for 37% of total emissions reduction (Figure 2.34). This CCS is used with iron-making processes, cement kilns, ammonia production, large CHP units and black liquor gasifiers in pulp production.

Figure 2.34 ▶ Industrial CO_2 emission reductions in the ACT Map and BLUE Map scenarios in 2050, compared to the Baseline scenario

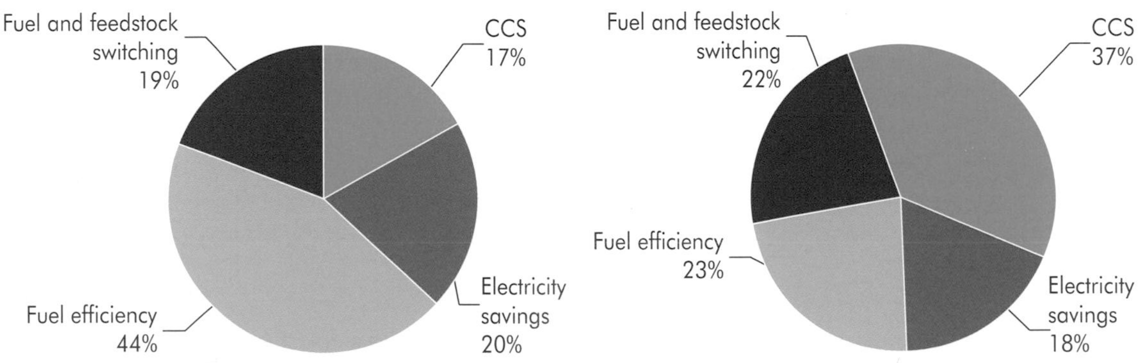

Note: Includes savings from coke ovens, blast furnaces and steam crackers, and CO_2 emission reductions in power generation due to reduced electricity demand in industry.

Key point

Efficiency gains account for 64% of the total CO_2 reduction in ACT Map, CCS gains ground in BLUE Map.

Table 2.9 lists the CO_2 reductions by industry sector. The savings compared to emission levels in 2005 depend on the growth of production and the potential to reduce emissions. The emission reductions compared to Baseline are similar, but the production growth rates are different and therefore the emission reductions compared to the base year of 2005 show a wider range.

Table 2.9 ▶ Industrial direct CO_2 emissions and reductions by sector in the ACT Map and BLUE Map scenarios, 2050

Reference	ACT	BLUE	ACT	BLUE
	Baseline 2050 (%)	Baseline 2050 (%)	2005 (%)	2005 (%)
Iron and steel	–20	–65	71	–26
Cement	–22	–68	38	–44
Chemicals and petrochemicals	–2	–53	101	–5
Other	–15	–53	69	–6
Total	**–16**	**–61**	**66**	**–22**

Note: Iron and steel includes blast furnaces and coke ovens. Industrial-process CO_2 emissions are included.

Industrial cogeneration of heat and power (CHP) doubles in the Baseline scenario and quadruples in the ACT Map and BLUE Map scenarios. In the IEA energy accounting system, the benefits of CHP are allocated to the power sector, where they show up as higher efficiencies in power plants (mainly in gas-fired power generation).

The marginal abatement cost in industry can be split into three main parts. First are energy efficiency options, many of which are cost-effective on a lifecycle basis provided they are introduced during the regular capital stock turnover cycle. Second is the industrial use of CCS, which is generally more costly than for coal-fired power plants, but which is essential for deep emission reductions in key industries such as iron and steel and cement-making. The third category includes more costly options for fuel and feedstock substitution, notably a switch to biomass. The shape of the curve (Figure 2.35) explains why emissions continue to rise in the ACT Map scenario and are only reduced below today's level in the BLUE Map scenarios.

Figure 2.35 ▶ Industrial sector marginal abatement cost curve for the BLUE Map scenario, 2050, compared to the Baseline scenario (direct and indirect emissions)

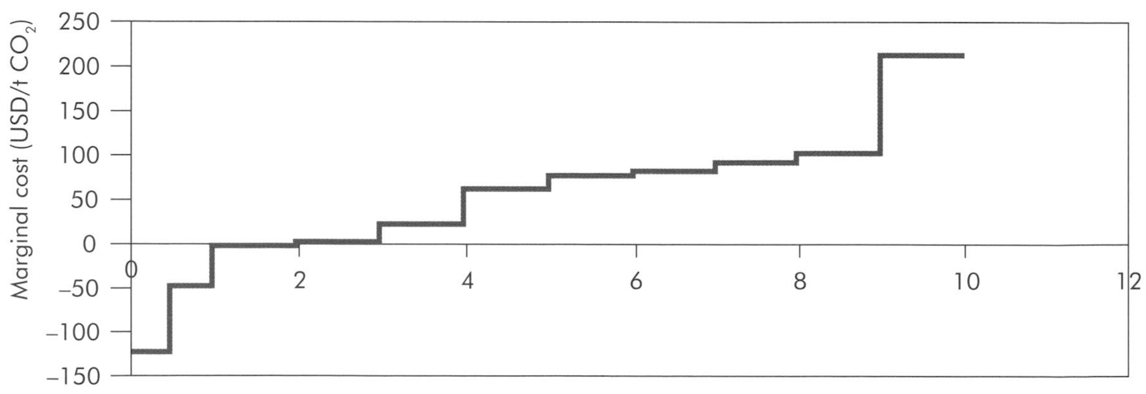

Key point

A significant potential exists in the USD 50/t to USD 100/t cost range, largely CCS-based.

Box 2.7 ▶ Carbon leakage and sectoral approaches

Government policies that lead to higher energy prices may cause industry to relocate to countries with lower energy prices. If this happens, CO_2 reductions in one country can result in increased emissions in another. The increase can exceed the reduction; for example, if an industry relocates to a country where process efficiency is lower. This may have potentially significant economic and environmental costs.

Modelling studies give different estimates of the likely impact of this relocation effect. Some energy-intensive industries are very sensitive to energy prices and have already relocated as a response to higher energy prices. Major energy and feedstock cost differences will mean that the growth of the petrochemical industry in the coming decades will be in the Middle East. Such relocation will happen irrespective of climate policies, but CO_2 pricing may accelerate it. Econometric models calibrated to past price sensitivities may underestimate the future impact of CO_2 policies on location choice and carbon leakage as markets are liberalised, logistics improve and developing countries have access to the latest production technologies.

In Europe, for example, the pulp and paper industry faces higher feedstock prices as renewables policies favour the use of wood for energy. Russia is planning an export tax on timber. These are cases where climate policies can already be seen to have an impact on location choices. In the United States, cement is already imported on a large scale from Asia into California, and similar effects are anticipated in Europe as production expands rapidly in North Africa and the Middle East. The case of cement is extreme, as this is a cheap and heavy material in which transportation costs matter. If carbon leakage can occur for cement, it is even more likely for other products. Therefore more analysis and monitoring is needed.

Many industries are increasingly competing on a global scale. Such effects need to be borne in mind by policy makers approaching the issue of industrial emission reductions. Increased emphasis should be given to energy efficiency (which increases competitiveness and is supported everywhere) and international sectoral approaches. The IEA is working with industry associations, other organisations and companies to develop these approaches further.

Global industrial energy use is currently 2 800 Mtoe, representing 35% of total final energy use. Energy consumption is dominated by a small number of energy-intensive sectors: iron and steel, chemicals and petrochemicals, non-ferrous metals, non-metallic minerals and pulp and paper account for more than two-thirds of current industrial energy use. This energy-intensive industrial production is also concentrated in relatively few countries. China accounts for about 80% of the growth in total industrial production over the past 25 years and today is the largest producer of commodities such as aluminium, ammonia, cement, and iron and steel. The United States, Western Europe and China are together responsible for half of global industrial energy use.

Industrial energy intensity has declined substantially over the last three decades across all manufacturing sub-sectors and all regions. However, the absolute levels of energy use and CO_2 emissions have continued to increase worldwide. Industrial final energy use increased by 72% between 1971 and 2005, at an average annual growth rate of 2%.

Recent analysis shows that there is a substantial potential for improving energy efficiency based on best practice technologies that are available today. Manufacturing industry can improve its energy efficiency by 18% to 26% based on proven technology. This estimate does not consider the economics of such change. Part of this efficiency potential will already be realized in the Baseline scenario (IEA, 2007c).

Figure 2.36 ▶ Trends in final energy intensity for key energy-intensive industry sectors under the different scenarios

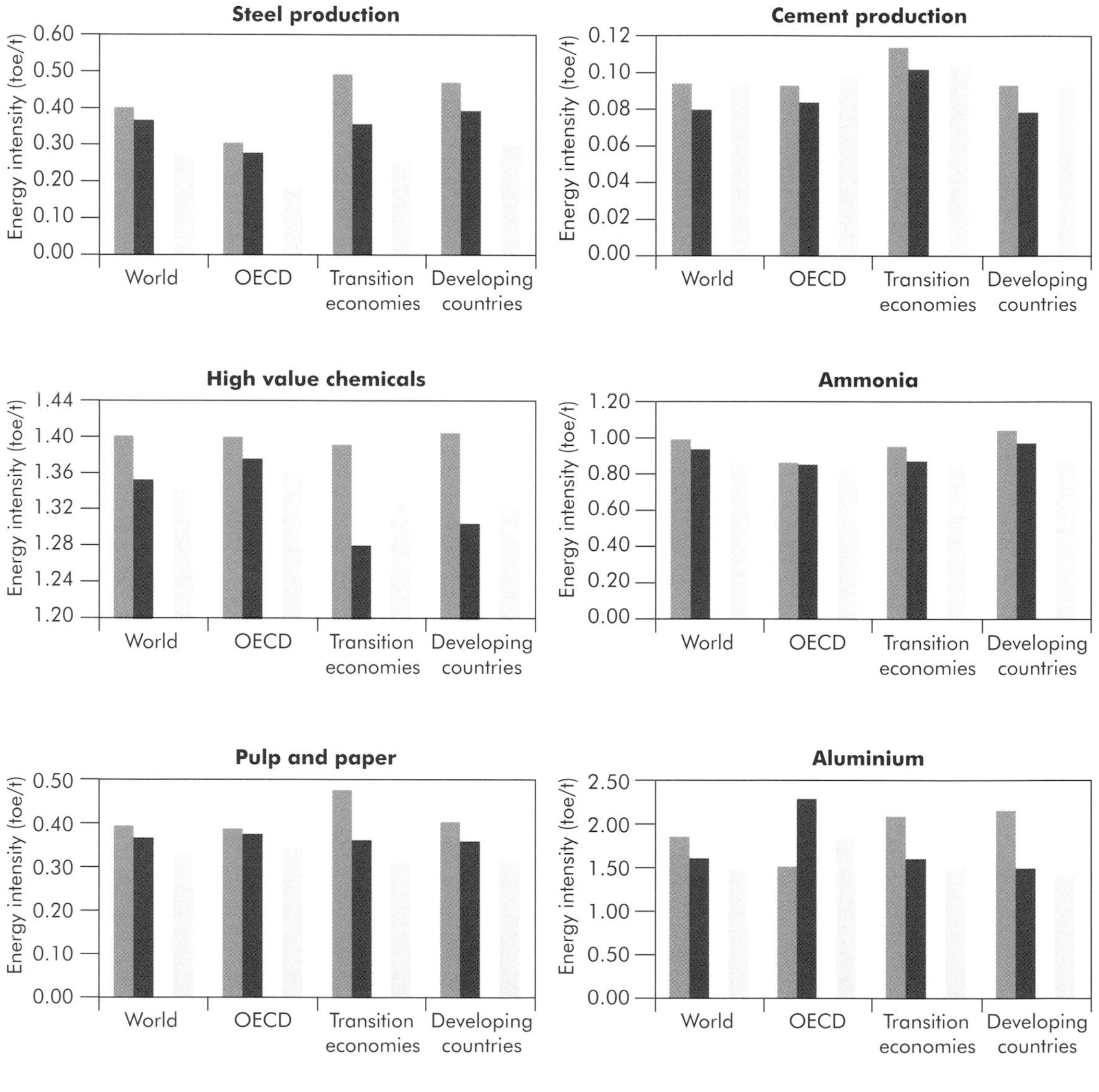

Key point

All energy-intensive sectors in all regions show substantial improvements in energy efficiency compared to today's levels.

In the Baseline scenario, industrial energy use (including industrial processes in the transformation sector) increases to 5 820 Mtoe by 2050, with China representing 28% of the total. The share of industrial energy use in OECD countries falls from 44% in 2005 to 27% in 2050. There are important energy-efficiency improvements under the Baseline scenario due to the natural replacement (*i.e.* retirement and refurbishment) of capital stock and the construction of new, more efficient plants to meet increasing demand for industrial products. As a result, the overall energy efficiency of industry improves by around 10%.

In the ACT Map and BLUE Map scenarios, no structural changes are assumed. But as a result of increased energy efficiency, energy use in 2050 is 550 Mtoe (9%) and 1 100 Mtoe (19%) lower than the Baseline. Over 60% of the energy reduction occurs in developing countries and nearly 30% in OECD countries.

The development of the energy intensity for key commodities is shown in Figure 2.36. In all cases it improves significantly – apart from the case of cement, where additional energy use for CCS exceeds all energy-efficiency gains. The efficiency potential for high-value chemicals is less than for other commodities because of the high share of feedstock energy, where no efficiency improvements are possible.

Sector results are discussed in more detail in Chapter 16.

Energy demand by fuel

In the Baseline scenario, total primary energy supply (TPES) grows at 1.6% on average per year, from 11 428 Mtoe in 2005 to 23 268 Mtoe in 2050 (Figure 2.37). This rate of growth is less than the 2.1% per year that occurred between 1971 and 2005, but it still represents an increase of 104% in primary energy demand between 2005 and 2050.

By 2050, coal becomes the predominant fuel and accounts for 37% of primary energy use. It surpasses oil demand in absolute terms between 2030 and 2050. Oil's share of TPES declines from 35% in 2005 to 27% in 2050. The share of natural gas declines 1%, to 20%. Non-fossil fuels account for just 16% of demand in 2050, down from 19% in 2005. Of the non-fossil fuels, nuclear's share declines from 6% in 2005 to 4% in 2050, and other renewables from 11% in 2005 to 10%, while hydro remains at 2%. It should be noted that the accounting for nuclear and renewables in primary energy terms does not properly reflect their importance for the energy system, as the conversion efficiencies from electricity to primary energy are somewhat arbitrary for these energy sources.

In the Baseline scenario, fossil fuel's share of total demand increases from 80% in 2005 to 84% in 2050, despite the growth in nuclear and renewable energy in absolute terms. It follows that concerns about energy security would continue, and significant climate change would be a consequence.

Figure 2.37 ▶ World total primary energy supply by fuel in the Baseline scenario

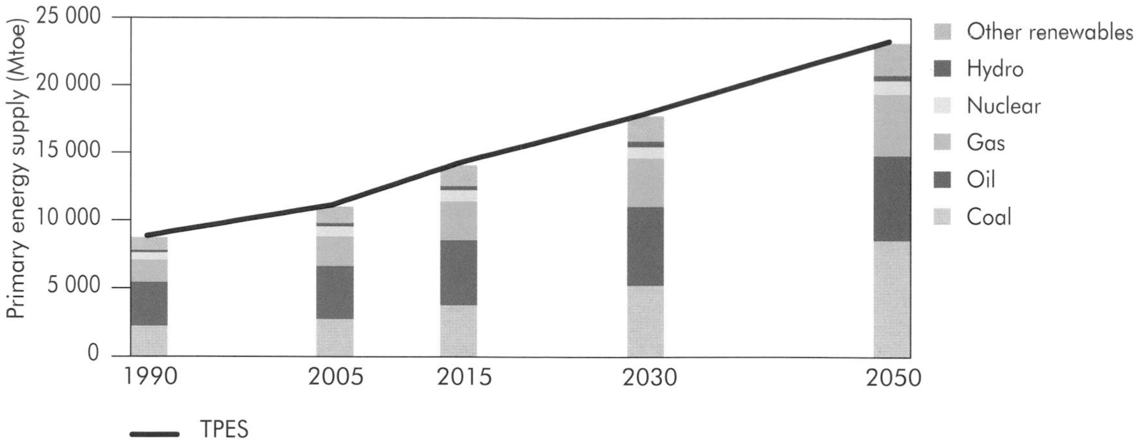

Key point

Primary energy use more than doubles between 2005 and 2050, with a very high reliance on coal.

The use of fossil fuels in 2050 is significantly lower in the ACT Map and BLUE Map scenarios than in the Baseline scenario. This ranges from 45% lower in the ACT Map scenario to 59% lower in the BLUE scenario (Figure 2.38). In absolute terms, total demand for fossil fuels in the BLUE Map scenario in 2050 is 13% below the level of 2005. But even in the BLUE scenarios, fossil fuels constitute a key component of the energy system. The reduction in fossil-fuel use can be attributed to energy efficiency gains and fuel-switching. The use of carbon-free fuels increases much faster than the total primary energy supply. Biomass exemplifies the magnitude of change: its use in 2050 reaches nearly the level of oil use today.

Figure 2.38 ▶ World fuel supply for Baseline, ACT Map and BLUE Map, 2050

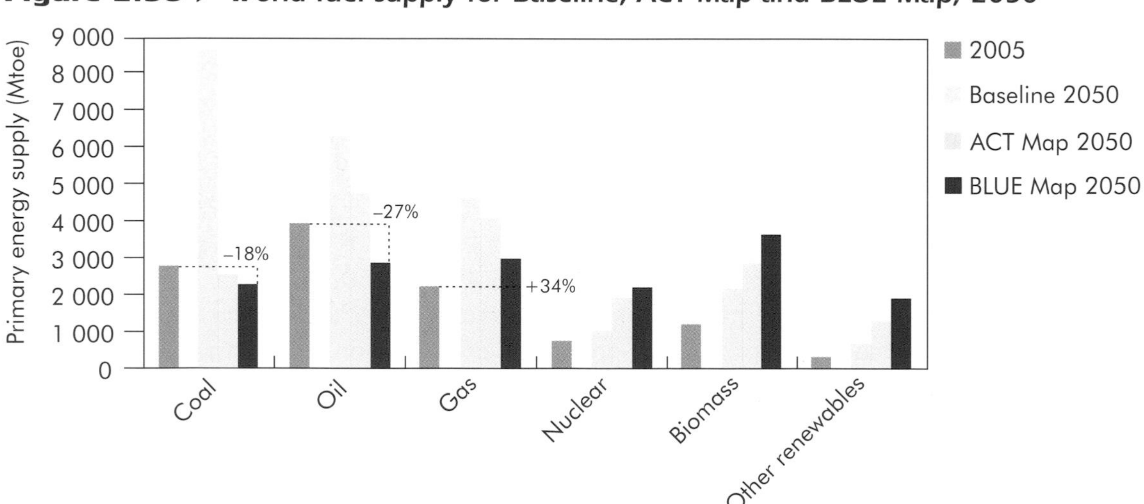

Key point

Fossil fuels continue to play a key role in the ACT Map and BLUE Map scenarios.

Coal

In the Baseline scenario, coal demand triples between 2005 and 2050 (Figure 2.39). Coal's share of total demand grows from 25% in 2005 to 37% in 2050. Between 2030 and 2050, coal eclipses oil as the single most important fuel. Coal's strong growth in the Baseline scenario is driven by three factors. First, high oil prices make coal-to-liquids (CTL) technologies more economical, and the production of synfuels from coal increases significantly after 2030. In 2050, nearly 1 800 Mtoe of coal is being consumed by CTL plants, predominantly in the OECD countries and a few developing countries. Second, high gas prices result in more new coal-fired electricity-generating plants being built. Third, energy-intensive industrial production grows rapidly in developing countries, especially China and India, which have large coal reserves, but limited reserves of other energy resources.

Figure 2.39 ▶ World coal supply by scenario, 2005-2050

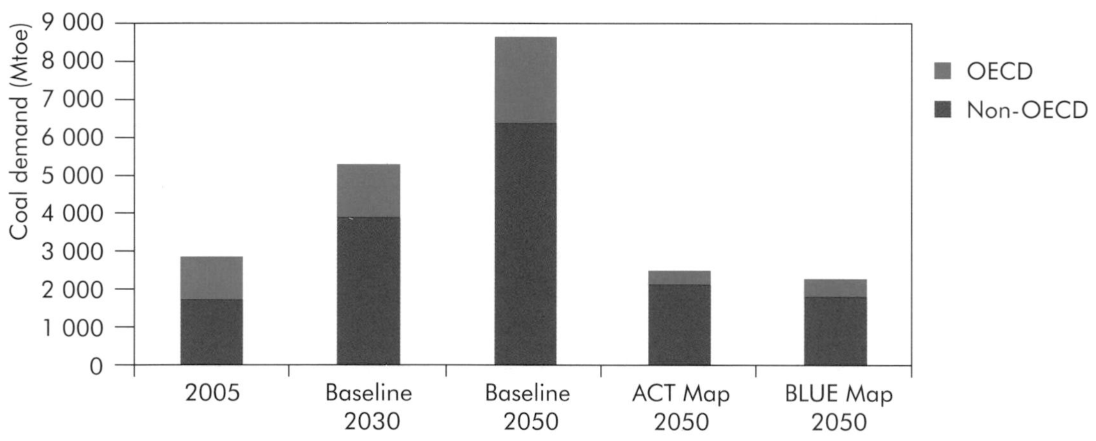

Key point

There is a strong reduction in coal demand in the Act Map and BLUE Map scenarios relative to the Baseline scenario.

Coal demand in the ACT Map scenario, at 2 466 Mtoe in 2050, is 15% lower than in 2005. This is the result of lower electricity demand in the ACT Map scenario, but is also a consequence of higher efficiencies and fuel-switching in power generation. In the BLUE Map scenario, coal demand in 2050 is 22% below the 2005 level. In percentage terms, coal use declines most in OECD countries. Coal use in 2050 in non-OECD countries is about equal to today's consumption in the BLUE Map scenario.

Oil

Oil demand in the Baseline scenario increases by 86% between 2005 and 2050, from 4 000 Mtoe in 2005 to 6 287 Mtoe in 2050. This is an increase from 85 Mb/d to 135 Mb/d. Such growth is unlikely to be capable of being met by conventional oil, which would account for about 92 Mb/d. A significant growth in the production of non-conventional oil is needed (heavy oil, tar sands, shale oil and arctic oil), to about 40 Mb/d. These resources account for 30% of total supply in 2050. A rising share of demand is also met by synfuels produced from coal and gas, which increase from very low levels today to 1 039 Mtoe in 2050 (14% of supply). Biofuels play some, albeit limited, role in the Baseline scenario.

Liquid fuel demand grows most rapidly in the transport sector, at 1.8% on average per year. In the buildings sector it grows by 1.3% per year and in the industrial sector by 1.1% per year.

Oil demand in the ACT Map scenario in 2050 is 30% less than in the Baseline scenario, reaching just 4 394 Mtoe. Primary oil supply (excluding synfuels) grows by 10% in the ACT Map scenario between 2005 and 2050. Synfuels from coal and gas are reduced by about two-thirds below the Baseline scenario and contribute 346 Mtoe in 2050. Total liquid fuel demand is 22% lower in 2050 in the ACT Map scenario than in the Baseline scenario.

In the BLUE Map scenario, the increased use of biofuels and improvements in the average fuel efficiency of transportation vehicles mean that oil demand is only 2 840 Mtoe in 2050, 55% lower than the Baseline scenario. Oil demand in 2050 drops about 27% below the current level. The supply security benefits of this development are obvious.

In the Baseline scenario, synfuels make up 14% and biofuels 1.7% of liquid fuels in 2050. In the ACT Map scenario, the share of synfuels drops dramatically, while biofuels account for 11% of supply.

Figure 2.40 ▶ World liquid fuel supply by scenario, 2005-2050

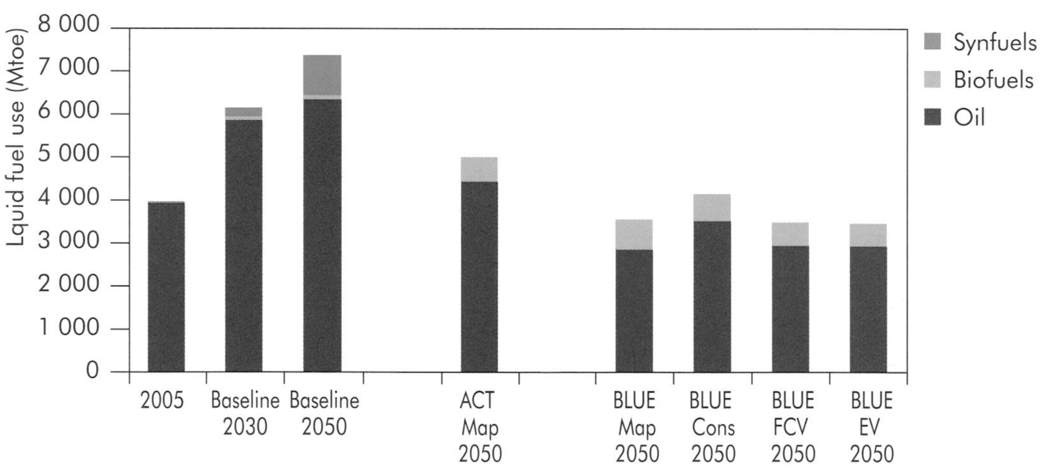

Key point

Primary oil demand in 2050 is below the 2030 Baseline level in all ACT scenarios, and below today's level in the BLUE scenarios.

While oil demand in the ACT Map scenario is 10% higher in 2050 than in 2005, it is 27% lower in the BLUE Map scenario. However, oil still accounts for the majority of fuel consumption in the transport sector in all of the ACT scenarios, and a substantial oil dependency remains.

Because of these significant demand reductions, there is less need for non-conventional oil and synfuels. This has important CO_2 benefits. The reduction in demand for oil in the ACT Map scenario – and even more in the BLUE Map scenario – has important supply security benefits.

In all of these scenarios, OPEC oil production in 2050 stays at least at the level of 2005. In the coming decades a substantial expansion of OPEC production will be needed in any scenario. Very large investments, especially in the Middle East, will be required to meet demand growth and to maintain secure supplies of transport fuels. Development of sufficient new oil supply is a key challenge in any of the scenarios.

Figure 2.41 ▶ World oil supply by scenario, 2005, 2030 and 2050

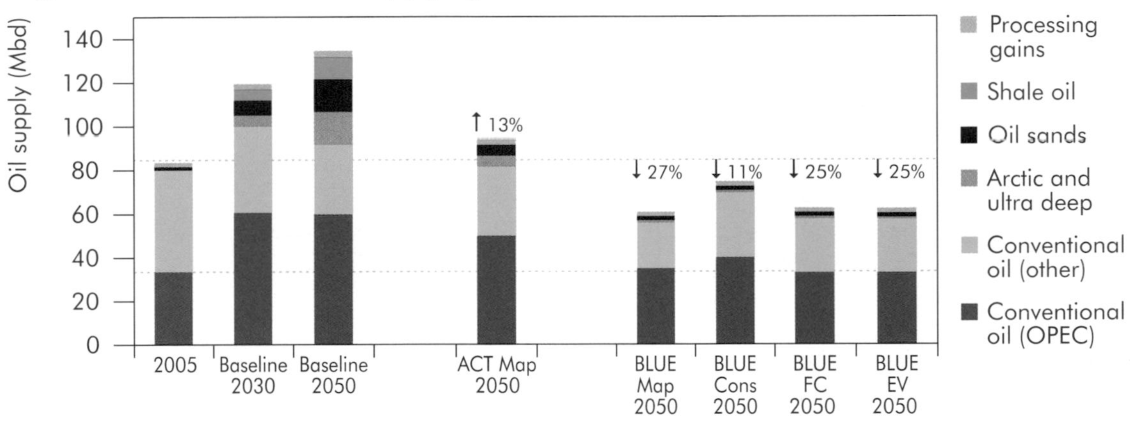

Key point

In the ACT Map scenario, oil demand in 2050 is below the 2030 Baseline level. Oil demand is below today's level in the BLUE scenarios.

Box 2.8 ▶ *World Energy Outlook 2008*: analysis of oil supply prospects

The 2008 edition of the IEA's World Energy Outlook will include an in-depth analysis of the medium- to long-term prospects for crude oil production. It will focus on the factors that will determine future production rates at the world's currently producing fields, the rate at which other fields that have already been discovered are developed, and the prospects for new discoveries. This analysis is intended to support the growing demand for more transparency in oil-reserve and production data and to provide insights into underlying trends in decline rates at the world's biggest oilfields, the adequacy of current investment plans, and the technical and economic feasibility of continuing expansion of global hydrocarbons production through to at least 2030.

The analysis will comprise a mixture of detailed quantitative analysis of historical data on resources and production; modelling and projections of oil and gas supply; and qualitative assessment of technological and structural factors, including opportunities for international oil companies to gain access to reserves. A central pillar of the work will be a detailed field-by-field analysis of trends in and prospects for production from more than 250 of the world's largest producing oilfields, with the aim of identifying the impact of geology and the application of technology on production and recovery rates. The work will also involve a bottom-up assessment of recent trends in upstream investment and near-term plans for such investment, including major new projects and capacity additions at existing and yet-to-be-developed fields.

The reduction of oil demand in both the ACT and BLUE scenarios can be largely attributed to the transport sector (Figure 2.42). This reflects the fact that oil demand for transport is rapidly rising in the Baseline scenario. The reduction of primary oil demand is less than the reduction in the demand for oil products as synfuel production is phased out in the scenarios (796 Mtoe less synfuel in 2050).

Figure 2.42 ▶ Reduction in oil demand by sector in the ACT Map and BLUE Map scenarios, 2050[5]

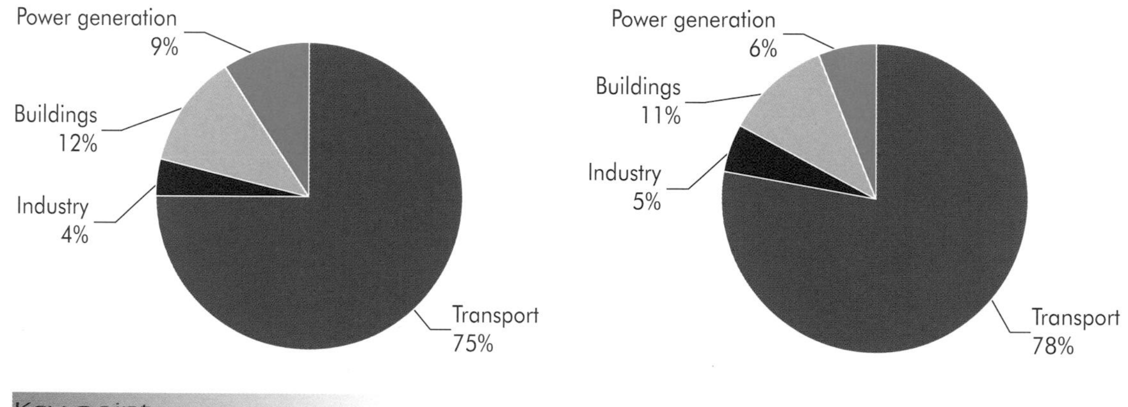

Key point

Savings below the Baseline scenario in 2050 in ACT Map are around half of current total oil demand.

In the Baseline scenario, non-OECD countries' share in oil demand rises from 47% in 2005 to 68% in 2050. In the ACT Map and BLUE Map scenarios, however, it is around 62% in 2050. This lower share can be explained by the higher efficiency improvement potential of non-OECD countries.

Natural gas

Primary demand for natural gas in the Baseline scenario grows at 1.3% on average per year between 2005 and 2050, rising from 2 354 Mtoe to 4 605 Mtoe (Figure 2.43). Global gas use by the electricity generation sector doubles, from 909 Mtoe in 2005 to 1 488 Mtoe in 2050. Natural gas used in other transformation activities grows at 1.6% per year, from 300 Mtoe in 2005 to 828 Mtoe in 2050. Most of this increase is for gas-to-liquids plants and refinery hydrogen production. Demand for natural gas in the final consumption sectors grows at 1.6% per year, with little difference between the sub-sectors at the global level.

5. Includes conventional oil, non-conventional oil, and synfuels from coal and gas.

Figure 2.43 ▶ World gas supply by scenario, 2005-2050

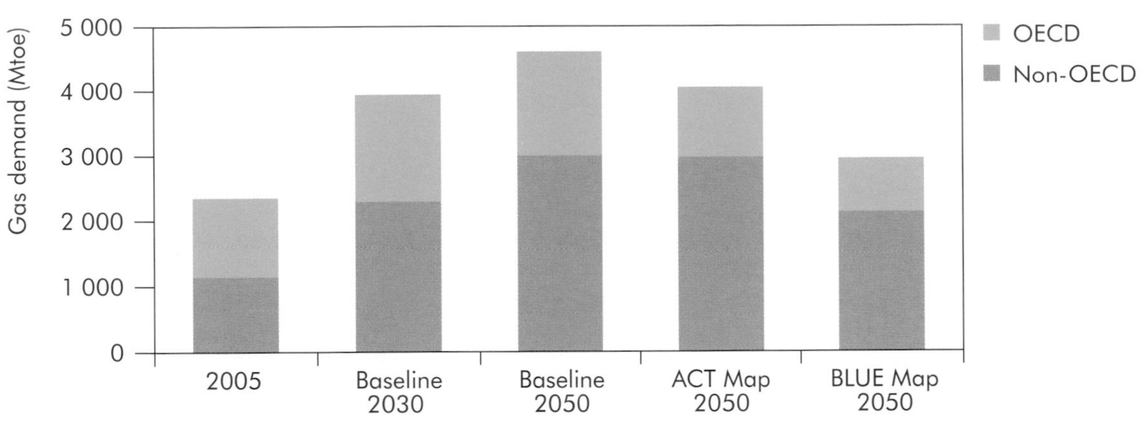

Key point

Despite significant reductions below the Baseline scenario in 2050, demand for natural gas in the ACT Map and BLUE Map scenarios is still significantly higher than today's level.

Global use of natural gas in the ACT Map scenario grows by 1.1% per year on average, with total consumption reaching 3 945 Mtoe in 2050. This is 660 Mtoe less than in the Baseline scenario in 2050, but still 68% higher than in 2005. Gas demand is 2 951 Mtoe in the BLUE Map scenario in 2050, 25% higher than today.

Primary demand for natural gas in developing countries increases by 230% in the Baseline scenario, from 660 Mtoe in 2005 to 2 351 Mtoe in 2050, or 2.8% per year on average. The share of non-OECD countries in world gas demand rises from 49% in 2005 to 65% in 2050 (Figure 2.44). It rises further to 74% in the ACT Map and BLUE Map scenarios. By 2050, developing countries will consume more gas than the OECD countries, with one-third of the growth in demand coming from electricity generation and the remainder from end-use sectors and fuel transformation. Between 2005 and 2050, demand nearly doubles in transition economies in the Baseline scenario and grows by almost half in the BLUE Map scenario.

Demand for gas in OECD countries grows at 0.6% per year, from 1 211 Mtoe in 2005 to 1 605 Mtoe in 2050. As in the developing countries, the bulk of the increase in OECD demand comes from end-use sectors.

Electricity

Electricity demand in the Baseline scenario increases on average 2.2% per year between 2003 and 2050, making electricity the fastest-growing component of total final demand. Electricity demand increases from 1 564 Mtoe (18 196 TWh) in 2005 to 4 293 Mtoe (49 934 TWh) in 2050. Electricity's share of final demand increases from 17% in 2005 to 25% in 2050. These trends are driven by rapid growth in population and incomes in developing countries, by the continuing increase in the number of electricity consuming devices used in homes and commercial buildings, and by the growth in electrically driven industrial processes. Electricity demand in buildings and in industry grows at a rate of 2.5% per year in the Baseline scenario.

Figure 2.44 ▶ Electricity demand by sector in the Baseline scenario, 2005-2050

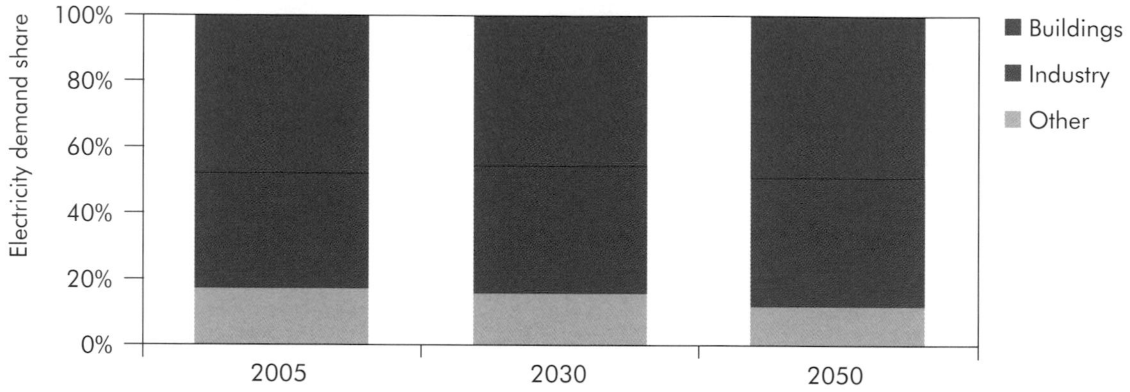

Key point

Demand continues to grow at similar rates in all end-use sectors.

Baseline electricity demand in developing countries grows on average 3.8% per year, two-and-a-half times as fast as in OECD countries. This is primarily due to higher population growth and rapid increases in GDP and per-capita incomes in developing countries. Between now and 2050, millions of people in developing countries will gain access to electricity.

In the ACT Map scenario, global electricity demand growth is reduced to on average 1.6% per year, with demand reaching 3 393 Mtoe (39 471 TWh) in 2050 (Figure 2.45). These reductions result in electricity demand growth in the ACT Map scenario being just half that of the Baseline scenario by 2050. Electricity demand in 2050 is 21% below the Baseline scenario level. Three-quarters of the reduction in electricity demand occurs in the buildings sector. These reductions in electricity demand contribute significantly to the total emissions savings attributable to end-use efficiency. In the low-efficiency scenario, electricity demand in 2050 is 14% higher than in the ACT Map scenario, at 3 662 Mtoe (42 599 TWh).

Further savings occur in the buildings sector and in industry in the BLUE scenarios, but these are outdone by increased electricity demand for plug-in hybrid electric vehicles and heat pumps. As a consequence, electricity demand in the BLUE Map scenario is 3 641 Mtoe (42 340 TWh) in 2050.

Figure 2.45 ▶ Electricity demand in the Baseline, ACT Map and BLUE Map scenarios, 2005 to 2050

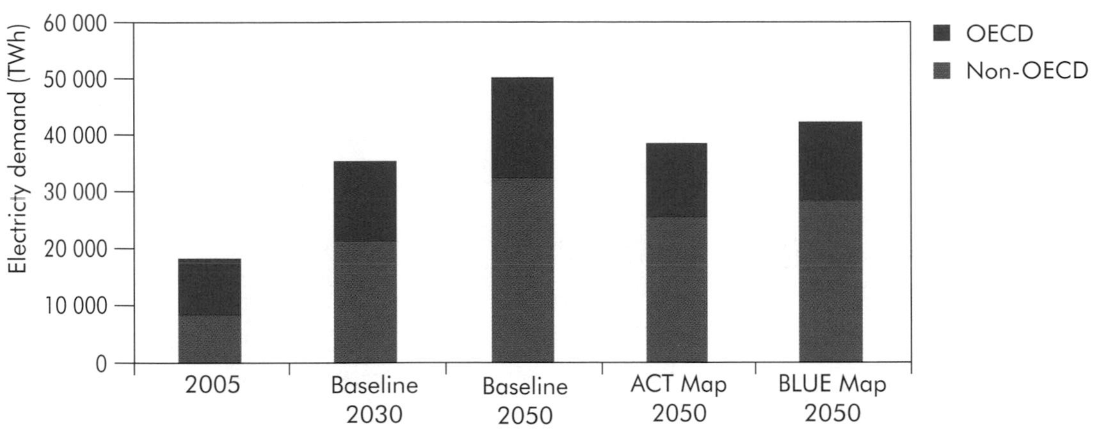

Key point

In the ACT Map scenario, electricity demand in 2050 is 27% lower than in the Baseline scenario. Demand rises again in BLUE Map due to electrification based on CO_2-free electricity supply.

Biomass

Biomass is by far the most important source of renewable energy today, accounting for about 9% of total primary energy use. However, most biomass is used in traditional domestic heating and cooking. Only about 10% of biomass is used on an industrial scale for the production of electricity or fuels.

The role of biomass more than triples in the ACT Map and BLUE Map scenarios. In these scenarios, bioenergy use in 2050 would approach the level of oil consumption today.

This development would require fundamental improvements in agriculture and forestry. The challenge is that the world population will grow by 50% during the same period, with food intake rising correspondingly. Therefore, total productivity of all land currently in production must triple. Such growth has happened in recent decades, but its continuation in the coming decades will require major efforts. Development and use of high-yield crops, water management, soil management and land-use policies and considerations of ecological sustainability all need to be closely coordinated. The recent problems with rain forest and bushland clearing for first-generation biofuel crops show that a focus on energy alone can yield undesirable outcomes. Energy crops and food crops need to be optimised.

About half of the primary bioenergy would be used for the production of liquid biofuels. The other half would be used for power generation, heating and industrial feedstocks.

Figure 2.46 ▶ Biomass use in the Baseline, ACT Map and BLUE Map scenarios, 2005-2050

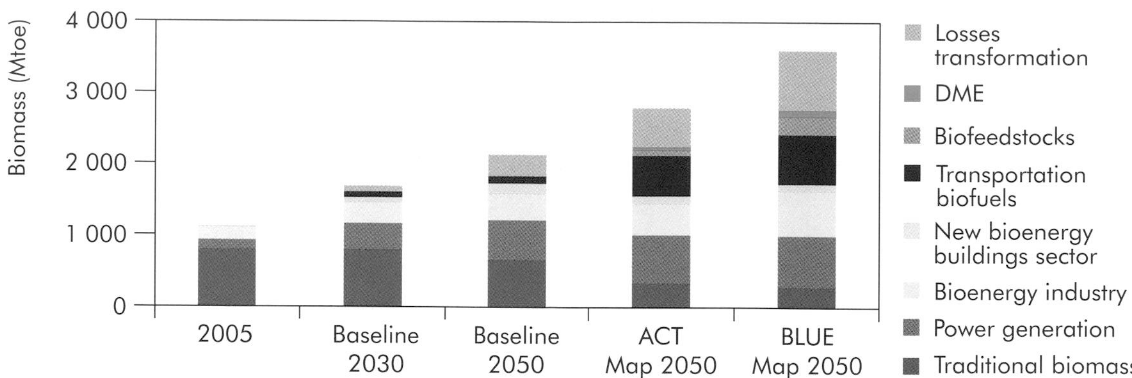

Note: Transformation losses in the production of liquid biofuels from solid biomass are indicated and accounted for in the energy balances.

Key point

Biomass use increases significantly in the ACT Map and BLUE Map scenarios.

Beyond 2050

The ACT Map and BLUE Map scenarios can offer technology pathways that may eventually stabilise CO_2 concentrations in the atmosphere. However, to effectively mitigate climate change, the progressive reduction in CO_2 emissions through to 2050 would have to continue into the second half of this century. While the ultimately sustainable level of energy CO_2 emissions is not yet clear, there is little doubt that the carbon intensity of economic activity will need to be reduced still further after 2050.

Energy technology development takes place on a timescale of decades, often followed by decades of gradual growth. Although it is possible to assess developments until 2050 based on technological information that is available today, such an approach reaches its limits beyond 2050. Developments beyond 2050 may have consequences for earlier investments in long-life energy infrastructure.

The development of the BLUE Map scenario, as described in this chapter, implies a heavy reliance on CCS between now and 2050, and therefore also a prominent role for CCS beyond 2050. This can be considered as part of a transition to a more sustainable energy system.

For the power sector, the main challenge is that the sector cannot rely on underground CO_2 storage forever. Limited regional storage potentials must result in a plateauing and eventually gradual phase out of CCS beyond 2050. Alternative solutions will be needed beyond 2050. This implies a continued shift from fossil-fuel-based power generation to renewables, and possibly some acceptable forms of nuclear energy – for example fusion. These changes in power production entail further changes in power transmission and distribution. Realisation of longer-range transmission systems will require new types of transmission systems with lower losses and lower costs, smaller land-use footprints, and reduced visual impacts. It will be crucial to develop efficient and affordable electricity storage technology further.

Decarbonising the end-use sectors, which is more difficult, would need to be achieved in the following decades. The more radical changes in the BLUE Map scenario could be regarded as providing an indication of the trends that may develop more strongly, and perhaps with more certainty, in the second half of this century. While electrification starts to play a role in the BLUE Map scenario in 2050, this will need to accelerate beyond 2050.

For the transport sector, the technologically "optimal" solution is not yet clear. User-friendly public transportation can play a more important role. High-speed trains, an example of such a gradual transition, began in the 1970s. Hydrogen would be another CO_2-free energy carrier. The development of a hydrogen infrastructure will depend on developments in the transportation sector. It seems unlikely that a hydrogen network will develop solely for stationary applications. Developments in the coming decade will show if hydrogen has a viable future. For the buildings sector, spatial planning can play a more important role on this long timescale. Compact cities will have a significant mitigating effect on transportation energy demand.

While carbon-free alternatives exist in the power sector, radical new process designs will be needed for certain industrial processes such as iron-making and cement-making. At present, these sectors lack a viable carbon-free alternative, and the ACT and BLUE scenarios imply a heavy reliance on CCS. In the longer term, radical new solutions will be needed, possibly based on affordable CO_2-free electricity, solar energy, or a radical change in the way structural materials are produced and used.

PART 2 THE TRANSITION FROM PRESENT TO 2050

3

Chapter 3 TECHNOLOGY ROADMAPS

Key Findings

- *Global emissions stabilisation and even a 50% reduction in CO_2 emissions by 2050 are technically feasible. But the technologies to deliver those outcomes remain far from economically viable in the current policy environment. A portfolio of technology options will be needed to combat future increases in CO_2 emissions and to offset the increase in energy demand.*
- *Without clear signals or binding policies from governments on CO_2 prices and standards, the market on its own will not be sufficient to stimulate industry to act with the speed or depth of commitment that is necessary. A clear, long-term vision is needed that can underpin investor confidence to further invest in innovative technologies.*
- *Technology roadmaps are highly dependent on policy targets. The BLUE scenario would entail a marked and unprecedented rapid shift from the Baseline scenario.*
- *More work is needed at all levels – including governments, industry, R&D institutions, financial investors, and institutions – to:*
  - *develop sound policies and measures to enable more continuous R&D investment in emerging clean technologies;*
  - *develop clear, long-term incentives to help establish investor confidence in innovative technologies;*
  - *identify policies and measures that will advance consumer awareness of clean technologies and their intended benefits;*
  - *identify future actions to alter consumer behaviour and preferences and to accelerate the adoption of clean technologies;*
  - *create the educational incentives and viable career paths that are necessary to ensure that skilled staff are available to make the transition to a more sustainable energy future; and*
  - *create the legal and regulatory framework needed to develop these technologies.*
- *Roadmaps offer a starting point for the further development of an international collaborative framework.*

Overview

Successfully achieving the outcomes of the ACT Map scenario will take a major, co-ordinated and sustained international effort. Achieving the outcomes of the BLUE Map scenario will be even more challenging. Yet the benefits of these efforts will be substantial in terms both of climate change and of improving energy security through lower energy consumption. They tackle the environmental consequences of industry that may otherwise impose constraints on economic growth world-wide.

The task is urgent, as it must be carried out before a new generation of CO_2-intensive capital stock becomes established. It will take decades to complete and require political fortitude and significant investment. Continued research and development of clean alternative technologies and improvements in process efficiency will be crucial to its success.

Achieving these objectives will require a transformation in how we generate power; how we build and use homes and communities, offices and factories; and how technologies are developed and deployed in the transport sector. It will also require a transformation in consumer awareness and behaviour. These in turn will depend on political courage and substantial public- and private-sector investment, alongside significant intellectual effort in the research, development and deployment of new energy technologies. Responding to market signals, the private sector will in practice deliver most of the required changes. But the market on its own cannot always deliver the desired results.

Governments have a major role to play in supporting innovative R&D; in developing policies to allow open markets; and in co-operating with industry and the financial sector to develop appropriate market conditions to allow technologies to surmount some daunting barriers. Industry looks to governments to share the political, and in some cases financial, risks linked with bringing many of these clean energy technologies to market. Governments need to create the economic environment, without picking any winners (still less losers), that will let technologies compete on environmental criteria and will make carbon-abating technologies competitive. Intergovernmental agreements on a global post-Kyoto framework will be an important part of this.

Action is also needed to increase public awareness, acceptance and understanding of the energy and climate challenge and to help the public to better understand their role in combating climate change and improving energy security.

The IEA can describe and recommend a way forward to achieve these outcomes. But they will only be achieved if government policy makers and industry leaders agree to:

- create policies that eliminate barriers to technological advancement;
- create market and financial incentives to allow the development and deployment of clean energy technologies;
- engage the power of the marketplace to drive future technology breakthroughs.

Roadmaps

This chapter presents 17 technology roadmaps, each outlining one technological approach that could be considered to help reach emissions stabilisation (ACT

Map scenario) or a 50% reduction in emissions level (BLUE Map scenario) by 2050. All countries have an important role to play in bringing these clean energy technologies to market. Developed countries will play the largest role in terms of RD&D, but many of these technologies will only be viable if they are deployed and commercialised in developing as well as in developed countries.

International co-operation will help to reduce the costs and speed up the development and deployment of these technologies. The roadmaps show that a great deal needs to be accomplished in the next 20 years if the technologies needed to reduce climate change and improve energy security are to have an impact. They can serve as a starting point for developing an international collaborative framework.

The ETP model encompasses a vast range of technologies (see Annex D). It was not feasible to create technology roadmaps for all of these. Rather, we have chosen to highlight 17 technologies which together represent over 80% of total CO_2 savings in the BLUE Map scenario. We can, depending on need, further refine and expand on these in future ETP reports. A number of enabling technologies, such as electricity storage and transmission, are treated within the eight power-generation roadmaps.

The technologies highlighted in the 17 roadmaps were selected as representing:

- the largest potential CO_2 reductions under the ACT Map and BLUE Map scenarios;
- technologies that are at advanced stages of RD&D, and in some cases deployment, with significant advancements expected between 2015 and 2030;
- a balanced portfolio of technologies, especially in regard to global and regional considerations.

Limitations of the roadmaps

The roadmaps developed for *ETP 2008* are examples of possible technology options. They should by no means be construed as being all-encompassing or as including all technologies. There are too many competing variables to assume these roadmaps could be applied across all technologies in every region of the world.

What is included in the roadmaps

Each roadmap provides the reader with a quick assessment of the relevant technologies and the steps that are needed to accelerate their adoption on the commercial marketplace under both the ACT Map and BLUE Map scenarios. The technology roadmaps are not dependent on each other and should be read individually.

Each roadmap includes:

- projections of the potential CO_2 reduction that could be reached by 2050 by adopting the technology, compared to the baseline scenario;
- projected distribution of the technology by region in 2050 for the ACT Map and BLUE Map scenarios;
- indicative estimates of global deployment needs (with regional details), total investment costs for RDD&D and total commercial investments needed to 2050, as a reference for global RDD&D planning;
- technology targets;
- a timeline indicating when the technology would need to reach certain RDD&D phases;
- the most important steps needed to bring the technologies to commercialisation;
- a brief outline of the key areas for international co-operation.

Our goal was to help guide policy and business decision-makers and encourage international co-operation and global efforts on energy-technology RDD&D. The roadmaps capture the essential RDD&D issues associated with these technologies and identify specific actions that are needed nationally and globally. It is our hope that they will spur discussions among governments, businesses and financial institutions on the feasibility and potential to collaborate to advance these technologies. It is not our intent to prescribe what must be done, only to identify possibilities that exist.

The technology roadmaps presented in this chapter are global roadmaps and hence may differ from national technology roadmaps. Where possible we have tried to take into consideration the content of those national roadmaps we are aware of.

How to use the roadmaps

The roadmaps were designed for policy makers and aim to help determine:

- how carbon targets could technically be met at least cost (rather than the policies needed to make this happen);
- what milestones are consistent with achieving significant outcomes to meet the ACT Map and BLUE Map objectives;
- who should be at the table (in terms of international collaboration, existing frameworks, IEA implementing agreements and industry);

- where deployment could occur;
- what funding is needed.

The investment cost figures given for deployment and commercial investments reflect total costs for all supply technologies, while in the case of demand side technologies they incorporate only the incremental cost for the various energy components. For example, in the case of hydrogen fuel cell vehicles the costs reflect only that of the fuel cell vehicle drive system and do not include the total cost of the vehicle. Greater detail on the system boundaries used in this cost analysis can be found in Chapters 5 and 6.

These roadmaps provide a snapshot of the technology outlook as we see it in 2008. They will need to be updated over time to reflect progress and developments in R&D, policy and the marketplace.

List of technology roadmaps

Power generation sector

CO_2 capture and storage (CCS) – Fossil fuel power generation

Nuclear power plants

Onshore and offshore wind energy

Biomass integrated gasification combined cycle (BIGCC) and co-combustion

Photovoltaic systems (PV)

Concentrating solar power (CSP)

Coal integrated gasification combined cycle (IGCC) systems

Coal ultra-supercritical steam cycles (USCSC)

Buildings sector

Energy efficiency in buildings and appliances

Heat pumps

Solar space and water heating

Transport sector

Energy efficiency in transport

Second-generation biofuels

Electric and plug-in hybrid vehicles

Hydrogen fuel cell vehicles

Industry sector

Carbon capture and storage (CCS) – industry, H_2 & fuel transformation

Industrial motor systems

Table 3.1 ▶ Emission reductions and RDD&D investment costs by technology in the ACT Map and BLUE Map scenarios

	CO_2 savings (Gt)		RDD&D (USD bn)	
	ACT Map	BLUE Map	ACT Map	BLUE Map
Power generation	**8.96**	**15.13**	**3 200-3 760**	**3 860-4 470**
CCS fossil fuel power generation	2.89	4.85	700-800	1 300–1 500
Nuclear power plants	2.00	2.80	600-750	650-750
Onshore and offshore wind energy	1.30	2.14	600-700	600-700
BIGCC and co-combustion	0.22	1.45	100-120	110-130
PV	0.67	1.32	200-240	200-240
CSP	0.56	1.19	300-350	300-350
Coal IGCC systems	0.66	0.69	350-400	350-400
Coal USCSC	0.66	0.69	350-400	350-400
Buildings	**6.98**	**8.24**	**320-400**	**340-420**
Energy efficiency in buildings and appliances	6.50	7.00	n.a.	n.a.
Heat pumps	0.27	0.77	70-100	90-120
Solar space and water heating	0.21	0.47	250-300	250-300
Transport	**8.20**	**12.52**	**260-310**	**7 600-9 220**
Energy efficiency in transport	5.97	6.57	n.a.	n.a.
Second-generation biofuels	1.77	2.16	90-110	100-120
Electric and plug-in vehicles	0.46	2.00	170-200	4 000–4 600
Hydrogen fuel cell vehicles	0.00	1.79	n.a.	3 500-4 500
Industry	**3.00**	**5.68**	**700-900**	**1 400-1 700**
CCS industry, H_2 and fuel transformation	2.00	4.28	700-900	1 400-1 700
Industrial motor systems	1.00	1.40	n.a.	n.a.
Total	**27.14**	**41.57**	**4 480-5 370**	**13 200-15 810**

Note: The table above shows the contribution of the 17 technologies where roadmaps have been created. It does not cover the CO_2-emissions-reduction of all technologies covered in the ETP analysis. For a full list of technologies please see ANNEX D.

Next steps

The roadmaps presented in *Energy Technologies Perspective 2008* could serve as a useful tool for further enhancing world-wide collaboration. What is needed includes:

- International agreement on an overall framework under which countries would share information and collaborate on joint RDD&D efforts, and appropriate joint funding levels and milestones;
- Further international collaboration to define the role of roadmaps and the appropriate elements they should contain, identify the appropriate technologies, share information on individual national efforts to develop technology roadmaps, and determine where possible overlap and gaps exists;
- Establishment of an international forum to allow for monitoring and information sharing.

The IEA could provide this central role through use of its existing worldwide network of co-ordinated R&D programmes.

CO_2 capture and storage: fossil fuel power generation

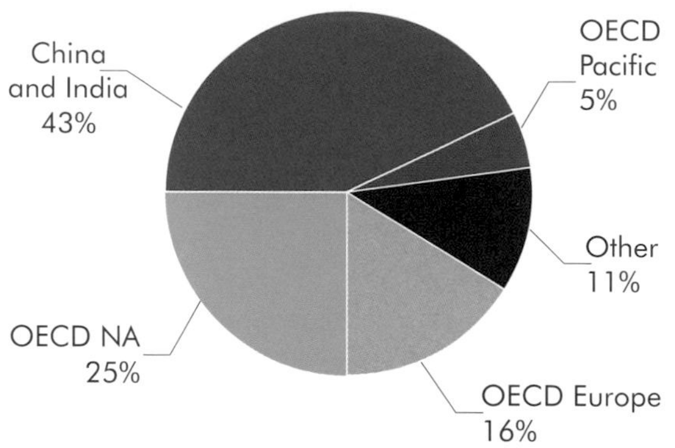

ACT 2.9 Gt savings 2050

China and India 43%
OECD Pacific 5%
Other 11%
OECD Europe 16%
OECD NA 25%

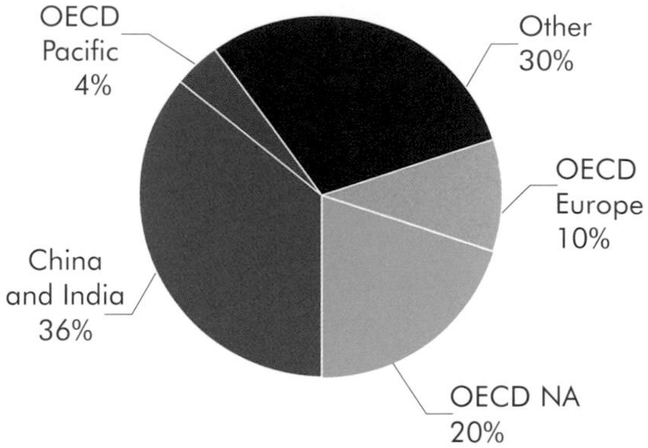

	Global Deployment Share 2030	RDD&D Inv. Cost USD bn 2005-2030	Commercial Inv. Cost* USD bn 2030-2050
OECD NA	35%	25-30	160-180
OECD Europe	35%	25-30	100-120
OECD Pacific	10%	7-8	30-40
China & India	15%	10-12	280-300
Other	5%	3-4	60-70

BLUE 4.9 Gt savings 2050

OECD Pacific 4%
Other 30%
OECD Europe 10%
OECD NA 20%
China and India 36%

	Global Deployment Share 2030	RDD&D Inv. Cost USD bn 2005-2030	Commercial Inv. Cost* USD bn 2030-2050
OECD NA	35%	30-35	350-400
OECD Europe	35%	30-35	150-200
OECD Pacific	10%	10-12	70-80
China & India	15%	12-14	400-450
Other	5%	4-5	250-300

* Excludes operating costs. Total including OPEX is USD 1.3-1.5 trillion for ACT and USD 4.0-4.5 trillion for BLUE.

Technology targets

	ACT: Emissions Stabilisation	BLUE: 50% Emissions Reduction
RD&D		
Capture technologies for three main options (post-combustion, pre-combustion, and oxy-fuelling)	Technologies tested in small- and large-scale plants. Cost of CO_2 avoided around USD 50/t by 2020. Chemical looping tested	
Demonstration targets	20 large-scale demo plants with a range of CCS options, including fuel type (coal/gas/biomass) by 2020	30 large-scale demo plants with a range of CCS options, including fuel type (coal/gas/biomass) by 2020
New gas-separation technologies: membranes & solid adsorption	New capture concepts: next-generation processes, such as membranes, solid absorbers and new thermal processes	
Technology transfer	Technology transfer to China and India	Technology transfer to all transition and developing countries
Deployment		
Regional pipeline infrastructure for CO_2 transport	Major transportation pipeline networks developed and CO_2 maritime shipping	
Deployment targets	Early commercial large-scale plants by 2015 (ZEP, ZeroGen, GreenGen)	30% of electricity generated from CCS power plant by 2050

Technology timeline

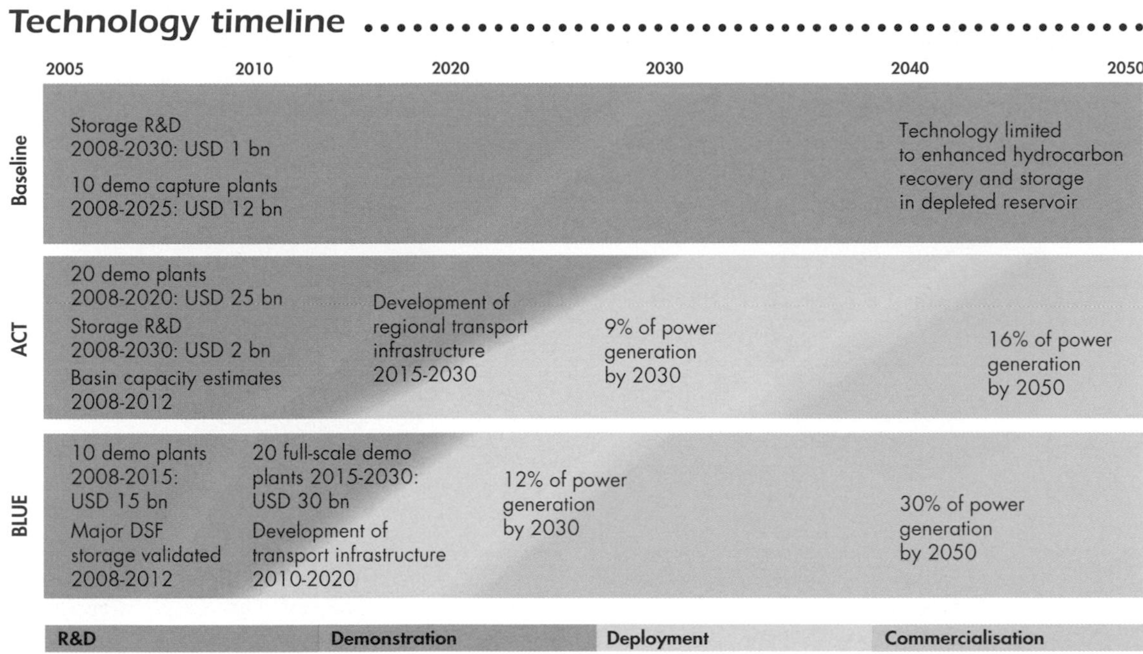

In this roadmap, commercialisation assumes an incentive of USD 50/t CO_2 saved.

Key actions needed

- Develop and enable legal and regulatory frameworks for CCS at the national and international levels, including long-term liability regimes and classification of CO_2.
- Incorporate CCS into emission trading schemes and post-Kyoto instruments.
- RD&D to reduce capture cost and improve overall system efficiencies.
- RD&D for storage integrity and monitoring. Validation of major storage sites. Monitor and valuation methods for site review, injection & closure periods.
- Raise public awareness and education on CCS.
- Assessment of storage capacity using Carbon Sequestration Leadership Forum methodology at the national, basin and field levels.
- Governments and private sector should address the financial gaps for early CCS projects to enable widespread deployment of CCS for 2020.
- New power plants to include capture/storage readiness considerations within design by 2015.

Key areas for international collaboration

- Development and sharing of legal and regulatory frameworks.
- Develop international, regional and national instruments for CO_2 pricing, including CDM and ETS.
- Raise public awareness and education.
- Sharing best practices and lessons learnt from demonstration projects (pilot and large-scale).
- Joint funding of large-scale plants in developing countries by multi-lateral lending institutions, industry and governments.
- Development of standards for national and basin storage estimates and their application.
- Organisations: CSLF, IEA GHG, IEA CCC, IPCC.

Nuclear power plants

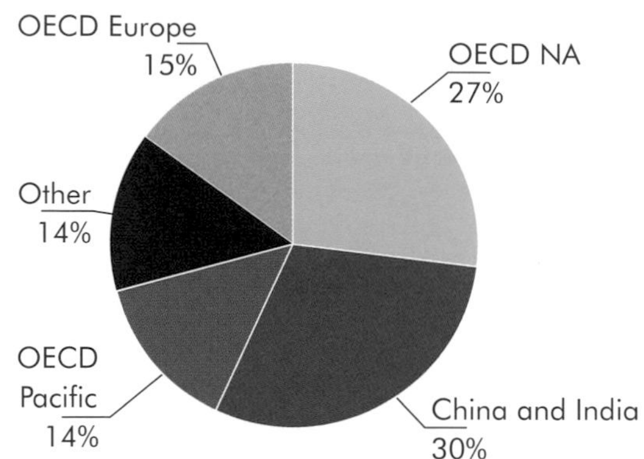

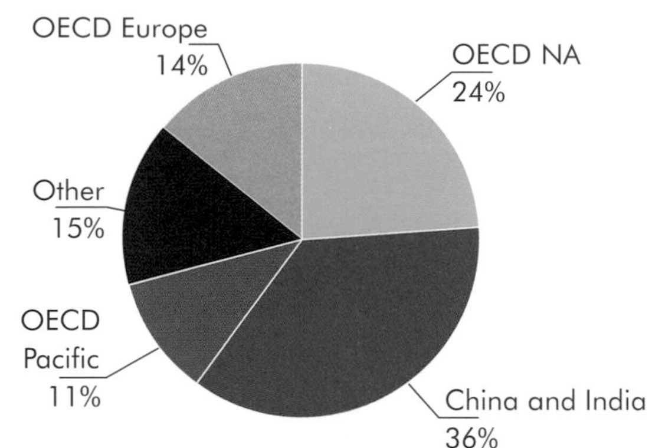

	Global Deployment Share 2035	RDD&D Inv. Cost USD bn 2005-2035	Commercial Inv. Cost USD bn 2035-2050
OECD NA	29%	170-220	210-250
OECD Europe	20%	115-150	110-140
OECD Pacific	15%	90-110	100-125
China & India	21%	140-160	225-275
Other	15%	90-110	100-130

	Global Deployment Share 2035	RDD&D Inv. Cost USD bn 2005-2035	Commercial Inv. Cost USD bn 2035-2050
OECD NA	26%	180-200	300-350
OECD Europe	18%	120-140	175-200
OECD Pacific	14%	90-110	140-160
China & India	26%	160-180	450-475
Other	16%	95-115	200-225

Technology targets

	ACT: Emissions Stabilisation	BLUE: 50% Emissions Reduction
RD&D		
Gen III and Gen III+ technology commercially available	Currently available	
Small and Medium Reactors (SMRs)	Prototype demonstration by 2030	Prototype demonstration by 2020
Gen IV reactors and fuel cycle (including H_2 production capabilities)	System design and prototype demonstration by 2030	System design and commercial implementation by 2030
Deployment		
Gen III and Gen III+	Gen III currently available. Gen III+ commercial deployment by 2025	
SMRs	Commercial deployment by 2030	Commercial deployment by 2020
Gen IV	Commercial deployment by 2045	

Technology timeline

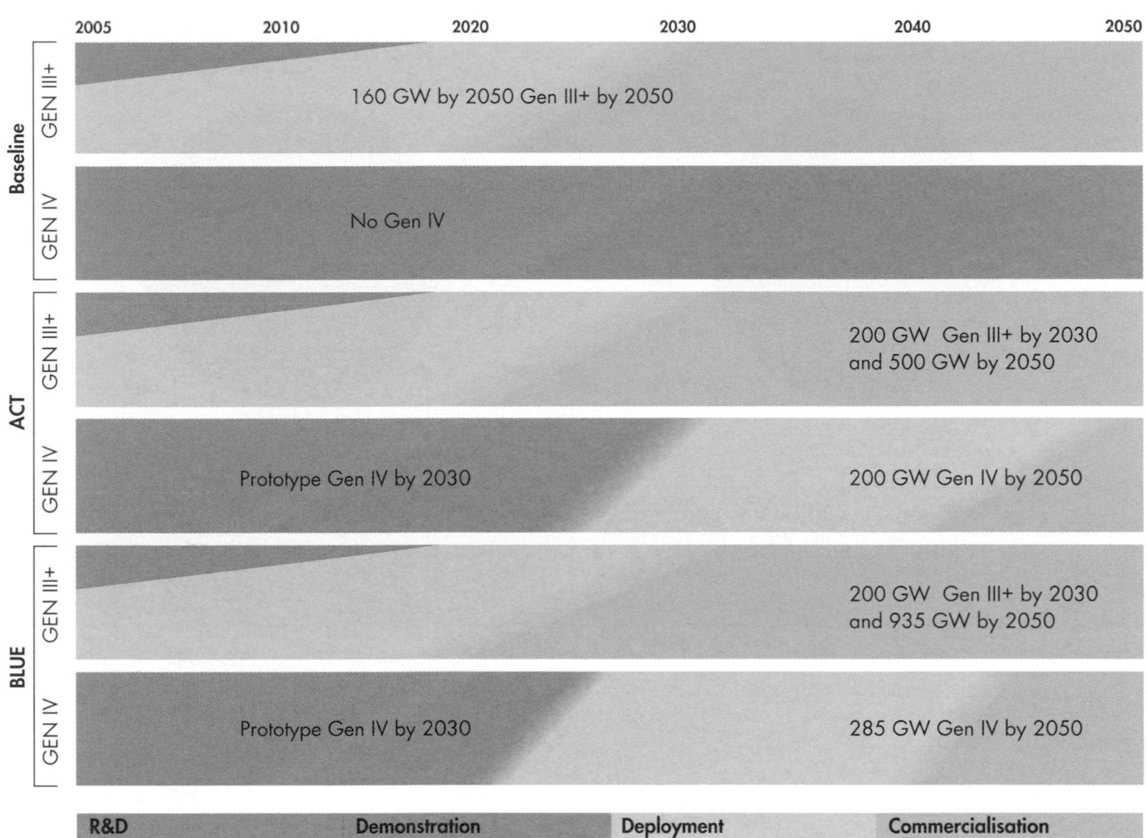

Key actions needed

- Development of Gen IV will help to reduce costs, minimise nuclear waste, enhance safety and hence improve public acceptance of nuclear.
- Small and Medium Reactor development; useful for smaller grid systems/ more isolated communities and ease financing difficulties.
- Continue effort to gain wider public and political acceptance. Public information programmes and National policies can help.
- Urgent need to regenerate a nuclear workforce to meet future demands.
- Need for continued effort to streamline licensing processes.
- Need to develop proliferation resistant fuel systems.
- Uranium exploration and mine development should be further increased.
- Fast reactors extend uranium resources by factor of 50 times or more.

Key areas for international collaboration

- Continued co-operation in the development of advanced systems (Gen IV) and the associated fuel cycles (e.g. P&T and actinide recycling). This includes sharing of expensive R&D facilities.
- Further development of international systems for non-proliferation (e.g. International Fuel Cycle, guaranteed fuel supplies, ratification of additional protocols to the non proliferation treaty).
- Development of internationally approved safety standards and designs.

Onshore and offshore wind energy

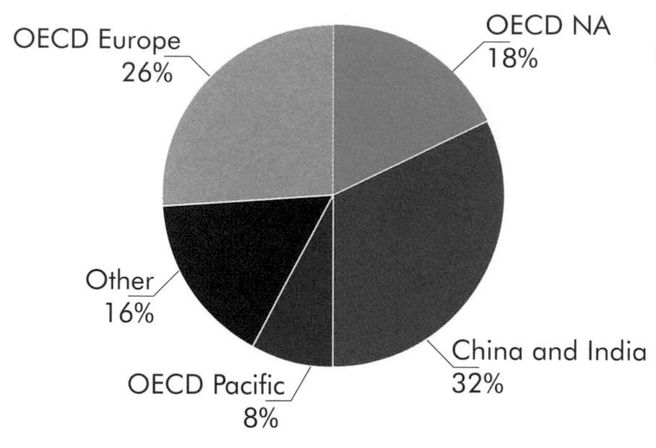

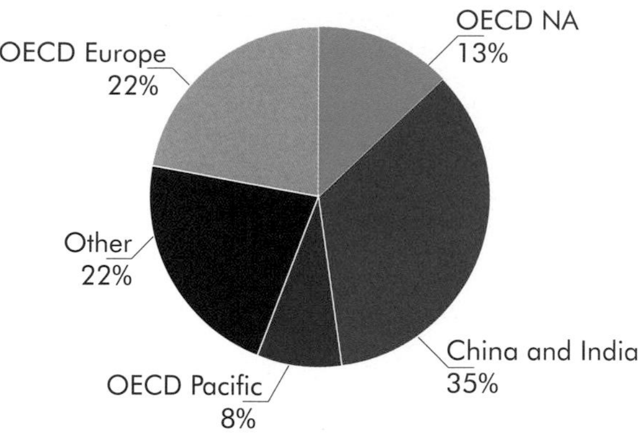

	Global Deployment Share 2030	RDD&D Inv. Cost USD bn 2005-2030	Commercial Inv. Cost USD bn 2030-2050
OECD NA	24%	140-160	75-85
OECD Europe	34%	200-220	100-110
OECD Pacific	10%	60-70	30-35
China & India	25%	150-170	130-140
Other	7%	45-55	65-75

	Global Deployment Share 2025	RDD&D Inv. Cost USD bn 2005-2035	Commercial Inv. Cost USD bn 2035-2050
OECD NA	24%	145-165	130-150
OECD Europe	38%	230-250	210-230
OECD Pacific	10%	60-70	70-80
China & India	19%	110-130	340-360
Other	9%	50-60	215-225

Technology targets

	ACT: Emissions Stabilisation	BLUE: 50% Emissions Reduction
RD&D		
High-resolution global mapping of and long term predictability of wind resource	Meteorological models for predictability. Micro-scale modelling for siting	
Reduce steel dependency	Develop alternative materials	
Reduce O&M "downtime" for offshore turbines	Secure, fast offshore access. Deep offshore support structures and corrosion resistance	Additional tasks as in ACT. Development of floating systems
Investment in RD&D	OECD private and public investment in RD&D should be in the region of USD 300 m per annum	
Deployment		
Available supply of turbines, components and support structures	Larger manufacturing facilities.	
Available transmission capacity. Optimise electricity network	Reinforce weak grids and interconnect. Dynamic line rating, HVDC (offshore)	Additional tasks as in ACT. Grid associated costs are shared across power sector
Maximum wind farm capacity factors	Match power curves to site wind regimes. Worldwide deployment onshore, offshore mainly in OECD	Additional tasks as in ACT. Additional offshore deployment in the developing world

Technology timeline

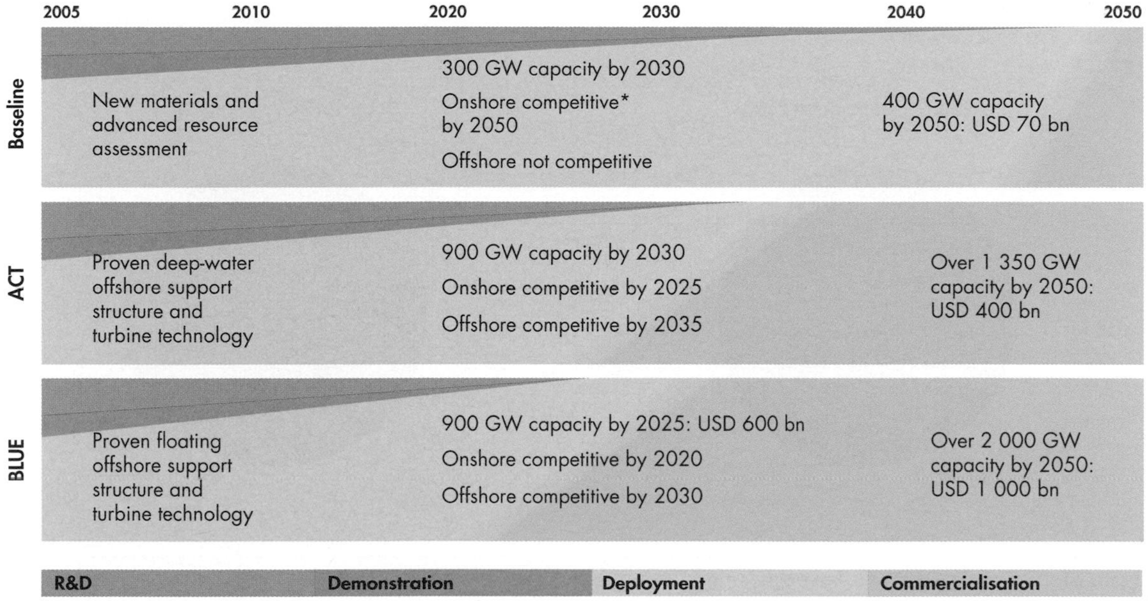

	2005–2010	2020–2030	2040–2050
Baseline	New materials and advanced resource assessment	300 GW capacity by 2030 Onshore competitive* by 2050 Offshore not competitive	400 GW capacity by 2050: USD 70 bn
ACT	Proven deep-water offshore support structure and turbine technology	900 GW capacity by 2030 Onshore competitive by 2025 Offshore competitive by 2035	Over 1 350 GW capacity by 2050: USD 400 bn
BLUE	Proven floating offshore support structure and turbine technology	900 GW capacity by 2025: USD 600 bn Onshore competitive by 2020 Offshore competitive by 2030	Over 2 000 GW capacity by 2050: USD 1 000 bn

R&D — Demonstration — Deployment — Commercialisation

* Already cost-competitive in good sites, but will take wider deployment to become competitive in general.

Key actions needed

- Internalisation of external costs of all technologies. Presently, the full cost to society of conventional technology is not reflected in price.
- Stable, predictable policy support to encourage investment.
- Fully competitive electricity markets, on a continental scale for aggregation of output from dispersed variable renewable generators, to smoothen aggregate variability profile.
- Reduce lead times for planning and construction of new transmission. In Europe they can be a long as ten years. The needs of large-scale wind power to be considered in the planning of new infrastructure development, onshore and offshore.
- Streamline and accelerate planning for new wind plants.
- Further measures to increase system flexibility (to enable higher share for variable renewables): development and cost reduction of storage technologies, encouragement of dispatchable plant in generation portfolio, interconnection of balancing areas, increased demand-side participation, and shorter scheduling periods (gate closure).
- Low-cost, long-range DC transmissions systems.
- Grid-associated costs are shared across power sector.

Key areas for international collaboration

- International co-operation should focus on identifying and building key interconnectors. Electricity prices vary from country to country, and sometimes regionally. Interconnection will benefit some at the expense of others. Need to find ways to overcome resistance to trade of electricity across borders.
- Offshore interconnection of wind farms.
- Establishment of continental scale, competitive electricity markets.

Biomass integrated gasification combined cycle and co-combustion

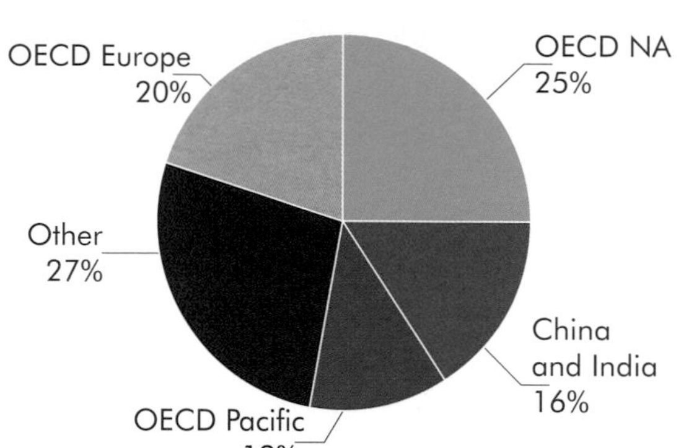

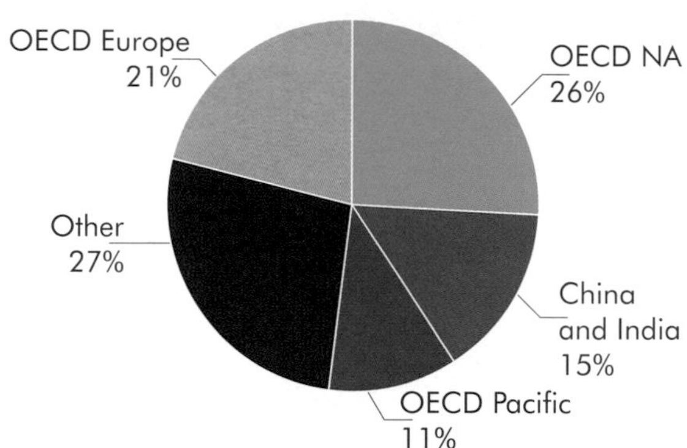

	Global Deployment Share 2050	RDD&D Inv. Cost USD bn 2005-2050	Commercial Inv. Cost USD bn
OECD NA	25%	25-30	n.a.
OECD Europe	20%	20-25	n.a.
OECD Pacific	12%	12-15	n.a.
China & India	16%	15-20	n.a.
Other	27%	25-30	n.a.

	Global Deployment Share 2030	RDD&D Inv. Cost USD bn 2005-2030	Commercial Inv. Cost USD bn 2030-2050
OECD NA	26%	30-35	40-45
OECD Europe	21%	25-30	60-65
OECD Pacific	11%	12-15	15-20
China & India	15%	15-20	20-25
Other	27%	25-30	40-45

Technology targets

	ACT: Emissions Stabilisation	BLUE: 50% Emissions Reduction
RD&D		
Gasification of biomass on a small scale needs to be more reliable and automated, needs continuous feed. RD&D needed for fuel and gas clean up	Plants more reliable by 2012 with gas clean-up mostly solved. Cost reductions from large-scale demo plants. Optimum biomass feed storage, drying and handling systems	Multi-fuel bio-refineries including BIGCC as part of the process need RD&D (USD 900 m). Biomass fuel standardised. Technology transfer to developing countries
Oxygen and air-blown plants demonstrated	Oxygen vs. air-blown benefits understood, but expensive vs. standard steam cycle systems	
Develop coal plants that can accommodate higher biomass shares	Maximise co-combustion.	
Develop co-gasification for NGCC	By 2020	By 2015
Deployment		
Efficient, reliable gasifiers with low air emissions need demonstration to gain additional learning experience	Early commercial BIGCC plants operating by 2015	Growth rate of 25%/yr after 2015 declining to 3-5% by 2040 as biomass becomes constrained. 1-2 plants built on avg. / month from 2020 to 2050

Technology timeline

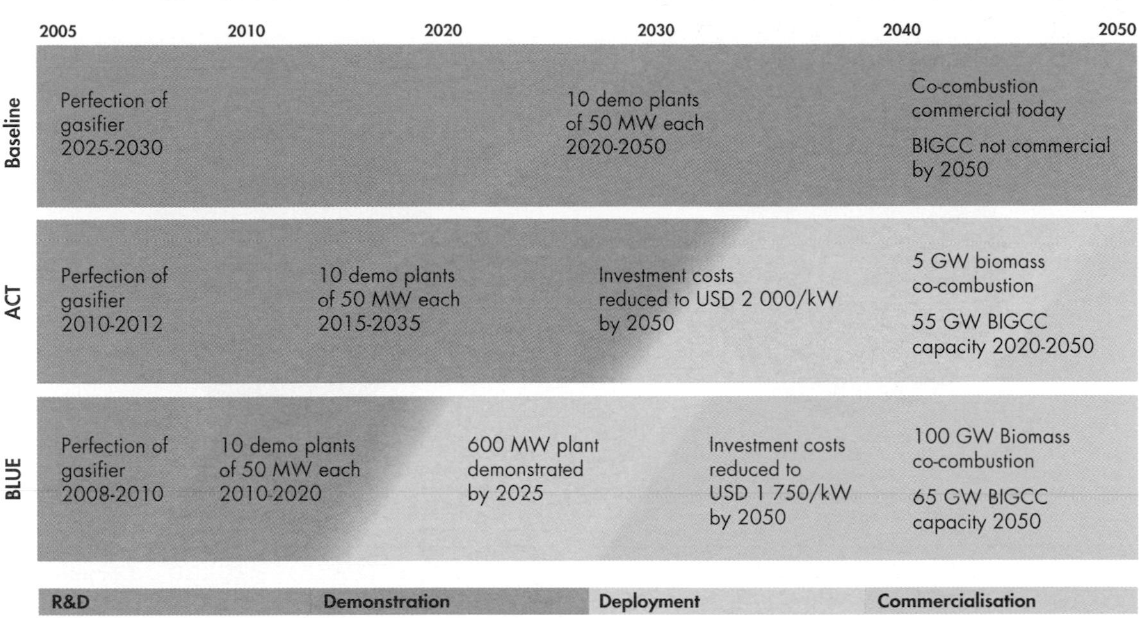

Timeline reflects Biomass Integrated Gasification Combined Cycle. Co-combustion technologies already commercial today.

Key actions needed

- Biomass resources need to be identified and secured for the long term by plant developers. Optimum plant locations identified by GIS process with transport infrastructure optimised.
- Co-combustion of biomass in coal-fired power plants should be encouraged.
- Reliability of gasifiers, especially the challenging gas clean-up process, needs demonstrating over the long term to give confidence to potential investors. Various biomass types, including black liquor and bagasse, should be considered.
- Gasifier development can be run in parallel with synthetic biofuels produced using the FT process and methanol/DME. Industry investment a key for success, building on knowledge of earlier plants.
- Technology transfer including data on fuel specifications and suitability needed for uptake in developing countries where local manufacture is encouraged.
- Full life-cycle analyses to be undertaken to ensure a sustainable system results.
- Once CCS has become fully commercial for coal plants, it can be tested for integration with BIGCC systems. First BIGCC plants with CCS in 2030 (BLUE).

Key areas for international collaboration

- A review of successes and failures of biomass gasification plants to date, to identify problems.
- Joint funding of large-scale plants in developing countries by industry and governments.
- International standards on fuel quality, air emissions and plant designs needed.
- Technology transfer for small- and large-scale plants undertaken collaboratively.

Photovoltaic systems

ACT 0.67 Gt savings 2050

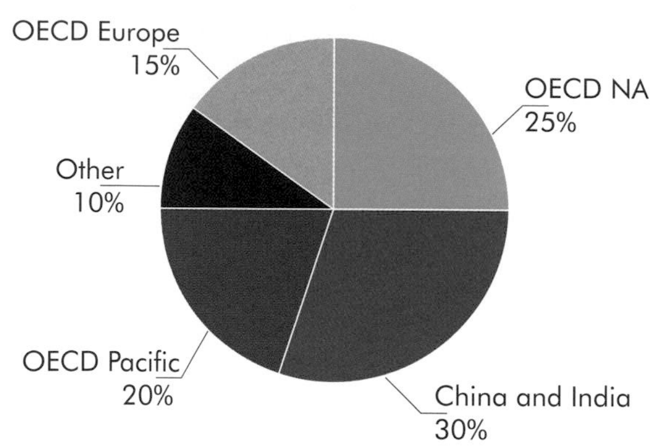

BLUE 1.32 Gt savings 2050

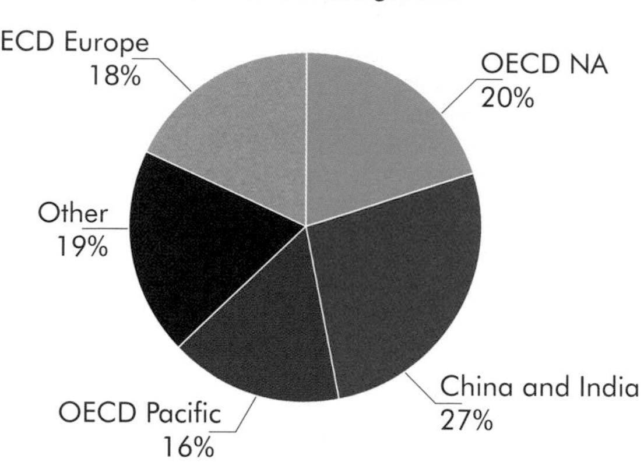

	Global Deployment Share 2035	RDD&D Inv. Cost USD bn 2005-2035	Commercial Inv. Cost USD bn 2035-2050
OECD NA	25%	45-55	120-130
OECD Europe	25%	45-55	75-85
OECD Pacific	30%	55-65	100-110
China & India	15%	25-35	150-160
Other	5%	10-12	50-55

	Global Deployment Share 2030	RDD&D Inv. Cost USD bn 2005-2030	Commercial Inv. Cost USD bn 2030-2050
OECD NA	25%	45-55	200-220
OECD Europe	25%	45-55	180 190
OECD Pacific	25%	45-55	250-260
China & India	20%	40-45	270-280
Other	5%	10-12	180-190

Technology targets

	ACT: Emissions Stabilisation	BLUE: 50% Emissions Reduction
RD&D		
Increase efficiency and reduce material intensity and costs of c-Si modules	c-Si module efficiencies above 20%. Cost-effective and alternative silicon feedstock supply developed	c-Si modules efficiency around 25%
Increase efficiency and lifetime of thin films	Thin film module performances15-18%, lifetime of 25-30 years	Thin film modules reach efficiencies of 20-25%, lifetimes of 30-35 years
Develop 2 types of 3rd generation devices: • Ultra-high efficiency cells • Ultra-low cost cells • Low-cost building integration	Third-generation technologies understood, demonstration plants in niche market applications	Third-generation devices fully developed and deployed: • Devices above 40% efficiency • Ultra-low-cost cells reach 10-15% efficiencies, lifetimes of 10-15 years
Deployment		
Building integration and storage	Fully integrated and multi-functional PV applications in buildings. Use of advanced storage facilities	
Cost target	Investment costs reduced to USD 2.2/W in 2030, 1.2/W by 2050	Investment costs reach USD 1.9/W in 2030 and USD 1.1/W by 2050

Technology timeline

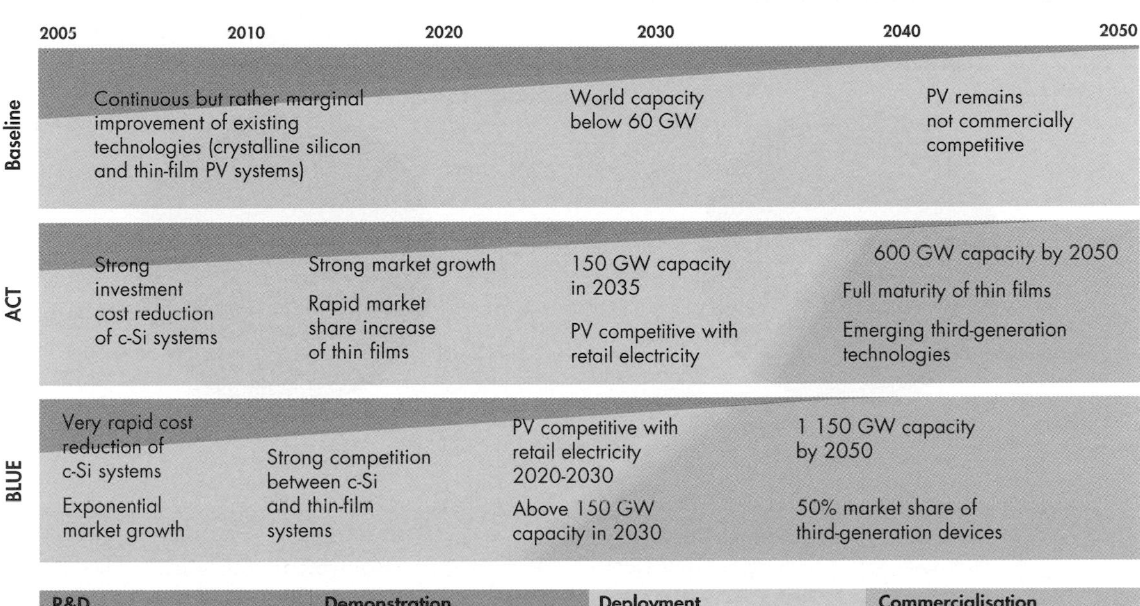

Key actions needed

- Double technology shift: from crystalline silicon (c-Si) to thin films, to third-generation novel devices.
- Sustained and effective incentives needed in the next 5-10 years to overcome the pre-competitive stage of PV systems.
- Guarantee long-term high purity silicon feedstock supply, develop alternative feedstock production routes.
- Guarantee sufficient public and private R&D funding for the development of third-generation novel devices (ultra-high efficiency and ultra-low-cost cells).
- Up-scaling of manufacturing capacity to the 1-10 GW/year scale per manufacturing plant.
- Develop standardised solutions for building integration in collaboration with the construction industry.
- Address technology transfer issues for application in developing countries, with specific respect to off-grid applications.

Key areas for international collaboration

- Development and application of international standards in measuring PV module and system performances under real and large-scale application conditions.
- Technological spill-over from other industry sectors (e.g. thin film and LCD screen production).
- Pre-competitive R&D collaboration in the field of 3rd generation devices: nanotechnologies, concentrators, dye-sensitised cells, organic cells.
- Management of end-of-life recycling of modules.
- Technology transfer for small & large-scale plants undertaken collaboratively.

Concentrating solar power

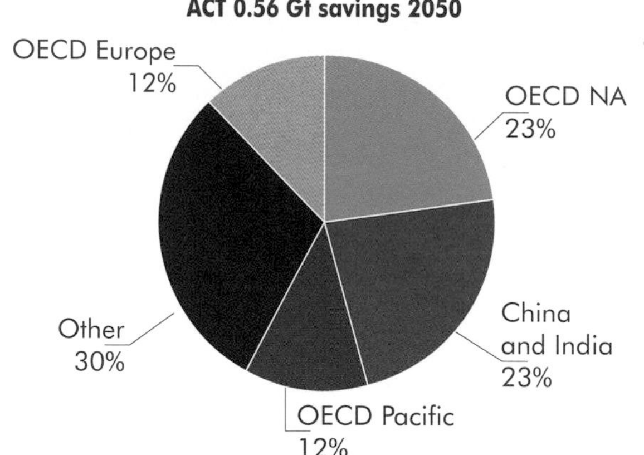

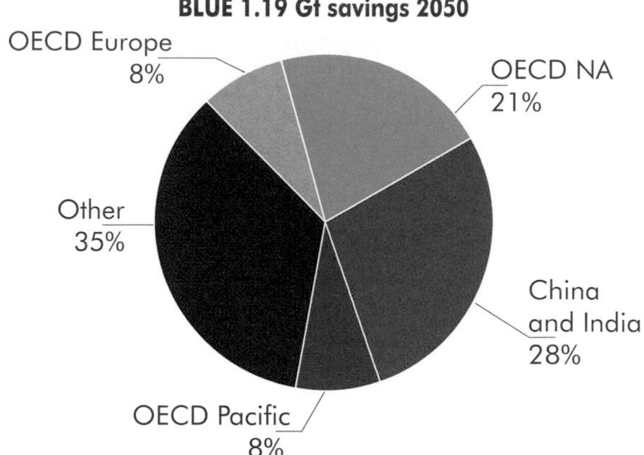

	Global Deployment Share 2030	RDD&D Inv. Cost USD bn 2005-2030	Commercial Inv. Cost USD bn 2030-2050
OECD NA	25%	65-75	45-50
OECD Europe	15%	40-50	25-30
OECD Pacific	15%	40-50	25-30
China & India	25%	65-75	45-50
Other	20%	55-65	50-55

	Global Deployment Share 2030	RDD&D Inv. Cost USD bn 2005-2030	Commercial Inv. Cost USD bn 2030-2050
OECD NA	23%	60-70	60-70
OECD Europe	14%	35-40	25-30
OECD Pacific	14%	35-40	25-30
China & India	24%	65-75	80-90
Other	25%	65-75	100-110

Technology targets

	ACT: Emissions Stabilisation	BLUE: 50% Emissions Reduction
RD&D		
System efficiency	Increase efficiency of systems to reduce costs	
Trough plants	Development of direct steam generation for trough plants	
Development of new technologies at system level for trough, dishes and towers	• Towers with air receivers to significantly increase working temperatures and conversion rates, demo by 2012 • Combined power and desalination plants, demo by 2012	Solar production of hydrogen and other energy carriers, demo by 2020
Low-cost, high efficiency thermal storage	Storage costs to fall to USD 0.05/kWh and efficiencies greater than 95%	
Deployment		
• Cogeneration power desalination • Troughs + direct steam generation • Troughs + molten salts	Commercial deployment by 2020	
Towers + air receiver + gas turbine	Commercial deployment by 2030	

Technology timeline

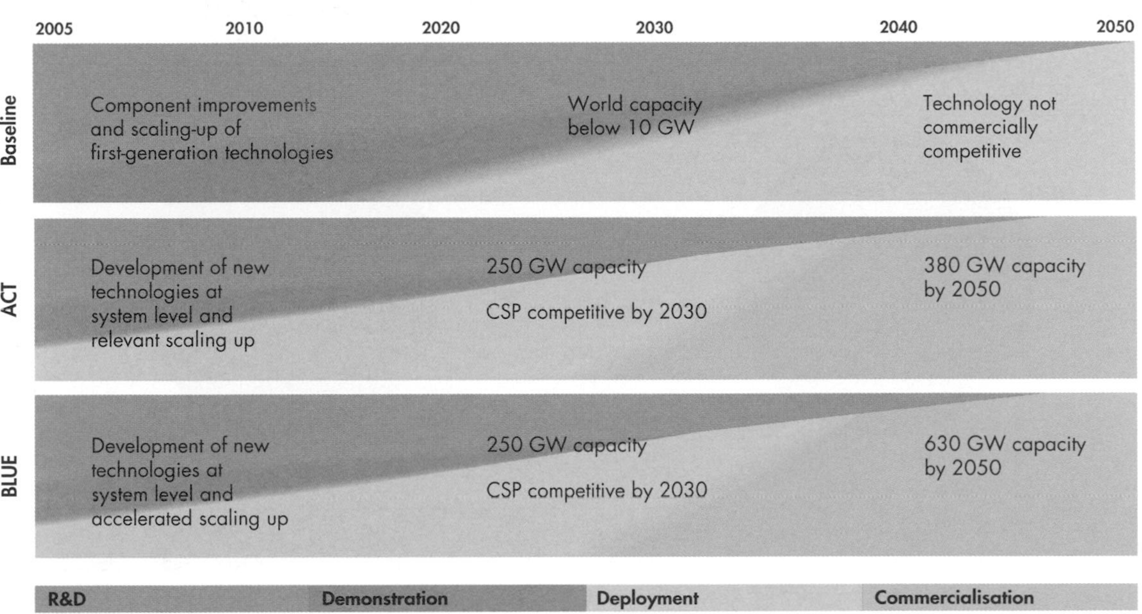

Key actions needed

- Economies of scale, mass production, learning by doing, and incremental improvements of all system components (mirrors, infrastructures, sun-tracking, heat receivers, pipes, balance of plants, etc.) will combine to improve performances and reduce costs.
- The emergence of heat storage, as an alternative to back-up with fossil fuels, significantly increases the value of the electricity produced in making power capacities guaranteed or even dispatchable.
- The development of incremental improvements such as direct steam generation, use of molten salts in troughs, cogeneration of heat for desalination and power, and cheaper dishes will further help increase performance and reduce costs.
- Development of towers with air receivers will significantly increase working temperatures and conversion rates and reduce costs even further, but still requires important R&D efforts.
- Low-cost long-range DC transmission systems.

Key areas for international collaboration

- Continuing co-ordination of R&D efforts, outreach efforts sharing and information exchanges through IEA's SolarPACES Implementing Agreement.
- Effective financing of CSP plants in developing countries beyond the global environment facility-supported plants.
- Developing efficient interconnection via high-voltage, direct-current lines to feed important consuming areas from neighbouring sunny regions.

Coal IGCC systems

ACT 0.66 Gt savings 2050

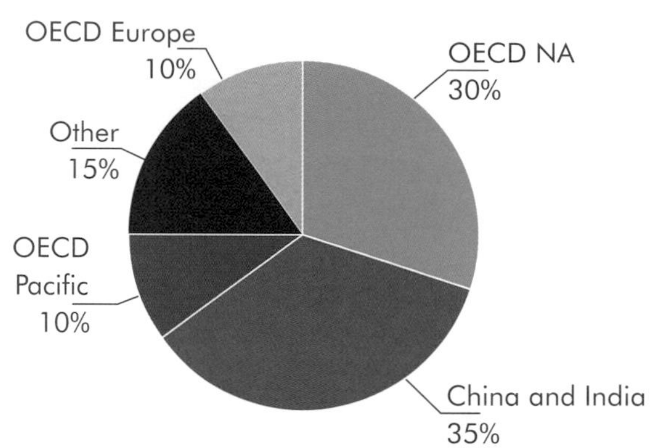

	Global Deployment Share 2030	RDD&D Inv. Cost USD bn 2005-2030	Commercial Inv. Cost USD bn 2030-2050
OECD NA	40%	145-155	100-110
OECD Europe	25%	90-100	30-40
OECD Pacific	20%	70-80	30-40
China & India	15%	50-60	120-130
Other	0%	0	50-55

BLUE 0.69 Gt savings 2050

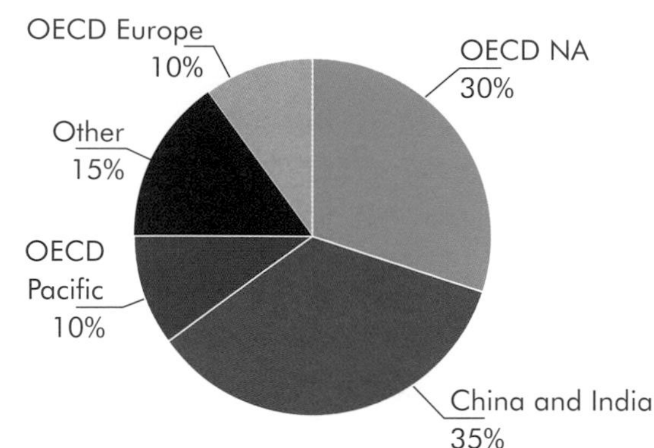

	Global Deployment Share 2030	RDD&D Inv. Cost USD bn 2005-2030	Commercial Inv. Cost USD bn 2030-2050
OECD NA	40%	145-155	100-110
OECD Europe	25%	90-100	30-40
OECD Pacific	20%	70-80	30-40
China & India	15%	50-60	120-130
Other	0%	0	50-55

Technology targets

	ACT: Emissions Stabilisation	BLUE: 50% Emissions Reduction
RD&D		
Ion transport membranes for Oxygen separation	O_2 production using 150 kWh/t, 90% efficient gasifier	
Coal pre-drying using waste heat	4% points efficiency gain for lignite, general application	
Efficient coal feeding at high pressure	Larger, higher pressure, low cost quench gasifiers	
IGCC-CCS integration (hydrogen turbines, physical absorption, etc.)	Different entrained-bed/fluidised bed gasifier designs for integration with drying units	
New higher efficiency turbines	50% efficient IGCC w/o CCS/45% efficient IGCC with CCS	
IGCC demos for different coal types (lignite, high-ash coal, etc.)	10 demonstration projects with integrated drying where necessary. Develop polygeneration	
Development of larger fuel cells for coal fuel gas	Proven 65% efficiency with natural gas on large scale. >50% efficiency with coal. Systems integration with gasifier and gas cleaning system. Testing at 1-50 MW scale by 2030	
Deployment		
Cost target	IGCC USD 1 400/kW	

Technology timeline

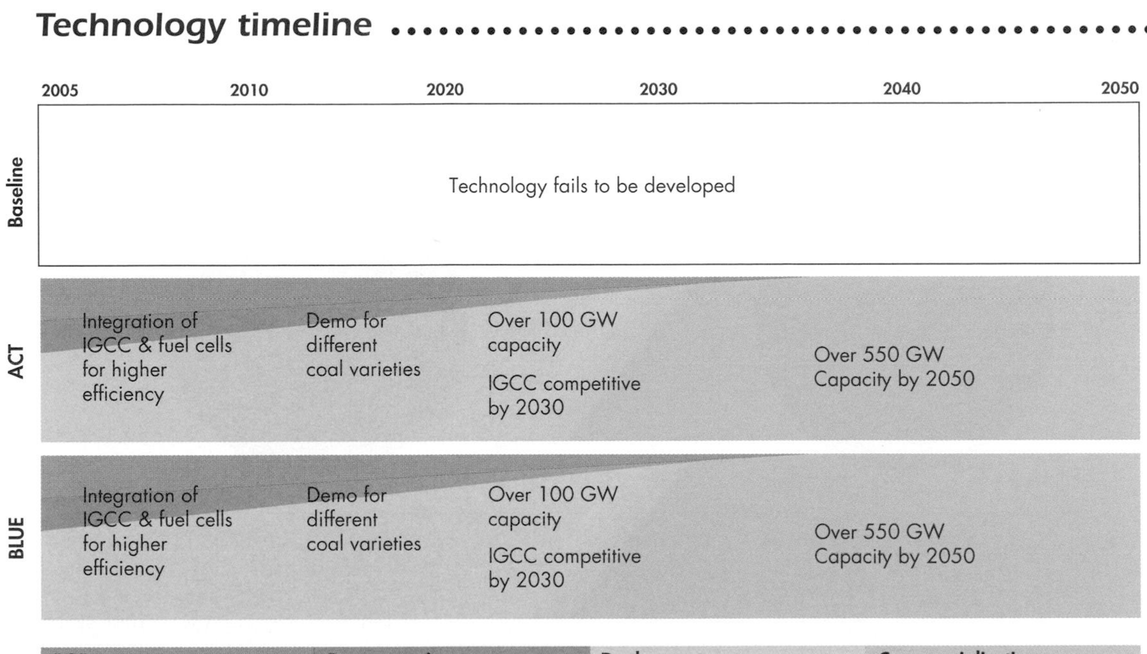

Key actions needed

- IGCC is an enabling technology for CCS.
- Costs need to come down closer to pulverised coal combustion costs.
- The energy needs for oxygen production need to be reduced.
- Gasification needs further development in terms of availability and ease of operation.
- More efficient gas turbines (higher turbine inlet temperatures are needed).
- Hydrogen turbines need further development.
- Systems heat integration needs further development.
- Polygeneration is still not well understood.

Key areas for international collaboration

- Hydrogen turbines for IGCC with CCS.
- Large scale low-cost ion transport membrane separation oxygen production technologies.
- 10 coal IGCC demonstration projects for different coal types using different types of gasifiers.

Coal ultra-supercritical steam cycles

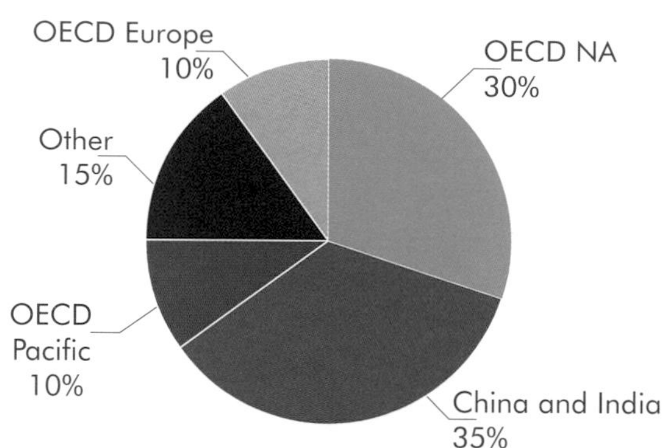

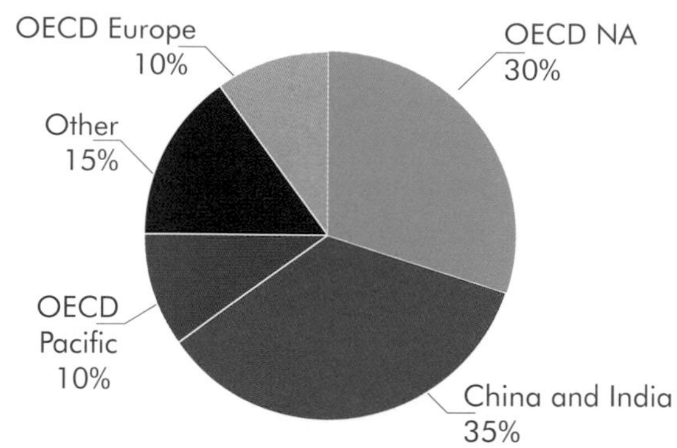

	Global Deployment Share 2025	RDD&D Inv. Cost USD bn 2005-2025	Commercial Inv. Cost USD bn 2025-2050
OECD NA	40%	145-155	100-110
OECD Europe	25%	90-100	30-40
OECD Pacific	20%	70-80	30-40
China & India	15%	50-60	120-130
Other	0%	0	50-55

	Global Deployment Share 2025	RDD&D Inv. Cost USD bn 2005-2025	Commercial Inv. Cost USD bn 2025-2050
OECD NA	40%	145-155	100-110
OECD Europe	25%	90-100	30-40
OECD Pacific	20%	70-80	30-40
China & India	15%	50-60	120-130
Other	0%	0	50-55

Technology targets

	ACT: Emissions Stabilisation	BLUE: 50% Emissions Reduction
RD&D		
Ten test plants at 700 degrees steam	By 2020	Skipped
Ten oxyfueling plants of at least 100 MW operational for several years	By 2025	By 2020
Pre-drying technologies for lignite integrated to full-scale plants	Widespread application and demos for other coal types	
Materials that can withstand > 700°C steam at >250 bar pressure	Materials feasibility proven 2015. Component testing finished 2020	Materials feasibility proven 2012. Component testing finished 2015
Beneficiation technology for high-ash coals	By 2020	
Ion transport membranes for O_2 separation	50% efficiency by 2025	52% efficiency by 2025
Burners and boiler designs for oxyfuelling	Pilots proven by 2015	Pilots proven by 2012
10 USCSC demo plants at > 700°C steam at >250 bar pressure	Oxygen production 150 kWh/t by 2025	Oxygen production 150 kWh/t by 2020
Deployment		
Cost target	USCSC USD 1 400/kW	

Technology timeline

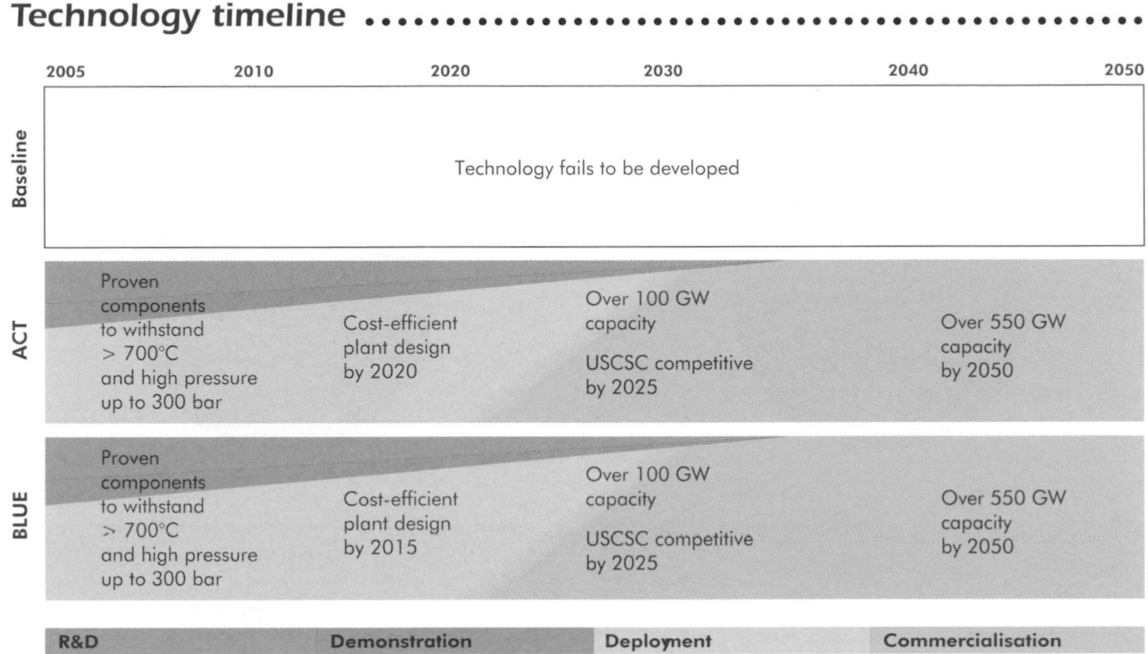

Key actions needed

- Develop new low-cost materials for high-temperature steam conditions (nanotechnology, new alloys).
- Fabrication (including welding) of high-temperature alloy tubes.
- Develop methods for more rapid testing of such materials.
- Develop oxyfueling as an enabling technology for CCS.
- Enhance the understanding of oxyfuelling retrofit options.
- Encourage the development of more manufacturing infrastructure to insure suppliers are able to meet future demand.

Key areas for international collaboration

- Fundamental materials research.
- Better understanding of fluid dynamics.
- Low-cost plant designs.
- Oxyfuelling pilot and demonstration plants.

Energy efficiency in buildings and appliances

ACT 6.5 Gt CO_2 savings 2050

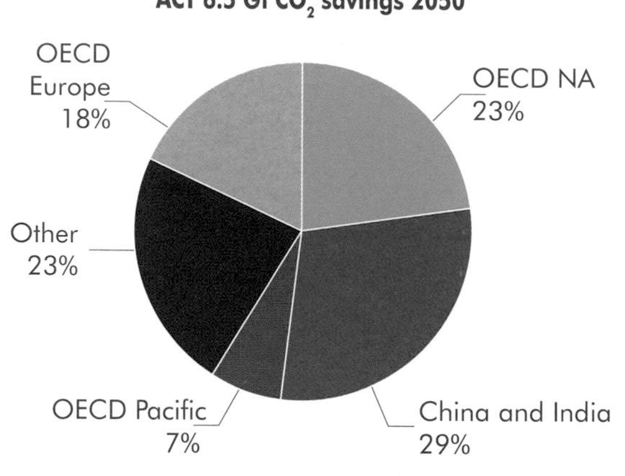

BLUE 7.0 Gt CO_2 savings 2050

OECD Europe 16%

OECD NA 24%

Other 21%

OECD Pacific 7%

China and India 32%

	Commercial Inv. Cost USD bn 2005-2050
OECD NA	1 100-1 200
OECD Europe	850-950
OECD Pacific	300-400
China & India	1 000-1 200
Other	1 800-2 000

	Commercial Inv. Cost USD bn 2005-2050
OECD NA	1 500-1 700
OECD Europe	950-1050
OECD Pacific	450-550
China & India	1 500-1 800
Other	2 200-2 500

Technology targets

	ACT: Emissions Stabilisation	BLUE: 50% Emissions Reduction
Diffusion		
Limit standby power use to 1-Watt.	Implemented in OECD countries between now and 2030; and globally by 2040	Implemented in OECD countries between now and 2020; and globally by 2030
Tighten or establish minimum energy efficiency standards for all major existing appliances	New appliances standards shifted to LLCC between now and 2020 in OECD and by 2030 globally	New appliance standards shifted to BAT between now and 2020 in OECD and globally by 2030.
Mandatory standards across full range of mass-produced equipment	Appliances brought under standards by 2030 in OECD and by 2040 globally	Standards for appliances by 2020 in OECD and 2030 globally. Continuous tightening required
Building codes	Cold countries at "low-energy" standard from 2015 and globally from 2030	Cold countries to meet "passive house" levels by 2015, and globally from 2030
Adopt best practice in lighting efficiency	Policy must shift to LLCC from 2015	Policy must begin shift to BAT from 2025 onwords
Promote low-energy houses and fuel switching	Simplified planning requirements to encourage low-energy buildings and alternative fuel sources (especially solar)	

Technology timeline

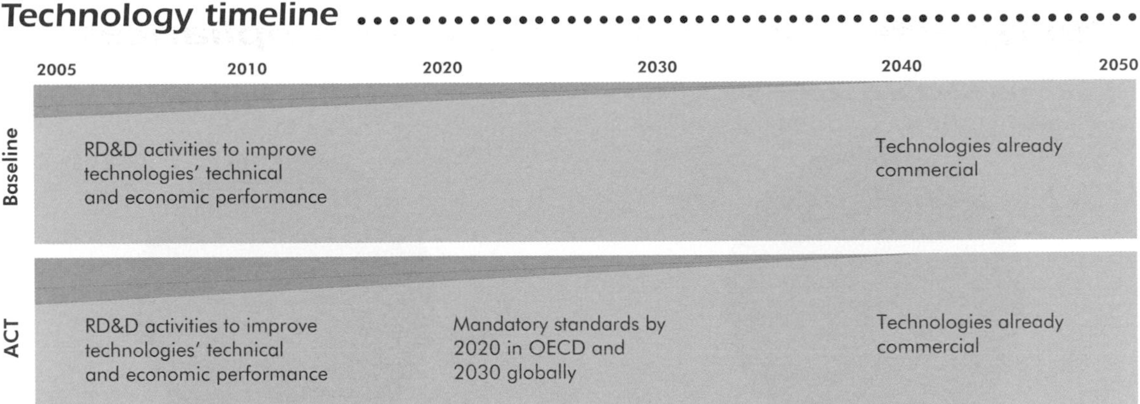

Key actions needed

- Monitor energy efficiency improvements in existing buildings and appliances. Need to collect consistent and comprehensive data on end-use consumption and energy efficiency worldwide.
- Implementation of mandatory minimum efficiency performance standards (MEPS), harmonised at a high level of efficiency and implemented worldwide, ongoing tightening will be required.
- International standards need to be reviewed regularly to ensure adequate vigor.

Key areas for international collaboration

- Establish a common set of efficiency "tiers" from which countries could draw when they establish minimum energy performance standards.
- Facilitate the rapid exchange of BAT in the buildings sector to ensure rapid uptake worldwide.
- Promote the diffusion of passive house design, construction techniques and energy technologies.

Heat pumps

ACT 0.27 Gt savings 2050

OECD Europe 28%
OECD NA 25%
Other 5%
OECD Pacific 11%
China and India 31%

BLUE 0.77 Gt savings 2050

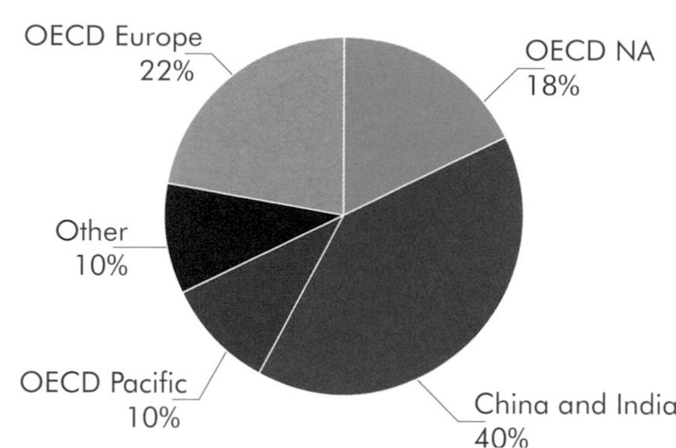

	Global Deployment Share* 2025	RDD&D Inv. Cost* USD bn 2005-2025	Commercial Inv. Cost USD bn 2025-2050
OECD NA	10%	5-10	400-500
OECD Europe	50%	32-36	500-600
OECD Pacific	40%	20-25	140-160
China & India	0%	8-12	800-1 000
Other	0%	0	50-75

	Global Deployment Share* 2015	RDD&D Inv. Cost* USD bn 2005-2015	Commercial Inv. Cost USD bn 2005-2050
OECD NA	20%	15-20	450-550
OECD Europe	35%	30-35	600-700
OECD Pacific	35%	30-35	175-200
China & India	10%	7-12	1 000-1 200
Other	0%	0	150-200

* Figures for deployment above are for geothermal heat pumps only.

Technology targets

HPT: Heat Pump Technologies	ACT: Emissions Stabilisation	BLUE: 50% Emissions Reduction
RD&D		
More efficient components and systems for heating and cooling applications, using environmentally neutral working fluids. More efficient integrated HPT systems for net zero energy buildings. High-efficiency, high-temperature HPT.	Increased penetration of HPT in retrofit markets. 15% of industrial waste heat upgraded by HPTs. 15% less energy used in commercial buildings by use of HPT.	Energy-efficient systems using environmental benign working fluids available by 2020. 25 % industrial waste heat upgraded by 2030. 25% less energy used in commercial buildings.
Deployment		
HPT included as an option in building codes to reduce GHG emission. Financing schemes in place to stimulate HPT diffusion	Policies to support wide adoption of HPT for heating and cooling by 2020. Majority of new buildings equipped with HPT systems, 25% retrofits by 2030	Majority of new buildings equipped with HPT, 75% retrofits by 2030.
Increased awareness of annual performance and benefits of HPT systems	75% of installers certified in 2015	100% of installers and equipment certified in 2020

Technology timeline

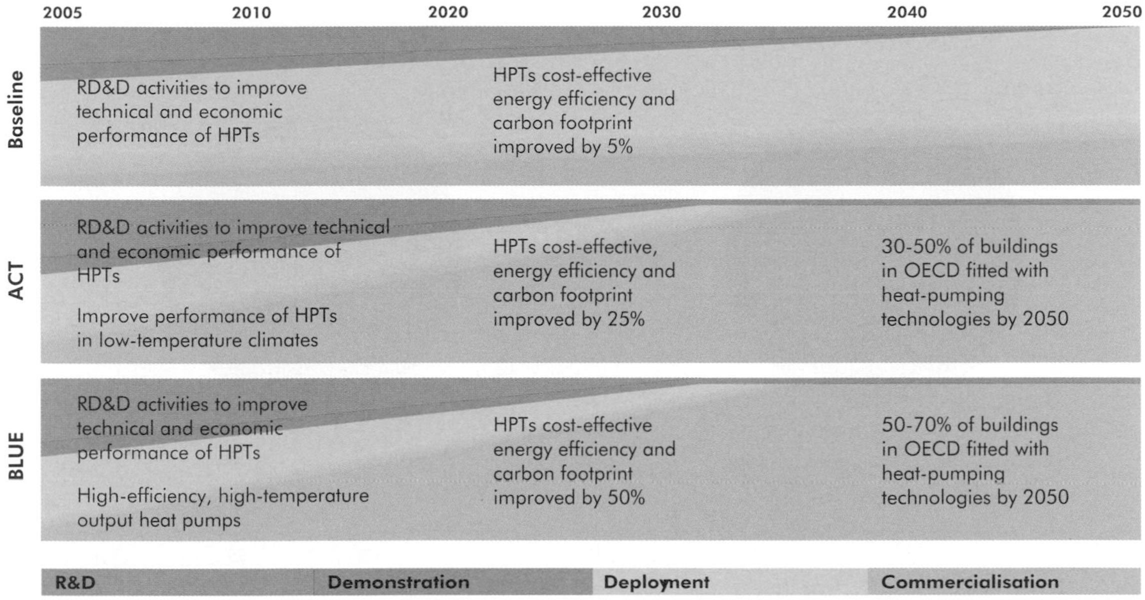

	2005–2020	2020–2040	2040–2050
Baseline	RD&D activities to improve technical and economic performance of HPTs	HPTs cost-effective energy efficiency and carbon footprint improved by 5%	
ACT	RD&D activities to improve technical and economic performance of HPTs Improve performance of HPTs in low-temperature climates	HPTs cost-effective, energy efficiency and carbon footprint improved by 25%	30-50% of buildings in OECD fitted with heat-pumping technologies by 2050
BLUE	RD&D activities to improve technical and economic performance of HPTs High-efficiency, high-temperature output heat pumps	HPTs cost-effective energy efficiency and carbon footprint improved by 50%	50-70% of buildings in OECD fitted with heat-pumping technologies by 2050

R&D | Demonstration | Deployment | Commercialisation

Key actions needed

- Further RD&D to develop more energy-efficient, sustainable and cost-effective heat-pumping technologies (heating and cooling) particularly for buildings and industrial applications.
- Development of higher efficiency low-temperature-environment heat pumps.
- Increased research, development, demonstration and the dissemination of objective information to increase awareness, acceptance and understand HPTs.
- Actions on policies to ensure all buildings codes promote energy conservation and efficiency measures.
- Actions to have policies in place in most countries that recognise the benefits of air, water and ground source heat pumps.

Key areas for international collaboration

International collaboration is needed

- To quantify and publicise the energy-saving potential and environmental benefits (local and global) of HPTs;
- To develop cost-effective, energy-efficient and sustainable heat-pumping technologies through RD&D;
- Develop policies to support deployment and to promote quality assurance of installation and systems;
- To exchange information and analyse the success of deployment & diffusion strategies.
- Organisations:
  IEA HPP: http://www.heatpumpcentre.org
  ASHRAE: http://www.ashrae.org
  AHRI: http://www.ahrinet.org
  EHPA: http://ehpa.fiz-karlsruhe.de
  HPTCJ : http://www.hptcj.or.jp
  IIR: http://www.iifiir.org

Solar space and water heating

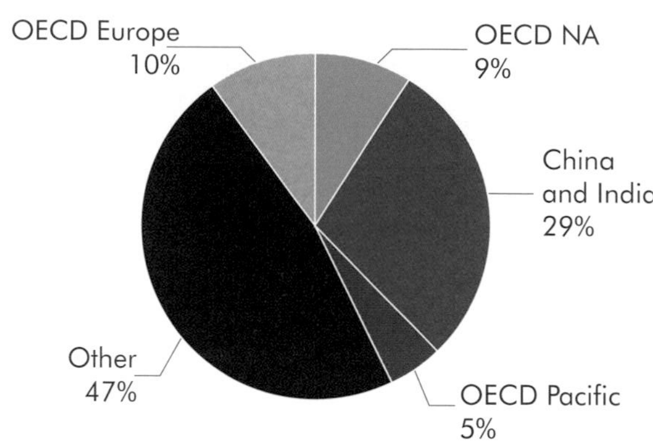

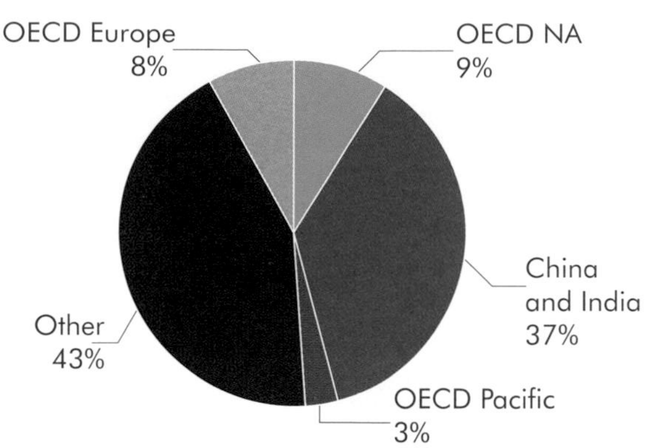

	Global Deployment Share 2030	RDD&D Inv. Cost USD bn 2005-2030	Commercial Inv. Cost USD bn 2030-2050
OECD NA	20%	50-55	30-35
OECD Europe	20%	50-55	30-35
OECD Pacific	15%	40-45	15-20
China & India	20%	50-55	90-100
Other	25%	65-70	140-150

	Global Deployment Share 2020	RDD&D Inv. Cost USD bn 2005-2020	Commercial Inv. Cost USD bn 2020-2050
OECD NA	20%	50-55	55-65
OECD Europe	20%	50-55	50-60
OECD Pacific	15%	40-45	20-25
China & India	20%	50-55	240-250
Other	25%	65-70	280-290

Technology targets

	ACT: Emissions Stabilisation	BLUE: 50% Emissions Reduction
RD&D		
Improve heat storage systems	Develop cheap, simple solar-assisted heating devices for mass production	District CHP schemes using combinations of solar/biomass/geothermal widely deployed
Deployment		
Affordable ownership to empower user choice	Policies to encourage widespread deployment to reduce costs with mass production	
Mandate for integrated renewable technologies	Combi solar thermal/cooling PV systems in place. Concentrating solar heat used by industry incorporating heat storage and bioenergy systems	
Utility related	Finance schemes by utilities to save grid upgrades	

Technology timeline

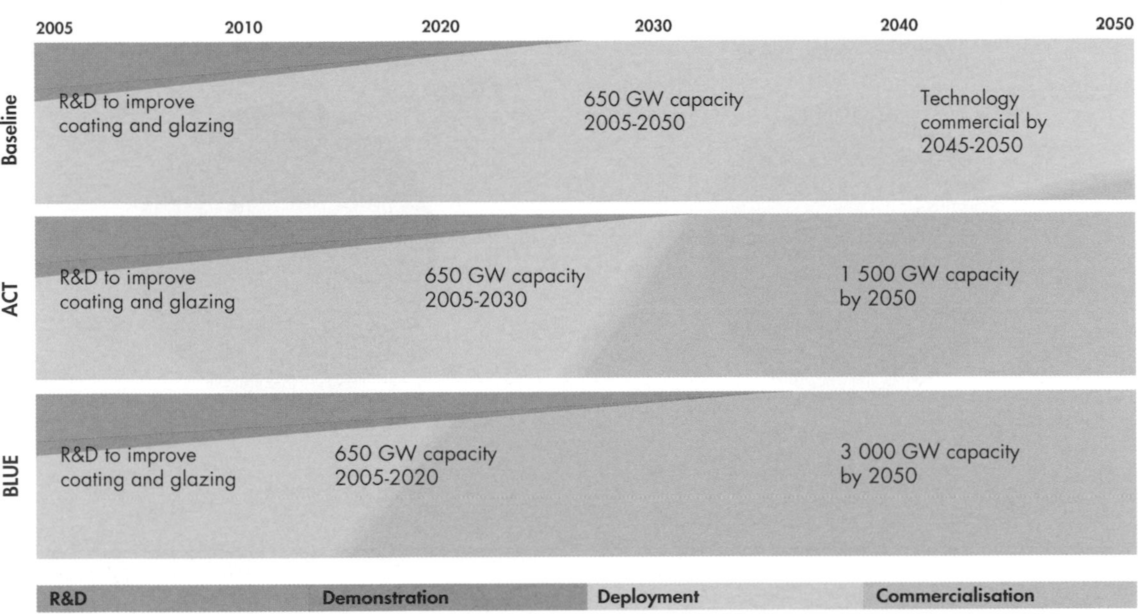

Key actions needed

- Solar heating technologies are already deployed but currently tend to be high-cost options in cold climates. RD&D is needed to help drive down unit costs and improve efficiency. This is particularly the case for solar thermal.
- Need for priority actions on policy development to ensure all new buildings are designed to need minimal heating over their lifetimes, this will help facilitate solar thermal. Retrofits are also to be encouraged where feasible. Capacity building, continued education of architects and builders is required.
- Ownership of small-scale systems is key for both industry and domestic sectors. Distributed systems, however, need micro-financing. There is an opportunity for utilities to look for new business, i.e. by leasing technologies, and to avoid costly grid upgrades as demand increases.
- The connection between energy-efficiency and supply is key for solar heating systems. Metering systems are needed to encourage awareness and provide better data for policy-making and planning.

Key areas for international collaboration

- Policy development for heating has been neglected, so opportunity exists to develop jointly.
- Joint RD&D with industry is encouraged to gain more rapid development.
- Heat metering, micro-finance schemes and capacity building of installers are areas to be addressed.

Energy efficiency in transport

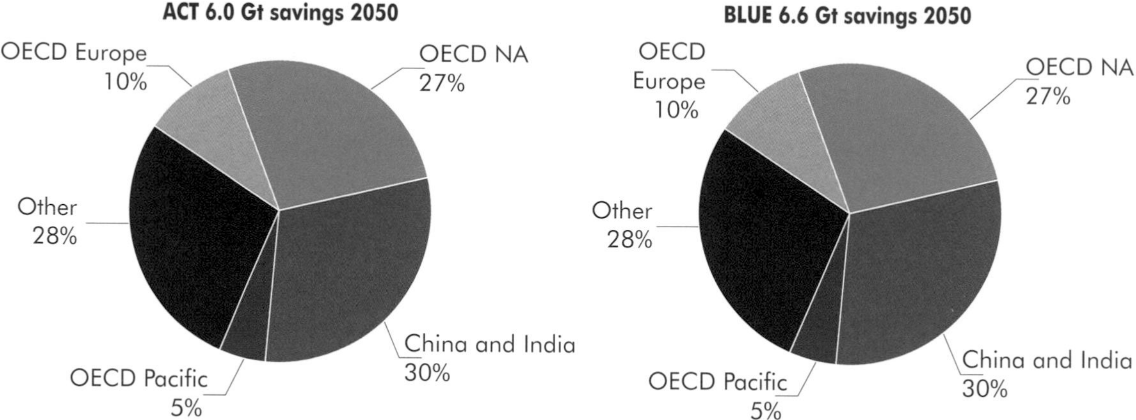

	Commercial Inv. Cost USD bn 2005-2050
OECD NA	1 200-1 300
OECD Europe	1 000-1 100
OECD Pacific	350-450
China & India	2 200-2 300
Other	1 500-1 600

	Commercial Inv. Cost USD bn 2005-2050
OECD NA	1 750-1 850
OECD Europe	1 500 1 600
OECD Pacific	500-600
China & India	3 100-3 200
Other	2 100-2 200

Technology targets

	ACT: Emissions Stabilisation	BLUE: 50% Emissions Reduction
RDD&D/Diffusion		
Introduce mandatory fuel efficiency standards for cars and small trucks	Fuel use or CO_2 emission standards for new LDVs by 2015 in OECD and 2020 globally, tightened over time to reach a 50% reduction in fuel use per km by 2050 compared to 2008. Complementary measures as needed to ensure vehicle size/weight/power do not increase and that no travel rebound effects occur from lower-cost driving.	
Standards and programmes for fuel efficient accessories	Labelling and regulations on component such as low-rolling resistance tyres, lighting and air-conditioning, by 2015/2020 for OECD/non-OECD	
Medium and Heavy-duty truck efficiency standards	Similar to LDV standards, but with related policies to promote logistic improvements, vehicle maintenance, and driving-style related savings. Policies in place by 2015/2020	
Efficiency improvements for other modes	Policies should be developed to cover rail systems, aircraft and shipping. International aircraft and shipping should be handled in a co-operative international framework approach. Voluntary or mandatory standards should be set internationally by 2015 or sooner.	

Technology timeline

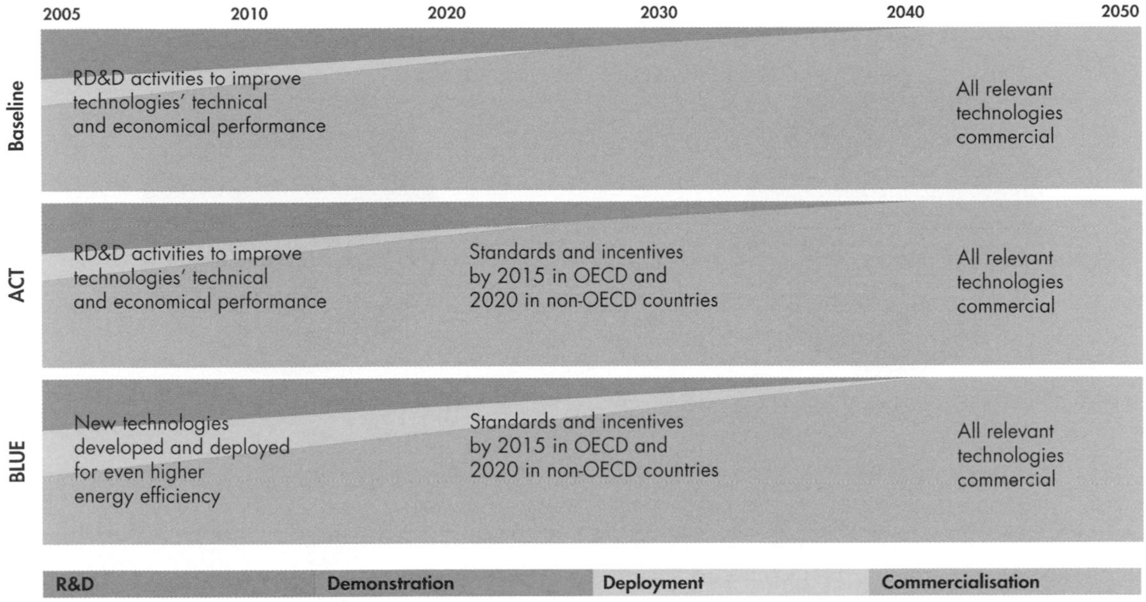

	2005–2010	2020–2030	2040–2050
Baseline	RD&D activities to improve technologies' technical and economical performance		All relevant technologies commercial
ACT	RD&D activities to improve technologies' technical and economical performance	Standards and incentives by 2015 in OECD and 2020 in non-OECD countries	All relevant technologies commercial
BLUE	New technologies developed and deployed for even higher energy efficiency	Standards and incentives by 2015 in OECD and 2020 in non-OECD countries	All relevant technologies commercial

R&D | Demonstration | Deployment | Commercialisation

In Baseline and ACT, deployment is primarily for hybrid vehicles and in BLUE is for hybrid vehicles and other advanced technologies such as light weighting.

Key actions needed

- Monitor energy efficiency trends, improvements and assess technical potential in a consistent manner around the world, for new and existing vehicle stock.
- Implementation, strengthening and updating of mandatory efficiency standards, providing strong, steady incentives into the future; over time these should be adopted in non-OECD countries and eventually harmonised at a high efficiency level.
- Incentives for introduction of new technologies and ensure they are used for fuel economy rather than increase size, weight or power; particularly hybrid and plug-in hybrid vehicles in near term; strong incentives for vehicle light-weighting are also needed.
- Standards needed for medium and heavy duty trucks; policies should address in-use performance via logistics and on-road efficiency.

Key areas for international collaboration

- Harmonise vehicle test procedures and, eventually, regulatory intensities.
- Establish a standardised set of test cycles and regulatory approaches from which countries could draw when they establish minimum energy efficiency standards.
- Introduction of advanced fuel economy technologies, such as hybrids and plug-in hybrids globally.
- International technical assessment and support for policy making for aircraft and shipping efficiency.

Second-generation biofuels

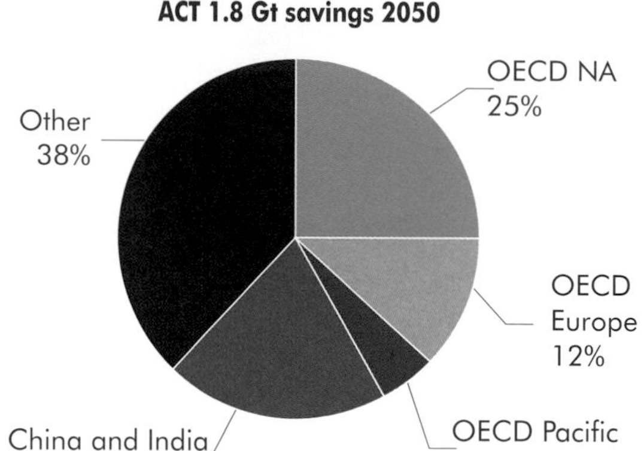

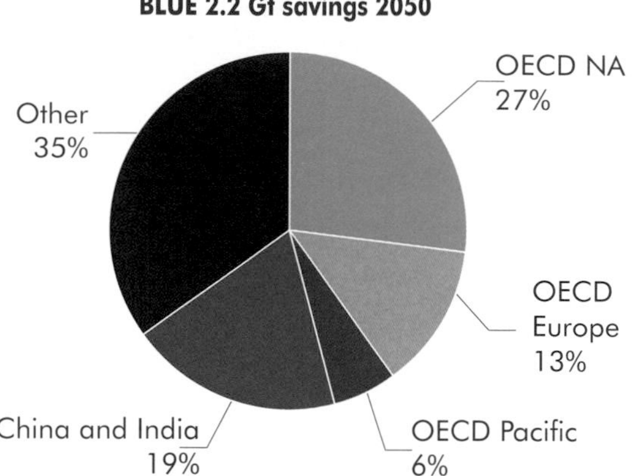

	Global Deployment Share 2035	RDD&D Inv. Cost USD bn 2005-2035	Commercial Inv. Cost USD bn 2035-2050
OECD NA	25%	25-30	1 300-1 500
OECD Europe	12%	15-20	850-950
OECD Pacific	5%	5-10	250-300
China & India	20%	15-20	800-850
Other	38%	30-35	450-500

	Global Deployment Share 2030	RDD&D Inv. Cost* USD bn 2005-2030	Commercial Inv. Cost USD bn 2030-2050
OECD NA	27%	30-35	1 100-1 300
OECD Europe	13%	15-20	900-1 000
OECD Pacific	6%	8-10	300-350
China & India	19%	15-20	1 400-1 600
Other	35%	30-35	1 400-1 600

Technology targets

	ACT: Emissions Stabilisation	BLUE: 50% Emissions Reduction
RD&D		
Cellulosic ethanol	Cut cost of ethanol production to USD 0.60 per litre gasoline equivalent (GE), mainly via better enzymes, by 2015-2020	
BTL (F-T) gasoline/diesel	Cut cost of BTL production to USD 0.70 per litre GE by 2015-2020 via optimisation of biomass handling, gasification, and synthesis gas production steps	
Deployment		
Cellulosic ethanol	Deployment begins by 2015, full commercialisation by 2035	Deployment begins by 2012, full commercialisation by 2030
BTL (F-T) gasoline/diesel	Deployment begins in 2015, full commercialisation by 2035	Deployment begins by 2012, full commercialisation by 2030

Technology timeline

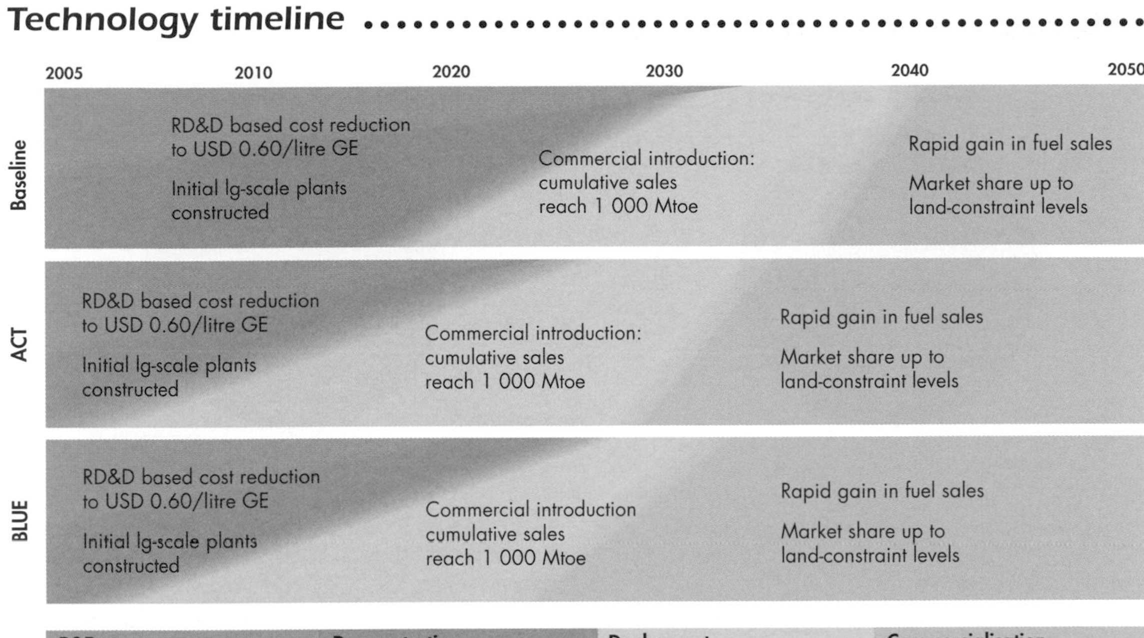

3

Key actions needed

- Both ligno-cellulosic ethanol and Fischer-Tropsch "biomass-to-liquids" are reaching the demonstration and, perhaps within a few years, the deployment phase, though basic R&D in some areas is still needed.
- Ligno-cellulosic demo. projects amounting to over USD 1 bn are expected in North America from 2008-2012; various technologies will be tested at scales less than half of expected future commercial size.
  - Similar trials are needed in other parts of the world; better data on feedstock availability and cost by region are needed; land use change analysis.
  - Pathways and strategies to get from demo. to deployment to commercialisation must be developed and clarified.
  - More work on co-products and bio-refinery opportunities.
- For BTL fuels, a small demo project in Germany has been announced, others expected (particularly in Europe) by 2010-2015.
  - Continued engineering research on feedstock handling, gasification/treatment, co-firing of biomass and fossil fuels.
  - Better understanding of cost trade-offs between plant scale and feedstock transport logistics.

Key areas for international collaboration

- Ongoing basic research collaboration (e.g. feedstock and enzyme research, feedstock handling/transport, process and plant scale optimisation).
- Global assessment of biomass availability / cost for production of 2nd generation biofuels.
  - Impacts on GHGs, sensitive eco-systems soils, food security, alternative uses of land ("land use change").
  - Assessment of economic viability of 2nd generation biofuels in the developing world.
- Better co-ordination of demo. projects, trials, deployment policies, biofuels trade.

Electric and plug-in vehicles

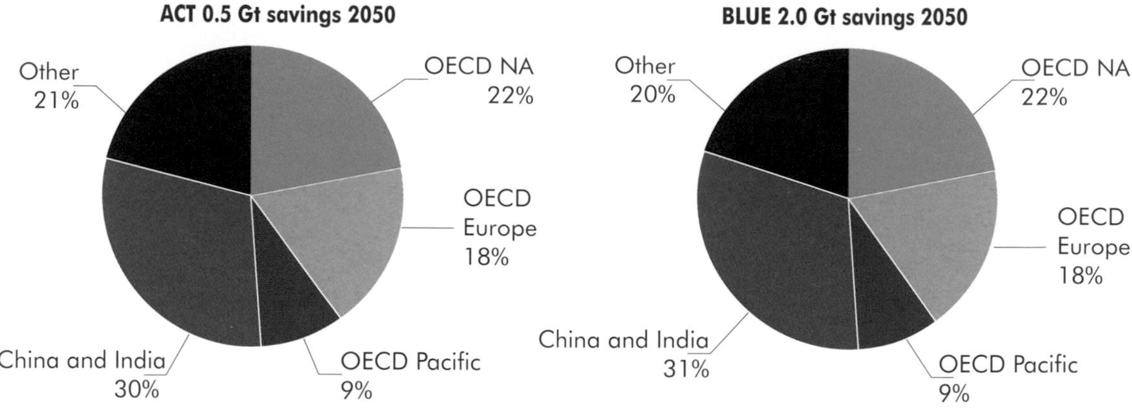

Plug-in hybrids, but not electric vehicles are deployed under ACT. Plug-in Commercial costs are about 10% higher than if they were regular hybrids.

	Deployment sales share of plug-in hybrid sales 2035	RD&D Inv. Cost USD bn 2005-2035	Deployment Cost USD bn 2005-2050
OECD NA	9%	10-12	40-50
OECD Europe	9%	8-10	30-40
OECD Pacific	9%	6-8	30-40
China & India	6%	6-8	20-30
Other	6%	8-10	10-20

Costs cover plug-ins and pure electric vehicles. Between 2020 and 2050, EVs cost, on average, about 20% higher than gasoline vehicles.

	Deployment sale share plug-ins (2035)/EVs (2050)	RD&D Inv. Cost USD bn 2005-2035	Deployment Cost USD bn 2005-2050
OECD NA	20% / 25%	20-25	950-1 100
OECD Europe	20% / 25%	15-20	800-900
OECD Pacific	20% / 25%	12-16	400-450
China & India	15% / 15%	12-16	1 050-1 200
Other	15% / 15%	15-20	750-850

Technology targets

	ACT: Emissions Stabilisation	BLUE: 50% Emissions Reduction
RD&D		
Plug-in hybrid system	Optimise configuration for maximum consumer acceptability at minimum cost	
Energy storage	Cut cost of battery storage to USD 300 per kWh by 2020, resolve technical issues. Long life span, deep cycling and rapid charging of batteries	Accelerated RD&D to cut cost of battery storage to USD 300 per kWh by 2015, resolve technical issues. Long life span, deep cycling and rapid charging of batteries
Deployment		
Plug-in hybrid vehicle	Semi-commercial deployment of plug-in hybrids up to 5% sales share in IEA countries by 2020	
Pure electric vehicle	No deployment assumed	Pure electric vehicle deployment begins in 2025, to achieve 5% sales share by 2030 (5 years earlier in "EV Success" scenario)

Technology timeline

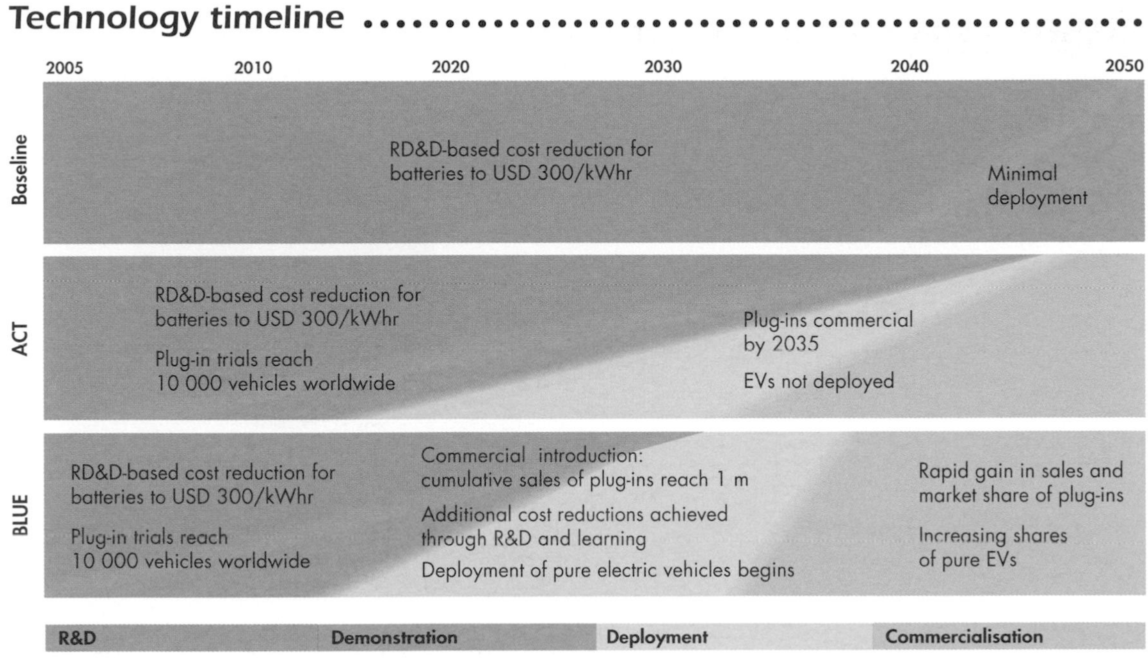

Key actions needed

- The primary hurdle for both plug-in hybrids and electric vehicles is the energy storage system. Despite slow progress, there now appears tremendous potential for key breakthroughs.
- A great deal of RD&D is now occurring in battery manufacturing companies. Governments need to re-double efforts to identify emerging, promising battery (and other energy storage) technologies and support research (whether commercial, scientific, etc.) to bring these technologies to market. Partnerships with vehicle manufacturers may be particularly useful as they have now taken an active stake in developing and commercialising new technologies.
- Most (but not all) recent efforts focus on further development of Li-ion batteries, e.g. Li-polymer, Li-sulfur, etc. Ultracapacitors and flywheels also deserve attention, as do systems that combine storage technologies, such as batteries with ultracapacitors.
- Research and consumer acceptance and early adopter markets.

Key areas for international collaboration

- International collaboration for Electric vehicles and component (especially battery) research already exists in a number of forms, including an IEA implementing agreement on Electric and Hybrid Vehicles. Emphasis is placed on energy storage and power densities of batteries and other storage systems, including ultra-capacitors and flywheels.
- International networks are critical in order to maximise the information sharing and learning. This is a critical time for battery development as a) recent breakthroughs, *i.e.* new types of Li-ion batteries, appear promising and b) consumers have become interested again in vehicle electrification.
- In general IEA countries need to ensure that their RDD&D programmes complement each other and provide assistance to companies to promote battery demonstration, deployment, and commercial production.

Hydrogen fuel cell vehicles

ACT 0 Gt savings 2050

Technology is not deployed under ACT.

BLUE 1.8 Gt savings 2050

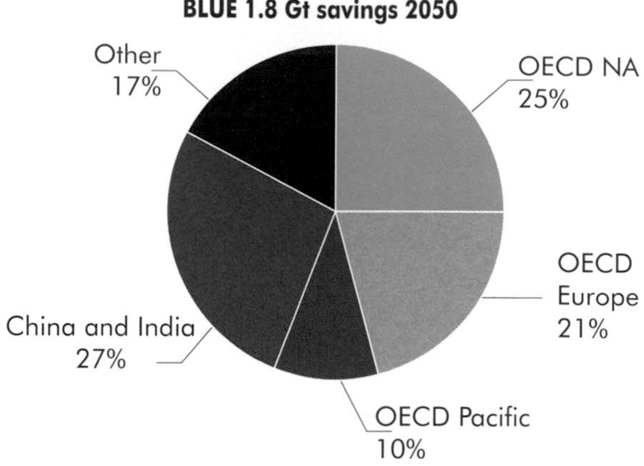

Though fuel cell vehicle costs decline over time, they average about 20% higher than gasoline vehicles, 2008-2050, as reflected in the Deployment cost column below.

	Deployment share of vehicle sales, 2050	RD&D Inv. Cost USD bn 2005-2035	Deployment Cost USD bn 2010-2050
OECD NA	50%	10-12	800-1 100
OECD Europe	50%	8-10	750-950
OECD Pacific	50%	4-5	350-450
China & India	35%	10-12	800-1 100
Other	35%	6-8	600-800

Technology targets

	ACT: Emissions Stabilisation	BLUE: 50% Emissions Reduction
RD&D		
Fuel Cell Stack System		Accelerated R&D activities USD 300/kW by 2020, lifespen 8 000 hrs and reduced catalyst needs
Energy (H_2) Storage		Achieve technical advances to store H_2 on board with a 50% cost reduction by 2020
Deployment		
Fuel Cell Stack System	No deployment assumed	Semi-commercial deployment begins in 2020, to 10% OECD sales share by 2030 helps bring cost to USD 50/kW by 2050
Energy (H_2) Storage	No deployment assumed	Continued cost reduction to 2050

Technology timeline

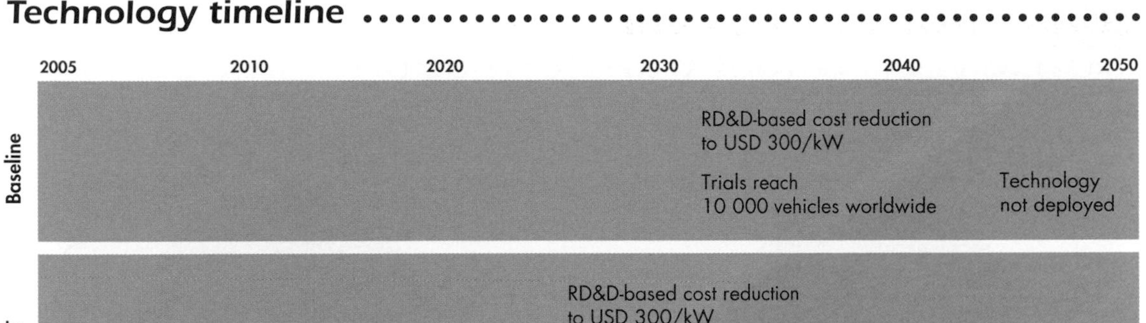

Key actions needed

- H_2 fuel cell vehicle (FCV) costs are currently very high, with a few manufacturers in 2007 offering very limited production runs at prices of USD 100 000. The two main cost components are the fuel cell stack and the H_2 storage, though various "balance of system" components (such as system controller, electronics, motor, and various synergistic fuel economy improvements) may also add considerable expense.
- Deployment in 2020 (initial medium-scale production and semi-commercial sales) assumes fuel cell system cost at USD 300/kW (compared with USD 500+ today). H_2 storage to reach at USD 500/kg, about half of current cost. These 2020 targets will require a doubling of RD&D efforts with greater attention to energy storage options.
- System expansion issues and fuel infrastructure investments, in co-ordination with vehicle sales need to be addressed – a global roadmap for fuel cell vehicle deployment should be in place by 2015.

Key areas for international collaboration

- International collaboration, is needed to co-ordinate research on key components.
- The IEAs Implementing Agreements on H_2 and fuel cell vehicles could be strengthened via stronger funding and more countries participating.
- Apart from technical research, work to begin co-ordinating fuel infrastructure development around the world is needed.
- On-going work on international standard setting, safety testing, etc. needs to continue apace.

CO_2 capture & storage: industry, H_2 & fuel transformation

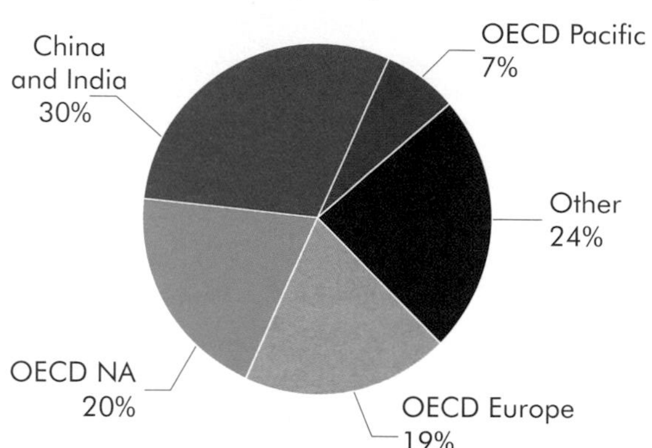

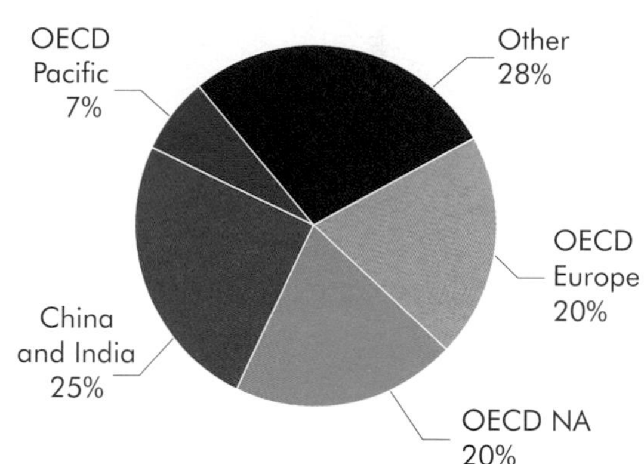

	Global Deployment Share 2050	RD&D Inv. Cost USD bn 2005-2030	Commercial Inv. Cost* USD bn 2030-2050
OECD NA	20%	10-12	125-150
OECD Europe	19%	8-10	125-150
OECD Pacific	7%	2-5	60-70
China & India	30%	6-8	200-300
Other	24%	3-4	150-200

	Global Deployment Share 2050	RD&D Inv. Cost USD bn 2005-2030	Commercial Inv. Cost* USD bn 2030-2050
OECD NA	20%	15-20	350-400
OECD Europe	20%	10-14	350-400
OECD Pacific	7%	5-7	150-200
China & India	25%	10-12	300-400
Other	28%	10-12	250-300

*Excludes operating costs. Total including OPEX is approximately USD 1.0–1.2 trillion for ACT and USD 4–4.5 trillion for BLUE.

Technology targets

	ACT: Emissions Stabilisation	BLUE: 50% Emissions Reduction
RD&D		
Development of various industry applications	Nitrogen free blast furnace and smelt reduction processes (enabling tech.), CCS demo for iron production processes, cement kilns with oxy-fuelling, black-liquor IGCC, fluid catalytic crackers equipped with high-temp. CHP and CO_2 capture. Cost of CO_2 avoided at a range of 50-100 USD/tonne by 2020	
Demonstration targets	5 large scale demo plants in various sectors by 2020	12 large scale demo plants in a range of capture and storage options, including fuel type (coal/gas/biomass) by 2020
New gas separation and capture technologies	Including next-generation processes, such as membranes, solid adsorbers and new thermal processes	
Technology transfer	Technology transfer to China and India	Technology transfer to all transition and developing countries
RD&D		
Development of a regional pipeline infrastructure for CO_2 transport	Major transportation pipeline networks developed, and CO_2 maritime shipping	

Technology timeline

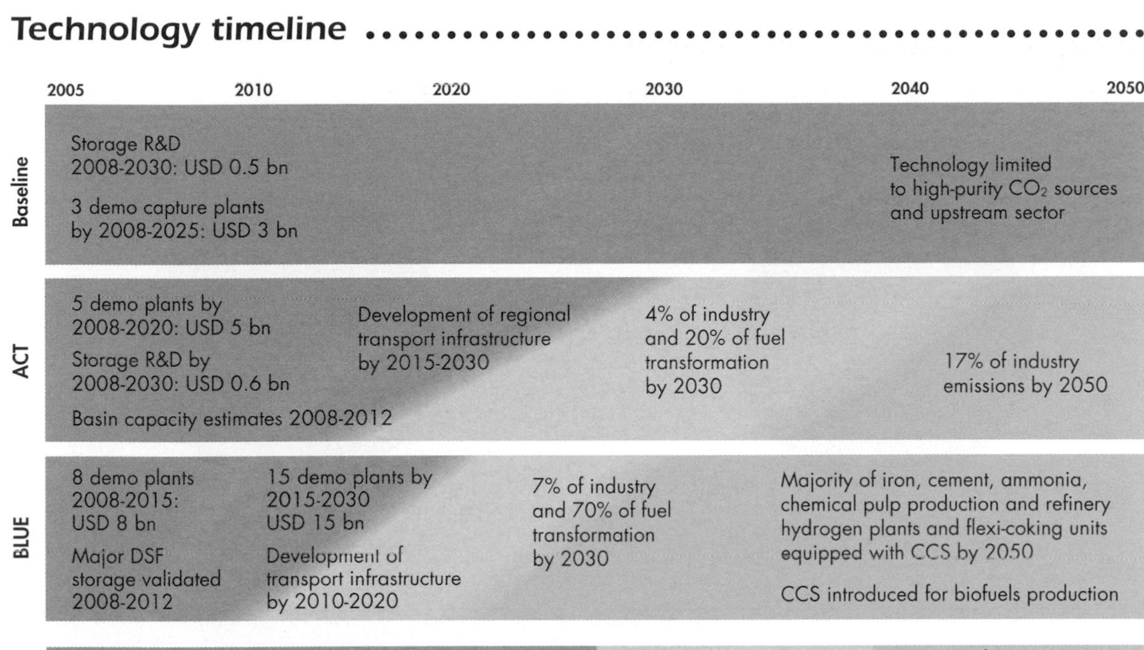

In this roadmap, commercialisation assumes an incentive of USD 50/t CO_2 saved.

Key actions needed

- Develop and enable legal and regulatory frameworks for CCS at the national and international levels, including long-term liability regimes and classification of CO_2.
- Monitoring and verification methods for site assessment, injection and closure periods.
- Incorporate CCS into Emission Trading Schemes and Clean Development Mechanisms.
- RD&D to reduce capture cost and improve overall system efficiencies.
- RD&D for storage integrity and monitoring.
- Raise public awareness and increase education about CCS.
- Assessment of storage capacity using CSLF methodology at the national, basin and field levels.
- Develop 5 large scale demonstration plants by 2020 with public-private partnerships.

Key areas for international collaboration

- Develop and sharing of legal and regulatory frameworks.
- Develop international, regional and national instruments for CO_2 pricing, including CDM and ETS.
- Raise public awareness and education.
- Sharing best practices and lessons learned pilot and large scale from demonstration projects.
- Joint funding of large-scale plants in developing countries by multilateral lending institutions, industry and governments.
- Develop standards for national and basin storage estimates and their application.
- Organisations: Carbon Sequestration Leadership Forum, IEA GHG.

Industrial motor systems

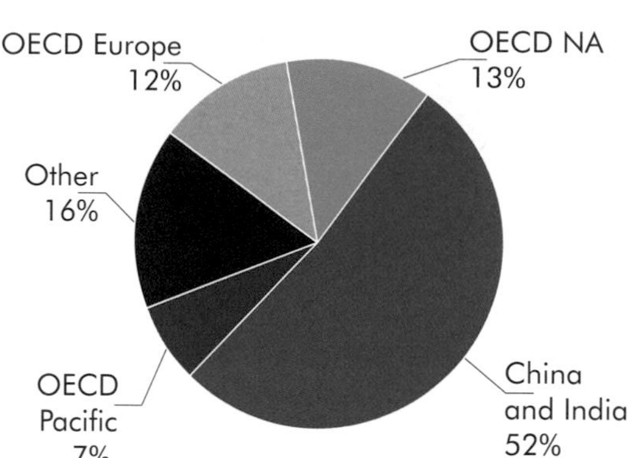

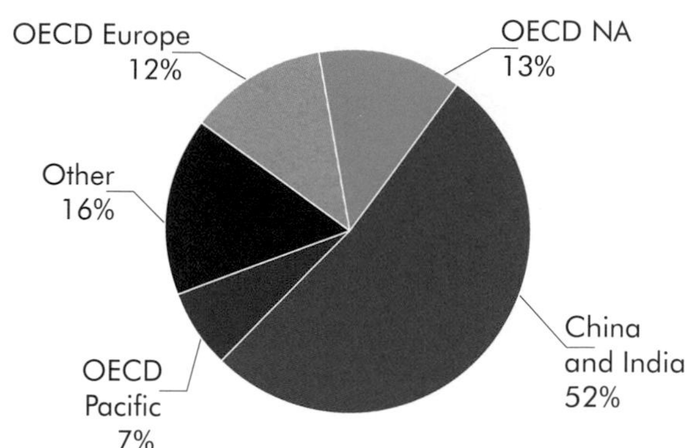

			Commercial Inv. Cost USD bn 2005-2050
OECD NA			400-450
OECD Europe			400-450
OECD Pacific			250-300
China & India			1 100-1 200
Other			550-600

			Commercial Inv. Cost USD bn 2005-2050
OECD NA			600-650
OECD Europe			600-650
OECD Pacific			400-450
China & India			1 600-1 700
Other			800-900

Technology targets

	ACT: Emissions Stabilisation	BLUE: 50% Emissions Reduction
Diffusion		
MEPS harmonised at a high efficiency level and implemented worldwide, to gradually phase-out low-efficiency motors (and other equipment such as pumps) from entering the market	Focus on implementation of energy-efficient motor systems	
Off-the-shelf energy-efficient motor systems	Work with equipment suppliers, plant designers and buyers to facilitate the implementation of maximum-efficiency systems	
Systems efficiency standards and regulations	Promote life-cycle costing	
Design tools for energy-efficient motor systems	Transfer design knowledge of motor systems to non-OECD countries	

Technology timeline

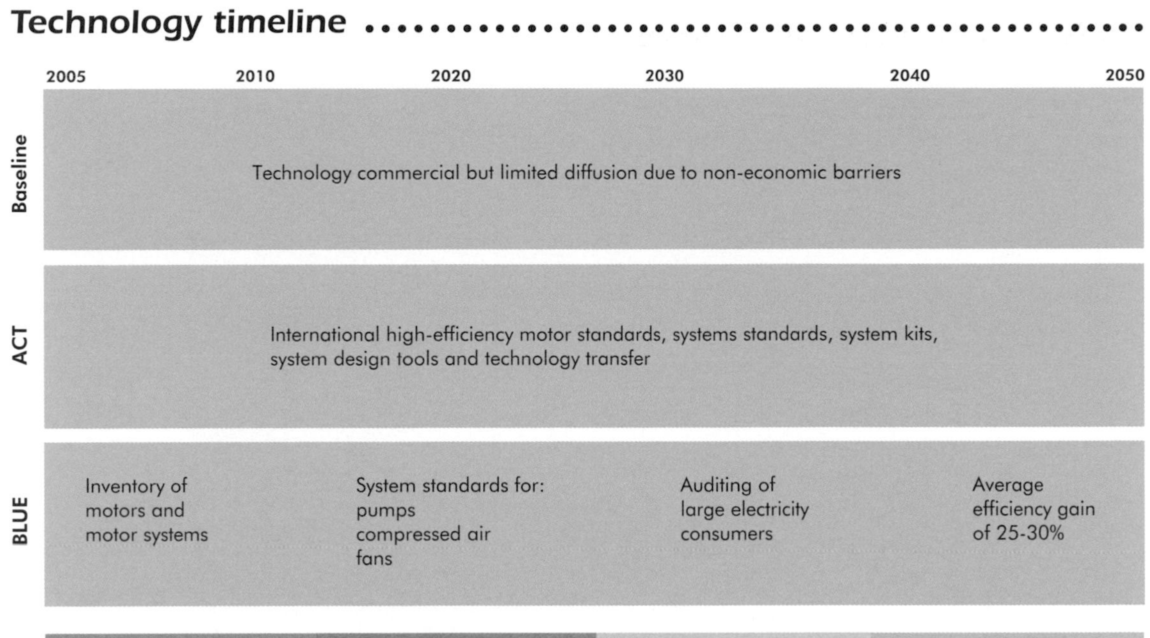

Key actions needed

- Consistent and comprehensive data on motor system efficiency worldwide is lacking. Collecting such data and better understanding the efficiency potentials is a first step.
- Proper design of motor systems to the load requirements can contribute to large energy savings. Use of adjustable speed drives shall be encouraged, where appropriate, to match the speed and the torque to the load requirements.
- The efficiency of industrial electric motors and motor systems must be addressed under a comprehensive market-transformation strategy. A portfolio, or menu, of policies and instruments is essential to address the multitude of barriers that stakeholders face.
- The equipment "dealer" must be leveraged to act as a partner in any market-transformation activity. This *may* require a monetary incentive, but can be based on tools, training, marketing and customer audits.

Key areas for international collaboration

- Harmonise international test procedures (*i.e.* IEC 60034-2) for electric motors.
- Establish a common set of efficiency "tiers" from which countries could draw when they establish minimum energy performance standards for motors.
- International standards for motor systems

Chapter 4 RESEARCH, DEVELOPMENT AND DEMONSTRATION

4

Key Findings

- *Achieving the ACT Map and BLUE Map scenario outcomes requires accelerated cost reductions and substantial technical improvements in both existing and emerging technologies. These will be dependent on significant increases in, and restructuring of, global RD&D efforts in both the public and private sectors.*

- *Public energy technology RD&D spending today, at approximately USD 10 billion a year, is at about half the level it was at 25 years ago. Although governments have made commitments to increase public investment in energy RD&D, this has not yet materialised.*

- *Private sector spending on RD&D of energy technologies today far exceeds public sector spending, at USD 40 billion to USD 60 billion a year. Private sector energy RD&D has also declined over the long term. Mobilising private RD&D is one of the keys to accelerating energy technology innovation.*

- *Governments have a crucial role to play in ensuring the technology development and innovation required by the ACT Map and BLUE Map scenarios. In addition to investment, governments have to establish processes to prioritise and evaluate national RD&D programmes. They must develop policies that can stimulate private sector investment in energy RD&D technology, and portfolios that will prioritise technologies offering the best prospects of reducing CO_2 emissions.*

- *No single policy tool will ensure that the RD&D activities needed in the scenarios occur. A portfolio of policy tools adapted to individual technologies and national systems will be required to make the scenarios come true.*

- *International co-operation and public–private partnerships are significant for future RD&D efforts. Governments need to help minimise unnecessary overlaps and maximise information exchange. RD&D collaborations between OECD and non-OECD countries can help to achieve cost effective and faster technology development.*

Introduction

This chapter explores the role of research, development and demonstration (RD&D) in helping to bring forward the innovative technologies that will be needed to significantly reduce CO_2 emissions. It looks at trends in energy technology RD&D spending, provides an overview of RD&D needed to bring forward key technologies in the scenarios, and outlines a range of policy measures that will be required to make our energy system more sustainable.

Phases of technology development

The generally recognised phases of the innovation process are shown in Figure 4.1 The transition between phases is not automatic – many energy technologies fail at each phase. And in practice the process is not necessarily linear. RD&D is only part of the innovation system required to develop and deploy new and improved technologies. RD&D happens continuously throughout the technology lifecycle: for example, feedback from the market and from technology users during the commercialisation and diffusion phases can lead to additional RD&D, driving continuous innovation.

Figure 4.1 ▶ **Schematic working of the innovation system**

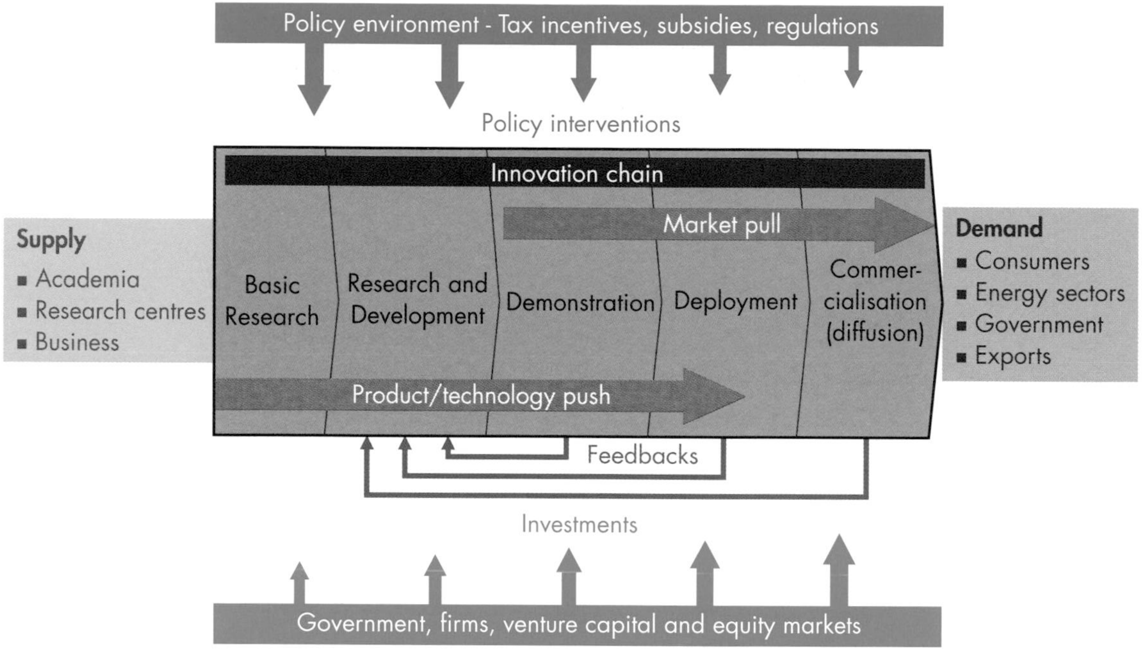

Sources: Adopted and modified from Grubb, 2004 and Foxon, 2003.

Key point

RD&D is only part of the innovation system.

The main focus of this chapter is on RD&D breakthroughs in the earlier phases of technology development, in particular those that help achieve the technological advances and cost reductions that can take technology through to initial deployment and commercialisation. Such breakthroughs may take the form of "revolutionary" innovations; but they may equally take the form of significant "evolutionary" innovations.

The role of government in energy technology innovation

Empirical research has found that total RD&D spending may be less than a quarter of the optimal level (Jones and Williams, 1997). Where RD&D investments are made, returns can be high: the average return on RD&D to firms is estimated to be around 20% to 30%. This is high compared to the 10% rate of return typically required by the private sector on capital investment. Returns to society can be even higher, at 50% or more (Johannsson and Goldemberg, 2002; Nadiri, 1993; Griliches, 1992). More generally, technical change has been recognised as the most significant force for economic growth (Scherer, 1999; Solow, 1957).

But three main market failures can discourage private sector RD&D investment (Johannsson and Goldemberg, 2002; Stiglitz and Wallsten, 1999):

- Innovations that can bring society-wide benefits are often not pursued by private firms because as others capitalise on their work, the original innovators are unable to appropriate enough of the resulting gains to justify their investments. This problem, known as spillover, is generally considered to be most serious in the fundamental or basic research phase of RD&D.
- Innovations that create potentially widespread but unvalued public benefits, known as externalities, are not pursued if there is no mechanism to effectively value that public good and reward the innovation for its contribution to the benefit achieved.
- Private sector risk thresholds are often much lower, and the timescale for expected returns often much shorter, than those required by many RD&D projects. In addition, given the need to protect their ideas, innovators may be restricted in the amount they can tell investors about an RD&D project. As a result, RD&D projects may be exposed to capital market imperfections which force them to pay higher interest rates on loans or to rely heavily on internal funding.

Such market failures undermine innovation in cleaner energy technologies such as those that will reduce pollution or CO_2 emissions. In most OECD countries there is consensus that the government should invest in basic scientific and technological research to complement the nearer-to-market technology investments that the private sector will be prepared to make. To induce private sector investment in innovation in the field of energy technology, governments need to create a framework that will value the public benefits that are achieved or to directly support RD&D investment and activities to help move innovations to a point where they are commercial.

RD&D trends

Government investment in energy RD&D

Government energy RD&D budgets in many member countries declined between the early 1980s and the 1990s from USD 18 billion in 1980 to USD 8 billion in 1997 (Figure 4.2). This decline was largely associated with the difficulties of the nuclear industry and with the decrease in oil prices from 1985 to 2002. Since 1999, government expenditures on RD&D have slightly recovered and stabilised: they were estimated to be around USD 10 billion in 2006. Remarkably, however, over the same timeframe energy RD&D as a share of total RD&D in OECD countries has declined from 11% in 1985 to 3% in 2005.

In most of the nine IEA countries recently surveyed, climate change has emerged as a key driver for public RD&D investments in energy (IEA, 2007c) along with energy security and economy.[1] Most countries foresee an increase in RD&D investments in the coming years (2008 to 2010), although generally modest in scale. Near-future investments seem likely to put most emphasis on cleaner coal use, energy efficiency and biofuels. European countries seem likely to prioritise energy efficiency

1. Austria, Denmark, Germany, France, Italy, Japan, the Netherlands, Switzerland, and the United States – these represent more than 75% of total public RD&D investments in OECD countries.

(in buildings in particular), renewables (biomass in particular) and CO_2 capture and storage (CCS); nuclear research is stable or declining. Several countries are putting more focus on the demonstration phase of the innovation chain.

Figure 4.2 ▶ Government budgets on energy RD&D of the IEA countries

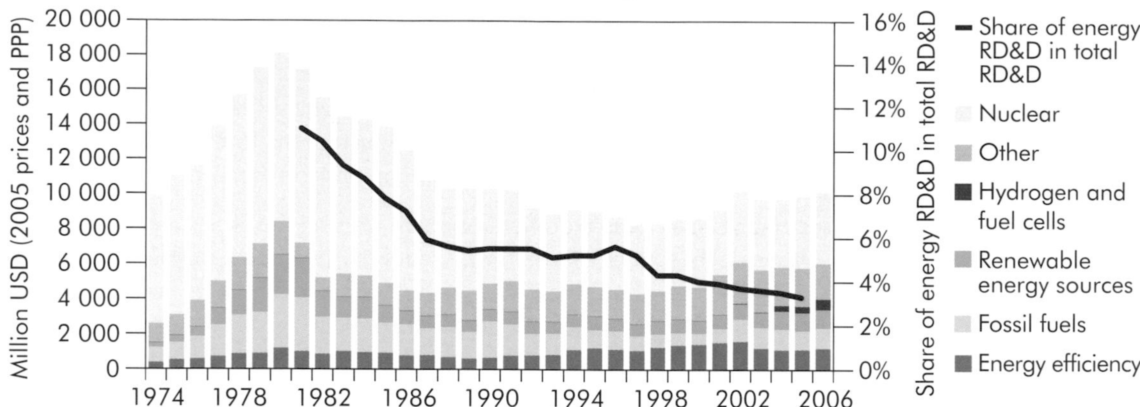

Note: RD&D budgets for the Czech Republic not included due to lack of available data.
Source: IEA 2007a, OECD 2007a.

Key point

Government expenditures on energy RD&D have declined compared to the level seen during the late 1970s and early 1980s.

Energy RD&D budgets as a percentage of GDP for selected countries are illustrated in Figure 4.3. In every case except that of Japan, relative energy RD&D budgets have declined over recent years. This is particularly so in several European countries. In Japan, energy RD&D represented 0.08% of GDP in 2005, whereas in many other OECD member countries it was below 0.03%. Although most European IEA member countries have signed up to the Barcelona goal to increase total public and private

Figure 4.3 ▶ Energy RD&D as a percentage of GDP

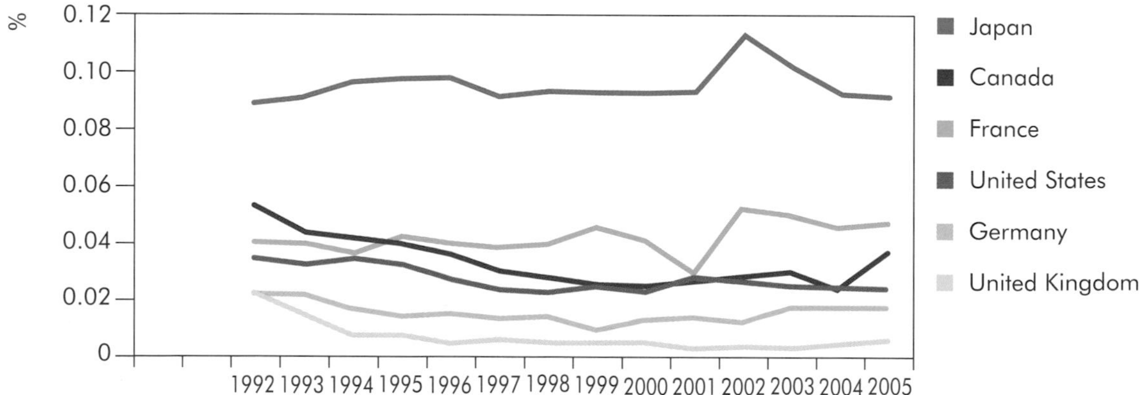

Note: Figures of France, Germany and the United Kingdom do not include the expenditures for the European Commission (EC) RD&D programmes.
Source: IEA, 2007a.

Key point

Energy RD&D shares of GDP are less than 1% and have declined for the last 15 years in many OECD countries.

research and development budgets to 3% of GDP by 2010, there is little sign that they are likely to achieve this. RD&D budgets need to be rebuilt and sustained if governments are to achieve the objectives that they consider necessary for energy sustainability.

Nuclear technologies still attract significant public RD&D spending in some of the largest IEA member countries (Figure 4.4). But the relative share of nuclear technologies decreased between 1992 and 2005. Government expenditure on fossil fuel research experienced the largest drop in share over the same period. The share of government budgets increased slightly for renewable energy and energy conservation technologies, and grew significantly for hydrogen and fuel cells and for power and storage technologies. Two countries (Japan and the United States) account for more than 70% of total energy RD&D government expenditure in IEA countries.

Figure 4.4 ▶ Technology shares of government energy RD&D expenditures in IEA countries

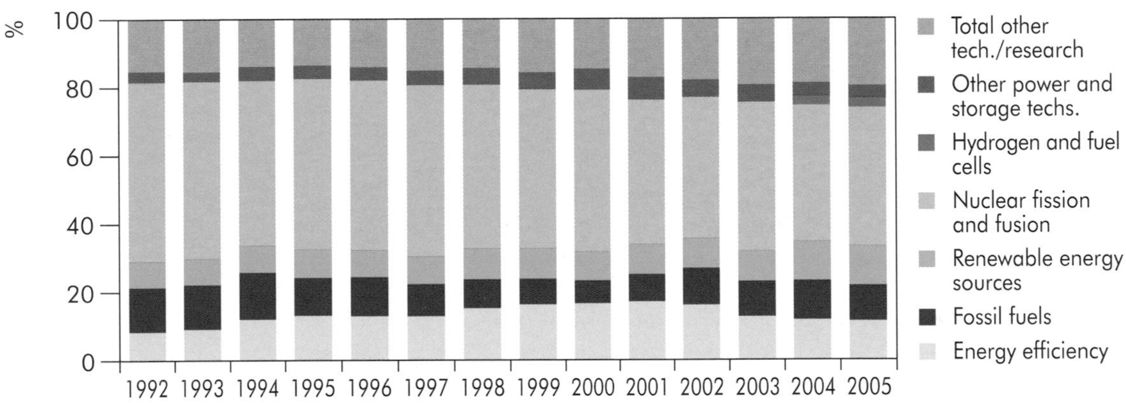

Source: IEA, 2007a.

Key point

The largest share of energy RD&D expenditures is for nuclear technologies. The shares of hydrogen and fuel cells, renewable energy and fossil fuels have increased in recent years.

A number of non-OECD countries, particularly those that are rapidly industrialising, are increasing their involvement in science and innovation. As they try to leapfrog in selected sectors, different countries have very different RD&D priorities, and the competition for scarce talent increases. A large proportion of the energy RD&D effort in these industrialising countries is currently being spent on adapting and improving technologies introduced from OECD countries. This is likely to change as these countries become progressively more sophisticated in their RD&D capacities and in their ability to innovate.

Figure 4.5 shows RD&D spending and human capital for selected OECD and developing countries as a function of government expenditure on R&D (GERD), and as a percentage of GDP and the number of researchers per 1 000 people in the labour force. These indicators show large differences between OECD and non-OECD countries. This suggests that there is room for non-OECD countries to strengthen both their RD&D spending and their RD&D human capital as their economies grow.

Figure 4.5 ▶ Total science and technology R&D expenditure (GERD) in 2004 in selected OECD and non-OECD countries

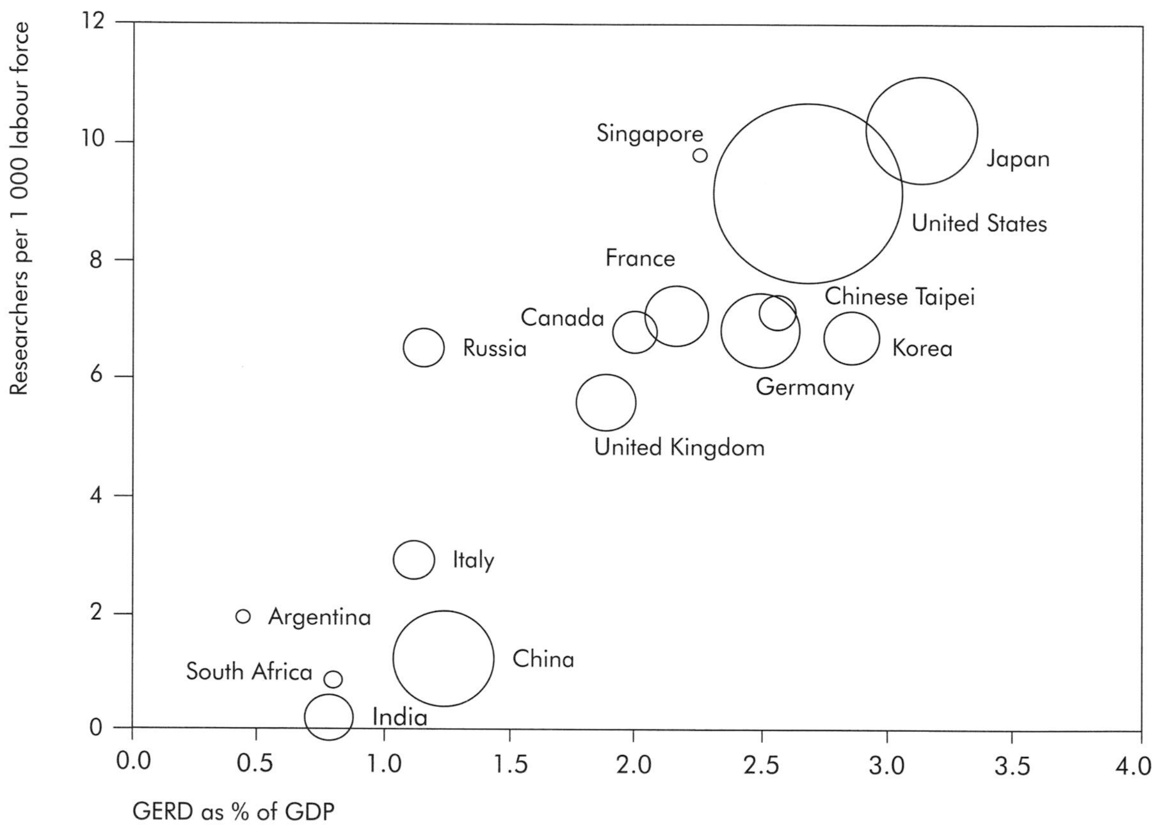

Note: Circles reflect size of spending in USD billion.
Source: OECD, 2007b.

Key point

There are large differences between OECD and non-OECD countries in terms of science and technology RD&D expenditure as a percentage of GDP.

Trends in private sector RD&D

Trends in private sector energy-related RD&D are more difficult to evaluate than those for government RD&D. There is a lack of comprehensive private sector RD&D data, mainly due to their proprietary nature. A good deal of energy RD&D is also conducted by heavily diversified large industrial firms and conglomerates such as Siemens, General Electric and Toshiba. This makes it difficult to identify how much of their overall RD&D is related to energy. Many non-energy product and process innovations also impact on energy applications (Sagar and Holdren,

2002). The increasingly complex pattern of the energy sector due to privatisation and the growing number of public–private partnerships in energy RD&D further complicates the collection of reliable data on private RD&D.

Investment in energy RD&D appears to be low compared with other market sectors. In information technology and pharmaceuticals, for instance, the private sector finances innovation through significant RD&D programmes, equivalent to around 10 to 20% of sector turnover (Neuhoff, 2005). In the power sector, by contrast, broadly the same technologies have dominated for almost a century. Private sector energy RD&D has fallen sharply following privatisation to around 0.4% of turnover in the late 1990s (Margolis and Kammen, 1999). RD&D as a share of total turnover (RD&D intensity) in the power sector is 0.5% – compared to 3.3% in the automobile industry, 8% in the electronics industry and 15% in the pharmaceutical sector (Alic, Mowery and Rubin, 2003).

In general, private sector spending on RD&D in energy-related sectors far exceeds that of government spending. Total private sector energy RD&D is estimated to amount to USD 40 billion to USD 60 billion a year, *i.e.* four to six times the amount of government RD&D.

Power generation sector

RD&D investment by the top ten private sector spenders in the power generation sector was approximately USD 2.4 billion in 2006, ranging between USD 2.2 billion and USD 2.6 billion since 2000 (extrapolated from DIUS [Department for Innovation, Universities and Skills, United Kingdom] and BERR [Department for Business, Enterprise and Regulatory Reform, United Kingdom], 1997 to 2007).[2]

Fossil fuel power generation

Spending on RD&D in the private fossil fuel power generation sector in the United States declined from USD 1 400 million to USD 729 million between 1994 and 2003, despite an annual market growth rate of 2% to 3%.[3] Increased competition and persistent regulatory uncertainty, both caused by a deregulated market, were the primary drivers of this decline (Nemet and Kammen, 2007).

Renewable energy power generation

In the renewable energy sector, the picture is mixed and changing. In the United States, for example, while installed capacity in wind and solar has grown by 20% to 30% a year, private sector spending on wind RD&D declined from USD 327 million to USD 268 million between 1994 and 2003 (Nemet and Kammen, 2007).[4]

2. The top ten RD&D spenders in the data set complied by the United Kingdom Department for Innovation, Universities and Skills include: British Nuclear Fuels (United Kingdom), Electricite de France (France), AREVA (France), Union Electrica Fenosa (Spain), Enel (Italy), Vattenfall (Sweden), Hydro-Quebec (Canada), Tokyo Electric Power (Japan), Kansai Electric Power (Japan), Kyushu Electric Power (Japan), Chubu Electric Power (Japan), Tohoku Electric Power (Japan), Shikoku Electric Power (Japan), Chugoku Electric Power (Japan), Korea Electric Power (South Korea) and Taiwan Power (Taiwan). The actual makeup of top ten changes year by year.

3. The original figure was USD 1 290 million, and 672 million in 2002 USD (Nemet and Kammen, 2007).

4. The original figure was USD 301 million, and 247 million in 2002 USD (Nemet and Kammen, 2007).

Conversely, nearly USD 1 billion was poured into alternative energy RD&D ventures in California alone in 2007 (Financial Times, 2008). In both Europe and Japan, however, private sector spending on renewable energy sector RD&D is increasing. For example, in the wind energy sector, Vestas Wind System in Denmark, almost doubled its RD&D spending from USD 56 million in 2001 to USD 106 million in 2006 (extrapolated from DIUS and BERR, 1997 to 2007).

Oil and gas sector

RD&D investment by the oil and natural gas industry, along with entrepreneurial start-ups funded by venture and equity capital, appears to be rising. The sector spent more than USD 6.5 billion on RD&D in 2006. Investment by the global top ten spenders in this industry amounted to USD 4.0 billion in 2000 and increased to USD 5.2 billion in 2006 (extrapolated from DIUS and BERR, 1997 to 2007).[5] In this sector, the focus of RD&D investment has changed in recent years. From the early 1980s, major oil and natural gas companies began to decrease their RD&D spending, as they sought to buy in technology from service companies rather than to develop it themselves. As oil and gas prices rise, it can be expected that private sector RD&D investment will increase – in the search for new ways to maximise production from (and identify and exploit) oil and natural gas reservoirs.

Automobile sector

It is not possible to isolate spending on energy-related RD&D in the automobile sector from wider RD&D spending on such things as safety, comfort or performance. But the sector is a big investor overall, and many non-energy developments (such as lighter, stronger materials) have energy spin-offs – for example, in terms of increased energy efficiency.

RD&D spending by the top ten global automobile manufacturer spenders between 1997 and 2005 increased from USD 38 billion to USD 52 billion and then fell to USD 47 billion in 2006.[6] Total spending by 75 global manufacturers and their sub-suppliers amounted to almost USD 73 billion in 2006. The top ten spenders carried out the bulk of the RD&D in the entire sector (extrapolated from DIUS and BERR, 1997 to 2007). Despite the very weak profitability of some companies in recent years, Ford, GM, DaimlerChrysler, Toyota and Volkswagen have maintained high levels of RD&D spending. Strong pressure to stay competitive by retaining market share and scale in the sector requires faster product development, on-going RD&D, and the exploitation of low cost manufacturing options in developing countries. Intensifying market competition in the area of environmental performance and improving fuel economy, as well as progressively tightening regulations, suggests that private funding for RD&D in this sector is likely at least to be maintained.

5. The top ten spenders include: Schlumberger (United States), Total (France), ExxonMobil (United States), Royal Dutch Shell (United Kingdom), BP (United Kingdom), Halliburton (United States), ChevronTexaco (United States), ENI (Italy), China Petroleum & Chemical (People's Republic of China), Petroleo Brasiliero (Brazil), Baker Hughes (United States), Gazprom (Russia) and Statoil (Norway). The actual makeup of top ten changes year by year.

6. The top ten spenders include: Ford (United States), General Motors (United States), DaimlerChrysler (Germany-United States, since 1998), Toyota (Japan), Honda (Japan), Nissan (Japan), Volkswagen (Germany), BMW (Germany), Renault (France), Peugeot (PSA, France), Fiat (Italy), Mitsubishi (Japan), Volvo (Sweden), Daimler (Germany, 1997) and Chrysler (United States, 1997). The makeup of top ten changes year by year, although the top ten spenders have stayed the same since 2001 (the first ten companies on this list).

Buildings sector

Private RD&D spending by the top ten mostly European and Japanese construction and building materials companies between 2000 and 2006 showed broadly stable spending between USD 1.5 billion and USD 1.7 billion (extrapolated from DIUS and BERR, 1997 to 2007).[7] The figures do not include RD&D on appliances by appliance manufacturers.

Manufacturing sector

Chemical industry

RD&D spending by the top ten global private chemicals companies between 2000 and 2006 showed a stable spending trend between USD 7 billion and USD 10 billion.[8] This amounted to around half to two-thirds of the total global spending in this sector of around USD 15 billion in 2006 (extrapolated from DIUS and BERR, 1997 to 2007).

Pulp and paper industry

Private RD&D spending by the top eight pulp and paper industry spenders between 2003 and 2005 showed a stable spending trend between USD 601 million and USD 636 million (extrapolated from DIUS and BERR, 1997 to 2007).[9]

Industrial metals

Private RD&D spending by the top ten global industrial metal companies between 2003 and 2006 showed a gradual increase from USD 1.7 billion to USD 2.2 billion (extrapolated from DIUS and BERR, 1997 to 2007).[10]

Industrial equipment industry

Eight large global industrial equipment manufacturers (Siemens, General Electric, Mitsubishi Heavy Industrials, United Technologies, Caterpillar, ABB, ALSTOM, and IHI) spent between USD 13 billion and USD 15 billion on RD&D between 2001 and 2006 (extrapolated from DIUS and BERR, 1997 to 2007).

It is not possible to assess from the available figures how much of this RD&D spending was targeted at energy efficiency. The proportion and focus of RD&D investment will vary from industry to industry. For example, while energy efficiency-

---

7. The top ten spenders include: Saint-Gobain (France), Asahi Glass (Japan), Hilti (Liechtenstein), Bouygues (France), JS (Japan), American Standard Companies (United States), Toto (Japan), Kajima (Japan), Taisei (Japan), Fortune Brands (United States), Nippon Sheet Glass (Japan), Sekisui Chemical (Japan), Tostem Inax (Japan, now JS), Shimizu (Japan), and Lafarge (France). The actual makeup of the top ten changes year by year.

8. The top ten spenders include: BASF (Germany), EI du Pont de Nemours (Du Pont, United States), Dow Chemical (United States), Syngenta (Switzerland), Sumitomo Chemical (Japan), Solvay (Belgium), Mitsubishi Chemical (Japan), Monsanto (United States), Asahi Kasei (Japan), Toray Industries (Japan), Mitsui Chemicals (Japan), PPG Industries (United States), Degussa (Germany) and Linde (Germany). The actual makeup of the top ten changes year by year.

9. The top eight spenders include: Stora Enso (Finland), Oji Paper (Japan), SCA (Sweden), Nippon Paper (Japan), International Paper (United States), Georgia-Pacific (United States), Weyerhaeuser (United States), and UPM-Kymmene (Finland).

10. The top ten spenders include: POSCO (South Korea), JFE (Japan), ThyssenKrupp (Germany), Nippon Steel (Japan), Alcan (Canada), Kobe Steel (Japan), Corus (United Kingdom), Sumitomo Metal Industries (Japan), Umicore (Belgium), Arcelor (Luxembourg), and Mitsubishi Materials (Japan). The actual makeup of the top ten changes year by year.

related RD&D is mostly performed by machine supply companies in the pulp and paper industry, product- and process-oriented RD&D in the iron and steel industry is performed by integrated large steel companies through co-operation with both machine suppliers and customers. Techno-economic differences between industrial energy efficiency technologies (*e.g.* industry-specific performance characteristics, the need for close compatibility with different production routes) make it difficult to stimulate industrial technology innovation (Luiten and Blok, 2004; Luiten, Blok and van Lente, 2006).

General trends in energy RD&D

Public spending on energy RD&D has declined significantly compared to the 1970s and the early 1980s, but has stabilised since the 1990s. Although in many sectors private sector RD&D spending has remained generally stable during the 2000s, the longer-term trend is downwards (Nemet and Kammen, 2007; Edmonds, *et al.*, 2007; Dooley, 1998).

Three main factors appear to have contributed to this apparent decline in public and private energy-related RD&D investment:

- Energy RD&D budgets were expanded greatly in the 1970s in response to the oil price shocks at the beginning of the decade, particularly due to the search for alternatives to imported oil. With the oil price collapse in the 1980s and the generally low energy prices in the 1990s, concerns about energy security diminished. This was mirrored in a reduction in RD&D efforts. Recent rises in oil prices have not yet led to any significant increase in energy RD&D.
- Following the liberalisation of energy markets in the 1990s, competitive forces shifted the focus from long-term investments such as RD&D towards making better use of existing plants and deploying well-developed, proven, technologies and resources. This was particularly the case for natural gas technologies for power and heat, which were themselves the product of RD&D and investment over the previous three decades.
- There has been a very large reduction in RD&D expenditure on nuclear power following many countries experiencing cost overruns and construction delays, together with the growth of public concerns about reactor safety, nuclear proliferation and nuclear waste disposal.

Technology RD&D needs

Achieving the very large global CO_2 emission reductions envisaged in the ACT Map and BLUE Map scenarios will require the progressive decarbonisation of power generation and substantial steps to reduce emissions in other manufacturing sectors and in transport. This is a huge challenge, which will require very high levels of innovation and investment if it is to be successfully delivered. In particular, achieving the outcomes envisaged in both the ACT Map and BLUE Map scenarios will be dependent on urgent action to rapidly advance a portfolio of current and breakthrough technologies.

Table 4.1 identifies the key technology priorities that will be needed to deliver the outcomes in the two main scenarios. It is descriptive, rather than exhaustive. The technologies listed are those which offer the greatest potential contribution to reducing CO_2 emissions, but require strong technology breakthrough and cost reduction efforts. Although currently known technologies are capable of delivering the emission reductions required, many of those technologies face significant technical and cost barriers. (For detailed technology development targets and RD&D breakthroughs for individual technologies, refer to Annex C as well as the respective technology chapters. For possible development approaches of selected technologies, refer to Chapter 3: Technology Roadmaps.)

Table 4.1 ▶ **Key technology priorities for RD&D in the ACT Map and BLUE Map scenarios**

Key RD&D technologies	
ACT Map and BLUE Map scenarios	**Additional for BLUE Map scenario**
Power supply	
Biomass supply	Deepwater offshore wind
CO_2 capture and storage (CCS)	High efficiency transmission and distribution (T&D) (including direct current [DC] transmission)
CCS coal: oxyfuel, post-combustion, pre-combustion	Hydrogen production and infrastructure
CCS gas: oxyfuel, post-combustion, chemical looping	Large-scale electricity storage (500 GW)
CCS: biomass	
Coal integrated gasification combined cycle (IGCC)	
Concentrated solar power (CSP)	
Enhanced geothermal system (EGS)	
Nuclear IV	
Offshore wind	
Photovoltaics	
Smart grids	
Stationary fuel cells for combined heat and power (CHP)	
Industrial	
Bio-refineries	
CCS: industry (iron/steel/ammonia/pulp and paper/cement)	

Table 4.1 ▶ **Key technology priorities for RD&D in the ACT Map and BLUE Map scenarios** (continued)

Key RD&D technologies	
ACT Map and BLUE Map scenarios	**Additional for BLUE Map scenario**
Feedstock substitution (biopolymer; naphtha products from biomass; monomer from biomass; and clinker substitute)	
Fuel substitution (industrial heat pumps; and electric heating technologies)	
Plastic recycling/energy recovery	
Process innovation (smelt reduction/direct casting in iron and steel; membranes in chemical and petrochemical; black-liquor gasification in pulp and paper; and inert anode for aluminium)	
Buildings/appliances	
Heat-pump technologies (air-source; geothermal; and water-source)	
Lighting system: light emitting diodes (LED)	
Liquid biofuels for cooking/heating	
Passive housing	
Solar heating	
Transport	
Hybrid/plug-in hybrid vehicles: low-cost high-density batteries	Electric vehicles: low-cost high-density batteries
Second-generation biofuels (advanced biodiesel, *i.e.* BTL w/ FT process; and cellulosic ethanol)	Hydrogen fuel cell vehicles

Priority near-term RD&D targets for the development of lower-carbon technologies

Figures 4.6 to 4.9 illustrate the important stages of development in the next 10 to 15 years for the key technologies. The positioning of the bars on the horizontal axes represents the near-term priority or priorities for each technology cluster. The thicker the bar, the greater the need for effort (not necessarily investment). The vertical axes show the expected CO_2 saving achieved by each technology cluster in the BLUE Map scenario compared to the baseline scenario.

Power generation technologies

Significant cuts in CO_2 emissions from the power generation sector can only be achieved with a significant increase in renewable energy generation and with extensive CCS and/or more nuclear generation.

Figure 4.6 ▶ Near-term technology development priorities and CO_2 mitigation for power generation technologies

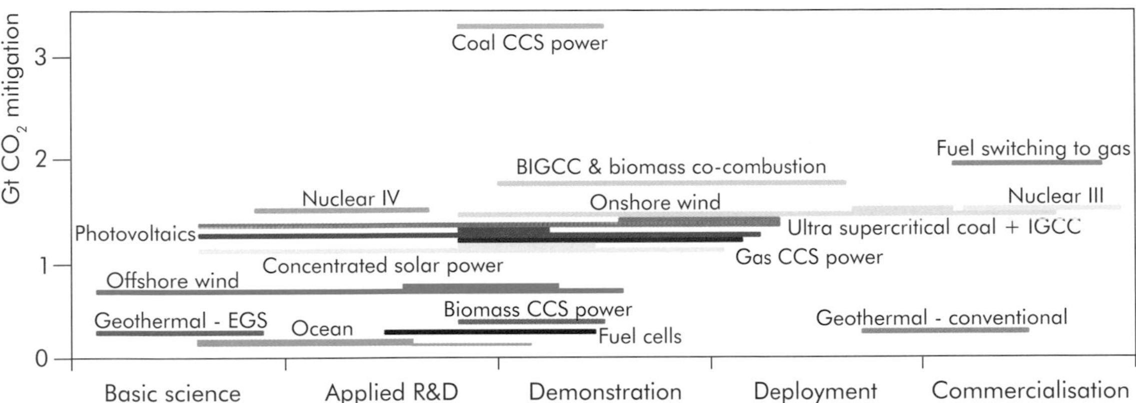

Notes: 1) See Annex C for detailed RD&D priorities for individual technologies. 2) Near-term indicates the next 10 to 15 years. 3) CO_2 emission mitigation in the BLUE Map scenario relative to the Baseline scenario.

Key point

A wide range of power generation technologies require strong RD&D efforts.

Both the ACT Map and BLUE Map scenarios require high shares of renewable generation (35% and 46% respectively). This will require significant RD&D breakthroughs in wind, solar, biomass, and (to a lesser extent) hydro and geothermal power generation. For CCS technologies, RD&D needs to be directed to reducing capture cost and improving overall system efficiencies, as well as storage integrity and monitoring. For nuclear technologies, although in principle the ACT Map and BLUE Map scenarios can be delivered with existing Generation III and Generation III+ technologies, RD&D is needed for Generation IV technologies and the associated fuel cycles which will help to reduce costs, minimise nuclear waste and enhance safety.

Industry

Successfully achieving the outcomes of both the ACT Map and BLUE Map scenarios is dependent on a wide range of innovative industrial technology developments – including materials and product efficiency, process innovation, fuel and feedstock substitution, and CCS. The near-term technology priorities in respect of key industrial energy technologies, and their relative contributions to CO_2 mitigation in the BLUE Map scenario, are illustrated below.

In the BLUE Map scenario, total fuel and electricity savings account for 41% of the CO_2 savings compared to the Baseline scenario. 37% of the reduction in 2050 will be expected to come from CCS. Changes in the energy-fuel mix and feedstock substitution account for 22% of all CO_2 emission reductions. These include switching to less carbon-intensive energy sources and feedstocks.

Figure 4.7 ▶ **Near-term technology development priorities and CO_2 mitigation for industrial energy technologies**

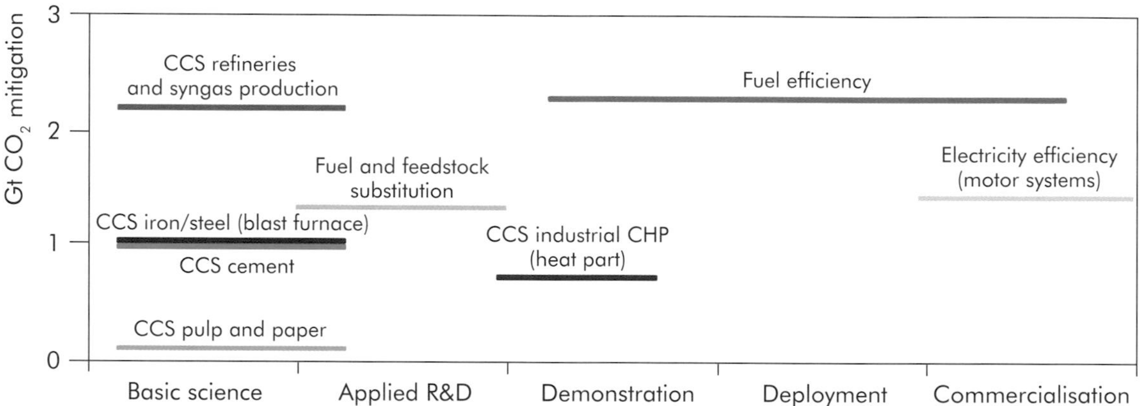

Notes: 1) See Annex C for detailed RD&D priorities for individual technologies. 2) Near-term indicates the next 10 to 15 years. 3) CO_2 emission mitigation in the BLUE Map scenario relative to the baseline scenario. 4) Only one-third of CCS in the cement industry is energy-related. The other two-thirds of captured and stored CO_2 derives from chemical reactions. 5) Industrial CHP-related CCS includes only heat-related and not power-related CO_2.

Key point

CCS as well as fuel and feedstock substitution technologie need strong RD&D efforts in the near term.

Buildings and appliances

For the buildings and appliances sector, delivering the outcomes in the ACT Map scenario will require innovation in heat pump technologies, building shell measures (insulation, windows, etc), energy efficient appliances and solar hot water heating. In the BLUE Map scenario, reducing thermal fuel consumption is a priority, *i.e.* heat pumps, modern biomass technologies, solar hot water heating and a shift to passive housing all become increasingly important. Cooling will be a rapidly emerging demand in developing countries, so building design and shell measures will need to reduce cooling loads, and the efficiency of air-conditioning will need to be improved.

Many of the technologies required in the buildings and appliances sector are already commercially available, and in some cases mature. The potential for RD&D breakthroughs is, therefore, limited. However, incremental technological improvements will be vital, not only to improve the performance of these technologies, but to reduce their cost. The main technology development emphasis for this sector is, therefore, on incremental cost reductions, improved performance and system integration.

Figure 4.8 ▶ **Near-term technology development priorities and CO_2 mitigation for buildings and appliances technologies**

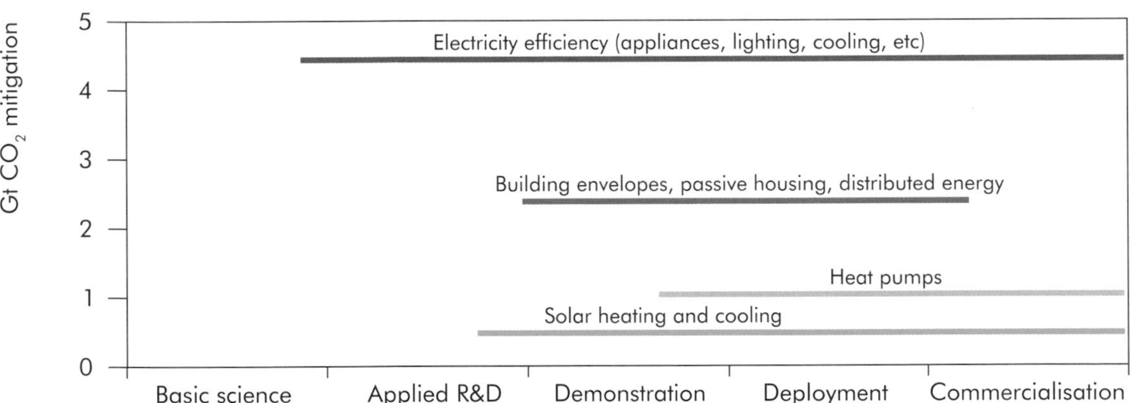

Notes: 1) See Annex C for detailed RD&D priorities for individual technologies. 2) Near-term indicates the next 10 to 15 years. 3) CO_2 emission mitigation in the BLUE Map scenario relative to the Baseline scenario.

Key point

The main emphasis in building and appliance technologies is incremental cost reductions, improved performance and systems integration.

Transport

In transport, further improvements in the fuel economy of light-duty vehicles (LDVs) provide most of the energy savings in the ACT Map scenario. Although engine-related and non-engine-related vehicle technologies have significant potential to improve fuel economy and reduce emissions, they require continuous improvement rather than RD&D breakthroughs. For RD&D breakthroughs, the most promising areas are concentrated on specific vehicle and fuel technologies. The most significant efficiency improvements needed to deliver the outcomes envisaged in the ACT Map scenario are the introduction of plug-in hybrids.

For the BLUE Map scenario and its variants, the transport sector will require new solutions. In this scenario, efficiency gains by gasoline and diesel vehicles provide about half the CO_2 reduction. The other half comes from the use of biofuels and introduction of electric vehicles (EVs) and fuel cell vehicles (FCVs). Both FCVs and EVs offer efficiency improvements of up to 50% over that achievable with full hybrids. This explains the large fuel consumption reductions under the BLUE scenarios. As for fuels, the biofuels account for 26% of total transport fuel demand in the BLUE Map scenario, which brings the use of conventional oil products to 35%

below the 2005 level. Hydrogen plays an important role as well, as FCVs sales and the construction of hydrogen infrastructure will begin after 2020 and grow steadily over time in this scenario. Figure 4.9 shows the near-term technology development priorities in this sector.

Figure 4.9 ▶ **Near-term technology development priorities and CO_2 mitigation for transport technologies**

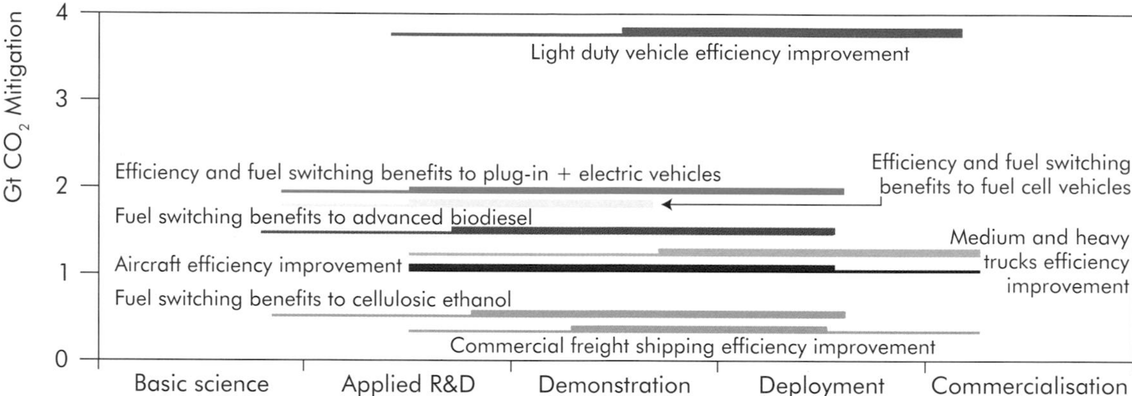

Notes: 1) See Annex C for detailed RD&D priorities for individual technologies. 2) Near-term indicates the next 10 to 15 years. 3) CO_2 emission mitigation in the BLUE Map scenario relative to the Baseline scenario.

Key point

For transport technologies, RD&D breakthroughs are needed on specific vehicle and fuel technologies.

RD&D policies needed to achieve technology priorities

The primary outcome sought in the ACT Map and BLUE Map scenarios – the mitigation of climate change – is a benefit that will be shared widely and globally. It is, in economic terms, a public good. The successful achievement of this outcome will require the value of that public good to be built, either directly or indirectly, into the commercial and innovation systems that will influence behaviours and results.

Public policy, therefore, needs to play a crucial role in energy technology development – in funding and prioritising research and development and in stimulating innovation and deployment.

Supply-push and market-pull: a policy portfolio approach

Over the years it has been recognised that the role of government is often most effective if it combines to support "supply-push" (*i.e.* a focus on RD&D and technology standards) and "demand-pull" (*i.e.* a focus on influencing the market through economic incentives such as regulation, taxation or guaranteed purchase agreements).

Governments and the private sector both play distinct roles in each of the five phases in the innovation chain. Governments tend to invest more than the private sector in the initial phases of the innovation chain. The degree of risk and speculation changes along the chain; accordingly the role of government changes due to changes in the degree and nature of the market failure. Private sector investment (coupled with government regulation) plays a stronger role in the later phases.

Private sector competition is a significant driver of technology innovation. However, government support is essential in many cases to initiate the process of technology innovation and to facilitate successful deployment. Government-funded energy RD&D can play a critical role in solving difficult technical problems that markets may fail to address. The specification of technology standards can also be important in inducing firms to innovate to achieve higher technology performance levels. Public funding for full-scale "in the field" demonstration projects can also, in many circumstances, be critical for learning.

To achieve the large scale of technological change required for the ACT Map and BLUE Map scenarios, a portfolio of policies is needed. A successful outcome is most likely to be achieved through a multi-faceted policy portfolio involving (IEA, 2007b):

- a clear definition of government's role in technology development;
- national energy strategies (policy directions and goals);
- accompanying technology and RD&D strategies;
- adequate and predictable funding;
- well-defined and transparent RD&D prioritisation and evaluation processes;
- the involvement of stakeholders, including the private sector, in RD&D priority setting and evaluation;
- effective linkages with national science, research and innovation strategies;
- effective linkages with policies for commercialisation and deployment;
- public–private partnerships;
- a clear strategy for international RD&D collaboration.

A complementary portfolio of "push" and "pull" policies is likely to be needed to maximise the overall impact of government actions. However, this section focuses more on "push" policies.

RD&D spending

An ambitious and sustained global effort of technology development is required if technologies are to be delivered within the timescales required for both the ACT Map and BLUE Map scenarios. But, as shown above, public and private sector investment in RD&D has decreased significantly since the 1970s, and has remained at relatively low levels in recent years. This trend needs to be reversed. The main tools available to governments in this respect include direct funding of basic research in universities and research institutions, patent protection to award a temporary monopoly to innovators to enable them to capitalise on their ideas, tax measures to support increased RD&D in the private sector, and other market measures that can indirectly stimulate private sector investment.

Estimating RD&D investment needs

It is clear that the current level of RD&D spending is far from enough to reach the targets of the ACT Map or BLUE Map scenarios, both of which require accelerated cost reductions and the technical improvement of existing as well as new technologies. The Stern report recommends a doubling of the public investment in energy RD&D (Stern *et al.*, 2006). Several other studies estimate that overall RD&D investments need to be increased from two to ten times the current spending levels (PCAST, 1997, 1999; Schock, *et al.*, 1999; Davis and Owens, 2003; Nemet and Kammen, 2007).

It is difficult to rationalise the case for any particular level of investment, and different studies use different methodologies. The study by Anderson for the Stern report estimates the necessary investment in innovation as the difference between the average incremental costs of investment in new technologies and that of mature technologies (Anderson, 2006). Schock, *et al.* (1999), however, value energy RD&D by estimating the cost of the insurance needed against four types of energy-related risks (oil price shocks, power supply disruptions, local air pollution and climate change), concluding that on this basis energy RD&D needed to be increased by a factor of four. Nemet and Kammen (2007) utilise the same methodology and conclude that three to ten times the current level of RD&D spending is needed.[11]

Such methodologies cast a useful light on the likely level of the shortfall in current RD&D expenditure. However, the empirical relationship between RD&D spending and outcomes – *i.e.* whether higher levels of spending will automatically lead to higher success rates of RD&D in terms of technology commercialisation – has not been clearly established. There is no such thing as a "right level of funding" in this respect. However, to achieve the ACT Map and BLUE Map scenarios, it is clear that:

- Innovation investments become much more expensive as the activities move from basic research through to demonstration. Compared to the estimated amounts required in the deployment phase, RD&D investments are much smaller as cost-reduction measures and can be considered an inexpensive insurance policy to hedge against the future risks of climate change.[12]

---

11. While Schock *et al.* treated stabilisation levels as an uncertain parameter between 650 ppm and 750 pm with a known probability density function (35%), Nemet and Kammen used a lower CO_2 stabilisation target of 550 ppm.

12. Chapter 5 estimates deployment costs for new cleaner technologies to be USD 4.8 trillion in the ACT Map scenario and USD 10.4 trillion in BLUE Map. Total learning investments (the additional costs beyond the cost of the incumbent fossil technology) during the deployment phase are estimated at USD 2.8 trillion for the ACT Map scenario and USD 7.0 trillion for the BLUE Map scenario.

- Current levels of investment are very unlikely to achieve the sort of step change in technology that is needed to deliver the sought outcomes. Even a doubling of current levels of investment may not be enough.

Governments can play an important role in augmenting and more effectively marshalling global RD&D investments. There is a need to encourage greater private sector energy RD&D and to ensure more effective co-ordination of RD&D efforts between the public and private sectors, particularly in areas where the private sector is unlikely on its own to invest sufficiently in innovation. There are potentially important synergies to be exploited here, particularly in terms of the ways in which publicly funded RD&D can stimulate private investment in RD&D.

RD&D priority setting: a technology portfolio approach

Innovation is, by its nature, unpredictable. Some technologies will succeed and others will fail. Uncertainties and risks inherent in developing low emission technologies can to some extent be smoothed by adopting a portfolio approach.

Empirical research on the ratio of successful returns to RD&D projects show highly skewed outcome distributions: a small percentage of "winners" yield above-cost returns, which to some extent at least offset the much larger number of "losers" that generate little if any returns (Grabowski and Vernon, 1990; Harhoff, 1999; Mansfield, 1977; Scherer, 1999). Developing a portfolio of projects can help to hedge such risks and uncertainties.

Governments can also help ensure that proper attention is paid to longer-term aims as well as to short-term ones. Markets will tend to deliver least-cost, short-term options at the expense of technologies that could ultimately deliver huge cost savings or other benefits in the longer term. An RD&D portfolio can mix technologies to optimise both short-term incremental innovation and longer-term, more radical innovation and development. There may also be efficiencies to be gained through collaboration to create international RD&D portfolios.

Technology portfolios need to be carefully selected against clear outcome-focused objectives. The progress made in each technology area should be the subject of continuous assessment and reassessment, and the mix adjusted as appropriate. Establishing an effective portfolio formation and management system is, therefore, crucial. Technology roadmaps can help portfolio making, implementation and adjustment.

Basic science

To develop many of these breakthrough energy technologies, advances in basic science will be necessary. Table 4.2 shows a selected list of key technology areas with basic research breakthrough opportunities. The list is by no means exhaustive. All these areas need to be supported through public initiatives such as funding and research programmes.

Table 4.2 ▶ Selected basic research opportunities for key technology challenges

Key technology challenges	Scientific disciplines	Basic research opportunities
Power supply		
Geothermal	Geology/Geophysics/ Geochemistry/ Materials science	Understanding of geologic formation properties and fluid conditions; Models of suitability for geothermal applications; and development of better materials for drilling, down-hole measurement and fluid handling
Deep offshore wind Ocean energy	Oceanography/ Marine science/ Ocean science	Understanding of wave behaviours/wave-stream flow and hydrodynamics; understanding the physical and environmental interaction of conversion process with wave, tidal current, temperature gradient and salinity gradient resources; understanding of offshore network interaction with ocean energy plants; and new materials for efficient osmotic processes
Photovoltaic (PV)	Chemistry/Physics/ Materials science	Comprehensive understanding of underlying properties for new PV materials and concepts
Ultra super critical steam cycle (USCSC)	Materials science/ Nanosciences	New low-cost materials for high temperature steam conditions
Electricity system	Chemistry/ Nanoscience	Discovery of high temperature superconductors
Industry		
Chemical/petrochemical process innovation in basic materials production processes	Agronomy/ Biochemistry	Discovery of genes responsible in rhizobia and legumes; and comprehensive understanding of natural mitrogen fixation process (recognition of signals exchanged between the plant and bacteria; structural chemical bases of rhizobia/legume communication; and signal transduction pathways responsible for the induction of the symbiosis-specific genes for nitrogen fixation)
Buildings and appliances		
LED	Chemistry/ Nanoscience	New light emitting substance discovery; and stability of organic LED
Cross-cutting		
Biomass and second-generation biofuels	Genomics	Development of better energy plants; and supply productivity increase
	Environmental science	Understanding of the net GHG impacts of different type of land use
Hydrogen production	Chemistry/Biochemistry/ Electrochemistry/ Nano and molecular science	Alternative catalysts for water splitting (photoelectrochemical and photocatalytic); bioreactors; and photosynthesis imitation at molecular level

Table 4.2 ▶ Selected basic research opportunities for key technology challenges (continued)

Key technology challenges	Scientific disciplines	Basic research opportunities
Hydrogen storage	Chemistry/Biochemistry/ Materials science	Solid storage in metal hydrides; chemical hydrides; and nanopore materials
Lightweight materials	Chemistry/Materials science	Identification of novel alloys; and new reinforcement materials in plastics
CCS	Geology	Understanding of geologic formation, suitability, long term stability and safety for CCS
Fuel cells and industrial electrolysis processes	Electrochemistry/ Chemistry/Materials science	New materials and catalysts for electrodes and electrolytes

Role of national and university laboratories in basic science

National and university laboratories are the most important players in basic research. While governments have been the main source of funding for basic research, industry has increasingly supported basic science research at universities since the 1990s (Bozeman, 2000; NSB, 1998). Governments can help develop relationships here, in support of mission-oriented basic research programmes.

The outcomes of basic science are highly uncertain. It is this that justifies government intervention and initialisation. Governments need to identify, at a national level, the priorities they want to attach to basic science in energy. Strategic RD&D and technology portfolio/roadmaps can play a particularly useful role here. Governments then need to consider how they can best achieve their aims – e.g. in national programmes or in university-based programmes, with or without private sector involvement as appropriate. Governments also need to consider whether the scale and expense of some programmes requires international collaboration, which can usefully be co-ordinated at a government-to-government or multilateral level.

International collaboration in the pre-competitive stage of basic research has the potential to benefit all participants through cost-sharing/cost-reduction, upscaling of research and the building-up of common pools of knowledge. Such collaborations have already happened in many areas, and many of the IEA Implementing Agreements are part of them. For such collaboration to materialise, governments need to take positive steps to co-ordinate with other countries, and to encourage their national laboratories and their foremost university laboratories to engage in the process. Where appropriate, private sector firms may also be encouraged to participate.

Applied R&D and demonstration

Role of industry in applied R&D and demonstration

Many of the technology breakthroughs identified earlier in this chapter will depend on developments in applied R&D and demonstration phases of the innovation chain, in which the private sector begins to play a particularly important role. Clear institutional signals from policy and regulatory regimes and markets must significantly help to stimulate such investment.

Industry consortia have been an important source of RD&D in various countries performing targeted RD&D to: raise industry-level competitiveness, realise economies of scale in RD&D, and reduce the costs of RD&D by cost-sharing. The formation of industry consortia, however, is normally influenced by long-term strategic considerations as well as industry and firm characteristics (Kogut, 1988; Sakakibara, 2000).[13] Therefore, each sector needs to carefully evaluate the advantages of such consortia formation.

Role of government

Governments need to play a critical role in mobilising private sector technological capacity and capability and increase applied R&D and demonstration investment, especially in long term. In particular, setting clear and consistent policy and regulatory frameworks for fair and competitive markets and regulating to improve technology standards can do much to reduce the risk and uncertainty in innovation. It is important that governments involve private sector stakeholders to develop effective institutional frameworks that will meet the private sector's needs while balancing them with public interests. As discussed below, numerous obstacles present themselves in the applied R&D and demonstration phases of innovation. Public–private partnerships at various levels can be critical in overcoming them.

Issues in applied R&D and demonstration

Applied R&D and bridging the gaps from basic research

While basic research enables applied R&D by providing a base of knowledge, skills and techniques for solving problems, applied R&D questions the basic sciences in relation to real world applications. Each can, and should, learn from the other. Since industry laboratories do not usually perform basic science research, knowledge needs to be transferred to industry to enable industries to do so. However, in many countries it is clear that there is significant under-exploitation of new and available knowledge: funding for basic scientific research and applied R&D has proven to be not enough to support commercialisation of technology in many sectors including energy. A number of barriers exist between these two communities, including different goals, incentives and time horizons; organisational barriers; and intellectual property issues. Although both national and university laboratories have increasingly developed mechanisms for transferring their scientific finding to industry, technology transfer from research laboratories into the private sector to develop useful products is often weak.[14]

13. Firms in oligopolistic industries, firms with weak appropriation conditions to original innovations and firms with better RD&D capabilities have a higher rate of participation in industry consortia (Sakakibara, 2000).

14. The term "technology transfer" is used in two ways. The first definition is the process of converting scientific findings from research laboratories into useful products by the private sector. The second definition involves cross-border transmission of technology from one country to another. Here, the term is used to describe the former.

Demonstration projects

Demonstrations help move cutting-edge technologies from the laboratory to the commercial market. After a concept has been proven in principle, pilot or full-scale demonstrations are needed to identify real-world performance issues. Technology demonstrations afford opportunities to reduce investment risks, clarify the parameters affecting a technology's cost and operational performance, and identify areas needing further improvement or cost reduction. The important issues in this phase are the high costs of demonstration and ensuring fairness of opportunity among all interested parties.

Gap between RD&D and deployment: the "valley of death"

Moving from publicly-funded demonstration to commercial viability is often the most difficult phase for many technologies, resulting in what Murphy and Edwards (2003) have called a "valley of death". It is at this point, where investment costs can be very high and where risks also remain significant, that projects can easily fail. Frequently, neither the public nor the private sector considers it their duty to finance commercialisation. This is where neither "technology-push" force nor "market-pull" force has sufficient strength to fill the gap. This funding gap is particularly problematic for technologies with long lead times and a need for considerable applied research and testing between invention and commercialisation, as is the case for many energy technologies (Norberg-Bohm, 2002).

Public–private partnerships: navigating applied R&D, demonstration and the "valley of death"

Applied R&D

Public–private partnerships in applied R&D can take two main forms: 1) government direct and indirect funding of private sector applied R&D, and 2) collaborations between governments and industry researchers. Public–private partnerships in applied R&D may, where effectively managed, be an efficient and targeted mechanism for stimulating priority private sector applied R&D by utilising limited resources more effectively. Indirect measures, such as tax credits and inexpensive loans from governments, can also support private sector applied R&D. In all cases of such support, policies need to be evaluated regularly to ensure that they are achieving their aims in a cost effective manner.

Direct government funding of private sector applied R&D raises a number of difficult issues which need to be carefully managed. In particular, project selection criteria need to be established and implemented in a manner that ensures that the process itself is competitive both among technologies and companies.

Government policy can also help encourage technology transfer from national and university laboratories. Governments can relax anti-trust regulations at the pre-competitive stage and permit the use of national laboratories as research partners to industry, subject to suitable safeguards. Governments can also expand their patent policies to permit the use and disposition of government patents and technology for commercial use. They can also allow industries and universities the use of title to inventions funded by governments as license inventions.

In addition, governments can encourage the development of public–private research consortia, for example, between business and research universities – including the setting up of university research centres. Such centres can be supported financially by government agencies, by private companies or by other outside organisations. Such arrangements, particularly where they are clearly focused on interdisciplinary technology generation, can be very innovative. Several countries have successfully generated "triangular" partnerships between public, private and research institutions.

Demonstration

Technology demonstration is costly. Governments may see an advantage in helping the private sector, in appropriate circumstances, with the cost of strategic large-scale demonstration projects. Open and competitive processes are necessary in this phase. Government leadership through technology demonstrations can strongly influence – not always for the best – the decisions of private sector investors and other non-government parties.

Navigating the "valley of death": toward successful technology transfer

Policy tools to address the funding gap in the "technology valley of death" and stimulate technology transfer include both economic incentives (such as tax credits, production subsidies, or guaranteed procurements) and knowledge access support (for example, the codification and diffusion of generated technical knowledge). Spin-off companies formed from public-private research consortia are often an important means of technology transfer and commercialisation. To support technology incubators and entrepreneur start-ups and spin-offs, governments can offer funding for technology transfer or establish specialised technology transfer centres. This is the phase where governments need to begin incorporating market-pull policy measures. On the market side, governments can stimulate the incorporation of clean-energy and/or environment-specific venture capital into the current capital market by reducing regulatory barriers and providing fiscal incentives.

Governments can also help create demand for new technologies by putting in place regulatory requirements (for example, building standards) that progressively challenge the supply side to respond to new demands. In this case, governments need to be careful to ensure that the regulatory objectives are likely to be attainable: frequent or unplanned changes in requirements can significantly increase regulatory risk for the private sector and discourage investment.

International collaboration

Competition among countries and among companies is the major driver of energy technology innovation. But there are still many areas where countries and the private sector can benefit from increased collaboration.

International collaboration in RD&D offers a number of important benefits:

- It can reduce the need to spend national public funds on technology – by pooling available budgets, creating economies of scale, and reducing the redundancy of

RD&D activities simultaneously under way in several countries – improving the overall cost effectiveness of global RD&D investment.

- In the pre-competitive stage, it can create a common pool of knowledge which can contribute to global industry-level competitiveness and knowledge accumulation. This can eventually be capitalised on by individual industry players to build national- and firm-level competitiveness.
- It can strengthen and accelerate technology deployment by combining different kinds of national comparative advantages – such as the science and technology strengths of an industrialised country, or lower labour costs for manufacturing in a developing country.

Many international energy technology collaborations already exist. Table 4.3 shows the existing IEA Implementing Agreements, their agendas, activities and achievements, and their fit to the key technology RD&D needs identified earlier in this chapter.

Table 4.3 ► Key RD&D technologies under the ACT Map and BLUE Map scenarios and existing IEA Implementing Agreements

ACT Map and BLUE Map key technology areas	IEA Implementing Agreement	Agenda/works/achievements related to key technology RD&D
Power supply		
Renewable		
Biomass: black liquor	Bioenergy	Workshops on production of synthesis gas that can subsequently be converted to a variety of motor fuels; and integration into modern, eco-cyclic, kraft pulp mill bio-refineries
Biomass: IGCC	Bioenergy	Demonstration of IGCC plants
CSP	SolarPACES	Design, testing, demonstration, evaluation and application; solar-driven thermo-chemical and photochemical processes for production of energy carriers; and advancement of technical and economic viability of emerging solar thermal technologies, and their validation
Geothermal: EGS	Geothermal	Address new and improved technologies of EGS; application of conventional geothermal technology to EGS; data acquisition and processing; reservoir evaluation and scenario simulation for sustainable strategies; and field studies of EGS reservoir performance
Hydro: small-scale	Hydropower	Address technological, organisational and regulatory issues related to small hydro projects
Ocean: tidal and wave	Ocean Energy Systems	Wave and tidal energy converters; develop international standards for wave and tidal energy technology; and priorities on deployment and commercialisation of ocean waves and marine current systems

Table 4.3 ▶ **Key RD&D technologies under the ACT Map and BLUE Map scenarios and existing IEA Implementing Agreements** (continued)

ACT Map and BLUE Map key technology areas	IEA Implementing Agreement	Agenda/works/achievements related to key technology RD&D
Onshore and offshore wind	Wind Energy Systems	Stimulate co-operation on wind energy research and development and to provide high quality information and analysis by addressing technology development and deployment and its benefits, markets, and policy instruments; design and operation of power systems with large amounts of wind power; integration of wind and hydropower systems; offshore wind energy technology development; and dynamic models of wind farms for power system studies
Photovoltaics (PV)	PVPS	Design and operational performance of PV power systems; and developing emerging applications, e.g. building integrated PV, hybrid systems, mini-grids, very large scale PV
Fossil		
CCS coal advanced steam-cycle with oxyfueling	GHG R&D Programme CCS Oxy-fuel Combustion Network	Demonstrate the techno-economic feasibility of technology as a CO_2 capture option for a power plant in the near future
Clean coal	Clean Coal Sciences	Promote research on coal from the science of coal combustion, conversion and utilisation to co-firing and bio-co-processing
	Clean Coal Centre	Undertaking in-depth studies on topics of special interest; assessing the technical, economic and environmental performance; identifying where further research, development, demonstration and dissemination are needed; reporting the findings in a balanced and objective way without political or commercial bias; and showing, where appropriate, worldwide opportunities for cross-border technology transfer
Fuel cells	Advanced Fuel Cells	Research, technology development and system analysis on molten-carbonate, solid oxide and polymer electrolyte fuel cell systems
Electricity system		
Energy storage	Energy Storage	Development of underground thermal energy storage systems in the buildings, industry and agriculture sectors; examination of the potential role of electrical storage technologies in optimising electricity supply and use; examination of the role of phase-change materials and thermo-chemical reactions in energy systems; and development of procedures and screening and decision tools to facilitate the adoption of energy storage
T&D system	Electricity Networks Analysis, Research and Development (ENARD)	Facilitate the uptake of new operating procedures, architectures, methodologies and technologies in electricity T&D networks, to enhance their overall performance in relation to the developing challenges of network renewal, renewables integration, and network resilience and distributed generation system integration

Table 4.3 ▶ **Key RD&D technologies under the ACT Map and BLUE Map scenarios and existing IEA Implementing Agreements** (continued)

ACT Map and BLUE Map key technology areas	IEA Implementing Agreement	Agenda/works/achievements related to key technology RD&D
Industry		
Process innovation in basic materials production processes		
Black-liquor gasification	Industrial Energy-Related Technologies and Systems	Black-liquor gasification research on refractory and metallic materials, gas clean-up, and black liquor delivery systems; and computational fluid dynamics study of black-liquor gasifiers
Separation technologies, including drying and membranes	Industrial Energy-Related Technologies and Systems	State-of-the-art of separation systems analysis tools and concepts; extend/combine previously developed methods and tools to address advanced separation systems design or retrofits; automate or guide the design/retrofit process to the extent practicable; and workshop on drying and membrane technologies
Buildings and appliances		
Heating and cooling: heat pumps	Heat Pumping Technologies	Quantify and publicise energy saving potential and environmental benefits; thermally driven heat pumps; future potential and needs for heat pump systems and cooling; retrofit heat pumps for buildings; and ground-source heat pumps
Passive housing	Solar Heating and Cooling Buildings and Community Systems	Sustainable solar housing with passive solar design, improved daylighting and natural cooling and solar/glare control; and cost-optimisation of the mix of concepts
Solar heating	Solar Heating and Cooling	Advanced storage concepts for solar thermal systems; solar heat for industrial process; and polymeric materials for solar thermal applications
Transport		
Vehicle		
Hydrogen fuel cell vehicles	Advanced Fuel Cells	Fuel cells for vehicles, including use as auxiliary power units (APU) and hybridisation of the fuel cell with on-board energy storage devices like batteries or super-caps
Plug-in/ electric vehicle	Hybrid and Electric Vehicles	Electrochemical power sources and energy storage systems (batteries, fuel cells, and supercapacitors) for electric and hybrid vehicles; and heavy duty hybrid vehicles
Hybrid vehicle		
Fuels		
Second-generation liquid biofuels	Bioenergy	Commercialising first- and second-generation liquid biofuels from biomass, especially bio-based ethanol and biodiesel
	Advanced Motor Fuels	Production and use of synthetic vehicle fuels made by FT technique including biomass as possible raw material, production technique, emissions from production and use, engine performance

Table 4.3 ▶ **Key RD&D technologies under the ACT Map and BLUE Map scenarios and existing IEA Implementing Agreements** (continued)

ACT Map and BLUE Map key technology areas	IEA Implementing Agreement	Agenda/works/achievements related to key technology RD&D
Cross-cutting		
Bio-refinery	Bioenergy	Co-production of fuels, chemicals, power and materials from biomass for transport sector, chemical sector, power sector, agricultural sector; and assess the worldwide position and potential of bio-refineries
	Industrial Energy-Related Technologies and Systems	Development of industry-based bio-refineries, including black-liquor gasification
General CCS	GHG R&D Programme CCS	Provide a central source of information on CO_2 capture and storage R&D; promote awareness of the extent of R&D that is now underway; facilitate co-operation between projects; technical workshops on CCS; and development of international networks on CCS (International Network for CO_2 Capture; International Network on Biofixation of CO_2 and Greenhouse Gas Abatement with Microalgae; Risk Assessment Network; Monitoring Network; Oxy-Fuel Combustion Network; Well Bore Integrity Network)
Hydrogen	Hydrogen	Development of advanced technologies; photoelectrolytic production of hydrogen; photobiological production of hydrogen; hydrogen from carbon-containing materials; solid- and liquid-state hydrogen storage materials; integrated systems evaluation; and direct methanol fuel cells
Renewable energy	Renewable Energy Technology Deployment	Technology improvement and cost reduction for all renewable energy technologies by facilitating international deployment efforts

Sources: IEA (2007d); IEA (2008) with links to the above individual IAs.

Table 4.3 shows that IEA technology agreements (implementing agreements) already address many of the key technologies discussed in the ACT Map and BLUE Map scenarios with various degrees. Also, Table 4.4 presents other current technology collaborations in the areas of CCS, nuclear fission and hydrogen technologies. Yet many important RD&D breakthroughs will be made outside these schemes and projects. Also, these projects do not cover a number of important technology potentials – including thin film technologies and third-generation concepts in advanced solar photovoltaic technologies; deep offshore technologies; and many areas in industrial technologies (such as smelt reduction, direct casting and inert anodes innovations in basic materials production processes; plastic recycling/energy recovery; and feed stock substitution such as biopolymer, monomers from biomass, and naphtha products from biomass through FT).

Table 4.4 ▶ Key RD&D technologies under the ACT Map and BLUE Map scenarios and selected international energy technology collaborations

ACT Map and BLUE Map key technology areas	Collaborations	Agenda/works/achievements related to the key technology RD&D
Power generation		
Fossil		
CCS coal and gas – oxyfueling	CANMET Energy Technology Centre R&D Oxyfuel Combustion for CO_2 Capture under CSLF	Pilot-scale project that will demonstrate oxyfuel combustion technology with CO_2 capture
Nuclear		
Generation IV	Generation IV International Forum	Advanced research and development; and technology roadmap
Cross-cutting		
General CCS	Carbon Sequestration Leadership Forum (CSLF)	International co-operation in research and development to make CCS technologies broadly available internationally; and identify and address wider issues relating to carbon capture and storage
Hydrogen	International Partnership for the Hydrogen Economy (IPHE)	Provide a mechanism for partners to organise, co-ordinate and implement effective, efficient and focused international RD&D and commercial utilisation activities related to hydrogen and fuel-cell technologies; and provide a forum for advancing policies and common technical codes and standards that can accelerate the cost effective transition to a hydrogen economy

Table 4.5 summarises a number of multilateral, large-scale collaborations which focus on multiple energy technologies. All have been, and will continue to be, important drivers for international energy technology innovation. They already cover many of the technology areas important for the delivery of the ACT Map and BLUE Map scenarios. Many existing bilateral collaborations are also important, particularly as they address technology problems that are region/culture-specific or share specific views on certain technologies.

The future of international collaborations and the involvement of developing countries

In the future, there may be opportunities to consolidate to reduce redundancy and unnecessary duplication among international collaboration schemes and between international schemes and national programmes. To do so, it will first be important to illustrate the current RD&D landscape to help identify any gaps between the required RD&D breakthrough needs and existing national and international RD&D programmes and projects, as well as any overlaps between existing programmes and projects. An important first step, therefore, will be the mapping of relevant institutions and their RD&D activities. This will also help governments to rationalise their own national RD&D programmes. Technology roadmaps are another possible tool for further enhancing international collaboration, as discussed in Chapter 3.

Table 4.5 ► ***Selected international energy technology collaborations with technology innovation focus***

Collaborations	Agenda/works/achievements
IEA Group of 8 (G8) Gleneagles Programme	Focus on climate change, clean energy and sustainable development, promoting energy sector innovation, better practice and use of enhanced technology, including: alternative energy scenarios and strategies; energy efficiency in buildings, appliances, transport and industry, including indicators; cleaner fossil fuels; carbon capture and storage; renewable energy; and enhanced international co-operation
Major Economies Meeting on Energy Security and Climate Change	1) Highlight the most urgent needs for research and development of clean energy technologies, focusing on four key areas: generating power from fossil fuels with lower carbon emissions; reducing carbon emissions in the transportation sector through vehicle and fuel technologies; addressing land use and the current unsustainable rate of deforestation; and accelerating and expanding markets for current efficiency and the use of nuclear, solar and wind technologies; and 2) identify areas for collaboration in key sectors and discuss challenges and opportunities for the development, financing and commercialisation of clean energy technologies, including discussing the approaches to reduce or eliminate tariff and non-tariff barriers for clean energy technologies and services
Asian Pacific Partnership (APP) on Clean Development and Climate	Accelerate the development and deployment of clean energy technologies by focussing on expanding investment and trade in cleaner energy technologies, goods and services in key market sectors (aluminium, buildings and appliances, cement, cleaner use of fossil energy, coal mining, power generation and transmission, renewable energy and distributed generation, and steel)
EU 7th Research Framework Programme	Accelerating the development of cost effective technologies, emphasising: hydrogen and fuel cells; renewable power generation; renewable fuel production; renewables for heating and cooling; CO_2 capture and storage technologies for zero emission power generation; clean coal technologies; smart energy networks; energy efficiency and savings; and knowledge for energy policy making
Nordic Energy Research	Further develop co-operation strategies for the Nordic region in energy and climate research: climate change and energy; energy efficiency (production, transmission and distribution, consumer level/end user, industry, transport); renewable energy (bioenergy, wind and PV); hydrogen technology (production, transport, storage, conversion, safety issues); energy markets; European research area; and policy studies

In some areas, it may be possible for RD&D to work together with other policy strands to accelerate technology development and diffusion, creating inter-sectoral collaborations. For example, coherent policies on urban development, public transport and health – together with strong efforts to promote RD&D in these areas – may help generate sufficient momentum to ensure the simultaneous and faster development of carbon-free power generation, "smart growth" urban development, and electric vehicles than could be achieved by any one part of the system alone.

Developing countries also offer particular opportunities here, as it is often easier for them to adopt new technologies as they grow. It is important to remain aware of the social and cultural needs of developing countries and their often unique technological capacities and capabilities. To achieve this will require stronger and wider collaborations with developing countries, as well as system development and, where necessary, financial support for cross-border technology transfer. However, increasing technological and economic competition between developed and developing countries will be a key issue. The development of strategies to handle and resolve contentious intellectual property right issues will also be vital.

Chapter 5 DEPLOYMENT AND TECHNOLOGY LEARNING

Key Findings

- *Deployment costs for new, cleaner technologies are estimated at USD 4.8 trillion under the ACT Map scenario (USD 3.2 trillion for power generation and USD 1.6 trillion for buildings, transport and industry technologies) and at USD 10.4 trillion under the BLUE Map scenario (USD 3.8 trillion for power generation and USD 6.6 trillion for buildings, transport and industry technologies).*

- *The total learning investment (the additional costs exceeding the cost of the incumbent fossil technologies) is estimated at USD 2.8 trillion under the ACT Map scenario and USD 7.0 trillion under the BLUE Map scenario.*

- *An economic incentive to reduce CO_2 would raise the cost of the incumbent technologies and so lower the financing needed to bring clean energy technologies to market. If a USD 50/t CO_2 price were applied today, deployment costs would drop to USD 2.3 trillion (ACT Map).*

- *Most IEA countries are entering a new investment cycle in power generation. This is an important opportunity to deploy cleaner and more efficient power generation technologies. Investment decisions taken over the next decade will lock in CO_2 emissions for the next 40 to 50 years.*

- *Early deployment of these technologies will take place primarily in the United States and Europe. But deployment in China and other major developing countries will also be critical if they are to reach commercialisation.*

- *Government intervention to remove barriers to the diffusion of energy-efficient technologies is crucial. Stringent codes and standards are the most effective way to bring these technologies to commercialisation.*

- *A flexible policy framework is required to accelerate the deployment of clean technologies. While policies should be continuous and predictable, governments must continually ensure the measures they contain are appropriate and serve the desired outcomes.*

- *More effective international co-operation is needed to minimise the costs and speed up the rate of deployment of new energy technologies.*

Overview

The IEA has shown in *Energy Technology Perspectives 2006* (ETP 2006) that CO_2 emissions could be brought back to today's level by 2050 by effectively deploying technologies that are already available or are under development. The new BLUE scenarios presented in Chapter 2 show how these could in fact contribute to halving today's emission levels by 2050. Through learning and deployment models and by examining barriers to deployment, this chapter considers the steps that are needed to bring these technologies to market, and the role that governments might play in accelerating that aim.

Deployment and the role of technology learning

Deployment describes the stage between research, development and demonstration (RD&D) and market uptake. At this stage, a technology is not yet economically competitive except possibly in particular niche markets. Production may be expanding, but it is still taking place on a small industrial scale. *Technology learning* occurs during deployment, as economies of scale are established and as progressive (possibly quite small) product improvements result in further cost reductions.

Figure 5.1 ▶ ***Stages in technology development***

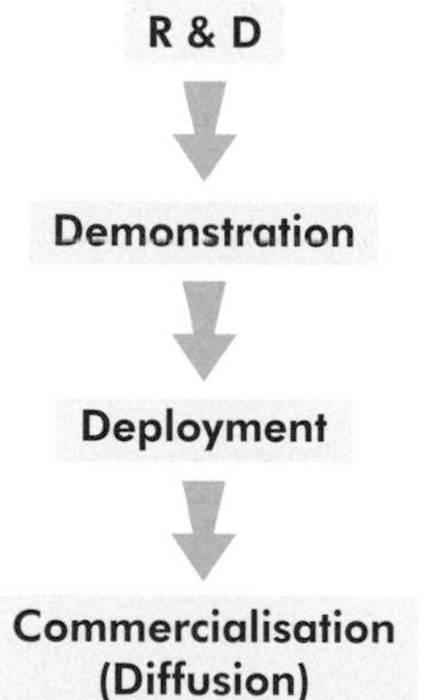

R&D seeks to overcome technical barriers and to reduce costs. Commercial outcomes are highly uncertain, especially in the early stages.

The technology is demonstrated in practice. Costs are high. External (including government) funding may be needed to finance part or all of the costs of the demonstration.

Successful technical operation, but possibly in need of support to overcome cost or non-cost barriers. With increasing deployment, technology learning will progressively decrease costs.

The technology is cost competitive in some or all markets, either on its own terms or, where necessary, supported by government intervention (e.g. to value externalities such as the costs of pollution).

Source: IEA 2006c.

As Figure 5.1 illustrates, new technologies typically go through several stages to overcome technical and cost barriers before they become cost-competitive. The deployment phase can be considerably more expensive than the RD&D phases.

Deployment versus diffusion (commercialisation)

Cost effective demand-side technologies already exist that could deliver two-thirds of the 44% reduction in CO_2 emissions expected from improved energy efficiency. The technologies required to deliver the remaining one-third depend on government support for deployment to become commercial. Many technologies that are cost effective, however, fail to penetrate the market because consumers focus on short-term costs rather than taking life-cycle costs into account. While government support for deployment is not needed in these cases, governments do need to promote technology diffusion as well as development, and to intervene through regulations to overcome additional barriers.

On the supply side, some carbon reduction technologies, such as CO_2 capture and storage, are an expensive addition to the cost of supply. These technologies will only become competitive if a value is attached to reducing CO_2 emissions. Governments must determine the most effective mechanisms for removing market and non-market barriers to diffusion, and support these with appropriate policy instruments.

Technology learning curves

5

Most new technologies, including energy technologies, initially have higher costs than incumbent technologies. But over time, the costs of the new technology may be lowered through *technology learning* – as its production costs decrease and its technical performance increases (BCG 1968; IEA, 2000). The rate of switching from older technologies to new technologies will depend on both relative costs and on the extent to which consumers' value the long term, often at that stage uncertain, benefit of the new technology.

The prospect that a given technology will be produced and sold on the market can stimulate private industry R&D ("learning-by-searching") and improvements in the manufacturing process ("learning-by-doing"). Feedback from the market may suggest avenues for improving a technology, further reducing costs or tailoring some of its features to consumers' needs ("learning-by-using"). Because these benefits can only be reaped once the technology is actually on the market, the rate of improvement of a technology is usually a function of its adoption rate.

Technology learning is an important factor in R&D and investment decisions in emerging energy technologies. Technology learning curves can be used to estimate the deployment and diffusion costs for new technologies and, thereby, provide policy makers with a tool to explore technology and policy options for the transformation of energy systems.

Using learning curves to estimate deployment/diffusion costs

Technology learning curves can be used to derive deployment and diffusion costs for new technologies. Learning curves show a constant reduction of the investment cost for each doubling of production. Based on this relationship, the initial cost and the cost of competing incumbent technologies it is possible to quantify the deployment costs of new technologies. Figure 5.2 demonstrates how these relationships can be used to estimate the learning investments (*i.e.* deployment cost) necessary for an energy technology to compete with an incumbent technology, here called the "break-even" point.

The blue line represents the learning curve or the expected reduction in the cost of the new technology as its cumulative capacity increases. The grey line represents the cost of the incumbent fossil technology. Where the blue and grey lines meet is the point at which the new energy technology becomes competitive with the incumbent technology: the break-even point.

This indicates the cumulative capacity needed for the new technology to become competitive. Deployment costs are the total amount that must be invested in cumulative capacity to reach the break-even point. Deployment costs can be viewed in terms of costs equalling those of the incumbent technology (represented by the yellow rectangle) and additional investment costs that go beyond the cost of the incumbent technology (the orange triangle). The additional costs required for the new technology to reach the break-even point and become competitive are the learning investments.

Figure 5.2 ▶ Schematic representation of learning curves, deployment costs and learning investments

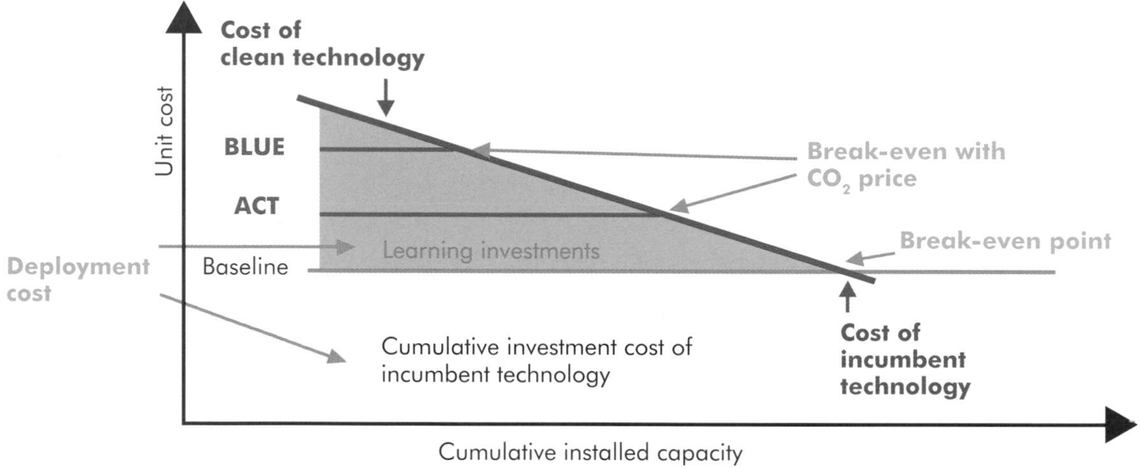

Source: IEA.

Key point

Increasing the CO_2 price reduces the learning investment needed to make the new technology cost-competitive.

The two red lines in Figure 5.2 illustrate how carbon prices of USD 50/t CO_2 (ACT Map scenario) and USD 200/t CO_2 (BLUE Map scenario) would reduce deployment costs for lower-carbon technologies. The CO_2 penalty increases the cost of the incumbent fossil technology, reducing the cumulative capacity needed for the clean technology to become competitive. The higher the carbon price, the lower the learning investments needed to bring a clean technology to market and the faster this technology will deploy.

Learning curves have been constructed for a wide range of energy technologies over many orders of magnitude (see *e.g.* IEA, 2000; McDonald and Schrattenholzer, 2001; Neij, *et al.*, 2003; Junginger, 2005; Nemet, 2006). Some of these findings in respect of supply-side technologies are summarised in Table 5.1.

Although the bulk of this literature has focused on energy-supply technologies, learning curve analysis has shown that "learning-by-doing" effects are also present in demand side technologies, as seen in Table 5.2. These curves are a useful tool for examining the potential to reduce costs in demand-side technologies (Newll, 2000; Laitner and Sanstad, 2004).

Table 5.1 ▶ **Observed learning rates for various electricity supply technologies**

Technology	Source	Country / Region	Period	Learning rate (%)	Performance measure
Nuclear					
	Kouvaritakis, *et al.*, 2000	OECD	1975-1993	5.8	Electricity production cost (USD/kWh)
Onshore wind					
	Neij, 2003	Denmark	1982-1997	8	Price of wind turbine(USD/kW)
	Durstewitz, 1999	Germany	1990-1998	8	Price of wind turbine(USD/kW)
	IEA, 2000	USA	1985-1994	32	Electricity production cost (USD/kWh)
	IEA, 2000	EU	1980-1995	18	Electricity production cost (USD/kWh)
	Kouvaritakis, *et al.*, 2000	OECD	1981-1995	17	Price of wind turbine(USD/kW)
Offshore wind					
	Isles, 2006	8 EU countries	1991-2006	3	Installation cost of wind farms (USD/kW)
Photovoltaics (PV)					
	Harmon, 2000	Global	1968-1998	20	Price PV module (USD/Wpeak)
	IEA, 2000	EU	1976-1996	21	Price PV module (USD/Wpeak)
	Williams, 2002	Global	1976-2002	20	Price PV module (USD/Wpeak)
	ECN, 2004	EU	1976-2001	20-23	Price PV module (USD/Wpeak)
	ECN, 2004	Germany	1992-2001	22	Price of balance of system costs
Biomass					
	IEA, 2000	EU	1980-1995	15	Electricity production cost (USD/kWh)
Combined heat and power (CHP)					
	Junginger, 2005	Sweden	1990-2002	9	Electricity production cost (USD/kWh)
CO_2 capture and storage (CCS)					
	Rubin, *et al.*, 2006	Global	na	3-5	Electricity production cost (USD/kWh)

Sources: McDonald and Schrattenholzer, 2001; Williams, 2002; Junginger, 2005; Rubin, 2006 and Isles, 2006.

Although useful in context, learning curves need to be used with caution. For example:

- They are often based on price, rather than cost, data.
- Careful analysis and further data collection is required to identify the right system boundaries to be used when applying learning curves.
- There is a need to understand the factors that might drive future cost reductions, as distinct from past cost reductions.

Table 5.2 ▶ Observed learning rates for various demand-side technologies

Technology	Country / Region	Period	Learning rate (%)
Ford model T	United States	1909-1923	13
Refrigerator	United States	1980-1998	12
Freezer	United States	1980-1998	22
Washing machine	United States	1980-1998	13
Electric clothes-dryer	United States	1980-1998	12
Dishwasher	United States	1980-1998	16
Air conditioner	United States	1980-1998	15
Selective window coatings	United States	1992-2000	17
Heat pumps	Germany	1980-2002	30
Heat pumps	Switzerland	1980-2004	24
Facades with insulation	Switzerland	1975-2001	17-21
Double-glazed coated windows	Switzerland	1985-2001	12-17
CFL	Global	1990-2004	10
Air conditioners	Japan		10-17

Sources: McDonald and Schrattenholzer 2001; Laitner and Sanstad, 2004; ECN, 2005; Jakob and Madlener, 2003; Ellis, 2007.

- It is important to examine the data carefully. For example, it has been shown that bottom-up engineering models have in some instances overestimated the cost of bringing energy-efficient appliances (which account for 7.5% of the potential 45% reduction in emissions from energy efficiency) to market (Ellis, *et al.*, 2007). These models did not take into account the impacts of "learning-by-doing", which offset many of the higher costs related to more efficient components. As these "learning effects" are not captured in engineering models, a combination of a top-down learning-curve analysis with a bottom-up engineering model is required to better estimate the costs of bringing technologies to market.

- Global learning rates are appropriate for most technologies where new knowledge spills over national boundaries. But where learning occurs locally (*e.g.* photovoltaics (PV) installations), a global curve may misrepresent learning. For certain technologies, national learning rates may be more appropriate.

Learning rates do not generally vary widely over time. However, technology characteristics sometimes change due to new regulations, and more intricate designs may raise costs. The choice of the initial starting point from which to collect data can have an important impact on the resulting learning rate.

It is important to take other factors into account – for example supply-chain effects, which can distort learning curves. Learning rates for PV and wind technologies are currently being affected by a shortage of silicon, steel and gear boxes, which has created temporary price bubbles. In PV, however, the current silicon shortage has also served to trigger innovations in thin-film technologies that require significantly less silicon. If this technology is successful, it is anticipated that a significantly lower learning investment will be needed to make PV competitive (Williams, 2002). PV cells using substitutes for silicon have also attracted considerable attention.

The key message from these observations is that it is important to understand the processes and changes underpinning learning curves, especially where they are used to influence policy choices.

Technology learning and diffusion

Modelling technology deployment costs is highly sensitive to assumed learning rates. An overly conservative estimate of the learning rate will reduce the projected deployment rate of a technology, and may lead to a technology being squeezed out by other, more competitive, technologies. But an unreasonably high estimate will lead to unrealistic estimates of potential cost reductions and an over-optimistic assessment of the deployment rate.

In the Energy Technology Perspectives (ETP) model, the total investment or deployment costs needed to bring down the cost of each technology to competitive levels have been estimated using learning curves. Tables 5.3 and 5.4 outline the boundaries used for this analysis and the learning rates applied. Learning rates were based on those observed by various technology experts. Some of these technologies are still relatively new and do not have significant data sets from which to derive a learning rate. In these cases, we have used a conservative rather than an optimistic figure to avoid under-estimating the likely technology deployment costs.

Table 5.3 ► **Applied learning rates for power generation technologies**

	Current inv. cost (USD/kW)	**Learning rate** (%)	**Estimated commercialisation under ACT Map**	**Cost target to commercialisation** (USD/kW)
Onshore wind	1 200	7	2020-2025	900
Offshore wind	2 600	9	2030-2035	1 600
Photovoltaics (PV)	5 500	18	2030-2035	1 900
Concentrated Solar Thermal	4 500	10	Not commercial	1 500
Biomass integrated gasifier/combined cycle (BIG/CC)	2 500 (2010E)	5	Not commercial	2 000
Integrated Gasification Combined Cycle (IGCC)	1 800	3	2030-2035	1 400
CO_2 capture and storage (CCS)	750 (2010E)	3	Post-2050	600
Nuclear III+	2 600 (2010E)	3	2025	2 100
Nuclear IV	2 500 (2030E)	5	Post-2050	2 000

Source: IEA estimates.

5

Table 5.4 ▶ Applied learning rates for buildings, industry and transport technologies

	Unit	Boundary	Current cost (USD)	Learning rate (%)	Cost target to reach commercialisation (USD)
Fuel cell vehicles	USD/kW	FCV drive system cost	750	22	50
Hybrid vehicles	Car	ICE+ electric+ battery	3 000	20	1 500
Lignocellulosic ethanol	USD/litre	Fuel cost	0.8	10	0.5
FT-biodiesel	USD/litre	Fuel cost	1	10	0.5
Plug-in vehicles	Car	Batteries for plug-ins	9 000	20	2 000
Geothermal heat pumps	USD/system	Heat pump + installation	15 000	15	7 000
Solar heating and cooling	USD/m^2	Panel	630	10	450
Feedstock substitution	Ethylene		1 300	10	650
CCS blast furnace	USD/t CO_2	CCS cost	150*	5	50
CCS cement kilns	USD/t CO_2	CCS cost	200*	5	75
CCS black liquor IGCC	USD/kW	Production cost	1 600	5	1 200

Note: A discount rate of 10% and an import fuel cost of USD 6.5-7/GJ were applied to calculate the annual cost of the incumbent technology (7 GJ was assumed for the energy saved).

* Cost per tonne of CO_2 captured.

Source: IEA estimates.

Deployment costs: investment implications of the scenarios

Deployment costs and learning investments

The total deployment costs from 2005 to 2050 for the new energy technologies are estimated to be USD 4.8 trillion in the ACT Map scenario and USD 10.4 trillion in the BLUE Map scenario.[1] Deployment costs represent the total costs of cumulative production needed for a new technology to become competitive with the current, incumbent technology. Learning investments under both scenarios are considerably less than the total deployment costs, at USD 2.8 trillion (ACT Map) and USD 7.0 trillion (BLUE Map) (Figure 5.3).

1. The estimated deployment figures are based on learning rates for capital costs.

Figure 5.3 ▶ **Deployment costs and learning investments, 2005-2050**

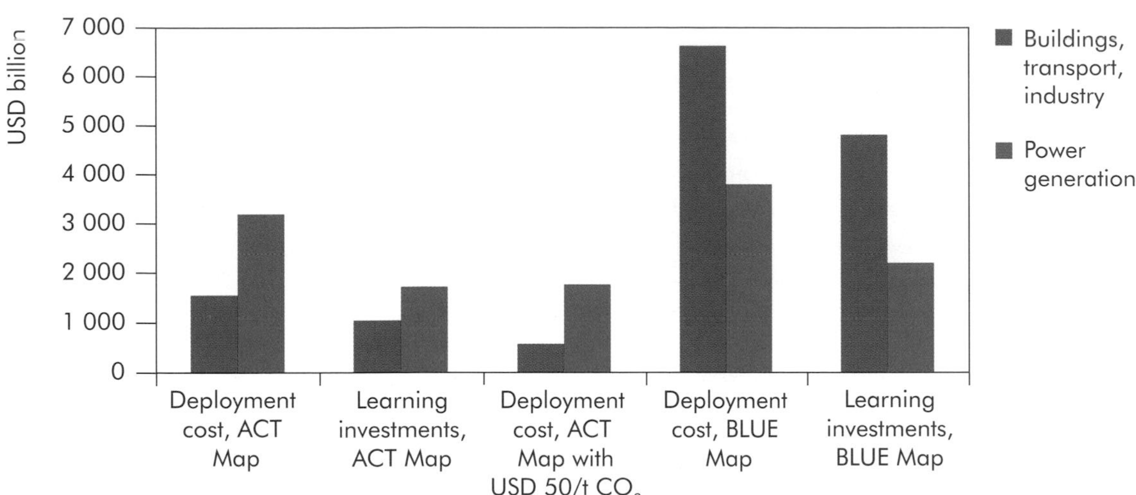

Note: Figures are not discounted.

Source: IEA estimates.

Key point

Learning investments under both scenarios are considerably less than the total deployment costs.

Figure 5.3 also shows the impact that a CO_2 incentive of USD 50/t CO_2 would have on the deployment costs of clean energy technologies in power generation and in the buildings, transport and industry sectors under the ACT Map scenario. The analysis assumes that the CO_2 incentive is in effect today – as this is not the case, these figures can only illustrate how a carbon price could reduce the financing needs to deploy cleaner technologies. (It is unclear when a global CO_2 price at such a level will be applied.) Although the overall costs of the new technology remains unchanged, as the carbon price raises the cost of the incumbent fossil technology, the new technology becomes competitive at a lower level of deployment.

Total deployment costs under the ACT Map scenario with a USD 50/t CO_2 price would fall by 63% for buildings, transport and industry (from USD 1.6 trillion to USD 0.6 trillion) and by 45% for power generation (from USD 3.2 trillion to USD 1.8 trillion). Given the current high CO_2 intensity of both end-use and power generation technologies, a CO_2 incentive will have a significant impact on reducing the investments needed to deploy cleaner energy technologies. The effect of a CO_2 credit of USD 200/t CO_2 has not been analysed for the BLUE Map scenario because of the great uncertainty as to when such a high CO_2 price will be applied globally.

Supply-side costs: investment needs

On the supply side, deployment cost estimates vary significantly among the baseline, ACT Map and BLUE Map scenarios. In the baseline scenario, total deployment costs for power generation technologies are estimated at USD 1.4 trillion. This is more than doubled in the ACT Map scenario, where total deployment costs amount to USD 3.2 trillion. In the BLUE Map scenario, total deployment costs, at USD 3.8 trillion, are two-and-a-half times those of the baseline scenario and 20% higher than those in the ACT Map scenario.

Deployment costs in the ACT Map and BLUE Map scenarios have been broken into two periods: from 2005 to 2030 and from 2030 to 2050. For both scenarios, more than two-thirds of the investments are required in the earlier period. In the ACT Map scenario, USD 2.3 trillion is needed by 2030, with a further USD 0.9 trillion needed between 2030 and 2050. In the BLUE Map scenario, USD 2.6 trillion is required by 2030 and USD 1.2 trillion from 2030 to 2050.

Figure 5.4 presents a breakdown of the deployment costs for power generation technologies for each of the three scenarios. A significantly higher investment is required for wind, solar thermal, nuclear Generation III and Generation IV, and CO_2 capture and storage (CCS) technologies in the ACT Map scenario than in the Baseline scenario. Deployment costs do not vary significantly between the ACT Map and BLUE Map scenarios – the difference can be attributed mainly to higher investment needs for tidal and geothermal power in the BLUE Map scenario. Total deployment costs for renewable power generation reach USD 1.4 trillion in the ACT Map scenario and USD 2.4 trillion in the BLUE Map scenario. In both scenarios, deployment costs for nuclear power are approximately USD 650 billion.

Figure 5.4 ▶ Deployment costs for power generation in the Baseline, ACT Map and BLUE Map scenarios, 2005-2050

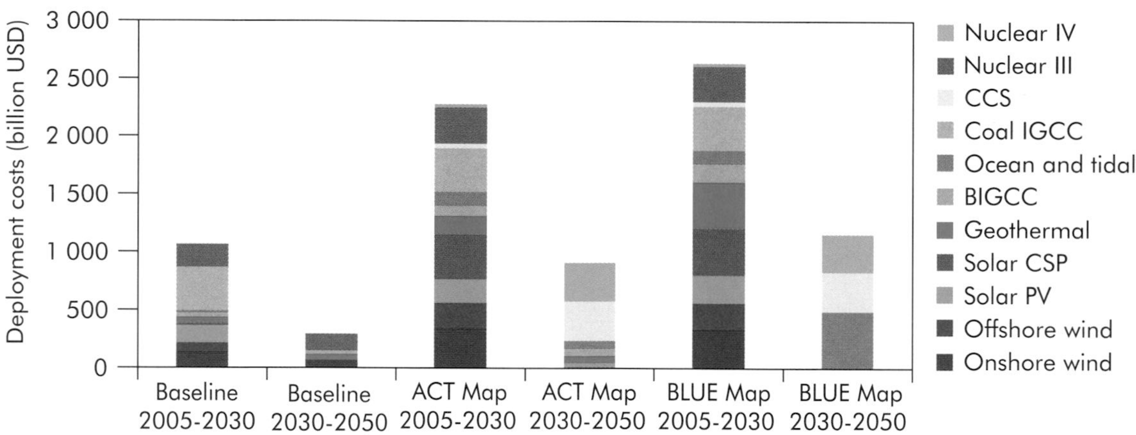

Note: Figures are not discounted.

Source: IEA estimates.

Key point

Deployment costs for power generation do not vary significantly between the ACT Map and BLUE Map scenarios.

Demand-side costs: investment needs

On the demand-side, Figure 5.5 shows estimated deployment costs for building, industry and transport technologies under the baseline, ACT Map and BLUE Map scenarios.

Deployment costs in the baseline scenario are estimated to be USD 0.77 trillion. These more than double for the ACT Map scenario, reaching USD 1.6 trillion. Of this total, USD 0.9 trillion is needed from 2005 to 2030 and a further USD 0.7 trillion from 2030 to 2050.

In the BLUE Map scenario, deployment costs increase more than eight-fold – to USD 6.6 trillion – of which almost USD 1.4 trillion is required by 2030, with a much larger USD 5.3 trillion needed between 2030 and 2050. More than half of the deployment investments for demand-side technologies are needed to deploy fuel-cell vehicle technologies, which alone require an estimated investment of USD 3.6 trillion.

In terms of individual technologies, hybrid vehicles account for the largest share of demand-side deployment costs in both the baseline and ACT Map scenarios: approximately USD 300 billion. Hybrid vehicles together with solar heating account for the largest share of deployment needs for the earlier 2005 to 2030 period, while in the later period deployment investments are dominated by CCS in industry as the other end-use technologies have reached commercialisation by 2030 to 2035. In the BLUE Map scenario, higher deployment investments are needed for fuel cell vehicles, CCS for cement kilns and CCS for blast furnaces. The total deployment costs for CCS in industry reaches USD 1.6 trillion in the BLUE Map scenario.

Figure 5.5 ▸ Deployment costs for demand-side technologies in the Baseline, ACT Map and BLUE Map scenarios

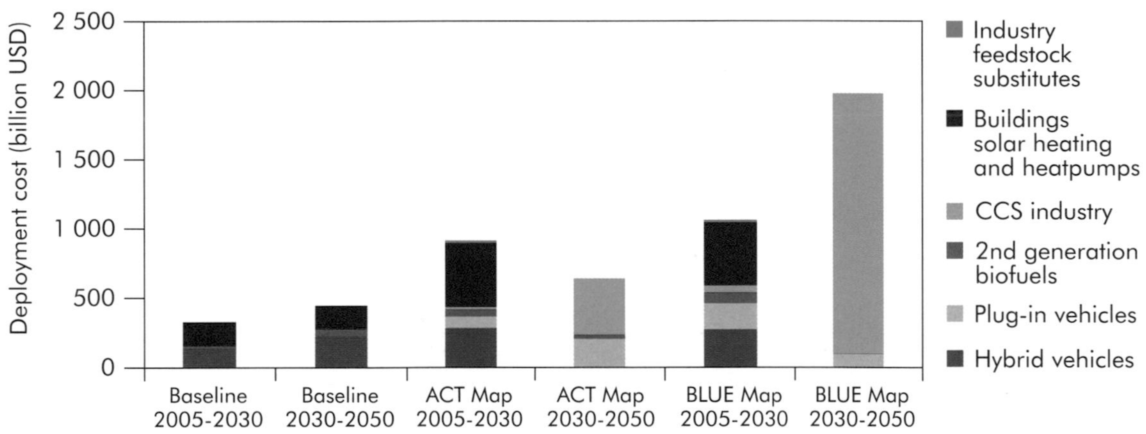

Notes: Figures are not discounted.
The figure above excludes investments for fuel cell vehicles under the BLUE Scenario, which total USD 0.36 trillion from 2005 to 2030 and USD 3.3 trillion from 2030 to 2050.
Figures above for BLUE Map do not include deployment costs for Electric Vehicles as estimates of future costs are highly uncertain for this technology and are estimated to range from USD 1.5 trillion to USD 3.0 trillion.
Source: IEA estimates.

Key point

Deployment costs for demand-side technologies more than double for the ACT Map scenario and increase more than eight-fold in the BLUE Map scenario.

Limitations of this analysis

In this analysis we have applied learning rates to a number of technologies that are still at the RD&D phase. But the evolution of investment costs is particularly difficult to predict at this stage, because unexpected measures, externalities or market changes could result in a significant increase in costs that lie outside the known boundaries of a given learning curve. Equally, however, the analysis does not take other potentially positive external benefits into account, such as reduced local air pollution or increased supply security.

Deployment costs may also be underestimated because this approach assumes 100% success and makes no allowance for the costs of false starts or failures. For example, in the field of car technologies, many options have been tried in the past three decades, but only very few have survived. The deterministic technology-learning model in this way underestimates the real costs of innovation.

The deployment costs shown in this analysis are undiscounted. Discounted costs would show significantly lower costs. However, the slower the technology develops, the lower the value of future discounted benefits once the technology becomes cost effective. In an extreme case, the cost may exceed the long-term discounted benefits.

Regional breakdown of deployment for key power-generation technologies

The ETP deployment analysis is undertaken on a global basis. In practice, though, the future potential for technological diffusion varies from region to region, according to the current state of deployment in the region and the capacity for technology exploitation. This section examines regional differences based on the findings of the ACT Map scenario.

Table 5.5 ▶ Regional deployment

	Wind		Photovoltaics (PV)		CO_2 capture and storage (CCS)		Nuclear		
	2005	**2030**	**2005**	**2035**	**2030**	**2050**	**2005**	**2020**	**2050**
OECD North America	13%	24%	27%	25%	35%	25%	34%	31%	27%
OECD Europe	69%	34%	19.5%	25%	35%	16%	32%	25%	15%
OECD Pacific	2%	10%	51.7%	30%	10%	5%	17%	17%	14%
China	3%	21%	0.0%	10%	12%	33%	2%	8%	23%
India	5%	4%	0.2%	5%	3%	10%	1%	3%	7%
Others	6%	7%	1.7%	5%	5%	11%	14%	15%	14%

Source: IEA estimates.

In general, our scenarios show that, with the exception of wind technology, the largest share of deployment for new power generation technologies is expected to take place in the United States. Europe will dominate deployment of wind technologies in the early phase, but widescale uptake will require a greater market uptake in the United States and China. As the fastest growing electricity market, deployment of all these new technologies in China will be crucial to reach the cumulative capacity needed for them to become competitive.

Onshore wind

With the exception of the current price bubble, the cost of wind production has declined significantly over the last decade. Wind prices are expected to fall again within the next two to three years, at which point installation costs for wind technologies will return to their former path of declining costs. The cost of generating electricity from onshore wind is expected to be competitive with fossil-fuel generation by approximately 2020, when the cumulative global capacity reaches over 650 GW. It is already competitive at good wind sites.

Deployment of onshore wind technologies will continue to be dominated by Western Europe until about 2020, when investments in onshore wind power in the United States and China are expected to pick up. Onshore wind installations in the United States will attain a capacity of 200 GW by 2025 and will then remain relatively constant; while in China onshore wind power will increase progressively to 250 GW by 2040.

Offshore wind

Offshore wind power-generation is dominated by Western Europe, which today accounts for 93% of total capacity. This technology is expected to reach commercialisation between 2035 and 2040, when it will reach approximately 250 GW. Higher capital cost requirements will limit the deployment of this technology to Western Europe, OECD Pacific and OECD North America.

Photovoltaics (PV)

Japan has the world's largest share of PV capacity today, with a total of 2.8 GW, equivalent to 47% of global capacity. Other significant regions are Western Europe and OECD North America (almost entirely in the United States). Our analysis shows that the deployment of PV will be strongest between 2030 and 2040, when costs become more competitive and rapid uptake in the United States and China helps to boost market uptake. The United States is expected to have the world's largest capacity of PV in 2045. At that point, the United States will account for 50% of an expected global capacity of 545 GW.

CO_2 capture and storage (CCS)

Under the ACT Map scenario, CCS deployment is expected to begin in 2020 – with the United States accounting for the largest share of deployment. By 2030, China is anticipated to have significant CCS capacity, and by 2050, China will account for the largest global share of CCS. Canada and India are also expected to have significant CCS capacity by 2030 and 2050 respectively. Unlike the other power generation technologies, which will become competitive as additional cumulative capacity is added, CCS will always require a carbon price of at least USD 50/t CO_2 to make it cost-efficient.

Nuclear

The regional deployment of new nuclear technologies (Generation III+ and Generation IV) will depend very much on local acceptance of nuclear power. Some countries currently have a ban on developing new nuclear generation capacities. The large up-front cost of nuclear power and the current uncertainties about the cost of Generation III+ and Generation IV technologies will limit its uptake in developing countries. Nuclear investments in these countries are likely to be based on older, proven technologies. In this analysis it is expected that Generation III+ technologies will be deployed until 2020 to 2030. After 2030, nuclear deployment will focus on Generation IV technology. The key regions for nuclear deployment will be Canada and the United States, China and India, Russia, Western Europe, and OECD Pacific.

Barriers to technology diffusion

Market and non-market barriers to new technologies need to be overcome if these technologies are to deliver their potential in regard to reducing carbon emissions. The main barriers to new technology deployment are listed in Table 5.6.

A recent IEA study, *Tackling Investment Challenges in Power Generation* (IEA, 2007) indicates that most IEA countries are entering a new investment cycle in power generation. This represents an important opportunity to deploy cleaner and more efficient power generation technologies, as the investment decisions taken over the next decade will lock in CO_2 emissions for the next 40-50 years.

According to the *World Energy Outlook 2006* (IEA, 2003a), OECD countries will need 466 GW of new power generation by 2015. This is 20% more than their existing capacity. Although improved energy efficiency could reduce this figure, many existing power plants are nearing the end of their operational lives and large investments are needed just to replace much of their production. *World Energy Outlook 2006* estimates that 200 GW will need to be replaced by 2015, and that one-third of existing capacity – or 872 GW – will need to be replaced by 2030.

Table 5.6 ▶ **Barriers to technology diffusion**

Barrier	Key characteristic
Information	Clear and persuasive information about a new product at the time investors are planning to invest
Transaction costs	The indirect costs of a decision to purchase and use equipment
Buyer's risk	Perception of risk (which may differ from actual risk)
Finance	Costs relative to alternative technologies; absolute costs; imperfections in market access to funds
Capital stock turnover rates	Sunk costs; tax rules that reward long depreciation periods; inertia
Excessive / inefficient regulation	Regulation must keep pace with developing policy objectives
Capacity	Capacity to introduce technology or use technology is not sufficient
Uncompetitive market price	For example, where scale economies and learning benefits have not yet been realised

Source: IEA, 2003b.

The rate of technology diffusion depends on a number of factors, including:

- the market growth rate, and the rate at which old capital stock is phased out;
- the rate at which new production capacity can come on stream;
- the extent of market fracturing;
- the availability of a supporting energy infrastructure (e.g., hydrogen supply);
- the viability and competitiveness of alternative options;
- the existence and phasing out of constraining standards and regulations, and the existence and phasing in of supportive standards and regulations;
- the rate at which skilled personnel can learn to produce, install and maintain such equipment;
- the market power of existing suppliers and their involvement in marketing new solutions;
- consumer information, interest and incentives;
- the existence of policies that support the introduction of a new technology;
- compliance with regulations and technical standards.

The relevance of these factors will vary for specific products. For individual products, the first five factors can be estimated on the basis of market characteristics, while the last six are often hard to quantify. However, policies can be put in place to mitigate the delays caused by these factors.

For this study, market growth and capital stock are considered the key constraining factors. As a consequence, technology uptake can take place at a faster rate in rapidly growing markets (such as those in developing countries). The rate of technology diffusion is higher for products with a short life-cycle than for those with longer long life-cycles.

Table 5.7 outlines the typical service life of a range of common energy-consuming goods. It shows that for most technologies, the timeframe for the diffusion of new energy technologies will be in the order of decades. Technology diffusion will often start slowly, until consumers are confident that the new technology is reliable.

Table 5.7 ▶ **Typical service life for energy-consuming capital goods**

Type of asset	Typical service life (years)
Household appliances	8-12
Automobiles	10-20
Industrial equipment/machinery	10-70
Aircraft	30-40
Electricity generators	50-70
Commercial/industrial buildings	40-80
Residential buildings	60-100

Source: Jaffe, 1999.

In the case of more energy efficient vehicle technologies, diffusion in many OECD countries will be limited by the trend towards heavier vehicles, such as SUVs, pick-up trucks, four-wheel drives and vans. These are relatively inefficient and will probably remain in circulation for the next 10 to 20 years. In the United States, these types of vehicles represented 41% of registered passenger vehicles in 2005 (Gallagher, 2007).

Technology diffusion rates are often overestimated. For example, it took ten years to reach one million cumulative hybrid vehicle sales, which remains a small fraction of the 70 million cars sold each year. In purchasing durable products, especially cars and home electronics and appliances, consumers attach relatively low weight to energy efficiency or environmental issues. In these areas, diffusion rates will be difficult to predict unless policies are implemented to promote the uptake of new technologies (such as minimum efficiency standards, building codes and tax incentives).

There is significant potential to speed up technology deployment in newly industrialised countries by focusing efforts on the relatively large market of first-time buyers. But costs will be a major barrier, as clean technologies are often more expensive. First-time buyers in these countries are generally constrained by limited budgets and high financing costs. To encourage investment in new technologies, steps may also need to be taken to avoid the dumping of less-efficient, older products in developing countries, as the industrialised world moves on to more-efficient products.

Overall, energy efficiency offers the highest potential for reducing future CO_2 emissions. The majority of the technologies needed are already available today at low or negative costs. Energy-efficient technologies that are already cost effective but are not being taken up require government intervention, through policies aimed at removing barriers to market uptake. Codes and standards are the most effective way to bring these energy-efficient technologies to commercialisation, but are rarely the most economically efficient way. A wide range of other policy instruments are available: such as public information campaigns, non-binding guidelines, labels and targets, and fiscal and other financial incentives. Greater international harmonisation of codes, standards and labelling schemes, together with the continuous development of international standards is also needed.

Policy options to accelerate deployment

No single policy or set of policies ensures that a technology will successfully make the hurdle from deployment to commercialisation. The choice of technologies is best left to industry, rather than governments. The role of governments should be to implement policies targeted at overcoming barriers to market uptake of new and improved energy technologies, which can deliver the overall outcomes the government is seeking (Sagar and van der Zwaan, 2006).

In terms of policy development, a number of key criteria must be met:

- Externalities must be addressed. For example, governments need to develop mechanisms to ensure a proper cost is attributed to the CO_2 impact of individual technologies.
- A flexible policy framework is needed that provides reliable support for clean energy technologies, but with room for modifications if necessary as a justified response to changing conditions.
- Direct support should be avoided. Industry should be encouraged to establish itself.
- Support policies should be proportionate. Overgenerous support policies can raise prices, be a disincentive for innovation, and lock in inappropriate technologies.

Businesses need clarity and consistency regarding long-term market rules so that they can make investment decisions based on calculated risks. Without regulatory certainty, the perceived risk level can undermine incentives for investing in projects that represent major up-front investment costs. Credible, long-term policy commitments can significantly reduce the risks of investing in new technologies.

Analysis of renewable energy policy effectiveness

The IEA is assessing the effectiveness of renewable energy policies in its ongoing Global Renewable Energy Markets and Policies Analysis Programme. The Programme's main message is that effective renewable policies reflect four fundamental principles:

- the need for a predictable support framework to attract investors;
- the removal of non-economic barriers, such as too much bureaucracy;
- a specified duration and declining level of support which, in order to control costs, should be maintained consistently over time;
- the tailoring of policy schemes to specific technologies so as to reflect their varying level of maturity.

Policies are needed to remove non-economic barriers to the diffusion of renewable energy. Administrative complexities or hurdles, grid-access issues that affect connection or public resistance to new technologies can still act as "showstoppers" in many cases, even where renewable energy technologies (RETs) are economically competitive with conventional energy technologies. Removing these barriers remains a key area for future policy work and public involvement.

Policy support mechanisms for RETs should be designed to be transitional, with decreasing support levels over time. Beyond the need to ensure the continuity of a renewable-energy policy, the support mechanisms have to be flexible enough to ensure that they keep up with technological improvements and do not exclude less competitive RET options that have a high potential for development in the longer term. In these respects, feed-in tariffs have generally been more effective than tradable green certificate-based (TGC) schemes in developing RETs, although at a relatively high price. Regular reviews of the mechanisms in place and of the progress achieved are crucial to ensure that renewable-energy penetration and deployment occurs smoothly and effectively.

Significant cost savings can be achieved when deployment can be focused at least initially on niche markets. These markets often provide high growth rates and require less learning investment, as the cost of the alternative, incumbent technology is often also higher. For example, Poponi (2003) found that the break-even price for PV systems in southern Italy was EUR 4/W, versus an average EUR 1/W for utility-owned systems.

International co-operation to promote technology deployment

Much of the deployment in clean energy technologies is expected to take place in OECD countries. But as investments in power generation are locked in for 40 to 50 years, it is important that fast-growing non-OECD countries also deploy these technologies. Technology collaboration between OECD and non-OECD countries would help to not only promote the uptake of cleaner technologies in non-OECD countries, but also to speed up the deployment phase, as manufacturing costs are generally lower in non-OECD countries. Non-OECD countries may also see opportunities to build a national industry from a new energy technology, which would justify the higher deployment costs.

Rapid demand growth in developing countries for a wide range of consumer goods provides a unique opportunity to deploy cleaner technologies. It is important to ensure that intellectual property rights are protected for business-based technology transfer to succeed.

Many developing countries are reluctant to impose tough standards and codes for fear of hurting local businesses. This often leads to the commercialisation of less-efficient technologies and creates barriers to the transfer of clean technologies. Sharing international best practices can help OECD and non-OECD countries identify appropriate standards and codes to encourage the market uptake of cleaner technologies.

The benefits of technology learning are typically shared on a global level. This emphasises the need for international collaboration on technology development and deployment.[2] In many cases, deployment costs can be lowered through international collaboration.

2. The IEA Implementing Agreements offer a good opportunity to improve international collaboration on technology development and deployment.

Chapter  INVESTMENT ISSUES

Key Findings

- The additional investment needs over the Baseline scenario to 2050 are USD 17 trillion in the ACT Map scenario and USD 45 trillion in the BLUE Map scenario, which is an increase of 7% and 18% respectively over the baseline. This represents an increase in the investment needs that is equivalent to 0.4% of cumulative GDP between 2005 and 2050 in the ACT Map scenario and 1.1% in the BLUE Map scenario. The BLUE Map scenario requires additional investment of around USD 1.1 trillion per year between 2010 and 2050. This is roughly the current annual output of the Italian economy.

- Total cumulative investment needs in the Baseline scenario are estimated to be USD 254 trillion between 2005 and 2050. Although extremely large in absolute terms, this is only 6% of cumulative GDP over the period. Demand-side investments dominate, with USD 226 trillion invested in energy consuming technologies between 2005 and 2050.

- The ACT and BLUE scenarios imply that energy consumers in industry, buildings and transport invest significantly more than in the baseline. Transport dominates investment needs in all scenarios and the additional investment needs in the ACT and BLUE scenarios, due to the growing sales of transport vehicles and their high unit cost. Transport accounts for around 78% of the additional investment needs in the ACT Map scenario and 70% in the BLUE Map scenario.

- The additional investment needs in the ACT Map and BLUE Map scenarios result in significant fuel savings between 2005 and 2050 – USD 34.7 trillion and USD 50.6 trillion respectively (undiscounted). Subtracting the fuel savings from the additional investment needs yields savings of USD 17.4 trillion (ACT Map) and USD 5.6 trillion (BLUE Map). Discounting back to 2005 at 3%, the additional investment needs and the fuel savings show a net discounted saving of USD 4.5 trillion in the ACT Map scenario, but an increase of USD 0.8 trillion in the BLUE Map scenario. At a 10% discount rate, the net increase is USD 0.7 trillion for the ACT Map scenario and USD 2.1 trillion for the BLUE Map scenario.

- Investment in the electricity sector (generation, transmission and distribution) is USD 1.1 trillion lower than the baseline in the ACT Map scenario, but USD 2.9 trillion higher in the BLUE Map scenario. In the ACT Map scenario, energy efficiency (through reduced generation, transmission and distribution needs) more than offsets the trend towards a more capital intensive generating system. However, the deeper cuts required in the BLUE scenario, as well as electricification mean this is not the case in the BLUE Map scenario.

- Investment in power generation plants increases by USD 0.7 trillion over the baseline in the ACT Map scenario and by USD 3.6 trillion in the BLUE Map scenario. This is an increase of 6% and 28% respectively. In both scenarios, the electricity system shifts to more capital-intensive renewables and nuclear generation, as well as

CCS-equipped thermal plant. The incremental investment over the baseline in CCS technologies in the BLUE Map scenario is estimated to be USD 1 trillion for power generation, with another USD 0.4 trillion invested in CCS in the industrial sector.

- *Electricity transmission network needs increase by USD 0.9 trillion and USD 1.4 trillion in the ACT Map and BLUE Map scenarios. In these scenarios, power generation and transmission investment together increases by between 10% and 30%. However, reduced electricity demand growth due to energy efficiency means that investment needs in the electricity distribution network are USD 2.7 trillion lower than in the Baseline scenario in the ACT Map scenario and USD 2.1 trillion lower in the BLUE Map scenario.*
- *Energy efficiency and fuel switching in the end-use sectors means that investment needs in the energy transformation sector are USD 1.9 trillion lower than in the Baseline scenario in the ACT Map scenario and USD 0.6 trillion lower in the BLUE Map scenario. The smaller reduction in the BLUE Map scenario is due to the greater investment needs in biofuels and hydrogen production reducing the net savings from less investment in conventional oil refineries.*
- *The additional investment needs over the baseline in transport of USD 17 trillion (ACT Map) and USD 33 trillion (BLUE Map) dominates total incremental investment. This represents an increase in transport investment of 8% in the ACT Map scenario and 15% in the BLUE Map scenario. Transport dominates total investment, due to the high unit costs of cars, trucks, ships and planes and the sheer quantity that are projected to be sold (an average of 106 million light-duty vehicles per year between 2005 and 2050).*
- *Investment by consumers in the residential sector is USD 2.2 trillion higher in the ACT Map scenario and USD 6.4 trillion higher in the BLUE Map scenario than the USD 9.1 trillion projected in the Baseline scenario. In the commercial sector, the increase over the baseline is USD 0.4 trillion and USD 1 trillion respectively. This represents increased investment in more energy efficient appliances and lighting, the additional costs of more energy efficient building shells, the increased capital costs of more efficient heating systems, and additional capital investment in the switch to lower-carbon heating fuels. In the ACT Map scenario, investment in the industrial sector is USD 0.6 trillion higher than the Baseline scenario total of USD 2.4 trillion and in the BLUE Map it is USD 2.5 trillion higher.*
- *Additional investment needs in clean energy technologies and energy efficiency in the ACT Map scenario are around 10 times the current estimated level of investment. In the BLUE Map scenario, it is around 18 times the current level of investment. Ramping up this investment in the demand-side will be critical to achieving the ACT Map and BLUE Map scenarios.*
- *OECD countries will need to invest USD 7.3 trillion more in the ACT Map scenario than in the Baseline scenario, compared to an additional investment of USD 10.3 trillion needed in non-OECD countries. In the BLUE Map scenario, additional investment in OECD countries is USD 18.4 trillion, or 2.5 times the level of the ACT Map scenario. For non-OECD countries, additional investment in the BLUE Map scenario is 2.6 times that of the ACT Map scenario, or USD 27 trillion. There*

is a significant ramping up in the Blue Map scenario of the additional investment needs in the period 2030 to 2050.

- *Achieving the incremental investment needs of the BLUE Map scenario will be challenging, but the global economy is projected to generate sufficient funds. Governments need to ensure that the right policies are in place to make sure this investment occurs in a timely fashion. Current financing mechanisms will need to be expanded, and new and innovative facilities will need to be created. International financial organisations are aware of the challenge, but need support from donors to expand programmes, pilot new large-scale financing mechanisms and partner with national or regional programmes to enhance their effectiveness or scale.*
- *The importance of demand-side investments is a paradigm shift: it will require a change in thinking and structure so as to focus on the financing needs of individuals in order to overcome capital constraints, high implicit discount rates and poor information about costs and benefits. The BLUE Map scenario will require well-designed efficiency standards, improved building regulations, carbon reduction incentives and new financing facilities.*
- *The challenge posed by greater up-front investment needs will be particularly significant for developing countries where rapid economic growth is driving investment in proven low-cost fossil-fuel technologies. They will also require assistance in capacity building to help improve their capital markets and in the development of financing schemes, especially for consumers.*

Investment needs in the Baseline scenario

In the Baseline scenario, total final energy consumption almost doubles between 2005 and 2050 because of increasing demand for goods, services and leisure activities that require energy as an input. This implies dramatic investment growth in energy consuming devices and processes, but also in the energy production and supply infrastructure that will be needed to service them.[1] In the Baseline scenario, the total investment required on the demand- and the supply-side is estimated to be USD 254 trillion between 2005 and 2050.[2] The vast bulk of this (USD 226 trillion) is accounted for by investments that energy consumers will make in capital equipment that consumes energy, from vehicles to light-bulbs to steel plants, as shown in Figure 6.1.[3]

1. All figures in this chapter are in USD 2005, evaluated at market exchange rates.
2. This doesn't include upstream investment in the production and transportation of coal, oil and gas. Estimating upstream investment in the coal, oil and gas industries beyond 2030 is highly uncertain. Upstream investment is therefore not included in the totals in the remainder of this chapter. However, including the upstream investments in the Baseline scenario between 2005 and 2030 raises total investment needs presented in this chapter from around USD 95 trillion to USD 117 trillion, of which supply-side only (IEA, 2007a) is USD 22 trillion (see Box 6.1).
3. See Annex B for a description of what is included in the investment figures calculated in this chapter.

Figure 6.1 ▶ **Investment needs in the Baseline scenario, 2005-2050**

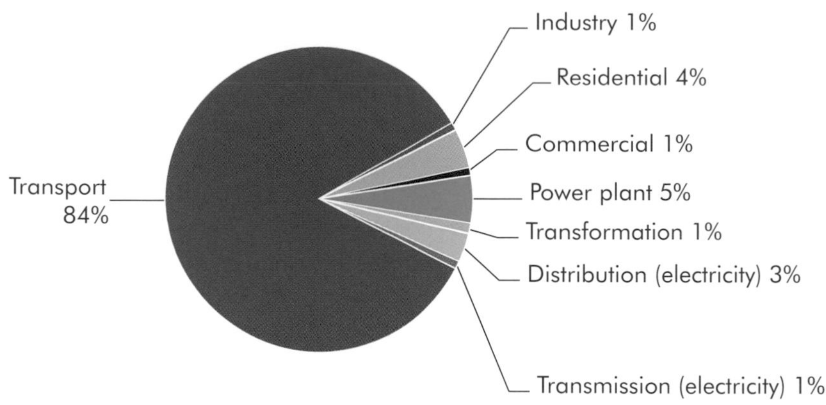

Key point

Investment in transport dominates total investment needs in the Baseline scenario, accounting for 84% of the total.

Additional investment needs in the ACT Map and BLUE Map scenarios

In the ACT Map and BLUE Map scenarios, overall investment needs increase over the baseline by USD 17.3 trillion and USD 45 trillion respectively (Figure 6.2).[4] These figures include the learning and deployment costs calculated in Chapter 5. In these scenarios, consumers invest in more energy efficient equipment, vehicles and industrial plants with CCS; while electricity generators invest in higher capital-cost renewable, nuclear and CCS-equipped plants. Many of these investments are economic over their life-cycle even without a CO_2 reduction incentive; as they yield fuel cost savings that when discounted exceed the additional initial investment. Increased energy efficiency also offers other investment benefits: in the ACT Map scenario, investment needs in the transformation sector are USD 1.9 trillion lower than in the Baseline scenario and USD 2.7 trillion lower for electricity distribution systems (Figure 6.2). For power plant, the additional per unit capital costs of power sector investment are offset to some extent by the lower electricity demand in this scenario.

In the ACT Map scenario, energy efficiency plays a relatively more important role than biofuels in driving down CO_2 emissions in the transport sector (there is no hydrogen). As a result, increased investment in biofuels is more than offset by the decline in conventional refinery investment that results from less growth in oil demand. In the BLUE Map scenario, investment needs for biofuels and hydrogen production are higher than the reduced investment in refineries due to lower oil demand through efficiency and fuel-switching. Transformation sector investment

4. Although the projection period extends from 2005 to 2050, no change occurs to investment between the Baseline scenario and the ACT Map and BLUE Map scenarios until 2010.

in the BLUE Map scenario is therefore higher than in the ACT Map scenario, but still lower than in the Baseline scenario. In the electricity distribution sector, lower investment is needed in both the ACT Map and BLUE Map scenarios than in the Baseline scenario; but the reduction in the BLUE Map scenario is smaller because of increased electrification.

Figure 6.2 ▶ **Additional investment in the ACT Map and BLUE Map scenarios compared to the Baseline scenario, 2005-2050**

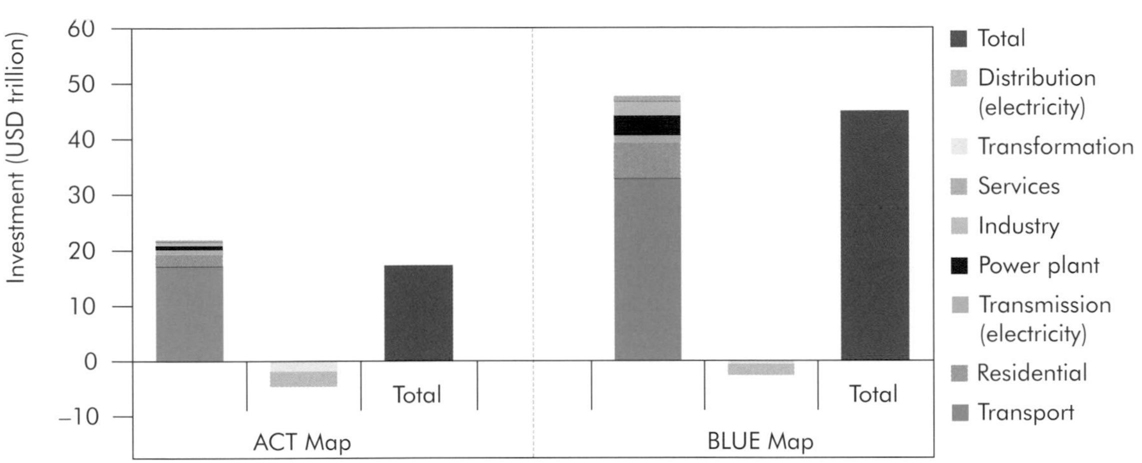

Key point

Transport dominates the additional investment needs in both the ACT Map and BLUE Map scenarios. Energy efficiency lowers investment needs in electricity distribution and energy transformation.

In both the ACT Map and BLUE Map scenarios, the transportation sector dominates the additional investment needs, as consumers invest in fuel-efficiency options (including improved internal combustion engines, power trains, aerodynamics, appliances, low-resistance tyres, hybridisation, fuel cells and onboard hydrogen storage). Transport accounts for around 78% of the additional investment in the ACT Map scenario for sectors needing additional investment, although this falls to around 70% in the BLUE scenario, as relatively more expensive options in other sectors are required.

As shown in Table 6.1, the ACT Map and BLUE Map scenarios represent a significant change in the patterns of investment that are needed. The additional investment needs in the ACT Map and BLUE Map scenarios stem from the increased capital costs of deploying more energy efficient equipment or capital plant, as well as from the increased costs associated with deploying renewable or low-carbon technologies. These investments yield significant savings in fossil-fuel consumption, but lead to increased bioenergy fuel costs. Many of the energy efficiency investments are competitive based on life-cycle costs. Overall, the undiscounted fuel savings total USD 34.7 trillion in the ACT

Map scenario and USD 50.6 trillion in the BLUE Map scenario (Figure 6.3).[5] The net total of undiscounted investment needs and fuel savings in the ACT Map scenario is a saving of USD 17.4 trillion, reflecting the significant share of low-cost or negative cost measures in this scenario.[6] In the BLUE Map scenario, the net savings are reduced to USD 5.6 trillion over the period to 2050. This is due to the significantly more expensive options that need to come into play to achieve the deeper emissions cuts in this scenario. It is important to note that these calculations are conservative, as they exclude fuel savings beyond 2050 that will occur as a result of investment before 2050.

Table 6.1 **Additional investment in the ACT Map and BLUE Map scenarios compared to the baseline, 2010-2050**

	Increase/Decrease from baseline	
	ACT Map (USD trillion)	**BLUE Map** (USD trillion)
Transformation	–1.9	–0.6
Power plant	0.7	3.6
Transmission (electricity)	0.9	1.4
Distribution (electricity)	–2.7	–2.1
Industry	0.6	2.5
Transport	17.1	32.8
Residential	2.2	6.4
Services	0.4	1.0
Total	**17.3**	**45.0**

Discounting the additional investment needs and the fuel savings these investments generate back to 2005 at a 3% discount rate yields a net discounted cost of USD -4.5 trillion in the ACT Map scenario and USD +0.8 trillion in the BLUE Map scenario. At a 10% discount rate, these costs rise to USD +0.7 trillion for the ACT Map scenario and +2.1 trillion for the BLUE Map scenario.

5. Fuel savings are evaluated using the Baseline scenario fuel prices. Using the BLUE Map scenario prices would reduce these savings by USD 4.5 and 7.1 trillion dollars respectively for the ACT Map and BLUE Map scenarios.

6. See *World Energy Outlook 2006* (IEA, 2006) for a discussion of the issue of discounting future costs and savings at the global level.

Figure 6.3 ▶ **Additional investment and fuel savings in the ACT Map and BLUE Map scenarios compared to the baseline, 2010-2050**

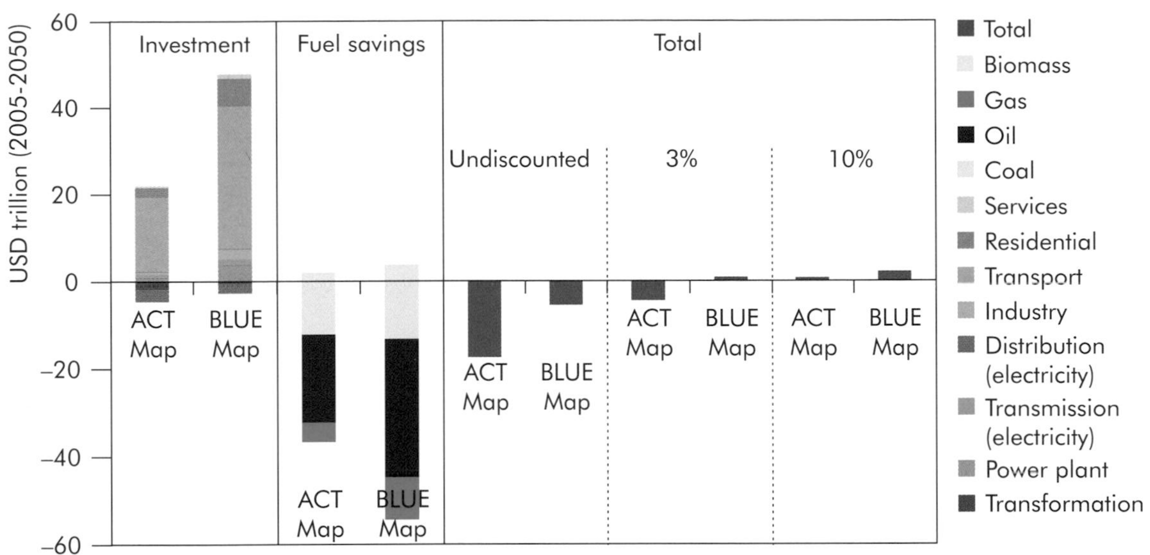

Key point

In the ACT Map and BLUE Map scenarios, fuel savings comfortably offset additional investment needs without discounting. Discounting at 10% implies a net additional cost in both scenarios.

Box 6.1 ▶ **Investment needs in *World Energy Outlook 2007*: modelling upstream investment in the coal, oil and gas sectors**

World Energy Outlook 2007 *estimated total investment in the upstream coal, oil and gas industries, as well as in power generation, transmission and distribution between 2006 and 2030 to be USD 21.9 trillion (IEA, 2007a). This chapter includes estimates of the investment needs for power generation, transmission and distribution to 2050, as well as investments in gas-to-liquids (GTL), coal-to-liquids (CTL), refineries and biofuels. However, the investment needs for the exploration, production and transport of coal, oil and gas are not included in the Baseline, ACT Map or BLUE Map scenarios presented in the main body of this chapter.* World Energy Outlook *2007 estimated upstream investment in the exploration, production and transportation of coal, oil and gas to be USD 10.2 trillion over the period to 2030. These costs are non-linear with relation to energy demand growth, and so are extremely difficult to estimate out to 2050 given the wide-range of uncertainties surrounding decline rates, capital costs, location of production growth, etc.*

Adding upstream investments in coal, oil and gas to the investment needs presented in the main body of this chapter for the period to 2030 increases the Baseline scenario total for both the demand and the supply side (including upstream) to USD 117.5 trillion. This figure is directly comparable with the supply-side-only investment figure in World Energy Outlook *2007 of USD 21.9 trillion to 2030. So in the period to 2030, including demand-side investment needs increases total investment needs to almost 5.4 times more than the supply-side only investments (Table 6.2).*

Table 6.2 ▶ **Comparison of WEO and ETP investment needs for the Baseline scenario to 2030**

	USD trillion *World Energy Outlook*	USD trillion *Energy Technology Perspectives*
Production and transport		
Coal	0.6	0.6
Oil	5.4	5.4
Gas	4.2	4.2
Electricity generation, transmission and distribution	11.6	11.6
Subtotal	**21.9**	**21.9**
Demand side	n.a.	95.6
Total	n.a.	**117.5**

Investment needs by sector

Transport

In the Baseline scenario, investment in planes, trucks, buses and light duty vehicles (LDVs) dominates total investment needs, accounting for USD 212 trillion or 84% of the total investment of USD 254 trillion. Of the transport sector total total, LDVs account for around 62% (USD 131 trillion) of the investment needs. A total of 4.8 billion LDVs will be sold between 2005 and 2050, implying average annual sales of 106 million LDVs per year in the Baseline scenario. Sales of hybrid, LPG and CNG powered vehicles reach 11.6 million per year in 2050, averaging 5.4 million units per year over the period.

After LDVs, shipping is projected to be the next single largest area of transport investment, as the global economy grows and the quantity of raw materials and finished goods transported between producers and their customers rises. Shipping companies will invest around USD 26.9 trillion in new ships between now and 2050, purchasing around 5 070 million tonnes of shipping over this period.

Purchases of heavy and medium trucks are estimated to cost around USD 39.7 trillion, with heavy trucks accounting for around USD 20.7 trillion. Total heavy truck sales are projected to be 157 million between 2005 and 2050, with around 57% of the sales occurring outside the OECD. Medium-freight truck sales total 312 million. Bus sales come to 69 million, with around four-fifths of these in non-OECD regions.

In the ACT Map scenario, investment needs over and above baseline are USD 17.1 trillion or an increase of 8%. Of this total, USD 15.1 trillion is in LDVs. In the LDV sector, investment in conventional vehicles is significantly reduced, being replaced by investment in more expensive hybrid and plug-in hybrid vehicles. Sales of hybrid vehicles reach 72% of new LDV sales in 2050. The additional cost of gasoline hybrid vehicles is assumed to fall to around USD 2 300 per vehicle in 2050. There are also additional investment needs for improvements to the internal combustion engine (although these are offset to some extent by engine downsizing) and other improvements in areas including aerodynamics, light weighting of vehicles and more efficient onboard appliances.

In the BLUE Map scenario, additional investment needs over the Baseline scenario are USD 32.8 trillion or an increase of 15%. In this scenario, even fewer conventional vehicles are sold as larger efficiency improvements and the further decarbonisation of LDVs is achieved by the penetration of electric vehicles (EVs) and hydrogen fuel cell (HFC) vehicles. The additional cost per vehicle of HFC, EV, plug-in hybrids and hybrids is expected to decline over time with deployment (Table 6.3). In the BLUE Map scenario, additional investment in LDVs reaches USD 20.4 trillion in 2050, for trucks and buses USD 9.3 trillion, with the balance attributable to aircraft and ships.

Table 6.3 ▶ **Additional cost per vehicle of hybrids, EVs and HFC vehicles in BLUE Map compared to conventional vehicle in the baseline**

	2015	2030 (USD per vehicle)	2050
Gasoline hybrid	2 800	2 300	2 300
Plug-in hybrid	5 300	3 600	3 400
HFC vehicle	45 000	9 000	6 400
EV	25 000	8 900	6 500

The overall comparison between the Baseline, ACT Map and BLUE Map scenario transport investment demands is shown in Figure 6.4, below.

Additional investment needs in the transport sector depend heavily on the assumptions made for learning rates for hybrids, electric vehicles and HFC vehicles. If either HFC or electric vehicles are more successful than the other is, investment needs could decrease by USD 2 trillion or increase by up to USD 7 trillion. This represents potentially a *decrease* in the additional LDV investment needs of 14% at one extreme or an *increase* of 31% at the other.

Electricity sector

In the Baseline scenario, investment in the electricity sector, including generation, transmission and distribution; is projected to be USD 24.8 trillion between 2005 and 2050. More than half of this (USD 12.9 trillion) is needed for new power-

Figure 6.4 ▶ **Additional investment in LDVs in the ACT Map and BLUE Map scenarios compared to the baseline, 2005-2050**

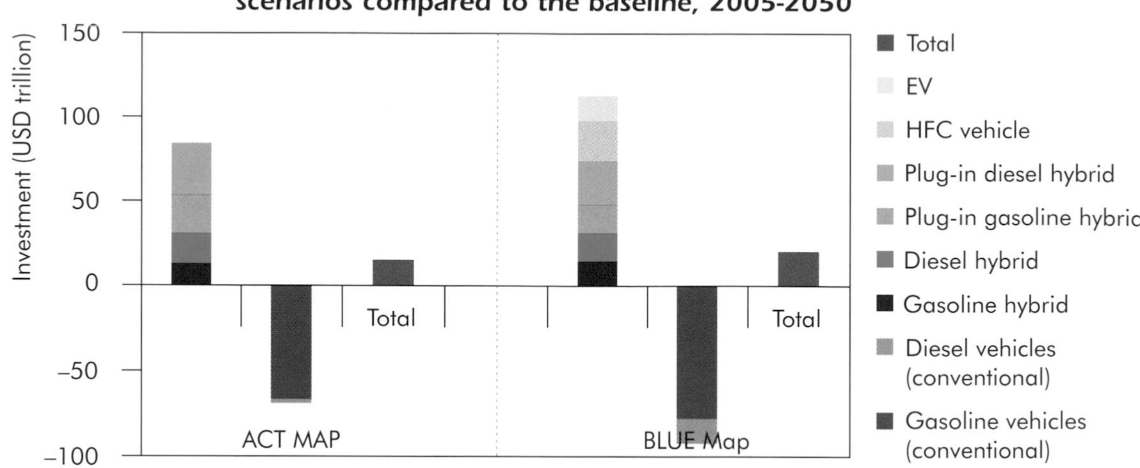

Key point

Increased investment in hybrids, HFC and electric vehicles is not offset by the reduced spending on conventional LDVs.

generation plants, with USD 8.3 trillion for maintaining and expanding the electricity distribution network and USD 3.6 trillion for the electricity transmission network (Figure 6.5). Investment in conventional technologies – gas, coal, biomass, hydro and nuclear – dominates the power generation sector total. Over 9 000 GW of gas-fired capacity is added in the Baseline scenario between 2003 and 2050, and just over 4 000 GW of coal-fired capacity.

Figure 6.5 ▶ **Electricity sector investment needs in the Baseline scenario, 2005-2050**

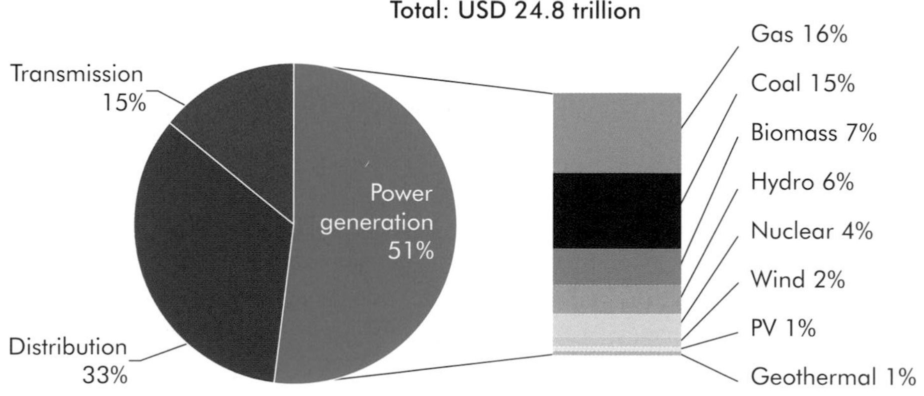

Key point

Power generation accounts for half of investment needs in the electricity sector in the Baseline scenario, of which gas-fired plant is the largest single investment.

In the ACT Map scenario, energy efficiency reduces electricity demand growth, reducing the need for new generation capacity and expansion of the transmission and distribution grids. There is also a switch to more capital intensive renewables, nuclear and CCS-equipped thermal technologies. The reduction in investment in conventional coal- and gas-fired electricity plant and the distribution network more than offsets the additional investment needs in renewable, nuclear and CCS technologies. Investment needs are therefore USD 1.1 trillion (–4%) lower in the ACT Map scenario, than in the baseline (Figure 6.6). In the BLUE Map scenario, there is a significant increase in the investment in renewables, nuclear and CCS technologies, as well as a reduction in savings in investment in the distribution network due to electrification. As a result, investment needs are USD 2.9 trillion (+12%) higher than in the Baseline scenario.

The additional investment needs for power generation plants over and above the Baseline scenario total USD 0.7 trillion (+6%) in the ACT Map scenario and USD 3.6 trillion (+28%) in the BLUE Map scenario. A 20% reduction in electricity demand growth as a result of improved energy efficiency in the ACT Map scenario (slightly less in the BLUE Map scenario) reduces the need for additional capacity, but this is offset by the increased capital costs of renewables, nuclear, and thermal capacity with CCS.

Figure 6.6 ▶ **Additional investment in the electricity sector in the ACT Map and BLUE Map scenarios compared to the baseline, 2005-2050**

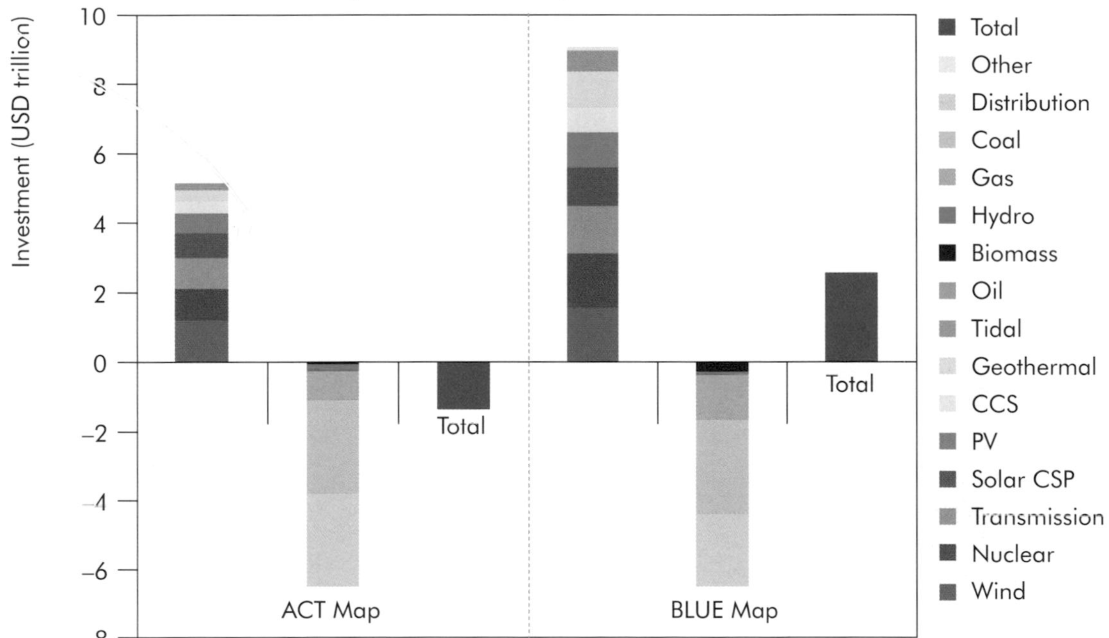

Key point

Additional investment in transmission, renewables, nuclear and CCS is greater than the reduced investment in coal, gas and the distribution network in the BLUE Map scenario.

The number of new-build coal-fired power plants without CCS drops by almost 90% in the BLUE Map scenario compared to the baseline. The number of coal-fired plants with CCS would grow by around 1 240 (500 MW units) in the ACT Map scenario and 1 400 in the BLUE Map scenario, including existing plant retrofits (over 300 units of 500 MW each). The prospects for gas-fired power plants are more stable, with only a modest reduction from the baseline in either the ACT Map or BLUE Map scenarios. Assuming that wind turbines average 4 MW in size, around 700 000 are required in the BLUE Map scenario (Figure 6.7), compared to 146 000 in the Baseline scenario. There is a significant increase in the level of physical investment on average over the period to 2050 compared to today's level of investment in renewables and CCS, with the exception of hydro. The ramp-up rates are achievable, but any delay in action would have a significant impact on the path of emissions.

Investment needs for transmission systems increase by USD 0.9 trillion in the ACT Map scenario and by 1.4 trillion in the BLUE Map scenario. The additional investment, despite the reduction in electricity demand, is necessary to provide transmission lines that will connect more remote renewables to the grid. The connection of intermittent renewables will also require some reinforcing of grids. Investment in the electricity distribution system is reduced by USD 2.7 trillion in the ACT Map scenario and by USD 2.1 trillion in the BLUE Map scenario, largely as a result of reduced electricity demand. The reduction is less in the BLUE Map scenario as electricification (particularly for plug-in hybrid vehicles and heat pumps for process, space and water heating) raises electricity consumption above the ACT Map level.

Figure 6.7 ▶ **Average annual power plant investment in the ACT Map and BLUE Map scenarios, 2010-2050**

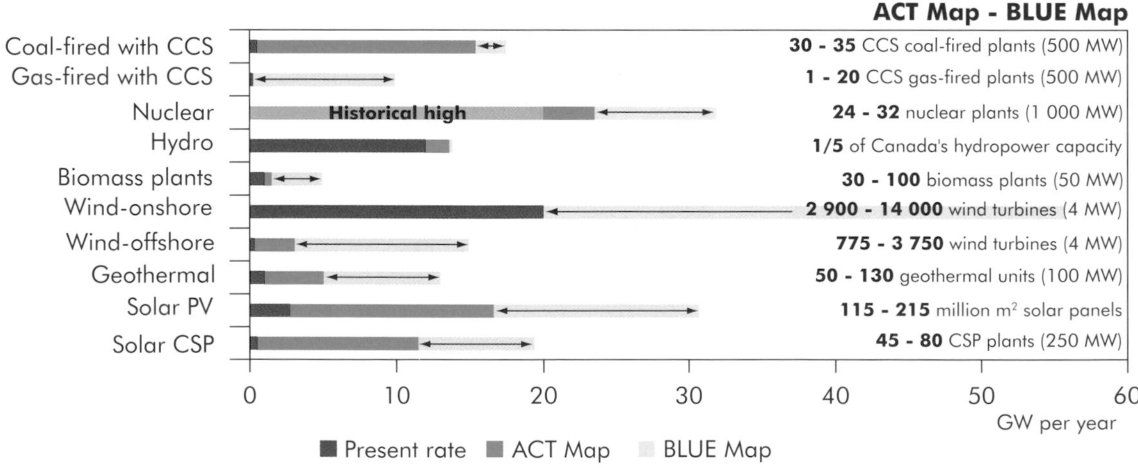

Note: Chapter 2 outlines a number of scenarios for power generation. In practice, individual countries will have considerable choice in the balance of low-carbon-generation options that they prefer, depending on local circumstances, resource availability etc.

Key point

Renewables will dominate new plant developments in the BLUE Map scenario.

Residential and services

In the Baseline scenario, investment by householders in energy consuming equipment is around USD 9.1 trillion. The number of households is projected to expand by nearly 1.1 billion between 2005 and 2050, with many of the new households being added in developing countries. Space heating and appliances account for around two-thirds of the total investment. Although space heating is concentrated in OECD countries, the high cost of heating systems means their share is still very significant at a global level. Investment in air-conditioners is set to increase rapidly over the outlook period, as incomes grow rapidly in developing countries with very high potential cooling loads.

Investment in energy consuming devices in the service sector is projected to amount to USD 1.5 trillion between 2005 and 2050. Space heating and water heating each account for around 15% to 16% of the investment projected in the service sector, much less than in the residential sector, as lighting, cooling and ventilation represent a much more significant share of the total investment needs of the service sector. This reflects the growth in service sector floor area in developing countries, and the fact that service-sector buildings tend to have higher occupancy rates during peak cooling periods.

In the ACT Map and BLUE Map scenarios, additional investment in the residential sector amounts to USD 2.2 trillion (+24%) and USD 6.4 trillion (+70%) respectively. Little change occurs in the lighting sector, as higher-cost compact fluorescent and other efficient lighting options need replacing less often. In the ACT Map scenario, appliances are shifted towards least life-cycle cost, whereas in the BLUE Map scenario there is a shift towards best available technology. Although the cost of this shift declines over time with deployment, it still implies a very significant increase in initial investment costs.

In the ACT Map and BLUE Map scenarios, significant investment in building envelopes helps to reduce incremental space heating investment needs and makes a significant contribution to containing overall investment levels. Reduced heat demand allows heating systems to be downsized. This offsets the cost of more expensive heating systems such as heat pumps, which for a residential unit may cost USD 3 500 more than a conventional gas boiler.

The BLUE Map scenario assumes a very significant shift to higher energy efficiency standards for building envelopes, both for new construction and for refurbishment. Given the very slow turnover of building stock, this will require a significant increase in energy efficiency refurbishment and reconstruction. Policies will therefore need to be put in place that result, directly or indirectly, in the increased level of energy efficiency refurbishment. This is likely to lead to the premature reconstruction/demolition of some lower-value housing stock to meet the higher energy efficiency targets. The need and potential impact of such policies is very much country-specific and depends on the balance between refurbishment and reconstruction costs versus the additional value gained. This is potentially a very difficult area for policy makers. Nevertheless, energy efficient refurbishments of the building envelope will be essential in the BLUE Map scenario, and could be difficult to achieve at a low cost.

Figure 6.8 ▶ **Additional investment in the residential and service sectors in the ACT Map and BLUE Map scenarios compared to the baseline, 2005-2050**

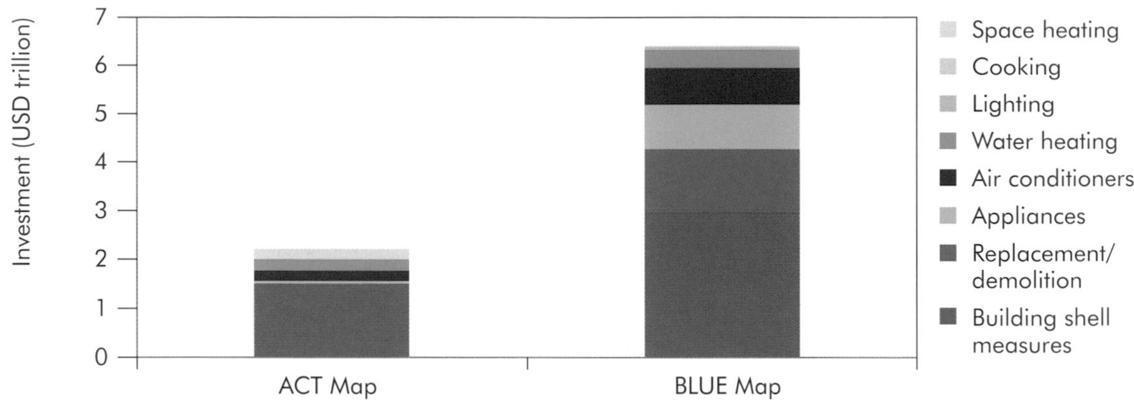

Key point

Additional investment needs are dominated by building shell measures, while the shift from ACT Map to BLUE Map requires a threefold increase in the additional investment.

In the services sector, additional investment of USD 0.4 (+25%) and USD 1 trillion (+63%) is required for the ACT Map and BLUE Map scenarios respectively. The investment needs are dominated by additional investment in the building envelope and in air conditioning and ventilation systems. Less investment is actually required in lighting in these scenarios, as longer-life lighting options reduce not only investment needs but also life-cycle costs, yielding strongly negative costs for CO_2 abatement.

Industry

In the Baseline scenario, investment in the industrial sector totals USD 2.4 trillion between 2005 and 2050. Investment is concentrated in the non-metallic minerals and chemicals sectors. Rapid growth in cement demand in developing countries and in the demand for chemicals is driving investment needs, as is the need for significant refurbishment of existing industrial capacity in all sectors over the period to 2050.

The ACT Map scenario (see Figure 6.9) envisages additional industrial investment between 2005 and 2050 of USD 0.6 trillion, primarily in the chemicals, non-metallic minerals and the residual industrial sectors. In chemicals, additional plastics recycling and more efficient crackers require significant investments, while in the non-metallic minerals sector, CCS and a more rapid shift to best available technologies increases costs. In the residual industrial sectors, energy efficiency investments, especially for industrial motors, are significant at around an additional USD 150 billion. Most of these investments are economic even without a CO_2 reduction incentive.

In the BLUE Map scenario, additional investment of USD 2.5 trillion is needed over and above the Baseline scenario. Chemicals demand an increased share of the additional investment needed over the Baseline scenario, primarily due to additional investment in plastics recycling. In the iron and steel sector, significantly increased investments are needed to increase heat recovery in the sintering process; to replace remaining beehive kilns; to install more CCS at blast furnaces and direct-reduced iron (DRI) gas-based plants; and to improve the use of cold dry quenching. In the pulp, paper and printing sector, additional investment in black liquor gasifiers and lignine drying push up investment needs compared to the ACT Map scenario.

Figure 6.9 ▶ **Additional investment in the industrial sector in the ACT Map and BLUE Map scenarios compared to the baseline, 2005-2050**

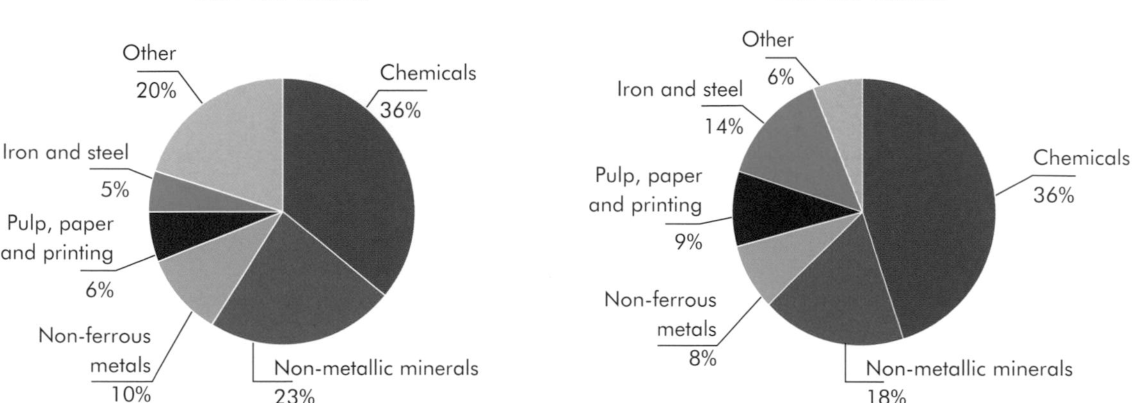

Key point

Around 60% of the additional investment over the baseline in ACT Map and BLUE Map occurs in the chemicals and non-metallic minerals sectors.

Transformation sector

In the Baseline scenario, the energy transformation sector requires USD 3.2 trillion of investment. Investment in refineries accounts for around USD 1.3 trillion. The capital-intensive expansion of coal-to-liquids (CTL), gas-to-liquids (GTL), and biofuel plants accounts for USD 0.5 trillion, USD 1.3 trillion and USD 0.1 trillion respectively. In the ACT Map and BLUE Map scenarios, there is virtually no investment in CTL or GTL. In the ACT Map scenario, fuel-efficiency improvements and the contribution of biofuels reduces oil demand growth and hence the need for significant refinery expansion. Total investment in the transformation sector is USD 1.9 trillion lower in the ACT Map scenario than in the Baseline scenario, as increased investment in biofuels does not exceed the reduced investment in refineries, CTL and GTL that occurs. In the BLUE Map scenario, oil demand is reduced even more – and after some initial investment to 2015, the refinery industry would start to disinvest. However, in the BLUE Map scenario the reduction compared to the Baseline scenario is only USD 0.6 trillion, as additional investment in biofuels and hydrogen production and infrastructure is significant in the BLUE Map scenario, totalling some USD 3 trillion between 2005 and 2050, or more than 26 times that of the Baseline scenario.

Figure 6.10 ▶ Additional investment in the energy transformation sector in the ACT Map and BLUE Map scenarios compared to the baseline, 2005-2050

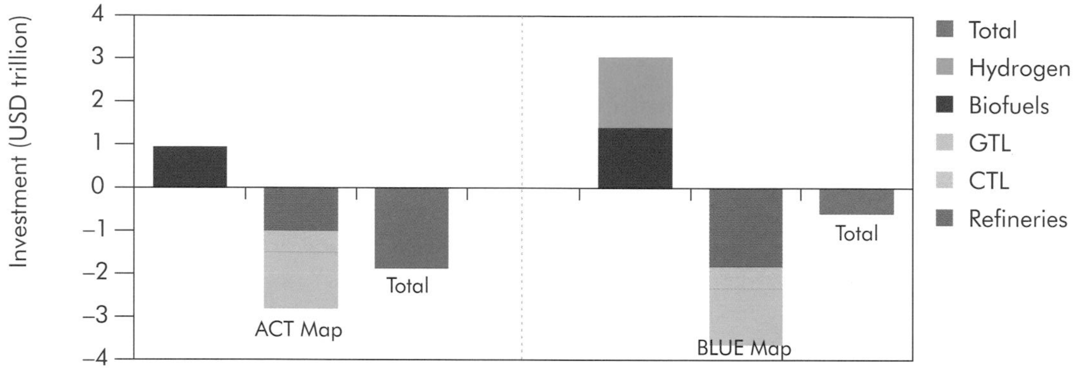

Key point

Less investment is required than in the Baseline scenario due to energy efficiency in end-use sectors.

Investment patterns over time

As regards timing, in the Baseline scenario, around 15% of investment needs are required in the period 2005 to 2015, 28% between 2015 and 2030 and 58% between 2030 and 2050. The average annual investment rises from USD 3.7 trillion in the first period, to USD 4.7 trillion in the second and USD 7.3 trillion in the final period as energy demand grows and significant replacement of earlier investment is required.

In the ACT Map scenario, the average annual additional investment needed over and above the Baseline scenario is relatively stable over the outlook period. This masks some counter-balancing effects, as the large investments made in energy efficiency begin to yield significant fuel reductions as time goes by – thereby reducing the need for investment in energy transformation and electricity transmission in the period 2030 to 2050 (Figure 6.11).

In contrast, in the BLUE Map scenario, successively larger average annual investments are needed in later periods as relatively more expensive energy efficiency and clean energy options are deployed. Between 2030 and 2050, the average annual additional investment in the BLUE Map scenario is 3.6 times as high as in the ACT Map scenario; mainly for the deployment of hybrid, electric and fuel-cell vehicles, and for renewables and nuclear plant for electricity generation, all of which accelerate between 2030 and 2050. Table 6.4 details the investments in

CO_2-free power generation over the period 2005 to 2050. This shows that annual investment needs increase significantly over time. Annual investments in the 2030 to 2050 period are around ten times today's level.

Table 6.4 ▶ **Investment in new CO_2-free power plants in BLUE Map (GW/yr)**

	2005-2015	2015-2025	2025-2035	2035-2050
Gas + CCS	0	5	17	18
Coal + CCS (including retrofit)	0	1	26	43
Nuclear	16	18	24	46
Wind	29	53	60	94
PV	2	6	28	58
Solar CSP	0	14	37	18
Biomass (including co-combustion)	8	12	20	25
Geothermal	2	10	11	19
Hydro	12	15	16	8
Total	**68**	**134**	**239**	**330**

The timing of the investments needed is different in the ACT Map and the BLUE Map scenarios. In the transformation sector, for example, both scenarios require slightly more investment to 2015 than does the Baseline scenario, predominantly because of increased investment in biofuels plant. Thereafter, additional investment needs are lower than in the Baseline scenario. However, the savings below the baseline between 2015 and 2030 in the BLUE Map scenario are around 40% smaller than in the ACT Map scenario and 75% smaller in the period 2030 to 2050. This is due to the higher biofuels and hydrogen production-plant investment.

For electricity generation plant, less investment is needed in the period to 2015 in both the ACT Map and BLUE Map scenarios compared to the baseline, as energy efficiency offsets the investment in more capital-intensive renewables. However, after 2030 there is a significant increase in investment needs in the BLUE Map scenario, as large amounts of renewable energy are deployed and as electrification reduces the contribution that energy efficiency makes to reduce the need for power-plant investment. Additional average annual investment over the baseline in the BLUE Map scenario between 2030 and 2050 is around six times higher than the additional needs in the ACT Map scenario for this period.

Investment needs in electricity transmission are lower than the baseline until 2015 in the ACT Map and BLUE Map scenarios, but are larger thereafter as the impact of more remote renewables and the need for grid strengthening come into play.

6

In the ACT Map scenario, higher average annual additional transmission network investment occurs between 2015 and 2030, while in the BLUE Map scenario, this occurs between 2030 and 2050. In terms of electricity distribution system investment, the needs compared to the baseline are reduced in each period in the ACT Map scenario. In the BLUE Map scenario, however, between 2030 and 2050, distribution investment rises to around the level of the baseline, as electrification returns growth in electricity demand in this period to a similar level to that in the Baseline scenario (note however, that between 2005 and 2050, distribution investment in total is still lower than the baseline).

In industry, the ACT Map and BLUE Map scenarios show increased demand for investment in each period, but the increase to 2015 is modest given capital stock turnover constraints. In later periods, more stock needs replacing at the same time that CCS technologies start to be widely applied. As a result, most of the industry investment needs (57% in the BLUE Map scenario) occur after 2030.

In the transport sector, the average annual investment need over the baseline is highest in the period to 2015 in the ACT Map scenario, before stabilising as deployment lowers the incremental cost of efficiency and hybridisation. In the BLUE Map scenario, deeper emissions cuts require much more expensive options to be taken up. As a result, the average annual additional investment in this scenario over the baseline increases significantly compared to the ACT Map scenario, and continues to increase over time as the greater deployment of still expensive options occurs after 2030. In the BLUE Map scenario, the average annual investment above the baseline in the period 2030 to 2050 is around 2.3 times higher than in the ACT Map scenario.

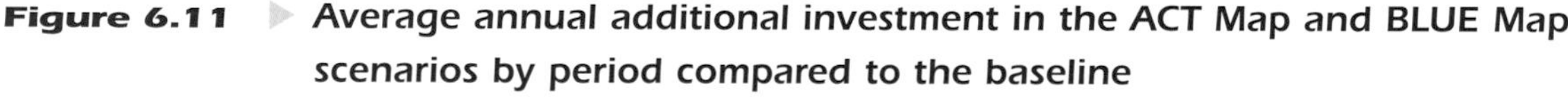

Figure 6.11 Average annual additional investment in the ACT Map and BLUE Map scenarios by period compared to the baseline

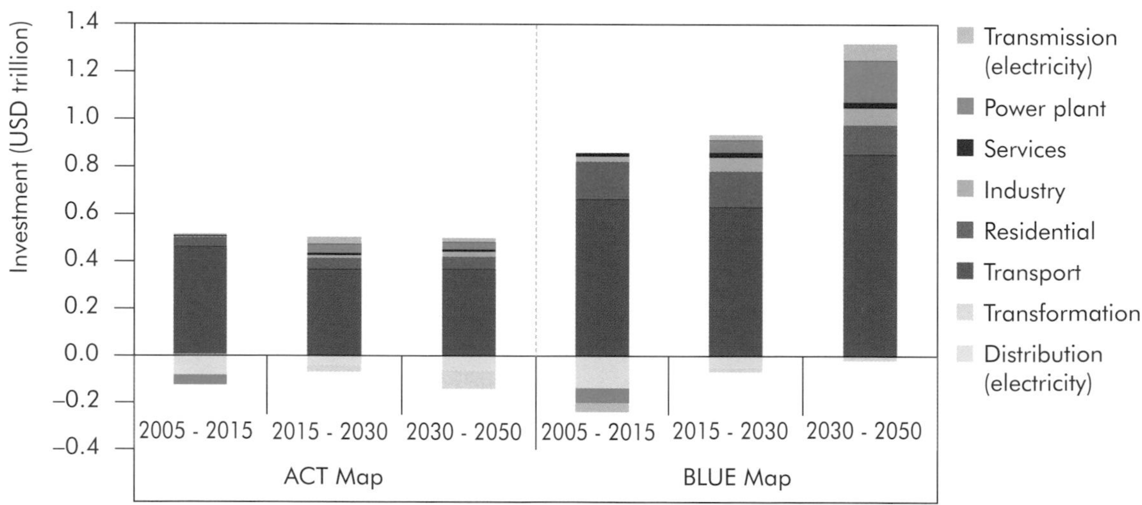

Key point

Average annual additional investment needs are quite stable in ACT Map, but need to increase over time in BLUE Map.

Regional differences

In the Baseline scenario, around 40% of the total investments to 2050 occur in OECD countries. In the period to 2015, investment in OECD countries is around 52% of the total. However, this share declines to 35% in the period 2030 to 2050, as the investment of developing countries in energy supply infrastructure and energy consuming equipment accelerates alongside their continuing rapid economic growth.

Investment in OECD countries is greater than in non-OECD countries in the residential and service sectors in the period to 2015 (Table 6.5). The OECD countries' share of investment is less than half of the total in the period 2030-2050 in every sector except electricity transmission and distribution and industry. Over the whole period from 2005 to 2050, non-OECD countries account for between 55% (in the power plant and residential sectors) and 72% (in the transformation sector) of the investment.

Table 6.5 ▶ **OECD countries' share of investment in the Baseline scenario**

	2005-2015	2015-2030	2030-2050	2005-2050
Transformation	30%	25%	29%	28%
Power plant	46%	49%	42%	45%
Transmission and distribution (electricity)	23%	24%	51%	34%
Industry	23%	24%	51%	34%
Transport	44%	43%	33%	39%
Residential	55%	47%	35%	41%
Services	59%	46%	41%	45%

The average annual investment in non-OECD countries in the period 2030 to 2050 averages 170% more than in the period 2005 to 2015. The average annual investment in non-OECD countries in the Baseline scenario by period is relatively stable in the electricity transmission and distribution sector and in industry. Investment in other sectors grows significantly, however. For example, average annual investment in transport from 2030 to 2050 is 215% higher than in 2005 to 2015. The same comparison for the residential and service sectors shows a growth of 111% and 193% respectively.

In the OECD countries, the increase in the average annual investment from the period 2005 to 2015 to the period 2030 to 2050 is only 32%, reflecting the much more modest growth in energy demand in these countries than in non-OECD countries. The only sectors in which OECD countries are projected to invest significantly more per year from 2030 to 2050 than in 2005 to 2015 are the electricity generation and transport sectors.

In the ACT Map scenario, the additional investment needs over and above the Baseline scenario are USD 7.3 trillion in OECD countries and USD 10.3 trillion in non-OECD countries (Figure 6.12). In the BLUE Map scenario, OECD countries invest USD 18.4 trillion and non-OECD countries invest USD 27 trillion over and above the Baseline scenario. Investment needs increase significantly in the transformation sector in the OECD countries between the ACT Map scenario and the BLUE Map scenario, as significant additional investment in biofuels and hydrogen production and the associated infrastructure is required. However, the increase in investment is largest in absolute terms in transport, where an extra USD 5.9 trillion is needed in OECD countries and USD 9.8 trillion is needed in non-OECD countries.

Figure 6.12 ▶ **Additional investment in the ACT Map and BLUE Map scenarios by region compared to the baseline, 2005-2050**

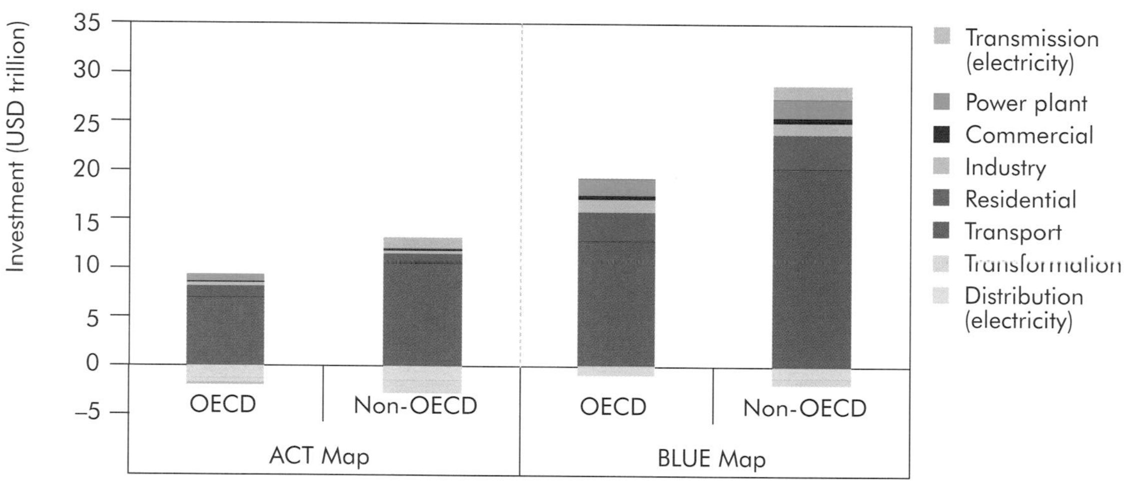

Key point

Around 60% of the additional investment needs over the baseline in the ACT Map and BLUE Map scenarios occurs in non-OECD countries.

Investment needs and global investment flows

The investment required to achieve the outcomes envisaged in the ACT Map and BLUE Map scenarios is very significant, both in absolute terms and compared to current levels. In 2006, investment in clean energy was estimated to total USD 70.9 billion. This was an increase of 43% over 2005 (UNEP and New Energy Finance, 2007). The average annual additional investment needs in the ACT Map scenario are 6 times higher than this, while in the BLUE Map scenario they average around 16 times this level each year from 2010 to 2050.

The global economy has the capacity to finance this additional investment. The total investment of USD 254 trillion between 2005 and 2050 in the Baseline scenario – or USD 5.6 trillion a year – represents around 6% of global GDP over that time.[7] In the ACT Map scenario, this increases by USD 0.4 trillion per year between 2010 and 2050, and in the BLUE scenario, it increases by USD 1.1 trillion. The total investment needs as a percentage of global GDP therefore increase by 0.4% in the ACT Map scenario and by 1.1% in the BLUE Map scenario.

Globally, total investment in the economy is estimated to have averaged around 22% to 23% of global GDP at market exchange rates since 1985. It is projected to grow to an average 24% to 25% of global GDP (Figure 6.13) between 2009 and 2012 (IMF, 2007).[8] With the exception of the United States, investment as a share of GDP is generally growing. Developing countries, particularly in Asia, also tend to have higher rates of investment, as these economies are rapidly expanding their infrastructure and industrialising. The additional investment needs in the ACT Map and BLUE Map scenarios, particularly when excluding what would be considered "consumption" expenditure in the analysis presented here, therefore appear to be well within the capability of the global economy to finance.

Figure 6.13 ▶ **Global economy-wide investment trends by region, 2001-2012**

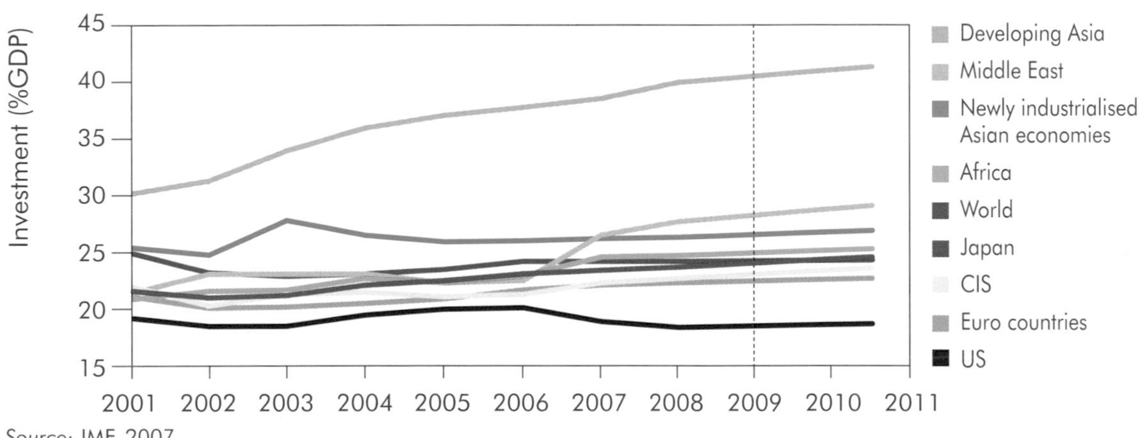

Source: IMF, 2007.

Key point

Since 2001, global investment as a share of GDP has been growing in most regions.

The key issue for policy makers, however, will be to ensure that the required investment in clean energy technologies and energy efficiency will actually occur, and in a timely fashion. Although over the period to 2050 there is sufficient global capacity to meet investment needs, in the short to medium term, ramping up investment in clean energy technologies could prove very challenging. This is critical, however, as any delays in investment in the ACT Map or BLUE Map scenarios would result in significantly higher CO_2 emissions in the early years and hence higher concentrations of GHGs in the atmosphere.

7. Unlike in other chapters, the comparison to global GDP in this chapter is based on GDP at market exchange rates. This is to ensure the direct comparison of monetary values between countries in this analysis.

8. NB many of the additional purchases required in the end-use sectors (such as televisions and dishwashers) that are treated as investments in this analysis are not classified as investment, but as consumption in official statistics.

Within the total level of investment, policy makers will also want to ensure that investment is directed to those cleaner energy developments that have the most economically effective impact on carbon emissions. Currently, wind dominates investment in clean energy, accounting for around 38% of total clean energy investment of USD 70.9 billion, with biofuels accounting for 26%, solar 16% and biomass and waste 10%. Given the low-cost potential of energy efficiency to reduce fuel bills, improve energy security and reduce CO_2 emissions, a disappointingly small proportion (just 6%) of investment is directed towards this area.[9]

Figure 6.14 ▶ Clean energy investment by technology, 2006

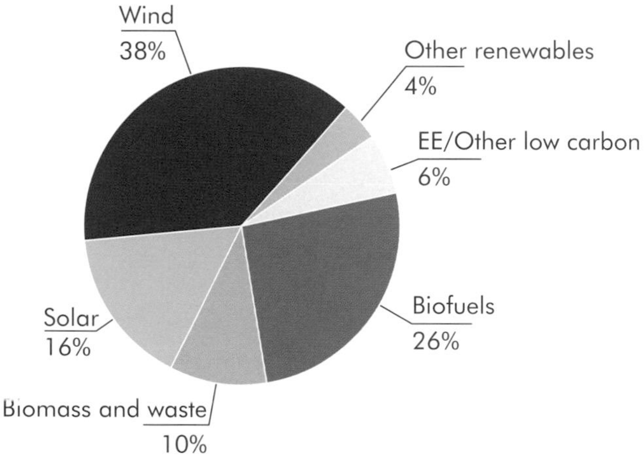

Total: USD 70.9 billion

Source: UNEP and New Energy Finance, 2007.

Key point

Wind, biofuels and solar are currently attracting the largest share of clean energy investment.

Figure 6.15 shows the total average annual investment from 2005 to 2050 for renewable electricity generation technologies, nuclear and CCS, as well as *incremental* average annual investment in energy efficiency for the final demand sectors[10] in the ACT Map and BLUE Map scenarios. In the Baseline scenario, average annual investment between 2005 and 2050 for the categories considered in Figure 6.15 is only 36% higher than in 2006. This is because this scenario assumes no new policies and supposes that the current high levels of investment in biofuels, solar and wind all decline over time. In the ACT Map scenario, average annual investment needs for 2005 to 2050 in energy efficiency and clean energy technologies is almost 10 times as high as in 2006. In the BLUE Map scenario,

9. Given the difficulty of tracking all utility and other energy efficiency programmes, this figure is probably a significant under-estimate of the true investment in energy efficiency.

10. This figure only includes a sample of the investment needs in this chapter, to ensure the data are directly comparable with the available historic data for 2006.

investment is 18.4 times as high as it was in 2006. The additional investment needs for energy efficiency in the residential, commercial and industry sectors in the ACT Map scenario is 17 times current estimated levels of investment, in the BLUE Map scenario it is 50 times current estimated levels.

Figure 6.15 ▶ **Average annual clean energy investment for selected technologies and sectors, 2006 and 2005-2050**

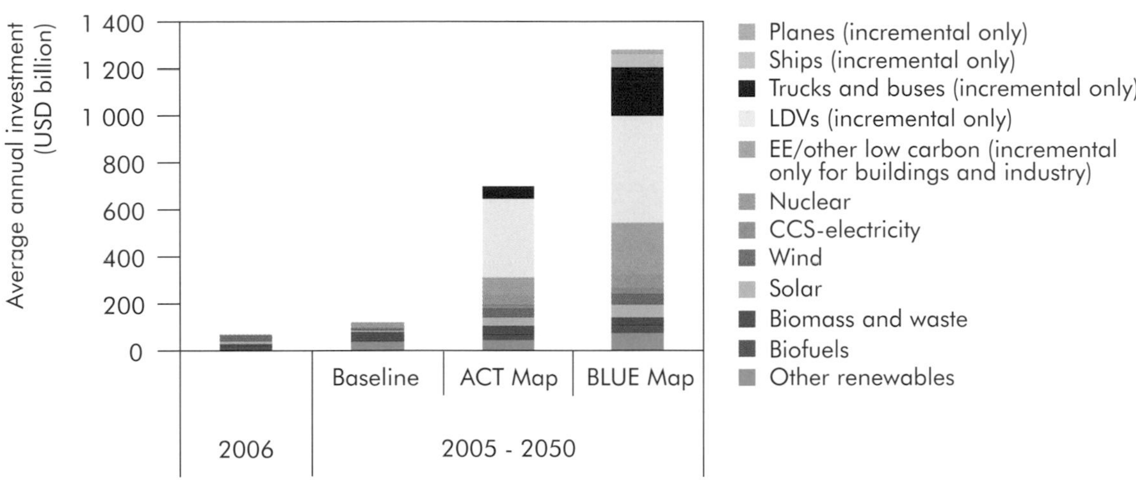

Sources: UNEP and New Energy Finance, 2007 and IEA.

Key point

Investment in clean energy technologies and energy efficiency in the ACT Map and BLUE Map scenarios is dramatically higher than current investment.

Bringing about a rebalancing of overall investment towards clean energy technologies and energy efficiency represents a significant challenge, particularly in the short to medium term. Those sectors that are likely to be the most capable of making the transition are the upstream sectors, although this may not always be the case. If policies create a secure and stable long-term market for clean energy technologies, then the upstream companies have the expertise, institutional capacity and financing ability to ensure that investment takes place. This is clear from the current surge in investment in biofuels production capacity and wind and solar. However, governments will also need to ensure that deployment policies and CO_2-reduction incentive mechanisms are put in place to ensure that low-carbon technologies that are currently more expensive than fossil-fuel options are taken up. For those technologies that are not as close to market deployment, RD&D support will also be critical.

Perhaps the most significant challenge lies in ensuring that investment in energy efficient end-use technologies occurs in a timely fashion. There are a number of barriers to this. These problems are not insurmountable, but they will require careful examination of different product markets and consumers so that policies can be tailored both to promote more efficient technology options and to ensure that consumers invest in those technologies in a timely manner. In OECD countries, multi-policy packages that address all of the barriers to energy efficiency uptake will be the most relevant and likely to succeed (IEA, 2007b). In developing countries, lack of access to credit and the high risks associated with debt when living close to the poverty line will often mean that poorer consumers are not in a position to choose least life-cycle cost products. Experience in developed and developing countries with the successful financing of energy efficiency programmes will need to be adapted to meet the specific needs of different countries in the ramp-up of investment that is required in the ACT Map and BLUE Map scenarios.

Financial barriers to investment in clean and efficient technologies

Like any other new technology, new supply- and demand-side energy technologies will face barriers in the development chain from R&D through to demonstration and to full commercial deployment. Chapter 5 examines the technical and deployment barriers, while the following section discusses the often-faced financial barriers.

The uptake of clean energy technologies and energy efficiency is likely to be inhibited by a number of financially related barriers, including:

- New technologies are often perceived to carry higher risks than mature technologies (including areas such as operation and maintenance costs, efficiency and economic life). Investors may also lack confidence in them.
- High initial costs compared to existing technologies can be a barrier for capital-constrained consumers, or where financial markets are immature or ill-adapted to clean energy technologies and energy efficiency investments.
- Information may not be available to consumers to enable them to make a valid comparison of investment options. The absence of international standards and codes can exacerbate this.
- Small investments may suffer from the fact that it is more difficult to develop appropriate financial packages for numerous small investments than for small numbers of large projects. In addition, smaller clean energy or energy efficiency projects are likely to carry higher transaction costs than larger investments.
- Markets, without regulatory intervention, generally fail to properly value the environmental benefits of clean energy technologies.
- New technologies may depend on significant parallel infrastructure investment or on the need for investment to adapt existing infrastructures.
- Tax policies tend to favour existing low-investment cost technologies, for example by enabling fuel expenditures to be deducted from tax in the year of use. Clean energy technologies tend to have a higher tax burden because they are more capital-intensive.

- "Split incentives" can occur between asset owners and users. This is the classic principal-agent problem: for example, where the owner of an apartment or building has an incentive only to minimise up-front capital costs, but not to minimise life-cycle costs of energy consumption – because energy-consumption costs are born by the tenant.

Many of these barriers are not just financial. They are also influenced by consumer behaviour and psychology. Achieving significant CO_2 emission reductions will be heavily dependent on these barriers being tackled, particularly in the BLUE Map scenario. Integrated policies will need to be designed to ensure that proper emphasis is placed on addressing these financial barriers.

Policy issues and options

Governments need to create a stable policy environment that promotes low carbon technologies and energy efficiency. This is critical in the ACT Map scenario, and even more so in the BLUE Map scenario. It will require unprecedented co-operation and co-ordination between developed and developing countries to ensure that an international framework is put in place to incentivise investment in low carbon technologies and energy efficiency. Setting stable long-term policy frameworks will help to reduce regulatory uncertainty and thus reduce the risk to individuals and businesses of investing in clean energy technologies and energy efficiency. However, good policy design is just as important as early implementation. Unnecessary volatility in the CO_2 reduction incentive would have a negative impact on investment decisions and lead to unnecessary delays in investment in clean-energy technologies. This could lock in dirty and inefficient capital equipment for as much as 40 years in the case of new investments in coal-fired electricity generation plant.

Another important goal is the reduction or elimination of subsidies to fossil fuels. These subsidies, often introduced with social or development goals in mind, are generally an inefficient way of meeting their declared goals, and encourage inefficiency and waste. Phasing out these subsidies should be a top priority; they can be replaced if necessary by more efficient, targeted social and development programmes. Although their absolute level is uncertain, fossil-fuel subsidies could be in the region of USD 600 billion annually (Upton, 2007). This is some 40% more than the annual additional investment needs of the ACT Map scenario and around half of the average annual additional investment needs of the BLUE Map scenario. The removal of these subsidy costs would provide a potentially major contribution to the investment needs of the ACT Map and BLUE Map scenarios.

The ACT Map and BLUE Map scenarios imply two significant new challenges if the necessary investment is to occur in a timely fashion. First, the importance of demand-side investment means that financing mechanisms and policies will have to be integrated into energy efficiency policy to influence the investment decisions of individuals and households. Second, the scale of clean energy and energy efficiency investment needed in non-OECD countries is such as to suggest a need both for a significant expansion of current funding arrangements and for new and innovative funding mechanisms.

In general, OECD countries are likely to have sufficient capital, or access to it, to finance their own needs in new technology investment, although ensuring that this actually occurs will require significant policy effort. The situation for many developing countries is often much more difficult. Although savings rates may be high, domestic and international investment is often not forthcoming. Better economic policy, improved regulation and more effective financial markets would all contribute to facilitating appropriate investment in developing countries. These countries will also require assistance in policy and capacity building, as well as in financing mechanisms and technology transfer.

The ACT Map and BLUE Map scenarios assume that, in parallel with climate change policy, economic and financial policies evolve to facilitate the needed investment. However, effort will be needed to bring this about. If successful, such changes will have significant economic and social benefits in developing countries, in addition to their environmental benefits.

End-use efficiency improvements in the transportation, industry, commercial and residential sectors reduce the need for investment in upstream energy supply, but these clean energy investment requirements shift the balance of investment from the supply-side to the demand-side. This represents a significant challenge, as demand-side policies often need to influence a wide-range of actors facing a myriad of individual circumstances.

Capital markets in developing countries differ in several important ways from those in developed countries. These differences are important in analysing options for providing credit to the poor. Many particular issues in developing countries prevent consumers from obtaining a loan to finance cleaner energy technologies, including limited collateral, limited investment options, high transaction costs, and isolated and thinly competitive financial markets. These issues are also often coupled with high delinquency and default rates.

International financial institutions have had many decades of experience in tailoring policies and programmes to help overcome these barriers in their efforts to improve investment in infrastructure, education and health services. Where strong partnerships have been formed with donors and recipient countries alike, there have been some significant success stories. Building on this experience and those of other organisations also active in these areas will be critical to ensuring that the essential investment is made in clean energy technologies and energy efficiency.

A wide range of funding mechanisms specifically facilitate investment in developing countries in clean energy options and carbon reduction and energy efficiency opportunities. Although they are substantial in size, it is nonetheless clear from the *Energy Technology Perspectives* scenarios that these existing financing mechanisms are too small to facilitate the scale of transition implied in the ACT Map and BLUE Map scenarios. Even so, these mechanisms can provide a nucleus of expertise and experience that could be used to significantly expand their size and role, as well as to help other organizations to engage in this area effectively.

The magnitude of the investment challenge is not lost on international financial institutions. They are active in trying to expand the financing capacity available for clean energy and efficiency investment. The World Bank has proposed two new funds, the Clean Energy Financing Vehicle (CEFV) and the Clean Energy Support Fund (CESF). The CEFV would blend public and private sources of financing. It would assist in scaling-up clean energy technologies, reduce the incremental costs of clean energy technologies and related energy infrastructure through increased deployment, and help stimulate investments in the carbon market. An initial capitalisation of USD 10 billion, with an annual disbursement of up to USD 2 billion, was suggested by the World Bank (2006). This would provide low-interest loans to cover the incremental capital costs with the carbon credits generated assigned to the CEFV. Initial equity could be provided via direct cash contributions from developed countries, although the fund itself would be expected to generate a reasonable rate of return to attract, over time, private capital.

The CESF would be a subsidy mechanism to support projects according to the amount of carbon emissions they reduced. It would operate on a grant financing basis, with funding provided by donors. The CESF would provide a subsidy based on the incremental costs required to achieve carbon savings. Eligible projects would be competitively selected to ensure the lowest subsidy is paid. The project's carbon credits would be pledged to the CESF.

PART 3 ENERGY TECHNOLOGY: STATUS AND OUTLOOK

Chapter 7 FOSSIL FUEL-FIRED POWER PLANTS AND CO_2 CAPTURE AND STORAGE

Key Findings

- *Already available clean coal technologies can make a significant contribution to containing the growth of CO_2 emissions from power generation. Use of advanced steam cycle or integrated gasification combined-cycle (IGCC) technologies could raise the average efficiency of coal-fired power plants from 35% today to 50% in 2050.*

- *The age of a country's power plants will be an important factor, as the current efficiency of most coal-fired power plants is well below state-of-the-art. A gradual replacement of smaller subcritical coal-fired units should be considered, along with retrofitting larger-scale plants to achieve higher efficiencies (preferably >40%) and to enable CO_2 capture and storage (CCS).*

- *New power plants should be designed to be suitable for CCS retrofitting, and located in places where they can be connected to suitable storage sites.*

- *Many components of the CCS chain (capture, transportation, storage) have been validated at an industrial scale for more than a decade. Costs across the whole chain have been rising since 2005 in most countries due to the general increase in material costs and engineering shortages. It is unclear whether such increases will continue.*

- *Near-zero emissions can be achieved using fossil fuels with CCS. A CO_2 reduction incentive of USD 50 per tonne will be necessary for wide-scale deployment of CCS in the power sector. Enhanced oil recovery (EOR) provides early opportunities for technology demonstration at a lower cost. In the BLUE Map scenario, nearly 20% of the emissions reduction will originate from CCS in the power sector.*

- *Full-scale deployment of CCS requires a significant effort in demonstration and the development of a suitable infrastructure. Development of the legal and regulatory frameworks, CO_2 reduction incentive pricing, financial support for RD&D, and public outreach are needed to enable CCS. From a technical viewpoint, CCS may become a mature technology for fossil-fuelled power plants by 2020.*

- *Combined heat and power (CHP) can significantly raise energy supply efficiency, but barriers need to be removed and appropriate policies are needed. With further research and demonstration, CHP can expand into new commercial and residential markets to lower the costs of high-temperature CHP, fuel cell CHP and micro-turbine CHP.*

- *Natural gas fuel cells for distributed generation or back-up power are currently used in demonstration projects or niche applications. Fuel cells and other emerging decentralised power generation technologies are expected to raise overall fuel efficiencies, but require further RD&D.*

Overview

The current mix of natural gas and coal in electricity generation varies by country and region depending on resource availability and domestic fuel prices. Overall, 40% of the world's electricity production comes from coal and 20% from gas. In South Africa and Poland the share of coal in power generation is above 90%. In China and Australia it is close to 80%, as in India, where it is more than two-thirds. Coal accounts for around half of electricity generation in the United States and Germany, one-third in the United Kingdom, one-quarter in Japan and one-sixth in Russia. Russia produces almost half of its electricity from gas, the United Kingdom close to 40% and the United States and Japan around 20%.

Carbon-dioxide emissions from fossil fuel-fired plants can be reduced by improving conversion efficiency – by modernising and refurbishing existing plants and deploying the best available technologies in new plants; by co-firing coal with biomass, adding biogas to natural gas and employing CCS; and by switching from coal to natural gas.[1] The best combination of mitigation measures depends on the existing power generation stock, the price of competing fuels and the cost of alternative technologies.

In the Baseline scenario, without a CO_2 reduction price incentive, coal dominates the power sector, with nearly 50% of the total power generation in 2050 (Figure 7.1).

Figure 7.1 ▶ **Share of power generation in the baseline, ACT Map and BLUE Map scenarios**

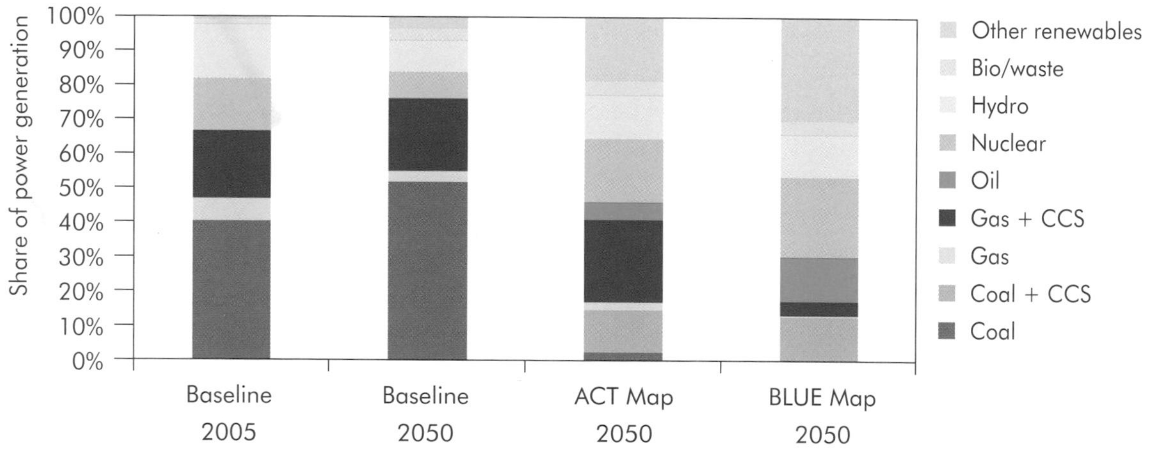

Source: IEA Statistics, IEA 2006.

Key point

In the baseline scenario, coal's share in power generation increases from 40% in 2005 to more than 50% in 2050. In the ACT Map and BLUE Map scenarios, all coal-fired power generation will incorporate CCS in 2050.

1. Efficiency figures in this chapter are based on lower heating values (LHV). LHVs, unlike higher heating values (HHV), do not include the latent heat of the moisture originally present in the fuel or from combustion of the coal hydrogen. European and IEA statistics are reported on an LHV basis, while United States statistics are reported on an HHV basis. On these bases, HHV efficiencies are about 2% lower than LHVs for coal-fired power plants and 5% lower for gas-fired combined-cycle plants.

Overview

The current mix of natural gas and coal in electricity generation varies by country and region depending on resource availability and domestic fuel prices. Overall, 40% of the world's electricity production comes from coal and 20% from gas. In South Africa and Poland the share of coal in power generation is above 90%. In China and Australia it is close to 80%, as in India, where it is more than two-thirds. Coal accounts for around half of electricity generation in the United States and Germany, one-third in the United Kingdom, one-quarter in Japan and one-sixth in Russia. Russia produces almost half of its electricity from gas, the United Kingdom close to 40% and the United States and Japan around 20%.

Carbon-dioxide emissions from fossil fuel-fired plants can be reduced by improving conversion efficiency – by modernising and refurbishing existing plants and deploying the best available technologies in new plants; by co-firing coal with biomass, adding biogas to natural gas and employing CCS; and by switching from coal to natural gas.[1] The best combination of mitigation measures depends on the existing power generation stock, the price of competing fuels and the cost of alternative technologies.

In the Baseline scenario, without a CO_2 reduction price incentive, coal dominates the power sector, with nearly 50% of the total power generation in 2050 (Figure 7.1).

Figure 7.1 ▶ Share of power generation in the baseline, ACT Map and BLUE Map scenarios

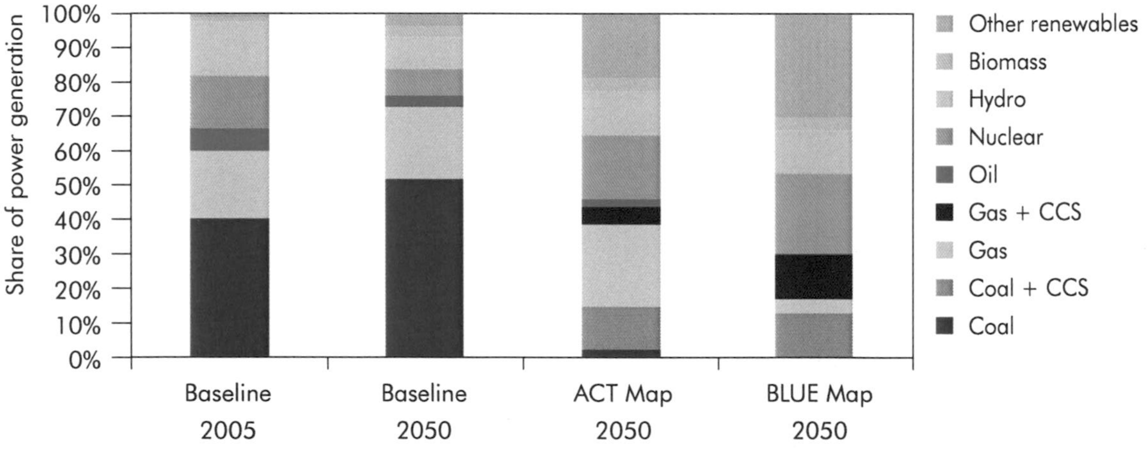

Source: IEA Statistics, IEA 2006.

Key point

In the baseline scenario, coal's share in power generation increases from 40% in 2005 to more than 50% in 2050. In the ACT Map and BLUE Map scenarios, all coal-fired power generation will incorporate CCS in 2050.

1. Efficiency figures in this chapter are based on lower heating values (LHV). LHVs, unlike higher heating values (HHV), do not include the latent heat of the moisture originally present in the fuel or from combustion of the coal hydrogen. European and IEA statistics are reported on an LHV basis, while United States statistics are reported on an HHV basis. On these bases, HHV efficiencies are about 2% lower than LHVs for coal-fired power plants and 5% lower for gas-fired combined-cycle plants.

Gas is the second largest fuel source with 23%. Hydropower and nuclear are the other key contributors. In the ACT Map scenario, the total fossil fuel share of power generation decreases from 72% to 43%, with the bulk of the difference made up from renewables and nuclear. There is also a significant shift in the coal/gas mix towards gas. The BLUE Map scenario has a total share of coal that is similar to that of the ACT Map, although in the BLUE Map scenario nearly 60% of coal-fired power generation and 41% of gas-fired power incorporates CCS.

In the Baseline scenario, CO_2 emissions from the power sector alone increase to 27 Gt in 2050, equal to the total CO_2 emissions in 2005 (Figure 7.2). In the ACT Map scenario, CCS in the power sector amounts to 2.9 Gt per year by 2050. In the BLUE Map scenario, 2050 emissions from the power generation sector drop to 2 Gt, a reduction of more than 80% from the 2005 level.

Figure 7.2 ▶ **CO_2 emissions from the power sector in the Baseline, ACT Map and BLUE Map scenarios**

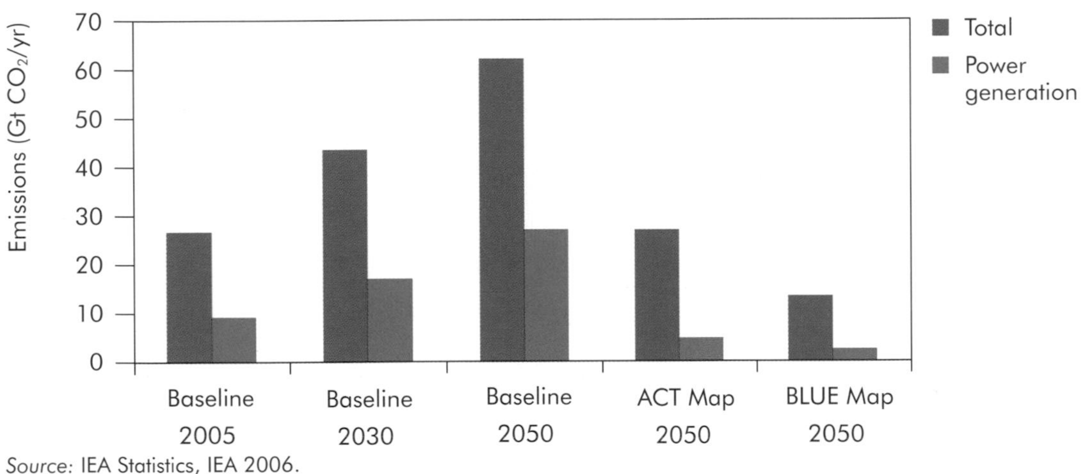

Source: IEA Statistics, IEA 2006.

Key point

In the Baseline scenario, CO_2 emissions from the power sector alone increase in 2050 to more than the total CO_2 emissions in 2005.

The current status of coal and natural gas-fired electricity generation

Power generation using natural gas is competitive with coal at today's prices for natural gas and coal in many regions of the world (for gas, typically USD 4 to USD 8 per GJ). However, fuel costs in natural gas combined-cycle (NGCC) plants account for 60% to 75% of total generation costs, as compared to plants powered by renewables, nuclear or coal, where fuel costs account for between 0% and 40% (Figure 7.3). Rises in gas prices in the United States and Europe in recent years have resulted in a switch from gas to coal-fired generation. A rapid development of natural gas-fired power generation could strain gas production and transmission systems and lead to further natural gas price increases.

Box 2.1 ▶ Coal-fired power generation in China

Installed power generation capacity in China has increased nearly ten-fold from 1985 to 2006, reaching 622 GW. This includes 100 GW of new capacity in 2006 alone. Installed coal-fired capacity in China is projected to increase under the IEA WEO Reference Scenario to 814 GW in 2015 and to 1 259 GW in 2030. The 4 × 1 000 MW Huaneng Yuhuan power plant in Zhejiang province (Eastern China) is the world's largest coal-fired plant using ultra-supercritical technology. It has a target efficiency of more than 45% (HHV). China also has, however, a very large number of small-scale subcritical power plants. 78% of the total electricity supply in 2006 was from coal-fired power plants (mostly based on pulverised coal). The average coal consumption of plants in China is more than 50 gce/kWh higher than for state-of-the-art USC units – this is equivalent to using 100 Mtce a year more than could be achieved with the best available technologies. China is the world's largest coal consumer, and if Chinese plants were as efficient as the average plant in Japan, coal demand would be 21% less in China.

Table 7.1 shows emissions relative to electricity generation in China's coal-fired plants. The expected introduction of large numbers of supercritical and ultra supercritical plants, along with the retirement of older small capacity units, is expected to improve average efficiency from 32% in 2005 to 39% in 2030, and should reduce emissions by 25% in 2030 compared to 2005.

Table 7.1 ▶ Coal-fired electricity generation and CO_2 emissions in China

Reference scenario	1990	2005	2015	2030
Generation (TWh)	471	1 996	4 326	6 586
Capacity GW	87	368	814	1 259
CO_2 (Mt)	598	2 424	4 328	5 997
Emissions Ratio (Mt CO_2/TWh)	1.27	1.21	1.00	0.91

Source: IEA 2007c.

Figure 7.3 ▶ Investment, O&M and fuel costs of natural gas and coal-fired power generation

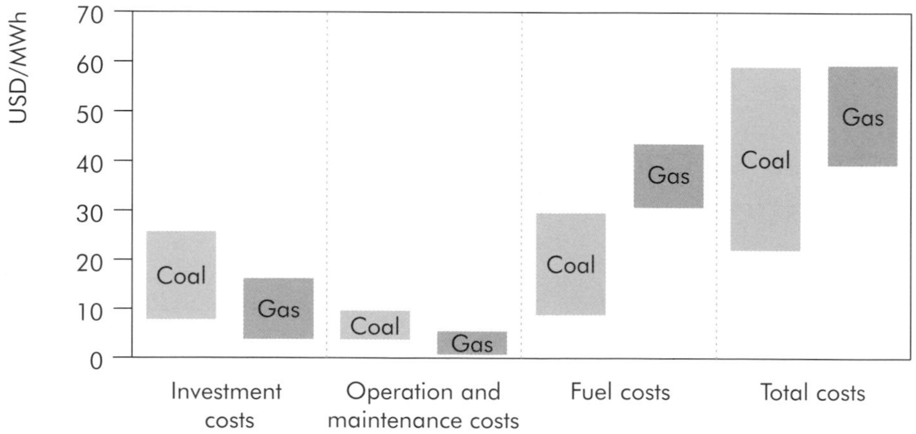

Sources: IEA Greenhouse Gas R&D Programme (IEA GHG); IEA Clean Coal Centre (IEA CCC).

Key point

Natural gas plants are more sensitive to fuel costs, while coal plants are generally more capital intensive.

Power generation efficiency

Coal

The efficiency of hard coal-fired power plants averaged about 35% from 1992 to 2005 globally. The best available coal-fired plants can achieve 47%. The efficiency of brown coal-fired power plants increased from 33% in 1992 to 35% in 2005.

In 2005, the average efficiency of hard coal-fired power plants ranged from 33% in China to 42% in Japan. The average efficiency of hard coal-fired plants in the United States has not changed significantly over the last 30 years, while the efficiency of plants in Western Europe and China has increased by about 6 percentage points. Relatively low coal prices in the United States provide little economic incentive to invest in more efficient technology.

The current efficiency of most coal-fired power plants is well below the levels that are already possible – and there is much potential for significant efficiency improvements in state-of-the-art technologies. Efficiency gains can be realised by improving existing plants or by installing new-generation technology. The cost to retrofit or replace an existing plant depends on the efficiency and age of the stock. The younger the plant, the more economical it is to retrofit an existing plant. The efficiency of power plants also depends on the quality of their fuel (especially in the case of coal), their environmental standards and their operation mode. All else being equal, power plants using high-ash, high-moisture coal (such as those used in India) have a lower efficiency than plants using low-ash, low-moisture coal. The cleaning of flue gases requires energy and, therefore, reduces power plant efficiency. Running plants below their rated output, a common practice in market-driven electricity supply systems, also substantially reduces plant efficiency.

Pulverised coal combustion (PCC) accounts for about 97% of the world's coal-fired capacity. Improving the efficiency of PCC plants has been the focus of considerable efforts by the industry as it seeks to stay competitive and to become more environmentally acceptable. PCC *subcritical* steam power plants, with steam pressure of around 180 bar, temperatures of 540°C and combustor-unit sizes up to 1 000 MW, are commercially available and in use worldwide. The average net efficiency (after in-plant power consumption) of larger subcritical plants burning higher quality coal is between 35% and 36%. New subcritical units with conventional environmental controls operate closer to 39% efficiency. The overall efficiency of older, smaller PCC plants that burn low quality coal, can be below 30%.

Supercritical steam-cycle plants with steam pressures of around 240 bar to 260 bar and temperatures of around 570°C have become the system of choice for new commercial coal-fired plants in many countries. Early supercritical units developed in Europe and the United States in the 1970s lacked operational flexibility and reliability and experienced maintenance problems. These difficulties have been overcome. In Europe and Japan, plants with supercritical steam operate reliably and economically at net thermal efficiencies in the range of 42% to 45%, and even higher in some favourable locations. *Ultra-supercritical* plants are supercritical pressure units with steam temperatures of approximately 580°C and above.

Integrated coal gasification combined-cycle (IGCC) plants are a fundamentally different coal technology, and are now expected to become commercially available. A small number of plants that were initially built with public funding as demonstrators are currently operating, with the best one achieving 42% electric efficiency. Future coal-fired steam units and IGCC plants are expected to achieve efficiencies above 50% in demonstrator projects within ten years.

For coal with high ash and sulphur content, fluidised bed combustion (FBC) in boilers operating at atmospheric pressure could be more efficient than PCC. FBC relies on two technologies: bubbling beds (BFBC) and circulating beds (CFBC), the latter being more commonly used for power generation applications. The power generation efficiency of larger CFBC units (200 MW to 300 MW) is generally comparable to that of PCC plants, because they use steam turbine cycles that operate under similar conditions.

Brown coal (lignite) is expected to increase its contribution to coal supply in some countries. It has a higher water content than hard coal, a lower heating value, and different boiler requirements. The optimal technology choice for hard coal and lignite may differ, as the availability and price of different coal types affects the power generation technology choice.

Gas

There is considerable scope to increase the efficiency of natural gas-fired generation, primarily by replacing gas-fired steam cycles with more efficient combined-cycle plants. Because open-cycle plants are used as peaking plants, their annual use is low – which makes their low efficiency more acceptable from a cost perspective. A natural gas combined-cycle plant consists of a gas turbine and a steam cycle. A gas-fired steam cycle has an efficiency similar to that of a coal-fired plant.

The average efficiency of natural gas-fired power plants increased from 35% in 1992 to 42% in 2005. Most of the improvement in efficiency was a result of the introduction of large combined-cycle units, which now account for 38% of global gas-fired capacity.

In 2005, the average efficiency of natural gas-fired power plants ranged from about 33% in Russia to 49% in Western Europe. Average efficiencies in Europe have increased since 1990 with the introduction of natural gas, combined-cycle units. The range of efficiencies among regions widened, mainly because of rapid efficiency gains in Western Europe. If Russian gas-fired plants had the same average efficiency as that of Western Europe, they would use one-third less gas for the same output.

Since the early 1990s, NGCC has been the preferred technology for new gas-fired generation plants. Efficiencies of the best available combined-cycle plants are 60%. The new Siemens-E.ON NGCC plant under construction is expected to be the first over 60%. Natural gas plant efficiency, however, falls considerably when plants are run at widely varying loads. This explains why reported fleet efficiencies fall below quoted design efficiencies.

Because of the long lifespan (up to 60 years) of power plants, the average efficiency of currently operating power plants that are not implementing appropriate plant operation and maintenance is substantially lower than that which could be achieved by the best available technology. Power producers primarily aim to minimise their production costs, not to maximise efficiency – and these two objectives do not always coincide.

CO_2 emissions

A comparison of average efficiencies with the best available power plant efficiency (as shown in Table 7.2) shows that fuel consumption and CO_2 emissions could be reduced considerably if the best available technologies were employed for retrofitting existing power plants.

Table 7.2 ▶ Performance summary for different fossil fuel-fired plants

Plant type		PCC	PCC	PCC	PCC	NGCC	IGCC
Fuel		**Hard coal**	**Hard coal**	**Hard coal**	**Hard coal**	**Natural gas**	**Hard coal**
Steam cycle		Sub-critical	Typical super-critical	Ultra-super-critical (best available)	Ultra-supercritical (AD700)	Triple pressure reheat	Triple pressure reheat
Steam conditions		180 bar 540°C 540°C	250 bar 560°C 560°C	300 bar 600°C 620°C	350 bar 700°C 700°C	124 bar 566°C 566°C	124 bar 563°C 563°C
Gross output	MW	500	500	500	500	500	500
Auxiliary power	MW	42	42	44	43	11	67
Net output	MW	458	458	456	457	489	433
Gross efficiency	%	43.9	45.9	47.6	49.9	59.3	50.9
Net efficiency	%	40.2	42.0	43.4	45.6	58.1	44.1
CO_2 emitted	t/h	381	364	352	335	170	321
Specific CO_2 emitted	t/MWh net	0.83	0.80	0.77	0.73	0.35	0.74

Source: Loyd, 2007.

More information on designs for high efficiency and the potential of efficiency improvements can be found in IEA, 2007b, 2008a and 2008b.

Efficiency improvements can significantly reduce CO_2 and other emissions. For a power plant with efficiency of 30%, an increase in efficiency to 45% brings about a 33% decrease in CO_2 emissions. Improvements in the average efficiency of coal-fired power plants are already feasible. Two-thirds of all coal-fired plants are over 20 years old. Such plants have an average net efficiency of 29% or lower, and emit at least 3.9 Gt CO_2 per year. If all of these were replaced by plants with efficiencies of 45%, CO_2 emissions would be reduced by 1.4 Gt per year.

Efficiency improvements also have the potential to reduce emissions of sulphur dioxide and, in certain cases, nitrous oxides (NO_X). Natural gas, combined-cycle plants have the lowest CO_2 emissions of all fossil fuel-based technologies, because of the low carbon intensity of natural gas and the high efficiency of the plants (Figure 7.4).

Figure 7.4 ▶ The impact of fuel and efficiency on the CO_2 emissions of power plants

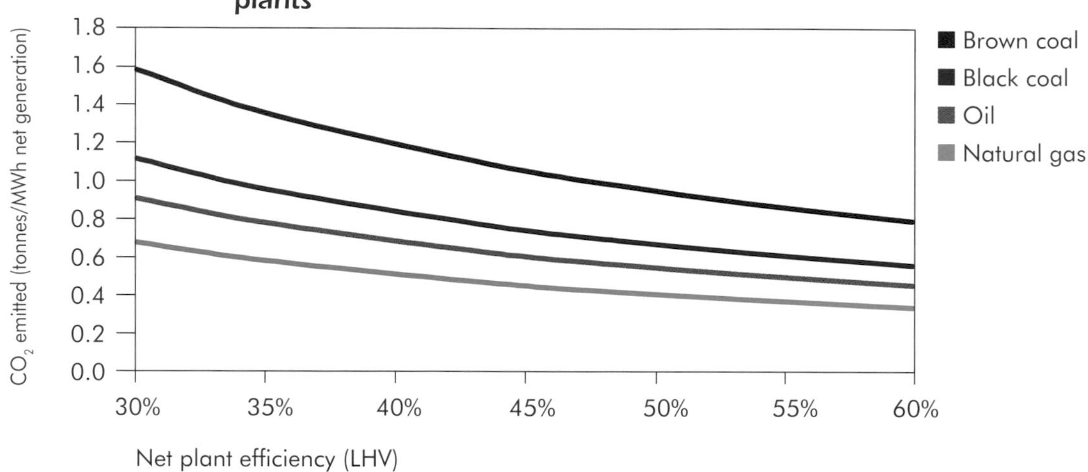

Source: Loyd, 2007.

Key point

CO_2 emissions per MWh net generated decrease by nearly 50% when net plant efficiency is doubled.

Age profile of the capital stock

The age of a coal-fired generation plant has a considerable impact on the potential for CO_2 emission reductions. Outage rates for coal-fired plants are generally about 5% for plants that are 10 to 20 years old. Unless the plant is refurbished, the rate increases to 20% for plants that are 40 years old. In the United States, repowering projects for existing coal plants have significantly extended plant lifetimes and in certain cases have resulted in substantial efficiency improvements. China is planning to repower existing plants by introducing CFBC steam boilers and by replacing pulverised coal subcritical boilers with supercritical plants. Measures to reduce pollutant emissions may also be detrimental to boiler life. Electricity market liberalisation has brought more start-and-stop cycles than were contemplated in original plant designs, which has considerably reduced boiler life (Paterson and Wilson, 2002).

Given a lifespan of 40 to 60 years, retrofits may be considered for many coal fired plants. In China, the bulk of coal-fired power plant stock is under 15 years old, so retrofitting existing stock may be a good option, as it may be in the United Kingdom, where 30-year old plants may be subject to life extensions. In Germany, about one-third of the stock is under 15 years old, and may be suitable for retrofitting, as in India where plants are on average 20 years old (IEA, 2008a). Construction of coal-fired stock in the United States peaked around 1970. Many of these plants will have to be replaced between 2010 and 2030 and may not therefore be candidates for retrofitting. Our scenario analysis indicates that at around USD 25 per tonne of CO_2, old plants may have higher operation costs than the total costs of a new plant with CCS.

Technology status/development

Advanced steam cycles

Supercritical and ultra-supercritical plants are defined by the steam temperatures they generate. Supercritical plants use steam temperatures of 540°C and above, while ultra-supercritical plants use steam at 580°C and above. Supercritical steam-cycle technology has been used in OECD countries for several decades. Typically, a switch from supercritical to ultra-supercritical steam conditions would raise efficiency by another 4 percentage points. Overall, the efficiency of ultra-supercritical pressure units could be in the range of 50% to 55% by 2020.

Supercritical technology is already used in a number of countries. In China, more than 18 GW of supercritical units were installed in 2006. There are ultra-supercritical plants in operation in Japan, Denmark and Germany. Ultra-supercritical units operating at temperatures of 700°C and higher are still in the RD&D phase. They will need to use nickel-based super-alloys for some components. These are already used in gas turbines, but larger components are needed for steam boilers and turbines, and the operating environment is different. International programmes such as the EC-supported AD700 project and the associated COMTES700 demonstration in Germany, as well as national programmes such as COORETEC in Germany, are seeking to develop the necessary materials and components (IEA, 2007b).

Because of fuel savings, the total investment cost for ultra-supercritical steam-cycle plants can be 12% to 15% higher than the cost of a subcritical steam-cycle and still be competitive. The balance-of-plant cost is 13% to 16% lower in an ultra-supercritical plant, because of reduced coal handling and reduced flue gas handling. The boiler and steam turbine costs can be as much as 40 to 50% higher for an ultra-supercritical plant. Studies in the United States of supercritical coal power plants indicate a relatively low learning rate of 5% for the capital cost.

In power plants based on steam cycles, the introduction of coal drying for lignite may improve efficiency by up to 4 percentage points. This technology is expected to be commercial by 2010.

The major barriers to advances in supercritical and ultra-supercritical steam cycles concern metallurgical and control problems. Developments in new steels for water and steam boiler tubes and in high-alloy steels that minimise corrosion are expected to result in a dramatic increase in the number of supercritical plants installed over the next few years. New control equipment and strategies will also allow these plants to be more flexible than in the past.

Fluidised bed combustion (FBC)

Two parallel paths have so far been pursued in FBC development – bubbling (BFBC) and circulating (CFBC) beds. Another promising option, particularly for CO_2 capture, is a circulating fluidised bed (CFB) power plant working with O_2 instead of air. In this case, solids are cooled down before their return to the bed. Consequently, the temperature can be controlled more effectively. This could lead to a significant reduction in flue gas recirculation, thereby reducing both investment and operating costs.

There are hundreds of atmospheric CFBC units operating worldwide, including a number of plants as large as 250 MW to 300 MW. Fluidised beds are particularly suited to the combustion of low-quality coals and most of the existing CFBC plants burn such materials. Moving to supercritical cycles is a logical step for very large CFBC units. A 460 MW supercritical unit is under construction at Lagisza, Poland, and is due for start-up at the beginning of 2009. This unit is expected to have a thermal efficiency of 43%. Designs for even larger 600 MW supercritical CFBC units have also been developed.

Other advantages of CFBC systems include fuel flexibility, good emissions performance and the ability to scale up from a few megawatt to over 500 MW. CFBC technology is a near-term solution, because it uses commercially available technologies including oxygen production and CO_2 stream gas processing.

FBC can also be employed at high pressure, in which case the boiler exhaust gases can be used to generate additional power. Heat is also recovered from the exhaust of the turbine. This approach has been applied in demonstrations at a small number of locations. The result is a form of combined gas and steam cycle that gives efficiencies of up to around 44%. The first of such units had a capacity of about 80 MW, but two larger units are operating in Karita and Osaki, Japan, the former using supercritical steam.

Second generation pressurised FBC cycles (such as hybrid systems incorporating higher-temperature turbines with supplementary firing of coal-derived gas after the combustor) have been considered in some locations, including Japan, but their development is unlikely.

Further work is required to understand the oxyfuel combustion conditions to further clarify the mechanisms involved in pollutant formation and carbonation due to high CO_2 concentrations. Design considerations, particularly for supercritical boilers, are also important areas of research. It is also necessary to learn more about fuel flexibility and options for cost-effective CO_2 sequestration.

Natural gas combined-cycle (NGCC)

Today, NGCC power plants are often preferred over conventional coal-fired plants due to:

- efficiency achievements topping 60%;
- lower capital costs of USD 600 to USD 750 per kW, compared with USD 1 400 to USD 2 000 per kW for a typical coal-fired plant;
- shorter construction times;

- lower emissions: NGCC plants emit less than half the CO_2 emissions of similarly rated coal-fired plants.

The efficiency of NGCC plants has improved with new gas turbine technology. The General Electric F-class combined-cycle gas turbine (in the 200 MW range) was first introduced in the 1990s. Many of its features derive from jet engine technology. Although commissioning problems have occurred, combined-cycle gas turbine designs have progressed, with advances in both cooling systems and materials, including higher compression ratios and higher firing temperatures. It is estimated that advanced NGCC plants will bring a further reduction of 3% to 6% in CO_2 emissions per kWh of electricity generated. Further efficiency gains are possible if fuel cells are integrated into the design, or if a bottoming cycle using waste heat is added, albeit at higher cost.[2] The IEA has published a case study on recently constructed NGCC plants (IEA, 2007b).

Natural gas turbines are also employed as peaking plants that generate electricity only during periods of high demand. Such single-cycle plants will probably co-exist with advanced NGCC plants, as low capital costs are more important than high efficiencies when the annual load factor is low.

Future R&D efforts are likely to focus on natural gas turbine design and additional efficiency improvements. Gas turbine R&D is aimed at higher firing temperatures and the use of reheat, which gives higher power outputs and efficiencies, but which may increase NO_X formation. A number of counter-measures are under consideration, including the use of novel gas turbine cycles. Many gas turbine manufacturers are also investigating the possibility of more advanced combustors, including catalytic combustors. Other R&D activities aim to increase the aerodynamic efficiencies of components, reduce the number of compressor and turbine stages, and improve turbine-stator and blade-cooling mechanisms.

Integrated gasification combined-cycle (IGCC)

Integrated gasification combined-cycle (IGCC) technology (Maurstad, 2005) comprises four basic steps:

- fuel gas is generated from the partial combustion of solid fuels such as coal at pressure in a limited supply of air or oxygen;
- particulates, sulphur and nitrogen compounds are removed;
- the clean fuel gas is combusted in a gas turbine generator to produce electricity;
- the residual heat in the hot exhaust gas from the gas turbine is recovered in a heat recovery steam generator – the steam is used to produce additional electricity in a steam turbine generator.

IGCC systems are among the cleanest and most efficient of the coal technologies. Gasification technologies can process all carbonaceous feedstocks, including coal, petroleum coke, residual oil, biomass and municipal solid waste. There are seventeen (totalling 4 000 MW) IGCC plants operating in the world today – of which five are using coal alone (IEA CCC, 2007).

2. A bottoming cycle uses a medium with a low boiling temperature, such as an organic solvent.

The net efficiency of existing coal-fired IGCC plants is around 40% to 43% (IEA, 2007b). Recent gas turbines would enable this to be improved, and future developments should take efficiencies beyond 50%. The investment cost of IGCC is about 20% higher than that of PCC. There is, however, more uncertainty in IGCC costs, as there are no recently built coal-fuelled IGCC plants and the existing ones were originally constructed as demonstrations. Availabilities have also not yet reached the demonstrated level of operating PCC units. Suppliers have plans to bring capital costs within 10% of that of PCC.

IGCC reference plant designs of 600 MW have been developed by supplier groupings to encourage market uptake by driving down costs and providing turnkey IGCC plants. This is aimed at facilitating planning and decision-making for power producers. Examples are those from GE-Bechtel and Siemens with ConocoPhillips. With IGCC now available as a commercial package, more orders could follow as utilities see the cost decreasing and availability improving. Subsidies or incentives may still be necessary to cover the higher cost compared with PCC.

IGCC fits well with CCS, and there are CCS projects planned in several countries – including Canada, Australia, Germany and the United Kingdom. Further programmes are being pursued through the United States DOE FutureGen and European Commission Hypogen initiatives and the GreenGen project in China. Inclusion of CCS will reduce efficiency, but the generation cost may be lower than for CO_2 capture on PCC.

Major R&D efforts are ongoing in the field of gasification systems, gas turbines and oxygen production. Research is being carried out to improve efficiency and availability and to reduce capital and operating costs. R&D is focusing on hot gas clean-up, development of large-scale gasifiers with 1 200 MWth to 1 500 MWth for a single train configuration (ZEP, 2006), novel air separation technologies, improved coal feeding systems, improved slag and fly-ash removal systems, system optimisation, and the integration of fuel cells.[3] Cogeneration of electricity and other products, such as hydrogen or other transportation fuels, is also being considered.

Studies have shown that second generation IGCC plants will need to have an investment cost around that of supercritical plants. Second generation IGCC plants are expected to have lower kWh costs than PFBC and supercritical plants. Their competitiveness relative to NGCC plants depends on the evolution in natural gas prices.

Combined heat and power (CHP)

Cogeneration, or combined heat and power (CHP), is the simultaneous utilisation of useful heat and power from a single fuel source. As Figure 7.5 illustrates, by using both heat and power, CHP plants can convert 75% to 80% of the fuel resource into

3. Existing technologies for the removal of contaminants from the generated syngas (before it is fed to the turbine) require significant cooling of the gas. Hot gas cleanup would significantly improve efficiency. Warm gas cleanup is also being explored as an option that could provide most of the benefits of hot gas cleanup while avoiding sorbent attrition costs that render hot gas cleanup uneconomic.

useful energy, with some plants reaching overall efficiencies of 90% or more (IPCC, 2007). In contrast to centralised generation plants, which can experience efficiency losses of 8% to 10% during transmission and distribution, most small decentralised CHP plants experience significantly lower transmission and distribution losses because they are sited near the end user.

Figure 7.5 ▶ Comparison of energy flows from CHP and separate production of heat and electricity

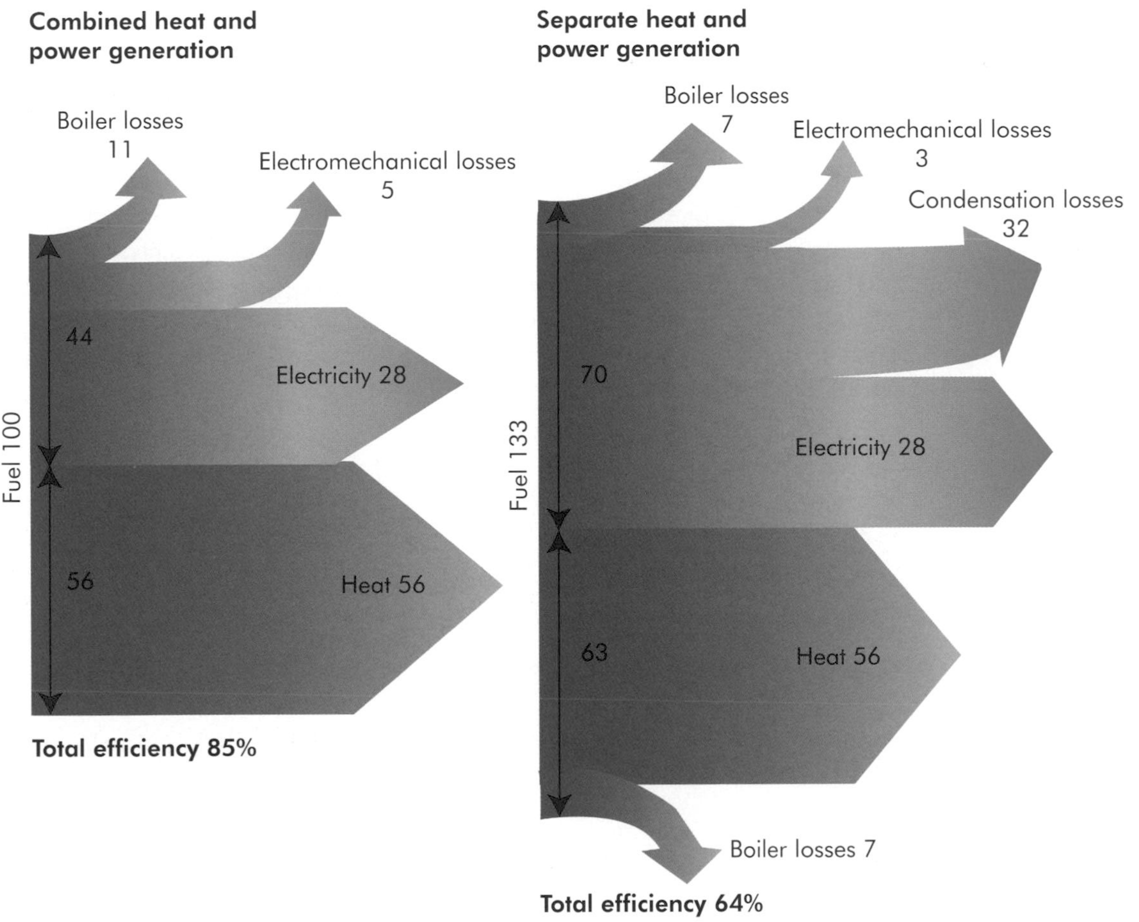

Source : Alakangas and Flyktman, 2001.

Key point

CHP can be more fuel efficient than producing the same amount of heat and electricity in two separate plants.

Almost any fuel is suitable for CHP, although natural gas and coal currently predominate. Some CHP technologies can be fired by multiple fuel types, providing valuable flexibility at a time of growing fuel choice. CHP plant sizes range from 1 kW to 500 MW. For larger plants (greater than 1 MW), equipment is generally tailored to the individual site, but smaller-scale applications can often utilise pre-packaged units. CHP plants are usually sized to meet the required heat demand, selling the excess electricity produced back to the grid.

The efficiency gains from CHP plants depend on the technologies used and the fuel or energy sources employed, and on the heating and power generation systems they replace. In recent years, many countries have begun to differentiate between high- and low-efficiency CHP (UK DEFRA, 2000). Efficiency is typically measured in power-to-heat ratios.

The amount of electricity produced globally from CHP has been gradually increasing, and has now reached more than 6 EJ per year, or more than 10% of total global electricity production. The amount of heat that is cogenerated is not exactly known, but it is in the range of 5 EJ to 15 EJ per year, which represents an important share of industrial, commercial and residential heat supply.

The penetration of CHP in the power generation sector varies widely from country to country. Whereas Denmark, Finland and the Netherlands already have high penetration rates, Russia and China have substantial lower-efficiency CHP capacity that offers significant opportunity for improvement. China also has tremendous growth potential given its increased attention to energy efficiency and its rapidly growing industrial base. Many other countries have significant potential to expand their use of CHP, but they must first address barriers such as unfavourable regulatory frameworks (buy-back tariffs, exit fees, back-up fees), challenges in locating suitable heat users, and cost-effectiveness (relative fuel and electricity prices) for smaller-scale CHP units (under 1 MW capacity).

While CHP facilities can be found in almost all manufacturing industries, the food, pulp and paper, chemical, and petroleum-refining sub-sectors represent more than 80% of the total current capacity. More than 50% of the electricity produced in CHP units in Europe is generated in public CHP plants that are connected to district heating schemes. Figure 7.6 shows the distribution of industrial CHP capacity in the European Union and the United States.

Figure 7.6 ▶ Distribution of industrial CHP capacity in the European Union and the United States

Share of total industrial CHP capacity
40%
35%
30%
25%
20%
15%
10%
5%
0%
Chemicals
Refining
Pulp and paper
Food
Primary metals
Textile
Minerals
Other
United States
EU 25

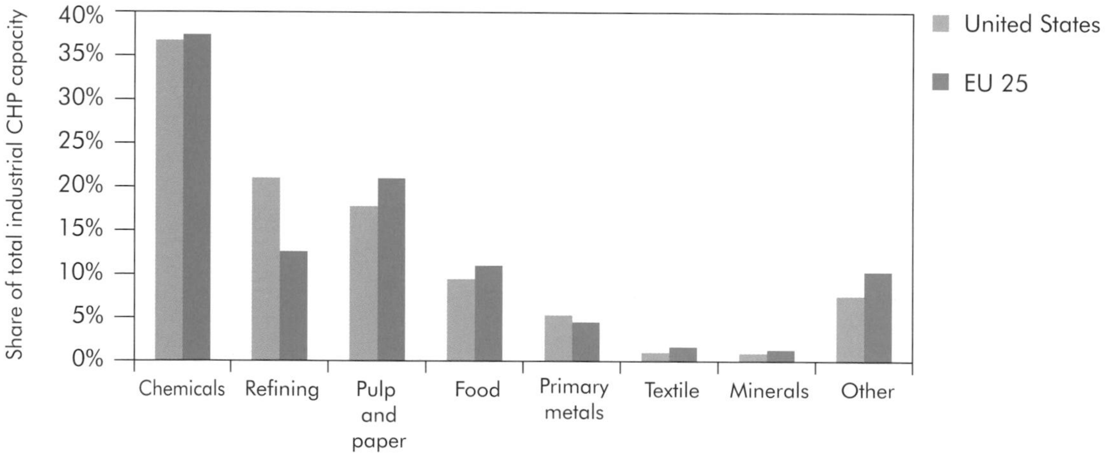

Note: In Eurostat statistics, utility-owned CHP units at industrial sites are classified as public supply. This may affect the distribution of capacity.

Source: IEA, 2007f.

Key point

Industrial CHP is concentrated in a few energy intensive sectors.

Large systems still account for the vast majority of CHP facilities. In the United States, more than 85% of existing capacity is 50 MW or larger. Reciprocating engines and smaller gas turbines dominate in smaller industrial CHP applications such as food processing, fabrication and equipment industries, while combined-cycle and steam turbine systems dominate the larger systems.

Natural gas fuels 40% of CHP generated electricity in the European Union and 72% of capacity in the United States. But coal, wood and process wastes are used extensively in many industries, especially in large CHP systems. As a result, combustion turbines are the dominant technology, representing 38% of CHP based power in the European Union and 67% of installed capacity in the United States. Boilers and steam turbines represent 50% of power generated by CHP in the European Union and 32% of installed CHP capacity in the United States.

The current industry standard has an efficiency of 34% to 40%. Industrial sized turbines are available that, with increased turbine inlet temperatures, demonstrate efficiencies of 40% to 42%. It is expected that the efficiencies of aero-derivative and industrial turbines can be increased to 45% by 2010.

Further efficiencies can be achieved through "repowering", in which the combustion air fans in the furnace are replaced by a gas turbine. The exhaust gases still contain a considerable amount of oxygen and can thus be used as combustion air for the furnaces, while the gas turbine can deliver up to 20% of the furnace heat. The repowering option has been used at two refineries in the Netherlands, with a total combined capacity of 35 MW.

Two different types of high-temperature CHP are available. In the first type, the exhaust gases heat the process feed directly in a furnace. In the second, exhaust heat is led to a heat exchanger, where thermal oil is heated as an intermediate. The heat content of the oil is transferred to the process feed and gives greater process flexibility. In the long term, probably after 2025, the integration of industrial processes with high-temperature solid-oxide fuel cells could lead to revolutionary design changes and to the direct cogeneration of power and chemicals. High-temperature CHP has a large market potential, especially in the chemical and refinery industries in relation to atmospheric distillation, coking and hydro treating, and the manufacture of ethylene and ammonia.

CHP integration allows increased use of CHP in industry by employing the heat in more efficient ways. The flue gas of a turbine can often be used directly for drying or process heating: for example, for the drying of minerals and food products. Tri-generation of electricity, heat and cooling has been used in food processing plants in Europe for margarine and vegetable oils, dairy products, vegetable and fruit processing, freezing, and meat processing.

Worldwide, CHP has very significant potential. In the United States alone, the future potential of large-scale conventional CHP systems has been estimated at 50 GW (IEA, 2007f), with potential energy savings of more than 1 EJ. But policies will be needed to support its diffusion, including the removal of direct and indirect subsidies for centralised power generation, the resolution of interconnection issues, the removal of unfavourable tariffs for power sales, and high back-up rates and exit fees.

To improve the performance of CHP technologies, and to demonstrate their reliability and reduce investment costs, R&D is needed in the following areas:

- High-temperature CHP: the inlet (and outlet) temperatures of gas turbines need to be increased, as well as the reliability of the turbines, to allow longer running times.
- Medium-scale applications: the integration of medium-scale turbines needs to be demonstrated at various scales and in various industrial settings. Development of integrated technologies to reduce the nitrogen oxides in flue gases would allow process integrated applications to be used in food industries.
- Biomass CHP, heat/cold storage system optimisation and integration of CHP with other forms of surplus and renewable heat in district heating and cooling systems.
- Performance improvement (technology and economics) for district heating and cooling networks.
- Small-scale systems: the efficiency of micro-turbines needs to be improved and their cost brought down through improved manufacturing techniques. Fuel cell research aims at bringing down the costs through improved durability and better materials (lower catalyst needs and improved lifetime) and through better manufacturing processes.

Table 7.3 ▶ Global technology prospects for CHP systems

Cogeneration (CHP)	2003-2015	2015-2030	2030-2050
Technology stage	R&D, demonstration, commercial	Demonstration, commercial	Commercial
Internal rate of return	10%	10-15%	10-15%
Energy reduction (%)	< 20%	10-20%	15-30%
CO_2 reduction (Gt/yr)	0-0.05	0.01-0.1	0.1-0.4

Fuel cells

Gasification-based power plants can improve their efficiency by incorporating fuel cells.

Fuel cells are electrochemical devices that generate electricity and heat using hydrogen (H_2) or H_2-rich fuels, together with oxygen from air.[4] These options are discussed in detail in IEA, 2007d.

4. The text on fuel cells comes from IEA, 2007d.

Figure 7.7 ▶ **Fuel cell concept**

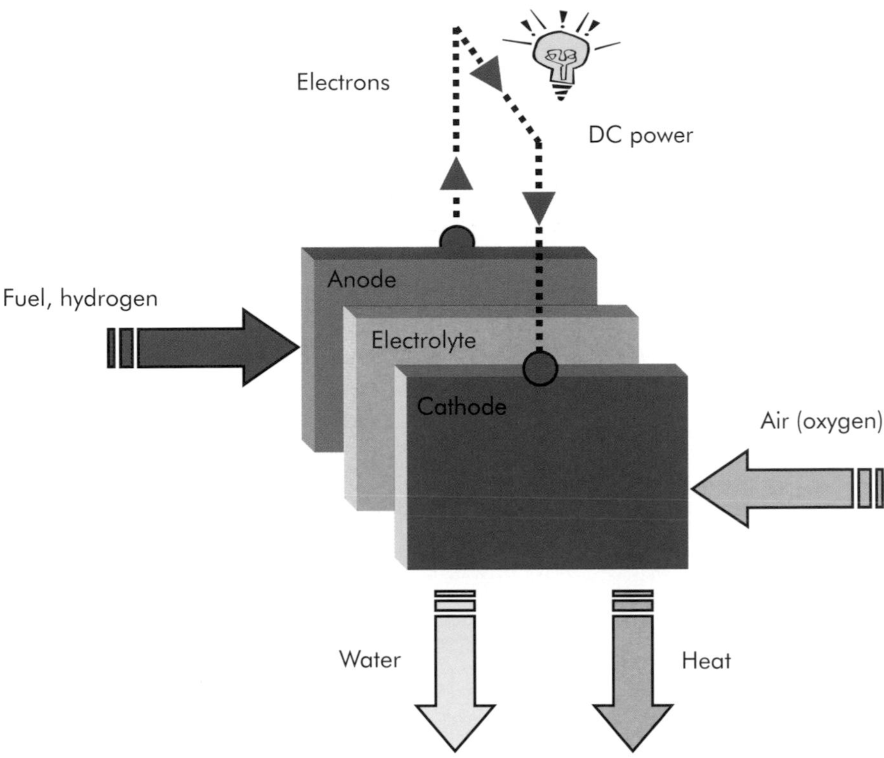

Source: IEA, 2005.

Key point

Fuel cells consist of two electrodes sandwiched around an electrolyte; they operate by feeding hydrogen to the anode and oxygen to the cathode.

7

Several thousand fuel cell systems are produced per year. Most are for small stationary units, although several hundred are for large stationary systems and several hundred more are for car and bus demonstration projects. Total installed FC power capacity is some 50 MW. There are around 3 000 stationary systems in operation worldwide. A number of additional small units are being installed for remote applications and for telecommunication power supplies.

Polymer electrolyte membrane fuel cells (PEMFC) are the choice technology for the transportation sector and for 70% to 80% of the current small-scale stationary fuel cell market. While phosphoric acid fuel cells were a pioneer technology for the large-scale stationary market, molten carbonate fuel cells (MCFC) and solid oxide fuel cells (SOFC) are now the reference options in this sector. They are used in niche markets for back-up, highly reliable or remote power generation. SOFCs represent 15% to 20% of the stationary market, but their share is expected to increase. Direct methanol fuel cells (DMFC) appear to be close to entering the market for portable devices. More R&D is needed on PEMFCs in the transport sector.

Table 7.4 ▶ **Fuel cells: performance and use**

		PEMFC	SOFC	MCFC	DMFC
Operating temperature (°C)		80-150	800-1 000	>650	80-100
Fuel		H_2	H_2, hydrocarbons	natural gas and other hydrocarbons	methanol
Electrical efficiency (%)		35-40	<45	44-50	15-30
Applications		vehicles, power	stationary power	stationary power	portable power
Lifetime (h)	**Vehicles**	2 000	6 000	8 000	data not available
	Power	30 000	20 000	20 000	
Target lifetime (h)	**Vehicles**	4 000	40 000	40 000	data not available
	Power	25 000	60 000	60 000	

Source: IEA, 2005.

For stationary MCFC and SOFC systems, the cost of prototype or small-scale 200kW to 300 kW units is between USD 12 000/kW to USD 15 000/kW, the FC stack accounting for 50% of this. Large-scale production and technology learning are expected to reduce the cost to between USD 1 500/kW and USD 1 600/kW. These systems could become economically competitive in a few years, notably for distributed power generation.

CO_2 capture and storage (CCS)

CO_2 (or carbon) capture and storage (CCS) involves three main steps. These have been used in the chemical processing and oil and gas industries for decades, but are not yet incorporated into large-scale power plants:

- CO_2 capture from a large-scale stationary source, such as a power plant or other industrial emission process. Includes gas processing, fuel transformation and compression.
- Transportation to an injection sink. Onshore and offshore pipelines, ships and trucks are the most common options.
- Underground geological injection. This involves injecting CO_2 in a supercritical state via wellbores into suitable geological strata such as deep saline formations, depleted oil and gas reservoirs, and non-mineable coal seams on land or under the sea floor (at depths generally exceeding 700 metres). Other methods, such as storage in ocean waters and mineral carbonation are still in the research phase and will require a considerable amount of testing and assessment of environmental risks, especially for ocean storage (IPCC, 2005). Most countries, including those in the European Union, exclude storage in ocean waters for environmental reasons.

Turning the gas into storable solids through chemical reaction with rocks would require very large quantities of reactant, and enormous storage space for the reaction product.

CO_2 capture

Capturing CO_2 from emission sources

Most man-made CO_2 emissions come from power generation and large-scale industrial processes. The cost of capturing CO_2 from these larger-scale emission sources is much less than from distributed sources, such as transport.

There are three main classes of CO_2 capture processes (Figure 7.8):

- With post-combustion processes, CO_2 is captured at low pressure from flue gas that generally has a CO_2 content of 2% to 25%. The challenge is to recover CO_2 from the flue gas economically. The separated gas has to be compressed before transportation.
- CO_2 can also be captured pre-combustion in coal or natural gas burning plants. Reacting the fuel with air or oxygen enables the capture of high concentrations of CO_2 (more than 95%).

Figure 7.8 ▶ Three main options for CO_2 capture from power generation and industrial processes

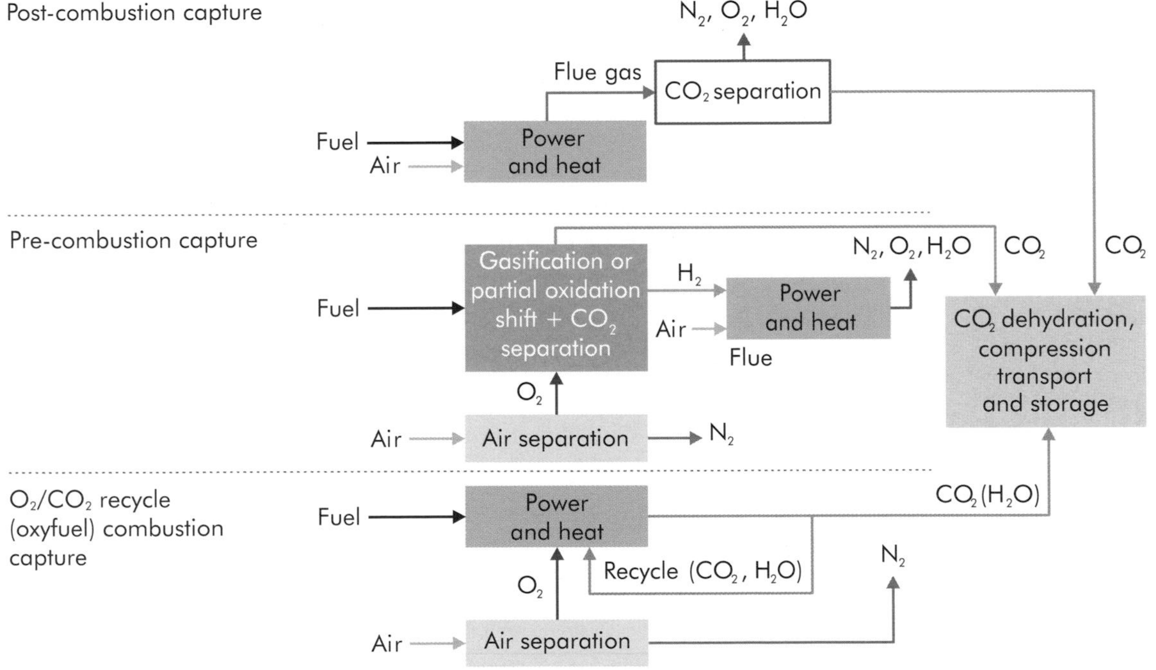

Source: IPCC, 2005.

Key point

CO_2 capture technologies fall into three main categories: post-combustion generates CO_2 with the lowest purity, while pre-combustion and oxyfuel combustion use air from which nitrogen and other gases have been stripped – hence they use mainly oxygen, to produce high purity CO_2.

Cost and potential for cost reductions from power plants

The bulk of the costs of CCS projects are associated with CO_2 capture. CCS costs between USD 40 and USD 90 per tonne of CO_2 emissions avoided, dependent on the fuel and the technology that the power plant uses. For the most cost effective technologies, capture costs alone are USD 25 to USD 50 per tonne of CO_2 emissions avoided, with transport and storage about USD 10 per tonne. Because CO_2 capture itself uses more energy and leads to the production of more CO_2, the cost per tonne of CO_2 emission reduction is higher than the per tonne cost of capturing and storing CO_2. The gap between the two narrows, however, as CO_2 capture energy efficiency increases.

In some circumstances, depending on factors such as oil prices, extraction economics and reservoir performance, the benefits from enhanced oil recovery (EOR) can offset part or all of the capture, transportation and injection costs. By 2030, costs for coal-fired plants could fall to below USD 35 per tonne of CO_2 captured, provided sufficient R&D and demonstration efforts are put in place and are successful (IEA, 2008c).

Using CCS with new natural gas and coal-fired power plants would increase electricity production costs by USD 0.02 to USD 0.04 per kWh. By 2030, the additional costs could drop back to USD 0.01 to USD 0.03 per kWh (Remme and Bennaceur, 2007).

Future cost projections for CCS depend on which technologies are used, how they are applied, how far costs fall as a result of RD&D and market uptake, and fuel prices.

Efficiency and retrofitting

Capturing CO_2 from low-efficiency power plants is not economically viable. The higher the efficiency of electricity generation, the lower the cost increase per kilowatt-hour of electricity. Future PCC systems employing super alloys, high temperature hydrogen gas turbines, and new CO_2 separation technologies should enable power generation efficiencies with CO_2 capture that are comparable with current conventional plants without capture (IEA, 2007b).

A case study of a new gas-fired power plant in Karstø, Norway, has compared the costs of an integrated system (where steam was extracted from the power plant) with those of a back-end capture system (with its own steam supply) designed as a retrofit after the power plant had been built. The analysis suggested that the retrofit would reduce efficiency by 3.3% more than the integrated option, at similar investment cost (IEA, 2004).

As most coal-fired power plants have a long lifespan, any rapid expansion of CO_2 capture into the power sector would include retrofitting. New capacity will be needed to offset the capacity de-rating caused by CO_2 capture.

Capture readiness

Financial and regulatory frameworks do not currently make CCS from fossil fuel-fired power plants economically justifiable. The option of retrofitting a new plant to be capture-ready when the appropriate economic conditions are in place is under evaluation, following the recommendations of the 2005 G8 Gleneagles Plan of Action (Mandil, 2007). The 2007 IEA Greenhouse Gas R&D Programme's study of capture-ready plants provides conceptual definitions and assesses the economic implications. The three elements under consideration are (IEA GHG, 2007a):

- plant space and access requirements for additional equipment needed to capture CO_2;
- a reasonable storage route for CO_2 (including a suitable storage reservoir in the vicinity) and feasible transportation options;
- an economic analysis of CCS options.

Transporting CO_2

Pipeline transport of CO_2 is generally more cost-effective than the alternatives (trucking/sea shipping), especially for distances less than 1 000 km. A network of CO_2 pipelines has been operating in the United States for more than two decades, with a proven track record of safety.

7

The cost of transportation depends on terrain and pipeline configurations, pressure requirements, distance and CO_2 volumes. For a 250 km pipeline carrying 10 Mt CO_2 a year, costs range from USD 1 to USD 8 per tonne of CO_2 onshore, and are 40% to 70% more offshore. Figure 7.9 compares the investment cost per kilometre expressed as a function of pipe diameter for onshore and offshore environments. Pipeline transportation is an established technology and no significant cost decrease is expected, except in the optimisation of the configuration and scheduling of the pipeline network.

Figure 7.9 ▶ Investment costs for CO_2 pipelines

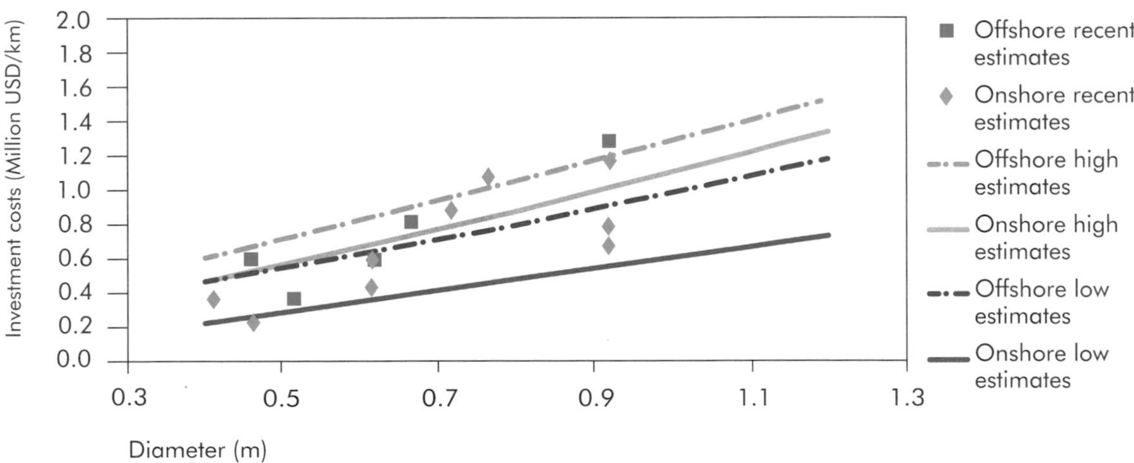

Note: Graph shows recent project costs vs. IPCC (2005) estimates.

Source: IEA, 2008c.

Key point

CO_2 transport costs have increased, especially in larger diameter pipelines, due to their steel component.

Geological storage

Geological storage options include:

- Deep saline formations.
- Depleted oil and gas fields. These are expected to be ideal CO_2 sinks, as the formations have generally been well characterised by the oil and gas industry, and they generally have excellent geological seals. But the permanence of storage over longer time-scales has yet to be demonstrated.
- CO_2 EOR. CO_2 has been used for almost three decades to enhance oil recovery (SPE, 2002). Up to an additional 5% to 23% of hydrocarbon recovery can be obtained, depending on CO_2 and oil miscibility and reservoir conditions.
- CO_2 enhanced gas recovery, through reservoir re-pressurisation. Only one commercial project has been implemented so far (the Gaz de France K12-B project). This technology is still considered speculative, as the additional amount of gas extracted can be very low.
- CO_2 enhanced coal bed methane recovery.

Other geological options include basalts, caverns and mines. But these techniques are generally limited by the available storage volumes, the absence of natural seals, low injectivity, or chemical interactions. Basalt formations have the advantage of being widespread, and these require further research.

Figure 7.10 shows the worldwide distribution of sedimentary basins.

Figure 7.10 ▶ Map of sedimentary basins and their storage prospects

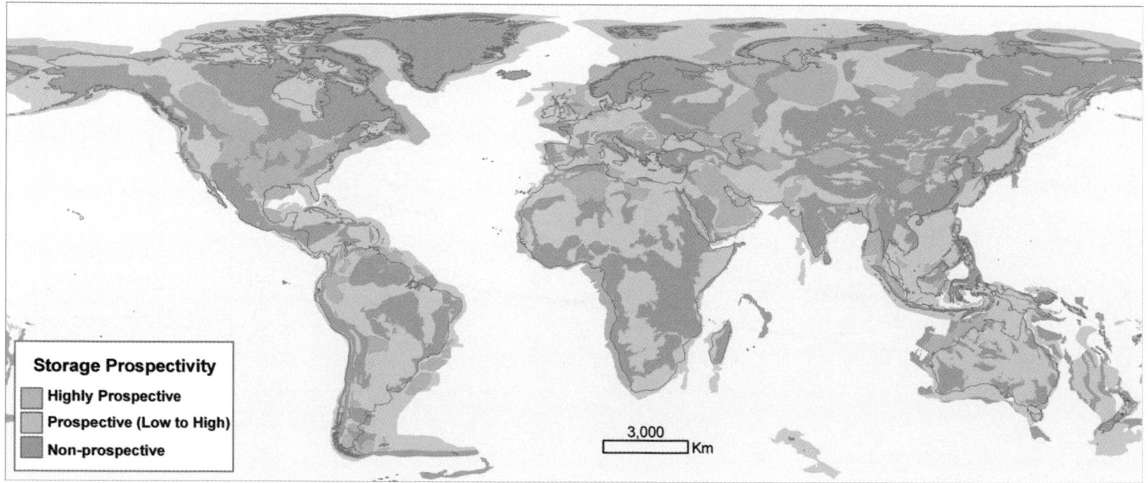

Source: Bradshaw and Dance, 2004.

Key point

Highly prospective for CO_2 storage basins are found mainly in the United States and Canada, Siberia, the Middle East and North Africa, as well as in offshore environments.

Table 7.5 gives a worldwide assessment of capacity by storage type.

Table 7.5 ▶ **Storage capacity (Gt CO_2)**

Storage option	Deep saline formations	Oil and gas fields (EOR, EGR, depleted fields)	ECBM
Lower estimate	1 000	600	3
Upper estimate	> 10 000	1 200	200

Source: IPCC, 2005.

Key point

The largest capacity of CO_2 storage exists in deep saline formations.

7

Factors that affect storage costs include infrastructure requirements (injection and monitoring wells and retrofitting facilities, especially in offshore environments), the volumes to be injected, injection depth and hydrocarbon economics. EOR allows the recovery of 0.1 tonne to 0.5 tonne of additional oil per tonne of CO_2 injected. Where EOR contributes to revenue generation, the cost of CCS can be negative. EOR storage costs are typically estimated to range from USD 35 to USD 40 per tonne of CO_2. Storage in saline aquifers is estimated to cost USD 0.5 to USD 10 per tonne of CO_2 and in depleted oil and gas fields, USD 1 to USD 40 per tonne of CO_2 (BERR, 2007; IEA, 2008c). Increases in material costs, combined with a lack of resources (drilling rigs and personnel), have contributed to CCS costs more than doubling in the period from 2004 to 2007. Monitoring costs depend on project uncertainties with regards to leakage risk and are generally less than USD 1 per tonne of CO_2 (IEA GHG, 2004).

Prospects for CCS

In the Baseline scenario, which assumes a negligible price for CO_2, CCS will mainly be limited to EOR and fuel-transformation applications. Figure 7.11 shows the amount of emissions abatement from CCS in the ACT Map scenario, which assumes an incentive of USD 50 per tonne of CO_2. The CCS potential is over 5.2 Gt of CO_2 per year in 2050, of which 68% is from the electricity sector. Retrofit represents nearly 40% of the total CCS potential. Gas processing and synthetic fuel production represent 17%, and industry CCS 5% of the total. The cumulative storage volume between 2010 and 2050 is less than 100 Gt. This represents only a small fraction of the capacity available (Table 7.5). Note that CCS deployment at the scale of 1.8 Gt by 2030 will be challenging, as it requires fast-tracking the RD&D phases, the validation of the technology options, and the development of large-scale regional transport infrastructures. As the curve flattens in 2040, the 2050 targets are achievable, the main issue is the phase-in of large-scale deployment.

Achieving 5 Gt of storage a year would present a formidable challenge in terms of investment and infrastructure. To achieve this, it would be necessary to inject 1.8 Gt per annum worldwide by 2030. This is equivalent to 1 800 Sleipner CO_2 projects. A major international collaboration effort would be required to meet this challenge.

Figure 7.11 ▶ **CO_2 capture and storage potential with a USD 50/tonne incentive**

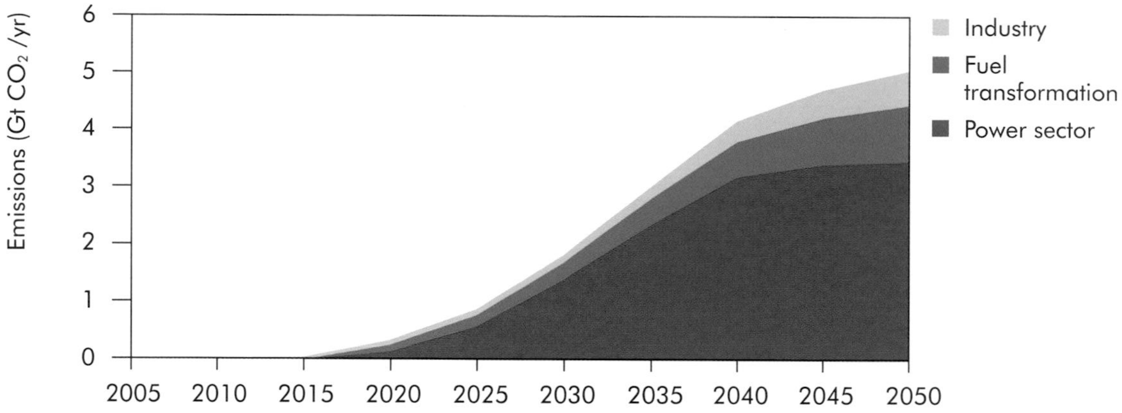

Source: IEA, 2008c.

Key point

By 2050, with a USD 50 per tonne of CO_2 reduction incentive, 5 Gtpa of CO_2 would be captured and stored, mainly from the power sector, but also from industry and synthetic fuels.

Current status of CCS: major projects

In 2007, four large-scale (over 0.5 Mt injected per year) anthropogenic CO_2 projects were in operation around the world: Sleipner (Norway), Weyburn (Canada-United States), In Salah (Algeria) and Snohvit (Norway).

Sleipner

The offshore Sleipner project, operated by StatoilHydro, separates CO_2 from produced gas with an initial CO_2 content of 9% to 12% and injects it into a saline aquifer. CO_2 injection of over 1 Mtpa began in 1996, and plans are to store more then 20 Mtpa during the life of the project. Extensive monitoring has been carried out, including the use of 4-D (time lapse) seismic monitoring to track the progression of CO_2 in the reservoir (NGU, 2006).

Weyburn

Over 1.7 Mtpa of CO_2 is captured from a North Dakota (United States) coal gasification plant, compressed and transported via a 330 km land pipeline to the Weyburn (Saskatchewan, Canada) field, operated by Encana, where it is used for EOR. Injection started in 2001, and over 120 million barrels of additional oil is expected from the process. A large-scale monitoring programme involving Canadian partners, the IEA Greenhouse Gas R&D Programme, and the European Union (DG Research) is studying the interaction between the injected CO_2 and the formations/wellbores (PTRC, 2004).

In Salah

The gas produced in Algeria's In Salah (and neighbouring) fields has a CO_2 content of (between 4% and 9%) that exceeds the amount allowed by the commercial specifications. A chemical solvent (ethanol-amino solution) is used to separate 1 Mtpa of CO_2. Four compression stages are then used to pressurise CO_2 and inject it into a 20 metre thick carboniferous reservoir containing water, underlying the gas producing zone. A total of 17 million tonnes of CO_2 will be stored, at an average CCS cost of USD 6 per tonne (Wright, 2006).

Snohvit

Located in the Barents Sea, the field, operated by StatoilHydro produces gas with a CO_2 content that is higher than commercial specifications. CO_2 is separated from natural gas onshore, at the Hammerfest facility which is located 160 km from the field. There, 0.7 Mtpa CO_2 is compressed and transported back offshore to an injection layer 2 600 m underneath the gas producing zone.

International efforts to accelerate deployment of CCS

A number of international initiatives have been launched by the public and private sectors to study, develop and promote CCS technologies. Given the magnitude of the challenge, including the cost of research, development and demonstration, international co-operation and sharing of best practices will be required to accelerate the pace of technology deployment.

International organisations

The Carbon Sequestration Leadership Forum (CSLF) is an international climate change initiative that focuses on co-operation to develop improved cost-effective technologies for the separation and capture of CO_2 for its transport and long-term safe storage. The CSLF aims to make these technologies broadly available internationally and to identify and address wider issues relating to CCS. This could include promoting the appropriate technical, political and regulatory environments for the development of such technology. The CSLF currently comprises 21 countries and the European Commission. A number of oil and gas companies participate as stakeholders in the CSLF workshops and work groups.

The IEA Greenhouse Gas R&D Programme (IEA GHG) is an international collaborative research programme. IEA GHG focuses its efforts on studying technologies to reduce greenhouse gas emissions. IEA GHG was established in 1991, with three key activities: evaluation of technologies aimed at reducing GHG emissions, dissemination of results of its evaluation studies, and facilitating RD&D. Over 20 countries and several oil and gas service companies and technology institutes participate in the programme.

Regional initiatives

Several programmes and initiatives have been developed in the last decade, involving public and private partners (in particular from the oil and gas sectors). These include:

- North America Regional Sequestration Partnerships;
- Canada CCS Technology Network;
- European initiatives: the Zero Emissions Technology Platform, the Carbon Capture and Storage Association, Competency networks including CO_2NET and CO_2GeoNet;
- Germany's R&D programme (COORETEC);
- Australia's CO_2CRC;
- APEC's capacity building, and the Asia-Pacific Partnership on Clean Development and Climate;
- China-related initiatives (Greengen, nZEC, MoveCBM).

Major R&D projects

Several major R&D projects with participation from universities, technology institutes, oil and gas and service companies, other industry sectors and governments are currently ongoing. These include:

- Stanford's GCEP on climate change, with USD 200 million funding over ten years;
- the Carbon Capture Project (CCP);
- projects that come under the EU Framework Programmes for RD&D (FP5-FP7), such as SACS, CASTOR, GeoCapacity, CO_2SINK, CO_2ReMoVe and ENCAP;

Additionally, three large-scale public co-funded initiatives have been announced in OECD countries:

- the United States based FutureGen aims at building a USD 1.5 to USD 2.0 billion, 275 MW coal-fired power plant with CCS and hydrogen generation by 2017;
- the EU-funded Hypogen is a EUR 1.3 to EUR 1.6 billion Quick Start initiative that plans over the next eight years to build a coal based, pre-combustion based plant with power and H_2 generation;
- the Queensland (Australia) ZeroGen project plans for an IGCC with 100 MW baseload electricity generation by 2012, with capture, pipeline transport and storage in the Northern Denison Trough.

Table 7.6 lists announced commercial power generation projects and Table 7.7 lists major storage and RD&D initiatives. These lists are changing rapidly, however, due to a number of project cancellations as well as new projects being announced.

Table 7.6 ▶ **Proposed full-scale (~100 MW and above) CCS projects for power generation**

Company/Project name	Fuel	Plant output/Cost	Technology	Start
BP-Rio Tinto DF2, Carson, United States	Petcoke	500 MW (USD 1bn)	IGCC + shift + pre-combustion, storage in the oilfield – EOR	2011
BP-Rio Tinto DF3, Kwinana, West Australia	Coal	500 MW	Coal gasification + storage in saline aquifer	2011
Centrica/Progressive Energy, Teeside, United Kingdom	Coal (petcoke)	800 MW (+H_2 to grid) (GBP 1 bn)	IGCC + shift + pre-combustion	2013
China Huaneng Group (CHNG), GreenGen, China	Coal	100 MW	IGCC + shift + pre-combustion	2015
E.ON Killingholme, Lincolnshire coast, United Kingdom	Coal	450 MW (GBP 1 bn)	IGCC+shift+pre-combustion (may be capture ready)	2011
Ferrybridge, Scottish and Southern Energy, United Kingdom	Coal	500 MW retrofit GBP 250 m, capture GBP 100 m	PC (supercritical retrofit) + post-combustion capture	2011
E.ON Kingsnorth (Kent), United Kingdom	Coal	2x800 MW (GBP 1 bn)	Supercritical retrofit	2012
FutureGen, United States	Coal	275 MW (USD 1.5 bn)	IGCC + shift + pre-combustion	2012-2017 (under restructuring)
Hypogen, EU	Coal	EUR 1.3 bn	Pre-combustion + H_2	2014-2016
GE/Polish utility	Coal	1 000 MW	IGCC + shift + pre-combustion	
Karstø, Norway	Natural gas	384 MW	NGCC + post-combustion amine, potential storage in the oilfield – EOR	2012 (capture)
Mongstad, Norway	Natural gas	280 MW 350 MW_{th}	CHP with post-combustion CCS Phase 1: Pilot capture Phase 2: Full-scale with transport and storage	Phase 1: 2010 Phase 2 2014
Nuon, Eemshaven, Netherlands	Coal/ biomass/ natural gas	1 200 MW	IGCC with option to capture	>2011 (decision in 2009)
Powerfuel, Hatfield Colliery, United Kingdom	Coal	~900 MW	IGCC + shift + pre-combustion	2010
RWE, Germany	Coal	450 MW (EUR 1 bn)	IGCC + shift + pre-combustion, storage in saline reservoir	2014
RWE, Tilbury, UK	Coal	1 000 MW (GBP 800 m)	PC (supercriticial retrofit) + post-combustion (may be capture ready)	2016

Table 7.6 ▶ **Proposed full-scale (~100 MW and above) CCS projects for power generation** (continued)

Company/Project name	Fuel	Plant output/Cost	Technology	Start
SaskPower, Saskatchewan, Canada	Lignite coal	300 MW	PC+Post-combustion or oxyfuel, storage in the oilfield – EOR	>2011 (on hold)
EPCOR, Alberta, Canada	Coal	500 MW	IGCC	2015
Siemens, Germany	Coal	1 000 MW EUR 1.7 bn	IGCC + shift + pre-combustion	2011
Stanwell, Queensland, Australia	Coal	100 MW	IGCC + shift + pre-combustion, storage in saline reservoir	2012

Source: IEA GHG R&D Programme, CSLF, IEA.

Key point

A large number of industrial size CCS prospects have been announced for the 2010 to 2016 time period, mainly in Europe.

Table 7.7 ▶ **Major projects for storage of CO_2**

Project name and location	Source of CO_2	Type of geological formation	CO_2 stored
Sleipner (Norwegian North Sea)	Stripped from natural gas	Saline reservoir	1 Mt/year since 1996
In Salah (Algeria)	Stripped from natural gas	Gas/saline reservoir	1.2 Mt/year since 2004
K12b (Netherlands)	Stripped from natural gas	Gas field – EGR	Over 0.1 Mt/year since 2004
Snohvit (Norwegian North Sea)	Stripped from natural gas	Gas/saline reservoir	0.7 Mt/year, started in Q4-2007
Gorgon (Australia – offshore)	Stripped from natural gas	Saline reservoir	129 Mt over the life of the project, starting between 2008-2010
Weyburn-Midale (Canada/United States)	Coal	Oil field – EOR	Over 1 Mt/year since 2000
Permian Basin, Rockies, and Western States (United States)	Natural reservoirs and industry	EOR	500 Mt injected since 1972 (no storage)
Frio Brine (United States)		Saline reservoir	3 kt injected in 2005-2006
Nagaoka (Japan)		Saline reservoir	10.4 kt in 2004-2005

Table 7.7 ▶ **Major projects for storage of CO_2** (continued)

Project name and location	Source of CO_2	Type of geological formation	CO_2 stored
Ketzin (Germany)		Saline reservoir	60 kt total, starting 2007
Otway (Australia)	Stripped from natural gas	Depleted gas field	50 kt/year, starting 2007
Callide (Australia)	Coal		Starting 2010 Over 30 kt/year
Lacq (France)	Steam boiler/ oxyfuel	Depleted gas field	2008, 150 kt over two years
Altmark (Germany)		EGR, depleted gas field	2008-2011, 100 kt
Quinshu (China)		ECBM micro-pilot	200 tonnes
Hazelwood (Australia)	Coal		50 t/day, starting 2008

Sources: IEA GHG R&D Programme; CSLF; IEA.

Key point

CO_2 injection associated with oil and gas operations represents the largest source of information currently available.

Barriers to large-scale deployment of CCS

A number of barriers need to be overcome for the large-scale deployment of CCS, including (IEA/CSLF-2007):

- **Legal and regulatory barriers:** legal guidelines regarding the injection of CO_2 and long-term liabilities must be established, a regulatory framework must be defined, and risk-management procedures that include monitoring and remediation must be developed.
- **Commercial and financial barriers:** a global market that can value CO_2 must be created. In addition, governments need to create a framework and an infrastructure for enabling efficiencies.
- **International mechanisms:** economic incentives for CCS need to be developed and agreed on.
- **Technical barriers:** RD&D must be accelerated, with the objective of improving reliability and reducing costs. Potential leakage routes and long-term isolation procedures need to be identified.
- **Public awareness:** education and outreach to all stakeholders are crucial.

7

Legal and regulatory barriers

A number of international frameworks relate to offshore storage. Some progress has been made recently in amending these to allow progress to be made with CCS. In November 2006, the Contracting Parties to the London Protocol adopted an amendment that allows for CO_2 to be stored in sub-seabed formations. And in June 2007, the OSPAR commission decided to amend the Convention to allow the storage of CO_2 in geological formations while banning the injection of CO_2 into the water column or its deposition at the seabed.

A few countries are in the process of passing legislation that enables CO_2 storage. The Netherlands is amending the 2003 Dutch Mining Act to enable CO_2 storage in depleted gas fields. Poland already has legislation (the Polish Mining Law) that allows the injection of CO_2 in the coal seams within the EU-funded RECOPOL project. Australia is moving ahead with the first release of CO_2 storage exploration acreage in 2008.

The 2006 to 2007 IEA-CSLF workshops on Near-Term Opportunities for CCS recommended that "governments should clearly define the liability regime for the operational, closure and post-closure phases of a storage project" (IEA, 2007g). The regime should also address:

- government assumption of long-term liability;
- the timing of the transfer of liability to governments for the post-closure phase;
- implications for the international movement of carbon dioxide (surface and sub-surface).

Financial mechanisms to enable CCS deployment

Fuller deployment of CCS requires a global and long-term value for CO_2 emission reduction at around USD 50/tonne of CO_2 (IEA, 2008c). CCS technologies are not expected to be deployed in the absence of a CO_2 emission reduction incentive, except for cases with substantial benefits from EOR.

National policies need to create a balanced policy framework that recognises the potential of CCS along with that of other climate mitigation technologies. Some experts question whether markets alone can deliver the outcomes that are sought in this area. If so, governments would need to consider direct measures to support the spread of CCS (IEA GHG, 2007b). If the CO_2 price offered by trading systems is low or unstable, CCS will depend on governments employing other supporting policies, such as:

- Public financial support (probably at the member state level):
  - direct investment support;
  - feed-in subsidies;
  - CO_2 price guarantees.
- low-carbon portfolio standard with tradable certificates (probably at the EU level);
- some form of CCS obligation;
- public-private partnerships.

International mechanisms

CCS is being considered as an emission mitigation option under the Clean Development Mechanism (CDM, 2006). At the twelfth COP/MOP in Nairobi (2006), a decision was postponed pending submission of further information to the UNFCCC. The final decision is expected to be taken in 2009. Issues raised in Nairobi included the technical capability of CCS, the effect of CCS on the Certified Emission Reduction (CER) market, the potential workforce and its expertise, standardisation and accreditation, trans boundary issues, and accounting for leakages (IEA GHG, 2007b). Further information on leaks and storage permanence, and on project boundary and liability issues can be found in a paper prepared for the Annex I Expert Group on the UNFCCC (Philibert, Ellis and Podkanski, 2007).

Technological issues

Reduction of CO_2 capture costs is one of the biggest challenges for CCS. For the power industry to significantly expand CCS deployment by 2020 within the cost limit of an additional USD 0.02 to USD 0.03 per kWh, a range of technological routes will need to be tested. To accelerate technology testing and the learning curve, the IEA and CSLF recommend that a minimum of 20 full-scale CCS projects be implemented worldwide by 2020. The European Union Zero Emissions Technology Platform aims to support the development of 10 to 12 demonstration plants within Europe by 2020.

All storage options – including deep saline aquifers and depleted oil and gas reservoirs – will need to demonstrate a high degree of CO_2 retention if they are to command public acceptance and be useful in mitigating climate change. CO_2 storage activities and sites will need to be monitored and their performance measured (Zakkour, 2005). Additional pilot projects are also needed to better understand and validate retention in various geological formations and to develop criteria to select and rank appropriate sites. Progress in modelling will allow increasingly accurate forecasts of the long-term fate of stored CO_2 – which cannot be tested in practice.

Public awareness

CCS stakeholders include politicians, policy makers and regulators, environmental NGOs, the public, the media, the relevant industries, financial institutions, and the insurance industry. Under the G8 Plan of Action, the 2006 to 2007 IEA/CSLF workshop series on Near-Term Opportunities for CCS addressed issues related to stakeholders' perceptions. But several surveys have confirmed that there is very limited public awareness of CCS (de Coninck, 2006; IEA, 2008c). This constitutes a serious barrier to deployment. In the absence of effective communication strategies, controversy and fears of leakages could pose obstacles to demonstration and deployment projects.

Chapter 8 NUCLEAR

Key Findings

- *Projected costs of generating electricity show that in many circumstances nuclear energy is competitive against coal and gas generation. As a result, a number of countries are reconsidering the role of nuclear energy, particularly in view of its advantages in reducing CO_2 emissions and in security of supply.*

- *The cost of capital has a significant effect on the cost of nuclear power, with the nature of risks affecting investment decisions being perceived differently for different types of generating plant. Governments can reduce these risks by streamlining planning and licensing regimes. Carbon pricing would increase the competitiveness of nuclear generation.*

- *Because fuel is a relatively small part of total generating cost, nuclear power is much less sensitive to variations in the price of uranium than conventional generation is to fossil fuel prices. Uranium is available from a diverse range of countries, and the major suppliers are politically stable. Reserves of uranium are not a limiting factor on nuclear generation.*

- *China, India, Russia, Japan, South Korea and Ukraine are, in total, planning nuclear capacity increases of 116 GW by 2020.*

- *Extrapolation of historic evidence suggests it would be theoretically possible in economic terms to construct nuclear plants at a rate that would meet at least 18% and possibly 30% of the IEA forecast of world generating capacity requirements. However, supply-chain and skill constraints are likely to provide a cap on the overall level of new construction.*

- *Small- and medium-sized reactor (SMR) designs are being developed to meet the needs of remote communities, often linked to district heating or cogeneration plants producing potable water from desalination.*

- *Evolutionary Generation III reactor designs such as those operating in Japan and under construction in Europe offer improved safety performance over existing designs, which already have a very positive safety record.*

- *While there is now a broad international consensus on geologic disposal of high-level waste, with the United States and Finland having identified suitable sites and several countries engaged with stakeholders to find acceptable locations, no high-level waste repositories have yet been opened.*

- *The need to maintain and develop a growing skilled and experienced nuclear workforce is being tackled. But provision for the number of skilled people needed for any significant new build programme is unlikely to materialise until the programme itself is more clearly defined.*

Overview

Nuclear power generation has the capacity to provide large-scale, virtually CO_2-free, electricity. The technology is already proven. It has the potential to play a very significant role in the decarbonisation of power generation. Under the ACT and BLUE scenarios, nuclear power generation becomes more prominent in both developed and developing countries. This switch to nuclear power will contribute 6% of CO_2 savings based on the construction of 30 GW of capacity each year between now and 2050. Currently China has very little nuclear power capacity. Under both the ACT and BLUE scenarios, China becomes the dominant user of nuclear power and India also increases its use of nuclear power. Growth in OECD countries is also significant (Figure 8.1).

The recent UN Intergovernmental Panel on Climate Change report (IPCC, 2007 Working Group III,) notes that "Given costs relative to other supply options, nuclear power … can have an 18% share of total electricity supply in 2030 … but safety, weapons proliferation and waste remain as constraints."

Figure 8.1 ▶ **Regional breakdown of nuclear power generation for the Baseline, ACT Map and BLUE Map scenarios**

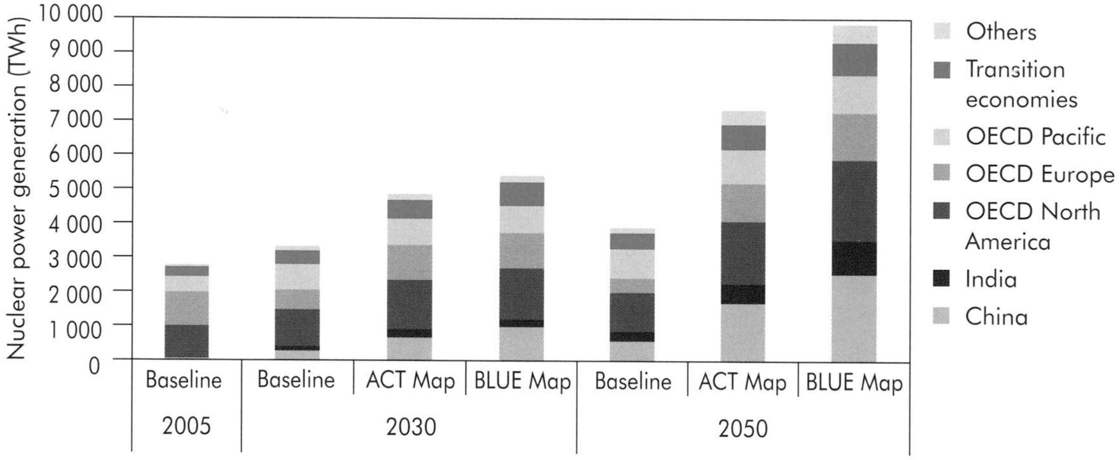

Key point

Growth in nuclear power generation will increase in both developing and developed countries.

The following sections examine these potential constraints, together with cost, to explore the prospects for nuclear energy.

The current status of nuclear power generation

In August 2007, there were 438 operating nuclear power plants in 30 countries. They had a total capacity of 372 GW (IAEA, database). Thirty-one reactors were under construction in Asia, Russia, Bulgaria and Ukraine, which will produce an additional 24 GW. Nuclear power supplied 2 700 TWh in 2006, 16% of the world's electricity and 25% of OECD countries' electricity generation. The global operating experience of nuclear power reactors now exceeds 12 000 reactor-years.

Almost 60% of global nuclear capacity is in the United States, France and Japan. The United States has 104 reactors, the largest number of any country (Figure 8.2). In 2006, France had the highest share of nuclear in its power generation mix, at 78%.

Figure 8.2 ▶ Nuclear share of electricity generation by country, 2006

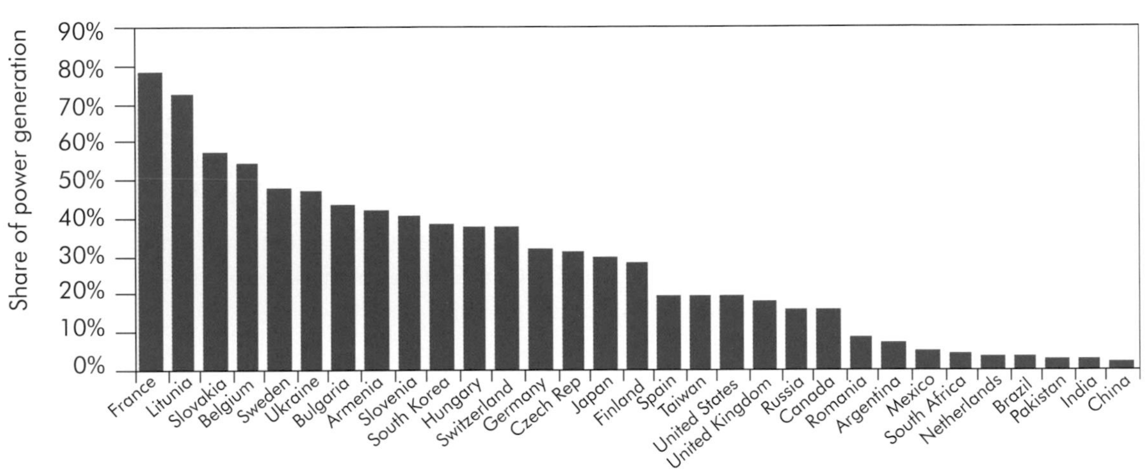

Source: IAEA, 2008.

Key point

Electricity generation from nuclear power is primarily in OECD countries.

Nuclear reactors that operate by fission are classified by neutron energy (thermal or fast), by coolant fluid (water, gas or liquid metal), by moderator type (light water, heavy water or graphite) and by reactor generation. Generation I prototype reactors were developed in the 1950s and 1960s. Very few are still operational. A large number of Generation II reactors were built in the 1970s as large commercial power plants, many of which are still operating today, often with licences for life extension to typically 60 years. In the United States, around 46 reactors have been granted life extensions, the most recent (Nine Mile Point Unit 2) to 2046. Twelve others are in the application process (NEI, 2008a). Generation III reactors were developed in the 1990s with a number of evolutionary designs that offered advances in safety and economics. Generation III+ reactors have further evolutionary and revolutionary aspects to their designs. Generation IV reactors offer the future prospect of further enhanced safety and economic advantages, while minimising waste production and improving proliferation resistance and physical protection.

Eighty-two percent of nuclear power plants use ordinary water as both moderator and coolant. Other water reactors, primarily in Canada and India, use heavy water as both moderator and coolant. Gas-cooled reactors are found mostly in the United Kingdom, where the coolant is carbon dioxide.

Nuclear electricity generation depends on the availability of uranium for fuel. The current demand for uranium (about 67 000 tonnes per year) means that known conventional resources (4.7 million tonnes) are sufficient at 2004 generation levels for 85 years. Geological evidence points to the existence of at least an additional 10 million tonnes of uranium, which would extend supply from 85 to 270 years (NEA, 2005). In addition, the reprocessing of spent fuel would enable existing supplies to be used more efficiently. The use of fast-breeder reactors would mean the world had almost unlimited stocks of readily available fuel. Fast-breeder reactors have received significant research funding over several decades, but there has been little commercial support because uranium has, until recently, remained relatively inexpensive. These reactors can extract some 50 times more energy per kilogramme of uranium than other reactor types.

Thorium can also be used to provide fuel for nuclear power plants, although the thorium fuel-cycle has received little attention due to the wide availability of uranium. India has shown most interest in developing the thorium cycle, driven by ample domestic thorium resources, a shortage of domestic uranium, and the country's inability (as a non-signatory of the Nuclear Non-Proliferation Treaty) to import nuclear raw materials. Thorium is thought to be about three times more abundant in the earth's crust than uranium.

The cost of nuclear power

Three main factors contribute to the direct costs of nuclear power: construction costs, operation and maintenance (O&M) and fuel costs, and so-called back-end (waste-management and decommissioning) costs.

To compare the cost of different technologies, a standardised methodology is used that produces a "levelised" cost expressed in currency units per kWh or MWh. This is the ratio of total lifetime cost to total expected output, expressed in terms of present value equivalent (NEA, 2005b). Levelised cost is equivalent to the average consumer price that exactly repays the investor and operator for the capital, O&M, fuel and back-end costs, with a rate of return equal to the discount rate.

Construction costs

Four variables primarily control construction costs: the length and complexity of the pre-construction period, capital costs (excluding interest), construction time, and the cost of capital.

The *pre-construction period* is the time taken to secure permits and planning approvals. Historically, this process has been lengthy in many countries, such as the United Kingdom, where the cost is estimated to be around 9% of total construction costs. Governments can reduce the length and, therefore, the cost of the pre-construction period through improvements to planning and licensing regimes. Introduction of National Generic Design Assessments and international co-operation among national regulators are examples of current initiatives to reduce licensing delays.

Reliable *capital cost* data are difficult to obtain. Most nuclear power cost studies base capital cost estimates (usually called overnight costs) on recent new-build experience or on vendor estimates. However, there is no internationally agreed-upon definition of capital cost, and opinions vary on the subject. Vendors have a commercial interest in minimising the apparent cost of new plants, and turnkey prices are inevitably commercially sensitive.

Long *construction times* increase interest costs. Since the 1980s, average worldwide construction times have steadily increased. Recent experience from Asia, however, where average construction times of 62 months are being achieved, has shown a marked reduction in time from construction start to commercial operation. Of the 18 units built in Asia between 2001 and 2007, three were connected to the grid in 48 months or less. The fastest was Onagawa 3, a Japanese 800 MW BWR (boiling water reactor) that was connected in 2002 after a 41-month construction period. In contrast, however, Finland's fifth nuclear power unit, currently under construction at Olkiluoto, has seen its completion date slip two years from 2009 to 2011, resulting in an expected construction time of 72 months. The delay has been attributed to difficulties in securing high-quality components, from concrete to heavy forgings. European suppliers are said to have lost their familiarity with the required nuclear standards. These issues illustrate the difficulties that can arise with first-of-a-kind construction.

The *cost of capital*, which depends on aspects of the financing scheme such as the ratio between debt and equity, the interest rate of the debt, and the internal rate of return required by shareholders, has a major impact on construction costs. A recent IEA/NEA study shows that levelised costs increase by some 50% to 60% as the discount rate increases from 5% to 10% (NEA, 2005b). A University of Chicago study shows that interest payments during the construction period can amount to 30% of overall expenditure for a five-year construction schedule, rising to 40% for a seven-year construction period (University of Chicago, 2004). The discount rate tends to be higher for nuclear than for fossil power plants. This is because investors and shareholders factor in what they see as higher risks resulting from more complex plants, potential construction delays, and regulatory and stakeholder intervention – and, therefore, require a higher interest rate and internal rates of return.

Building larger units to provide economies of scale and building significant numbers of standardised and simplified designs would lead to reductions in capital costs as a result of learning from experience. This would reduce construction times and increase investor confidence, thereby reducing the risk premium from the cost of capital.

Operating (O&M and fuel cycle) costs

O&M costs relate to the safe running and upkeep of a power station during its lifetime. They generally include the costs of safety inspections and safeguards as well as labour, insurance, and security costs; corporate overheads; and the costs of maintaining a level of spare generation capacity. Extensive data are available on O&M costs. These show a wide degree of variability that reflects, for example, differences in labour costs, plant sizes and age distributions in different countries, as well as differences resulting from government versus private security. The French and Japanese nuclear industries are both mature, with similar numbers of reactors, but 2010 O&M costs in Japan are projected to be 2.3 times higher than in France and Finland. For fossil fuel plants, O&M costs are almost the same in Japan and France. Nuclear O&M costs are particularly influenced by changing regulatory requirements. However, IEA/NEA studies from 1983 to 2005 show that O&M costs have now broadly stabilised.

O&M costs also include the cost of insurance borne by the operators. Operators' insurance costs are expected to rise in the future, following the 2004 revisions to the Paris and Brussels Conventions (NEA, 1982), which led to a substantial increase in the minimum cap on operator liability for an occurrence at a nuclear site.

Fuel-cycle costs, from uranium production to eventual radioactive-waste disposal, represent a relatively small component of nuclear power costs. And the base cost of uranium is only a small component of fuel-cycle costs. Nuclear fuel supply is a mature industry and costs have been broadly stable for many years (Sustainable Development Commission UK, 2006). Although the spot price of uranium has risen sharply in the past two years, relatively little uranium is traded in this manner. Data supplied to IEA/NEA from ten countries show that, at a 10% discount rate, fuel-cycle costs are expected to average 12% of levelised costs (UK Environmental Audit Committee, 2006).

Overall operating costs for nuclear plants in the United States have been falling steadily in real terms since the mid-1980s – as shown in Figure 8.3. In 2003, average United States nuclear production costs (O&M plus fuel costs) were USD cents 1.72/kWh. In Europe, production costs of EUR 0.01/kWh have been achieved in Finland and Sweden. The combined O&M and fuel cost for France's fleet of 58 reactors is EUR 0.014/kWh (Stricker and Leclerq, 2004).

Figure 8.3 ▶ **Average United States nuclear electricity production costs**

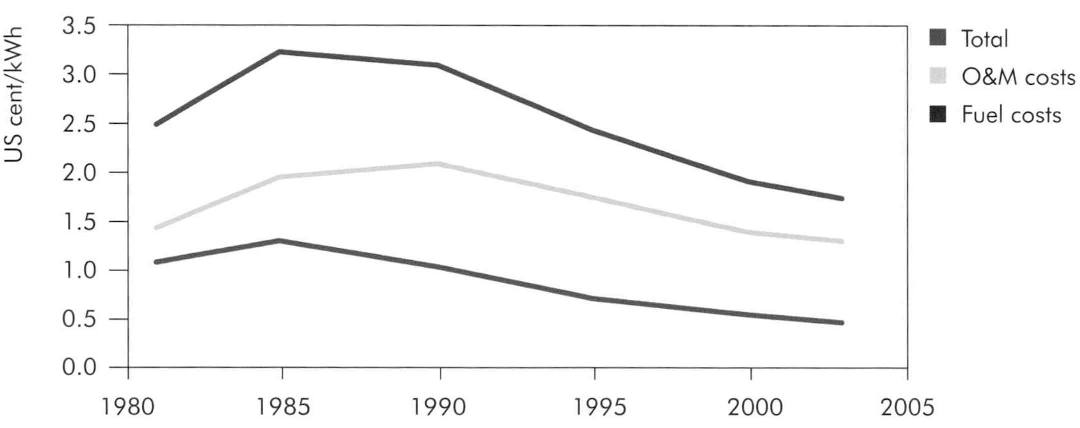

Source: Stricker and Leclerq, 2004.

Key point

Nuclear production costs for United States nuclear reactors continue to decline.

Back-end costs

Waste management and decommissioning liabilities are regarded by some stakeholders as major impediments to nuclear power generation. For the first generation reactors (many of which were effectively prototypes, with little if any provision for back-end costs) these costs are potentially significant and subject to considerable uncertainty. However, back-end costs for future nuclear plants, provided that radioactive waste disposal facilities are available and that regulatory requirements (including definitions of clearance levels) do not change, are predictable. In the United States, several large nuclear power reactors (e.g. Trojan, Maine Yankee, Millstone) have been decommissioned and the resultant waste disposed of: the costs of such routine decommissioning are well known.

Decommissioning and the majority of associated waste management costs are not incurred until the end of the reactor's life, allowing the operator to accumulate funds from revenues. As a result, levelised costs are not particularly sensitive to back-end costs. A United Kingdom Department of Trade and Industry (DTI) study shows that if back-end waste management costs were to double, the levelised cost would increase by only 0.8% (DTI, 2007).

Cost reduction opportunities: existing plants

Generators can recover the high construction costs of nuclear power stations more quickly by increasing output. Energy availability factors for nuclear plants worldwide have risen steadily over the past decade. Some countries have achieved very high energy-availability factors: between 2003 and 2005, Finland achieved 94.2% and a further four countries exceeded 88%. As a result, while generating capacity rose by only 1% per year in this period, nuclear electricity production has increased by 2% to 3% per year (World Nuclear Association, 2005) (see Figure 8.4).

Figure 8.4 ▶ Historic trend of global nuclear capacity and electricity production

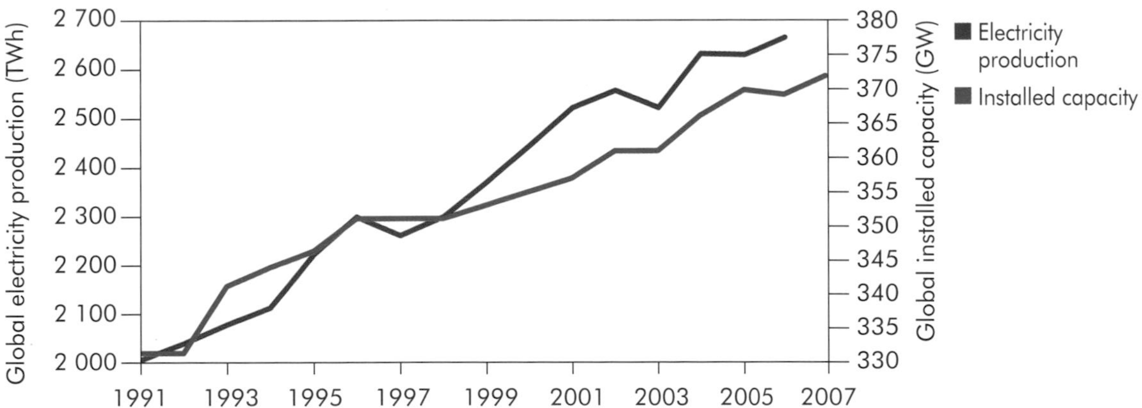

Source: World Nuclear Association, 2005.

Key point

Electricity from nuclear generation exceeds installed capacity.

For some existing plants, unit cost reductions have been achieved by up-rating the power output, in some cases by as much as 20%. In the United States, 113 up-rates of reactors were made between 1977 and 2007, increasing output by 4 900 MW (NEI, 2008b). A further 1 470 MW of up-rating is expected by 2011. In some countries, operating licences are time-limited and owners have sought extensions. In the United States, nearly half of the operating reactors have been granted life extensions, the most recent to 2046.

New nuclear power plant costs

Table 8.1 summarises the results of some recent studies of the overnight capital and levelised cost of new nuclear electricity-generating plants. Data presented in the NEA study are based on questionnaire responses from ten OECD countries using a 10% discount rate.

Table 8.1 ▶ **Results of recent studies on the cost of nuclear power**

Study	Cost of capital (%)	Overnight cost per kW	Levelised cost per MWh
Massachusetts Institute of Technology (MIT, 2003)	11.5	USD 2 000	USD 67
General Directorate for Energy and Raw Materials, France (DGEMP, 2004)	8	EUR 1 280	EUR 28
Tarjanne and Luostarinen (2003)	5	EUR 1 900	EUR 24
Royal Academy of Engineering (2004)	7.5	GBP 1 150	GBP 23
University of Chicago (2004)	12.5	USD 1 500	USD 51
Canadian Energy Research Institute (2004)	8	CAD 2 347	CAD 53
Department of Trade and Industry, UK (DTI, 2007)	10	GBP 1 250	GBP 38
IEA/NEA (2005)	10	USD 1 089-3 432	USD 30-50

Source: NEA, 2005b.

The data from the studies in Table 8.1 are presented graphically in Figure 8.5. Three of the cost estimates stand out as being particularly high. The United Kingdom Department of Trade and Industry study (DTI, 2007) is discussed in more detail below. Japanese levelised costs are very similar for coal, gas and nuclear power generation. Coal and gas costs in Japan are, like nuclear costs, the highest of all the IEA/NEA responses: this reflects exchange-rate effects and the high cost of labour and commodities in Japan. The Massachusetts Institute of Technology (MIT, 2003) study provides results applicable in the United States context, taking into account the corporate tax regime in place in the United States; the NEA study (2005) does not consider corporate tax.

Figure 8.5 ▶ **Levelised cost of new nuclear power generating plants**

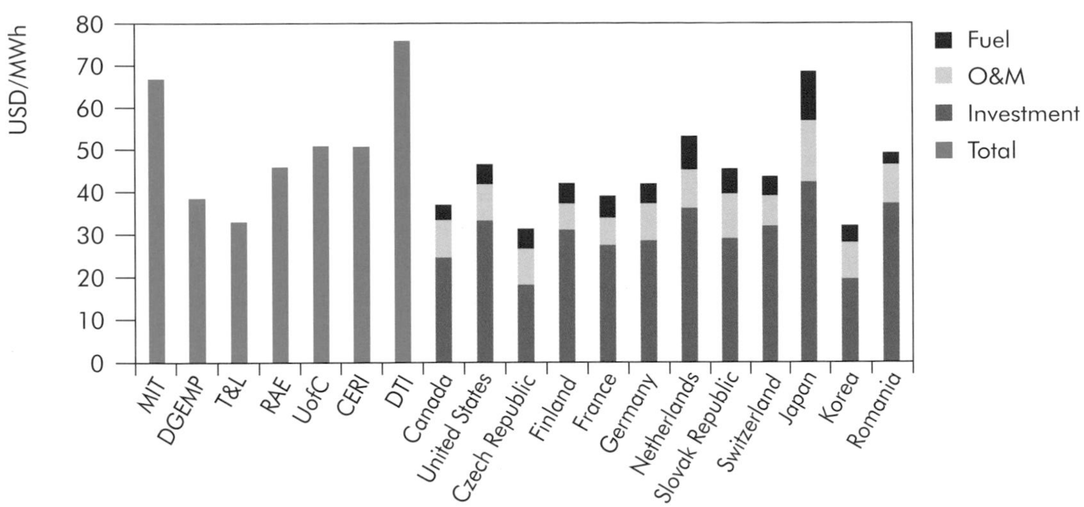

Note: Individual studies (left) and responses to NEA questionnaire (right).
Source: NEA, 2005b.

Key point

For future plants, most predicted levelised costs are in the range USD 30/MWh to USD 50/MWh, as shown by countries supporting the 2005 IEA/NEA study. However, country-specific issues are significant in determining these costs.

8

Figure 8.5 also shows the breakdown of each country's expectations of projected levelised cost at a 10% discount rate, from the IEA/NEA study. Broadly, investment costs represent around 70% of total costs while O&M and fuel-cycle costs contribute around 20% and 10% respectively. The total levelised cost (at 2004 prices) is projected to be in the range USD 30/MWh to USD 50/MWh in all countries except Japan and the Netherlands. In Japan, the total cost is expected to be USD 69/MWh.

Of the 12 countries considered in the study, in Canada, the Czech Republic, France and the Slovak Republic, and for two of the four German plants studied, nuclear was cheaper than coal by a margin of more than 10%. In Canada, the Czech Republic, France, Germany, the Netherlands, the Slovak Republic and the Republic of Korea, and for two of the three Swiss plants studied, nuclear was cheaper than gas by a margin of 10% or more. Since 2004, fossil-energy prices have risen considerably, suggesting that nuclear power should now be even more cost-competitive. Further, external costs are potentially significant in assessing the economics of nuclear power relative to other forms of generation. These include security of supply and reductions in atmospheric emissions, particularly CO_2. As nuclear energy is virtually CO_2 free, any value attributed to the cost of carbon would also add to nuclear's competitiveness.

Nuclear power cost sensitivity

The predicted costs of nuclear generation vary widely, depending on the input assumptions made. It is, therefore, crucial that assessments of nuclear power costs consider the sensitivity of the outcome to variations in these input assumptions.

The most recently published assessment of future nuclear levelised generating costs that includes a sensitivity analysis produced in May 2007 by the United Kingdom Government's Department of Trade and Industry (DTI, 2007).

The projected overnight construction costs in the DTI study are based on the Finnish Olkiluoto project, a 1 600 MW European Pressurised Water Reactor (EPR) being constructed under a turnkey (fixed-price) contract, and on a French programme equivalent to 10 GW of new reactor build. The projections included a number of adjustments (e.g. to allow for specific commercial issues and national regulatory requirements) to arrive at what DTI considered was a conservative approach to the question of costs and cost sensitivities.

The central forecast overnight construction cost on this basis was GBP 1 250/kW (USD 2 500/kW at July 2007 exchange rates). The DTI also brought together a number of 2006 private-sector market estimates of levelised new-build nuclear generation costs in a United Kingdom context, the average being GBP 30/MWh (USD 60/MWh at July 2007 exchange rates).

The assumptions adopted by DTI for their central-, low- and high-cost cases are set out in Table 8.2. These led to a range of nuclear generating costs of:

- high-cost: GBP 44/MWh (USD 88/MWh);
- central-cost: GBP 38/MWh (USD 76/MWh);
- low-cost: GBP 31/MWh (USD 62/MWh).

The DTI study regards the high cost case as unlikely, noting that its central case leads to a levelised cost already significantly greater than the average of market estimates (DTI, 2007). The high-cost case reflects a 30% overrun in construction costs, or an increase in the cost of capital to 12%. The low-cost assumptions are similar to forecasts made by the French Ministry of the Economy for a programme of ten reactors (General Directorate for Energy and Raw Materials, 2004).

Table 8.2 shows the relative significance of various factors in determining the cost of nuclear-generated electricity. The most important are overnight cost and the cost of capital. Factors with little impact on the levelised cost of nuclear power are the pre-development period, the early load factor, operational lifetime, fuel cost, and waste disposal and decommissioning costs. Although the DTI study only partially explored the sensitivity to construction-period and O&M costs, the evidence suggests these are also significant. The major significance of the cost of capital is consistent with the IEA/NEA study, which showed that levelised costs increase by some 50% to 60% as the cost of capital increases from 5% to 10%.

A recent study by the Keystone Center evaluating the life-cycle levelised cost for future nuclear power plants in the near term estimated costs to be in the range of USD 80 MWh to USD 110 MWh (Keystone Center, 2007). This range is slightly higher than the high-cost range of the DTI estimate.

Table 8.2 ▶ Sensitivity analysis for key parameters in the cost of nuclear power

Key item	Comment	Central assumption	Lower-cost assumption	Levelised cost GBP/ MWh	Higher-cost assumption	Levelised cost GBP/ MWh
Central case				38		38
Pre-development cost	Data from UK Environmental Audit Committee	GBP 250 m	GBP 100 m	36	GBP 300 m	38
Pre-development period	Five years to obtain site licence; three years for sitting inquiry	8 years	7 years	38	9 years	38
Construction cost[1]	Total cost GBP 2.8 b includes GBP 500 m IDC[2] plus GBP 10/kW onsite waste storage every 5 years	GBP 1 250/kW	GBP 850/kW	31	GBP 1 400/kW GBP 1 625/kW	40 44
Construction period	Vendor estimates 5 to 5.5 years	6 years			10 years	41
Load factor first five years	Vendor expectations >90%	80%	90%	37	60%	39
Operational life	Vendors expect 60 years	40 years	60 years	37	30 years	39
O&M cost	Equivalent to GBP 90 m/year, vendor estimates GBP 40 m/ year	GBP 7.7/MWh	GBP 4.4/ MWh[3]	35		
Fuel supply cost	All in cost equivalent to GBP 4.4/MWh	GBP 2 400/kg	GBP 2 000/kg	37	GBP 3 000/kg	39
Waste disposal cost	Assumes geologic disposal; fund growth 2.2% in real terms	GBP 276 m at EOG			GBP 320 m after 40 years	38
Decommissioning cost	Assumes GBP 400 m/ GWE, vendor estimates GBP 325 m-GBP 400 m/GWE, fun growth 2.2% in real terms	GBP 636 m at EOG			GBP 950 m after 40 years	38
Cost of capital	Post tax real discount rate	10%	7%	31	12%	42

Source: UK Government's Department of Trade and Industry (DTI), May 2007.

1. The higher-cost assumption includes the effect of two construction costs.

2. IDC: interest during construction.

3. The DTI study units for O&M costs in the central case differ from those in the low-cost case.

External costs

In addition to the direct costs of nuclear operations, it is also important to assess external costs – *i.e.* those costs that are not internalised in the market prices paid by consumers, but are paid by society as a whole. Such costs affect the real competitiveness of alternative generation options from a sustainable development perspective. In the case of electricity generation, external costs include the impact of pollutant releases and greenhouse gas emissions, as well as social costs such as accident risk aversion.

In this context, nuclear power offers a number of security-of-supply advantages. The fuel – uranium – comes from diverse, politically stable countries. One tonne of uranium produces the same energy as 10 000 to 16 000 tonnes of oil. This high energy-density makes uranium easier to stockpile and to transport, making it much less sensitive to supply disruptions than fossil fuels.

In terms of carbon emissions, nuclear power also offers significant benefits. In the United States alone, each year of nuclear generation saves the emission of 700 million tonnes of CO_2, 3 million tonnes of sulphur oxides and 1 million tonnes of nitrogen oxides (NEI, 2008c).

Most of the potential health and environmental costs of nuclear energy are already internalised through safety and radiation protection norms and standards. The internalisation of other external costs where possible, across all forms of electricity production, through the use of mechanisms to value the cost of avoided carbon emissions, for example, is likely to strengthen the relative competitiveness of nuclear energy.

Safety

A continuing concern for some members of the public and for some policy makers is the safety of nuclear generation. Two significant accidents have occurred during 12 700 reactor-years of civil nuclear power generation. These were at Three Mile Island (USA, 1979), where the reactor was severely damaged, but radiation was contained and there were no adverse health or environmental consequences, and Chernobyl (Ukraine, 1986), where the destruction of the reactor by steam explosion and fire killed around 40 people directly and had significant health and environmental consequences.

Since these two incidents, the nuclear industry has continued to develop and refine nuclear safety and design features in all nuclear generating plants, and to improve reactor operator training worldwide. One example is the industry's efforts to achieve optimum safety in OECD nuclear plants using a "defence-in-depth" approach, with multiple safety systems supplementing the natural safety features of the reactor core. Three Mile Island demonstrated the importance of these inherent safety features. In contrast, the Chernobyl reactor did not have a containment structure (unlike the water-cooled reactors used in the West or in post-1980 Soviet designs). An OECD expert report concluded, "the Chernobyl accident has not brought to light any new, previously unknown phenomena or safety issues that are not resolved or otherwise covered by current reactor safety programmes for commercial power reactors in OECD Member countries" (NEA, "Risks and Benefits of Nuclear Energy", 2007).

Another example is the industry's practice of improving certification and training programmes for nuclear power plant operators, along with improving dialogue with national regulatory bodies.

The Energy Related Severe Accident Database (ENSAD), established by the Paul Scherrer Institute in Switzerland, contains data on over 18 000 accidents, from 1969 onwards, of which 35% are energy related. More than 3 000 of these are rated as severe (with five or more prompt fatalities). Figure 8.6 shows frequency/consequences curves for this data, for OECD countries (NEA, 2007). The data for LPG, coal, oil and natural gas are data from real accidents, for full life-cycle analysis (including exploration, extraction, processing, storage, transport and waste management). During this period there has only been one severe hydropower accident in OECD countries, resulting in 14 prompt fatalities. There have been no OECD nuclear accidents in this "severe" classification. While this record of the OECD countries is commendable, public concern over nuclear safety continues to be an ongoing hurdle for the nuclear industry.

Figure 8.6 ▶ **Comparison of frequency-consequence curves for full energy chains in OECD countries for the period 1969-2000**

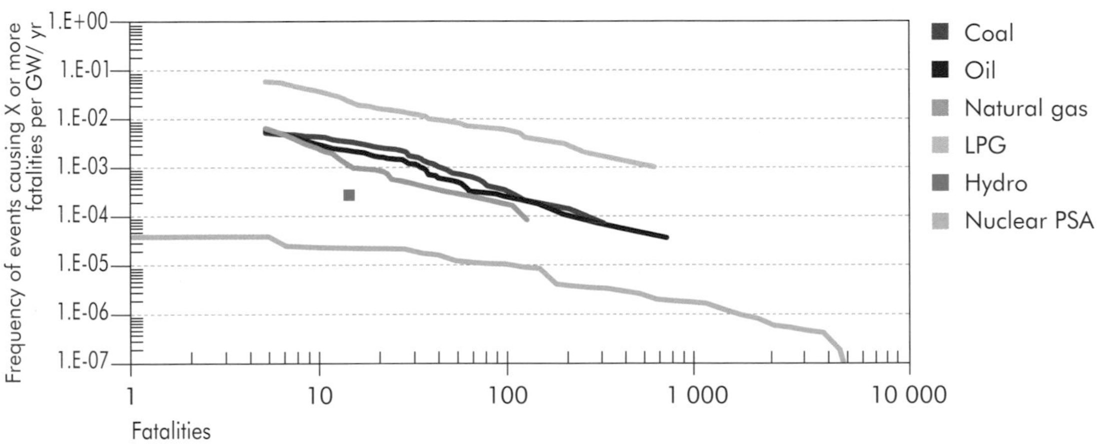

Source: NEA, 2007.

Key point

OECD nuclear energy accident rates compare favourably with other energy industries.

Figure 8.6 also shows the probabilistic safety analysis (PSA) for a Swiss nuclear power plant. Note that this line is not directly comparable, in that it is for the latent deaths (c.f. prompt deaths for other data) from theoretically possible releases, rather than actual releases or accidents). From this figure, it is clear that nuclear energy compares much more favourably against other energy sources than the public might believe. The data shows that in OECD countries, both hydro and nuclear have been very safe sources.

This particular plot could be subject to criticism from a number of positions. In choosing OECD countries, it ignores Chernobyl, for example. But Chernobyl, severe as it was, only caused about 40 prompt deaths. The biggest energy-related accidents elsewhere were caused by oil (Philippines, 1987: 3 000 fatalities; Afghanistan, 1982: 2 700 fatalities), hydro (India, 1980: 1 000 fatalities) and LPG (Russia, 1989: 600 fatalities). It could also be criticised for ignoring the latent death estimates from Chernobyl; but in that case comparison should also include latent deaths from both operation and accidents. And fossil technologies come out quite badly in terms of latent deaths as a consequence of air pollution.

Proliferation of nuclear weapons

Over the past 35 years, the International Atomic Energy Agency's (IAEA) safeguards system under the Nuclear Non-Proliferation Treaty has continued to serve the international community in helping prevent the diversion of civil uranium into military uses. The Nuclear Non-Proliferation Treaty, to which 187 states are party, came into force in 1970; it was extended indefinitely in 1995. The safeguards arrangements are backed up by diplomatic, political and economic measures, and complemented by controls on the export of sensitive technology.

Shortly after the Nuclear Non-Proliferation Treaty was set up, international agreements established two mechanisms for controlling nuclear exports: the Zangger Committee in 1971 and the Nuclear Suppliers Group in 1975. These engage exporting countries in international efforts to prevent the international trade of items that could be used directly to pursue production of nuclear weapons. States outside the Treaty are required to institute IAEA safeguards before being allowed to import such items. The Nuclear Suppliers Group has voluntarily agreed to co-ordinate export controls to ensure that transfers of nuclear material or equipment are not made to states that do not agree to IAEA inspections, or where safeguards are not in place.

International events over the past two decades have shown the need for reinforcement of the Nuclear Non-Proliferation Treaty, particularly where undeclared facilities are involved. In 1997, the IAEA Board of Governors agreed a model protocol to aid the IAEA's ability to detect undeclared nuclear activities. Some aspects of this strengthened Treaty can be implemented through IAEA's existing legal authority; others require further authority which can be conferred through an Additional Protocol agreed between each state and IAEA. The Additional Protocols, once they are in force, provide credible assurance that there are no undeclared nuclear materials or activities in the states concerned. As of July 2007, 121 states have signed or ratified Additional Protocols.

Notwithstanding the success both of the Nuclear Non-Proliferation Treaty and voluntary export controls, the potential for diverting nuclear fuel into weapons programmes is seen as one of the disadvantages of nuclear energy. One example is a study by The Keystone Center that questions the IAEA and the international community's effort to demonstrate that the enforcement mechanisms are effective. The Keystone study finds the IAEA safeguards to be currently insufficient to provide timely detection when weapons quantities of highly enriched uranium (HEU) and plutonium are diverted. This is because the time required to convert different forms of nuclear material to the metallic components of a nuclear explosive device are short compared to the IAEA timeliness detection goals used to define the frequency of inspections (The Keystone Center, 2007).

Despite these concerns, the IAEA has proposed the development of multilateral nuclear approaches to increase non-proliferation assurances for nuclear energy fuel-cycle facilities. International fuel-cycle centres, under arrangements that would guarantee supplies of nuclear fuel, could create additional non-proliferation assurances while allowing developing countries access to nuclear energy. Such facilities would reinforce existing market mechanisms.

High-level waste disposal

Radioactive wastes are generally classified according to their activity content and thermal heat load. In many countries, disposal of low- and intermediate-level wastes to repositories is routine. High-level waste (HLW) contains more than 95% of the radioactivity produced by reactors. It requires cooling as the process of natural radioactive decay continues to generate heat, typically for a period of several decades.

Reactor operations create radioactive fission products and transuranic elements; these are contained within the spent fuel. Some countries reprocess spent fuel to recycle uranium and plutonium. The fission products and transuranic elements are separated and become HLW that will eventually be disposed (other than plutonium), usually after vitrification. In countries where spent fuel is not reprocessed, the spent fuel element itself is classified as HLW and is appropriately packaged. Commercial reprocessing plants currently operating in France, the United Kingdom and Russia have a capacity of some 5 000 tonnes of fuel per year, and the global cumulative operating experience is some 80 000 tonnes over 50 years (WNA, 2007). A 1 000 MW light-water reactor produces about 25 tonnes of spent fuel per year; where spent fuel is reprocessed, about three cubic metres of vitrified waste is produced per year. Nuclear power utilities internalise almost all of their waste-management costs, including processing, storage and provision for ultimate disposal of HLW or direct disposal of spent fuel.

There is consensus among international experts that deep geological disposal provides an appropriate and safe technological route for the final disposal of high-level waste. This is a consequence of the many years of work by many institutions around the world, a free exchange of information and knowledge among these institutions, and a strong tradition of open documentation available for peer and public review. No geological repository for spent fuel or HLW has yet been built, primarily because of public concern over safety and the consequent socio-political issues associated with the siting of repositories. Only two countries, Finland and the United States, have settled on sites for their repositories. Some countries, such as Japan, Sweden and the United Kingdom, are seeking volunteer communities to host HLW disposal sites. As an interim strategy, spent fuel is currently stored in either spent-fuel pools or dry-cask storage on site.

France plans to have a disposal facility working in 2025, Japan in about 2035, and the United Kingdom in 2045. Other countries, such as Finland and Sweden, plan direct disposal of spent fuel in geological formations without reprocessing.

Although the technology is well developed, there is a need for continued high-quality scientific and technical work on specific sites, and to increase technical confidence through the further reduction of uncertainties. This further refinement, testing, demonstration, implementation and quality control, as well as research into the economic costs of once-through fuel cycles versus reprocessing/recycle systems, is likely to need to extend over two or more decades.

If spent fuel is reprocessed using current technology, the uranium and plutonium are removed for recycling and the activity of the vitrified waste product is dominated by the minor actinides. If these long-life isotopes could be separated (partitioned) and then turned into very much shorter half-life isotopes (transmuted), the radiotoxic inventory would be reduced. The radioactivity of the waste would then fall to below that of the original uranium ore in a period of around 300 years, which would make it more straightforward to dispose of HLW (CEA, 2002). Although the current design of HLW disposal facilities has risk targets of typically one in a million per year to the most exposed member of the population, some thousands of years into the future, public acceptance of waste-disposal facilities would be improved if partitioning and transmutation were employed. Acceptance of future nuclear power programmes, to a significant extent predicated on a satisfactory solution to HLW management, would be also strengthened.

A number of countries are researching partitioning and transmutation technologies. French R&D is particularly advanced in this area (CEA, 2005) and has been subjected to international peer review (NEA, 2006). Results obtained to date show that partitioning of the minor actinides americium, curium and neptunium from PWR fuel, together with the fission products caesium and iodine, is possible on a laboratory scale and that industrial deployment could be successful. However, this remains to be demonstrated on a commercial scale.

Transmutation of the minor actinides to shorter-lived isotopes will probably involve either fast reactor or accelerator technologies – thermal reactors cannot practically do this for all the necessary isotopes. Progress is likely only with substantial international co-operation. There are significant problems associated with handling large quantities of pure americium and curium, however, and in creating fuel for fast-reactor transmutation, or targets for accelerator transmutation. Commercial application of these technologies is still a considerable way off.

New nuclear build and construction rates

Nuclear power continues to be an energy option for many countries, as shown in Figure 8.7 (WNA, 2006-2007). This includes only those countries where more than one new plant is either planned or proposed. In this context, planned means that approvals and funding are in place or construction is well advanced (even though it may be suspended indefinitely). Proposed means there is a clear intention to build, but it is still without funding or approval.

Significant numbers of new reactors are planned or proposed for China, India and Russia, and Japan, South Korea, South Africa, Ukraine and the United States also have build programmes. China, India and Russia are reported to be planning nuclear capacity increases by 2020 of 40 GW, 16 GW and 22 GW respectively; governments have approved sites for many of these nuclear units. The governments of Japan and South Korea have also approved plans for additional nuclear capacity, primarily for energy security reasons (Japan, 9 GW by 2015; South Korea, 12 GW by 2017). A further 16 GW of nuclear capacity by 2030 has been approved by the government of Ukraine.

In the United States, the Nuclear Regulatory Commission has established a new process for licensing commercial advanced reactors, intended to eliminate the costs and delays that resulted from the 1960s process that was used to license the plants in operation in the United States today.

Figure 8.7 ▶ **Plans and proposals for new nuclear power reactors**

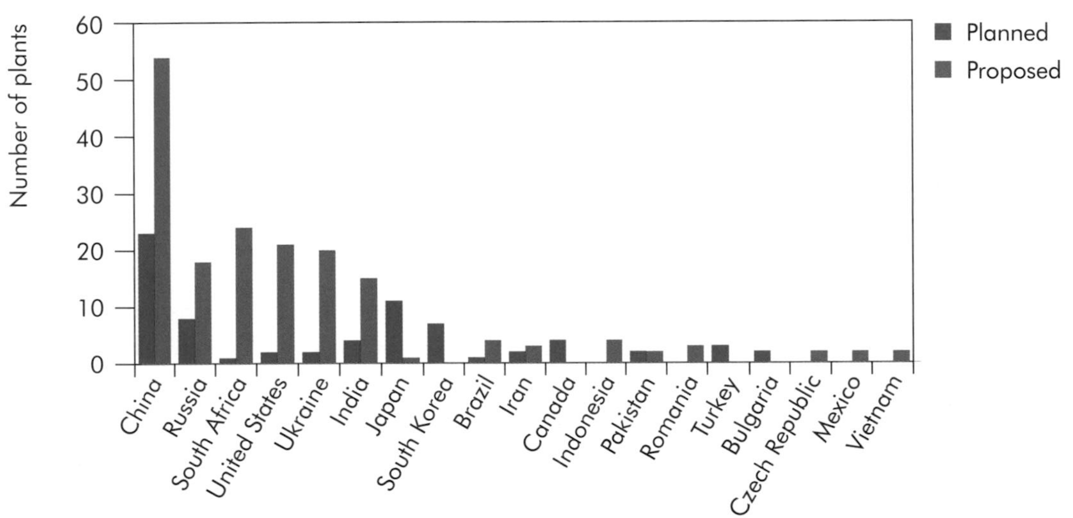

Note: May 2007.

Source: WNA, 2006-2007.

8

Key point

Many governments are considering or planning new nuclear power capacity.

The IEA Reference Scenario (WEO 2006) predicts that 52 GW of additional nuclear generating capacity will be built globally between 2004 and 2030 – a modest build rate of 2 GW per year. The IEA also projects that a total of 5 087 GW of global electricity-generating capacity (including replacement capacity) will be built by 2030 – *i.e.,* 195 GW per year. This section explores the extent to which nuclear power might be able to make a bigger contribution to that overall growth – for example, if there was a radical increase in the share of nuclear capacity to reduce CO_2 production or to increase security of supply.

Figure 8.8 shows that between 1970 and 1990, new nuclear plants were adding around 17 GW every year to global electricity-generating capacity. In the 1980s, 218 power reactors started operations, at an average of one every 17 days. This was mostly in France, Japan and the United States. The average output of these new plants was 925 MW. The build rate was continuing to accelerate up to the point of the Chernobyl accident in 1986, at which point it decelerated rapidly.

Figure 8.8 ▶ **Global nuclear generating capacity**

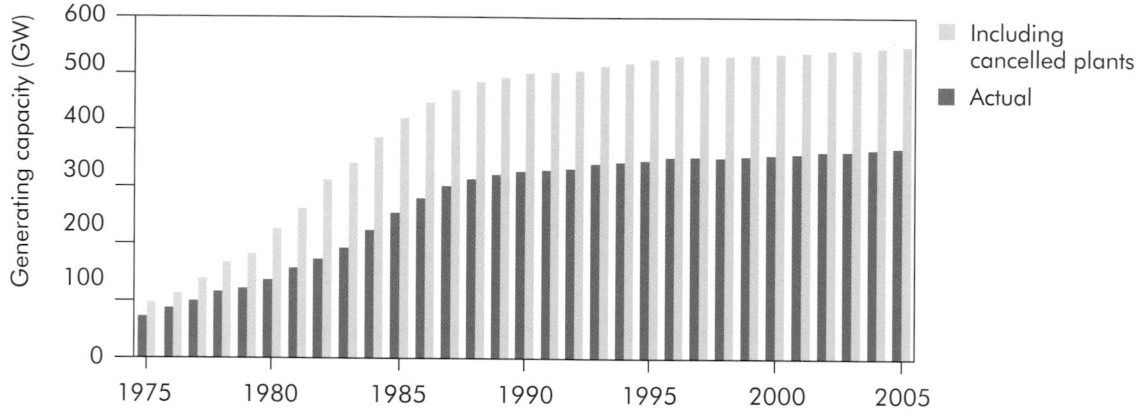

Source: IAEA, 2006.

Key point

In the 1980s, power reactors were grid-connected at the rate of one every 17 days (between 1977 and 1993, France alone constructed 3.6 reactors per year).

Figure 8.8 also shows the additional global nuclear electricity generating capacity that was planned but never built. Had it been, between 1970 and 1990 the world would have seen an additional 11 GW of nuclear generation commissioned every year. In the United States, 122 plants, capable of generating 134 GW, were cancelled between 1972 and 2006, after construction permits had been granted. Worldwide the total was 165 (WNA, reactor database). Of these 165 cancelled plants, construction had started on 62 (IAEA, 2006), and some were complete.

Figure 8.9 shows the number of global new reactor grid connections annually from 1955 to the present day, together with a five-year moving average. Annual grid connections peaked in 1984 and 1985 at 33 per year; the five-year moving average peaked around 27 per year.

In rough terms, the world's *industrial capacity* should be in constant proportion to the national gross domestic product (GDP). At constant money values, global GDP in 2005 was twice that in 1980. Globally, 17 GW per annum of nuclear generation was actually constructed, and around 28 GW per annum was ordered, between 1970 and 1990. The increase in global economic activity suggests that – all other things being equal – the world today should have the economic capacity to construct nuclear power stations at twice that rate – between 35 GW and 56 GW per year.

In France alone, 58 nuclear power reactors came into operation between 1977 and 1993 – an average of 3.6 reactors per year. World economic activity in 2005 was about 30 times that of France in 1985. A global scaling-up of the French programme would suggest an economic capacity to construct today some 100 reactors every year (160 GW per year if the reactors were EPRs).

Figure 8.9 ▶ **Global annual grid connections on five-year moving average**

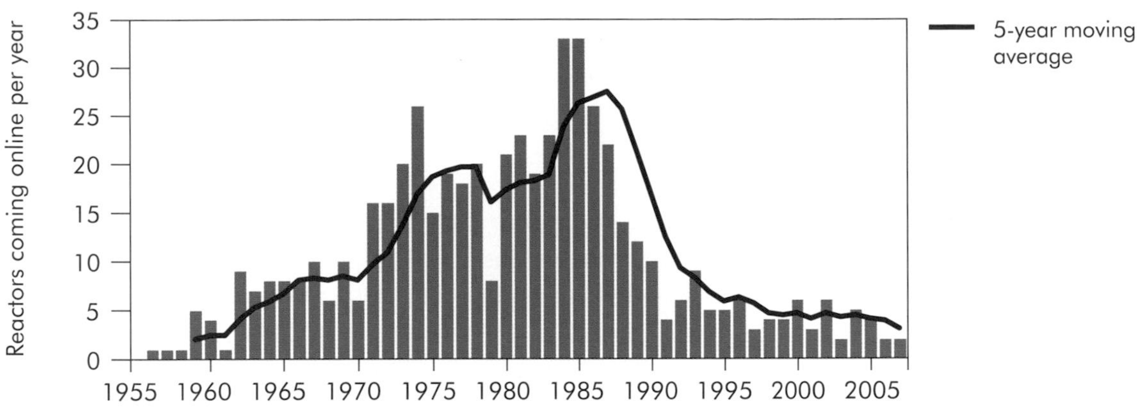

Source: IAEA, 2006.

Key point

Nuclear grid connections peaked in the mid 1980s.

These extrapolations suggest a global capability to construct nuclear plants at a rate that would meet at least 18%, and possibly 30%, of the IEA Reference Scenario (WEO, 2006) demand for new electricity generation capacity (including replacement build) by 2030. Extrapolation of French nuclear power history alone suggests this figure could be up to 80%.

These are of course theoretical economic capacities. They do not consider the rate at which such capacity could be developed, and from a base that is considerably lower than the peak build rate in the 1980s. Given the time needed to build up global industrial or supply chain capabilities, and the potential unavailability of appropriate skills, it may be that the nuclear generation shares suggested here could not be achieved by 2030. It is probable that the market for materials and skills will only respond when it is clear the demand is there. The following sections examine these aspects in more detail.

The world's ability to construct large numbers of reactors simultaneously will depend on, among other things, the capacity of the *global supply chain*. The United Kingdom nuclear industry estimates that a new nuclear power station would require around 2% of the United Kingdom's national construction capability, well within normal levels of demand variation (UK Nuclear Industries Association, 2006).

However, the Nuclear Energy Institute (NEI) has identified several potential manufacturing constraints that could hinder the construction of new nuclear power plants. For example, only one company, in Japan, has the capability to produce the ultra-large forgings that are needed for the largest reactor pressure vessels, and the company has a three-year order backlog. This could inhibit the expansion of nuclear power around the world unless new forging capacity is brought on-line. The NEI study identified ultra-large forgings as the first major pinch point that the industry will encounter before 2010, but concluded that constraints on supplies of nuclear-grade pumps, valves and heat exchangers could also arise in subsequent years (NEI, 2007).

The United Kingdom's Department of Trade and Industry has identified, in addition, a European shortage of heavy-lift cranes (DTI, 2007). DTI also notes the small global manufacturing base for large-generator transformers, large diesel generators for emergency core cooling, and sulphur hexafluoride for switchgear. Some of these supply issues will affect construction of fossil-fuelled electricity generation plants as well as nuclear plants.

As regards *nuclear skills*, the nuclear industry now faces two problems:

- Retention of existing skills and competences for the long life-cycle of existing plant.
- Development and retention of nuclear skills and competences, both in the area of decommissioning and radioactive waste management (often seen as unattractive activities by young people) and in support of potential new nuclear power build.

A large part of the current nuclear workforce received their education and started their careers during the rapid build-up of the nuclear programme in the 1960s and 1970s. This means that this workforce is now close to retirement, or has already left the industry. NEI recently estimated that 26% of engineers working in United States nuclear utilities will be eligible for retirement in the next five years.

Several studies have been undertaken to examine the concern that nuclear education and training has been decreasing. The Nuclear Energy Agency (NEA) of the OECD has quantified the status of nuclear education in member countries, confirming that, in most countries, nuclear education had declined to the point that expertise and competence in core nuclear technologies was becoming increasingly difficult to sustain (NEA, 2000). The need to maintain core skills and competences was generally recognised, but given that public funding has decreased, this responsibility was increasingly falling on the nuclear industry (NEA, 2004a).

The precise need for skilled and experienced personnel in the nuclear field will depend to a large extent on the scale of any new nuclear build programme. However, even without significant new build, governments and industry need to consider how to replace their current aging workforce in order to continue operating and, eventually, safely decommission existing reactors. Some governments have started this process and there is evidence that the shortfall in training is starting to be addressed (see Figure 8.10).

Figure 8.10 ▶ Nuclear engineering degrees from United States universities

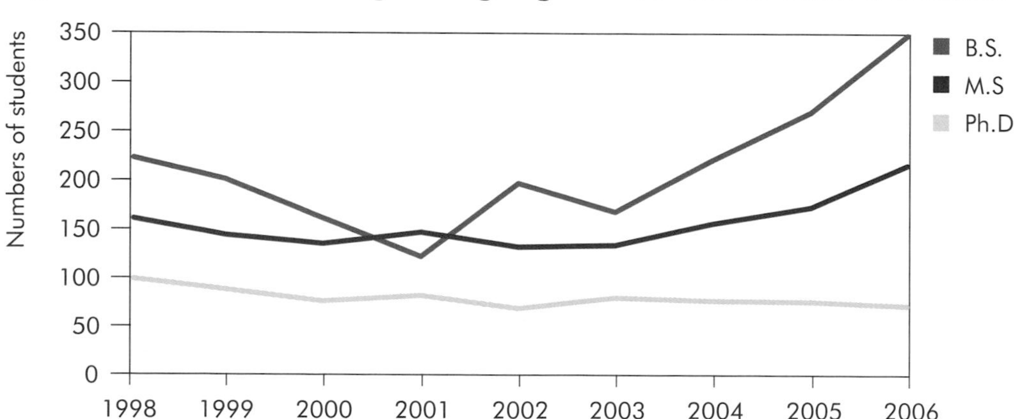

Source: Oak Ridge Institute for Science and Education, 2007.

Key point

Nuclear engineering degrees in United States universities are increasing.

Future technology options

Small- and medium-scale nuclear plants

The principal drivers behind the projected large increase in global energy needs are population growth and economic expansion in today's developing countries.

Most current reactor designs have large power outputs, typically 1 000 MW to 1 700 MW. These large reactors are unsuited to many developing countries, or isolated communities, where there is limited or localised electric grid capacity with few interconnections. Two-thirds of Russia's territory is off-grid and can be expected to remain so for decades. India, a developing country that is successfully embracing nuclear power with domestically produced 200 MW and 490 MW pressurised heavy water reactors, has identified 80 000 centres of population that are likely never to be connected to the grid. In addition, current nuclear plants have a large capital cost relative to fossil power plants.

Consequently, some 60 different small and medium-sized reactor (SMR) designs are being considered globally (IAEA, 2007).[4] Commercial deployment is generally expected to be between 2010 and 2030. Their reduced size and complexity means lower capital cost (although probably higher overall cost per unit of electricity generated) and shorter construction times. This is especially important for developing economies, where capital funds may be limited. SMRs allow flexibility to install generating capacity in small increments to match increasing power demand. Some SMRs have reduced specific power levels (*i.e.* power per unit reactor volume) that allow plant simplifications, enhancing safety and reliability (IAEA, 2005). This is especially advantageous in countries with limited nuclear experience and allows plants to be sited closer to population centres, reducing the need for long transmission lines.

In many countries, SMRs are likely to be a preferred option for non-electric applications that require proximity to the customer: such as desalination, district heating and, eventually, hydrogen production. Some have already been used for these purposes.

SMR designers aim for inherent and passive approaches to safety, for example providing very small reactivity margins. Many of the water-cooled SMRs being considered have integral reactor designs with all the steam generators and coolant pumps inside the pressure vessel, so that no primary circuit piping is required to connect the components. Some have the control rod drive mechanisms within the pressure vessel to remove the potential for control rod ejection accidents.

Half the SMR designs under consideration are planned without on-site refuelling. These SMRs would be factory fuelled, thereby reducing the generator's obligations for spent fuel and waste management and assuring more effective proliferation safeguards. For such reactors, fuel-cycle facilities could be centralised at a very limited number of facilities worldwide. Accountancy could be performed on entire cores during shipment and operation under international safeguards oversight.

4. IAEA classifies small-sized reactors as those having a power output of less than 300 MW, and medium-sized reactors as those producing 300 MW to 700 MW.

Other designs consider extended refuelling intervals with vendor-supplied fuel services. Current reactor designs could achieve infrequent refuelling through reduced core power density and use of burnable poisons, boosted by higher fuel enrichment. One alternative to higher enrichment is a design where fresh fuel particles or pebbles are stored outside the core (but inside the pressure vessel) and gradually moved into the core to compensate for reactivity reductions.

SMR designs targeted at near-term deployment include:

- Integral type PWRs, such as the SMART (Republic of Korea), IRIS (Westinghouse, leading a multilateral consortium) and CAREM (Argentina) designs.
- Factory fabricated loop type PWRs (*e.g.* the Russian KLT-40 design for barge-mounted nuclear power plants based on experience from nuclear icebreakers and submarines).
- Gas-cooled pebble bed modular reactors (PBMR) such as those being developed by South Africa which, with a gas outlet temperature of 900°C, can be directly linked to gas turbines.

Alternative uses of nuclear power

To date, nuclear energy has been applied primarily to the production of electricity. However, there are other potential uses. The extent to which they become important will affect future expansion of nuclear energy programmes as much as its development for electricity generation. Four potentially large-scale alternative uses exist: for hydrogen for use in transport, for district heating, for desalination and for process heat. Other, smaller scale, non-electric uses include isotope production for a wide range of medical and industrial applications.

In the short term, *hybrid electric vehicles* have the potential to increase the demand for base load power from grid systems. However, *hydrogen* has the potential to be a major transport fuel in the longer term. Nuclear energy can be used today to make hydrogen electrolytically – in the future, high-temperature reactors may be used to make it thermo-chemically (NEA, 2004b). Research into the use of nuclear power to generate hydrogen is expected to lead to commercial production around 2020. Investment is driven, particularly in the United States, by a desire to reduce dependence on imported oil. Future energy demand for hydrogen production could be significant.

It is estimated that one-fifth of the world's population does not have access to safe drinking water (GTZ, 2001). Where drinking water cannot be readily obtained from streams and aquifers, *desalination* of seawater or mineralised groundwater is required. Most desalination today uses fossil fuels. Total world capacity is approaching 30 million m^3/day of potable water, in some 12 500 plants; half of these are in the Middle East and the largest produces 454 000 m^3/day.

The use of nuclear power for desalination is a proven technology (IAEA, 1997). It looks set to expand as the world's population grows, but large-scale deployment of nuclear desalination on a commercial basis will depend primarily on economic factors. The IAEA is fostering research and collaboration on the issue, with more than 20 countries involved. France and Libya have signed a memorandum of understanding to co-operate on a project to build a nuclear-powered desalination plant in Libya.

District heating using steam from electricity-generating plants is a safe, widely used, mature technology, particularly in the Russian Federation. Over approximately 500-reactor-years of operational experience, no incidents involving radioactive contamination have ever been reported for any heat-supplying reactor (IAEA, 2000).

Future prospects

Most commentators consider that water-cooled reactors will continue to be the primary form of nuclear power generation until the middle of the century. Between 2010 and 2020, nuclear power could expand significantly, especially in developing countries, through the adoption of Generation III and Generation III+ LWR designs, including the Westinghouse AP 1000, the General Electric ESBWR, the AREVA EPR, the General Electric ABWR, and the Mitsubishi Heavy Industries APWR. These designs offer improved safety characteristics and better economics than the earlier Generation II water reactors currently in operation. Four ABWRs are already in operation in Japan. In Europe, a 1 600 MW EPR is being built at Olkiluoto in Finland, with a second planned at Flamanville in France. There are a significant number of expressions of interest in new nuclear build projects in the United States, but no firm orders have yet been placed.

Gas-cooled reactors offer some inherently better safety characteristics and higher thermal efficiencies than water-cooled reactors. Third-generation gas-cooled reactors, such as the pebble-bed modular reactor (PBMR), offer enhanced operational and safety features and are expected to become available in the next decade. These are generally considered Generation III+ designs. A PBMR demonstration is planned to be operational in South Africa in the next few years, with commercialisation from 2015.

A large number of longer-term reactor designs are under development. All such developments are expensive, and international co-operation is needed to maximise the effectiveness of scarce R&D funding. Three major international initiatives are already under way:

- Twelve countries and organisations – Argentina, Brazil, Canada, China, France, Japan, Russia, South Africa, Switzerland, the United Kingdom, the United States, and Euratom – have joined together to form the Generation IV International Forum. The Technical Secretariat of the Forum is provided by the OECD Nuclear Energy Agency (NEA). The Forum aims to develop a future generation of nuclear energy systems that will provide competitively priced and reliable energy while satisfactorily addressing the issues of improved nuclear safety, waste minimisation and improved physical protection and proliferation resistance.
- The International Project on Innovative Nuclear Reactors and Fuel Cycles (INPRO), undertaken under the auspices of the IAEA, is another major initiative to support the safe, sustainable, economic and proliferation-resistant use of nuclear technology.

The INPRO initiative's participants come from Argentina, Armenia, Belarus, Brazil, Bulgaria, Canada, Chile, China, the Czech Republic, France, Germany, India, Indonesia, Japan, Kazakhstan, the Republic of Korea, Morocco, the Netherlands, Pakistan, the Russian Federation, Slovakia, South Africa, Spain, Switzerland, Turkey, Ukraine, the United States and the European Commission.

- In February 2006, the United States launched the Global Nuclear Energy Partnership to expand the development of nuclear technologies while avoiding proliferation concerns. It has allocated USD 166 million to the Department of Energy's 2007 budget for this initiative, which it expects to pursue with international partners. The partnership had grown to 19 members by late 2007 (Australia, Bulgaria, Canada, China, France, Ghana, Hungary, Italy, Japan, Jordan, Kazakhstan, Lithuania, Poland, Romania, the Russian Federation, Slovenia, South Korea, Ukraine and the United States).

Fast reactors hold out the prospect of the near indefinite recycling of spent fuel. Several countries have invested significant funds into this technology, mostly using sodium coolants. While many Generation IV fast-breeder designs use sodium, others employ lead or lead/bismuth coolants to avoid the potential for fires and water reactions associated with sodium. Fast reactors operate at higher temperatures than current water-cooled reactors, so allowing significant increases in thermodynamic efficiency. In the future, gas-cooled fast reactors may allow the benefits of gas reactors to be coupled to those of fast-breeders – these include low specific power density and high outlet temperatures suitable for direct connection to a gas turbine.

Fusion is a nuclear process that releases energy by joining light elements – it is essentially the direct opposite of fission. In principle, fusion holds the promise of a long-term, sustainable, economic and safe energy source for electricity generation, with relatively inexpensive fuel. Over the past two decades, the operation of a series of experimental devices has enabled considerable advances in this technology. Production of fusion energy has been established, though only for a few seconds. The fusion reaction produces no greenhouse gases and no radioactive fission products or actinides. The cost of fusion electricity will depend upon the extent to which fusion physics, technologies and materials are further optimised in the next few decades. Fusion is being developed in the context of a long-standing international co-operation programme and significant fractions of energy R&D budgets are allocated to researching its feasibility and potential.

Caderache in France has been chosen as the location of the USD 10 billion International Thermonuclear Experimental Reactor (ITER) project. Seven partners are involved: the European Union, China, India, Japan, Korea, Russia and the United States. ITER is designed to demonstrate the scientific and technological feasibility of fusion energy and aims to provide the know-how to build the first electricity-generating power station based on magnetic confinement of high temperature plasma. It will test the main features needed, including high-temperature tolerant components and large-scale, reliable superconducting magnets. ITER's operating conditions will be designed close to those required in a fusion power system. The project aims to show how they can be optimised, and how design margins can be reduced to increase efficiency and control cost.

Fusion is not likely to be deployed for commercial electricity production until at least the second half of the century.

Chapter 9 BIOMASS AND BIOENERGY

Key Findings

- *Bioenergy is the largest renewable energy contributor to global primary energy today and has the highest technical potential of all renewable energy sources according to both the ACT Map and BLUE Map scenarios for 2050.*

- *Biomass used inefficiently for traditional domestic cooking and space heating accounts for around two-thirds of total current demand. By 2050, a transition towards more efficient use in improved conversion technologies could occur, including liquid biofuels such as dimethyl ether (DME).*

- *The amount of biomass available from both residues and energy crops by 2050 will be dependent on the efficiency of the world agricultural and forestry systems. Sustainably produced resources will be in demand for heat and power applications, to produce bio-chemicals, liquid biofuels for transport and other bio-materials. Future supply levels and priorities for the use of biomass resources are very difficult to predict with confidence.*

- *In the BLUE Map scenario, biomass use increases nearly four-fold by 2050, accounting for around 23% of total world primary energy (150 EJ/yr, 3 604 Mtoe/yr). This makes it by far the most important renewable energy source. Such a level would require in the region of 15 000 Mt of biomass to be delivered to processing plants annually. Around half of this will come from crop and forest residues, with the remainder from purpose-grown energy crops. These will require the equivalent of around half the land area currently used for agricultural production in Africa.* 9

- *Around 700 Mtoe/yr of the total biomass will be consumed to produce transport biofuels, and a similar amount to generate 2 450 TWh/yr of power. This includes biomass co-fired with coal and used in combined heat- and power-generation systems (CHP). The remaining 2 200 Mtoe will be used for bio-chemicals, heating and cooking (including solid biomass combustion and DME production), and in industry (including process steam from CHP plants and black liquor).*

- *Advanced combustion technologies, such as circulating fluidised bed (CFB) boilers and co-firing biomass with coal for steam turbines of up to 100 MW capacity, could generate electricity at around USD 60/MWh to USD 80/MWh, or less where the heat can be used in CHP projects. This would be cost-competitive with other technologies.*

- *The potential growth of biomass gasification technologies is difficult to predict, but could be significant. Given continued high RDD&D investment and greater experience, costs are likely to decline by 25% to 50% due to higher efficiencies. Considerable RDD&D investment is needed. It will not be possible to meet the projected 2050 demand for biomass for both Fischer Tropsch synthetic diesel and bioenergy power plants unless gasification of biomass becomes a mature and cost-effective technology.*

- *Biofuels could play an important role in reaching very low GHG emissions levels from the transport sector by 2050, especially advanced biodiesel for heavy goods vehicles, marine vessels and aeroplanes. In the BLUE Map scenario, 26% of total transport fuel demand is met by biofuels, requiring up to 4% of the current global pasture and arable land. Over time, second-generation biofuels (from non-food biomass feedstocks) will displace first-generation biofuels (produced primarily from grain and vegetable-oil feedstocks). Though these advanced biofuels may provide large CO_2 reductions compared to petroleum fuels, there remain many uncertainties such as land use change effects. The main constraint on the use of biofuels will be the amount of land that could be brought into production in a sustainable way, without compromising food security and environmental constraints.*

Introduction and scenario results

Biomass – *i.e.*, organic materials grown, collected or harvested for energy use – is a source of renewable hydrocarbons that can be converted to provide energy carriers (heat, electricity and transport fuels) as well as materials and chemicals. When made from biomass, these conversion products are known as bioenergy, biofuels, biogas, bio-materials and bio-chemicals.

The total annual demand for biomass has increased steadily over recent years (Figure 9.1), particularly in OECD countries. Total biomass use is uncertain, but currently probably accounts for over 10% of global primary energy consumption (45 ±10 EJ/yr; 1 070 ± 240 Mtoe/yr). Approximately two-thirds of this biomass is consumed in developing countries as traditional, non-commercial biomass (fuel wood, crop residues, dung, etc.) for domestic cooking and heating. The current demand for biomass to provide electricity and heat for buildings and industry is around 8 EJ/yr (190 Mtoe/yr) and around 1.7 EJ/yr (40 Mtoe/yr) for liquid transport biofuels.

Figure 9.1 ▶ **Global primary biomass use from 1971 to 2005**

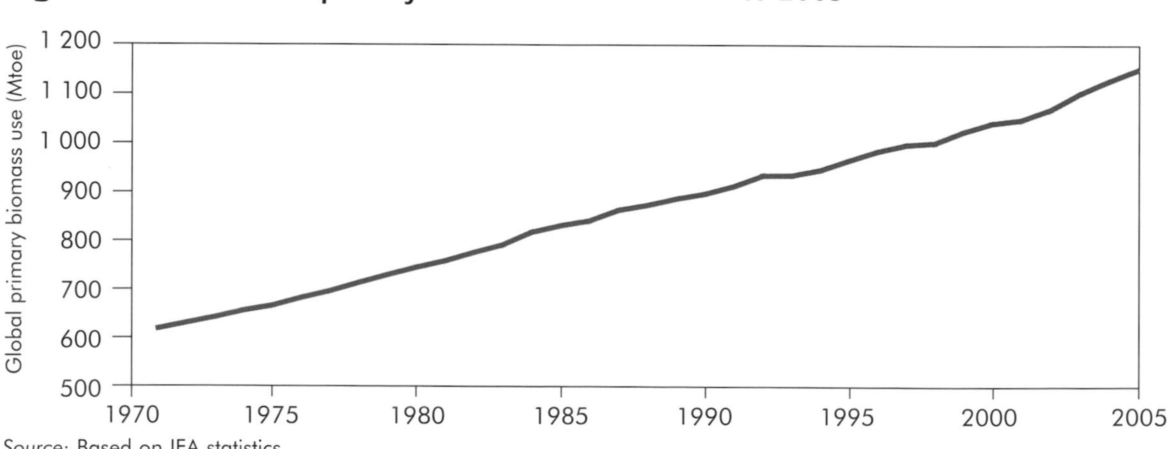

Source: Based on IEA statistics.

Key point

Biomass demand continues to increase, mainly for traditional cooking and heating in developing countries.

The small-scale use of biomass for cooking and heating in households is widespread in most parts of the world. Some countries, such as Nepal, are dependent on traditional biomass to meet up to 90% of their total energy demand. The efficiency of many stoves and open fire places could be improved significantly by introducing better designs. This would reduce the amount of biomass needed to provide the same energy services and reduce air emissions, thereby improving the health of the users by avoiding smoke and carbon-monoxide inhalation. With fewer people living in rural areas and greater uptake of more-efficient stoves, small-scale biogas systems, and biomass-based liquid cooking fuels such as DME or ethanol gels, the overall efficiency of small-scale biomass use is expected to increase through to 2050. The use of existing biomass supplies for modern bioenergy plants to produce process heat, power and liquid fuels would help some countries to better meet their sustainable development goals.

At a larger scale, biomass is consumed to provide heat in buildings and industry. Data is uncertain, but excluding traditional uses, in 2005 biomass and waste possibly contributed 1.4% (4.5 EJ; 105 Mtoe) of direct heat in the global industrial and residential sectors (IEA, 2007a) with heat from combined heat and power (CHP) plants possibly providing an additional 2 EJ to 3 EJ (47 Mtoe to 70 Mtoe). Biomass also supplied around 1% (0.8 EJ; 19 Mtoe) of transport fuels and over 1% (0.8 EJ; 230 TWh) of electricity generation (IEA, 2007b). By 2050, given supportive policy developments, these shares could rise significantly (IEA, 2006).

Estimates of future biomass supply and demand vary widely. The scope for biomass to make a significantly larger contribution to primary energy in the next 30 to 40 years is subject to its sustainable production, improved efficiency in the supply chain, the successful development and deployment of new thermo-chemical technologies, and improved bio-chemical conversions (in for example, anaerobic digestion and ethanol-fermentation plants). The demand for large volumes of traditional solid biomass is likely to be at least partly displaced by more convenient liquid fuels or the use of other energy sources, particularly as people move progressively from rural areas into cities. The greater uptake of improved cooking stove designs, community biogas plants, Stirling engines for CHP, and larger-scale heat plants to support rural development in developing countries should improve the overall conversion efficiency of biomass use. New approaches, such as combining biomass conversion with carbon capture and storage (CCS) or ways of encouraging soil carbon uptake, may further contribute to global CO_2 reductions.

Scenarios

In the BLUE Map scenario, up to 150 EJ/yr (3 605 Mtoe/yr) of primary biomass is projected to be potentially available for energy purposes in 2050 (Figure 9.2). This equates to around 15 billion tonnes of biomass that must be produced each year from a range of sources.

The BLUE Map scenario envisages biomass use increasing up to four-fold by 2050, to reach around 20% of total world primary energy (Figure 9.3). This includes the production of around 700 Mtoe/yr of transport biofuels and 2 450 TWh/yr of power generation, including CHP electricity and co-firing (co-combustion) with coal or gas.

Figure 9.2 ▶ **Biomass use allocation in the BLUE Map scenario, 2050**

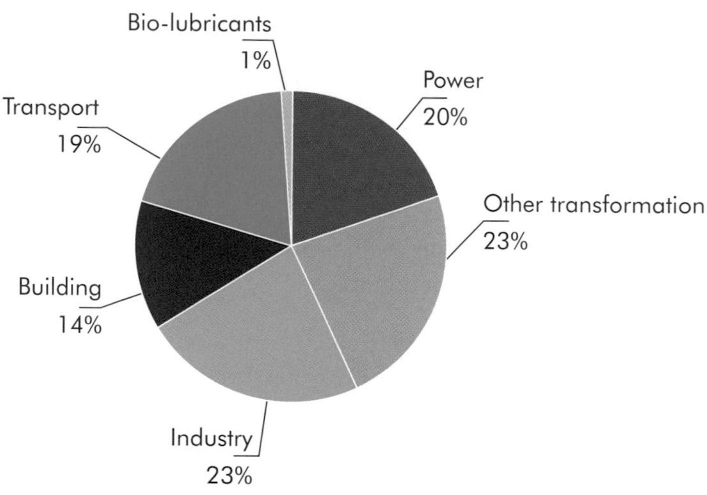

Key point

Biomass can provide useful energy services in many sectors.

Figure 9.3 ▶ **Biomass use by region in the Baseline, ACT Map and BLUE Map scenarios**

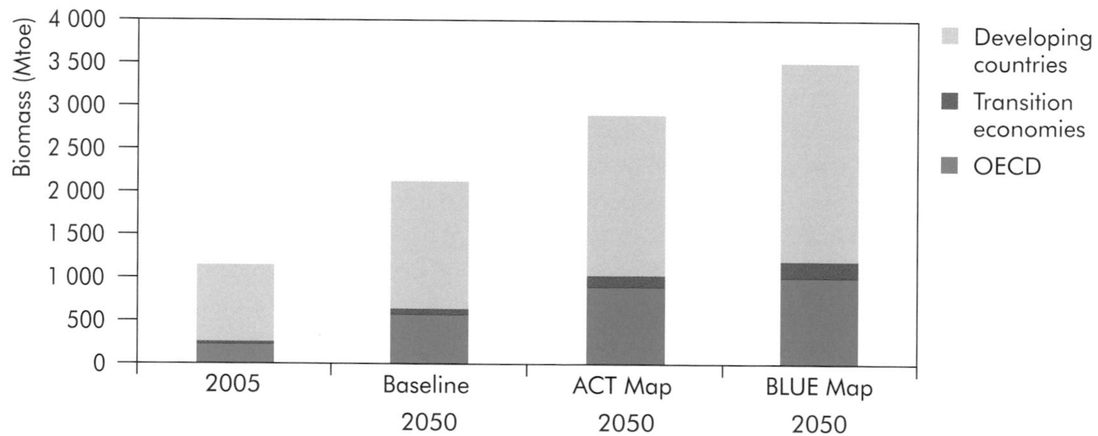

Key point

Biomass use grows significantly in all scenarios, particularly in developing countries.

In the power sector, about 21% of the projected biomass consumption is used for co-firing, mostly with coal. In industry, 200 Mtoe of liquids produced from biomass, mostly methanol, are projected to be used for the production of petrochemicals, and 45 Mtoe for bio-lubricants. A further 150 Mtoe of biomass-derived liquids is projected to be used in the buildings sector, largely as substitutes for traditional biomass and liquefied petroleum gas (LPG) presently used for cooking. The conversion of biomass to liquids creates a significant conversion loss, accounted for in the category "other transformation" in Figure 9.2. The remaining biomass (around 980 Mtoe) is projected to be used to provide direct heat in the industry and buildings sectors.

Biomass could also be used in industrial CHP units to produce a range of high-value products alongside heat and power. Stand-alone biomass integrated-gasification, combined-cycle plants (BIGCCs) for power generation are unlikely to gain a significant market position unless their costs can be driven down with the aid of supporting policies and RD&D investment over the next decade or so.

The projected 150 EJ/yr of biomass supply in 2050 is lower than that of a number of other assessments (for example, IEA Bioenergy, 2007) but higher than others. It assumes that land-use constraints and the demand for sustainable production and certification schemes will limit the volumes of biomass that might otherwise be produced.

Costs

Bioenergy costs are expected to reduce over time due to both technology learning and economies of scale in larger commercial plants. Current bio-electricity generation costs of around USD 62 to 185 per MWh could reduce by 2050 to between USD 49 to 123 per MWh (IEA Bioenergy, 2007). Transport biofuels could reduce from current costs of USD 10 to 31 per GJ to from USD 7 to 12 per GJ. Heat production is expected to remain at around today's cost of USD 4 to 19 per GJ over the forecast period. Table 9.1 shows the typical capacities, efficiencies and costs for a range of technologies.

The actual cost per unit of energy produced from a plant partly depends on the plant's capacity factor (percentage of total number of available hours that the plant is operated per year), maintenance costs, etc.

Policy options

The amount of feedstock available for bioenergy will depend upon a wide range of government and local policies, including those in relation to:

- land use and land-use change;
- avoidance of deforestation and protection of conservation areas;
- biodiversity;
- reclamation of degraded lands;
- genetically modified crops;
- soil carbon uptake;
- water use and quality;

- treatment of wastewater and solid wastes;
- local air pollution;
- sustainable development goals;
- health improvements;
- support for rural industries;
- transport;
- the provision of low-cost energy to stimulate economic growth.

The future uptake of biomass for energy will be determined, at least in part, by the impact such policies have on bioenergy projects. Policies supporting a greater uptake of bioenergy could be offset by others constraining it. For example, the growing demand for biofuels has already led to increased deforestation and the deterioration of wetlands and peat soils, which has actually increased CO_2 emissions (Fargione, *et al.*, 2008). It has also led to an upward pressure on food prices.

Table 9.1 **Typical plant size, efficiency and capital cost for a range of bioenergy conversion plant technologies**

Conversion type	Typical capacity	Net efficiency	Investment costs
Anaerobic digestion	< 10 MW	10-15% electrical 60-70% heat	
Landfill gas	< 200 kW to 2 MW	10-15% electrical	
Combustion for heat	5-50 kW_{th} residential 1-5 MW_{th} industrial	10-20% open fires 40-50% stoves 70-90% furnaces	USD~23/kW_{th} stoves USD 370-990/kW_{th} furnaces
Combustion for power	10-100 MW	20-40%	USD 1 975-3 085/kW
Combustion for CHP	0.1-1 MW 1-50 MW	60-90% overall 80-100% overall	USD 3 333-4 320/kW USD 3 085-3 700/kW
Co-firing with coal	5-100 MW existing >100 MW new plant	30-40%	USD 123-1 235/kW + power station costs
Gasification for heat	50-500 kW_{th}	80-90%	USD 864-980/kW_{th}
BIGCC for power	5-10 MW demos 30-200 MW future	40-50% plus	USD 4 320-6 170/kW USD 1 235-2 470/kW future
Gasification for CHP using gas engines	0.1-1 MW	60-80% overall	USD 1 235-3 700/kW
Pyrolysis for bio-oil	10 t/hr demo	60-70%	USD 864/kW_{th}

Note: BIGCC plants linked with CCS are not included, as their potential capacities and cost ranges are not yet known.
Source: Based on IEA Bioenergy, 2007.

Biomass supply and demand: by use and region

Due to different predicted outlooks concerning land availability and crop yields, environmental requirements, and the future availability of woody biomass and crop residues, estimates of the biomass energy resources that can be produced sustainably from waste and energy crops and agricultural, forest and industrial residues vary widely – 125 EJ to 760 EJ by 2050 (IPCC, 2007); 40 EJ to 1 100 EJ (Hoogwijk, *et al.*, 2003; IEA Bioenergy, 2007); 104 EJ (Parikka, 2004); and 78 EJ to 450 EJ (Haberl, Erb and Krausmann, 2007).[1]

Land availability depends primarily on the net balance of changing population growth, the potential for increasing crop productivity, and changing food patterns – especially concerning the share of meat in the human diet, which affects land requirements significantly.

Competition for land and water to produce food, fibre and energy crops will drive up costs. Initially it will make sense to make maximum use of forest and process residues and to move towards integrated crop production. Ideally, specialist energy crops will be grown on marginal or degraded lands to avoid deforestation or the use of pasture and arable land (Searchinger, *et al.*, 2008).

IEA Bioenergy (2007) estimates that by 2050, over 100 EJ/yr of biomass could be supplied from agricultural residues and wastes, for costs ranging from USD 2 to USD 3 per GJ depending on the source and transport distance. An additional 125 EJ/yr of biomass could come from high-yielding perennial crops if grown efficiently on present pasture and arable land, at costs of approximately USD 3 to USD 5 per GJ. Meeting these levels, along with satisfying increased future demands for competing products such as food and fibre, will require higher average crop yields (including from genetically modified crops) and improved land management. A further 75 EJ/yr could come from growing energy crops on 60 Mha of degraded and marginal lands, giving a total resource of 300 EJ/yr.

9

Regional analysis by the VTT Technical Research Centre of Finland (VTT, 2007a) projects a more moderate potential of 83 EJ/yr. The VTT report estimates that agricultural and forestry residues and wastes will be the most cost-competitive types of biomass (Figure 9.4), with only around 30% of total bioenergy coming from specialist energy crops. Only current technologies and crop yields were used in this assessment, and population growth was taken to be zero.

The 150 EJ of biomass consumed per year in the BLUE Map scenario lies in between the IEA Bioenergy and the VTT estimates for 2050. Approximately 75 EJ/yr of this biomass is projected to come from agricultural and forest residues, with the remaining 75 EJ/yr derived from energy crops. This would require 375 Mha to 750 Mha of land, assuming an average biomass yield of five to ten tonnes of dry matter per hectare across all soil types and climates.[2] Any degraded land that could be reclaimed for crop use could have an impact on future land use by reducing competition for land. The potential to produce algae in concentrated ponds and to reclaim desert lands for crops, if proven feasible, will similarly affect future land use. These aspects, however, are not considered further here.

1. For comparison, the world primary energy consumption in 2005 was 480 EJ (IEA, 2007b).
2. By way of comparison, around 6 000 Mha (60 Mkm^2) of land (40% of the total land area) is currently used for agricultural production, of which 1 150 Mha are within Africa (FAOSTAT, 2007).

Figure 9.4 ▶ **Regional technical biomass resource potentials in 2050 (Mtoe/yr)**

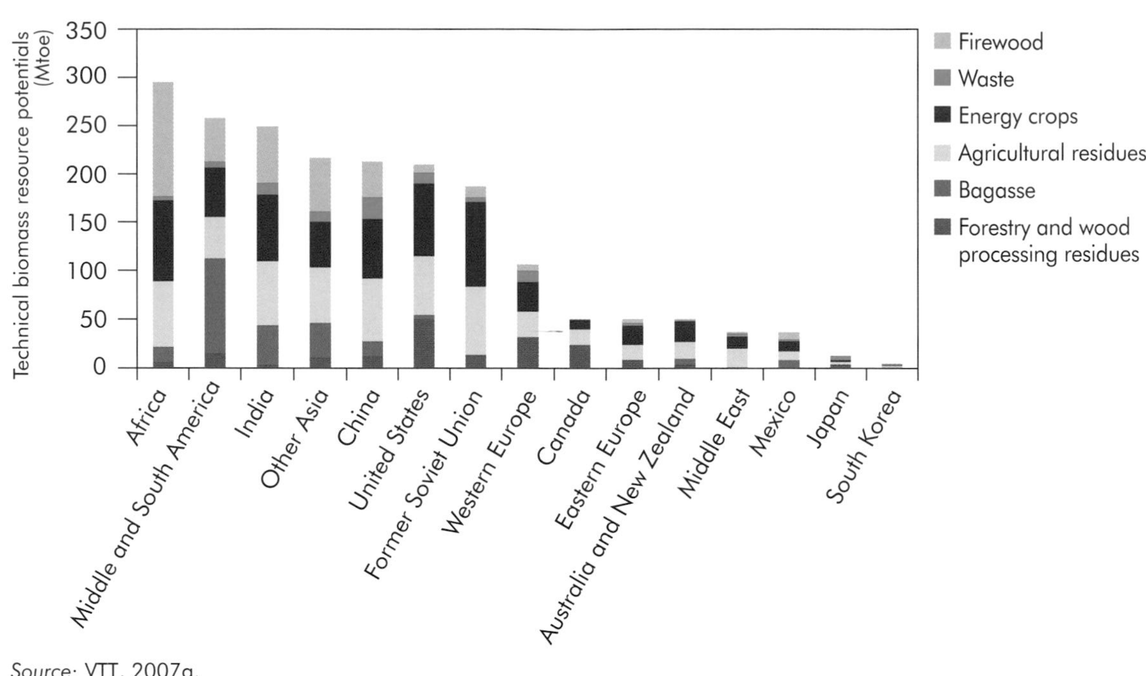

Source: VTT, 2007a.

Key point

The potential of biomass using a range of sources is considerable in many regions of the world.

Crop yields and plant breeding

The average yield per hectare of agricultural crops has increased progressively since the "green revolution" began in the 1960s (Figure 9.5). This is a result of improved land-management, conventional plant-breeding techniques and the selection of improved varieties and hybrids. Increasingly mechanised irrigation and drainage and improved post-harvest handling and storage methods have also contributed to raising yields, as have more intensive inputs of fertilisers and agri-chemicals. Future land availability for energy crops will depend on the rate of further crop yield improvements. Nutrient recycling and the success and acceptance of genetically modified species will also have an impact on land use and crop yield, as will future water availability and its use and the impacts of climate change.

Harvesting, logistics and pre-treatment of biomass

Biomass tends to be bulky, to deteriorate over time, and to be difficult to store and handle. Compared to coal and oil, biomass has a lower energy density (GJ per unit of weight or volume), which makes handling, transport, storage and combustion more difficult.

Figure 9.5 ▶ **Increased yield production per hectare for a range of staple food and fibre crops, 1961-2005**

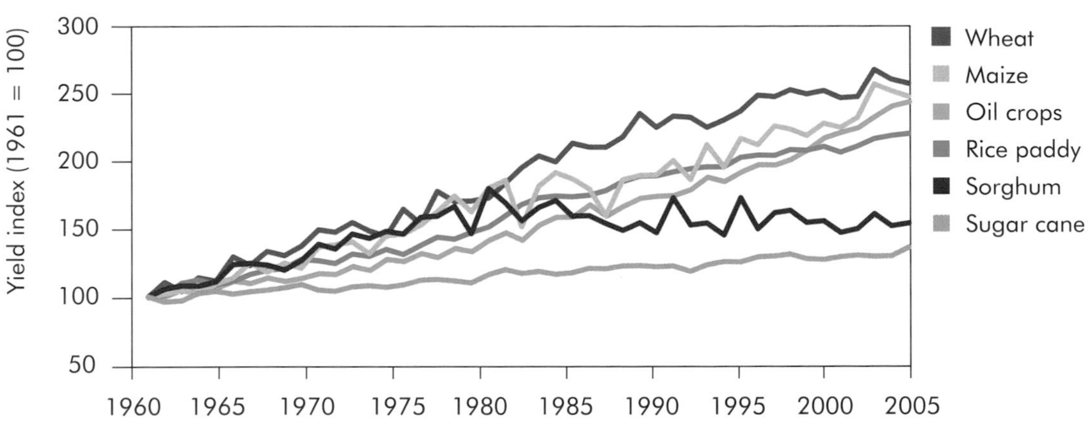

Source: FAOSTAT, 2007.

Key point

If average food-crop yields per hectare continue to increase, they will mitigate the increasing competition for land by energy crops.

Box 9.1 ▶ **Biomass versus food and fibre**

Recent analysis suggests that increased bioethanol production from corn in the United States has caused world corn prices to rise and has reduced reserves to very low levels (Searchinger, et al., 2008). Increasing demand for palm oil for biodiesel is also claimed to have pushed up world prices and led to significant additional rain-forest clearing in Indonesia and Malaysia. These and other similar claims may be partly true, but below-average cereal yields and droughts have also contributed to increased grain prices, and only around 10% of harvested palm oil is used for biofuel production. The Malaysian government has denied that any further deforestation is occurring and argues that the improved gene stock of palm trees (which are replanted in a 25-year rotation after older trees have grown too tall to harvest) has led to increased yields per hectare. Indonesia has, however announced plans to convert 1 million to 2 million hectares of forest into oil palm plantations.

Land displacement can also be an issue. For example, recent increases in corn prices have encouraged farmers in the United States to grow more corn and fewer soybeans. As a result, the demand for soybean imports has increased and is being met largely from increased production in Brazil. As soy is grown in the region adjacent to the Amazon rain forest, it is claimed that expansion of this crop is resulting in further forest-clearing.

The carbon debt arising from land-use change can take many years, even centuries, to pay back by using the biomass produced to displace fossil fuels (Fargione, et al., 2008). Producing biomass for energy purposes at the expense of either food or fibre supplies, or by increasing deforestation, is of little global benefit. Biomass production needs to be sustainable: by being integrated with food and fibre crop production or by being grown on surplus or marginal land. More research is needed to understand where and how these conditions can be met in practice.

Supply chain costs can add significantly to delivered biomass costs and can result in the economic failure of bioenergy projects (IEA, 2007c). Larger plants can achieve economies of scale, but this can be more than offset by the increased transport distances needed to obtain the required volume of biomass.

Well-designed fuel supply chains are needed to supply reliable and competitive biomass, especially at large-scale bioenergy production plants. Harvesting of biomass – with its low specific density, high moisture content and limited storage capability – often requires new types of machinery, new logistics and a new management approach. In a fuel chain supplying just one large plant, hundreds of farmers and forest-owners and numerous machinery contractors may be involved in providing biomass supplies, making consistency more difficult to achieve. Pre-treatment of the biomass can help to provide a homogeneous product with uniform particle size and moisture content.

The location of the chipping/crushing process in woody biomass production systems largely determines the form of the biomass during transportation and the need for further processing later in the delivery chain (Figure 9.6). Chipping in the forest requires specialist mobile equipment, which can be expensive. Alternatively, whole tree or branch materials can be hauled to a chipping site closer to the access road. Chipping at a processing plant enables better control of the procurement and chipping process. It is also less labour-intensive and permits better control of fuel quality. However, investment costs are high, and only large plants can afford the stationary chipper/crusher. The cost of shipping large volumes of low bulk density biomass is a main constraint to such central processing.

In recent years, new bundling processes have been developed to help in this respect. With many indirect cost savings and better supply security, bundling has proven to be an effective solution for large-scale operations with a central chipping plant. Current technology, however, is costly. It remains more common for forest biomass to be chipped in the forest using mobile equipment, with the chips then transported to the plant.

Costs of delivered biomass vary with country and region due to factors including variations in terrain, labour costs and crop yields. On average in Europe, the cost of operating a forwarder is USD 67 to 104 per hour; chipping is USD 148 to 213 per hour; transport is USD 91 to 143 per hour, and loading/unloading is USD 40 to 83 per hour (Asikainen, et al., 2007).

Biomass production costs vary according to the size of the clear-cutting area, distance to the road, optional roadside storage, transport distance and stumpage fees, but can be reduced over time with experience (Table 9.2). The cost of producing woody biomass has declined by over 30% in 20 years. The largest influence was the development of new forwarding and chipping technologies, together with improved management of both crop production and logistics.

Agricultural biomass use has traditionally been limited mainly to local heat production from the combustion of straw, bagasse, rice husks, coconut shells, etc. Small to medium CHP plants are increasingly being built at sugar mills and at other food-processing plants that have significant biomass waste streams.

Figure 9.6 ▶ **Biomass fuel-chain options from forest to power plant**

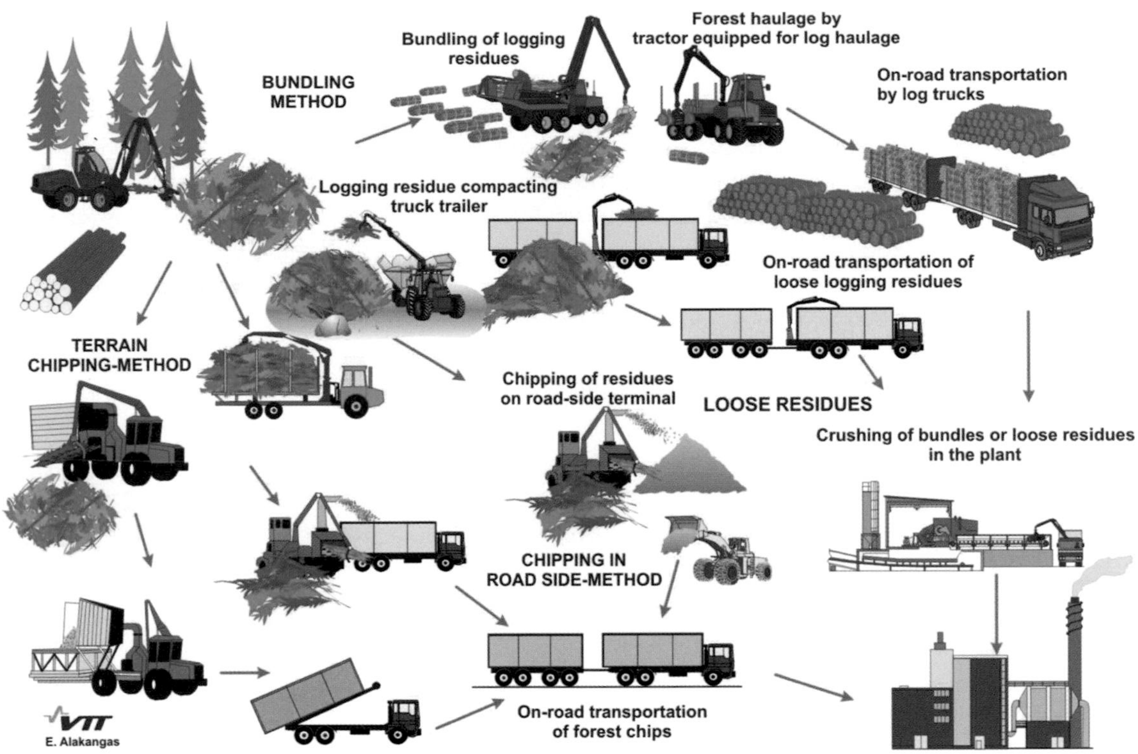

Source: VTT, 2007.

Key point

The choice of fuel supply chain and the location of the chipping operation can affect the delivered cost of biomass from forest arisings.

Table 9.2 ▶ **Production costs of forest biomass in Sweden in 1983 and 2003**

	Primary forest fuel production cost USD/GJ		Cost reduction 2003 vs 1983 %
Year	1983	2003	
Forwarding	2.16 (28.3%)	0.91 (17.7%)	58
Chipping	2.53 (33.3%)	1.70 (33.0%)	33
Transportation	65 (21.6%)	1.39 (27.2%)	15
Stumpage fee and other costs	1.27 (16.7%)	1.14 (22.1%)	10
Total	7.61	5.14	32

Source: Junginger, *et al.*, 2005.

9

In addition, biogas produced from the anaerobic digestion of animal manure, green crops and other forms of organic waste can be used for heat and power generation as well as for transport fuels – after scrubbing to remove CO_2 and H_2S.

The use of residues and waste as biomass can reduce farmers' costs and provide them with additional income. Cereal straw and other farm residues are already used in Denmark, Spain and Romania, for example, to produce significant heat and power production. In Brazil, Australia, South Africa and elsewhere, sugarcane bagasse is used for heat and power, both for use at the mill and for export to the grid. Vegetative grass crops such as *Miscanthus* and reed canary grass can be grown for combustion in commercial grate boilers for heat production. The co-firing of straw with coal is well demonstrated in fluidised-bed boilers. Small-scale (<500 kW) power generation plants based on the steam cycle have also been built, but they are relatively inefficient and hence have relatively high power-production costs. Further RD&D in CHP would help reduce costs. In all cases, storing the biomass is important so that the bioenergy plant can be operated all year round, or at least for as long a season as possible, to spread the investment costs.

The main barriers include fuel logistics, fuel quality fluctuations (due to variations in rainfall, for example) feedstock price fluctuations and delivery costs. Technical improvements in harvesting, storage, transport, fuel preparation and other measures are still possible for virtually all biomass feedstocks.

Some of the main supply-chain issues relating to the greater use of forest and agricultural residues are summarised in Table 9.3.

Table 9.3 ▶ **Technical and non-technical barriers, and RD&D goals to overcome them to increase the use of forest and agricultural residues**

Technical barriers	**RD&D goals: technical**
Lack of a cost-effective harvesting technology for forest residues	Technology transfer, learning from Finnish and Swedish experience of forest residues
Poor application of biomass production chains for local conditions	Optimisation of production chains and logistics to suit local conditions
Non-technical barriers	**RD&D goals: non-technical**
The insufficient availability of low-cost biomass	Products from agricultural fibre and fibre containing waste from pulp and paper mills
Competition for biomass with the pulp and paper industry and other wood-product processors	
Uncertainties concerning subsidy levels in the longer term	
Unsustainable harvesting that reduces the amount of nutrients needed for future production	Development of ash-recycling technologies

Source: VTT, 2007.

Energy crops

Crop cultivation for non-food applications is increasing. For example, in Sweden, over 15 000 ha of *Salix* (willow) have been cultivated to supply wood for co-firing or for biomass CHP and district heat boilers. In Finland, around 16 000 ha of reed canary grass have been cultivated for similar purposes.

Crop yields are highly dependent on local climatic conditions and soil types. Where an average crop yield of around 10 to 12 tonnes of dry matter per hectare per year is feasible, energy yield would typically be 180 to 220 GJ/ha. However, such yields can rarely be reached in practice on a widespread commercial scale.

The use to which the biomass is put also affects the energy that can be obtained from it. Growing 1 million hectares of an energy crop would give a potential primary energy resource of about 200 to 250 PJ/yr for heat and power generation. Growing crops for conversion to a liquid transport fuel on the same area would yield considerably less energy – for example, about 30 to 50 PJ/yr if oilseed rape is cultivated for biodiesel, or 90 to 120 GJ/ha if vegetative grasses or short-rotation forests are grown for second-generation biofuels.

Harvesting costs depend on the crop type. If existing farm harvesting equipment can be used, the cost is far less than if specialist harvesters need to be developed (as they do, for example, for short-rotation coppice *Salix*). For vegetative grasses, harvest methods that give low losses and high bale-densities are essential to reduce overall costs. A large commercial processing plant of 400 000 t/yr would require feedstock to be brought in from a radius of 100 km or more to ensure 24-hour operation, seven days a week. Current available baling methods result in relatively low-density bales. Denser bales are being sought to reduce transport costs (Figure 9.7), but to be economically viable they need to be capable of being produced without significantly higher energy inputs. 9

Figure 9.7 ▶ **Transport costs of reed canary grass over varying distances when using several alternative forms for transport**

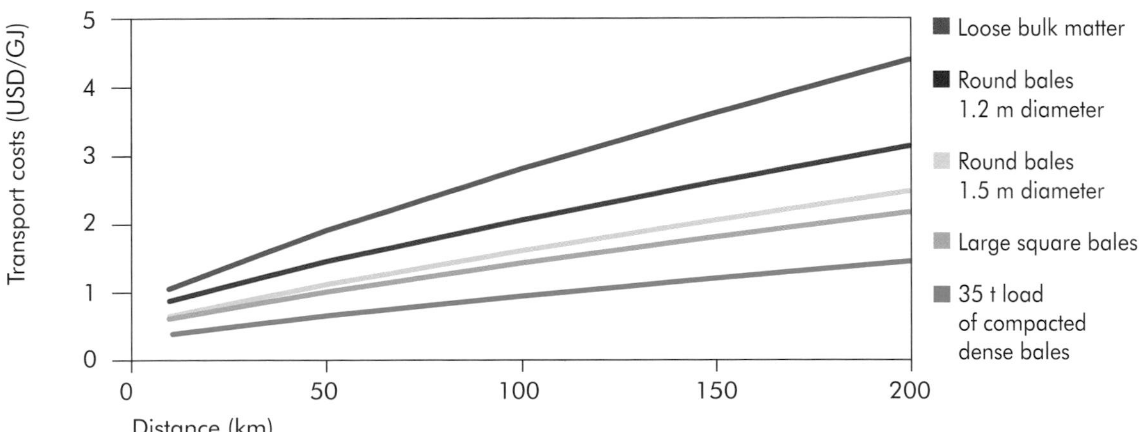

Source: Based on Lindh, *et al.*, 2007.

Key point

Further RD&D of biomass handling and transport could help reduce the delivered costs in energy terms.

Bigger bioenergy plants are being built to exploit economies of scale and take advantage of the improved availability, reliability and delivery of biomass resources. Plant capacity tends to be limited by the local availability of biomass. The high cost of transporting biomass feedstocks, even when traded internationally, may under some circumstances be outweighed by lower investment costs/MW and the increased conversion efficiencies of larger-scale commercial plants. Sugarcane mills have consumed 300 000 t or more of biomass per year for many years, using efficient delivery systems. There is no reason why bioenergy plants could not develop similar supply chains.

Competition for land is a potentially major constraint on the medium- and long-term development of energy crops. Other barriers to increasing production include the availability of new types of harvesting equipment and the costs of transport and delivery systems (Table 9.4). RD&D investment may help remove a number of these barriers.

Table 9.4 ▶ **Technical and non-technical barriers, to increased production and use of energy crops, and RD&D goals to overcome them**

Technical barriers	RD&D goals: technical
Lack of know-how in moving from food-crop production to energy-crop production Scale-up of ligno-cellulosic crop production	Whole chain system analysis: focusing on ligno-cellulosic feedstock production. Plant breeding advances, including genetically modified organisms (GMOs)
Non-technical barriers	**RD&D goals: non-technical**
Sustainability is unproven, especially for ligno-cellulosic crops Unpredictable economic conditions and legislation	Evaluation of environmental impats Demonstration of scale-up.Experimental farm based ligno-cellulose

Source: VTT, 2007.

Biomass potential

The economic potential of biomass is dependent on a very wide range of economic, practical and political variables. It is, therefore, difficult to establish with any degree of confidence the extent to which bioenergy could become a feasible option for climate-change mitigation. More work is needed to develop integrated land-use, energy-economy models that could provide a more comprehensive assessment of the prospects for biomass in the future sustainable global energy supply mix. Refining the modelling of interactions between land used for bioenergy and land used for food and materials production, and establishing the potential synergies between different land uses more clearly, would facilitate an improved understanding of the prospects for large-scale bioenergy deployment and biomass management in general.

Current expectations in the BLUE Map scenario are that, for a cost of up to USD 200/t CO_2eq avoided, a potential 150 EJ/yr of sustainably produced biomass would be used by the energy sector in 2050. In the ACT Map scenario, the demand for biomass is 120 EJ/yr, although this is still well above the Baseline scenario level of around 90 EJ/yr. Depending on how the available biomass is allocated to produce heat, power, transport fuels, bio-chemicals or bio-materials, and what fossil-fuel substitution would actually result, this biomass could offset somewhere between 5 Gt CO_2eq and 10 Gt CO_2eq in 2050.

Biomass conversion technologies

Around 400 GW of modern biomass heat-production equipment, consuming around 300 Mt/yr of biomass, currently produces around 4.5 EJ/yr (105 Mtoe/yr) of direct heat (assuming a 75% conversion factor). By 2005, over 40 GW of biomass-fired power generation capacity had been installed worldwide, generating 230 TWh/yr of electricity (IEA, 2007b). Assuming 60% average capacity factor and 25% average conversion efficiency, this would consume approximately 240 Mt/yr of biomass. For liquid biofuels, around 120 Mt of biomass resources were consumed in 2005, to produce around 19 Mtoe of biofuels, with an average conversion efficiency of around 50%.

Power generation: combustion

Grate boilers

Grate firing is the oldest combustion principle and was the most common design of small-size boilers until the beginning of the 1980s. It remains popular for relatively small boilers (less than 5 MW) in countries using fuels such as wood pellets, straw, plywood and chipboard residues, and municipal solid waste. Grates and stokers are rarely installed in combustion plants of over 50 MW capacity.

The capital cost of grate boilers varies with design and location, giving different costs per unit of energy (for both electrical and thermal outputs of CHP plants). An analysis of six such plants in Europe shows a close relationship between plant size and investment cost (VTT, 2007). Costs per unit of installed electricity-generation capacity dropped quickly as the plant size increased to around 20 MW (Figure 9.8). If heat capacity is added, this correlation becomes weaker, as plant size has no impact on the overall fuel-to-heat conversion efficiency. However, larger plants tend to have a more favourable power-to-heat ratio, up to 1:2.

Fluidised bed combustion

Bubbling fluidised bed (BFB) and circulating fluidised bed (CFB) combustion technologies became fully commercial in the 1970s. BFB combustion resembles grate firing, but offers better temperature control. BFBs are most suitable for non-homogeneous biomass. CFB combustion resembles pulverised fuel combustion, but better control of the furnace temperature allows the fuel to be ignited without necessitating a high-temperature flame. In BFB boilers, the bed particles stay in the bed, whereas in CFBs the gases carry the particles away from the bed into the furnace, from where they are later recirculated back into the bed (Figure 9.9). The bed material improves the mixing of air and fuel in the combustion system and hence improves the heat transfer.

Figure 9.8 ▶ **Relationship betwen investment costs and total heat and power output capacity of grate boilers and fluidised beds**

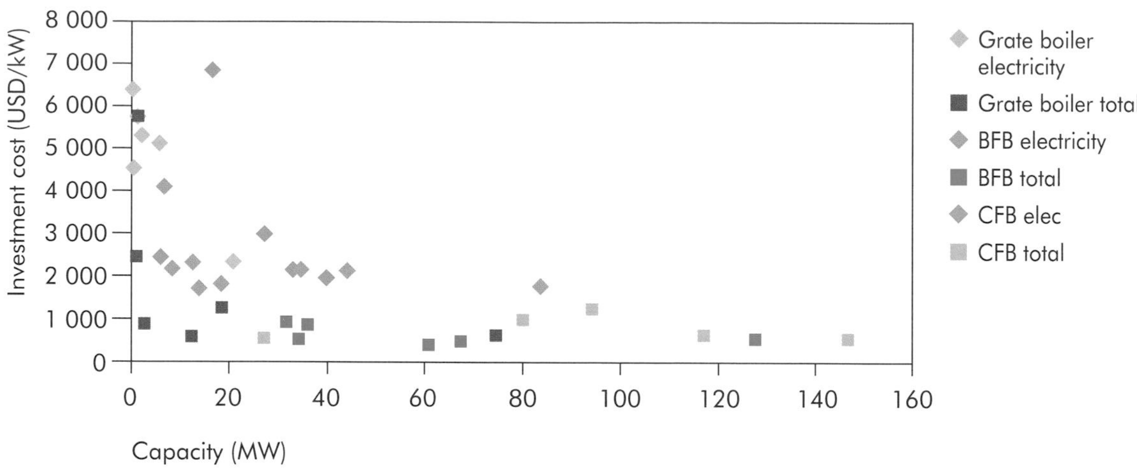

Source: Based on VTT, 2007.

Key point

Larger-scale biomass combustion plants for both heat and power benefit from economies of scale in terms of investment costs per unit of capacity (USD/kW).

Figure 9.9 ▶ **An example of a multi-fuel, circulating fluidised bed boiler**

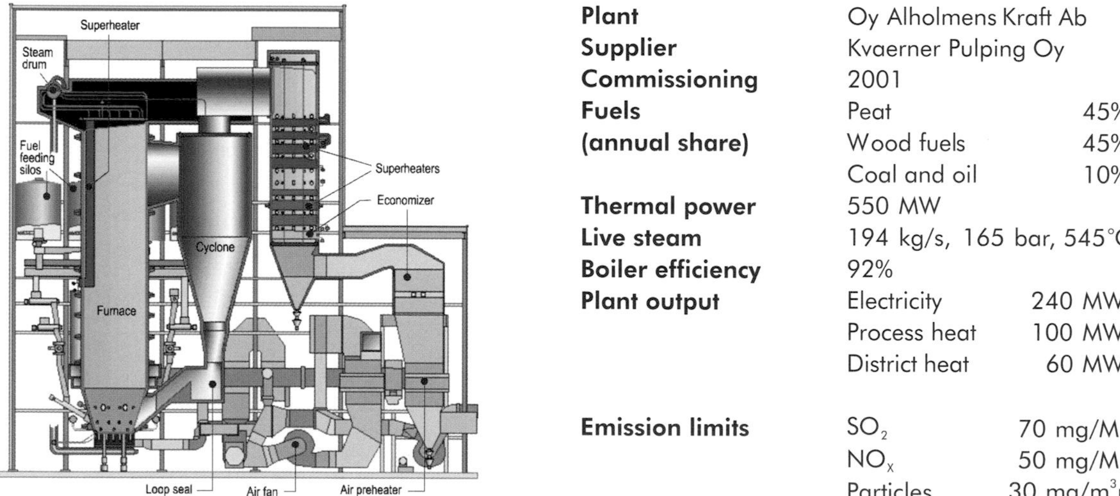

Plant	Oy Alholmens Kraft Ab	
Supplier	Kvaerner Pulping Oy	
Commissioning	2001	
Fuels	Peat	45%
(annual share)	Wood fuels	45%
	Coal and oil	10%
Thermal power	550 MW	
Live steam	194 kg/s, 165 bar, 545°C	
Boiler efficiency	92%	
Plant output	Electricity	240 MW
	Process heat	100 MW
	District heat	60 MW
Emission limits	SO_2	70 mg/MJ
	NO_x	50 mg/MJ
	Particles	30 mg/m^3n

Note: Bed material from the furnace is collected in the cyclone for recycling and the heat is taken off for industrial and domestic uses. Future unit sizes of such CFB boiler designs could reach from 600 MW to 800 MW.

Source: VTT, 2007.

Key point

Biomass CFB boilers are complex, but scaleable to gain greater benefit of size – though this is partially offset by the higher costs of transporting biomass fuel over greater distances.

The choice between grate and fluidised bed firing depends on the fuel type, ash content and quality, and the amount of physical impurities in the fuel. Fuels with a low ash melting point cannot be burned in a fluidised bed. Heavy physical impurities such as metal particles in municipal solid waste fuels cannot be fluidised, because they sink onto the air distribution plate, disturb the fluidisation and are difficult to remove from the furnace. However, new solutions for keeping the bed operational with municipal solid waste fuels have been developed and implemented successfully.

Costs

Costs vary with size and design for both BFB and CFB systems. An analysis of eight existing BFB bed boiler plants for electricity generation in the 8 MW to 87 MW output range, built or reconstructed between 1993 and 2002 in Finland and Sweden, suggested there was no significant reduction of unit capacity cost for this size range (VTT, 2007; see Figure 9.8). The total efficiency of these plants is in the range of 85% to 90%, with the plants achieving a power-to-heat ratio of up to 1 to 2.2. The investment cost range per unit capacity of CFB plants is around USD 400 kW_{e+th} to USD 750/kW_{e+th}, based on five existing plants built between 1990 and 2002, which is similar to that for BFBs. They had similar efficiencies, although the CFB plants surveyed were a slightly smaller range (at 7 MW to 42 MW) than the BFBs (VTT, 2007).

9

Co-firing in utility boilers

Co-firing biomass residues with coal in traditional coal-fired boilers for electricity production can make a significant contribution to CO_2 emission reductions. Biomass co-firing has been successfully demonstrated for most combinations of fuels and boiler types in more than 150 installations worldwide. About a hundred of these are operating in Europe, mainly in Scandinavian countries, the Netherlands and Germany, around 40 in the United States and a few in Australia. A number of fuels, including crop residues, energy crops, and herbaceous and woody biomass, have been co-fired. The proportion of biomass in the fuel mix has ranged between 0.5% and 10% in energy terms, with 5% as a typical value.

Additional capital costs for plant conversion and fuel handling commonly range from USD 100 to USD 300 per kW. For regions that have access to both coal-fired power facilities and suitable biomass resources, this is a highly cost-effective option for the use of biomass, as it enables:

- a reduction in the CO_2 emissions of the coal plant;
- the best use to be made of the infrastructure associated with large coal-based power plants;
- lower investment costs than for new biomass boilers;
- higher energy-conversion efficiency than would be obtainable in dedicated, smaller-scale, biomass facilities;
- reductions in the risks associated with unreliable biomass supplies and smaller storage areas than dedicated biomass plants;

- greater flexibility to purchase fuels according to their changing price levels;
- reduced sulphur and nitrogen-oxide emissions.

Co-firing of 5% to 10% biomass in pulverised coal boilers has been successfully carried out using pellets or direct feeding of pulverised or fine-crushed biomass. For a large-scale plant, the availability of biomass within a given economic collection radius is often the limiting factor with regard to the amount of biomass in the mix.

Co-firing of woody biomass can result in boiler efficiency reductions, typically of about 1% with 10% biomass fuel in the co-firing. This implies the combustion efficiency for biomass is 10% lower than for coal when fired in the same installation.

Worldwide, 40% of electricity is produced using coal. Each percentage point that could be substituted with biomass for co-firing would result in a reduction of about 60 Mt of CO_2 a year. Such an approach could achieve CO_2 reductions for approximately half the cost – in terms of USD/t CO_2eq avoided – of any other process, including the use of dedicated biomass power plants. In the absence of the advanced, sensitive flue gas cleaning systems commonly used in industrialised countries, co-firing of biomass in traditional coal-based power stations would typically result in lower emissions of dust, nitrous oxides and sulphur dioxide, due to the lower concentrations of nitrogen and sulphur components in the fuel. The lower ash content of biomass also results in lower quantities of solid residue that need to be disposed of.

Co-firing of forest and agricultural industry residues has additional benefits of particular interest to many developing countries. It adds economic value to these industries, which are commonly the backbone of rural economies in developing countries, and helps to engage them with larger-scale businesses such as utilities and chemical processors. The use of biomass residues also provides significant environmental relief from the popular on-site burning of unwanted residues. The incremental value added to the residues from field and forest industries generally represents a significant marginal increase in income for the rural populations involved. Many developing countries are located in climatic regions where biomass yields are high or large amounts of residues are available. Where biomass displaces imported coal or oil for heat and power generation, this will also represent a favourable shift in the trade balance.

Co-firing of the organic component of municipal solid waste is also being actively considered. Blending non-toxic waste materials with other biomass could regularise the fuel supply and enhance prospects for co-firing. Certain combinations of biomass and waste give specific advantages in terms of combustor performance, flue gas cleaning and ash behaviour.

Most BFB and CFB boilers can be designed to handle biomass as well as pulverised coal. In most designs, similar methods are used to feed the coal and biomass into the boiler, although the volume of biomass that can be used depends on the burner design (Table 9.5). Large supercritical, fluidised bed boilers with a power-generation efficiency of 50% could become a future option for co-firing.

Table 9.5 Comparison of typical parameters of biomass fuels when co-fired in different conversion systems

	Co-firing in fluidised bed boiler	Co-firing in pulverised fuel boiler	Separate gasifiers
Max biomass share (% of heat capacity)	20-100	0-5 (through grinder) 5-15 (separate feeding)	10-30
Biomass moisture (%)	< 55	< 40	< 50
Biomass particle size (mm)	**< 50**	**< 5-10**	**< 50**
Suitability for agricultural biomass	Good	Limitations	Good
Suitability for RDF*	Good	Limitations	Good
Max Cl-concentration (%)	**< 0.1**	**Depends on sulphur**	**Possible to remove by filtration**
Influence on SO_2 emissions	Can be larger than the amount from biomass	Equals the amount from biomass	Equals the amount from biomass
Influence of NO_x emissions	Lowers	No significant influence	Can be used for reburning
Ash treatment	**Ashes mix**	**Ashes mix**	**Bio-ash separate**
Influence on boiler usability	Can have negative effect	Can have negative effect	No effect
Investment costs	Small	USD 50-150/ kW_{th}	USD 300-800/kW_{th}

*RDF = refuse-derived fuel.

Source: Helynen, *et al.*, 2002.

To obtain an acceptable outcome when co-firing biomass and coal, however, the following factors need to be taken into account:

- The particle size of the biomass needs to be small enough to guarantee a long enough retention time in the boiler for complete combustion.
- In many pulverised coal boilers, the combustion temperature is 1 000°C to 1 250°C. To prevent slagging in the boiler, it is important that the biomass selected has an ash melting point higher than this.
- Cereal straw and green plant components may contain relatively high chlorine concentrations, which can cause corrosion at high temperatures and require careful monitoring for dioxin emissions.
- Biomass will change the ash composition. This can cause problems in the utilisation of coal ash in some applications.

Power generation: gasification

In fuel gasification, biomass feedstock is partially oxidised at high temperatures using restricted oxygen to form a mixture of CO, H_2, CH_4 and higher hydrocarbon gases that can then be combusted. Fuels can be gasified in many different designs of gasifier, the content of the synthesis gas mixture depending on the gasification method used. The gas mixture may contain different amounts of condensing liquids, tars formed during pyrolysis, carbonised residues, ash, impurities, and CO_2. Gasification technologies have been developed which can produce fuel gas from biomass feedstocks for use in engines, gas turbines and co-firing in boilers. Most gasifiers are based on combustion technologies using air, oxygen or water.

With air, reactive biomass can normally be gasified at relatively low temperatures of around 800°C to 1 000°C. Less air is required than for coal gasification, where higher temperatures are often used. In air gasification, the nitrogen in the air (around 50%) will dilute the product gas and lower the calorific value to between 3 MJ/Nm^3 and 7 MJ/Nm^3. Air gasification is best applied to reactive fuels and small- and medium-size applications (< 200 MW).

With oxygen, the product gas has a higher heat value, of about 7 MJ/Nm^3 to 15 MJ/Nm^3. However, oxygen production with current technology uses a lot of electricity: the oxygen plant itself represents a significant portion of the total capital investment of the plant as a whole. Oxygen blown gasifiers will result in higher chemical efficiency than air gasifiers. This will increase the efficiency of, for example, the gas turbine of a gas combined-cycle power plant, and hence compensate for the oxygen production costs. Oxygen-blown gasification is best suited to large plants above 200 MW and applications where high-temperature gasification is needed.

With steam, in processes based on indirect heat input, the main goal is to produce the gas with a medium-high heat value without expensive oxygen production. The gasifying agent is commonly superheated steam or recycled product gas.

Atmospheric fluidised and fixed-bed gasifiers are typically limited to niche markets. Pressurised gasification has not yet been successfully demonstrated in large-scale integrated gas combined-cycle (IGCC) plants, although these could be more competitive than traditional boiler/steam turbine cycles.

The cost savings can be significant with pressurised reactors, particularly in large-scale gasification plants using gas cleaning equipment. Pressurised gasification is usually beneficial when the high pressure can also be used in the energy production process.

The longest experience of biomass use in boilers designed for pulverised-coal combustion is that of the Kymijärvi plant in Finland, where in 1989 an atmospheric pressure, air-blown circulating fluidised bed gasifier was connected to the existing coal-fired boiler. The produced gas is used as fuel for burners located in the main boiler. This gas accounts for 350 GWh/yr of generation, around 15% to 20% of the plant's total fuel input from coal, natural gas and biomass.

Small-scale gasification plants

Gasified solid biomass can be used to provide higher power-to-heat ratios in small-scale CHP plants (<15 MW_{th}) connected to an internal combustion engine that drives a generator. Demonstration plants are widespread, but investment and operation costs have still to be reduced if the technology is to gain a large market share. At a small scale, the most competitive processes are based on fixed-bed gasification using the counter-flow design, which has been in commercial use since the 1980s. Fuel is fed into the reactor from the top, and the gasification agent (air or oxygen) is introduced from the bottom (Figure 9.10). Because the gas needs to flow up through the fuel bed, only a relatively homogeneous mix of biomass fuel with a particle size of a few centimetres across, such as wood chips, can be used.

Figure 9.10 ▶ Demonstration gasifier CHP plant in Finland

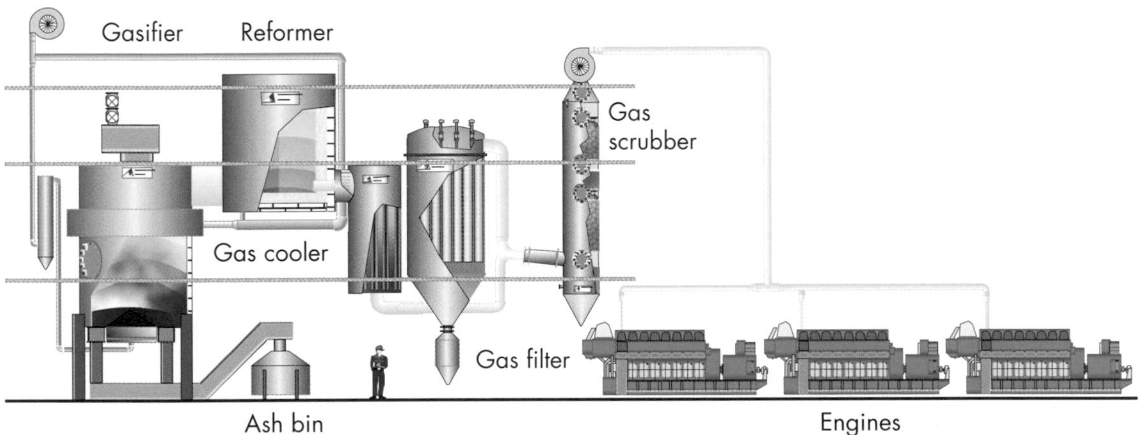

Note: This is a fixed-bed gasifier with a ceramic-lined reactor and gas cooling and cleaning system connected to three gas engines. Fuel capacity is 7.2 MW; power output 1 836 MW; district heat output 4.3 MW; and investment costs around USD 6 million.

Source: VTT, 2007.

Key point

Gasifiers have potential, but remain costly options and are largely at the demonstration phase compared with fluidised beds or combustion/steam turbine systems.

Economics

Currently at an early stage of demonstration, stand-alone systems have proven costly and largely unreliable. Several pilot plants have been shut down. The need to deliver fuel of a consistent quality and with a low moisture content has made cost reductions difficult. Data on four European gasification plants show that there are large variations in efficiencies and costs of different plant designs (Table 9.6). This is expected for new technologies at an early stage of development, however, as breakthroughs in designs and materials are still being sought. The data is included here as it exemplifies the difficulties in obtaining sufficiently accurate information from plant manufacturers and developers, where confidentiality and intellectual property are paramount. Assessing future costs and learning rates for such technologies with any degree of accuracy is challenging.

9

Table 9.6 ▶ **Gasification plant parameters and costs from existing demonstration and commercial plants**

	Plant 1 (UK)	Plant 2 (Austria)	Plant 3 (Denmark)	Plant 4 (Finland)
Built (reconstructed)	1997 (2002)	2001	1993 (2000)	1976 (1997)
Plant status	Demonstration	Demonstration	Commercial	Commercial
Main fuel	Wood chips	Wood chips	Wood chips	Multi-fuel
Net electrical output (MW)	0.096	1.85	1.45	200
Useful heat output (MW)	0.32		2.8	250
Electrical efficiency (%)	28	23	32	35
Overall efficiency (%)	72	79	90	85
Total capital cost (USD million)	0.26	12	6.3	15*
Cost per unit output (USD/kW_{e+th})	620	6 670	480	32*

*The investment cost includes only the cost of the gasifier and the fuel feed into it.

Source: European Bio-CHP, 2006.

Three of the plants produced useful heat as well as electricity. The ratio of electrical output to useful heat output depends on the chosen cycle. Higher power-to-heat ratios (approaching 1:1) are reached with combined cycles (as in the Finnish plant), although in the future even higher ratios might be expected if using fuel cells.

Combined heat and power (CHP)

In the most efficient generation-only plant, typically only around 30% of the fuel energy in the biomass is converted into electric power, the rest is lost into the air and water as low-temperature waste heat. One of the main ways to increase the efficiency of power generation and the competitiveness of bioenergy is to use this heat. Combined heat and power (CHP or cogeneration) plants generally have overall efficiencies of 80% to 90%.

CHP is typically the most economic choice for power production using biomass where there is a demand for heat for hot water or as process steam (Table 9.7). While it is normally more costly to build CHP plants than to have separate power and heating plants, CHP plants are cheaper to operate as less fuel is required. The overall lifetime costs of heat and power production with CHP are accordingly lower.

The economics of a biomass-fired CHP plant (and the profitability of the investment in the plant) depend to a great extent on local conditions: such as heat consumers, the volume and permanence of the heat load, and the price of available fuels.

Table 9.7 ▶ **Investment cost estimates and efficiencies for biomass CHP plants currently operating in Sweden for industrial or district heat**

Combustion technology	Main fuel	Net electricity (MW)	Net heat (MW)	Efficiency (%)	Investment costs (USD/kW_{e+th})
Industrial plants					
Fluidised bed	Wood	0	6.4	88	737
Grate	Wood	1	7	85.6	600
Fluidised bed	Wood	8	31	85.1	547
Fluidised bed	Wood	15	55	84.9	494
Fluidised bed	Wood	30	97	86.8	467
Fluidised bed	Wood	50	160	86.7	447
District heating					
Fluidised bed	Wood	3	9.5	83.5	654
Fluidised bed	Wood	6	17	84.4	623
Fluidised bed	Wood	17	40	85.4	540
Fluidised bed	Wood	60	120	85.7	448

Sources: Savolainen, Tuhkanen and Lehtilä, 2001; Alakangas and Flyktman, 2001.

District and industrial heat loads

Waste heat from the generator can be used to raise the temperature of water to between 120°C and 200°C for industrial processes or to between 70°C and 120°C for district space heating. In Nordic district heating systems, the outgoing flow water temperature varies with heat demand, while the return water temperature is maintained at around 50°C. Technically, all condensing power plant types can be modified for CHP. There is, however, a cost in terms of reduced generation efficiency – of around 0.1 MW to 0.15 MW for each MW_{th} of heat recovered.

In industrial applications, the heat is usually consumed as steam with pressures/ condensing temperatures ranging from 3 bar/130°C to 16 bar/200°C. Pulp and paper mills, sawmills, sugarcane plants and rice mills, for example, have traditionally used most of their biomass residues for steam and electricity production on-site. Sawmills are ideal candidates for CHP because drying the sawn timber creates a constant heat load, and bark and sawdust are available as biofuels. Biomass CHP plants are also used in large dairy factories, where milk-drying creates a relatively constant heat load. CHP is less efficient in plants where production is stopped at nights or over weekends, as the minimum heat load can often be too small, or the maximum load time too short, for the plant to be run efficiently.

In the Nordic countries, oil, natural gas and coal have been replaced by biomass for CHP since the 1970s. Low market prices for electricity in the 1980s reduced this trend, but promotion incentives have boosted the construction of bioenergy plants since the 1990s. In Finland, biomass-based fuels are used almost entirely in heat and CHP production in nearly 100 plants, with total capacity over 1 500 MW. Most pulp mills using debarked logs have installed CHP plants that use the bark as fuel together with other forest residues. The Alholmens Kraft CHP plant in Pietarsaari is the largest biomass-fuelled power plant in the world, producing 100 MW_{th} process steam for the adjacent paper mill, 240 MW for a utility generating electricity, and 60 MW_{th} heat output for district heating.

Fluidised bed boilers offer several benefits when using agricultural residues, such as straw, bagasse or rice husks. Although these require specialised manufacturing materials and construction, they have been used successfully. Increasing the superheated steam temperature and the pressure of steam boilers improves the power-to-heat ratios of biomass CHP plants. The largest plants are designed for 165 bar/545°C, but supercritical values will be introduced in future fluidised-bed boilers.

Large-scale versus small-scale CHP

For small-scale biomass technologies (under 10 MW), the main options for electricity and CHP are:

- combustion and steam boiler, with the steam used in steam turbines or engines;
- gasification and gas combustion in a boiler, with the steam used in steam turbines;
- gasification, with the gas used in a converted spark ignition engine, gas engine or gas turbine;
- pyrolysis oil, used in diesel engines;
- heat production to use with Stirling engines;
- heat production to use with the Organic Rankine Cycle process;
- landfill gas or anaerobic reactor biogas used in gas engines.

A comparison of two existing large- and small-scale combined heat and power plants in Europe showed little difference in heat costs but some economies of scale for power generation (Table 9.8).

Carbon-dioxide mitigation

Biomass integrated-gasification, combined-cycle (BIGCC) technologies have the potential to contribute CO_2-eq savings by 2050 of between 0.22 Gt/yr (ACT Map) and 1.46 Gt/yr (BLUE Map), assuming successful development and deployment of the technology. Linking BIGCC plants with CO_2 capture and storage (CCS) physically removes the CO_2 from the atmosphere. If the captured CO_2 is locked in geological reservoirs or other deposits, and the biomass is replaced by growing future crops or replanting forests, such an approach could actively reduce atmospheric concentrations of CO_2.

Table 9.8 ▶ **Comparisons of large and small CHP Plants**

	Plant 1	Plant 2
Plant output, power/heat (MW)	17/40	3.5/16
Overall efficiency	86.5%	86.5%
Boiler type	Fluidised bed	Fluidised bed
Primary fuel	Wood	Wood
Application		
Utilisation period of maximum load	6 000 hours/year	6 000 hours/year
Operating life, interest	20 years, 6%	20 years, 6%
Investment cost (USD million)	40.1	14.8
Fuel price (USD/MWh)	16	16
Value of produced heat (USD/MWh)	25	25
Value of produced electricity (USD/MWh)	104	110

Source: EUBionet 2, 2006.

9

Bioenergy CCS is most practical when the biomass is co-fired in coal-fired plants integrated with CCS systems. It would also be technically feasible for stand-alone biomass heat, power, CHP, BIGCC or biofuels plants to have CCS systems attached. But as these are normally relatively smaller plants, this is unlikely to be economic unless CO_2 prices are very high.

A more practical approach for biomass CCS might be to increase the carbon content of soil by the physical addition of char. This could be accomplished at a small scale in rural villages, or at a larger scale through a commercial pyrolysis or BIGCC plant. Char is produced during the gasification process by controlling the air/oxygen input. When incorporated into the soil, the carbon increases its water and nutrient holding capacity. With increased water and nutrients available to plant roots, crop yield is improved (Read, 2005).

The technical potential for biomass CCS is theoretically large, but due to high uncertainties at this early stage of development, none of the scenarios included it as a marketable technology at any material level.

Biofuels for transport

To achieve a very low carbon intensity in the transport sector, a shift away from fossil fuels to one or more low-GHG fuels, including electricity, hydrogen and biofuels, will be necessary. The prospects for the use of electricity and hydrogen for transport fuel are discussed in Chapter 15.

The production of transport fuel from biomass, in either liquid or gas form, holds the promise of a low net fossil-energy requirement and low life-cycle greenhouse gas emissions. However, there are many hurdles still to overcome and it remains unclear what level of biofuels production can be achieved globally on a sustainable basis by 2050. Issues such as food security and land competition with biofuels, and the potential impacts of biofuels on water resources, biodiversity and other aspects of the environment, are becoming major concerns that could severely limit the role of biofuels if not fully addressed. The successful development of advanced biofuels technologies, using non-food biomass feedstocks, could help overcome most barriers and achieve sustainable, very low CO_2, cost-effective biofuels.

Energy Technology Perspectives 2006 (IEA, 2006) provided a detailed description of the various process technologies associated with the different biofuels. This chapter focuses primarily on issues surrounding cost, technology challenges and obstacles to commercialisation.

Biofuels can be divided into a number of categories, including by type (liquid and gaseous) and by the feedstock or conversion process used (Table 9.9). Liquid biofuels such as ethanol and biodiesel are likely to dominate over gaseous fuels

Table 9.9 ▶ **A typology of liquid biofuels**

Fuel	Feedstock***	Regions where currently mainly produced	GHG reduction impacts vs. petroleum fuel use	Costs	Biofuel yield per hectare of land	Land types
1st generation ethanol	Grains (wheat, maize)	US, Europe, China	Low-moderate	Moderate-high	Moderate	Croplands
	Sugar cane	Brazil, India, Thailand	High	Low-moderate	High	Croplands
2nd generation ethanol	Biomass (cellulose)	None used but widely available	High	High	Medium-high	Croplands, Pasture lands, Forests
1st generation biodiesel (FAME)	Oil seeds (oilseed rape, soybean,)	US, Europe, Brazil	Moderate	Moderate-high	Low	Croplands
	Palm oil	Southeast Asia	Moderate	Low-moderate	Moderate-high	Coastal lands, Forests
2nd generation biodiesel*	Any biomass (via F-T**)	None used commercially	High	High	Medium-high	Croplands, Pasture lands, Forests

*Also termed biomass-to-liquids (BtL).
** Fischer-Tropsch process converts gasified biomass (or coal) to liquid fuels via a hydrocarbon chain building process.
*** A range of other crop feedstocks can also be used including sugar beet, cassava, jatropha, sunflower oil and sorghum, as well as purpose-grown vegetative grasses such as *Miscanthus* and reed canary grass, and short-rotation forest crops including *Salix* and *Eucalyptus*. These are not listed because they are less dominant.

Box 9.2 ▶ Biofuel from algae

A potential source of biofuels is algae. In the past few years a number of research and commercial start-up efforts have been initiated, indicating that there is now hope that biofuels from algae can become a viable commercial fuel in the near-to-medium term.

Like plants, algae require sunlight, carbon dioxide and water to grow via photosynthesis. Many types of algae produce oils that could be used as fuel, and certain types of algae could, under the right conditions, produce very large volumes of biofuel per unit of land area devoted to their production – perhaps hundreds of times more than oil crops.

Cultivating specific algae strains that are suitable for biodiesel production is challenging, due to the various trade-offs involved in selecting the strains and setting their growing conditions. Those that reproduce the fastest tend to be relatively low-oil-producing strains, with high-oil-producing strains tending to reproduce at the slowest rates.

Algae are typically cultivated in ponds and tanks. However, such "open" systems are vulnerable to being contaminated by other algal species and bacteria. As oil-producing algal strains are not the fastest to reproduce, it can be difficult to prevent other faster-growing strains from invading and disrupting cultivation of the desired strain. The number of species that have been successfully cultivated for a given purpose in an open system is relatively small.

Covering a pond with a greenhouse, or using tubes that allow sunlight to enter while also enabling the circulation of nutrients and carbon dioxide creates a "photo bioreactor". This is typically a smaller system, but it solves many of the problems associated with an open system. It allows a wider selection of viable species to be used and provides much better control of growing conditions, and hence results in higher oil yields.

Closed systems are more expensive to build and operate, but their costs can be reduced by locating production near existing factories that emit large quantities of carbon dioxide. This can increase algae yields while reducing direct carbon dioxide emissions. Production of co-products such as fertilisers can also offset costs.

Few cost estimates for closed systems are available. To reach commercial viability, however, costs will need to be substantially reduced (Briggs, 2004). Given the early stage of this research and its rapid expansion, cost reductions may indeed be possible.

such as methane and hydrogen for many years, due to their better compatibility with internal combustion engine vehicles and existing infrastructure. The conversion process is classified according to whether it uses "first-generation" biofuels (*i.e.* those already under commercial production, based on food-crop feedstocks) or advanced-technology "second-generation" biofuels (mainly ligno-cellulosic feedstocks such as straw, bagasse, vegetative grasses and wood). There are also "third-generation" biofuels under development, including oils from algae and other alcohols such as bio-butanol, but due to the lack of production experience to date, it has been assumed that these will make little contribution before 2050.

The characteristics of the different types of biofuels vary substantially. Second-generation technologies hold the promise of high-yielding, low-GHG-emitting and sustainably produced liquid fuels derived from forest and agricultural residues and purpose-grown energy crops. It is likely that commercial production of second-generation biofuels to produce gasoline or diesel substitutes from a range of ligno-cellulosic feedstocks (using either thermochemical-based biomass-to-liquid technologies or biochemical-based pathways) will eventually complement and perhaps supersede current first-generation biofuels from grains and oil-seed crops.

For light-duty vehicles (*e.g.* cars, small vans and SUVs), other propulsion technologies are likely to compete with the internal combustion engine in future, including electric motors and fuel cells. It is possible that the greatest demand for biofuels in the medium-long term will come from heavy-goods vehicles, marine vessels and aviation, where developing new power systems could be more challenging. Second-generation biofuels, in particular "biomass-to-liquids" (BtL) from biomass gasification and Fischer-Tropsch synthesis, could be important for diesel-fuel dominated transport modes in the coming decades, since BtL diesel is a high-quality fuel and, for example, fully substitutable for current aviation fuels.

Transition to second-generation biofuels

In a situation analogous to the refining of oil to produce multiple, higher-value chemicals and plastics, it is recognised that second-generation biofuels are also likely to be produced in conjunction with a series of value-added by-products – including bio-chemicals and bio-materials, and other forms of bioenergy (*e.g.* electricity and heat). This would allow a more comprehensive "biorefining" of biomass to serve multiple purposes.

Success in the development of second-generation biofuel technologies will be dependent on a number of factors:

- Continuing strong public and private support for research and development around second-generation biofuels, with particular emphasis on developing links among industry, universities, and government. Policies should be part of a comprehensive strategy for bioenergy development, and should be harmonised with rural employment and agricultural assistance.

- Demonstration and pre-commercial testing of second-generation biofuel technologies. This could reduce the risks to investors and create a more likely environment for the participation of financial institutions.

- Development of concrete measures of environmental performance, including net energy balance and net greenhouse-gas emissions, water and ecosystems impacts, and other attributes. Such "scorecards" should be used to develop incentives for second-generation biofuel production. As part of this strategy, life-cycle assessment tools should be further developed and used to confirm performance and to award credits to producers.

- A better understanding of the ligno-cellulosic biomass resources that could be utilised for second-generation biofuel production or bio-refinery applications. A full global mapping that helps identify optimal growing areas and promising non-crop sources (such as agricultural and forestry wastes) needs to be developed. Near-term successful deployment of second generation technologies could trigger exploitation of biomass resources (such as forests) in an unsustainable manner without proper planning and management strategies.

- The full range of impacts of biofuels – cost, environmental, and social among others, are potentially widely variant depending on fuel, feedstock and production technique. The potential co-benefits – including energy security, rural employment and diversification, local air pollution and environmental change – should not be overlooked. Thus, much more research into biofuels is needed, especially before countries become "locked in" to certain production approaches.

The IEA has developed a set of projections of costs and potential market penetration of the two major second-generation conversion technologies under development (enzymatic hydrolysis of cellulosic materials and gasification/F-T liquefaction) using a wide variety of biomass materials. The rate at which the cost of production declines will depend on feedstock prices, economies of scale realised from commercial plant development, and the benefits of experience and learning as cumulative production rises. Current costs and projected long-term "best-case" costs are shown in Figure 9.11. At an optimistic learning rate, both ligno-cellulosic ethanol and BtL biodiesel production costs drop rapidly after 2010 and reach a near-long-run cost level by 2030. At a more pessimistic learning rate, costs come down more slowly and permanently remain about USD 0.15/lge (litre gasoline equivalent) higher than the optimistic cost curve.

Figure 9.11 ▸ **Second-generation biofuel production cost assumptions to 2050**

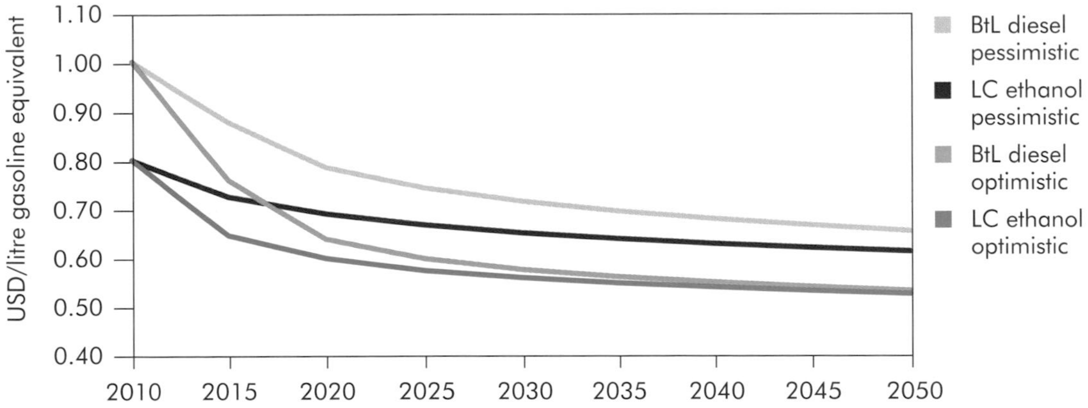

Note: BtL = Biomass-to-liquids; LC= ligno-cellulose.

Key point

Given appropriate RDD&D support, the currently high production costs for second-generation biofuels could decline to between USD 0.50 and USD 0.70 per litre gasoline equivalent through plant scale-up and learning experience.

Biofuels production scenarios

Fairly dramatic increases in production for second-generation ethanol and BtL diesel are assumed in the BLUE Map scenario. The total cumulative production by 2030 is several orders of magnitude above its starting point, allowing for a great deal of experience to be gained over time. Total transport fuel demand by 2050 is projected to be 3 273 Mtoe in ACT Map and 2 656 in BLUE Map. On this basis, biofuels would provide approximately 15% of the total in ACT Map and 23% in BLUE Map. In both scenarios, this is less than the share provided by oil, but more than that provided by electricity and hydrogen (see Transport Chapter).

Table 9.10 ▶ Second-generation biofuels production projections in the ACT Map and BLUE Map scenarios (Mtoe)

	2010	2015	2030	2050
ACT Map				
LC ethanol	0.0	1.5	46	140
BtL biodiesel	0.0	0.3	49	333
BLUE Map				
LC ethanol	0.0	3.0	62	121
BtL biodiesel	0.0	0.2	102	491

Note: LC = ligno-cellulose; BtL = biomass-to-liquids.

The incremental investment costs used in the BLUE Map scenario for the production and distribution of biofuels were calculated relative to the gasoline/diesel capacity that would otherwise have been built. The incremental investment costs (compared to displaced gasoline and diesel fuels), using intermediate biofuels cost assumptions, reflect the high capital costs of new facilities in the early years of production, followed by negative costs once the fuels become cheaper than gasoline and diesel (by 2025 for LC ethanol and 2030 for BtL diesel). Ultimately, the total (undiscounted) incremental investment costs are significantly negative over the 40-year period.

Production and land requirements for biofuels

The IEA has estimated current and future biofuel yields by feedstock type and region, based on various estimates of yields and land requirements in recent literature (Table 9.11). Simple assumptions were used regarding future yield improvements, on the basis of historic crop yield improvements and potential future improvements (including those from possible developments in genetic modification). These point estimates should be taken as rough averages; in reality there is a wide range in yield for any given feedstock/fuel/region combination.

Table 9.11 ▶ **Feedstock yield assumptions for land-use estimates**

Region – Biofuel	Feedstock	Yields, 2005 (l/ha)		Average	Resulting yields in 2050 (lge/ha)
		Nominal	Gasoline/diesel equivalent		
Europe – ethanol	Wheat	2 500	1 650	0.7%	2 260
Europe – ethanol	Sugar beet	5 000	3 300	0.7%	4 520
Europe – FAME biodiesel	Oilseed rape	1 200	1 080	0.7%	1 480
US/Canada – ethanol	Corn	3 000	1 980	0.7%	2 710
US/Canada – FAME biodiesel	Soybean/oilseed rape	800	720	0.7%	990
Brazil – ethanol	Sugarcane	6 800	4 490	0.7%	6 140
Brazil – FAME biodiesel	Soybean	700	630	1.0%	990
Rest of world – ethanol	Sugarcane	5 500	3 630	1.0%	5 680
Rest of world – ethanol	Grain	2 000	1 320	1.0%	2 070
Rest of world – biodiesel	Oil palm	2 500	2 250	1.0%	3 520
Rest of world – biodiesel	Soybean/ oilseed rape	1 000	900	1.0%	1 410
Second generation					
World – ethanol	Ligno-cellulose	4 300	2 840	1.3%	5 080
World – BtL biodiesel	Biomass	3 000	3 000	1.3%	5 360

Note: FAME = Fatty acid methyl esters; lge/ha = litres gasoline equivalent per hectare; l/ha = litres per hectare; ethanol converted to gasoline equivalent (ethanol 67% the energy content of gasoline), biodiesel converted to diesel equivalent (biodiesel 90% the energy content of diesel, except BtL biodiesel with 100% the energy content of petroleum diesel).

There is significant variation in our yield estimates across the various feedstocks, fuels and locations considered. Brazilian sugarcane-to-ethanol has the highest yield, whereas United States and European biodiesel from soybean and oilseed rape are lowest. The more intensively biofuels are produced in regions with soils and climates that support high-yield feedstocks and approaches, the less total land will be required to produce a given amount of fuel. On the other hand, some of the highest yielding land is also excellent land for food crops, so land competition for different uses becomes a concern.

Putting these yield estimates together with the projected future demand for biofuels in the BLUE Map scenario, the land area that will be required to produce the biofuels can be estimated (Figure 9.12).

Figure 9.12 ▶ **Demand for biofuels and land requirements in the BLUE Map scenario**

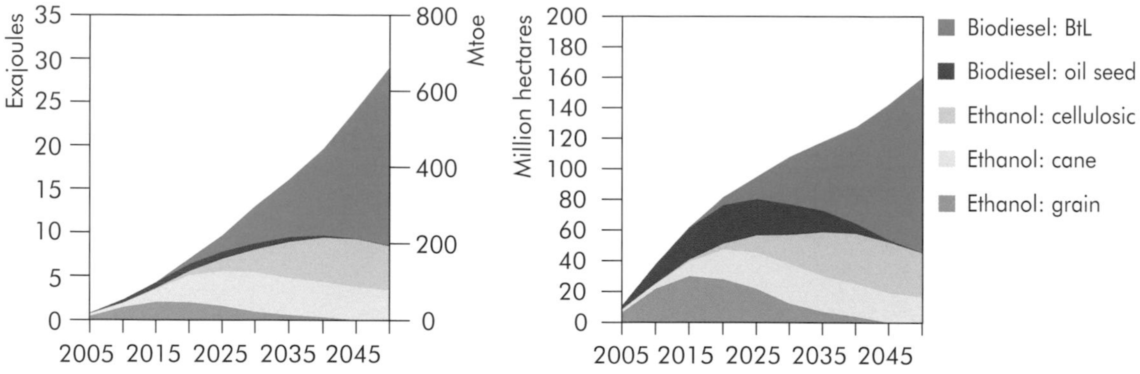

Key point

As second-generation biofuel production increases, more land will be needed for feedstock production. As first-generation grain feedstocks are phased out, a change in land-use patterns could result.

By 2050, about 160 Mha of land would be needed to produce the volumes of biofuel required to meet the demand expected in the BLUE Map scenario. This is included in the 375 Mha to 750 Mha required for total biomass production outlined above. It is around 3% to 4% of the 6 billion hectares of agricultural area in use today. However, if concentrated in certain countries and regions, particularly if in food-producing areas, it could have substantial impacts in terms of crop displacements and other land-use changes. For example, rapid increases in the production of biofuels in the United States and the European Union in recent years appear to have contributed to rises in prices of certain agricultural commodities (such as corn in the United States and rapeseed oil in the European Union) as competition for crops and land has increased.

These estimates neglect the possibility of producing biofuels (particularly second generation biomass-based fuels) from non-crop sources such as agricultural, forestry, and other waste biomass. Clearly use of such feedstocks would have the major advantage of causing few impacts on land use. The more that such sources can be utilised, the lower the net land requirement for producing biofuels. Net CO_2 emissions reductions could also be bigger.

Given the many uncertainties associated with the use of biofuels and their impact on the environment and our agricultural systems, it is important to manage these changes very carefully and to seek the most environmentally friendly and least land-intensive approaches. Sustainably produced second-generation biofuels will be essential if we are to shift towards a sustainable transport system at reasonable cost, especially given the limited alternatives for shipping and air transport. Ligno-cellulosic feedstocks can come from crop and forest residues, or they can be cultivated on marginal or degraded land – thereby avoiding competition with food production. Biofuels policies will have to be co-ordinated internationally and be integrated with agricultural and forestry policies in order to ensure their sustainability.

Chapter 10 WIND POWER

Key Findings

- *Wind power has grown rapidly since the 1990s. Global installed capacity at 94 GW in 2007 was 50 times that of 1990. Wind turbines provided 152 TWh in 2006, just under 1% of global electricity supply. European and United States markets continue to dominate, while India and China are experiencing impressive growth.*

- *Wind power is a robust technology that has made great strides since its first deployment spurt of the 1980s. The outlook is for continued double-digit percentage annual growth. Wind power provides 9% of global electricity generation in 2050 in the ACT Map scenario and 12% in the more ambitious BLUE Map scenario.*

- *Wind turbines need no fuel, incur almost no CO_2 emissions and, upon completion of the permitting processes, can be installed relatively quickly. Significant technology advances are expected to continue, partly driven by the move to large offshore installations.*

- *The cost of wind power has been reduced by a factor of four since the 1980s, driven largely by technological advances, scaling up turbine size and increased manufacturing capacity. However, turbine prices have risen about 20% since 2004, due to commodity and component market tightness and increased demand.*

- *Turbine output varies with the wind resource. This variability can be challenging for grid systems at high penetration levels, the degree depending on the flexibility of the electricity system as a whole. The deployment of new technologies for storage, network operation, transmission and the more efficient use of existing infrastructure needs to be accelerated.*

- *Onshore wind is considered commercial at sites with good wind resources and grid access. Much of the onshore wind resource remains untapped. Today, five countries account for 73% of global installed wind capacity: Germany, United States, Spain, India and China.*

- *Offshore wind is in a pre-commercial development phase, but deployment is progressing. The advantages of offshore compared with onshore wind include higher capacity factors, wind speeds yielding as much as 50% greater output, and lower visual impact. Though presently considerably more expensive, cost improvements are expected for offshore wind.*

- *Although wind power is increasingly commercial, much RD&D remains to be done if wind is to deliver its full potential to provide ample electricity supply in a carbon-constrained world. Priority areas include resource assessment in complex terrains and production forecasting. Storage, grid integration, power-system design and regulation are also important research areas. Still at a relatively early stage in R&D, but with important potential, are new offshore foundation concepts that include floating wind turbines systems.*

Wind power overview

Figure 10.1 ▶ **Global installed wind power capacity** (Annual and cumulative)

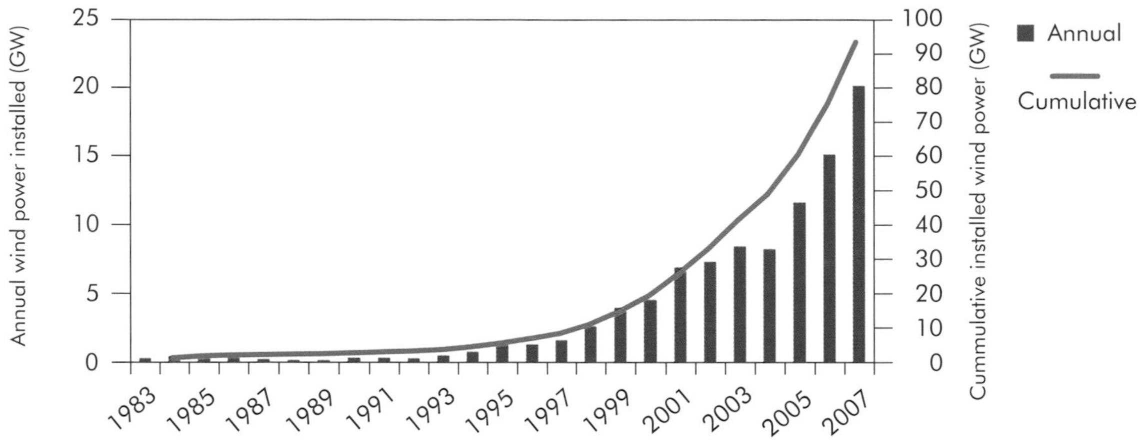

Sources: BTM Consult, 2008; Global Wind Energy Council, 2008.

Key point

Wind power capacity in 2007 was more than fifty times greater than in 1990.

Global wind power installed capacity in 2007 was 94 GW (Figure 10.1). These are predominately onshore installations. Since 2001, installed wind capacity worldwide has grown by 20% to 30% a year. Despite supply chain constraints, in 2007 alone more than 20 GW of wind power capacity was added, with a value of about USD 31 billion.

The bulk of global wind power capacity is installed in the 20 IEA member countries that participate in the collaborative R&D implementing agreement known as IEA Wind (Table 10.1). They account for about three-quarters of the world's wind-generated electricity supply. In these countries, wind's contribution to national electricity demand ranged from less than 1% in ten countries to almost 17% in Denmark.

Altogether, there are wind farms in more than 40 countries worldwide, 13 of which have more than 1 000 MW of installed capacity. Figure 10.2 shows the global share of wind power capacity. The top ten countries in terms of installed capacity are highlighted in Table 10.2.

Table 10.1 ▶ Electricity generation from wind power in selected IEA countries, 2006

Country	Total installed wind capacity MW	Offshore installed wind capacity MW	Annual increase in capacity MW	Total number of turbines	Average new turbine capacity kW	Wind-generated electricity GWh/yr	National electricity demand TWh/yr	% of National electricity demand from wind %
Australia	817	0	109	544	1 750	2 504	208.0	1.20
Austria	965		146					
Canada	1 460	0	776	1 186	1 230	3 800	*550.0*	0.69
Denmark	3 137	432	8	5 274	1 287	6 108	36.4	16.78
Finland	86	0	4	96	2 000	154	90.0	0.17
Germany	20 622	7	2 207	18 685	1 848	30 500	540.0	5.65
Greece	749	0	142	1 051	1 146	*1 580*	*51.1*	3.10
Ireland	744	25	251			1 617	28.9	5,59
Italy	2 123	0	405	2 575	1 148	3 215	338.0	0.95
Japan	1 574	1	494	1 358	1 159	1 910	882.6	0.22
Korea	175	0	77	118		247	381.2	0.06
Mexico	86	0	83	105				
Netherlands	1 559	108	335	1 792	2 248	2 747	116.0	2.37
Norway	325	0	57	163	2 280	671	112.0	0.55
Portugal	1 698	0	634	964	2 400	2 926	*49.0*	5.97
Spain	11 615	0	1 587	13 842	1 375	23 372	268.0	8.72
Sweden	571	23	62	812	1 879	986	150.0	0.66
Switzerland	12	0	0	34	20	15	58.0	0.03
United Kingdom	1 963	304	631		2 103	4 591	408.8	1.12
United States	11 575	0	2 454		1 600	31 000	4 027.0	0.77
Total	**61 855**	**900**	**10 461**	**48 599**	**1 697**	**117 886**	**8 280.2**	**1.42**

Note: blue = estimated value; underscore = value from 2004/2005.

Source: IEA Wind, 2007a.

10

Figure 10.2 ▶ **Share of global installed wind power capacity, 2007**

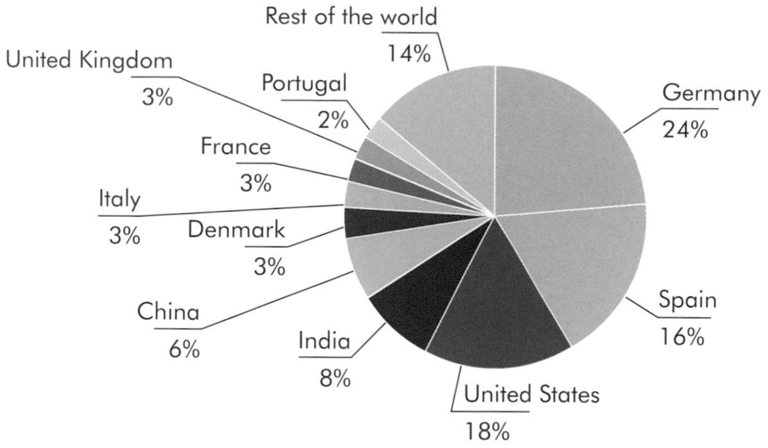

Sources: IEA statistics; Global Wind Energy Council, 2008.

Key point

Ten countries account for 86% of global installed wind capacity.

Table 10.2 ▶ **Top ten countries in installed wind power capacity**

Country	MW	%
Germany	22 247	23.6
United States	16 818	17.9
Spain	15 145	16.1
India	8 000	8.5
China	6 050	6.4
Denmark	3 125	3.3
Italy	2 726	2.9
France	2 454	2.6
United Kingdom	2 389	2.5
Portugal	2 150	2.3
Rest of the world	13 018	13.8
Total top ten	81 104	86.2
Global total	**94 122**	

Sources: IEA statistics; Global Wind Energy Council, 2008.

Europe is the leading market in wind power, with 57 GW of installed capacity (Figure 10.3). Yet, North America and Asia are developing wind power at a tremendous pace. The United States reported a record 5 244 MW new wind capacity installed in 2007, more than double the new capacity of 2006. India is the fourth-largest market, adding 1 730 MW in 2007. China built 3 449 MW in 2007, more than doubling its installed wind-power capacity.

Figure 10.3 ▶ Global distribution of wind power development, 2000 to 2007

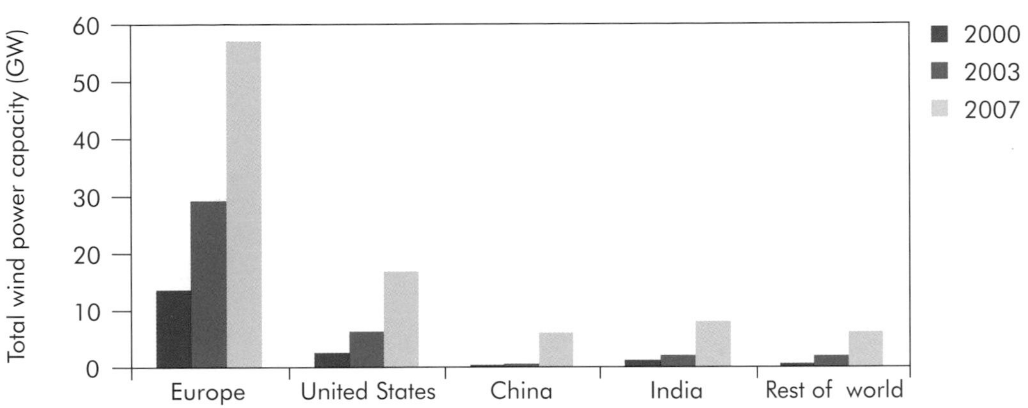

Sources: BTM Consult, 2008; Global Wind Energy Council, 2008.

Key point

Wind power capacity is increasing around the world.

10

Scenario highlights

In the ETP scenarios, global wind power capacity increases from 94 GW today to 1 360 GW in 2050 in the ACT Map scenario, and to more than 2 010 GW in 2050 in the BLUE Map scenario (Figure 10.4).

In the ACT Map scenario, electricity production from wind contributes 2712 TWh/yr in 2030 and 3 607 TWh/yr in 2050. In the BLUE Map scenario – which assumes higher CO_2 incentives and a more optimistic outlook concerning cost reductions, the pace of offshore developments, and innovative storage and grid design and management – wind power adds 2 663 TWh/yr in 2030 and 5 174 TWh/yr in 2050. Wind power constitutes 12% of global electricity production in 2050 in the BLUE Map scenario compared to 2% in the baseline, reducing emissions by 2.14 Gt CO_2/yr. Just over 700 000 turbines of 4 MW size are required in the BLUE Map scenario, compared to 146 000 in the baseline scenario.

Wind power production is expected to grow significantly in OECD countries, but also in emerging economies such as China and India. In the BLUE Map scenario, China leads in wind power generation in 2050 (Figure 10.5).

Figure 10.4 ▶ Global installed wind power capacity by scenario

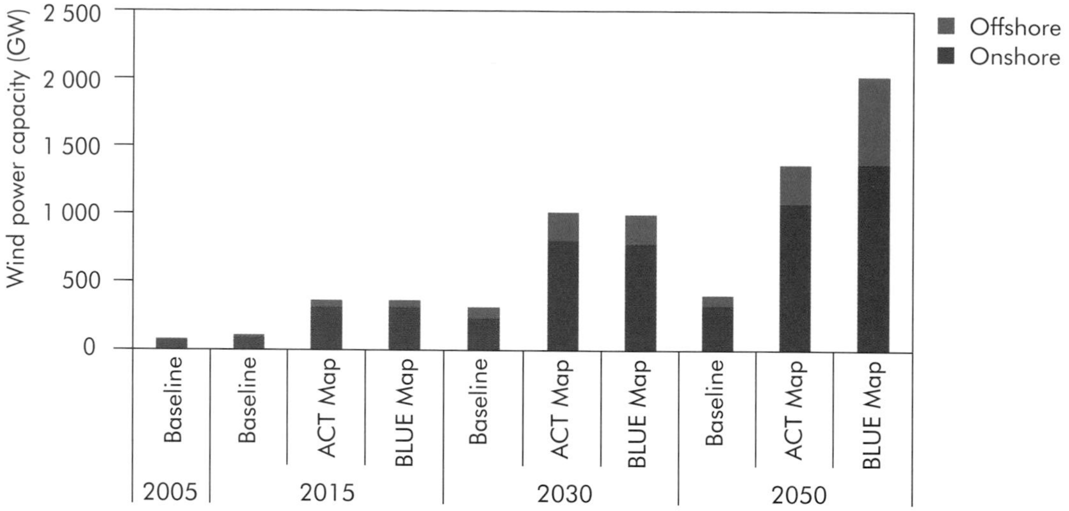

Wind power capacity (GW)
2 500
2 000
1 500
1 000
500
0
Offshore
Onshore
Baseline
Baseline
ACT Map
BLUE Map
Baseline
ACT Map
BLUE Map
Baseline
ACT Map
BLUE Map
2005
2015
2030
2050

Key point

Wind power capacity increases significantly in both the ACT Map and BLUE Map scenarios.

Figure 10.5 ▶ Wind power generation by region, BLUE Map scenario, 2050

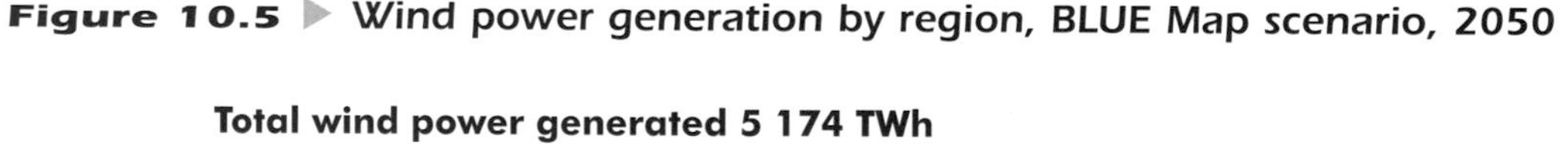

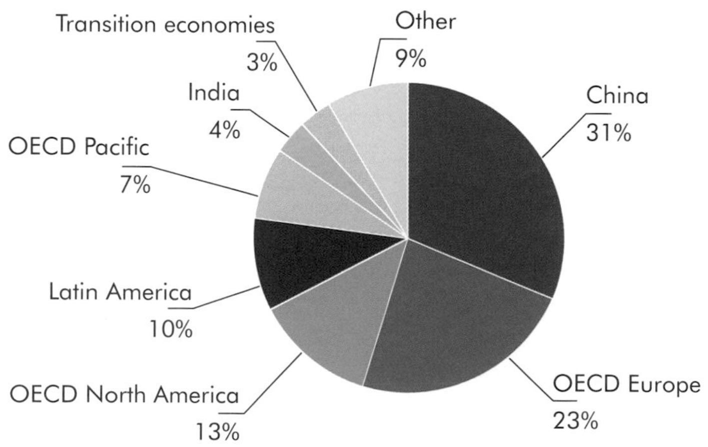

Key point

China and Europe account for more than 50% of electricity from wind power in 2050.

Technology developments

Wind power technology development has been very successful. From the 1970s to the early 1990s a variety of concepts competed. Today's standard is a three-bladed horizontal axis, upwind and grid connected wind turbine. Figure 10.6 illustrates how turbine size has increased since 1980. The largest wind turbines today are 5 MW to 6 MW units with a rotor diameter of up to 126 metres. Turbines have doubled in size nearly every five years, but a slowdown in this rate is expected in the near term, as transport and installation constraints start to limit these continuous increases.

Figure 10.6 ▶ Development of wind turbine size, 1980 to 2005

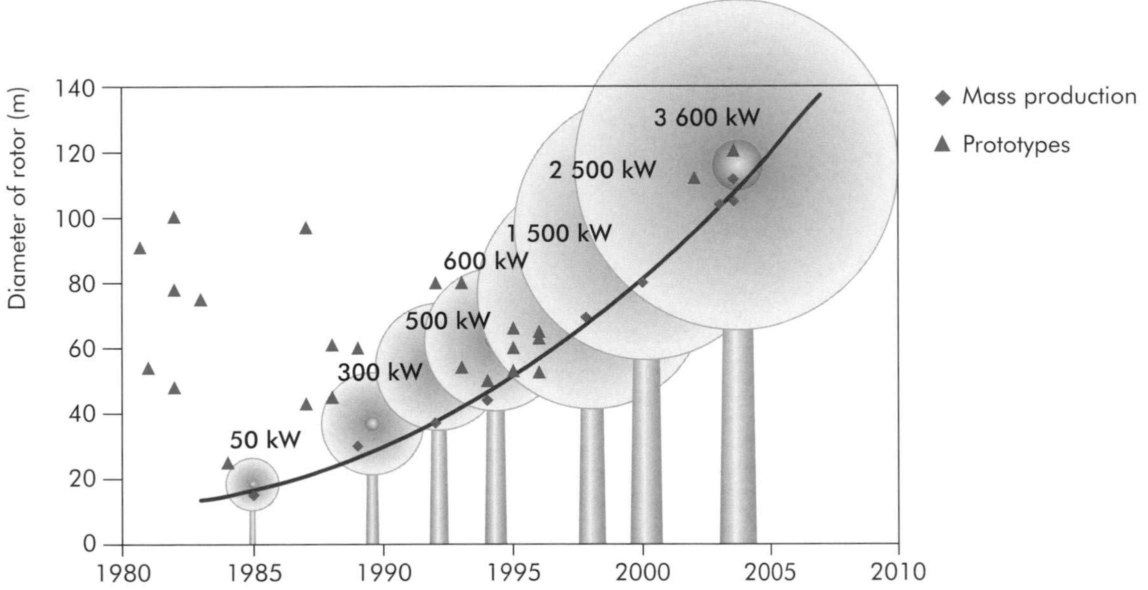

Source: German Wind Energy Institute (DEWI), 2006.

Key point

Scaling-up wind turbine rotor diameters has increased output.

In the 1970s, the reliability and availability of the first generation of wind turbines were quite low. Today the availability in mature markets is around 99%, as a result of extensive testing and certification (Jensen, *et al.*, 2002).

Cost developments

Onshore wind power installed costs in 2006 ranged from a low of USD 1 224/kW in Denmark to a high of USD 1 707/kW in Canada (Figure 10.7). Since 2004, turbine prices, constituting about 75% of project costs, have increased about 20%. Operation and maintenance costs for service, consumables, repair, insurance, administration and site lease for new large turbines in 2006 ranged from 2% to 3.5% of capital cost – or from about USD 13/MWh to USD 24/MWh.

Figure 10.7 ▶ **Average installed costs of onshore wind projects in selected IEA countries, 2003 to 2006**

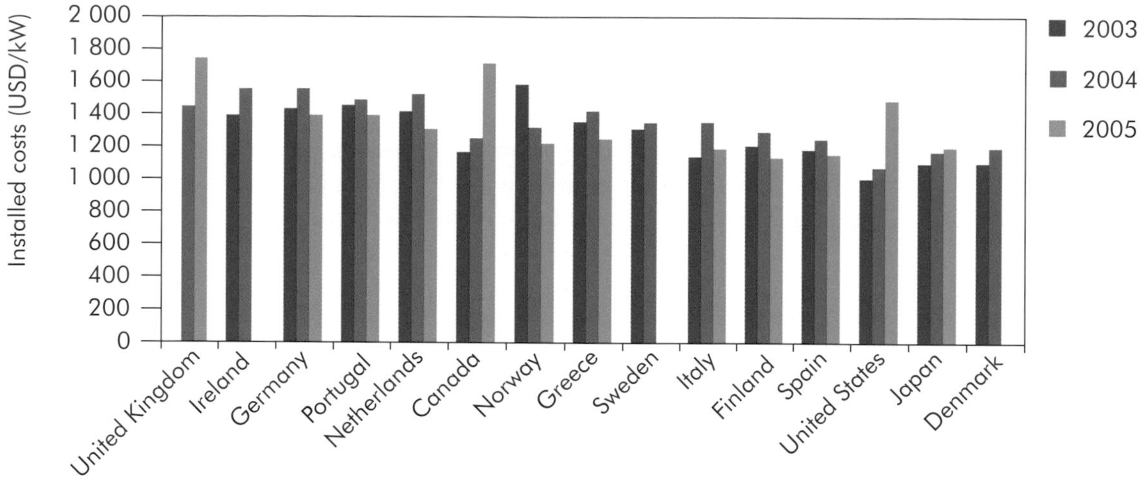

Note: Costs include turbines, roads, electrical equipment, installation, development and grid connection.
Source: IEA Wind, 2007a.

Key point

Wind turbine prices have increased 20% since 2004.

Offshore costs are largely dependent on water depth and the distance from shore. Recent offshore costs in the United Kingdom, where 90 MW of capacity was added in 2006, ranged from USD 2 226/kW to USD 2 969/kW. The costs of offshore foundations, construction, installations and grid connection are significantly higher than for onshore wind farms. Offshore turbines are typically 20% more expensive, and towers and foundations cost more than 2.5 times the price of an onshore project of similar size.

Market overview

In the 1980s there were two major markets for wind turbines: Denmark and California. In Denmark, where the government successfully and flexibly employed demand-pull and technology-push policy instruments, wind capacity has increased steadily. By contrast, very rapid deployment in California from 1982 peaked in 1986 and then collapsed in 1987, when financial incentives were withdrawn. United States and Danish (exporting) manufacturers were badly hit. Danish wind turbine manufacturers, however, were able to fall back on a relatively stable domestic market.

Since the mid 1990s, Germany has been the world's largest wind power market. With more than 22 GW of installed capacity, it is estimated that wind power in Germany accounted for 70 000 jobs and contributed USD 7 060 million to the country's GDP in 2006. Spain also launched aggressive development and deployment measures in the mid 1990s: it is now home to the world's second largest turbine manufacturer and is the third largest market in terms of installed capacity.

The United States is leading the market in terms of annual installations, and with more than 16 GW installed, it ranks second largest in the world. India and, more recently, China have also been witnessing impressive growth and now rank fourth and fifth in installed capacity.

The global market for wind power has created an international industry with an estimated annual turnover of more than USD 31 billion in 2007. It has fostered a substantial manufacturing industry with about 200 000 employees.

The boom in demand for wind power technology has led to supply constraints. Prices have increased by about 20% since 2004. Factors contributing to the bottlenecks include uncertainty about policy frameworks and incentive schemes which has inhibited investment in production facilities; price increases in raw materials such as copper and steel; and the lead time for component suppliers to ramp up to meet the demand for gearboxes, blades, bearings and towers for large machines. Industry sources expect the tightness in the supply chain to be resolved by 2009–2010.

Six leading wind turbine manufacturers accounted for about 90% of the global market in 2006. Turbine manufacturing continues to expand in Europe and new production plants are being opened in India, China and the United States. Four leading wind turbine companies opened manufacturing facilities in the United States in 2006, including India's Suzlon. There are now 40 turbine manufacturers operating in the Chinese market, and one of them, Goldwind, has reached the top ten in terms of market share worldwide (Table 10.3).

Table 10.3 ▶ Global top ten wind-turbine manufacturers

	Cumulative installed capacity 2005 MW	Capacity supplied in 2006 MW	Market share 2006 %	Cumulative installed capacity 2006 MW	Cumulative global market share %
VESTAS (Denmark)	20 766	4 239	28.2	25 006	33.7
GAMESA (Spain)	7 912	2 346	15.6	10 259	13.8
GE WIND (United States)	7 370	2326	15.5	9 696	13.0
ENERCON (Germany)	8 685	2 316	15.4	11 001	14.8
SUZLON (India)	1 485	1 157	7.7	2 641	3.6
SIEMENS (Denmark)	4 502	1 103	7.3	5 605	7.5
NORDEX (Germany)	2 704	505	3.4	3 209	4.3
REPOWER (Germany)	1 522	480	3.2	2 002	2.7
ACCIONA (Spain)	372	426	2.8	798	1.1
GOLDWIND (China)	211	416	2.8	627	0.8
Others	6 578	689	4.6	7 267	9.8
Total	**62 108**	**16 003**	**107**	**78 110**	**105**

Note: Country designation refers to the corporate base.

Source: BTM Consult, 2007.

10

Environmental factors

Wind power generates no CO_2 emissions other than small amounts in the production and installation of turbines and has low water needs. But as with other sources of energy, it has environmental impacts, particularly at a local and regional level. The three main environmental concerns are visual impact, noise and the risk of bird collisions and wildlife disruption.

Wind turbines can often be seen from some distance and are viewed by some as obtrusive. This can cause opposition to the siting of wind farms. Several design tools, such as photo-montage and animation, have been developed to help developers to minimise visual impacts.

Wind turbines generate two types of sound: aerodynamic noise from the blades and mechanical noise from the rotating machinery. Mechanical noise has been minimised using well-proven engineering techniques. Careful design, siting and operation should ensure that aerodynamic sound is not a nuisance.

There has been a great deal of research into the effect that wind turbines have on the routes of migratory birds or on sites of special significance to bird and wildlife populations. It has been found that most of these problems can be avoided through sensitive siting.

Offshore wind developments may pose additional environmental impacts due to their size and the sensitivity of the marine environment. Denmark conducted an environmental monitoring programme before, during and after construction of two large offshore wind farms from 1999 to 2006. This experience indicates that, if properly sited, offshore wind development can be engineered and operated without significant damage to the marine environment (Danish Energy Authority, 2005). The tools developed for this programme, particularly for the study of the behavioural responses of marine mammals and birds, will be useful for researchers at other offshore sites. They can be readily transferred to estuarine or open sea sites and can be applied in the study of a wide range of wildlife and bird species.

Onshore wind power

Overview

Today, most of the world's wind power capacity is land based. The size of onshore wind turbines has increased steadily over the past 25 years. Large turbines can usually deliver electricity at a lower average cost than smaller ones, as the costs of foundations, road building, maintenance, grid connection and other factors are largely independent of the size of the turbine. Large turbines with tall towers use wind resources more efficiently.

Figure 10.8 shows the development of the average size of onshore wind turbines sold by year for a number of countries. In Spain, the average size installed in 2006 was 1100 kW, well below that of Germany (1 634 kW) and the United States (1466 kW). In India, the average size installed in 2006 was approximately 800 kW, significantly below the level of other countries. This difference is mainly because Indian manufacturers only recently began producing megawatt-scale turbines.

Figure 10.8 ▶ **Development of average wind turbine size in leading wind countries**

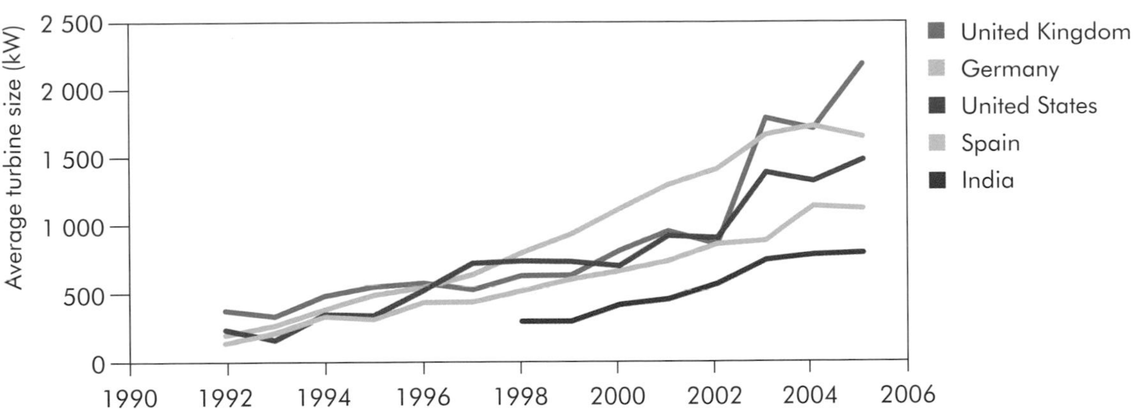

Source: BTM Consult, 2007.

Key point

Turbines continue to increase in size.

Efficiency improvements

Power from wind turbines is mainly determined by the wind regime at the site, turbine height and the efficiency of the turbine. Increasing the height of the turbines has yielded higher output. Methods for measuring and evaluating wind resources have improved substantially in recent years, which have enhanced turbine siting. Germany and Denmark have developed many of their best sites already, so new onshore developments in these countries may be at sites with lower average wind speeds. The re-powering of many early wind farms with larger units has yielded higher outputs on prime sites.

The efficiency of electricity production, measured as annual energy production per unit of swept rotor area (kWh/m^2), has improved significantly over time. Better turbine siting, more efficient equipment and higher hub heights have increased overall efficiency by 2% to 3% annually over the last 15 years.

Onshore wind power costs

Investment costs

Three major trends have dominated the cost of onshore wind turbines in recent years:

- turbines have become larger and taller;
- efficiency of turbine electricity production has increased steadily;
- investment cost per kW installed power decreased until 2004.

Energy output from a wind turbine is proportional to the swept area of the rotor. So are manufacturing costs.

Capital costs

The capital costs of wind energy projects are dominated by the price of the wind turbine (*ex works*). Table 10.4 shows the cost structure for a medium-sized onshore turbine (850 kW to 1 500 kW).[1] The turbine's share of total cost is typically around 74% to 82%.

Table 10.4 ▶ Cost structure for a typical medium-size onshore wind installation

	Share of total cost %	Typical share of other costs %
Turbine *(ex works)*	74-82	–
Foundation	1-6	20-25
Electric installation	1-9	10-15
Grid-connection	2-9	35-45
Consultancy	1-3	5-10
Land	1-3	5-10
Financial costs	1-5	5-10
Road construction	1-5	5-10

Note: Based on data from Germany, Denmark, Spain and United Kingdom for 850 to 1 500 kW turbines.

Source: Lemming, *et al.*, 2008.

Operation and maintenance costs

The main components of operation and maintenance (O&M) costs are maintenance and repair, spare parts, insurance, and administration costs. Over the life of a turbine, O&M costs can constitute about 20% to 25% of the total cost per kWh produced. In a turbine's early years, the share can be 10% to 15%, increasing to between 20% and 35% in later years. Manufacturers are attempting to lower O&M costs by developing new turbine designs that have less down-time and require fewer service visits.

So far, only a limited number of modern wind turbines have reached their expected lifetime of 20 years and these are almost entirely small machines. Experience in Germany, Spain, Denmark and the United Kingdom, however, suggests that average O&M costs are likely to be about US cents 1.5/kWh to US cents 1.9/kWh of produced wind power over the life of a turbine.

Onshore wind power production costs

Costs per kWh as a function of the local wind conditions are shown in Figure 10.9. They range from US cents 8.9/kWh to US cents 13.5/kWh at sites

1. *Ex works* means that no balance-of-plant costs, *i.e.* site works, foundation or grid connection costs, are included. *Ex works* costs include the turbine as provided by the manufacturer, including the turbine, blades, tower and transport to the site.

with low average wind speeds, to between US cents 6.5/kWh and US cents 9.4/kWh at sites with high average wind speeds – such as those on the coasts of the United Kingdom, Ireland, France, Denmark and Norway. At a medium wind site, such as inland sites in Germany, France, Spain, Portugal, Netherlands, Italy, Sweden, Finland and Denmark, average costs are estimated to be US cents 8.5/kWh.

Figure 10.9 ▶ **Wind power production costs as a function of the wind regime**

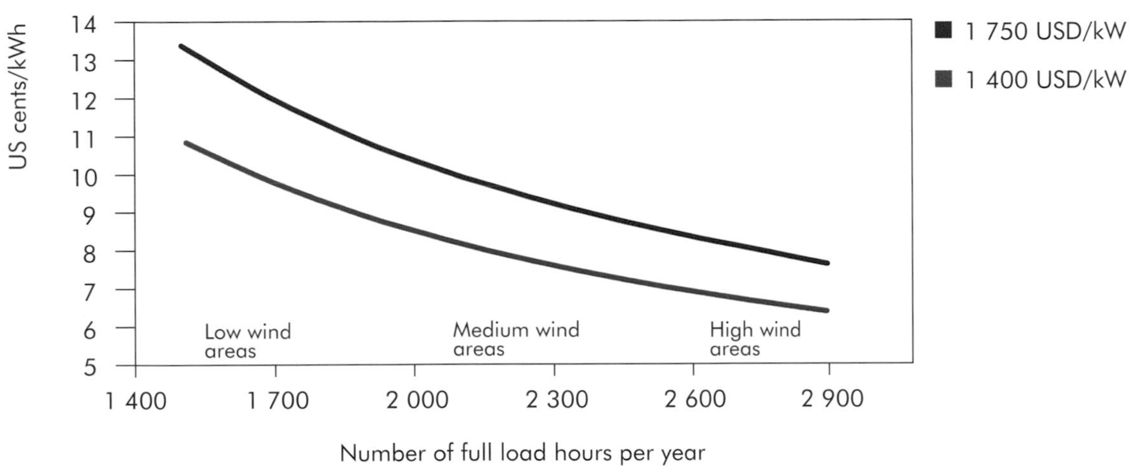

Note: The number of full-load hours is used to represent the wind regime. Full-load hours are calculated as the average annual production divided by the rated power of the turbine.

Source: Lemming, *et al.*, 2008.

Key point

The quality of the wind resource critically influences production costs.

About 75% to 80% of total wind-power production costs are capital costs. This makes wind power relatively capital-intensive compared to conventional fossil fuel-fired generation technologies, in which 40% to 60% of total costs are related to fuel and O&M costs.

Outlook for cost reductions

Further cost reductions in onshore wind power are expected over time. Given likely levels of demand, and assuming there are no capital price reductions before 2010, a learning rate of 10% a year is maintained, and cumulative capacity doubles every three years, costs are projected to decline as shown in Figure 10.10. This suggests that costs in 2015 would be about US cents 5.3/kWh at a high wind site and US cents 6.3/kWh for a medium wind site.

Figure 10.10 ▶ Onshore wind power cost estimates in 2015

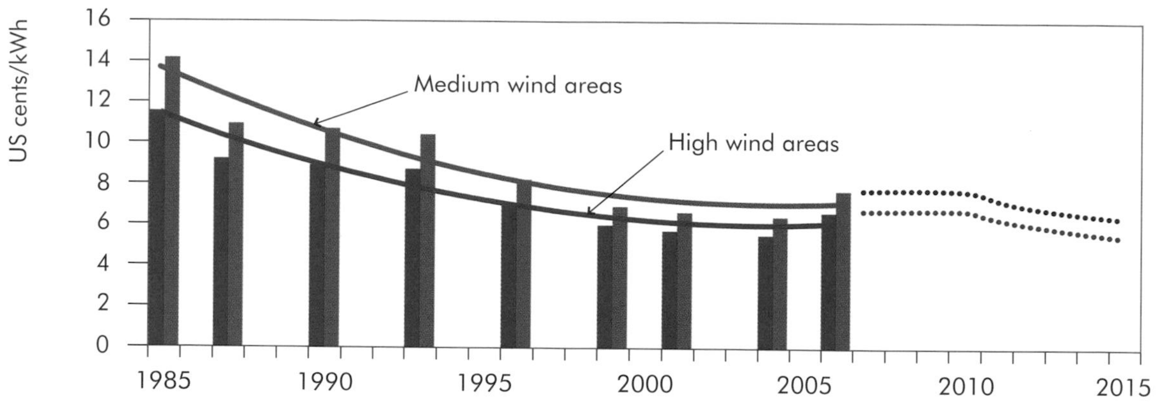

Note: Based on an average 2 MW turbine with present production costs of US cents 7.6/kWh installed in a medium wind area (average wind speed of 6.3 m/s at a hub height of 50 m).

Source: Lemming, *et al.*, 2008.

Key point

Onshore wind power costs look set to decline after 2010.

Offshore wind power

Overview

Offshore wind power technology is less mature and currently about 50% more expensive than onshore wind installations, yet offshore installations produce up to 50% more output than onshore machines due to better wind conditions. New approaches in foundation technology, larger turbines, more efficient and reliable components and learning from early projects have increased the attractiveness of offshore wind energy in recent years. Offshore wind faces the challenges of technological performance in harsh conditions; a shortage of auxiliary services, e.g. installation vessels; competition for space with other marine users; environmental impacts; and grid interconnection.

Five countries have offshore wind power capacity. Between them, they had more than 900 MW of capacity by the end of 2006 (Table 10.5), with an additional 200 MW installed in 2007. Most of this capacity is in relatively shallow water (< 20 metres deep) and is close to the coast (< 20 km). Offshore wind farms have used 2 MW or larger turbines since 2000.

Today, the high cost of offshore developments, difficulties in siting approvals, spatial planning uncertainties, constraints in the manufacturing supply chain and the availability of installation vessels are causing some delays. Nonetheless, several projects in Denmark, Germany and the United Kingdom are expected to be completed in the near term. The world's largest offshore wind farm, the

London Array, received planning approval in December 2006 and the first phase of development is expected in 2009. Situated more than 20 km offshore, with 1 000 MW of capacity, it will be capable of powering one-quarter of London households.

Table 10.5 ▶ **Installed offshore wind power capacity, 2006**

Country	Capacity installed in 2005 MW	Cumulative installed capacity 2005 MW	Capacity installed in 2006 MW	Cumulative installed capacity 2006 MW
Denmark	0	423	0	423
Ireland	0	25	0	25
Netherlands	0	18.2	108	126.8
Sweden	0	23.3	0	23.3
United Kingdom	90	214	90	304
Global total	**90**	**703.5**	**198.0**	**902.1**

Sources: BTM Consult; Danish Energy Authority.

Offshore wind power costs

10

Investment costs

Offshore costs are largely dependent on wind speeds, weather and wave conditions, water depth, and distance to the coast. The most recent offshore cost information is from the United Kingdom, where present investment costs range from USD 2 225/kW to USD 2 970/kW. Recent evidence suggests that costs are likely to rise in the near future.

The relatively high cost of offshore wind farms is partly offset by higher electricity production – due to higher wind speeds for longer periods. A land-based turbine is usually run about 2 000 to 2 300 full-load hours per year (~25% capacity factor) whereas a typical offshore installation will run for 3 000 to 3 300 full-load hours per year (~34% capacity factor) (Lemming, Morthorst and Clausen, 2007).[2]

Investment costs range from USD 1.5 million/MW (Middelgrunden) to USD 3.4 million/MW (Robin Rigg), partly reflecting differences in water depth and distance to shore (Table 10.6). Average costs for near-term offshore wind farms are expected to be higher – in the range of USD 2.5 million/MW to USD 2.8 million/MW for shallow, near-shore wind farms.

2. Full-load hours for Danish offshore wind farms are in the range of 3 500 to 4 000 hours per year (Danish Energy Authority, 2005).

Table 10.6 ▶ **Recent offshore wind installations**

	Year in operation	Number of turbines	Turbine size	Capacity MW	Investment cost million USD (current prices)	Million USD/MW
Middelgrunden (Denmark)	2001	20	2	40	59	1.5
Horns Rev I (Denmark)	2002	80	2	160	340	2.1
Samsø (Denmark)	2003	10	2.3	23	38	1.6
North Hoyle (United Kingdom)	2003	30	2	60	151	2.5
Nysted (Denmark)	2004	72	2.3	165	310	1.9
Scroby Sands (United Kingdom)	2004	30	2	60	151	2.5
Kentish Flats (United Kingdom)	2005	30	3	90	199	2.2
Barrows (United Kingdom)	2006	30	3	90	–	–
Burbo Bank (United Kingdom)	2007	24	3.6	90	226	2.5
Lillgrunden (Sweden)	2007	48	2.3	110	246	2.2
Robin Rigg (United Kingdom)	2009 (expeted)	60	3	180	615	3.4

Source: Lemming, *et al.*, 2007.

The main differences in cost between land-based and offshore wind are due to foundations and grid connections. The investment costs for two recent Danish offshore developments are shown in Table 10.7. The total cost of each of the two wind farms is about USD 325 million.

Table 10.7 ▶ **Offshore wind power investment costs: Horns Rev and Nysted, Denmark**

	Investment costs USD 1 000/MW	Share %
Turbines, *ex work*, including transport and erection	1020	49
Transformer station and main cable to coast	340	16
Internal grid between turbines	105	5
Foundations	440	21
Design, project management	125	6
Environmental analysis	75	3
Miscellaneous	12	<1
Total	**2 117**	**100**

Note: Exchange rate USD 1 = 5.96 Danish kroner.

Source: Lemming, *et al*, 2007.

Offshore wind power production costs

Figure 10.11 shows the estimated power production costs for selected offshore wind farms. Data assume annual operation and maintenance costs of USD 20/MWh averaged over the lifetime of the turbine, a normal wind year, full utilisation rate and a discount rate of 7.5%.

Figure 10.11 ▶ Estimated production costs for selected offshore wind farms

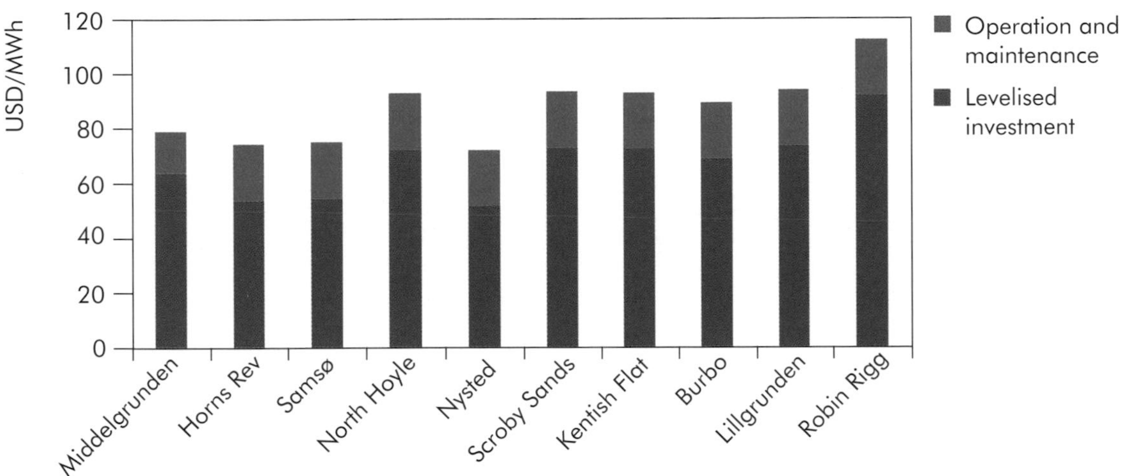

Note: 2006 prices.

Source: Lemming, *et al.*, 2007.

Key point

Recent offshore wind developments show upward pressure on investment costs.

Outlook for cost reductions

New offshore and onshore projects in 2006 and 2007 have had significantly higher costs than their predecessors due to supply chain constraints and material cost increases. Offshore developments have also suffered from the cost overruns and equipment failures that are not unexpected for an emerging technology operating in harsh environments. Cost reduction efforts aim to improve the reliability and performance of turbines and electrical equipment in the marine environment. They also aim to increase turbine size.

The United Kingdom's Offshore Wind Programme estimated the future cost of offshore wind generation and the potential for cost reduction (DTI, 2007). It identified the cost of raw materials, especially steel which accounts for about 90% of the turbine, as a primary cost driver. Major savings can be realised if turbines are made of lighter, more reliable materials and if the fatigue resistance of major components such as gearboxes can be improved. The study projected that offshore wind costs would rise from USD 3 million/MW to USD 3.3 million/MW in 2011 and then fall by around 20% by 2020 (2006 prices).

Table 10.8 sets out cost ranges for offshore wind power from 2006 to 2050 based on the assumption that turbine costs remain relatively high, due to demand, but that the considerable cost-reduction potential in foundations and transmission cables enables an overall learning rate of 10% from 2006 to 2030.

Table 10.8 ▶ Offshore wind turbines estimated cost ranges, 2006 to 2050

	Investment costs million USD/MW			O&M	Capacity factor
	Minimum	Average	Maximum	USD/MWh	%
2006	2.3	2.6	3.0	20	37.5
2015	1.9	2.3	2.6	16	37.5
2020	1.7	2.0	2.3	15	37.5
2030	1.5	1.8	2.0	15	37.5
2050	1.5	1.7	1.9	15	37.5

Source: Lemming, *et al.*, 2007.

Further technology development

Further technological advances are needed to exploit new resource opportunities and bring costs down. This includes incremental development in the design and construction of wind power components and cost reduction through increased production volumes, as well as innovations in materials and designs. Research needs to focus on aerodynamics, structural dynamics, electrical and structural design, control, materials, grid integration, storage and hybrid concepts.

Wind turbine technology

UpWind – the largest EU-supported wind energy R&D initiative – looks at the future design of very large turbines (8 to 10 MW) and wind farms of several hundred megawatts. The challenges inherent in development at this scale necessitate the highest possible standards in design; full understanding of external design conditions; the use of materials with extreme strength to mass ratios; and advanced control and measuring systems. The aim is a high degree of reliability, and, critically, reduced overall turbine mass. UpWind intends to contribute to the development of the concepts, tools and components that the industry needs to design and manufacture this new breed of wind turbines and components.

Superconducting generators

A Denmark Technical University/Risø project is seeking to develop a 10 MW generator based on high-temperature superconductor materials. The generator is expected to achieve a 50% to 60% reduction in weight and size compared to current models, together with a multi-pole design that makes direct-drive possible and avoids the use of gearboxes, resulting in reduced O&M costs.

Smart rotors

Smart rotors seek to alleviate the load by applying load control devices that do not adversely affect reliability or maintenance needs. Delft Technical University (NL) is advancing the investigation and proof-of-concept of such blades. Installation in their wind tunnel in 2007 showed that load reductions of 60% are possible.

Novel concepts

Subterranean storage techniques are being investigated as a means of storing energy from wind turbines in the form of compressed air to balance large penetrations of wind energy (Succar and Williams, 2008). Compressed Air Energy Storage (CAES) uses electricity to compress air when demand is low. The compressed air is then stored in a geologic formation. When demand rises, the flow is reversed and the air flows into a natural-gas-fired turbine, boosting its efficiency by more than 60%. A coalition of local utilities in Iowa (US) is due to start construction of a 268 MW CAES plant linked to 75 MW to 100 MW of wind capacity in 2009, with operation scheduled for 2011. In Texas (US), TXU Corporation. and Shell WindEnergy are developing a 3 000 MW wind farm which they propose to connect to a CAES system that will pump air into underground salt domes.

Kite concepts – or "flying windmills" – are a novel design concept in which turbines are tethered to the ground and tap jet stream wind currents. The advantages would be using almost constant wind sources without the expense of towers. The downsides include the weight and hazard of the cable and rotor/generators. Other questions concern the implications of bad weather and competition for air space. Researchers and companies in Canada, Italy, Netherlands and United States are testing prototypes that include a helicopter-like craft, an airborne turbine with a loop of kites and a horizontal rotor in a helium-suspended apparatus that is tethered to a transformer on the ground.

New offshore concepts

Offshore wind turbines can take advantage of stronger and less turbulent winds, avoid logistical constraints in transporting large turbines and blades and to a large degree address concerns of visual impact. Commercially available technology today uses mono-piles, jackets or tripods to anchor the turbines to the sea bed. Their cost of installation increases dramatically in deep water, which limits offshore sites to water depths of less than 50 metres. The harsh marine conditions in which offshore wind power operates calls for highly reliable designs and several new concepts for offshore turbines are under development and testing.

Turbine and platform design and water depth

Floating platform concepts may be of interest where load centres are located near deep water sites with good wind conditions. For remote deep water locations, the cost of transmission and of the floating foundation may be a deterrent.

A large-scale prototype submerged deepwater platform, which will be anchored in 108 metre depth water about ten miles off the coast of southern Italy, has been launched recently by Blue H Technologies. It uses submerged tension-legged platforms, developed by the oil industry, to create a platform large and stable enough to support a tower and a wind turbine. This significantly reduces the overall weight of the structure, which is a huge cost component of offshore wind units. It can be assembled onshore and then towed out to the site to take advantage of stronger and more regular winds.

In Norway, two projects, Hywind (Statoil-Hydro) and Sway (Statoil, Statkraft, Lyse Energi, Shell), are developing floating offshore wind farm concepts for deep water (200 to 300 metres). Both are based on wind turbines rated at 3 to 5 MW or larger and the sub-sea structure is made of concrete. The main difference between the two concepts is the mooring principle. Recently, Hywind has received NOK 59 million in financial support from the Norwegian Government for a prototype to be installed in 2009. The Sway project has raised funds for a prototype from private investors. Norway sees a theoretical potential for offshore floating wind power of about 14 000 TWh and estimates potential development of 140 TWh of floating turbines with grid connection.

Japan is also pursuing offshore wind technology innovation. Ryukyu University has developed the "hexa-float" system, which is made of concrete with 10 metre sides. A 10 kW prototype is planned. Also under consideration is a stable floating platform for two turbines in a diamond shape and a spar type floating structure.

A project to consider technology needs for water depths from 20 to 35 metres is underway in the United States through the Offshore Wind Energy Consortium, which is financed by the United States Department of Energy, General Electric and the Massachusetts Technology Collaborative. In March 2006, GE announced a USD 27 million partnership with the United States Department of Energy to develop 5 MW to 7 MW turbines by 2009.

Hybrid

Poseidon's Organ is a concept for a hybrid power plant in which a floating offshore wave power plant also serves as a foundation for wind turbines. The concept has been tested in wave tanks and a demonstration model is to be launched in early 2008 off the coast of Lolland in connection with Denmark's first offshore wind farm at Vindeby. A full-size plant with three 2 MW wind turbines is under consideration in Portugal.

As offshore oil and gas fields decline, their production facilities may be transformed to hybrid energy facilities by adding wind, wave and solar devices. An early example is seen at the Beatrice oil field off the coast of Scotland. The prototype installation consist of two 5 MW wind turbines at water depths of 42 metres. Power from the wind turbines will meet about one-third of the needs of the oil-production platform.

Wind power research, development and demonstration

RD&D has made an essential contribution to the cost and performance improvements in wind generation to date. Continued RD&D is needed to provide further reductions in cost and uncertainty in order to exploit the potential of wind power.

Government support for RD&D has played a critical role in wind turbine and system component technical advancements and deployment, as well as resource assessment. It continues to do so in a number of areas, e.g. turbine test sites and certification. Over the period 1974 to 2006, government RD&D budgets for wind power in IEA countries were about USD 3.9 billion (2006 prices and exchange rates), which represents an estimated 10% share of renewable energy R&D budgets in IEA countries. In 2006, the overall portion for all renewable technologies was 10.7% of total energy R&D budgets in IEA countries.

RD&D international frameworks

The incentives for stakeholders to collaborate include the need to learn from the technical and operational solutions and failed approaches of others. Collaboration is also vital to improve the reliability of tools such as models of wind farm dynamics and grid operation, to develop standardised approaches across market areas and to provide technical expertise for regulatory and standards-setting processes. Two examples of active collaborative RD&D are IEA Wind and the European Commission Framework Programme.

The European Commission has launched a process to develop a renewable energy roadmap to help achieve its renewable energy targets. A part of this effort, the European Wind Energy Technology Platform (TPWind) was launched in October 2006.[3] This is an industry led collaboration with public and private sector stakeholders which aims to accelerate innovation to reduce costs.

IEA Wind aims to advance wind power through international co-operation.[4] It is an implementing agreement that has been successfully conducting wind power RD&D for more than 30 years. Participants include 20 countries, the European

3. www.windplatform.eu.
4. www.ieawind.org.

Commission and the European Wind Energy Association. Current areas of focus are shown in Table 10.9. IEA Wind is developing a new strategic plan and setting RD&D priorities to 2020.

Table 10.9 ▶ Wind Energy Systems Implementing Agreement, current tasks

Task	Objective
Base technology information exchange	Further development of wind energy conversion systems through co-operative action and information exchange.
Wind energy in cold climates	Gather and share information on wind turbines operating in cold climates.
Horizontal axis wind turbines	Compare theoretical aerodynamics model predictions of wind turbine blade and structural performance and load with actual measurements.
Dynamic models of wind farms in power systems	Address effects on power systems of interconnecting and operating large number of wind turbines.
Offshore wind energy technology development	Address relevant issues of offshore wind development, including deployment in deep water.
Integration of wind and hydropower systems	Conduct co-operative research concerning the generation, transmission and economics of integrating wind and hydropower systems; provide a forum for information exchange.
Design and operation of power systems with large amounts of wind	Investigate impacts of large amounts of variable wind power on power system operation.
Cost of wind energy	Assess methodologies for estimating cost of energy and establish a method of assessing its impact on R&D.

(More information on these tasks is available at www.ieawind.org)

RD&D priorities

Priority areas for wind power RD&D efforts include:

- increase value and reduce uncertainties:
  - improve the accuracy of forecasting power performance;
  - reinforce engineering integrity;
  - improve and validate standards;
  - storage techniques.
- Continue cost reductions:
  - improve site assessment and identification, especially offshore;
  - better models for aerodynamics and aero elasticity;
  - more intelligent and lighter structures and advanced materials;

- more efficient generators and converters;
- new drive train concepts;
- new concept rotors for larger diameters.

■ Enable large-scale development:
- improve power quality;
- electric load flow control and adaptive loads.

■ Minimise environmental impacts:
- compatible use of land and aesthetic integration;
- flora, fauna and sound studies.

Priorities specific to offshore wind power RD&D efforts:

- substructures including floating foundations;
- operation and maintenance to improve reliability; remote sensors with intelligent software;
- optimisation of transport and logistics;
- cabling technologies, including High Voltage Direct Current technology.

System aspects

Electricity networks, and the power markets they underpin, have evolved to link large, centralised electricity producers to consumers. Dispersed, variable, wind electricity is a departure from this pattern. Large wind energy shares are possible, but they will require market and network design and operation to evolve to keep costs down while maintaining system reliability. For example in 2006, 17% of Denmark's electricity demand was met by wind energy (IEA Wind, 2007a). This would not have been possible without the opportunity provided by the Nordic Power Market to export surplus production and to import electricity during periods of low wind output.

Variability is not in itself a threat to system reliability, nor is it new to system operators; demand fluctuates continually. It becomes a challenge when the scale of supply variation approaches that of demand variation. Variability can be considerably smoothed out, especially in the short-term, when the output of widely dispersed wind power plants is aggregated. The concept of a universal "ceiling" on the energy share of wind energy, due to its variability, is simplistic and fails to take into account the diversity of power systems and their different constraints and degrees of flexibility.

Short-term forecasting of wind power production has made much progress, but is still less accurate than forecasting demand. While the overall shape of production can be predicted most of the time, significant deviations will occur. Recent experiences in West Denmark point to an average absolute prediction error of 6.2% of installed capacity in day-ahead forecasts, corresponding to 28% of yearly wind energy (IEA Wind, 2007b). Shortening forecast periods – trading closer to real time – increases accuracy.

Wind energy potential increases with the flexibility of the power system. Measures to increase flexibility include additional, flexible capacity in the generation mix, increasing the size of balancing areas, trading closer to real time (short gate-closure), improving communications between generators and system operators, encouraging demand-side flexibility and developing storage.

Public opposition can delay new transmission infrastructure by more than ten years. This can have a direct effect on the development of wind farms. Recent improvements in power system technology could reduce the need for new infrastructure, but their uptake is slow. Rewiring with lines that can operate at higher temperatures (150°C versus 80°C) and real-time monitoring of weather-related changes in the temperature of existing lines to measure the effect on transmission capacity at any given moment and dynamically rating the line accordingly can increase carrying capacity by up to 50%. Other advanced technologies include high voltage direct current cabling and power electronic devices to control load flow. Wind power penetration can be further increased through the clustered management of wind farms (Estanqueiro, *et al.*, 2008).

New, large-scale storage technologies including batteries in the megawatt scale and compressed-air energy storage also have potential, alongside existing technologies such as pumped hydro storage. Large-scale storage can benefit systems as a whole, reducing the need for new generation capacity to meet demand peaks, as well as increasing flexibility.

Additional costs of wind integration

There is wide consensus that the additional system integration costs associated with wind variability are very small at low penetrations. The main cost drivers – on top of those of conventional technologies – increase with penetration, however, and can be grouped into three categories:

- measures to ensure instantaneous balance of supply and demand;
- grid extension and reinforcement;
- measures to ensure long-term system adequacy.

The first category includes the additional system balancing costs arising from managing output fluctuations in the short term. They vary considerably across systems, depending on plant mix, fuel costs, cost of reserve provision, market operation, forecast quality and other factors. Recent estimates of balancing costs at wind penetrations of about 20% range from USD 1 to USD 5 per MWh of wind energy (IEA Wind, 2007b). Co-operation among system operators, interconnection of balancing areas and improvements to market operation can reduce costs by enabling imbalances to flow to the points in the system where it will cost the least to cover the shortfall.

Regarding grid extension and reinforcement, recent estimates made by national system operators in Germany, United Kingdom, Netherlands and Portugal suggest costs to be in the region of USD 60 to USD 190 per kW of wind capacity (IEA Wind, 2007b). These cost estimations are based on today's technology and system operations and make little allowance for innovation in system management.

When wind plants are unavailable supply has to come from elsewhere on the system, *i.e.* wind power has a relatively low "capacity credit". Capacity credit is a measure of how much conventional capacity wind energy displaces. This falls as penetration increases, *i.e.* the incremental amount of conventional plant displaced becomes smaller with each additional wind plant unit. It will also vary according to quality of the resource, season, structure and operation of the power system, and whether capacity is located on- or offshore. Capacity credit will be higher in systems where output and demand peaks coincide, and in more extensive power systems where wind output is dispersed and less correlated.

This low capacity credit can be expressed as a cost: that of the additional flexible generation capacity, storage or cross-border transit required to supplement wind plant when it is unavailable. This approach is controversial. A recent European study that adopts this approach suggests a cost of USD 2.6 to USD 9.9 per MWh, corresponding to capacity credit in the range of 27% or less (Auer, *et al.*, 2007). As with short-term balancing, relative dispatch costs are important when comparing alternative reserve and storage options (Succar and Williams, 2008).

Chapter 11 SOLAR

Key Findings

- *Solar power provides 6% of global electricity production in the ACT Map scenario and 11% in the BLUE Map scenario, from photovoltaics (PV) and concentrated solar power (CSP) in roughly equal proportions. Solar power has significant potential for many countries, both developed and developing.*
- *PV is a fast-growing market, especially in some industrialised countries, and is expected to significantly expand in emerging economies such as China and India.*
- *Grid-connected, building-integrated systems are the most dynamic sector in the PV market. These are mostly in industrialised countries, but are expected to significantly expand into emerging economies such as China and India as well.*
- *Off-grid PV systems for water-pumping and rural electrification constitute up to 10% of the total PV market. Such applications remain important in remote areas and are likely to continue to be so in developing countries. Today, PV is profitable only in remote off-grid areas, but their costs are decreasing rapidly as subsidised markets expand and R&D efforts improve performance.*
- *Between now and 2050, PV generation costs in the ACT and BLUE scenarios could drop to around USD 0.05 per kWh in sunny areas.*
- *The key technology developments needed for PV are: to increase the efficiency and reduce the material intensity and costs of c-Si modules; to increase the efficiency and lifespan of thin film modules; and to guarantee sufficient public and private R&D funding for the development of third-generation novel devices (ultra-high efficiency and ultra-low cost cells).*
- *CSP is experiencing a revival, and prospects for development loom large in Sunbelt countries.*
- *In the Sunbelt, CSP is cheaper than PV for large on-grid plants.*
- *A CSP plant with heat storage and/or fuel back-up can, providie utilities with guaranteed capacities and, if needed generate continously.*
- *In arid areas with high direct insolation, CSP delivery usually matches demand peaks that are driven by air-conditioners.*
- *CSP can provide combined heat and power, particularly in desalination plants.*
- *CSP plants situated in locations with excellent solar resource (e.g. in North Africa) can provide guaranteed electricity to less-sunny neighbouring areas (e.g. Southern Europe) at a cost that is competitive with other solar options, the transmission costs being more than offset by the lower cost of production.*
- *CSP technologies today have a cost somewhere between those of PV and wind. Costs are decreasing as markets expand and R&D efforts improve performance.*

- *Between now and 2050, CSP generation costs in the ACT and BLUE scenarios could drop to USD 0.035 per kWh in areas with very high direct irradiation.*
- *The key technology development needs for CSP are to increase the efficiency of mirrors, heat receivers, heat storage systems and balancing mechanisms and to ensure sufficient funding for the development of the next generation of towers (with pressurised air receivers and gas turbines).*

Introduction

Solar energy is the most abundant energy resource on earth (see Figure 11.1). The solar energy that hits the earth's surface in an hour is about the same as the amount of energy consumed by all human activities in a year. Its low energy density and intermittency, however, make it difficult and expensive to exploit on a large scale. Solar energy currently provides less than 1% of the world's total commercial energy.

Figure 11.1 ▶ Total energy resources

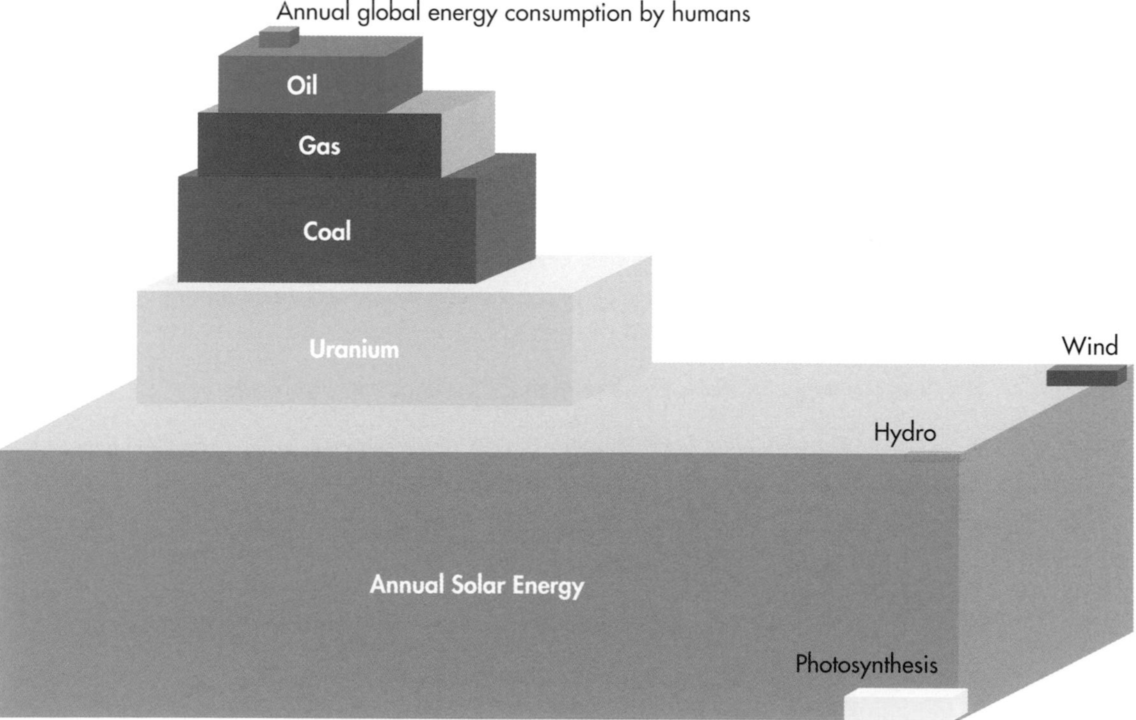

Source: National Petroleum Council, 2007 after Craig, Cunningham and Saigo.

Key point

Solar energy is plentiful.

Solar energy can be harnessed in several ways. Solar heat can be used directly to supply heat to the residential sector and in industrial processes. Overall, heat needs comprise more than 40% of global energy demand (Philibert, 2006). Solar energy can also produce power, either through the concentration of solar rays or through direct conversion to electricity in photovoltaic cells. It can also be used to produce various fuels, notably hydrogen, and to produce metals from metal oxides.

As shown in Figure 11.2, solar energy is projected to grow up to a thousand-fold from today's level by 2050, to 2 319 TWh/yr in the ACT Map scenario and to 4 754 TWh/yr in the BLUE Map scenario. Both scenarios assume that sustained and effective incentive schemes will be in place in many countries in the coming five to ten years, during which solar energy is likely to remain at a pre-competitive stage. Both scenarios also assume that incentive schemes for solar – especially PV – are supported long enough to allow the technology to deploy and for investment costs to decrease. The baseline scenario assumes this is not the case: as a result solar technologies make a negligible contribution in this scenario.

Figure 11.2 ▶ **Solar electricity generation in the different ETP scenarios**

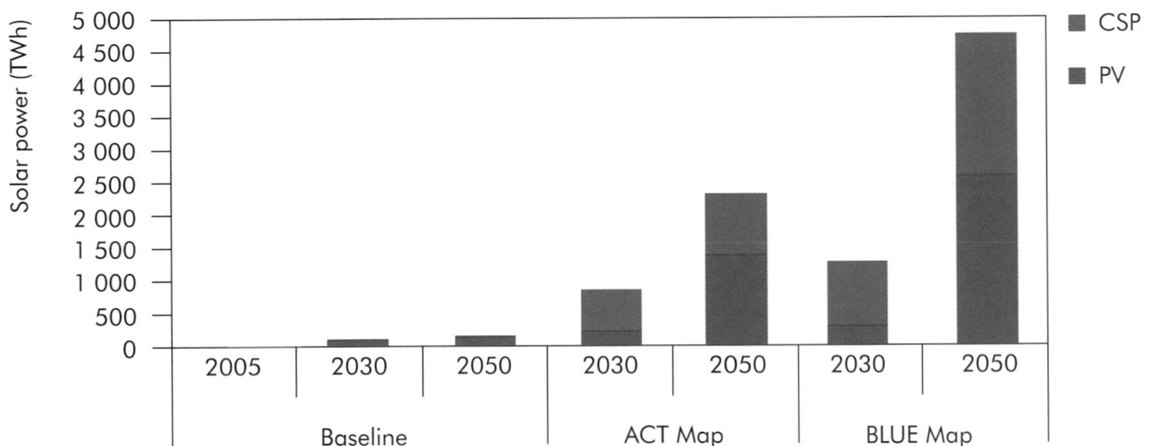

Key point

Solar electricity will grow strongly in the ACT Map and BLUE Map scenarios, mostly after 2030.

In terms of regional distribution, PV is projected to grow very significantly in solar-rich OECD countries (particularly in North America), but also in emerging economies such as China and India. Concentrated solar power (CSP) is expected to be deployed widely in those regions as well, and even more so in the Sunbelt regions of Latin America and Africa. Figure 11.3 shows the projected regional solar electricity generation from PV and CSP in the Blue scenario in 2050.

Figure 11.3 ▶ **Solar electricity generation in different world regions in the BLUE Map scenario**

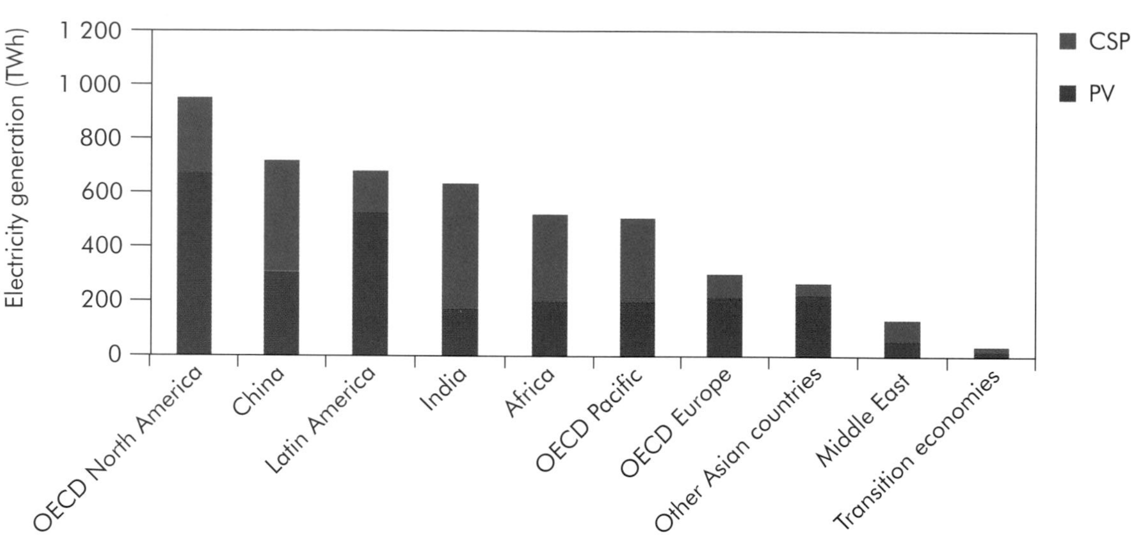

Key point

Solar is a key option for both industrialised and developing countries.

Photovoltaics

Photovoltaic (PV) systems directly convert solar energy into electricity. The basic building block of a PV system is the PV cell, which is a semiconductor device that converts solar energy into direct-current (DC) electricity. PV cells are low-voltage (around 0.5 V) and high-current (around 3 A) devices. Combining cells in a series forms a PV module. The typical peak power of a commercial module with an area of 0.4 m^2 to 1.0 m^2 is 50 Wp to 150 Wp (peak watts) although in some architectural applications, modules can produce as much as 300 Wp. PV systems are highly modular, *i.e.* modules can be linked together to provide power in a range of from a few Wp to several dozen MWp.

Current situation and market trends

PV systems can be grid-connected or stand alone (off-grid). They can be ground-mounted (*e.g.* in centralised electricity production facilities) or integrated into buildings. Until the mid-1990s, most systems were stand alone, as these offered in many places the most economically viable solution for rural electricity supply. However, since then the number of grid-connected systems for distributed generation has been increasing exponentially (as shown in Figure 11.4). The large majority of grid-connected systems are integrated in buildings.

Off-grid PV systems for transmission, water-pumping and rural electrification constitute up to 10% of the total PV market. Such applications remain important in remote areas and are likely to continue to be so in developing countries.

According to the IEA Photovoltaic Power Systems Programme (IEA PVPS), the total cumulative PV installed capacity in IEA PVPS member countries reached 5.7 GW at the end of 2006, an increase of 36% over 2005.[1] This represents around 87% of total world capacity (6.6 GW). Since 2000, total cumulative PV capacity has increased by a factor of eight. As shown in Figure 11.4, 90% of present total installed capacity is composed of grid-connected systems. 93% of this is from distributed generation systems in buildings.

Figure 11.4 ▶ Cumulative installed grid-connected and off-grid PV power in IEA-PVPS reporting countries

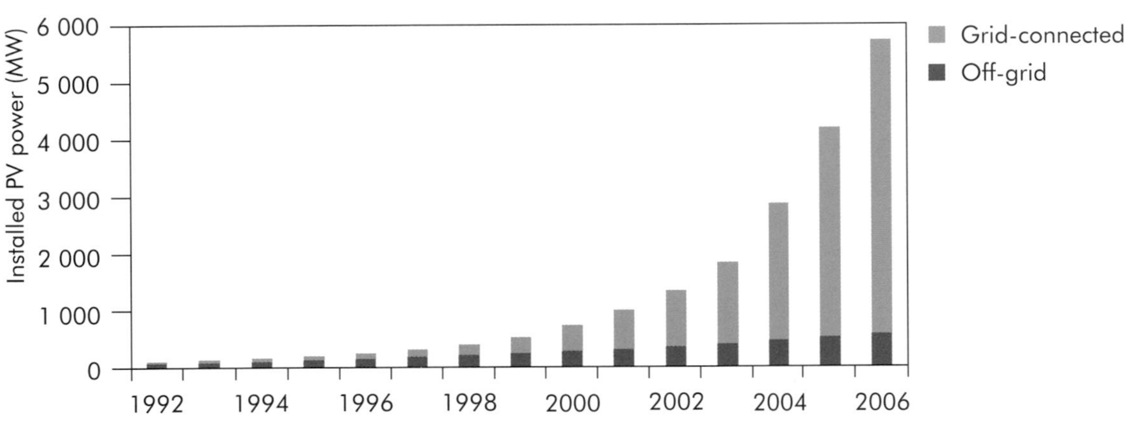

Source: IEA PVPS, 2007.

Key point

An exponential growth has occurred over the last 15 years.

Three countries (Germany, Japan and the United States) account for approximately 70% of global cumulative capacity. These countries are also the three largest PV-manufacturing nations, accounting for 63% of global PV production (EPIA and Greenpeace, 2007). In future, both non-IEA emerging economies – notably China and India – as well as other IEA countries (e.g. Australia, Korea and Spain) are expected to become important global players in PV, both in terms of installed capacity and in manufacturing. China has already become a major PV manufacturer, reaching a 15% share of global PV cell production by the end of 2006 (EPIA and Greenpeace, 2007).[2]

1. The IEA PVPS member countries are: Australia, Austria, Canada, Denmark, Finland, France, Germany, Israel, Italy, Japan, Korea, Mexico, the Netherlands, Norway, Portugal, Spain, Sweden, Switzerland, the United Kingdom and the United States.
2. The five largest PV-manufacturing companies at the end of 2006 were: Sharp (Japan, 17.1% of world production), Q-cells (Germany, 10%), Kyocera (Japan, 7.1%), Suntech (China, 6.3%) and Sanyo (Japan, 6.1%).

The PV market has been expanding rapidly and is expected to grow even more quickly in the next few years. In 2006, modules with a total capacity of 1.5 GW were sold. Production capacity was almost twice as high, but was limited in practice by a shortage of purified silicon feedstock. The market forecast for 2007 is around 2.5 GW.

The outlook for the next three years is very positive for a number of reasons:

- While market growth has recently occurred mostly in three countries, several effective incentive schemes are now in place. As a result, investments in PV are expected to expand in many more countries.
- Several plants producing hundreds of MW modules per year are being built. The first 1 GW manufacturing plant is planned in Japan. A significant growth in the world's capacity to manufacture thin-film modules is also expected.
- As a result of very significant investments in the supply chain, the shortage of purified silicon is expected to end in 2008.

A market of 6 GW/yr in 2010 is assumed in the ACT Map scenario and of 10 GW/yr in the BLUE Map scenario. While the latter represents a six-fold market increase in just four years, this is considerably less than the latest industry projections – which forecast an annual PV cell/module production of almost 23 GW/yr by 2011 (PHOTON, 2007).

In the ACT Map scenario, global yearly electricity generation from PV is expected to reach 1 383 TWh in 2050. In the BLUE Map scenario, generation is almost double that of the ACT Map scenario, *i.e.* 2 584 TWh, corresponding to 6% of total world electricity generation.

Technology description/status

Crystalline silicon

Today, more than 90% of PV modules are based on wafer-based crystalline silicon (c-Si). This is expected to remain the main PV technology until at least 2020. It is a well established and reliable technology that uses abundant resources of silicon as primary feedstock material. The resource effectiveness and cost efficiency of c-Si module production can still, however, be substantially improved.

To produce c-Si modules typically involves growing ingots of silicon, slicing the ingots to make solar cells, electrically interconnecting the cells, and encapsulating the strings of cells to form a module. Modules currently use silicon in one of two main forms: single crystalline silicon (sc-Si) or multi-crystalline silicon (mc-Si). Single crystalline silicon modules have a higher conversion efficiency (15%, expected to increase to between 25% and 28% by 2050) than multi-crystalline silicon modules, but they are more expensive (Table 11.1). Recently, ribbon technologies have been developed that have potentially similar efficiencies as mc-Si but a much better utilisation rate of silicon feedstock.

Thin films

Thin films are based on a completely different manufacturing approach. Instead of producing an ingot and then cutting it into wafers, thin films are obtained by depositing extremely thin layers of photosensitive materials on a low-cost backing such as glass, stainless steel or plastic. The first thin film produced was amorphous silicon (a-Si). More recently, other thin-film technologies have been developed in the area of II-VI semiconductor compounds, *i.e.* Cadmium Telluride (CdTe) and Copper-Indium-Diselenide (CIS). Adding small amounts of Gallium to a CIS layer (to produce CIGS modules) improves the efficiency of the device. Thin films range from 40-60 μm of amorphous silicon down to less than 10 μm of CdTe.

The main advantages of thin films are their relatively low consumption of raw materials, the high automation and resource-efficiency of production, their suitability for building integration, and their better appearance and reduced sensitivity to overheating. The current main drawbacks are lower efficiencies, limited experience of lifetime performance and (still) small production units.

Thin films are generally less efficient than c-Si modules. However, recent commercial CIS modules have reached 11% efficiency, very close to the typical efficiency of mc-Si modules. The New Energy and Industrial Technology Development Organization (NEDO, 2004) has indicated a target module efficiency of 22% for CIS modules in 2030. However, material shortages (especially of indium and tellurium) might limit diffusion of these technologies in the very long-term (Hoffmann, 2004a).

Table 11.1 summarises the current efficiencies of commercial, best prototype and laboratory modules for each specific type of PV technology.

Thin films are expected to increase their market share significantly by 2020. In the medium term, it is likely that modules that combine crystalline and thin-film technology will appear on the market. These devices will take advantage the best of both technologies, *i.e.* high efficiencies and lower material consumption, larger deposition areas, and continuous automatic manufacturing processes. According to both NEDO (2004) and Hoffmann (2004a), by 2030 such Si thin-film modules might reach an efficiency as high as 18%, thus representing viable additional solutions for cost-effective power applications.

Table 11.1 ▶ Present module efficiencies for different PV technologies

	Wafer-based c-Si		Thin films		
	sc-Si	mc-Si	a-Si a-Si/mc-Si	CdTe	CIS/CIGS
Commercial module efficiency (%)	13-15%	12-14%	6-8%	8-10%	10-11%
Maximum recorded module efficiency (%)	22.7%	15.3%	–	10.5%	12.1%
Maximum recorded laboratory efficiency (%)	24.7%	19.8%	12.7%	16.0%	18.2%

Sources: Adapted from Frankl, Menichetti and Raugei, 2008 and EPIA and Greenpeace, 2007.

Key point

Efficiencies of both crystalline silicon and thin film modules will significantly increase.

11

Third-generation devices and long-term PV technology roadmap

The long-term PV market will look very different from today's market. All major PV technology roadmaps forecast that the share of c-Si PV systems will significantly decline after 2020 in favour of a stronger diffusion of thin films (Hoffmann 2004b; NEDO, 2004; PVNET, 2004; PV-TRAC, 2005; Frankl, Menichetti and Raugei, 2008; EUPVPLATF, 2007).

A third generation of new concept PV devices is expected to emerge in the 2020-2030 timeframe. Under most favourable circumstances, these novel devices are forecast to account for half of the PV market by 2050. Figure 11.5 summarises the expected two-stage technology shift from present silicon-based to thin film to novel PV devices.

New concept PV devices are likey to be of two main types:

- ultra-low cost, low-medium efficiency cells and modules:
- ultra-high efficiency cells and modules.

In the first group of devices, the technology closest to pilot production is the dye-sensitised nanocrystalline solar cell (DSC) concept, which has shown an efficiency of 10.5% in the laboratory (NEDO, 2004). According to Hoffmann (2004a), commercial modules might reach 10% efficiency by 2030. The Japanese are more optimistic, forecasting this objective to be reached by 2020. The New Energy and Industrial Technology Development Organization expects DSC modules to achieve 15% efficiency by 2030 (NEDO, 2004).

Figure 11.5 ▶ The shift of PV technology market shares until 2050

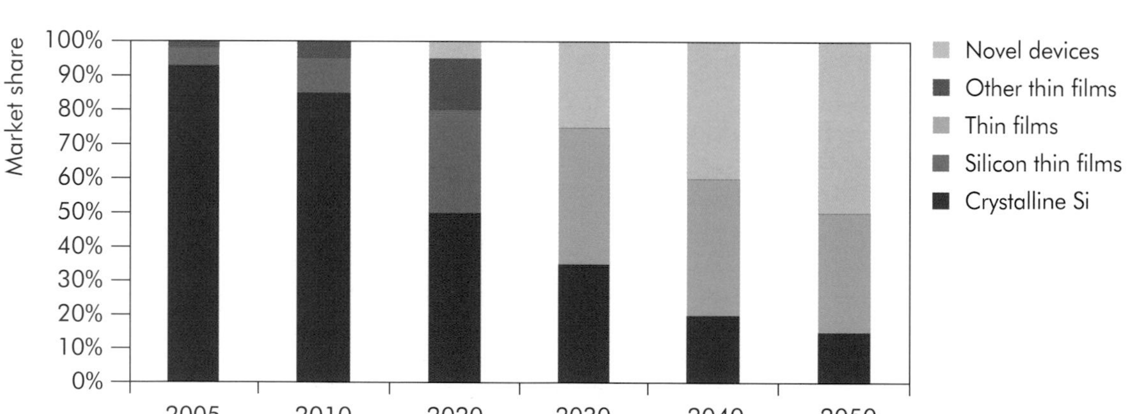

Source: Frankl, Menichetti and Raugei, 2008.

Key point

PV technology market shares will be very different in 2050.

In the same area, organic solar cells have recently been invented with efficiencies of around 2% (Grätzel, 2000). While it is too early to make any reasonable predictions about the role of these cells in the future PV market, they may represent a low cost option for special applications that do not have space problems.

The second type of novel technologies comprises a set of third-generation PV cells that will use advanced solid-state physics such as hot electrons, multiple quantum wells, intermediate band gap structures and nanostructures. The theoretical limit of these cells is considerably higher than that of conventional cells. But at this stage it remains impossible to predict the efficiency range that will be actually reached in industrial production. The Photovoltaic Technology Research Advisory Council (PV-TRAC, 2005) reports that PV modules may ultimately reach efficiencies of 30% to 50%, while Hoffmann (2004a) considers it possible that modules will reach an efficiency range of 30% to 60%. Goetzberger (2002) predicts an upper limit of 42%.

It is expected that all three categories of PV technology will co-exist in the long-term, each one responding to specific application needs and market segments. The main expected features of the different types and applications of PV devices in 2050 are summarised in Table 11.2.

Costs and potential for cost reduction

The investment costs of PV systems are still high. This represents the most important barrier to PV deployment. PV systems do not have moving parts, so operating and maintenance costs are much less significant – at around 0.5% of capital investment per year.

PV costs have in the past decreased with a learning rate of 15% to 20% (Neji, 2007).[3] This resulted in a significant decrease in costs from the early 1990s until 2004. However, since 2004, PV prices have increased, driven by increasing demand for PV (especially in Germany and Japan) and a shortage of purified silicon. Crystalline silicon modules are currently back to 2004 (nominal) prices and are expected to decrease further as new manufacturing plants and silicon-purification facilities come on line.

At present, PV modules account for roughly 60% of total system costs, with mounting structures, inverters, cabling, *etc.* accounting for the rest. Total PV-system costs were around USD 6.25/W by the end of 2006, although some PV systems were sold at USD 5.5/W in Germany.[4] They are expected to drop to USD 5.0/W to USD 5.6/W in 2008 and to USD 3.75/W to USD 4.4/W by 2010.

The increasing penetration of thin film modules in the market will help to drive down total PV-system costs. Thin film modules are produced at around USD 2.25/W today (as compared with USD 3.75/W for c-Si) and their cost is expected to reduce further to USD 1.5/W to USD 1.9/W by 2010. In the ETP low-carbon scenarios, PV-system costs are assumed to reach USD 4.4/W by 2010 and to achieve a learning rate of 18% from 2010 onwards. Both scenarios assume that effective incentive schemes

3. A learning rate of 20% means a 20% reduction in costs per each doubling of cumulative installed capacity.
4. All figures are in USD 2005 rates.

Table 11.2 ▶ **Technology and market characterisation of different PV technologies in 2050**

	Wafer-based c-Si		Thin films		New concept devices	
	Cz, Fz	**mc, ribbon**	**CIS, CdTe a-Si/μc-Si thin Si films**	**Pin-ASI and ASI-THRU**	**Ultra-high efficiency (3rd generation, quantum wells nanostructures concentrators)**	**Ultra-low cost (dye-sensitised cells organic cells)**
Module eff (%)	**24%-28%**	**20%-25%**	**CIS: 22%-25% Si: 20%**	**6-8%**	**> 40%**	**10%-17%**
Module lifetime (years)	40-50 years	40-50 years	30-35 years	30 years	>25 years	10-15 years
Provided service	High power at premium price	Cost-effective power applications	Additional solutions for cost effective power applications	Low cost / low eff "Solar electricity glass"	High power supply	Colour to PV Low material cost option
Market segment	Niche markets, space	Mass market ("The PV workhorse")	Mass market	Mass market	Niche market / mass market	Mass market
Applications	All applications with surface constraints (e.g. specific BIPV) Ground-mounted, very large-scale PV	All	All Special added value in BIPV (e.g. semi-transparency, screen-printing, etc.)	Consumer products Special applications Large surface buildings	All applications with surface constraints Ground-mounted, very large-scale PV	All

Sources: Adapted from Frankl, Menichetti and Raugei, 2008; NEDO, 2004; Hoffmann, 2004a; PVNET, 2004; and PV-TRAC, 2005.

Key point

In 2050, three categories of PV technology will co-exist, each one responding to specific application needs and market segments.

will be in place in many countries in the coming five to ten years, during which PV is likely to remain at a pre-competitive stage on the electricity market. A sustained high learning rate until 2050 is justified by the double technology shift expected in PV systems – from present c-Si to thin films to third-generation novel devices. Mass-scale integration in buildings is assumed to significantly reduce costs related to mounting structures. With these assumptions, the total system investment costs of PV systems are expected to fall to USD 2.2/W in 2030 and USD 1.24/W in 2050 in the ACT Map scenario and to USD 1.9/W in 2030 and USD 1.07/W in 2050 in the BLUE Map scenario.

The cost of the electricity generated from PV modules depends on the amount of local solar irradiation, the system lifetime and the discount rate. Figure 11.6 shows the expected PV electricity generation costs in 2050 as a function of the number of full-load hours for each of the ETP scenarios. As shown in the figure, PV electricity-generation costs are expected to be in the range of USD 0.05/kWh to USD 0.07/kWh in good irradiation places (above 1 600 kWh/kWp*yr).

Electricity produced in PV building-integrated systems is fed directly into the distribution grid. Its generation costs therefore compete with electricity retail prices.

Figure 11.6 ▶ PV electricity generation costs in 2050 as a function of electricity output

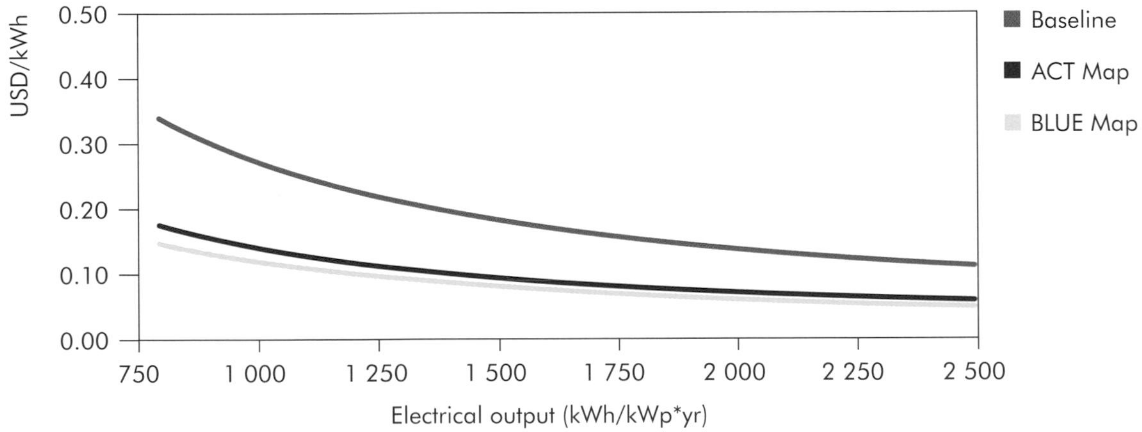

Note: For a lifetime of 35 years and an interest rate of 10%.

Key point

PV generation costs could be as low as five US cents per kWh by 2050 in good solar irradiation regions.

Future R&D efforts

C-Si modules

Present c-Si modules base their success on the reliability of the product and the production process, on the advantage of using a well-known technology that exploits experience in the electronics industry, and on the availability of feedstock. But further technological development is needed to achieve higher efficiencies and much larger production volumes, and to reach the target cost of less than USD 1.25/W. The Photovoltaic Technology Research Advisory Council (PV-TRAC, 2005) and the European Photovoltaic Technology Platform (EUPVPLATF, 2007) suggest that future R&D should consider the following areas:

Materials:

- the availability, quality and price of silicon feedstock (including developing solar-grade silicon);
- advanced wafer manufacturing processes (epitaxial deposition);
- the substitution of critical materials, for cost (silver) or environmental (lead, etc.) reasons, and designs that incorporate recycling.

Equipment:

- crystallisation and wafer-manufacturing processes (including ribbons) for markedly reduced silicon and energy use per watt;
- the development of lower cost, standardised, fully automated process equipment.

Device concepts and processes:

- the optimisation of processes developed originally for laboratory uses, and their adaptation to industrial scale;
- process development for thin and/or large-area wafers, including low-waste processes;
- reduction of the energy consumption of processes (including feedstock production);
- new module designs for easy assembly, low cost and 25-40 year lifespans;
- advanced cell designs and processing schemes for higher efficiencies (up to 22% on a cell level, 20% on a module level).

Thin-film technologies

PV-TRAC (2005) and EUPVPLATF (2007) also identify the following main research areas as most promising for the fuller implementation and exploitation of thin film technologies:

Materials and devices:

- increase of module efficiencies from the current 5% to 12% to >15%;
- understanding of fundamental properties of materials and devices, especially interfaces;
- development of new multi-junction structures;
- development of low cost, high-performance materials for thin film cell designs;
- reduced materials consumption (layer thickness and yield), use of low cost, low-grade materials;

- reduction or avoidance of the use of critical materials, substitution of scarce or hazardous materials, and recycling options;
- alternative module concepts (new substrates and encapsulation);
- ensuring stable module operation for 20 to 30 years with less than 10% decrease in efficiency.

Processes and equipment

- development of processes and equipment for high yield, low cost, large area manufacturing;
- ensure the uniformity of film properties over large areas and understand the efficiency gap between laboratory cells and large-area modules;
- increase stability of the process and yield;
- development of process monitoring;
- adopt successful techniques to industrial conditions in view of productivity and labour;
- reduction of energy pay-back time of modules (from the present 1.5 years to 0.5 years for central European climatic conditions).

New concept PV devices

New concept PV devices are still at the fundamental research stages. Achieving the full potential of these technologies will require a thorough understanding of the underlying chemistry, physics and materials properties. Strategic research areas identified by PV-TRAC (2005) include:

Organically sensitised cells and modules:

- stability (from a few months or years [estimated] to over ten years);
- efficiency (from 5% to 10% for modules);
- fully solid-state devices.

Inorganically sensitised cells (extremely thin absorber cells):

- efficiency (from very low to between 5% and 10%).

Other nano-structured devices with potential for very low costs:

- efficiency (from very low to between 5% and 10%).

Polymer and molecular solar cells:

- efficiency (from between 3% and 5% to 10%);
- stability (from very low to over ten years).

Development of stable, high-quality transparent conductor and encapsulant materials

Novel conversion concepts for super-high efficiency and full-spectrum utilisation:

- spectrum conversion;
- multi-band semiconductors;
- "hot-carrier" devices.

Concentrated solar power

Concentrated solar power (CSP) uses direct sunlight, concentrating it several times to reach higher energy densities and thus higher temperatures. The heat is used to operate a conventional power cycle, e.g. through a steam turbine or a Stirling engine, which drives a generator.

The technology has two basic features:

- It is best suited for areas with high direct solar radiation. These areas are widespread, but not universal.
- Because it uses a thermal energy intermediate phase, it has the potential to deliver power on demand, e.g. by using stored heat in various forms. Heat storage also offers the potential for continuous solar-only generation. Alternatively, CSP can work in tandem with burning fuel in a hybrid plant, using the same steam generators, turbines and generators to produce electricity on a continuous basis.

Firm capacities have a particularly high value for utilities. As a result, in carbon constrained scenarios where nuclear power or CO_2 capture and storage is limited, the market share of CSP increases and overtakes PV technologies. This value may be further increased as a result of the usually good match of CSP peak production with the peaks in electricity demand – for example, for air conditioning in arid and semi-arid regions, which are also where the most suitable conditions for CSP are found. In these areas, CSP electricity is much cheaper than PV, although it is not yet competitive with fossil fuel or even wind power.

Expansion of CSP technologies will be limited by the regional availability of good-quality sunlight. A yearly direct insolation of 2 000 kWh/m^2 is often considered a minimum requirement. The Middle East, North Africa, South Africa, Australia, south-western United States, parts of South America, and central Asian countries from Turkey to parts of India and China figure among the most promising areas (see Figure 11.7). Large engineering and industry groups, notably in Germany (e.g. Flabeg, Fichtner, Schott) and Spain (e.g. Abengoa, Acciona, ACS Cobra, Iberdrola), are now active in these markets.

Figure 11.7 ▶ **The most promising areas for CSP plants**

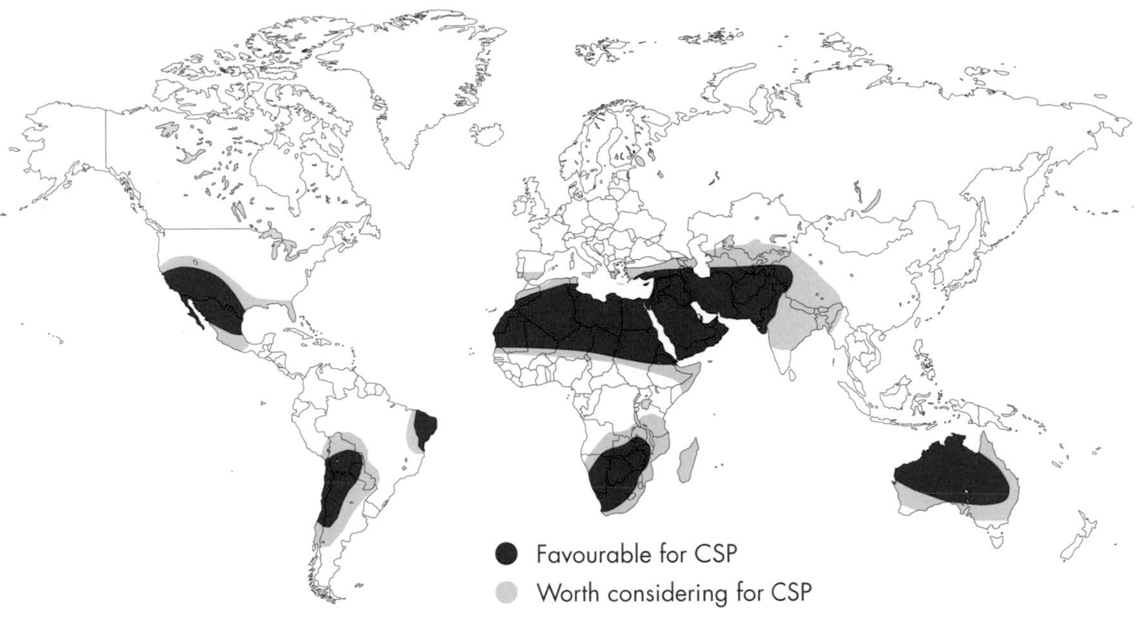

Source: Pharabod and Philibert, 1991.

Key point

CSP use is best suited for high irradiative areas.

CSP plants are large, running typically to several hundred Megawatts. Given their size, CSP plants need to be linked to the transmission network. With modern DC lines, exporting electricity from Northern Africa to Europe would cost USD 30 per MWh – less than the cost difference of solar electricity between the two zones (DLR, 2006). Overall, space is not a constraint (although it may be a material constraint in specific locations). According to the United States Department of Energy, enough electric power for the entire United States economy could be generated by CSP plants over an area of roughly one hundred square miles (DOE, 2002).

CSP technologies use conventional technologies and materials (glass, concrete, steel and standard utility scale turbines). Production capacity can be rapidly scaled to several hundred megawatts per year using existing industrial technologies.

In addition to producing electricity, CSP has a wide range of other current or potential uses, including providing direct heating/cooling for buildings or industrial processes, use in water desalination, or to produce fuels such as hydrogen. Where water supplies are limited and plant cooling is necessary, dry coolers may be required. However, in arid countries cogeneration of heat for desalination and power may be possible. This would greatly increase the overall efficacy of the plant (DLR, 2007).

Box 11.1 ▶ Thermal storage

The penetration of a number of renewable energy sources is limited by their intermittency. Electricity storage usually involves 40% to 50% conversion losses, and is often limited by geographic factors. An alternative is to store heat for conversion to electricity at times when the intermittent renewable is unavailable. Thermal storage losses can normally be held to less than 7% per unit of energy stored.

Adding storage to a solar plant, even in relatively small amounts, can allow producers to guarantee power supplies. This can considerably increase the value of the electricity produced. An alternative option is to add fossil fuel back up that uses the same steam cycle as the CSP plant. The fact that CSP needs only an additional burner makes this a much more economic option for CSP than for other renewables.

In individual circumstances, there may be a case for storing sufficient heat either to extend production (e.g. for a few hours after sunset to better match local peak loads) or to enable continuous production. In addition to increasing the value of the electricity produced, thermal storage may help reduce overall costs by optimising the capital invested in the turbine plant.

The cost reduction, however, is limited by the mere cost of storage, and the fact that the largest part of the cost of a CSP plant is that of the solar field, not that of the conventional part. Running continuously necessitates a much larger solar field – for a given power capacity – than running only during day-time.

Technology description/status

There are three main types of CSP technology: troughs, towers and dishes. The solar flux concentration ratios typically obtained are 30 to 100, 500 to 1 000, and 1 000 to 10 000 suns for trough, tower, and dish systems respectively (see Figure 11.8).

They work as follows:

Troughs: parabolic trough-shaped mirror reflectors linearly concentrate sunlight onto receiver tubes, heating a thermal transfer fluid. Fresnel collectors are a less effective but significantly cheaper form of trough in which the absorber is fixed in space above the mirror field, which is made up of segments that focus collectively on a receiver (Mills, 2004).

Towers: numerous heliostats concentrate sunlight onto a central receiver on the top of a tower. This is sometimes coupled with a second concentration step.

Dishes: Parabolic dish-shaped reflectors concentrate sunlight in two dimensions and run a small engine or turbine at the focal point.

Figure 11.8 ▶ Troughs, towers and dishes

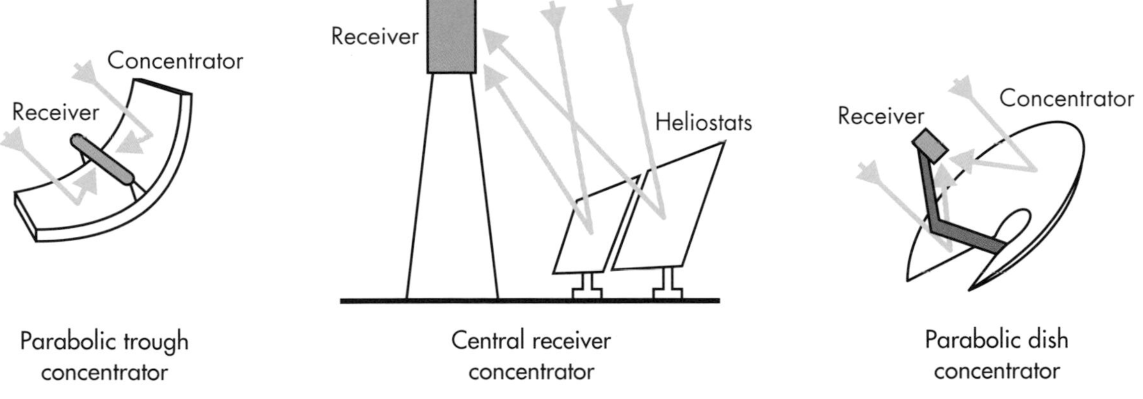

Source: Ferrière, 2005.

Key point

There are three key types of CSP devices.

Box 11.2 ▶ The early days of CSP

The first large CSP plant was built in 1912 in Meadi, 25 km south of Cairo. It had five 60-metre-long parabolic, mirror-equipped troughs with a four-metre aperture. This installation had a hot-water storage tank for night-time operation and ran a low pressure steam engine driving a 40-kW pump. The plant allowed 24 000 litres of Nile water per minute to be transported to the fields for irrigation.

Several IEA countries joined forces in 1977 through an IEA Implementing Agreement, now called SolarPaces, in which they shared the costs and efforts to demonstrate CSP technologies at the Plataforma Solar de Almería in Spain. Current membership of SolarPaces includes Algeria, Australia, Brazil, Egypt, the European Commission, France, Germany, Israel, Mexico, the Russian Federation, South Africa, Spain, Switzerland, the United Kingdom and the United States.

From 1984 to 1990, Luz International Ltd built nine solar electric generating systems (SEGS) in the Californian Mojave desert, totalling 354 MW of grid electricity. These ventures were aided by federal and state tax incentives and attractive mandatory long-term power purchase contracts.

Luz went bankrupt in 1991, when falling fossil-fuel prices coincided with the withdrawal of tax credits and a change in the mandatory purchase contracts. However, all nine SEGS plants are still in profitable commercial operation, with a history of increased efficiency and output as operators improve the procedures they use. Working temperatures were raised from about 300°C to about 400°C from the first to the last SEGS plants built.

Up to 2003, these nine plants combined produced more electricity than all PV devices in all IEA member countries (IEA, 2005, page 72). The plants are backed up by fossil fuel burning to guarantee supply in peak hours – hours that account for the bulk of the plant's financial revenues.

Sources: IEA, 2005; Pharabod and Philibert, 1991.

11

Usually based on trough or tower designs, CSP on-grid generation is evolving towards larger installations. In addition, some developers are now proposing large plants made of many dishes. New concepts, such as compact Fresnel linear collectors and multi-tower arrays, may emerge as ways to effectively utilise available roof surfaces for distributed power generation in sunny cities (Mills, 2004).

Troughs

Troughs represent the more mature technology, with a proven commercial record and 354 MW in operation in California since the 1980s, in nine SEGS plants (see Box 11.2). In the United States, one new plant came on line in 2007: Nevada Solar One, with a 64 MW capacity. Most projects under construction (such as those in Algeria and Spain) or under consideration in various countries are based on troughs.

Various heat transfer fluids have been proposed for trough plants, including mineral oils, molten salts and water/steam (*i.e.* direct steam generation). Current designs use molten salts for heat storage, but phase-change materials and concrete structures may prove more effective in the future.

Hybrid plants use both fossil fuel and solar energy. This allows continuous generation. In Integrated Solar Combined Cycle plants, the solar heat (at around 350-400°C) feeds the bottom cycle of a combined cycle plant. But in practice, the solar component is minor – ranging from 10% to 28% of the capacity, depending on the solar resource.

Trough plants are usually considered as offering a maximum concentration of 200 suns, maximum temperatures of 400°C, a solar-to-thermal efficiency of 60%, and a solar-to-electric efficiency of 12%. Better performance may require moving from linear concentration to point concentration, which will require double-axis sun-tracking, with either towers or dishes.

Towers

Towers typically use a large field of flat, double-axis tracking heliostats, often with a secondary reflection for greater concentration. There has been a wide variety of experimental installations, notably in Italy, Spain, France, Ukraine, Japan and the United States. There are many different designs with respect to the heat transfer fluid (including molten salts and saturated steam), heat storage and thermodynamic cycles. Molten salts have been used in Solar Two in the United States and in Themis in France, and will be used in the Solar Tres project under development by Sener in Spain. The 11 MW tower plant now on-line near Seville in Spain uses saturated steam as a heat fluid, and so will its two 20 MW sisters under construction by Solucar. Atmospheric air has also been tested for heat transfer in experimental devices, and pressurised air could be used in efficient combined-cycle systems.

Larger tower projects are being considered in South Africa by Eskom (100 MW in a single tower), while in Israel and the western United States, Luz-2 and its parent company Bright-Source are considering 100 MW to 200 MW plants on the basis of distributed power towers (DPT) of 20 MW each, linked by pipes to a single power generation unit.

Dishes

There are a few dozen dish units in operation in different sites. These are usually associated with a Stirling engine, and are mostly in the 10 kW capacity range. Two California utilities, Southern California Edison and Pacific Gas and Electric, have signed power purchase agreements with Stirling Energy Systems for hundreds of megawatts to be delivered by solar dishes. A 300 MW plant would consist of 12 000 Stirling solar dishes on approximately three square miles.

Costs and potential for cost reduction

Investment costs today for trough plants are in the range of USD 4 to USD 9/W, depending on local construction costs, on the desired yearly electrical output, and on local solar conditions. Capital costs for a 10-MW tower start at USD 9/W or above, but would be lower for a bigger plant. Capital costs for dishes are above USD 10/W, but might fall with mass production.

Plants under construction are expected to generate electricity at a cost of between USD 125/MWh and USD 225/MWh, mostly depending on the location.

There is considerable scope to reduce costs on all elements of CSP through RD&D. For example, the performance of trough plants with direct steam generation could be improved by using larger turbines to allow for better conversion rates and smaller mirror surface. Thinner mirrors to prevent dust deposition, storage in concrete and phase-change materials, and the creation of higher temperatures in the solar field are other potential sources of savings (Ferrière, 2005). However, this potential will only be reached if there is an active marketplace which can support technology learning.

Box 11.3 ▶ The GEF-funded CSP projects

The Global Environment Facility's Operating Programme No. 7 has identified CSP technologies as one of the most promising options for renewable bulk power production. GEF's CSP portfolio comprises four projects, in India, Egypt, Morocco and Mexico. All these projects are large integrated solar combined-cycle power plants (ISCC). Although initiated about 15 years ago, none has yet been implemented.

There are many reasons for this. A common feature, though, is the risk aversion of the private sector for a new technology, especially in projects involving government-owned utilities, which are seen to be vulnerable to changes in government.

Source: Philibert, 2004.

The United States Department of Energy has recently set the objective of CSP being competitive against carbon-constrained base load power by 2020. The industry considers that learning and economies of scale could achieve this in the next 10 to 15 years, provided global CSP capacities of 5 000 MW are built. Detailed analyses have confirmed that future costs may lie in the range of USD 43 to USD 62 per MWh for trough plants, and USD 35 to USD 55 per MWh for tower plants (Sargent & Lundy LLC Consulting Group, 2003). Cost reductions from current levels would come from increased volume production, plant scale-up, and technological advances. Significant cost reductions could be achieved with technology improvements limited to current demonstrated or tested technologies and the deployment of 2.8 GW trough plants and 2.6 GW tower plants; further reductions would be dependent on more active R&D programmes and the deployment of 4.9 GW trough plants and 8.7 GW tower plants.

Future R&D efforts

In addition to the technology improvements already outlined in this chapter, a number of other opportunities offer themselves, including direct steam generation for trough plants; using pressurised air with solar hybrid-gas turbines; combining power and desalination plants; and solar-assisted or solar-only production of hydrogen or other energy carriers.

Direct steam generation for trough plants

The replacement of expensive heat carriers such as mineral oil with water reduces investment and operating costs and increases efficiency. The particular challenge here is that the superheated steam may create unacceptable material stresses. Fundamental investigation of flow patterns and heat transfer in horizontal tubes has, however, shown that, provided a minimum mass flow is kept in the tubes, acceptable flow conditions can be achieved (Pitz-Paal, Dersch and Milow, 2005).

Towers using pressurised air with a solar-hybrid gas turbine

High-temperature solar heat, further heated by fossil fuel burning if necessary, can be used to run a gas turbine. This achieves high power conversion efficiencies. The French Pegase project on the existing tower plant Themis is seeking to validate an intermediate-scale (1.4 MW) demonstration of this concept, including components for the solar central receiver using air temperatures above 800°C. Luz II is developing a similar concept, with expected thermal-to-electric conversion efficiencies of above 50%, for the second generation of its distributed-tower power technology.

Power and desalination plants

Various semi-arid areas favourable for CSP plants are increasingly using desalination to satisfy growing fresh-water requirements. Multieffect distillation matches extremely well with power plants. If the solar plant's Rankine power cycle is designed to deliver exhaust steam from the turbine at 70°C (instead of the conventional 35°C), the resulting reduced efficiency in electricity production would be more than compensated for by the use of the heat for desalination purposes. Approximately 21 000 cubic meters of fresh water per day can be produced for every 100 MW installed.

Solar hydrogen and metals production

There are at least four thermochemical routes for solar hydrogen production, as shown in Figure 11.9. The hydrogen would come from water in the solar thermolysis and the solar thermochemical cycles, from fossil fuels for the solar cracking process, and from a combination of fossil fuels and water for the solar reforming and solar gasification processes. All of these routes would involve endothermic reactions that make use of concentrated solar radiation as the energy source of high-temperature process heat.

Figure 11.9 ▶ Solar hydrogen production

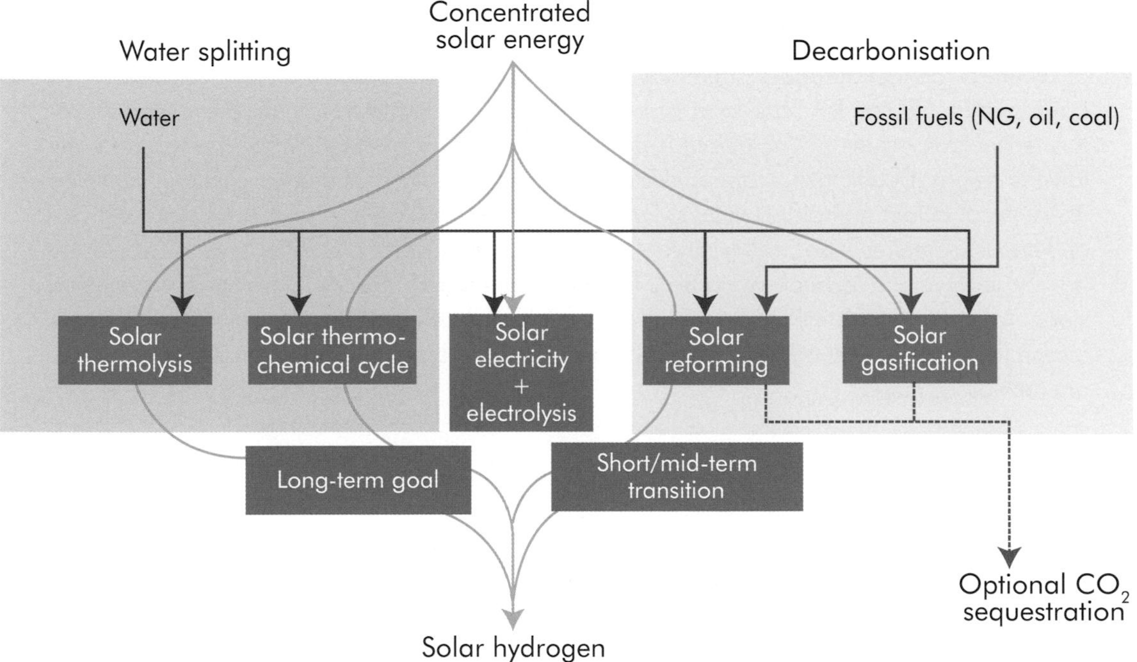

Source: Steinfeld, 2005.

11

Key point

Various routes exist for hydrogen production from solar energy.

Some of the routes shown would require break through improvements, for example in materials capable of withstanding the very high temperatures required for water thermolysis. Other routes, for example, solar-assisted fossil fuel steam reforming, are closer to maturity. Concentrated solar technologies could also be used to produce metals through solar thermal, carbothermal or electrothermal reduction of metal oxides, thus reducing the CO_2 emissions of extractive metallurgical industries. These metals may themselves be used as energy carriers, producing electricity in fuel cells or hydrogen via a water splitting reaction. Other energy carriers can be produced in solar power plants using reverse endothermic-exothermic reactions, such as methane reforming methanation, and ammonia dissociation synthesis (Steinfeld and Palumbo, 2001).

Box 11.4 ► The solar chimney concept

A solar updraft tower power plant – also called a solar chimney – is a solar thermal power plant that combines a solar air collector and a central updraft tube to generate a solar-induced convective flow, which drives pressure-staged turbines to generate electricity. An experimental demonstration plant with a peak output of 50 kW was built in 1981 at Manzanares in Spain, with funds provided by the German Ministry of Research and Technology. The tower was 195 m high.

Solar updraft towers can use all available solar light and can thus be installed in a great variety of climates. Thermal storage is offered by the ground itself and can be enhanced by water-filled bags in the collector for base-load power production. Economies of scale are important for this technology, as the power output is a function of the size of the collector multiplied by the tower's height. Doubling both the collector area and the height of a solar chimney multiplies its electrical output fourfold. Hence, solar chimneys have to be large, with towers at least one or several kilometres high, if they are to produce cheap electricity. Smaller systems would not be competitive. The technology cannot, for obvious technical reasons, develop in incremental steps. To make very slender and very tall chimneys technically and economically feasible, some researchers are considering using inflatable materials. The technical and practical obstacles here are, obviously, huge.

Chapter 12 HYDRO, GEOTHERMAL AND OCEAN ENERGY

Key Findings

Hydropower production can double in the next 40 years

- *Hydropower accounts for about 90% of all renewable power generation today.*
- *Important technical potentials remain in Asia, Africa and South America. A realistic potential is 2.5 to 3 times the current production.*
- *Hydropower production doubles in the ACT Map and BLUE Map scenarios between now and 2050, reaching 5 000 TWh to 5 500 TWh per year from 1 700 GW of capacity.*
- *Pumped storage has a potential of around 1 000 GW capacity. This is about ten times its current capacity. Pumped storage may be particularly useful in balancing grids.*
- *Future hydropower production may be affected by climate change. The potential impacts are not yet well understood and should be investigated in detail.*
- *The main challenges for hydropower projects are competition for scarce water and land resources in most parts of the world, and the social and environmental impact of hydro schemes. These challenges are likely to limit the potential of large schemes.*
- *Small hydro schemes still have considerable potential. RD&D into ways of exploiting smaller flows and reservoir heads will help maximise this potential.*

Geothermal power generation deserves more attention

- *The potential of geothermal energy is huge. High-quality resources are already economically viable today.*
- *10 GW of geothermal electrical capacity are currently installed worldwide.*
- *Enhanced geothermal system (EGS) technologies have the potential to economically produce large amounts of power almost anywhere in the world. Several pilot projects are now being conducted in the United States, Australia and Europe. Costs need to be reduced by 80% to make EGS economical without feed-in tariffs or subsidies.*
- *To improve the viability of EGS requires more cost-effective deep-well drilling and construction, more effective reservoir fracturing and stimulation techniques, and tailored surface-conversion technologies.*
- *Geothermal power production increases twenty-fold to 200 GW in 2050 in the BLUE Map scenario.*

Ocean energy is just emerging

- *Almost all ocean energy power generation today is based on using barrages to harness tidal energy. The prospects for further expansion are limited. No offshore tidal projects are yet planned. Tidal currents may pose opportunities at suitable sites.*
- *There has been a lot of progress in wave energy. But capacity is still very small, at less than 1 GW installed capacity in total.*
- *Costs need to come down to a third or a quarter of their current levels, and reliability must be improved.*
- *Ocean power production will stay below 50 GW in the BLUE Map scenario in 2050.*

This chapter discusses hydropower, geothermal and ocean energy. The expansion potential is significant for all three options. But while hydropower is already well established, geothermal and ocean power options still need further development.

Hydropower generation doubles in the ACT Map and BLUE Map scenarios, reaching 5 000 TWh to 5 500 TWh per year in 2050. Most of this growth is in Latin America, China, Eastern Europe and Turkey and Africa (see Figure 12.1). There will be scope for further expansion beyond 2050, but competing water and land uses will increasingly limit that scope. The share of hydropower in the power mix remains roughly constant at 16% of global electricity production. This is nearly half of all renewable electricity production in 2050.

Figure 12.1 ▶ Hydropower production in the Baseline, ACT Map and BLUE Map scenarios, 2050

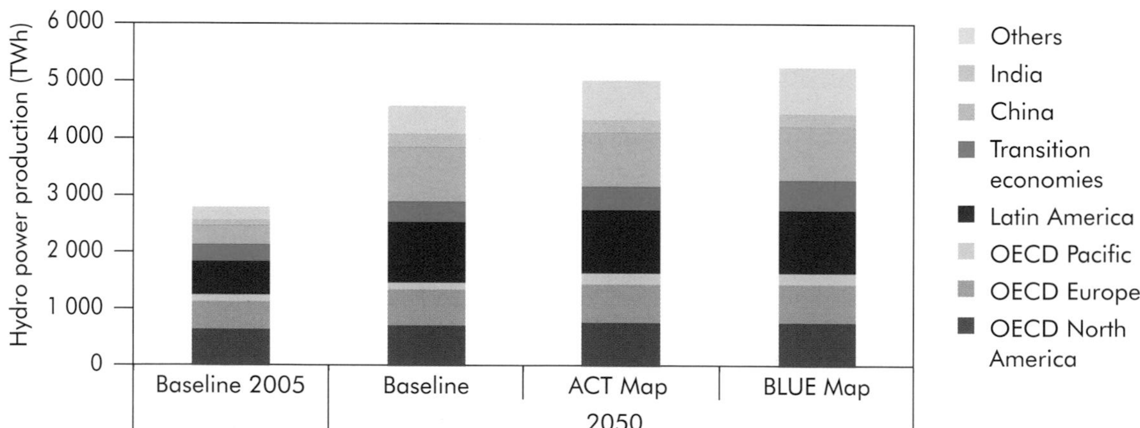

Key point

Already in the Baseline, hydropower shows significant growth.

Geothermal power production capacity amounts to 10 GW today, and is projected to increase twenty-fold in 2050 in the BLUE Map scenario, producing about 900 to 1 100 TWh a year – or 2% to 3% of total power generation. A significant share of the growth will be based on enhanced geothermal systems (EGS) currently under development. Geothermal production will be concentrated in countries where continental plates meet – *i.e.* around the Pacific, in the Great Rift Valley in Africa, and in places such as Iceland and Turkey.

Figure 12.2 provides an overview of national/regional geothermal power production for the different model scenarios.

Figure 12.2 ▶ Geothermal power productions in the Baseline, ACT Map and BLUE Map scenarios, 2050

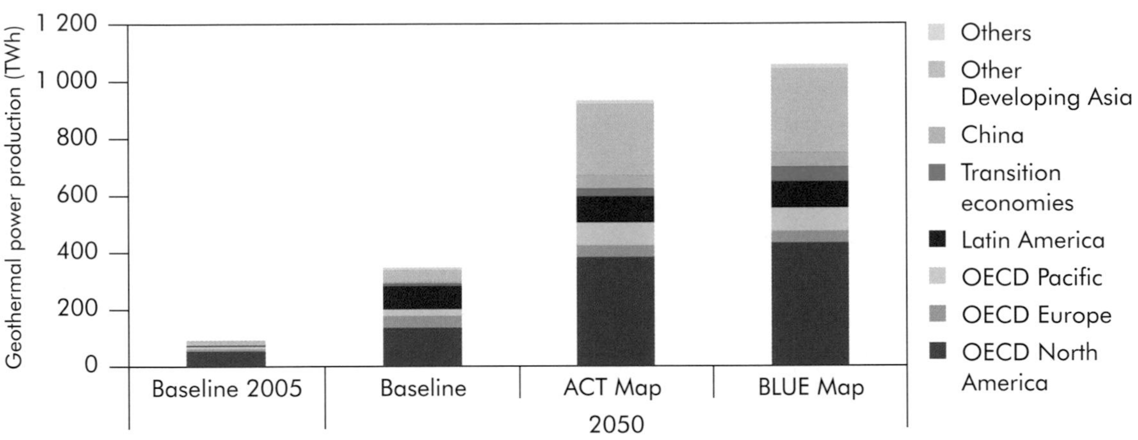

Key point

Rapid growth in geothermal power production in ACT Map and BLUE Map scenarios.

12

Ocean power technologies are still at a relatively early stage of development. Robustness and reliability under extreme weather conditions is still a challenge and significant further development is still needed. The total capacity of ocean power today is less than 1 GW. In the BLUE Map scenario, this rises to around 50 GW in 2050.

Hydropower

Status

Hydropower is an extremely flexible power technology. Hydro reservoirs provide built-in energy storage, and the fast response time of hydropower enables it to be used to optimise electricity production across power grids, meeting sudden fluctuations in demand or helping to compensate for the loss of power from other sources.

Large-scale hydropower projects can be controversial because they affect water availability downstream, inundate valuable ecosystems, may require relocation of populations, and require large DC transmission lines. New, less-intrusive low-head turbines are being developed to run on smaller reservoirs. Hydropower usually depends on rainfall in the upstream catchment area. Reserve capacity may be needed to cover for periods of low rainfall. This adds to costs.

Small-scale hydropower is normally designed to run in-river. This is an environmentally friendly energy conversion option, because it does not interfere significantly with river flows. Small hydro is often used in self-standing applications to replace diesel generators or other small-scale power plants or to provide electricity to rural populations.

The IEA estimates that the world's technically feasible hydro potential is 14 000 TWh per year. About 6 000 TWh per year is considered to have realistic potential (Taylor, 2007). Around 808 GW of capacity is in operation or under construction worldwide. Most of the remaining potential for development is in Africa, Asia and Latin America. Worldwide, the technical potential of small hydropower is estimated at 150 GW to 200 GW. Only 5% of the world's small-scale hydropower potential has yet been exploited.

OECD countries today produce roughly half of the hydroelectricity produced worldwide. The share from non-OECD countries is likely to increase, however, because most realistic large hydro potential in OECD countries has already been developed, while significant capacity remains to be developed in non-OECD countries. China will add some 18.2 GW of capacity by 2009 with the completion of the Three Gorges Dam.

Hydropower generation produces no CO_2 emissions other than those emitted in dam construction. Some reservoirs emit methane from decaying organic material, although this is rare (Scanlon, 2007) and can be avoided by proper reservoir design.

Hydropower can also be generated from pumped storage systems consisting of two or more reservoirs at different heights. Energy is stored when the water is pumped from the low to the high reservoir and released when the water flows back from the high to the low reservoir. Typical electricity storage efficiency is about 80%. New pumped storage can be combined with various renewable electricity sources. It can also reduce costs in nuclear-based electricity supply systems with limited load-following capacity.

Pumped storage capacity worldwide today is about 100 GW, about 2% of total power generation capacity. No new capacity was added between 1990 and 2000, although approximately 9 GW of new storage capacity is currently planned in the European Alps (Schwab, 2007). Globally, there is potential for approximately 1 000 GW of pumped storage capacity, equal to about half of all realistic hydropower potential (Taylor, 2007).

Costs

Existing hydropower is one of the cheapest ways of producing electricity. Most plants were built many years ago and their initial costs have been fully amortised. For new large plants in OECD countries, capital costs are about USD 2 400 per kW and generating costs around USD 0.03 to USD 0.04 per kWh. In developing countries, investment costs are routinely below USD 1 000/kW. Small hydropower generating costs are around USD 0.02 to USD 0.06 per kWh. Such systems commonly operate without major replacement costs for 50 years or more. The cost of pumped storage systems depends on their configuration and use. They may be up to twice as expensive as an equivalent unpumped hydropower system. Depending on cycling rates, their generating costs may be similar to those of unpumped systems.

Future R&D efforts

Like other energy technologies, hydropower technologies need to improve efficiencies, reduce costs and improve dependability. For large-scale hydropower, there are specific challenges in integrating with other renewables, developing hybrid systems and developing innovative technologies to minimise environmental impacts. Although small-hydro technology is mature and well-established in the market, there is a need for further R&D to improve equipment designs, investigate different materials, improve control systems and optimise generation as part of integrated water-management systems. One priority is to develop cheaper technologies for small-capacity and low-head applications, to enable the exploitation of smaller rivers and shallower reservoirs. Table 12.1 sets out the R&D priorities for large and small hydropower schemes.

Table 12.1 ▶ **Technology needs for hydropower**

Large hydro	Small hydro
Equipment Low-head technologies, including in-stream flow Communicate advances in equipment, devices and materials	**Equipment** Turbines with less impact on fish populations Low-head technologies In-stream flow technologies
O&M practices Increasing use of maintenance-free and remote operation technologies	**O&M practices** Develop package plants requiring only limited O&M
	Hybrid systems Wind-hydro systems Hydrogen-assisted hydro systems

Source: IEA, 2005.

Challenges to future deployment

Concerns over undesirable environmental and social affects have been the principal barriers to hydro schemes worldwide. Proper siting, design and operation can mitigate many of these problems, but more difficult challenges arise when human populations are forced to relocate. In some developing countries, the economic well-being and health of affected populations have declined after relocation.

Protection of fisheries is also often an issue. Flows need to be maintained in rivers to ensure the life and reproduction of indigenous fish and the free passage of migratory fish. To date, there is no universally accepted method of establishing an agreed minimum flow rate that can satisfy both developers and regulators.

In the last few years, more emphasis has been put on the environmental integration of small hydro plants into river systems. The technology is generally commercially and technically mature, although improvements are possible to make it suitable for export to rapidly expanding non-OECD markets. Innovations in civil engineering design and electro-mechanical equipment are possible, as well as in instrumentation and systems to mitigate environmental effects.

An emerging issue is the possible impact of climate change on hydropower production. Changes in climate can affect local rainfall runoffs in terms of their total annual quantity and distribution. Evidence indicates that a number of hydropower producers have had to adjust their production forecasts downward due to changing runoff projections. While less runoff may be compensated by more rainfall elsewhere, the impacts can be substantial on the scale of individual basins. As a dam may have a lifetime of 100 years or more, this change may affect its economics. This issue is, therefore, potentially important and deserves more attention.

Geothermal

Status

High-temperature geothermal resources can be used in electricity generation, while lower-temperature geothermal resources can be tapped for a range of direct uses such as district heating and industrial processing. This section deals only with the use of geothermal heat for electricity generation.

Geothermal power plants can provide extremely reliable base-load capacity 24 hours a day. Deep geothermal heat is produced from the decay of radioactive material. The heat is moved to the surface through conduction and convection. The temperature gradient in the earth's crust is typically 30°C/km, but can be much higher (to over 150°C/km). In total, 5 billion EJ of heat is stored in the earth's crust, approximately 100 000 times the world's annual energy use today (Bjarnason, 2007).

Geothermal power plant grew at a broadly constant rate of about 200 MW/yr from 1980 to 2005. Total capacity reached around 10 GW in 2007, generating 56 TWh/yr of electricity. Several countries such as Indonesia, Mexico, New Zealand, Nicaragua and the United States are now accelerating development.

There are three types of commercial geothermal power plants: dry steam, flash steam and binary cycle. Dry-steam sites use direct-steam resources at temperatures of about 250°C. Only five fields of this nature have been discovered in the world to date.

Underground reservoirs that contain hot, pressurised water are more common. Flash-steam power plants use resources that are hotter than 175°C. Before fluids enter the plant, their pressure is reduced until they begin to boil, or flash. The steam is used to drive the turbine and the water is injected back into the reservoir.

Binary-cycle plants have typically used geothermal resources with temperatures as low as 85°C. But in 2006, an organic Rankine cycle binary plant using water at a temperature of 72°C was commissioned at Chena Hot Springs, Alaska, making this the lowest temperature geothermal resource ever used for commercial power generation. The plants use heat exchangers to transfer the heat of the water to a fluid that vaporises at lower temperatures. This vapour drives a turbine to generate power. This type of geothermal plant has environmental advantages in that the hot water from the reservoir fluid, which tends to contain dissolved salts and minerals, is contained within an entirely closed system before it is injected back into the reservoir. Hence, it has practically no emissions. Binary power plants are the fastest-growing geothermal generating technology.

Large-scale geothermal power development is currently limited to tectonically active regions such as areas near plate boundaries, rift zones, and mantle plumes or hot spots. These active, high heat-flow areas include countries around the "Ring of Fire" (Indonesia, the Philippines, Japan, New Zealand, Central America, and the western coast of the United States) and rift zones (Iceland and East Africa). These areas are likely to be the most promising for large developments in the near term. If current enhanced geothermal systems (EGS) R&D efforts are successful, geothermal potential could lead to an expansion in other regions.

Costs

Exploration, well-drilling and plant construction make up a large share of the overall costs of geothermal electricity. Drilling costs can account for as much as one-third to one-half of the total cost of a geothermal project. The IEA Geothermal Energy Implementing Agreement, which provides a framework for international collaboration on geothermal issues, is pursuing research into advanced geothermal drilling techniques and investigating aspects of well construction with the aim of reducing costs.

Capital costs are closely related to the characteristics of the local resource system and reservoir, but typically vary from USD 1 150 per kW installed capacity for large, high-quality resources to USD 5 500 per kW for small, low-quality resources.

Generation costs depend on a number of factors, but particularly on the temperature of the geothermal fluid. Plants in the United States report current operating costs of USD 0.015 to USD 0.025 per kWh at the Geysers field in California, or USD 0.02 to USD 0.05 per kWh for other flash and binary systems, excluding investment costs. New constructions can deliver power at USD 0.05 to USD 0.08 per kWh, depending on the source. Similar costs are reported in Europe, where generation costs are USD 0.06 to USD 0.11 per kWh for traditional geothermal power plants (liquid/steam water resources).

New approaches are helping to exploit resources that would have been uneconomic in the past. This is the case for both power generation plant and field development. The costs of conventional geothermal energy have also dropped substantially since the 1970s and 1980s. Overall, costs fell by almost 50% from the mid-1980s to 2000. These large cost reductions, however, were achieved by solving initial problems of science and technology development. Although future cost reductions may be more difficult to attain, work underway in the United States and in Europe and Australia holds great promise.

Future R&D efforts

Current R&D is focused on ways to enhance the productivity of geothermal reservoirs and to use more marginal areas, such as those that have ample heat but are only slightly permeable. EGS techniques (formerly referred to as hot dry rock, or HDR, geothermal power production) aim to exploit these heat sources. Most are in the research phase although some pilot projects (e.g. at Landau, Germany) are becoming a commercial reality.

Vast amounts of heat are available almost anywhere worldwide at depths of 3 km to 10 km. To extract energy from hot impermeable rock, water is injected from the surface through boreholes to widen, extend and sometimes create fractures (cracks) in hot rock. In operation, water injected from the surface heats as it flows through these cracks in the hot rock. When it returns to the surface, it is used to generate electricity in a binary generator. The water is then recirculated to continuously repeat the cycle. New approaches of R&D and improved conventional approaches or producing smaller modular units will allow economies of scale in plant manufacturing.

EGS seeks to enable the exploitation of geothermal resources that are currently unattainable. Australia has a goal of providing 6.8% (5.5 GW) of its baseload power via EGS by 2030. The United States has an estimated EGS potential of 100 GWe in the next 50 years. Parts of China and India also have estimated EGS potentials of 100 GW. Germany may have a potential of up to 300 000 TWh from EGS, while Switzerland envisages an eventual 50 EGS plants – each with 50 MW (2.5 GW total) – to provide 33% of its electricity.

One line of R&D is aiming to develop deeper wells in volcanically active areas. A conventional well may yield 5 MW, while a deep 5-km well of the same flow rate would yield ten times as much power, because the steam conditions are much more favourable (430-550°C, 230-260 bar: Bjarnason, 2007). However, drilling costs rise exponentially with drilling depth as shown in Figure 12.3. Drilling to a well depth of 5 km has historically cost about USD 5 million, and drilling costs have roughly doubled in the past four years. The drilling market may ease in time, but is unlikely to do so in the short term.

EGS demonstration projects have also highlighted several problems. An EGS project in Basel, Switzerland was suspended in December 2006 after causing a small earthquake (measuring 3.4 on the Richter scale). Similar induced seismic effects have been observed for a number of other projects (Bromley and Mongillo, 2008). The European research project in Soultz-sous-Fôrets in the Alsace region of France has had problems with well productivity in one of its three wells. To date, improving permeability by massive hydraulic injections is still largely a matter of trial and error.

Figure 12.3 ▶ **Completed well costs as a function of depth**

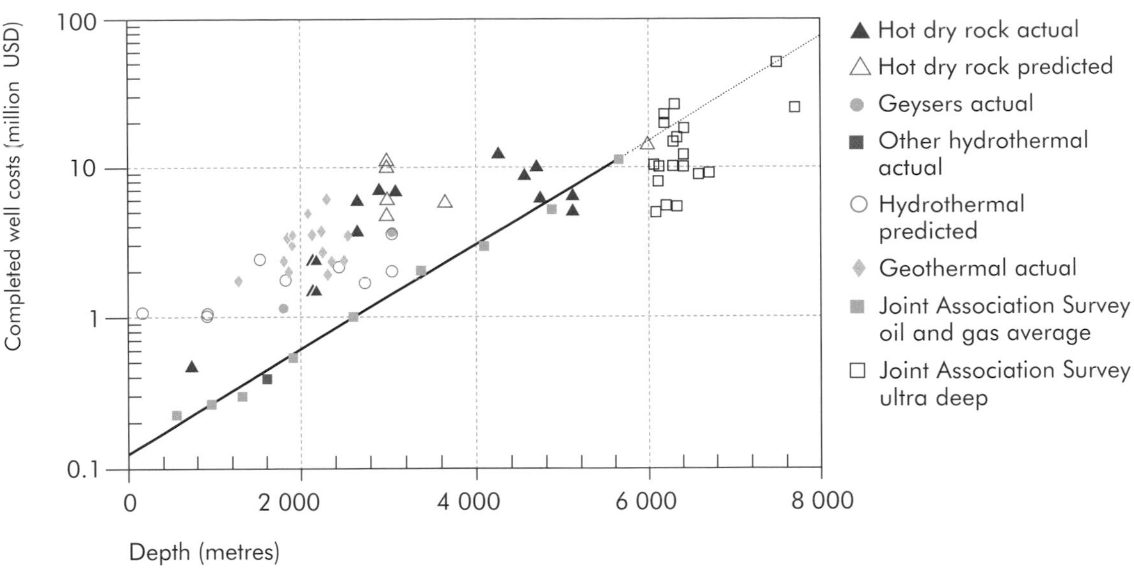

Note: The vertical axis is a logarithmic scale.
Source: Augustine, Tester and Anderson, 2006.

Key point

Completed well costs rise exponentially with well depth.

EGS projects require considerable pumping energy. The pumps for a low-grade reservoir, where the temperature of the produced fluid decreases from 200°C to 150°C over the project life span, typically require 20% to 45% of the gross energy produced (Heidinger, Dornstädter and Fabritius, 2006). At present, average investment costs amount to USD 13 000 per kW.

To accelerate the exploitation of geothermal resources and enhance its attractiveness to investors, several technical issues need further government-funded research and close government collaboration with industry. Higher flow rates and higher temperatures are the two keys to substantial cost reductions (Kaltschmitt and Frick, 2007). Further research in the exploration and enhancement of reservoirs and in drilling and power-generation technology, in particular for the exploitation of low-temperature geothermal resources, will be important in realising potential in this area.

Challenges to future deployment

The geothermal potential of large parts of the world is not yet fully characterised. China has just commissioned a study to assess its potential.

Challenges to expanding geothermal energy utilisation include long project development times, the risk and cost of exploratory drilling and, to a much lesser extent, the possibility of undesirable environmental effects. Some aquifers can produce moderately to highly saline fluids that are corrosive and present a potential pollution hazard, particularly to freshwater drainage systems and groundwater. Re-injection and corrosion management are, therefore, important.

Geothermal energy carries a relatively high commercial risk because of the uncertainties involved in identifying and developing reservoirs that can sustain long-term fluid and heat flow. It is difficult to fully characterise a geothermal reservoir before making a major financial commitment. A number of countries with geothermal resources have developed policies to underwrite risks at both the reservoir assessment and drilling stages. For these countries, it would be impossible to attract private investment without these measures.

Another potential challenge for EGS is the large quantity of recirculating water required in the process. A small 5-MW plant could use 8.5 mega litres (8 500 t/d, or 350 t/hr) of water per day, while a full-scale commercial plant could use ten times that amount. Coupling more water-efficient cooling systems with the closed EGS circulation systems will mitigate this requirement.

Ocean energy

Status

Ocean energy technologies for electricity generation are at a relatively early stage of development. Approaches to using ocean energy fall into several categories (Table 12.2), primarily focused around wave energy, tidal energy, temperature and salinity gradients, and marine biomass.

Wave energy and tidal current energy are the two main areas under development. Currently more than 25 countries are involved in developing different ocean energy systems (IEA, 2006).

The technology required to convert *tidal* energy into electricity is very similar to that used in hydroelectric power plants. Electricity can be generated by water flowing into and out of gates and turbines installed along a dam or barrage built across a tidal bay or estuary where there is a difference of at least five metres between high and low tides. Given tidal patterns, tidal power plants have periods of maximum generation roughly every six hours. Turbines can be used to pump extra water into the basin behind the barrage during periods of low electricity demand, replicating some of the characteristics of a pumped-storage hydroelectric facility.

There is 270 MW of tidal capacity in operation globally. A new tidal energy plant of 254 MW is under construction in Korea. The cost of this plant is about USD 1 000/kW. The United Kingdom is planning a feasibility study into the Severn Barrage.

The environmental impacts of dammed tidal energy projects are often unacceptable. Offshore tidal projects with reduced environmental impacts could be combined with wind turbines to reduce the cost. Tidal current systems are also under development. However, their use will be limited to locations with strong currents and sufficient flow. New projects with tidal current turbines comprised of modules of up to 2 to 3 MW in size have been planned in the United Kingdom, Canada and the United States.

Planned new wave energy capacity in the coming years is small, in the order of 10 MW per year. At this stage, several demonstration power plants with an individual turbine/generator capacity of up to 0.3 MW are operational. The potential for wave energy depends on average wave heights. The wave potential tends to be higher towards the poles, but is site dependent. The European Atlantic coast, the North American Pacific coast and the Australian south coast have significant potentials.

Table 12.2 ▶ Status of ocean (marine) renewable energy technologies

Sub-sector	Status
Waves	Several demonstration projects (up to a capacity of 1 MW) and a few large-scale projects are under development. The industry aims to have the first commercial technology in operation in 2008.
Tidal and marine currents	Three demonstration projects (up to a capacity of 300 kW)) and a few large-scale projects are under development. The industry aims to have the first commercial technology in operation in 2008.
Tidal barrages (based on the rise and fall of the tides)	Plants in operation include the 240 MW unit at La Rance in France (built in the 1960s), the 20 MW unit at Annapolis Royal in Canada (built in the 1980s) and a unit in Russia. Another 254 MW project is under construction in Korea. Tidal barrage projects can be more intrusive to the area surrounding the catch basins than wave or marine-current projects.
Ocean thermal energy conversion (OTEC)	Several desalination projects using temperature gradients are in place in India. In addition, several projects that use ocean water for heat pumps for heating or cooling are in operation around the world.
Salinity gradient/osmotic energy	A few preliminary laboratory-scale experiments have been developed, but they have limited R&D support. A 10 kW demonstration project has been planned in Norway.
Marine biomass	Negligible developmental activity or interest.

Note: In addition to the potential for grid-connected electricity-generation, there are potential synergies from the use of ocean renewable energy resources. Examples include: off-grid electrification in remote coastal areas; aqua-culture; the production of compressed air for industrial applications; desalination; integration with other renewables, such as offshore wind and solar PV, for hybrid offshore renewable energy plants; and hydrogen production.

Source: Bhuyan and Brito-Melo, 2007.

12

Oscillating water turbines can be integrated in breakwater systems or stand-alone units that convert water pressure into air pressure and use the compressed air to drive a Wells turbine. Such projects are planned in breakwaters in Spain and Portugal, with 0.3 MW rated power. A 3.9 MW project is targeted for Scotland in 2009 (Weilepp, 2007). Portugal is also very active in developing wave energy, with a goal of having 23 MW of wave energy capacity by the end of 2009. The first installed 2.3 MW machine was a Pelamis wave device, installed in 2008, which costs USD 6 000/kW. Although a number of other technologies are under development, fewer than ten of these conversion systems have reached full-scale development (Khan, *et al.*, 2008). It is unlikely that the technology will play an important role before 2030.

Ocean thermal-energy conversion (OTEC) may become important in the long term (after 2030) for certain countries. Relevant technological developments are taking place in Japan and India. Salinity gradient and marine biomass systems are currently the object of very limited research activities. Neither seems likely to play a significant role in the short or medium term.

Costs

A cost breakdown for typical mature ocean energy projects is shown in Figure 12.4. Civil works typically represent more than half of the total investment cost for shoreline and near-shore installations. The cost structure is different for deep-water devices. Because most of these technologies are still at the RD&D and demonstration stage, current cost data are not very informative. They are typically in the range of USD 150/MWh to USD 300/MWh. Tidal barrage systems are cheaper, but are not representative of the new ocean energy technologies.

Figure 12.4 ▶ Typical future investment cost for shoreline and near shore ocean energy installations

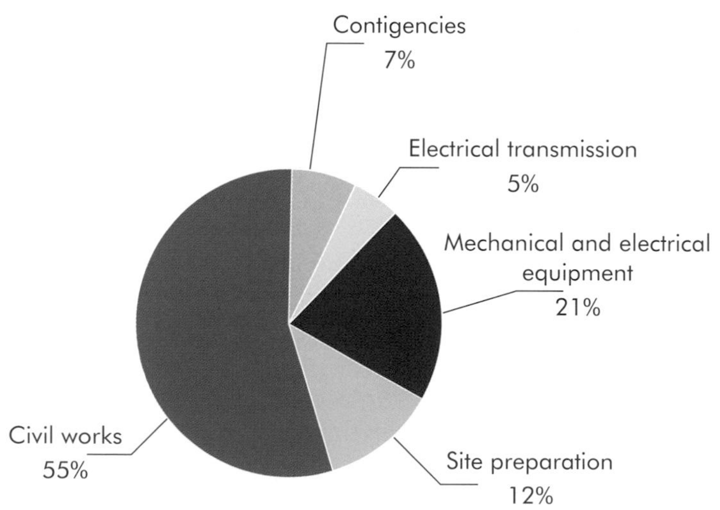

Source: Boud and Thorpe, 2006.

Key point

Civil works cost dominate total cost.

Opportunities for cost reductions depend on the choice of maintenance location (onshore or *in situ*); the distance from shore; the type and availability of the required vessels; and the frequency and duration of maintenance visits as well as the proportion of planned to unplanned maintenance.[1]

Future R&D efforts

At present, RD&D aims to overcome technical barriers related to wave and tidal, OTEC, and salinity-gradient technologies. The focus is on moorings; structure and hull design methods; power take-off systems; deployment methods; and wave behaviour and the hydrodynamics of wave absorption. Research on tidal-stream current systems can be divided into basic research that focuses on areas such as water stream flow patterns and cavitations, and applied science, which examines supporting structure design, turbines, foundations and deployment methods.

Research efforts on turbines and rotors will need to focus on cost-efficiency, reliability and ease of maintenance, particularly in developing components (*e.g.* bearings) that can resist hostile marine environments. Control systems for turbine speed and rotor pitch will also be important to maximise power output. The main challenge for salinity gradient systems is to develop functioning and efficient membranes that can generate sufficient energy to make an energy system competitive.

Challenges to future deployment

A factor common to all marine technologies is that pilot projects need to be relatively large-scale if they are to withstand offshore conditions. Such projects are costly and carry high commercial risks. These considerations have inhibited early development of these technologies. It is only in recent years that adequate government funding has been made available to support sizeable pilot projects. Once successful pilot projects are completed and confidence in the concept grows, commercial financing for even larger projects may become easier to obtain.

Although the prospects for tidal barrages are good in certain locations, their site-specific environmental effects need careful assessment. The technology reduces the range of the tides inside the barrage. This may affect the mud flats and silt levels in rivers, which would cause changes in the wildlife living in and around the estuary. It could also change the quality of the water retained by the barrage.

Non-technical challenges include the need for resource assessment and to develop energy-production forecasting and design tools as well as test and measurement standards. Environmental effects pose another challenge. Potential developments include arrays of farms of ocean energy systems and dual-purpose plants that combine energy and other structures.

1. See www.thecarbontrust.co.uk/ctmarine3/Page1.htm.

Cost overview

Table 12.3 provides an overview of cost estimates for the electricity generation technologies discussed in this chapter. There is a wide range of costs for each renewable technology, due mainly to varying resource quality and to the large number of technologies within each category. Investment comprises all installation costs, including those of demonstration plants in certain categories. Discount rates vary across regions. Because of the wide range in costs, there is no specific year or CO_2 price level for which a renewable energy technology can be expected to become competitive. A gradual increase in the penetration of renewable energy over time is more likely. Energy policies can speed up this process by providing the right market conditions and accelerating deployment so that costs can be reduced through technology learning.

Table 12.3 ▶ Key cost and investment assumptions of hydro, geothermal and ocean energy

	Investment cost			Production cost		
	2005 (USD/kW)	2030 (USD/kW)	2050 (USD/kW)	2005 (USD/kW)	2030 (USD/kW)	2050 (USD/kW)
Geothermal						
– hydrothermal	1 700-5 700	1 500-5 000	1 400-4 900	33-97	30-87	29-84
– hot dry rock	5 000-15 000	4 000-10 000	3 000-7 500	150-300	80-200	60-150
Large hydro	1 000-5 500	1 000-5 400	1 000-5 100	30-120	30-115	30-110
Small hydro	2 500-7 000	2 200-6 500	2 000-6 000	56-140	52-130	49-120
Tidal barrage	2 000-4 000	1 700-3 500	1 500-3 000	60-100	50-80	45-70
Tidal current	7 000-10 000	5 000-8 000	3 500-6 000	150-200	80-100	45-80
Wave	6 000-15 000	2 500-5 000	2 000-4 000	200-300	45-90	40-80

Note: Using 10% discount rate. The actual global range is wider as discount rates, investment cost and resource quality varies. Excludes grid connection cost.

Sources: IEA data; Carbon Trust, 2006; EPRI, 2005.

Chapter 13 ELECTRICITY SYSTEMS

Key Findings

- *The characteristics of the electricity system can significantly affect the cost of emission mitigation options. Investment costs for transmission and distribution systems are of a similar magnitude as production plant investments.*
- *Variable renewable output needs to be supplemented by reserve capacity, storage or increased trade with adjacent areas. In the short term, variability will reinforce the role of natural gas.*
- *In the longer term, more attention should be focused on increasing the flexibility of the power system through energy storage, improved use of interconnection, and improved market practices.*
- *The cost of storage or backup capacity typically adds USD 0.01 to USD 0.02 per kWh to the cost of variable renewables. However, these costs only come into play at very high supply shares when there are no lower-cost system management options.*
- *Direct current (DC) transmission systems make economic sense for long-range and for sub-sea transportation. Such connections might enable the use of better quality renewable resources. In the case of wind electricity, transportation over 2 000 km would add 50% to the supply cost (USD 0.02 to USD 0.03 per kWh). If this enables the use of a resource with high availability instead of one with average availability, it can make economic sense. Moreover, such regional interconnection allows renewable electricity systems to be developed that require less backup or storage.*
- *Transmission and distribution (T&D) losses need to be given more attention, especially in developing countries where important opportunities exist to reduce these losses. The average loss through transmission and distribution varies among countries, representing from 5% to 25% of total power production.*

Overview

Much more electricity is produced than is ever used. Transmission and distribution (T&D) losses and direct use in power plants equates to 14.3% of the electricity produced worldwide (8.8% is lost through T&D, which includes commercial and technical losses: *see* Table 13.1).

While losses are significantly higher in developing countries, in absolute terms, the United States and Europe lose the most electricity – because of the sheer size of their electricity markets. The two most efficient countries are Canada and Japan, with losses of only 9% to 11% (Table 13.1). Total losses worldwide exceed China's electricity production. The variation of losses in percentage terms suggests that important efficiency gains can be achieved.

Table 13.1 ▶ Country average variations in direct use in power plants and transmission and distribution (T&D) losses as a percentage of gross electricity production, 2005

	Direct use in plant	T&D losses	Pumped storage	Total
	(%)	(%)	(%)	(%)
India	6.9	25.0	0.0	31.9
Mexico	5.0	16.2	0.0	21.1
Brazil	3.4	16.6	0.0	20.0
Russia	6.9	11.8	–0.6	18.1
China	8.0	6.7	0.0	14.7
EU-27	5.3	6.7	0.4	12.5
United States	4.8	6.2	0.2	11.2
Canada	3.2	7.3	0.0	10.5
Japan	3.7	4.6	0.3	8.7
World	**5.3**	**8.8**	**0.2**	**14.3**

Note: T&D losses include commercial and technical losses. Commercial losses refer to un-metered use.
Source: IEA statistics.

Unlike other energy carriers, electricity can only in rare circumstances be stored in large quantities (and always in other energy forms). As a consequence, supply and demand must always be balanced in real time. Night demand is generally significantly lower than daytime demand. And in most countries, electricity demand is highly seasonal. Typically, peak national grid demand can be two to three times as high as minimum demand.

To cope with these differing demands grid systems need to be supplied by different types of generation plant. They need base-load plants – plants that can provide consistent levels of supply over long periods. They need shoulder-load plants – plants that can provide supply in periods of extended high demand through periods of the year. And they need peak-load plants – plants that can provide highly flexible supply to meet fluctuations in demand, sometimes of very short duration, when all other plants are fully loaded.

Base load is generally supplied by plants with high capital costs and low operating costs, such as coal and nuclear power plants. A natural-gas combined cycle (NGCC) plant or a gas turbine has much lower capital costs, however. Its output can also be varied quickly. It is accordingly suitable for both shoulder and peak demand.

The need to deliver consistent demand-driven supply poses particular challenges for variable renewables such as wind and solar energy. These are currently addressed by: providing flexible, backup systems based on storable fuels such as fossil fuels or biomass; assuring a wider dispersion of plants regionally, to reduce the risk and scale of variability; and developing technologies that can produce electricity across a wider range of weather conditions.

Load duration curves and their impact on CO_2 mitigation cost

Plant loading can have a significant impact on the cost of mitigating CO_2 emissions. Load duration curves can be split into base load and peak load. Base load is generally served from either fossil-fired generation or nuclear generation. Peak load is usually served by natural-gas combined cycle and gas turbine generation.

Load duration curves for three European countries and for the mid-Atlantic United States are shown in Figure 13.1. In all four cases, the minimum demand is about half the peak demand. This demand is supplied by base-load plants, usually coal and nuclear plants. The other half is provided by plants that operate part-time. About 20% of the total demand is met by plants that operate less than 10% of the time. NGCC plant is most effective at meeting supply at these lower load levels.

Figure 13.1 ▶ Hourly load curve for France, Germany, Italy and the Mid-Atlantic United States

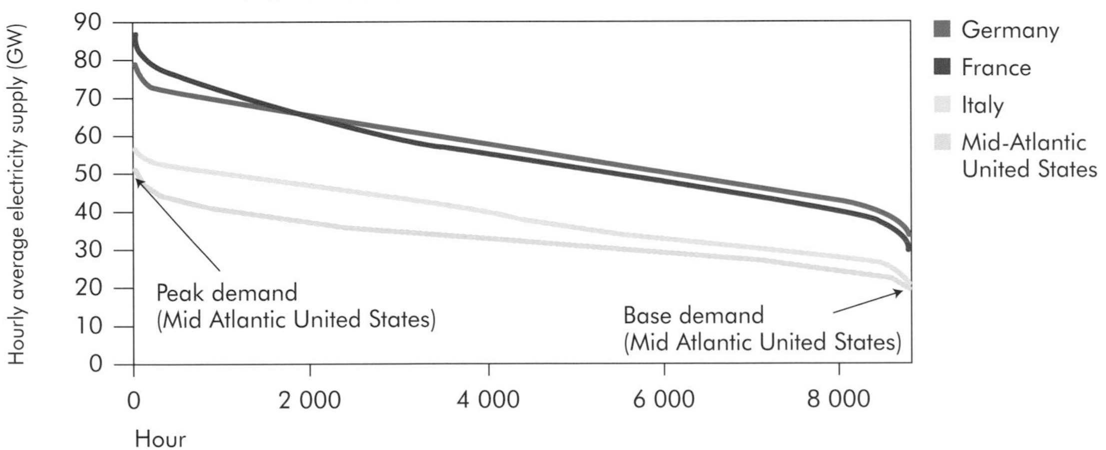

Note: The load curve shows hourly supply ranked from highest to lowest.

Key point

Electricity demand varies significantly during the year.

The characteristics of the load duration curve affect the cost of CO_2 mitigation. A plant that operates only part-time may require the same capital investment as a plant that operates full time, but the CO_2 reduction per year will be much smaller. This is exacerbated by the fact that a base-load plant is likely to be coal-fired, while a peaking plant could be gas-fired. For example, the cost of CO_2 capture and storage (CCS) is significantly higher for a NGCC plant than it is for a coal-fired plant – typically twice as high. More than half of the CCS costs are capital costs. If a plant is operated only half of the time, CCS costs will be 50% higher than they

13

would be for a plant that is operated full time. In effect, the cost of mitigating CO_2 emissions is likely to be much higher for shoulder- and peak-load plants than for base-load plants. In practice, reducing CO_2 emissions from shoulder and peak power plants is likely to cost significantly more than USD 50/t CO_2.

Transmission and distribution technology

Electricity is transported from generation plants to users through transmission and distribution (T&D) lines (grids). These grids are economically efficient in that they enable demand and supply to be "smoothed out" over large areas. In France, for example, the grid enables the total supply capacity to be only one-quarter of the total demand potential, as not all users draw their maximum potential demand at the same time. But the transportation of electricity entails significant losses and is costly. Most grid-management systems aim to transport electricity over as short a distance as possible. In many large countries, the overall system consists of a number of separate grids, sometimes with quite different characteristics, that can be linked together. In such systems, each grid is optimised separately, so that it may not be possible to match high demand in one part of the country with underused plant in another part. The linking of separate national grids can further compound these effects.

T&D is an important component of the cost of electricity supply – for low-voltage electricity users, it accounts for around USD 5.5/MWh to USD 8/MWh of their electricity price (Figure 13.2). This is equivalent to between 5% and 10% of the delivered cost of electricity. In most countries these costs are averaged among all customers, to the benefit of those in remote areas or areas of low demand density.

Figure 13.2 ▶ Transmission and distribution grid costs in selected countries by voltage

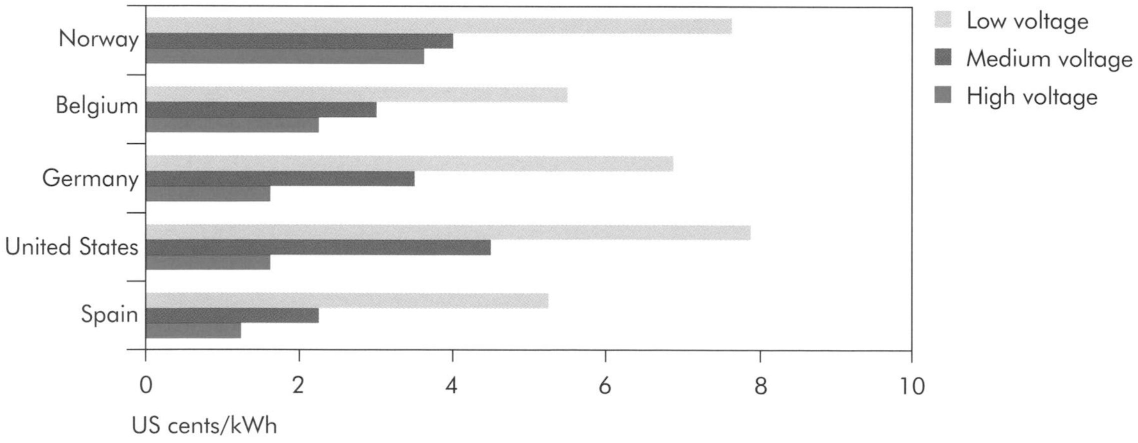

Source: Vattenfall, 2007.

Key point

Transmission and distribution costs are significant and vary by country and by market segment.

Electricity is mostly transported over long distances as alternating current (AC) at voltages ranging from 150 kV to 765 kV. This choice was made more than 100 years ago, because it is easier to transform AC supply than direct current (DC) supply. Losses in high-voltage AC overhead transmission lines amount to 15% per 1 000 km at 380 kV and 8% per 1 000 km at 750 kV (Table 13.2).

Table 13.2 ▶ Cost and performance parameters of high-voltage AC and DC transmission systems

Parameter	Unit	HVAC		HVDC	
Operation voltage	kV	760	1 160	± 600	± 800
Overhead line losses	%/1 000 km	8	6	3	2.5
Sea cable losses	%/100 km	60	50	0.33	0.25
Terminal losses	%/station	0.2	0.2	0.7	0.6
Overhead line cost	M EUR/1 000 km	400-750	1 000	400-450	250-300
Sea cable cost	M EUR/1 000 km	3 200	5 900	2 500	1 800
Terminal cost	M EUR/station	80	80	250-350	250-350

Source: DLR, 2006.

With the development of high-voltage valves, it has become possible to transmit DC power at higher voltages and over longer distances with lower transmission losses – typically of around 3% per 1 000 km. Today, most sub-sea cables (such as those between Norway and the Netherlands) use DC supply, because losses from an AC cable would be excessive. DC cables can also be run closer to the ground than can AC cables.

Given these advantages, a large number of high-voltage DC (HVDC) systems have been installed over the last 50 years. Today about 2% of all electricity is transmitted along HVDC lines, in more than 90 projects all over the world. Ultra-high-voltage DC systems – capable of carrying 800 kV over long distances – are likely to be developed in the near future. Such projects have already been awarded in China. However, AC-DC transformer stations are expensive. Once the transmission distance becomes very long (>500 km), the economics of construction and operation favour DC over AC transmission (Rudervall, *et al.*, 2000).

HVDC systems offer a number of additional advantages over AC systems:

- They are easier to control, and therefore better for T&D utilities as a means of meeting contracted technical and cost objectives.
- They require less land for the transmission system itself. In very sensitive environmental areas, such as national parks, they are sometimes the only viable option.

These advantages suggest that HVDC will increasingly become the system of choice where new T&D systems are being built. On any given right-of-way (ROW), with modern technology, significantly more power can be transmitted at EHV and UHV using DC instead of AC. However, DC also has disadvantages. For example, synchronisation is not possible, which means that a failure on one line cannot receive help from elsewhere.

A major problem for new transmission is public resistance to new overhead power lines. Advances in new technologies in cables and insulation – as well as in installation and maintenance tools – have in recent years been driving down the cost of underground DC transmission. In many cases, this is now cost-competitive with overhead systems. Modern DC technology allows for underground DC transmission to be integrated with AC grids, and in Europe, about 2% of the high/extra-high voltage network is underground. While its technological feasibility is proven, the economics pose an important barrier, as an underground DC line costs 5 to 25 times as much as an overhead line (ICF, 2003). Underground high-voltage AC lines are limited by engineering constraints.

If this trend towards HVDC continues, it may facilitate new transmission systems, which would open up new opportunities for renewables in geographically or environmentally sensitive areas.

Distribution

Transformers are needed to step voltage down from high to medium voltage, and subsequently to low voltage, supply for use in industry or domestically. Power transformers are extremely efficient. Losses are less than 0.25% in large units and less than 2% even in the smaller transformers used for local distribution. However, overall losses are considerable, as there can be as many as five transformation steps between a power station and the consumer. When transformers are very lightly loaded, for example, when offices closes for the evening or during school holidays, these losses are increased.

Losses due to transformers in a power network can exceed 3% of the total electricity generated. Technologies to reduce these losses are already available, however. A fundamentally new type of core material, amorphous iron, produced by cooling molten metal alloy very rapidly, has recently become available. Losses in the amorphous iron core are less than 30% those of conventional steel cores. Replacing even recent-model transformers can reduce losses by up to 75%, while replacing transformers that are more than 30 years old can reduce losses by 90%. The size of the transformers being installed in the network, and the way in which they are loaded, can also increase savings.

Losses in distribution power lines also depend on the geographical spread of the system. In extreme cases, such as in rural India, these losses may exceed 30% (Suresh and Elachola, 2000). In such systems, a larger number of lower-capacity substations, together with the conversion of single-phase supply to three-phase supply, would reduce these losses substantially. During periods of peak load, losses may even exceed 45%, so designing systems with sufficient "slack capacity" is also important. Obviously this slack capacity adds to the upfront investment cost, and a trade-off between investment and distribution costs is needed.

Important losses may also occur in the electricity system beyond the consumer's meter. In particular, the use of AC/DC transformers for electronic equipment has increased rapidly in recent years. These transformers are often switched on permanently while the equipment is only used intermittently. It is estimated that losses beyond the meter may amount to 5% to 10% of total electricity use. So far, these losses have received little attention.

In conclusion, transmission and distribution losses deserve more attention. Especially in developing countries, important opportunities exist to reduce these losses. It is estimated that average global losses can be reduced from 18% to 10%. The savings at today's electricity production levels would equal half of China's electricity generation in 2005. However, part of these savings is accounted for by improved measuring of consumption, so these are not technical savings. More analysis is recommended to maximise these efficiency gains at acceptable cost.

Electricity storage systems

Electricity cannot be stored directly (except for in small-scale capacitors), but it can be transformed into other types of energy that can be stored. In batteries, for example, electricity is transformed into chemical energy. In pumped-storage hydropower systems, it is transformed into potential energy. Electricity can also be converted for storage as compressed air or in flywheels. The cost and capacity of storage options vary widely (Figure 13.3). (The cost data have changed rapidly in recent years, however, notably for Li-ion batteries, which is not accounted for in Figure 13.3.)

Figure 13.3 ▶ Indicative cost of different electrical energy storage technologies

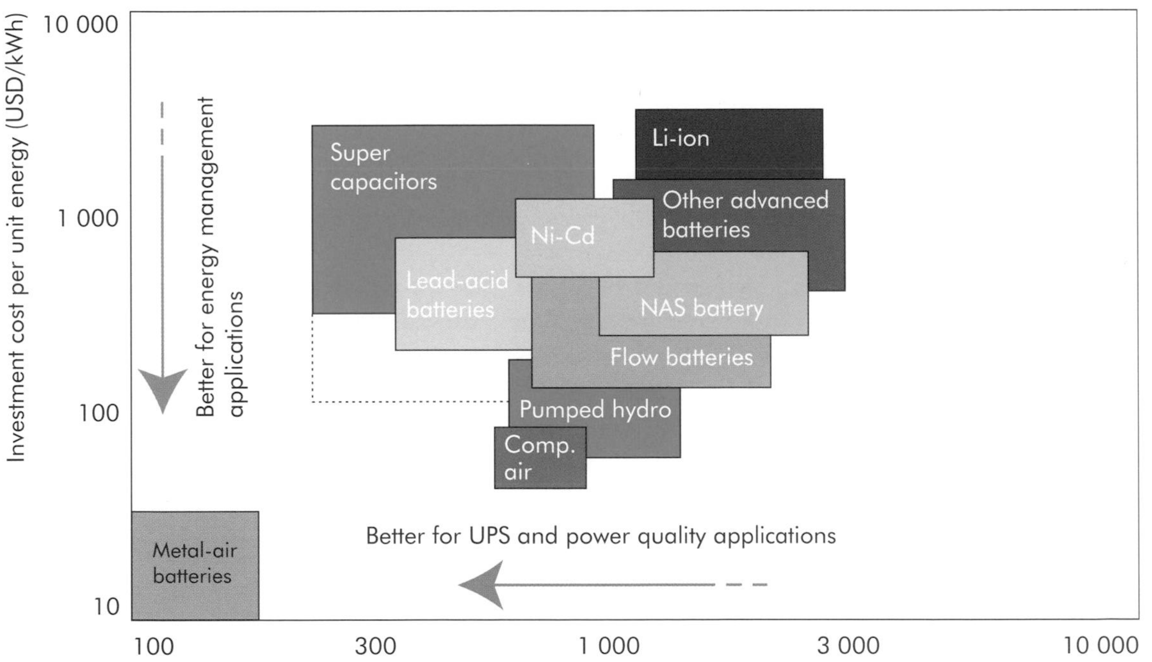

Source: Thijssen, 2002.

Key point

Unit capital cost of storage options varies by 1 to 2 orders of magnitude.

13

Battery electricity storage is efficient, but it is only applicable on a relatively small scale. Lithium ion (Li-ion) batteries typically cost about USD 500/kWh. Even with full usage, delivered costs are around USD 0.20/kWh. These costs are too high, and would be so even if the battery cost was to come down to USD 150/kWh.

Improving electricity storage technologies also reduces the cost of frequency regulation and so improves power electronics.

Figure 13.4 ▶ Storage options categorised by storage time and size

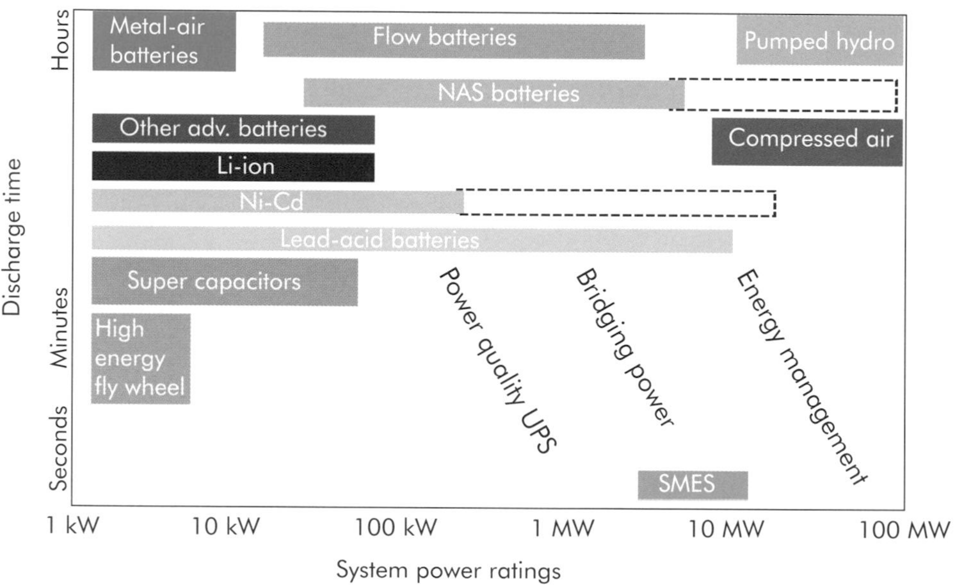

Source: Thijssen, 2002.

Key point

Discharge time and systems rating are the main technical characteristics used to measure storage options.

Different storage options also have different power ratings and discharge times (Figure 13.4). Pumped storage is the most widely applied electricity storage option today. This is covered in more detail in Chapter 12. The efficiencies of various power options range from 40% to nearly 100% (Figure 13.5). While hydrogen fuel cells can be applied over a wide power range, this option is less efficient than alternative options. Pumped storage has an efficiency ranging from 55% to 90%; CAES achieves about 70% efficiency.

New storage systems are under development. This includes underground, compressed-air energy storage systems (CAES). This technology uses underground cavities or aquifers to store air under pressure in periods of excess electricity supply. During periods in which demand exceeds supply, the air is released and drives a turbine to generate electricity. Two CAES demonstration plants have been operational for some decades. The efficiencies that can be achieved are somewhat lower than for pumped storage. Synergies with oil and gas well-drilling and CO_2 storage that are based on very similar technology may also be possible. The big problem with CAES to date is finding suitable storage caverns. Aquifer storage may overcome this problem (Shepard and van der Linden, 2001).

Figure 13.5 ▶ **Storage efficiencies and power ratings**

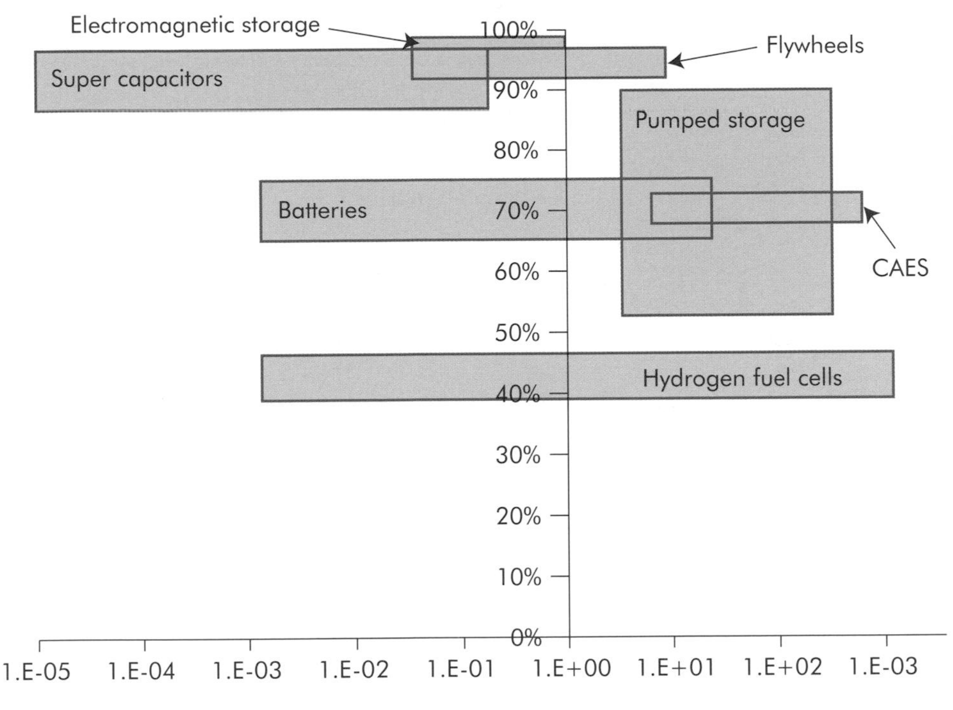

Source: Vattenfall, 2007.

Key point

Hydrogen fuel cells are less efficient than alternative options across a wide range of power ratings.

Superconducting magnetic energy storage (SMES) is a technology currently under development. It stores electrical energy in superconducting coils. This offers properties not exhibited by other storage technologies, in that it can control both active and reactive power simultaneously and can charge/discharge large amounts of power quickly. It can also tolerate repeated use. Current research is focusing on grid tests to establish the practicality and cost of the technology and to develop appropriate network control systems. A compact superconducting flywheel storage system is also under development that can charge/discharge power over a longer period than SMES, and with lower energy loss than conventional mechanical flywheels, with the aim of making network control systems more sophisticated (NEDO, 2006). While SMES prototypes have been available for some time, they are not yet commercially viable. Conventional low-speed flywheels are commercially available as an energy storage alternative.

Hydrogen is an energy carrier that can be produced from electricity via electrolysis. It can be used in periods of excess demand to generate power. However, the efficiency of this cycle is not very high. The efficiency of electrolysis is at best 70%, and the efficiency of power generation 60%. This gives the storage system an overall efficiency of 42%. Clearly, hydrogen storage makes sense only for very cheap electricity or under special conditions such as in remote areas. Solution-mined salt caverns, manmade caverns, aquifers or depleted oil and gas reservoirs could also be used for hydrogen storage for electricity production, although the need to maintain the purity of the hydrogen makes oil and gas reservoirs less suitable than rock or salt caverns. Aquifer storage, which entails no mining costs, is by far the cheapest option. The production of hydrogen, its storage and its subsequent use as transportation fuel may make economic sense if economic fuel-cell vehicles and the necessary hydrogen infrastructure become available.

Storage and variability

Variable supplies, such as wind power, increase the need for reserves during periods of low output. One option is to use storage as a backup.

Table 13.3 compares the cost of three supply/storage systems for delivering base-load electricity. In the Baseline scenario, NGCC is the cheapest option. In the ACT Map scenario, the cost of the wind turbine plus NGCC is almost equal to the stand-alone NGCC. In the BLUE scenario, the wind + CAES system has the lowest cost.

Table 13.3 ▶ Cost comparison of three base-load supply systems

	Investment (USD/kW)	Fuel (USD/kW/yr)	Baseline (USD/yr)	CO_2 (t/yr)	ACT Map (USD/yr)	BLUE Map (USD/yr)
3 wind turbines + 2 CAES units	4 000	0	600	0	600	600
1 wind turbine + 1 NGCC	1 500	229	454	2.0	503	848
1 NGCC	500	341	416	2.9	490	1 005

Note: Assumes 33% availability of wind turbines, USD 1 000/kW for wind turbines, USD 500/kW for CAES, 15% annuity, USD 6.5/GJ gas.

The comparison in Table 13.3 refers to an island operation. In practice, however, a transmission system with hundreds or thousands of power plants reduces the need for backup capacity. Therefore, in most cases storage is not the least-cost response to variability. Other options include distributed generation, discussed below. Nevertheless, when high shares of renewables are reached, storage becomes increasingly relevant. From the analysis in Table 13.3, it is clear that storage systems are likely to become increasingly economic where CO_2 prices are high. This is the case for the BLUE scenarios.

Variability can be made more manageable through wider distribution of plants, demand management, and a technology portfolio approach that includes various different technology options, all of which help to "flatten" the supply curve. Supply variability becomes less of a challenge as the power system itself is made more "flexible" – for example, by including fast-response gas plants in the generation portfolio, increasing interconnection, and trading closer to real time.

Distributed generation

Given the high cost and inefficiency of T&D systems, decentralised power generation has received considerable attention. The term is loosely applied to systems that generate electricity and are sited close to the centres of demand. This includes stand-alone systems that are not connected to the grid (e.g. industrial plants or individual houses), small generating units that are grid-connected, and small grids that operate as "islands". In practice, a mix of centralised and distributed generation is the most likely situation.

Distributed generation units are smaller than centralised units, which raises the investment cost per unit of capacity. This is partially offset be the cost savings for T&D investments. However, the technologies for decentralised generation are often radically different than for centralised units. Certain renewables are typically more suited to decentralised power generation given the low density of the resource used: such as PV, landfill gas, wind (in some cases), or biomass residues in industry. Other forms of renewable energy are remote, require large-scale development and must be connected to the transmission system.

Smaller-scale electricity generation units are usually less efficient than centralised large-scale units. But if residual heat can be used for heating or cooling purposes, it raises the overall efficiency. Industrial combined heat and power generation and district heating and cooling are well-established concepts that deserve further expansion.

Having a large number of decentralised units imposes additional costs to effectively and safely manage the grid. Nevertheless, they can improve the quality of the electricity and the system's reliability if they are placed near load centres. This offsets the greater management effort.

Regions with an established electricity supply infrastructure must be differentiated from those without such a system. Decentralised power generation for small stand-alone electricity systems may have better prospects in parts of Africa or India, for example, where the grid is either non-existent or unreliable, than in regions with a well-established grid and centralised production.

The general benefits of decentralised generation are unproven. They have a potentially important role to play in rural and remote areas. In the BLUE Map scenario, decentralised, building-integrated PV systems account for a significant share of power generation. As 80% of the world population will live in cities by 2050, the market for decentralised power generation will depend on its success in urbanised environments. Without much more effective and much less expensive energy storage, and without higher energy efficiency, it is unlikely that decentralised generation will play a significant part overall in electricity usage in the period through to 2050.

Chapter 14 METHANE MITIGATION

Key Findings

- *Energy related methane emissions amounted to 2.5 Gt CO_2 equivalents in 2005, which equals 8% of total energy related greenhouse gas emissions.*
- *Growth in global methane emissions has slowed in recent years. This trend is expected to reverse over time given anticipated growth in the energy and waste sectors in countries such as China, India, Russia and the Ukraine.*
- *Reducing energy-sector methane emissions can offer important near-term greenhouse-gas reduction opportunities at a cost of less than USD 10/t CO_2eq. In the short term (up to 2015), this could make a larger contribution to overall emission reductions than efforts to reduce CO_2 emissions.*
- *Methane emissions will be significantly reduced as energy production and consumption moves away from fossil fuel based energy resources toward less carbon intensive energy resources.*
- *Emissions triple in the Baseline scenario, but can be kept at today's level in the ACT Map scenario if options up to a cost of USD 50/t CO_2 equivalents are implemented. Further emission reductions are technologically feasible but more costly. The main challenge is emissions from gas supply systems.*

Overview

Methane, the major component of natural gas, is also a potent greenhouse gas. It is 21 times more effective than CO_2 at trapping heat in the atmosphere over a 100-year time period.[1] Methane is the second-most significant greenhouse gas after CO_2, accounting for 16% of total climate forcing. The chemical lifetime of methane in the atmosphere is approximately 12 years. This relatively short atmospheric lifetime makes it an important candidate for mitigating global warming in the near term. Several studies (Fisher, *et al.*, 2007) have assessed the importance of mitigating methane emissions early, due to the immediate climate impacts that are realised.

14

This chapter presents the IEA's first analysis of the role of energy sector methane emissions in climate change. Including energy sector methane mitigation technologies in the ETP model show that methane mitigation offers the most significant potential to reduce greenhouse gas emissions in the near-term. This is due in part to the fact that, while methane is a greenhouse gas, it also has significant value as a commodity. With rising fuel prices in recent years, the value of methane as a fuel makes a number of reduction opportunities economically viable.

Methane is emitted from a variety of human-related (anthropogenic) and natural sources. Slightly over half of the total emissions result from human activity

1. The global warming potential of methane in the IPCC's Third Assessment Report (2001) is 23 over 100 years.

(UNEP, 2002). Anthropogenic sources include fossil fuel production, agriculture (enteric fermentation in livestock, manure management and rice cultivation), biomass burning and waste management. Methane emissions vary significantly from one country or region to another, depending on factors such as climate, industrial and agricultural production, energy resources and usage, and waste management practices. Methane emissions from energy- and waste-related activities – the focus of this chapter – comprised approximately 36% of the global anthropogenic methane emissions in 2000.

Figure 14.1 ▶ Global greenhouse gas emissions in 2000 and anthropogenic methane sources

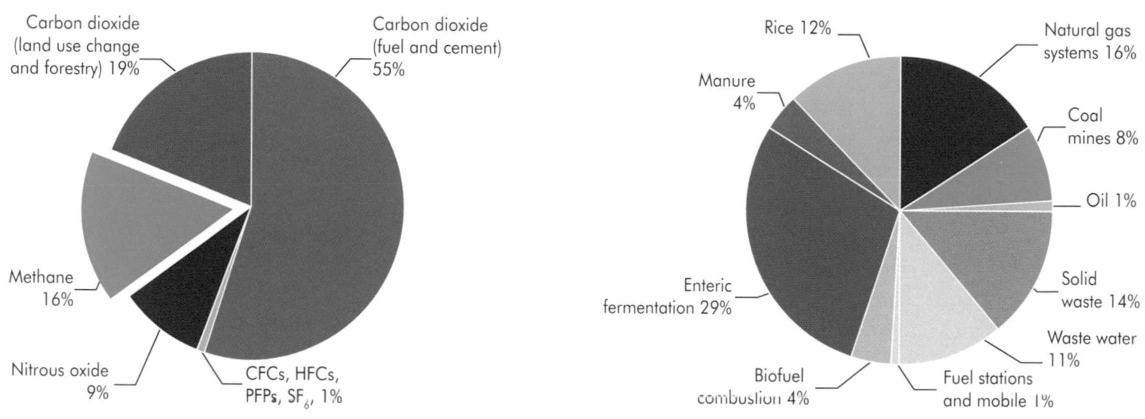

Source: US EPA, 2006.

Key point

Methane is the second most important greenhouse gas.

Since the mid-1700s, global average atmospheric concentrations of methane have increased 150%, from approximately 700 to 1 745 parts per billion by volume (ppbv) (IPCC, 2001). Although methane concentrations have continued to increase, the overall rate of growth during the past decade has slowed, largely due to mitigation efforts in several nations, including the European Union, the United States, Canada and Japan (US EPA, 2006). In the late 1970s, the growth rate was approximately 20 ppbv per year. In the 1980s, growth slowed to between 9 ppbv and 13 ppbv per year. From 1990 to 1998, methane grew by up to 13 ppbv per year (IPCC, 2001).

Current major sources of anthropogenic methane and emission reduction options

Natural gas and oil supply

Natural gas and oil systems account for 17% of total global methane emissions. Methane emissions mainly occur in these systems as the result of equipment or pipeline leaks and routine process- or maintenance-related venting activities. As the gas moves through system components under extreme pressure, methane can escape into the atmosphere through, for example, worn valves, flanges, pump seals, compressor seals, or joints or connections in pipelines. Methane emissions can also occur from standard oil and gas processes, such as releases from pneumatic controls operated by high-pressure natural gas.

As shown in Figure 14.2, Russia, the United States, Iran, Mexico and Ukraine contribute the most methane emissions from the natural-gas sector. Emissions are expected to increase over the next 15 years at an average annual rate of almost 3%, reflecting a projected increase in natural gas use as a share of total energy consumption (US EPA, 2003). Developing countries are expected to account for the largest percentage increases in emissions, as a result of increases in their production and consumption of natural gas.

Figure 14.2 ▶ Methane emissions from natural gas systems

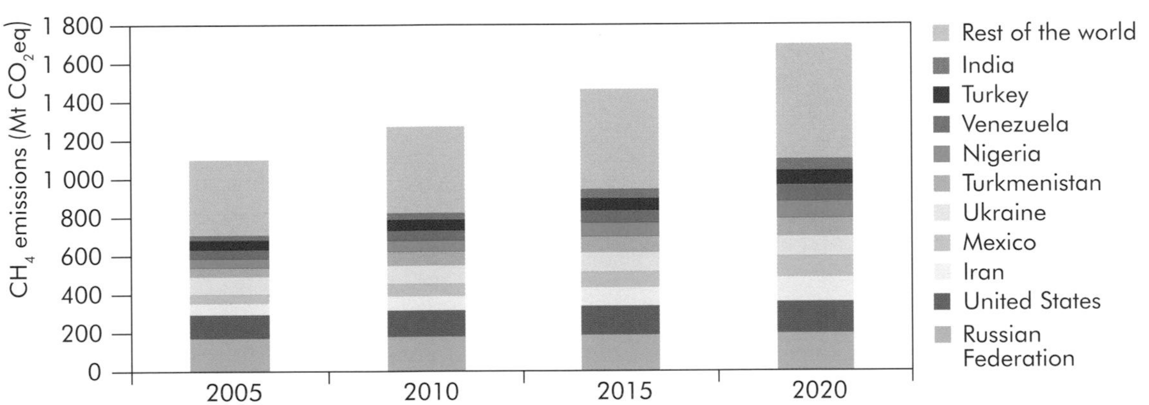

Source: US EPA, 2006.

Key point

Methane emissions from the gas sector are expected to increase more than 50% from 2005 to 2020. Iran, Mexico, Turkmenistan and India are projected to have the largest growth in Baseline emissions.

In oil and natural-gas systems, opportunities to reduce methane emissions generally fall into one of three categories:

- technology or equipment upgrades, such as low-emission regulator valves, that reduce or eliminate equipment venting or fugitive emissions;
- improvements in management practices and operational procedures to reduce process venting;
- enhanced leak detection and measurement programmes that take advantage of improved measurement or emission reduction technologies.

Figure 14.3 ▶ Selected national trends for oil system methane emissions

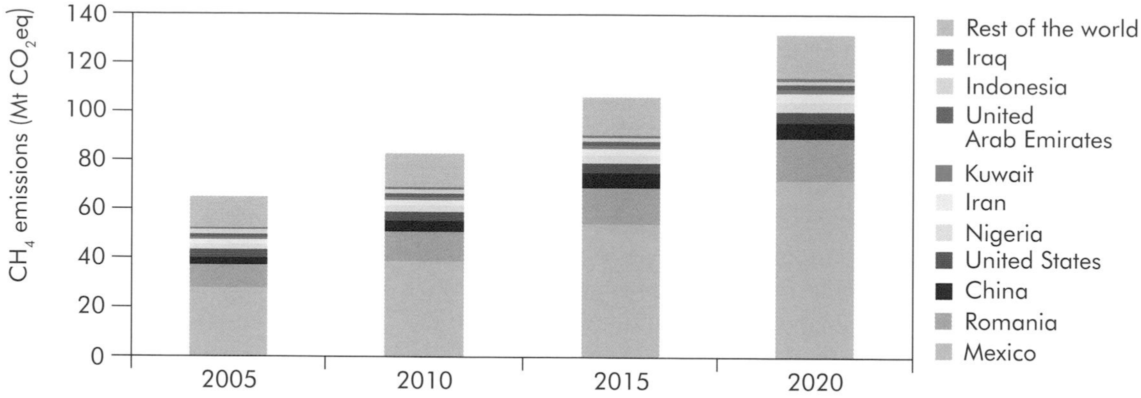

Source: US EPA, 2006.

Key point

While small today, methane emissions from oil systems are expected to increase in a number of countries, including Mexico, Romania and China.

Cost effective opportunities for reducing methane emissions in the oil and gas sector vary greatly from country to country based on major emission sources and physical and institutional infrastructure. Many abatement options and technologies, however, are capable of generic application. For example, directed inspection and maintenance (DI&M) programmes use a variety of leak detection and measurement technologies to identify and quantify leaks. This allows operators to identify the largest methane leak sources, leading to more accurate, efficient and cost-effective leak repairs. DI&M programmes can be applied to gas production, processing, transmission, and distribution operations wherever they take place. In countries with large oil and gas infrastructures, such as Russia and the United States, the wider application of these programmes has the potential to yield both substantial methane emission reductions and gas savings.

Coal mines

Coal mining contributes 8% of total global anthropogenic methane emissions, with the largest emissions coming from China, the United States, India, Australia, Russia, Ukraine and North Korea (Figure 14.4). Methane is a component of underground coal seams that is adsorbed onto the surface of coal and may accumulate in interstitial spaces. It is released during coal-mining operations. Many factors affect the quantity of methane released, including the gas content of the coal, the permeability and porosity of the coal seams, the method of mining used, and the production capacity of the mining operation. More than 90% of fugitive methane emissions from the coal sector come from underground coal mining. Abandoned (closed) underground coal mines also emit methane, depending on the extent to which the mine has been sealed or the extent to which it has flooded.

Coal methane emissions are projected to grow 20% from 2000 to 2020, as technology improvements enable the extraction of coal from increasingly greater depths. China is projected to have the largest increase in coal methane emissions (from 31% to 42% of worldwide emissions). This is a result of China's rapid economic growth, as it is projected to almost double its coal consumption by 2025 (United States Energy Information Administration, 2004).

Figure 14.4 ▶ Methane emissions from coal mines

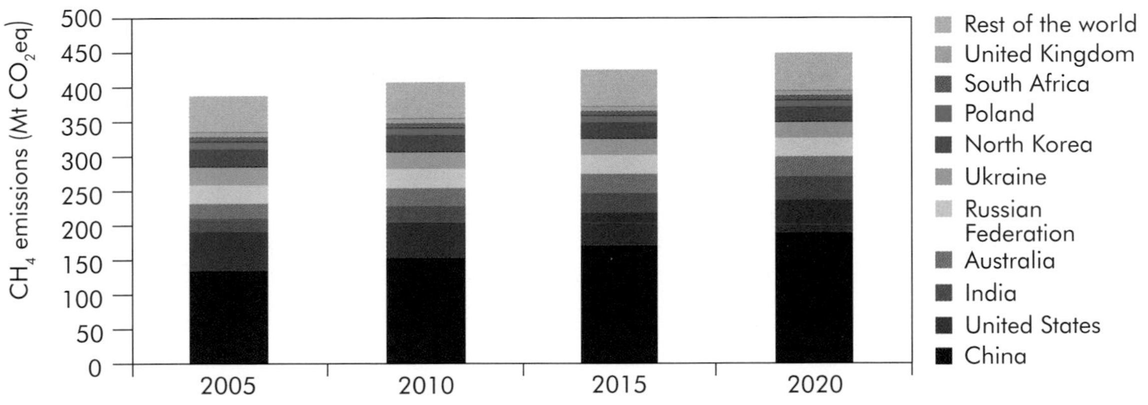

Source: US EPA, 2006.

Key point

China, India and Australia are expected to have the largest increases in coal mine methane emissions by 2020.

At active underground mines, methane must be removed for safety reasons. This is done primarily with large-scale ventilation systems that move massive quantities of air through the mines. These ventilation systems release large amounts of methane at very low concentrations. At some active mines, methane is also removed from the mine through degasification systems (also referred to as gas drainage systems) that employ vertical or horizontal wells to recover methane. Degasification wells may also be used to recover methane gas from abandoned underground mines.

There are a variety of profitable uses for coal mine methane (CMM).[2] The best use at a given location is dependent on factors such as project economics, the quality of methane and the availability of end-use options. CMM end-use options include injection into natural-gas pipelines, electricity generation, co-firing in boilers, district heating, vehicle fuel, and manufacturing and industrial uses (such as feedstock for carbon black and methanol and dimethyl ether production). For low-concentration methane in mine ventilation air, oxidisation technologies have been developed that produce thermal energy for heat, electricity, and refrigeration.

2. Coal mine methane should be distinguished from coal bed methane: coal mine methane is the gas that is released immediately prior to or during coal mining activities, and thus has climate change impacts; coal bed methane is harvested as a natural gas resource.

Solid waste management

Municipal solid waste management contributes 13% of total global methane emissions. Methane is produced through the natural process of the bacterial decomposition of organic waste under anaerobic conditions in sanitary landfills and open dumps. Methane makes up approximately 50% of landfill gas (LFG), the balance being mostly CO_2 mixed with small quantities of other gases. If LFG is not actively collected, it escapes into the atmosphere.

The United States, China, Russia, Canada and Southeast Asia are the main contributors of methane emissions from solid waste management. As shown in Figure 14.5, methane emissions from landfills are expected to decrease in industrialised countries and increase in developing countries. Industrialised countries' baselines are expected to decline as the result of expanded recycling and composting programmes, increased regulatory requirements to capture and combust LFG, and improved LFG recovery technologies. Developing countries' LFG emissions are expected to increase due to expanding populations, combined with a trend away from open dumps to sanitary landfills with increased anaerobic conditions conducive to methane production.

Figure 14.5 ▶ **Methane emissions from solid waste management**

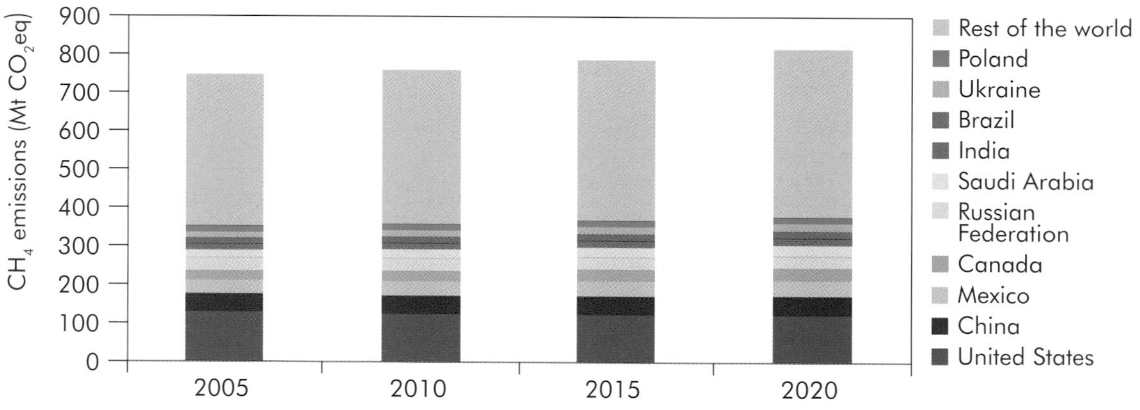

Source: US EPA, 2006.

Key point

While OECD countries have stabilised methane emissions from solid waste management, non-OECD countries are expected to see increasing emissions as they transition from open dumps to sanitary land-filling practices.

LFG can be extracted from landfills using a series of wells and a vacuum system that directs the collected gas to a point to be processed. From there, the LFG can be used for a variety of purposes, for example to produce electricity or as an alternative fuel for local industrial customers or other organisations that need a constant fuel supply. Such "direct use" of LFG is reliable and requires minimal processing and minor modifications to existing combustion equipment. A third emerging option is to create pipeline-quality gas or alternative vehicle fuel.

Modelling approach and results

Characterisation of scenario analysis

Additional analysis has been carried out to study the potential contribution of methane mitigation in the energy and waste sectors to overall greenhouse gas reductions. This analysis is based on three scenarios: the Baseline scenario, the ACT Map scenario, and a methane-mitigation variant scenario known as ACTM. In the ACTM variant, a CO_2 incentive is imposed on CO_2 and methane emissions in OECD countries. This incentive starts from USD 10/t CO_2eq in 2010, reaches USD 50/t CO_2eq in 2025, and remains constant thereafter. In non-OECD regions, the same profile has been assumed, but is introduced (depending on the region) 10 to 20 years later. The ACT Map scenario excludes energy- and waste-sector methane mitigation options, while the ACTM scenario includes these options. In addition to the ACTM scenario with a CO_2 incentive of USD 50/t CO_2eq, further variants of the ACTM scenario with CO_2 incentive levels of USD 10/t CO_2eq and USD 25/t CO_2eq have been analysed (ACT10M, ACT25M) to explore the possibility that mitigation may be cost-effective at these lower CO_2 incentive levels.

Modelling of methane mitigation

Methane sources included in this analysis are: emissions from coal mining; emissions from oil production; and emissions from gas production, transportation and distribution. Estimates of the emission factors relevant to different activities are based on data provided by the United States Environmental Protection Agency (US EPA, 2006). These emission factors and the underlying activities determine methane emissions in the Baseline and ACT Map scenarios, where emissions abatement options are not available. All scenarios also include an estimate for emissions from solid waste management, based on regional projections (US EPA, 2006).

The ACTM variants include specified methane emissions mitigation measures in the coal, oil, gas and waste sectors. The costs and potentials for the different mitigation measures are based on an assessment by the United States Environmental Protection Agency, which includes data and analysis from several international sources (de la Chesnaye, and Weyant, 2006; US EPA 2006). Figure 14.6 illustrates the modelling approach that was utilised for the coal sector. The choice and degree to which a mitigation option is implemented is determined by the model, driven by factors such as the investment and operating costs of the option, the price of natural gas and the CO_2 incentive.

Figure 14.6 ▶ Modelling of methane mitigation options from coal mining

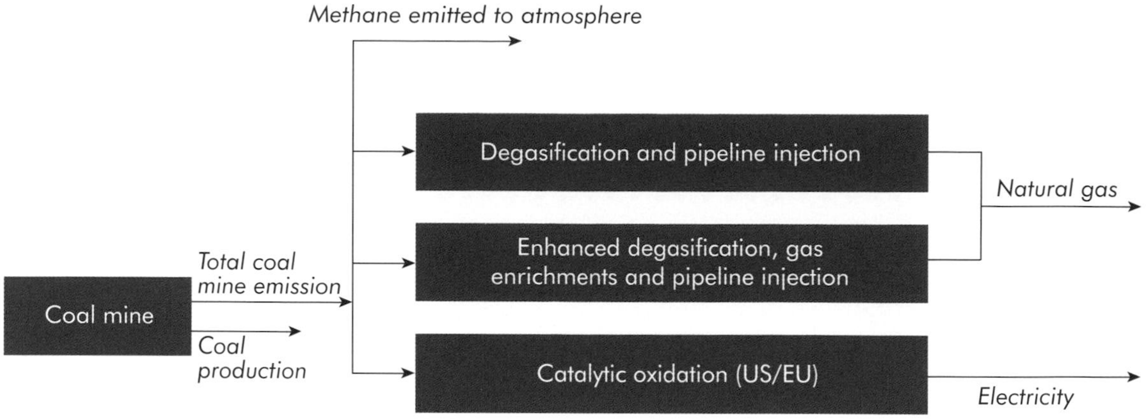

Methane emitted to atmosphere
Degasification and pipeline injection
Enhanced degasification, gas enrichments and pipeline injection
Catalytic oxidation (US/EU)
Natural gas
Electricity
Coal mine
Total coal mine emission
Coal production

Source: US EPA, 2006.

Thirty-three mitigation measures have been included for the natural-gas sector, two for the oil sector, five for the coal mining sector and five for the solid waste sector.

Scenario results

Global methane emissions more than triple in the Baseline scenario – from 2 140 Mt CO_2eq in 2010 to 7 420 Mt in 2050 (Figure 14.7). This growth is mainly driven by emissions from rapid growth in gas production and transportation in the former Soviet Union, the Middle East and Africa, and to a smaller extent by coal-mining activities in Asia, especially China. An important conclusion is that, while global growth in methane emissions has slowed in recent decades, this trend is not expected to continue without additional greenhouse gas mitigation measures, as the coal and natural-gas sectors are growing rapidly in developing regions and economies in transition.

Even though methane mitigation options are not included in the ACT Map scenario, methane emissions are projected to be significantly reduced in this scenario, especially after 2030. This is due to the CO_2 incentive, which results in reduced consumption of natural gas (-16% relative to the baseline) and coal (-62% relative to the baseline), both driven by a shift to less carbon-intensive resources.

In the ACTM variants, methane mitigation options are available after 2005. In all ACTM variants, significant methane reductions occur before 2015: a 37% reduction (925 Mt CO_2eq) compared to the Baseline scenario. These early methane-emission reductions are realised, as shown in Figure 14.8, primarily in the gas (496 Mt CO_2eq), coal (214 Mt CO_2eq) and waste sectors (365 Mt CO_2eq). After this initial reduction, methane emissions begin to rise again until 2050. This growth in emissions is seen in all scenarios.

Beyond 2015, the plot of methane emissions is very similar in all the ACTM variants. This suggests that most methane mitigation options are viable at an incentive of USD 10/t CO_2eq. Above that incentive level, there may also be increased competition from other greenhouse-gas mitigation options in the medium term, as expected cost decreases occur in key technologies such as CO_2 capture and storage and renewable electricity and heat generation. Increasing the incentive from USD 25/t CO_2eq to USD 50/t CO_2eq yields an additional methane reduction of only 550 Mt CO_2eq, mainly from the oil and gas sectors.

Figure 14.7 ▶ Global methane emissions in the Baseline, ACT Map and ACTM scenarios

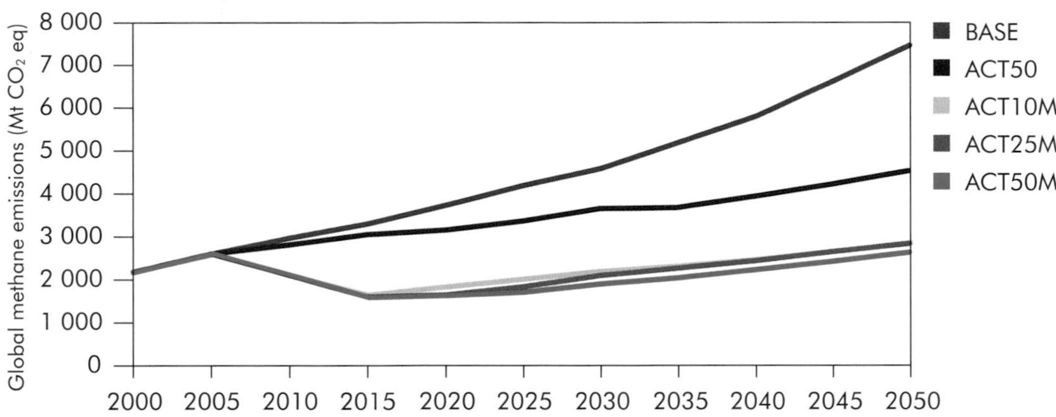

Source: IEA analysis.

Key point

The most dramatic methane-emissions reduction opportunity is expected to occur in the near term i.e., before 2015. After this initial reduction, without further action, methane emissions grow in all scenarios.

Figure 14.8 ▶ Global methane emissions by sector in the Baseline, ACT Map and ACTM scenarios

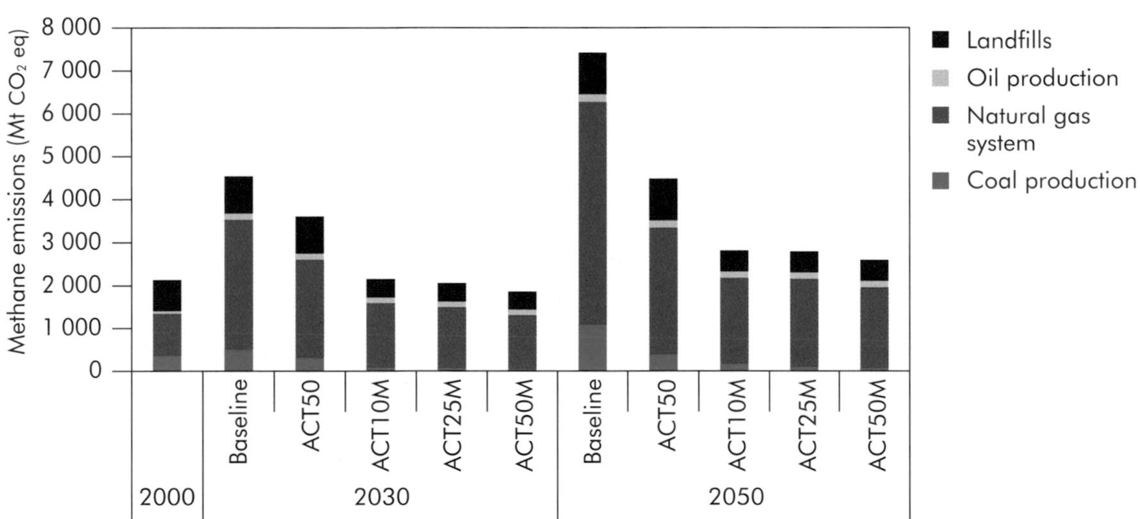

Source: IEA analysis.

Key point

Natural gas and coal mining are expected to make the largest contributions to future growth in methane emissions in all scenarios.

14

Challenges to deployment

This analysis highlights the opportunities for methane mitigation measures in the near-term, confirming other global analyses (de la Chesnaye and Weyant, 2006). However, as described below, methane mitigation technologies face challenges to deployment. This analysis also demonstrates that, due to the growth in coal and gas use, the trend of the past few decades of methane emissions stabilisation is not expected to continue, barring additional policy intervention.

One of the main challenges for the future development of methane mitigation projects is to increase awareness of the existence of methane emissions and the value of the lost fuel, particularly in countries such as China, Ukraine, India and Russia, which have rapidly growing energy and waste sectors. There are also legal and regulatory barriers to overcome in the areas of methane ownership at coal mines and landfills, reducing gas flaring and utilising associated gas, and obtaining access to the electricity grid to sell back power that is generated at landfills or coal mines. Efforts are underway to address these barriers. A number of countries have begun to regulate gas flaring in the oil and gas sector, with some success. In addition, a number of coal-mine methane projects in China have been negotiated under the auspices of the United Nations Framework Convention on Climate Change, (UNFCCC) Clean Development Mechanism (CDM). Also in China, regulations require LFG energy recovery for CDM project certification (*i.e.* LFG cannot simply be flared and qualify under CDM). As a result of China's success in attracting greenhouse-gas investors, other developing countries have begun to explore their methane emissions reduction opportunities. Separately, several countries have combined efforts via the international Methane to Markets Partnership, and are partnering with the private sector to identify and finance projects around the world, as well as to identify appropriate public policies to address key barriers (see box, "the Methane to Markets Partnership").

The Methane to Markets Partnership

Methane to Markets

The Methane to Markets Partnership is an international initiative that advances cost effective, near-term methane recovery and use as a clean energy source. The goal of the partnership is to reduce global methane emissions in order to enhance economic growth, strengthen energy security, improve air quality, improve industrial safety and reduce emissions of greenhouse gases. The partnership currently focuses on four sources of methane emissions: agriculture, coal mines, landfills, and the oil and gas industry. The partnership includes 21 countries with large sources of methane or special expertise and interest in developing methane projects. Partner countries account for approximately 60% of global methane emissions from the targeted sources. The partnership includes over 650 project network members. These are public and private organisations with experience or an interest in projects concerning methane recovery and use. In October 2007, Methane to Markets hosted the first International Project Expo in Beijing, China, which featured 91 new methane projects seeking investors (see www.methanetomarkets.org).

Chapter 15 TRANSPORT

Key Findings

- *Transport accounts for more than half the oil used worldwide and nearly 25% of energy-related CO_2 emissions. According to the ETP Baseline scenario, world transport energy use and emissions will increase by more than 50% by 2030 and will more than double by 2050. The fastest growth is expected to come from air travel, road freight and light-duty vehicle (car, small van and SUV) travel. Regionally, growth will be led by the developing world, especially China and India, as a function of expected high rates of income growth and increases in vehicle ownership.*

- *In the Baseline scenario, nearly all future fuel use in transport will continue to be fossil fuel. While conventional oil production is expected to peak and begin to decline, the shortfall is likely to be made up with non-conventional oil (such as tar sands) and fossil resources such as gas-to-liquids and (especially in China) coal-to-liquids. On average, these fuels are likely to be significantly more carbon intensive than oil. Such a future will be even less sustainable than present practice and creates even greater urgency to shift to a more sustainable, low-carbon transport system.*

- *The sector presents enormous challenges for achieving deep cuts in fuel use and GHG emissions. Critical technologies such as fuel cells and vehicle on-board energy storage (e.g. via batteries, ultra-capacitors and H_2 storage) are not yet technically mature or cost-effective, and it may be many years before they can deliver CO_2 reductions at a reasonable cost. However, there are a variety of other technologies that are already commercial and measures that are cost-effective. These should be pursued vigorously in the coming 5 to 15 years while ongoing efforts continue to bring down the cost of future technologies.*

- *Improving the fuel economy of light-duty vehicles (LDVs), is one of the most important and cost effective of available measures. With strong policies, available technologies have the potential to reduce the energy use per kilometre of new LDVs by up to 30% in the next 15 to 20 years, at very low cost after taking into account fuel savings. This is due to the availability of low-cost "incremental" technologies to improve engine/drive-train efficiency, tyres, aerodynamics and accessories such as air conditioning. Additional reductions (up to a 50% reduction in fuel intensity) are possible through hybridisation and the use of light-weight materials. But strong policies such as efficiency standards must also be put in place and tightened over time, in order to ensure that vehicles do not continue to increase in average size, weight and power.*

- *Increased investments in advanced public transit systems, such as "bus rapid transit", can help cities ensure that their residents have low cost, high quality mobility options. In particular, they can put the developing world's large cities on trajectories leading to much more sustainable transport systems (e.g. patterned after European rather than North American cities). Such cities typically already have high shares of public transit use, but these systems are often inadequate, spurring demand for private vehicles. The provision of better systems and infrastructure, along with effective urban and regional planning programmes, will require strong municipal governance along with technical and financial assistance from national governments and international bodies.*

- *In terms of freight movement, medium duty, urban-use trucks can benefit from substantial efficiency improvements, including hybridisation. Along with improved routing and logistics systems, they could achieve a cost-effective reduction in energy use per kilometre of up to 40% by 2030. Heavy-duty long-haul trucks already benefit from a very efficient propulsion system (diesel engines). However, these trucks can reduce their energy intensity by up to 40% via a combination of engine efficiency as well as cab and trailer (weight and aerodynamic) improvements, along with changes in usage patterns (e.g. reductions in empty travel). To achieve these improvements, governments will likely need to enact truck fuel efficiency regulations, which to date has only occurred in Japan.*
- *Rail accounts for a small share of transport energy use and GHG emissions (about 3%), but it holds the potential for significant growth in the future, particularly in the developing world. As an example, we estimate that if 25% of all air travel in 2050 under 750 kilometres were shifted to high-speed rail travel, around 0.5 Gt (gigatonnes) of CO_2 per year could be saved. Similarly, if 25% of all trucking over 500 kilometres were shifted to rail, about 0.4 Gt of CO_2 could be saved per year. This would require a dramatic increase in rail infrastructure investment around the world.*
- *International shipping accounts for about 80% of maritime energy use (domestic commercial shipping and recreational boating account for most of the rest). Strong growth in international shipping is expected as global trade continues to expand. Existing ships can be outfitted with energy-saving devices and be operated more efficiently, including the emergence of high-tech parachute-type sails to assist propulsion. Over the longer term, new ship designs can also help. Together, a package of measures appears capable of cutting average energy intensities by up to 30% by 2050. Alternative fuels – such as biofuels or possibly hydrogen – could also help. But achieving such changes will likely require strong international agreements and policies.*
- *Airlines and aircraft manufacturers have a strong incentive to improve aircraft energy efficiency, as fuel costs represent a significant (and rising) share of their operating expenses. New aircraft models incorporate many cost effective efficiency technologies and future aircraft are expected to keep improving. However, there are a number of measures available which, along with improvements in air-routing systems, could boost average fleet efficiency by up to 20% by 2050 beyond the 30% improvement expected in the Baseline scenario.*
- *Alternative fuels are likely to play an important role in getting to very low GHG emissions levels in transport by 2050. Over the next 10 to 15 years, the most cost-effective are likely to be biofuels, particularly cane ethanol from Brazil and perhaps from other developing countries. As described in Chapter 9, over time, second-generation biofuels such as ethanol from ligno-cellulosic feedstocks and synthetic diesel (and other fuels) from biomass gasification via Fischer-Tropsch processes may become important GHG reduction options, if sustainability concerns can be addressed.*

- *It is unlikely that a commercial, widespread system of hydrogen fuels for most modes of transport will emerge much before 2030, due to technical hurdles, high costs and extensive infrastructure requirements. High, sustained levels of RD&D appear critical to speeding this process. Certain modes, such as buses, offer some special opportunities, but also some disadvantages such as their small scale. If fuel cell vehicles can begin to be deployed by 2020, along with a massive fuel infrastructure investment effort, they could reach close to 100% of LDV sales in OECD countries by 2050, given a strong enough policy push. This would result in strong reductions in fuel use (due to efficiency benefits) and shifts to H_2 on the order of 500 Mtoe by 2050.*

- *Vehicle electrification is re-emerging as a potentially viable long-term option. Plug-in hybrids offer a potential near-term option as a means of transition to full electric vehicles. But battery costs are still two to three times as high as they will need to be to be commercially viable. Whether this can be achieved via large-scale battery production and learning from applications such as plug-ins is a critical uncertainty. In our scenarios, both plug-ins and pure electric vehicles show relatively high costs-per tonne of CO_2 reduction unless battery costs are reduced dramatically, to at least USD 300/kwh. More support is needed for battery RD&D and for the deployment of plug-in hybrid vehicles.*

- *If electric vehicles become more prevalent, more power generation will be needed. In the "EV Success" case, total transport electricity demand reaches 650 Mtoe in 2050, about 20% of total world electricity demand and probably requiring over 2 000 GW of additional capacity. In early days of plug-in hybrid and EV sales, much of the demand may involve night-time recharging with existing capacity, though as the stock of these vehicles grows, and particularly if quick-recharging technology emerges, substantial daytime charging will also occur, likely increasing peak demand in most regions. More research is needed in this area on a region-by-region basis.*

- *In the BLUE Map scenario, transport-wide CO_2 emissions are reduced overall to about 30% below the 2005 level by 2050 (i.e. about 70% below the Baseline scenario in 2050). As reflected in the ACT Map scenario, some of the reductions, particularly improved efficiencies, can be achieved quite cost-effectively. But the marginal costs may rise rapidly as countries turn to fuel switching to second-generation biofuels, hydrogen or electricity for major GHG reductions. In the BLUE Map scenario, the increasing use of fuel cell and electric vehicles after 2025 could provide CO_2 reductions with a cost as high as USD 500 per tonne, in the absence of improvements to reduce technology costs significantly. Increased RD&D over the next 15 years into energy storage systems, fuel cell systems and advanced biofuels systems appears critical to bringing down the longer-term costs of CO_2 reduction in transport.*

Overview

Since 1990, the transport sector's CO_2 emissions worldwide have increased by 36%. In 2005, transport accounted for 23% of global energy-related CO_2 emissions, up from 21% in 1990. On a well-to-wheels basis (*i.e.* including emissions from feedstock and fuel production and distribution to vehicles), transport GHG emissions account for close to 27% of total emissions.

This chapter provides an overview of the status and prospects for technologies that could help reduce transport CO_2 emissions. It reviews the current status of those technologies by mode (LDVs, trucks, aviation, etc.) and explores some of the technological and policy developments that will be necessary to achieve a low-CO_2 transport future at reasonable cost. It also outlines the key assumptions behind the *Energy Technology Perspectives* (ETP) transport scenarios.

For each mode, technologies are available that can improve efficiency, enable the use of alternative fuels and, in some cases, provide opportunities for modal shifts or for reductions in travel with minimal loss (or possible gain) in consumer utility. This analysis does not include changes that would be likely to reduce utility (*e.g.* by forcing reductions in travel), such as via higher fuel taxes.

A substantial potential for CO_2 reduction via low-cost (or net negative cost) improvements in energy efficiency appears to exist for light-duty vehicles and other transport modes. However, the costs of some technologies and options, especially related to fuel switching, are currently high. They may remain high for many years unless strongly supportive actions are taken in the near term. Policies that are designed to influence the vehicle and fuel mix – by incentivising low-carbon vehicles and fuels, for example – are likely to play an important role in bringing technologies into the market. In addition, continuing R&D is necessary to improve technologies and lower their costs as far as possible. As new technologies start to enter the market, technology learning (see Chapter 5) will continue to play a critical role in achieving cost-effective CO_2 reductions.

Current status and trends

Despite rising oil prices and concerns about the climate, energy use for transport is increasing around the world. High growth rates are forecast for most travel modes for decades to come. Two main factors influence the sector's emissions: changes in the volume of travel and changes in the efficiency of the mode of transport used. Regarding volume, between 1990 and 2004, travel in light-duty vehicles in OECD countries increased by about 20%, from about 13 000 to 15 000 kilometres per person per year. Truck travel (tonne kilometres per capita) increased by 36%. Air travel has grown by over 5% worldwide per year since 1990. While these growth rates are likely to slow down over time, there are no indications that they will reverse. In the developing world, precise growth rates are often uncertain, but given the still very low average rates of automobile ownership, and high expected GDP growth rates, vehicle travel is expected to show strong growth for many years to come.

Increases in transport efficiency have only partially offset this growth in volume. And the rate of efficiency improvement has been declining. As a result, in recent years transport energy use and GHG emissions have steadily increased. Across IEA countries, the average energy intensity of the car stock decreased by around 10% between 1990 and 2004 (although there are wide variations by country). Across all truck classes, average energy intensity per tonne kilometre of travel decreased by a similar percent. These improvements, while significant, were below 1% per year, and hence well below the rates of travel growth. Air travel efficiency has shown the best performance of any mode, with the stock of commercial aircraft achieving about a 30% improvement in OECD countries. But this is still well below the increase in the volume of air travel over that time period.

IEA trends in energy intensity by mode for passenger and freight transport are shown in Figure 15.1. This shows the very slow improvements in average efficiency apart from in passenger air travel over recent years. It also highlights the much higher energy intensities of some modes compared to, for example, mass transit modes (buses and rail) and bulk freight modes (shipping and rail).

Figure 15.1 ▶ Average energy intensities of the passenger travel and freight movement in IEA countries, 1990-2004

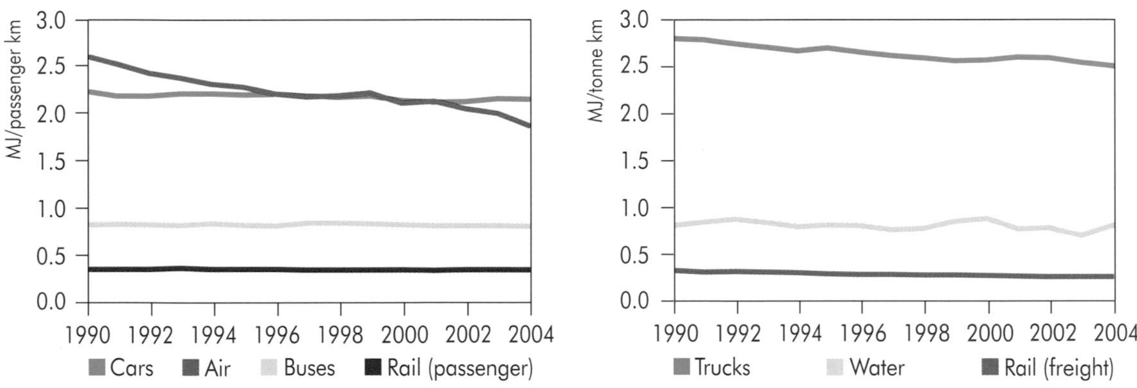

Key point

Though energy efficiency has improved only slowly for most modes, some modes are far more efficient than others.

Achieving deep reductions in transport greenhouse gas emissions over the next 50 years will be heavily dependent on the achievement of much greater rates of efficiency improvement and lower growth rates in travel, especially for the more energy-intensive modes. Passenger and freight shifts to more efficient modes will also have a contribution to make. And potentially very-low-carbon fuels such as biofuels, electricity and hydrogen will almost certainly be needed in order to achieve significant reductions in the carbon intensity of transport fuel use.

Scenario results

As part of the *Energy Technology Perspectives 2008* scenario development process, given the high degree of uncertainty surrounding key technological developments, a multi-scenario approach was used to depict several possible futures that could achieve the target GHG emissions reductions implicit in the BLUE scenario. Three sets of assumptions were made in these BLUE scenario variants: (a) the technological and economic success of fuel-cell vehicles ("FCV success"), (b) the success of electric vehicles ("EV success"), and (c) the long-term potential (given both technology and land use constraints) for the production of biofuels for transport. The assumptions used in each variant are shown in Table 15.1.

Table 15.1 ▶ Assumptions in ETP transport scenarios

		Baseline	ACT Map
Definition		Baseline projection	Based on ETP 2006, strong but co effective measures
LDVs	**New LDV fuel economy improvement**	10-25% lower fuel use in 2050, depending on region	50% reduction in new LDV fuel/km 2050 (includes hybrids but no EVs FCVs.)
	Gasoline and diesel hybrids	5-15% market share in 2050 depending on region	75-95% market share in 2050 depending on region
	Electric plug-in hybrids	none	Beginning in 2020, hybrid vehicles re 20% travel on electricity by 2050
	Electric vehicles	none	none
	Fuel cell vehicles	none	none
	Travel	Total woldwide LDV travel about triples between 2000 and 2050	15% lower in 2050 than Baseline du modal switch and telematic substituti
Trucks		20% on-road efficiency improvement by 2050	Average 35% efficiency improveme including 50% hybridisation by 205
Buses		10% improvement by 2050 including 5% hybrids	40% improvement by 2050 including 50% hybrids
Rail		5% more efficient in 2050	15% more efficient in 2050
Air		Aircraft stock 30% more efficient in 2050	Stock 35% more efficient in 2050 an 5% routing improvement
Water		10% more efficient in 2050	20% more efficient in 2050
Travel (non-LDV)		Baseline travel (more than doubles for most modes)	Up to 10% reduction for air, trucking 2050; up to 25% increase for buses, rail due to mode switching
Biofuels		Stays below 100 Mtoe, mostly first generation	About 570 Mtoe in 2050, mostly 2nd generation
Low GHG hydrogen		No H_2	No H_2
Low GHG electricity		30 Mtoe (mainly for rail)	130 Mtoe mostly for plug-ins

BLUE Map	BLUE conservative	BLUE FCV success	BLUE EV success
ͻreater use of biofuels, eployment of EVs, FCVs	Stronger efficiency gains than ACT, more biofuels, no pure EVs or FCVs	By 2050, FCVs dominant for cars and light/medium trucks	By 2050, EVs dominant for cars and light/medium trucks
)% reduction in new LDV fuel/km by 2050 from FCVs and EVs	60% reduction in new LDV fuel/km by 2050	70% reduction in new LDV fuel use by 2050 from FCVs	70% reduction in new LDV fuel use by 2050 from EVs
ıbout 70% market share 2030, dropping to 35% '050 due to EVs and FCVs	About 75% sales share in 2030, rising to 100% in 2050	About 60% sales share in 2030, dropping to 10% in 2050 due to FCV sales	About 60% sales share in 2030, dropping to 10% in 2050 due to EV sales
eginning in 2015, hybrid vehicles reach 60% electric share by 2050	Beginning in 2015, hybrid vehicles reach 40% electric share by 2050	Beginning in 2020, hybrid vehicles reach 20% electric share by 2050	Beginning in 2015, hybrid vehicles reach 75% electric share by 2050
Reach 20% of LDV sales in 2050	none	none	Reach 90% of LDV sales in 2050
each 40% of LDV sales in 2050	none	Reach 90% of LDV sales in 2050	none
Same as ACT Map	Same as ACT Map	Same as ACT Map	Same as ACT Map
ːVs and EVs each reach up to 25% of stock by 2050	Average 45% efficiency improvement; hybrids reach 80% of stock by 2050; no FCVs or EVs	FCVs reach 60% of medium truck stock by 2050, 30% of heavy	EVs reach 50% of medium truck stock by 2050, 25% of heavy
0% improvement by 2050 including 75% hybrids	Same as BLUE Map	Same as BLUE Map	Same as BLUE Map
;0% more efficient in 2050	25% more efficient in 2050	Same as BLUE Map	Same as BLUE Map
Stock 45% more efficient in 2050 and 10% routing improvement	Stock 40% more efficient in 2050 and 10% routing improvement	Same as BLUE Map	Same as BLUE Map
;0% more efficient in 2050, 30% biofuels	30% more efficient in 2050, no biofuels	Same as BLUE Map	Same as BLUE Map
Jp to 15% reduction for air, ucking; up to 35% increase for buses, rail due to mode switching	Same as BLUE Map	Same as BLUE Map	Same as BLUE Map
ıbout 700 Mtoe in 2050, all 2nd gen, mostly BTL	about 650 Mtoe in 2050, all 2nd gen, mostly BTL	About 540 Mtoe in 2050, mostly BTL	About 520 Mtoe in 2050, mostly BTL
260 Mtoe in 2050	No H_2	570 Mtoe in 2050	No H_2
320 Mtoe in 2050 for plug-ins and pure EVs	170 Mtoe in 2050 for plug-ins	100 Mtoe in 2050 for plug-ins	650 Mtoe in 2050

15

The ACT Map scenario envisages a strong push for faster improvements in technical efficiency and in the uptake of advanced biofuels to help cut the growth of carbon-intensive fossil energy use in transport. All ACT Map measures are estimated to cost less than USD 50 per tonne of CO_2 saved by 2050, and most achieve this by or before 2030. In the BLUE Map scenario, this push is even stronger, allowing the penetration of electric and fuel cell vehicles that could cost up to USD 500 per tonne of CO_2 saved, but below USD 200 if cost reduction targets can be achieved. In all scenarios, a small contribution is assumed from modal shifts and reductions in travel growth in the most energy intensive modes linked to technical innovations and investments: such as investments in bus rapid transit systems and high-speed rail.

A comparison of fuel use in the three main *Energy Technology Perspectives* (ETP) scenarios is shown in Figure 15.2 (other BLUE scenario variants are shown in Figure 2.21 in Chapter 2). The reduction in fuel use between the different scenarios is substantial by 2030 and about twice as large by 2050. Fossil fuel (*i.e.* oil, gas-to-liquids, coal-to-liquids) changes from being the dominant fuel type in the Baseline scenario to accounting for less than half of the total fuel used in the BLUE Map scenario in 2050.

Figure 15.2 ▶ Energy use by year and scenario

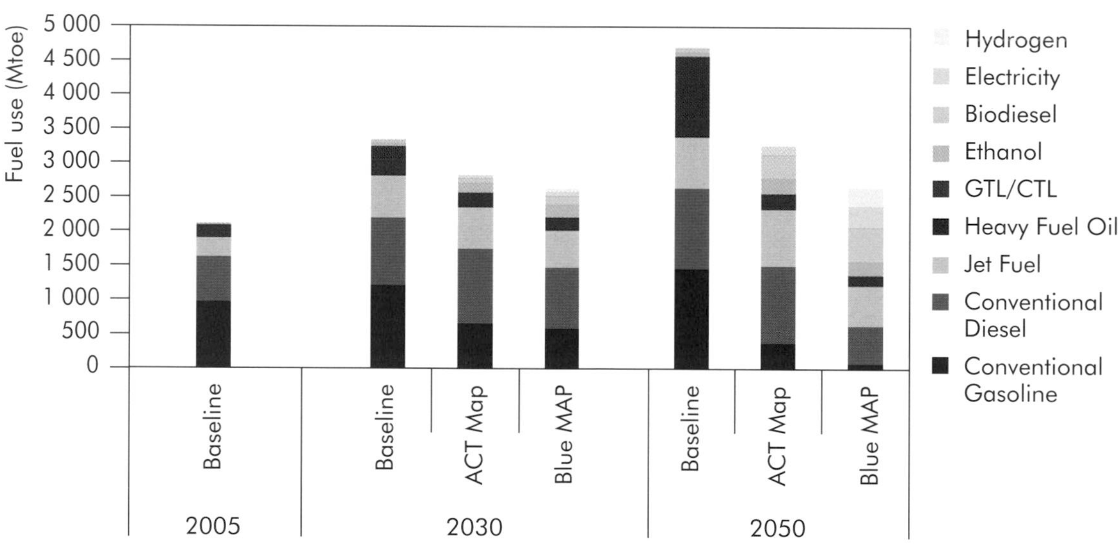

Key point

Reductions in fuel use from efficiency improvements dominate in the ACT Map scenario, while in the BLUE scenario, efficiency improvements are complemented to a greater degree with increased use of alternative fuels.

In the BLUE Map scenario, nearly all biofuels after 2020 are assumed to be advanced "second-generation", low-GHG types, and hydrogen and electricity come increasingly from near-zero-GHG-generation sources. As a result, the GHG profiles of the variant scenarios closely track their relative fossil-fuel use levels. Figure 15.3 shows, by case, region and year, the CO_2-equivalent greenhouse gas emissions on a life-cycle or "well-to-wheels" basis, *i.e.* showing upstream as well as vehicle emissions. (CO_2 emissions reductions by BLUE variant case and source of the reduction are shown in Figure 2.24 in Chapter 2).

CO_2 emissions in 2050 are cut by about 45% in the ACT Map scenario, and by about 70% in the BLUE Map scenario, compared to the Baseline scenario. All major regions show fairly similar cuts in CO_2, since by 2050 they have fairly similar stocks of vehicles and benefit from similar improvements in vehicle efficiency and the introduction of low-GHG alternative fuels. Hydrogen fuel cell vehicles and electric vehicles are assumed to penetrate with a five- to ten-year lag in non-OECD countries compared to OECD countries, but by 2050 their overall penetrations are fairly similar. Regional reductions for other BLUE variants are similar to those in the BLUE Map scenario.

Figure 15.3 ▶ CO_2 emissions for all scenarios in 2050

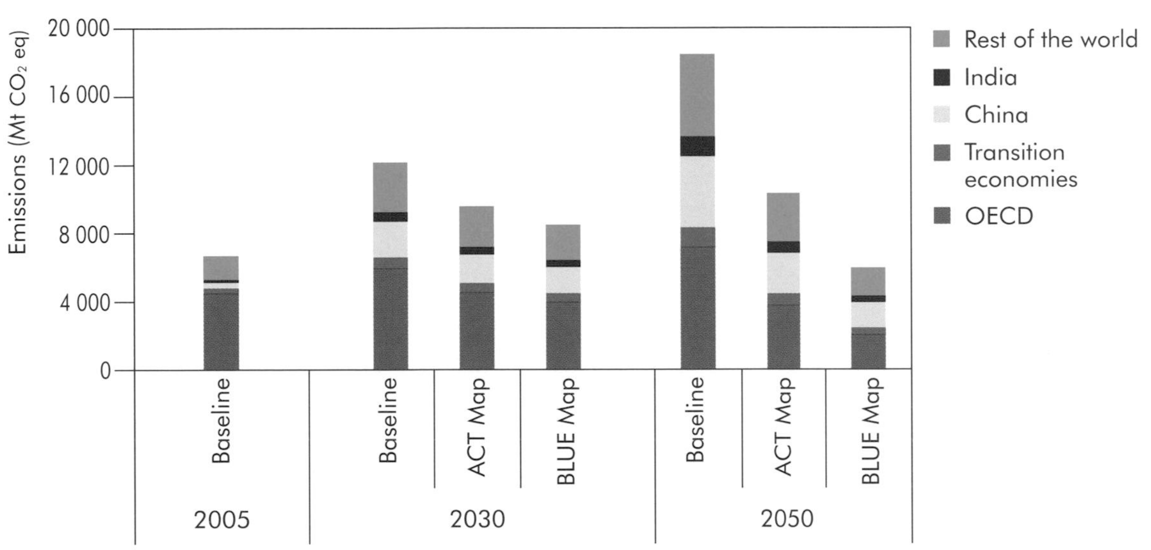

Note: The H_2 and electricity contributions include both the fuel-switching benefits and the vehicle efficiency benefits. The efficiency part of the bar includes only improvements to conventional gasoline and diesel vehicles.

Key point

By 2050, reductions in CO_2 in ACT Map and BLUE Map represent similar percentages in each region, relative to the Baseline scenario.

The extent to which different scenarios play out will depend on both the success of different technologies in terms of reaching technical and cost reduction targets, and the success of policies to deploy them (introduce and sustain them in the market until they reach a fully commercial status). To achieve the outcomes envisaged in the BLUE variants, society may need to accept fairly high costs during deployment periods, unless major technical breakthroughs are achieved. Once deployment does begin, cost reduction through scale and experience (as captured in the ETP analysis using estimated learning curves) will likely be needed to reach full commercialisation. This is further discussed in Chapters 4 and 5.

Alternative fuels: status and prospects

To achieve very low carbon intensity in transport, it will be necessary to shift away from fossil fuels to one or more low GHG fuels, *i.e.* biofuels, and to electricity and hydrogen from low-GHG sources. Biofuels are discussed in Chapter 9.

Electricity

Currently, the primary use of electricity in transport is in passenger rail systems. Electricity's share of transport fuel is below 1%. However, electricity is likely to play an increasing role in transport as in other sectors. In the future, electricity could be used to help power most types of vehicles, particularly cars, some types of trucks and most rail systems. For light-duty vehicles, electricity is increasingly used on board to power accessories and even core functions like steering. It is also generated on board, *e.g.* by the engine in hybrid vehicles. In the longer run, however, as electricity storage systems on vehicles improve, vehicles may be plugged into the grid to recharge. Such vehicles will be able to operate for some percentage of the time completely or primarily on grid electricity (discussed below in Light-duty vehicle section).

If electricity can be produced sustainably (*i.e.* with low net GHG emissions) and if electricity storage systems on vehicles improve, then together they can contribute to decarbonising transportation. The extent of this decarbonisation will depend on the availability of low carbon electricity, the extent of technological developments in vehicles and storage systems (*e.g.* batteries), as well as on a shift to transport modes and vehicle types that can use electricity as a fuel.

For long-haul trucking and international shipping, it appears unlikely that electricity will be important as a fuel unless batteries become far more advanced, since current batteries do not come close to the range needed in these modes. For most types of aircraft, electricity is not considered a serious option for primary propulsion.

Electricity costs per kilometre of vehicle travel are likely to be fairly low, given the expected cost of generating even low-CO_2 electricity and the high efficiency of vehicles running on batteries. Electricity use by vehicles is discussed in the light-duty vehicle section of this chapter. Electricity generation issues and technologies are discussed in a number of preceding chapters.

Hydrogen

Like electricity, hydrogen is an emerging fuel for transport. And like electricity, its use will depend on new types of vehicle propulsion and energy storage systems. Unlike electricity, however, there is no major hydrogen production or distribution system anywhere in the world today.

In transportation, hydrogen can be used directly in internal combustion engines. But it is most likely to be used in conjunction with fuel cell propulsion systems. These are very efficient devices that allow the generation of electricity which can then be used to power electrical motors. Fuel cells are currently very expensive, however, and they are not technically mature. The same is true for vehicle on-board storage of hydrogen. Fuel cells are discussed later in the chapter.

One way to reduce the costs associated with producing and storing hydrogen might be to produce it on-board vehicles using conventional fuels. While this is possible (*e.g.* by on board reforming of liquid or other gaseous fuels such as methane), it has so far proven too cumbersome and expensive, at least for light-duty vehicle applications. It will also result in CO_2 emissions if powered by a fossil fuel. As a result, on-board hydrogen generation appears unlikely to be attractive on technical, economic or environmental grounds.

For hydrogen to play a significant role, there will need to be massive changes to both vehicle design/production practices, and to fuel production/distribution/delivery systems. The use of hydrogen and fuel cells appears most likely for cars, buses and urban-duty trucks (*e.g.* delivery trucks), at least in the near-medium term. The rail sector could also be a user of hydrogen, possibly using larger fuel cells developed for stationary applications. Applications for long-haul trucks, shipping and aircraft are possible, but they are likely to suffer from difficulties with extended range requirements in relation to refuelling, or (especially in the case of shipping) competition with relatively efficient diesel engines and inexpensive fuel.

The use of hydrogen would provide a variety of benefits: very high fuel efficiency; near-zero pollution from vehicle operation (for hydrogen coupled with fuel cells and electrical motors); and near-zero greenhouse gases if the hydrogen is produced from low-GHG sources or with carbon capture. However, its drawbacks include a shorter range than for liquid fuelled vehicles, possibly long refuelling times and, most importantly, higher costs. Given oil prices assumed in these scenarios, hydrogen fuel costs are likely to be two to three times the cost of gasoline or diesel per unit of energy produced. However, much of this cost can be offset by the greater efficiency of fuel-cell vehicles. Vehicle costs are discussed in the following sections.

About 40 million tonnes of H_2 per year (less than 0.5% of world energy use) is currently produced for refinery and industrial uses by natural gas reforming, coal gasification or water electrolysis (CAN-Europe, 2003). These are established technologies for hydrogen production. However, to produce high volumes of cost effective hydrogen for energy use, these technologies would need to be significantly more efficient and less expensive. RD&D efforts are focussed on high efficiency gas reforming, coal gasification in IGCC plants, and electrolysis at high temperature and pressure. A number of new technologies, such as the use of solar and nuclear heat to split water, biomass gasification, and photo-biological processes, are also being developed. They are at different levels of development, but none is close to being commercial.

In addition, the prospects for producing hydrogen from renewable electricity are limited, even in the long term. While a substantial part of the electricity supply may be based on renewables by 2050, the availability of surplus renewable electricity for hydrogen production will probably be limited to a few world regions. If the hydrogen were produced from fossil fuels, CCS would be necessary.

Small-scale, decentralised, natural gas reforming (without CO_2 capture) and electrolysis appear to be the technologies of choice to produce hydrogen in the early market introduction phase. Most current RD&D focuses on decentralised production technologies, as these do not require any costly infrastructure for hydrogen transportation and distribution. However, decentralised technologies are relatively inefficient and expensive. In addition, CCS is not cost efficient with decentralised natural gas reforming, and electrolysis is even more expensive.

Current decentralised hydrogen production costs more than USD 50/GJ (USD 1.60/Lge), but various centralised production options promise, in the long run, hydrogen at USD 10/GJ to USD 15/GJ (USD 0.35/Lge to USD 0.50/Lge). While retail H_2 prices will be sensitive to feedstock (*e.g.* natural gas and electricity) prices, the cost of natural gas reforming may be reduced to less than USD 15/GJ H_2 by 2030 and electrolysis to less than USD 20/GJ H_2 (USD 0.70/Lge). The projected cost of hydrogen from coal gasification in centralised IGCC plants with CCS is even lower – below USD 10/GJ. Long-term costs for high-temperature water splitting could range from USD 10/GJ (using nuclear) to USD 20/GJ (using solar heat). Higher costs are projected for other technologies (IEA, 2005).

In addition to production facilities, infrastructure will need to be developed to distribute, store and deliver H_2 to vehicles. The overall investment cost for this infrastructure, worldwide, is likely to be in the trillions of US dollars. Overall, the retail price of hydrogen for transportation users, reflecting all feedstock related, capital (infrastructure) and operating costs appears likely to remain well above USD 1.00 per litre of gasoline equivalent for the foreseeable future.

There is no precedent in the transport sector for such a shift to an entirely new system of vehicles and fuels. It is unlikely, in the absence of very strong policy interventions and financial support from governments around the world, that market forces will be sufficient to deliver such an outcome. A basic problem is that the development of such infrastructure will be heavily dependent on the demand for H_2 in transportation, and the demand for H_2 in transportation will be heavily dependent on the availability of the appropriate infrastructure.

Recognising these concerns and uncertainty, significant penetration of hydrogen and fuel cell vehicles is characterised in only one scenario variant – BLUE FCV success. In BLUE Map, a much slower build-up of H_2 infrastructure and fuel-cell vehicles is assumed, reaching 25% of global LDV sales by 2050. In the BLUE conservative variant, fuel-cell vehicles do not reach the deployment stage, reflecting an implied failure to reduce costs sufficiently through RD&D or to successfully co-ordinate deployment of vehicles and hydrogen fuels.

Light-duty vehicles

Status and trends

Light-duty vehicle (car, sport-utility vehicle and small van) sales have increased dramatically in recent years, particularly in developing countries such as China and India. In OECD countries, car ownership rates continue to rise with incomes (Figure 15.4).

Figure 15.4 ▶ Car ownership per capita v. expenditures, various OECD countries, 1990-2004

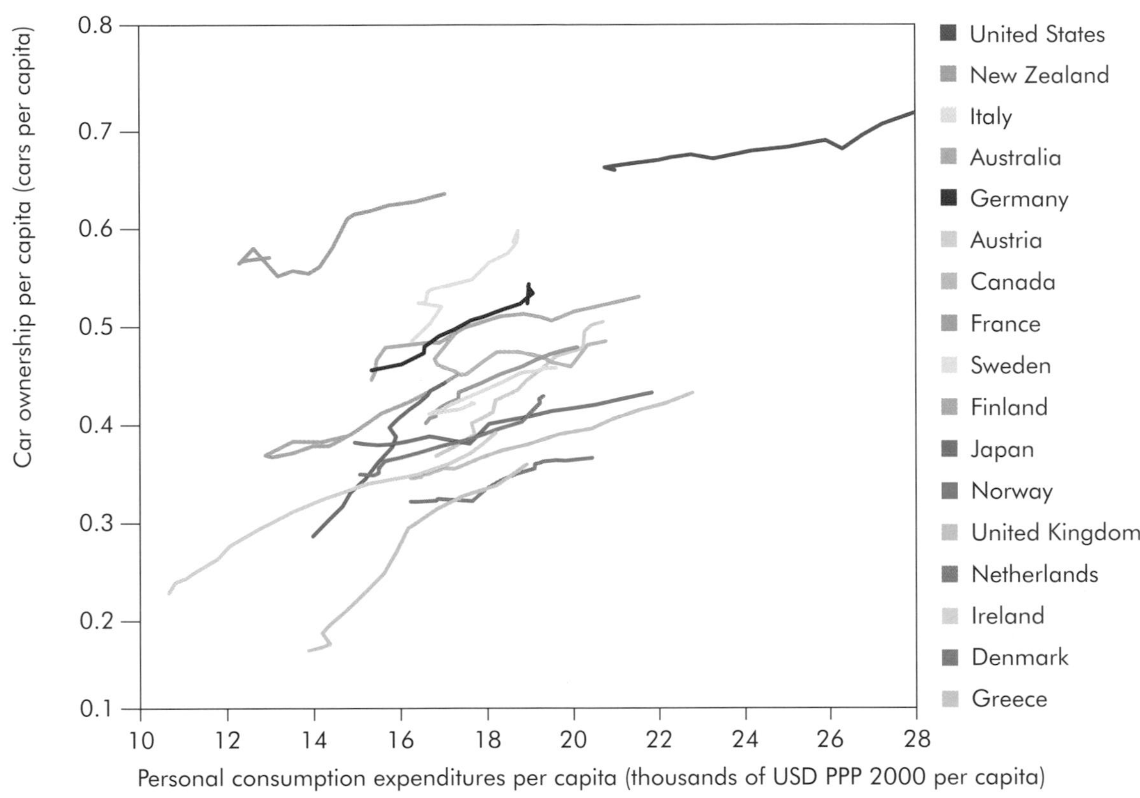

Key point

Many OECD countries still show strongly increasing car ownership rates; developing countries will for many decades to come.

Through much of the 1980s and 1990s, new car fuel economy remained fairly constant across most OECD countries, although it began to show steady improvements in Japan and most European countries in the late 1990s in response to new national and regional policies. This has increased the disparity in fuel economy between North American, European and Pacific OECD countries. In 2004, there was more than a 50% variation in the average fuel consumption of new LDVs across various OECD countries (Figure 15.5).

The average fuel economy of new LDVs projected to 2050, by region and scenario, is shown in Figure 15.6. In the Baseline scenario, fuel economy is projected to improve in all regions, although it is very difficult to predict average rates of improvement beyond the next few years. The ETP projections are a function of recent trends, current policy directives and assumptions about future technological improvements. Fuel economy requirements in Japan and China, expected requirements in the European Union, and recently passed legislation in the United States are all likely to result in substantial improvements in new car fuel use per kilometre even in the Baseline scenario, at least through the period 2015 to 2020. India is also expected to show strong improvements, in part due to expected strong sales of small cars. Other countries also improve, but at slightly slower rates.

After 2020, fuel-economy trends are projected to be nearly flat since, without new policies, any gains from technology improvement are once again likely to be offset by increases in vehicle size, weight and power.

Figure 15.5 ▶ New light-duty vehicle fuel economy (litres/100 kilometres) in various OECD countries, 1990-2004

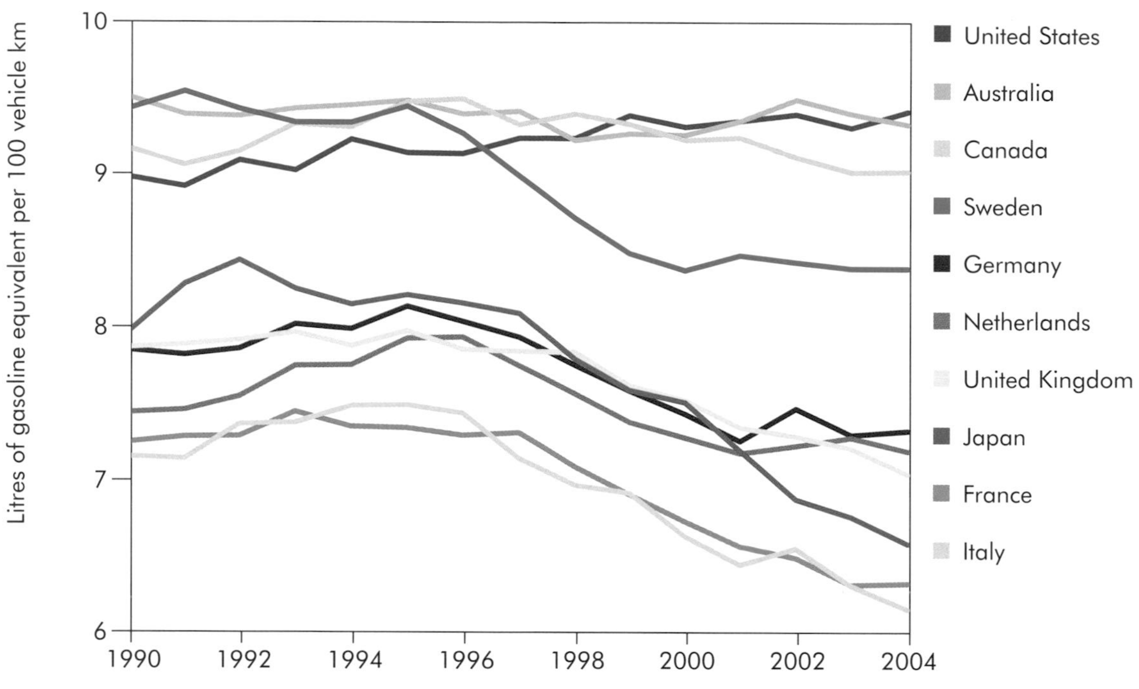

Key point

Regions and countries that have had strong fuel economy policies in recent years, such as the European Union and Japan, have shown strong declines in the fuel intensity of new vehicles.

Figure 15.6 ▶ Gasoline LDV fuel economy projections by region and scenario (litres/100 km)

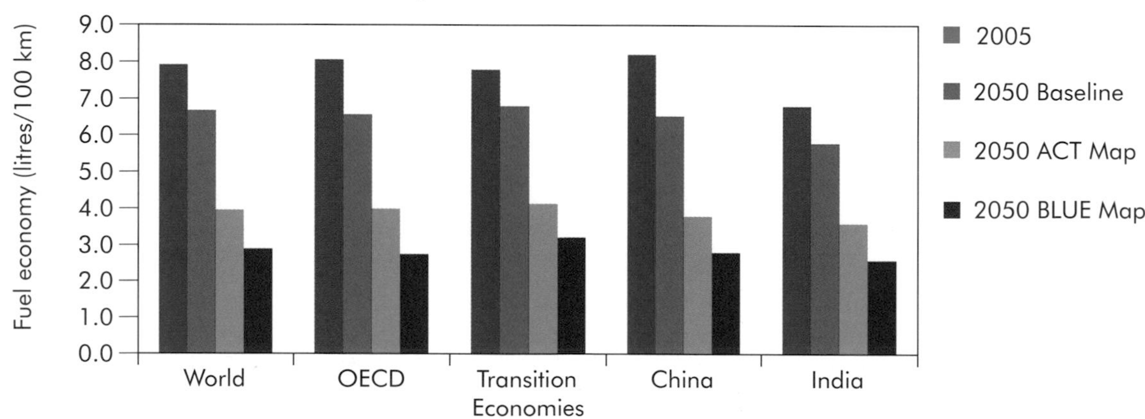

Key point

50% reductions in new-car fuel intensity are achieved in the ACT Map scenario in most regions by 2050; even greater reductions are achieved in the BLUE Map scenario, thanks to electric and hydrogen fuel cell vehicles.

The ACT Map scenario envisages much stronger efficiency programmes than in the Baseline scenario, resulting in greater use of advanced vehicle technologies and, in particular, much stronger sales of hybrid-electric vehicles (Figure 15.7). Sales of plug-in hybrids are also assumed, beginning in 2020 and increasing slowly over time, reaching 10% of vehicle sales after 2030. The BLUE Map scenario reflects strong sales of plug-in hybrids, electric vehicles and fuel cell vehicles, each reaching a 25% share of the market for new vehicles in OECD countries by 2050, the remainder being hybridised gasoline and diesel vehicles. Together with these power-train shifts, non-engine improvements such as the increased use of lighter materials, improved aerodynamics, and better tyres and accessories are estimated to result in large efficiency gains. Hybrids are assumed to be about 50% more efficient (less energy intensive) than today's average new LDVs, and conventional (non-hybridised) gasoline vehicles about 30% more efficient, given strong improvements in engine/drive-train technologies. With the sales of very efficiency electric and fuel cell vehicles in BLUE Map, an overall reduction in new light-duty vehicle energy intensity of close to 70% can be achieved.

Figure 15.7 ▶ Light-duty vehicle sales shares by scenario, in 2050

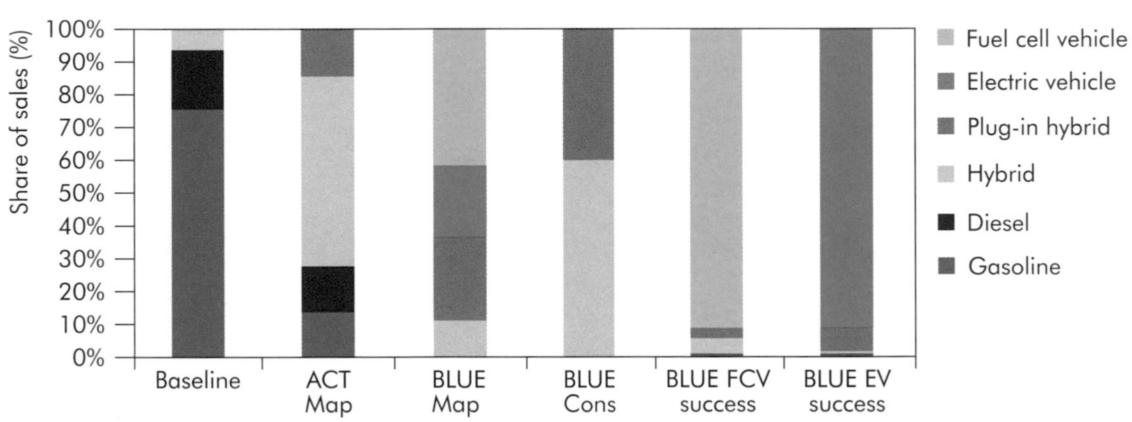

Key point

Moving from the Baseline to the ACT Map and the BLUE scenarios, an increasing share of hybrids, plug-in hybrids, and finally electric and fuel cell vehicles is seen.

LDV technology

A wide range of technologies are available to make vehicles more fuel efficient in the future. However these same technologies may also allow vehicles to be made larger, heavier and/or more powerful, while keeping fuel use fairly constant. An important assumption for the ACT Map and BLUE scenarios is that all new vehicle technologies result entirely in fuel economy improvements, while keeping average LDV size, weight and power constant (or in some cases smaller) in the future. For this assumption to be valid, it will be imperative that governments implement policies that strongly encourage or require fuel economy improvements and discourage the production and purchase of large and more powerful vehicles. These policies could include regulatory fuel economy targets, fuel-consumption-based tax systems, or other approaches to ensure that the potential fuel economies are achieved in practice.

Non-engine components

Most fuel efficiency improvements in conventional vehicles are expected to derive from technologies and changes to vehicle design that are already commercially available today. Incremental fuel economy technologies and their estimated costs and benefits are shown in Table 15.2.

Improvements in most vehicle accessories (e.g. lighting, air conditioning) are not properly captured in the fuel economy test procedures in OECD countries, so there is little incentive for manufacturers to make such improvements (ECMT/IEA, 2005). Modifications in test procedures, or the introduction of additional test cycles (e.g. with air conditioners and/or lights turned on) could help encourage such improvements. For aftermarket products such as replacement tyres and lubricating oils, information to consumers on the relative efficiency impacts of different options may help encourage efficient choices; if not, policies directed at the manufacturers of these products may be needed.

Box 15.1 ▶ Material substitution

There are many potential opportunities to lower vehicle mass through the use of substitute materials in vehicle and engine components. Examples include the use of aluminium and magnesium alloys rather than steel for wheels and engine components, the use of high-strength steel rather than iron or conventional steel components, and the increased use of plastics and other light-weight materials.

Advanced light-weight materials could eventually yield substantially more fuel economy gains than assumed in the BLUE Map scenario. Some substitute materials require significant design revisions (e.g. in all-aluminium vehicles, or in vehicles built using large amounts of composite materials). In such circumstances, costs are likely to rise (especially in an industry that has built cars using steel for several decades). This is one of the reasons why some very-low-mass cars that rely largely on composite materials, such as the "hypercar" developed by Amory Lovins (Lovins, 2004), have not succeeded to date.

Longer term, composites may become commercial if their higher costs are offset by savings resulting from high-priced fuel, or from declining costs in large-scale production. If so, and if issues associated with the inherent weaknesses of carbon-fibre structures – like their sensitivity to transversal loads – were to be solved, carbon-fibre vehicles could become an important contributor to the reduction of fuel consumption and GHG emissions, and yield light-duty vehicles that offer well below half of today's average energy intensity.

In all BLUE Map variants, lighter materials, including high-strength steel and aluminium, are assumed to progressively deliver a weight reduction reaching 25% by 2050 at an estimated cost of about USD 1 000 per vehicle. Taking into account improvement from other technologies, this is estimated to result in an additional reduction in fuel consumption of around 10%.

Powertrain options

A number of different powertrains are currently in wide commercial use and more may be commercialised in the future. Each of these powertrains can be associated with a range of potential fuel efficiency improvements and corresponding costs. Table 15.2 provides IEA estimates of fuel economy improvement (reductions in fuel use per kilometre) associated with different technologies, and their application to different configurations of vehicle (gasoline versus diesel, conventional versus advanced versus hybridised). Here "advanced" refers to vehicles that use advanced engine designs, whereas the non-engine improvements are the same as for "conventional" vehicles.

Virtually all the technologies listed in the table are commercial today, at least in some vehicle market segments. Their costs are likely to be offset by the fuel savings they offer. This is particularly true in an analysis using social costs and benefits, and therefore taking into account most or all of the fuel used over a vehicle's life. This can represent several times more fuel (and fuel savings) than is typically considered by consumers when choosing among vehicles that have different fuel economies.

Table 15.2 ▶ Potential fuel economy improvements from engine and non-engine component technologies

	Gasoline vehicle			Diesel vehicle		
	Conventional	Advanced	Hybrid	Conventional	Advanced	Hybrid
Non-engine improvements	1.5 – 13%	1.5 – 13%	1.5 – 13%	1.5 – 13%	1.5 – 13%	1.5 – 13%
Tyres	0.5 – 4%	0.5 – 4%	0.5 – 4%	0.5 – 4%	0.5 – 4%	0.5 – 4%
Improved aerodynamics	0.5 – 4%	0.5 – 4%	0.5 – 4%	0.5 – 4%	0.5 – 4%	0.5 – 4%
Lights	0 – 2%	0 – 2%	0 – 2%	0 – 2%	0 – 2%	0 – 2%
Better appliances	0.5 – 4%	0.5 – 4%	0.5 – 4%	0.5 – 4%	0.5 – 4%	0.5 – 4%
Material substitution (25% lower weight)	10 – 11%	10 – 11%	10 – 11%	10 – 11%	10 – 11%	10 – 11%
Variable valve timing/ higher compression ratio, no throttle		6 – 8%	5 – 6%	7 – 9%	7 – 9%	2 – 3%
Turbocharging		2 – 3%		3 – 4%	3 – 4%	
Direct injection		3 – 5%	1 – 2%	5 – 7%	5 – 7%	7 – 8%
Improved combustion		2 – 3%	2 – 3%		1 – 2%	3 – 4%
Start/stop (lower idling)	0.5 – 3%	0.5 – 3%			0.5 – 2%	
Continuously variable transmission (to replace automatic transmissions)	5 – 6%	5 – 6%		5 – 6%	5 – 6%	
Hybrid system			16 – 18%			15 – 17%
Range of improvement compared to base gasoline vehicle	14 – 27%	28 – 45%	40 – 52%	30 – 43%	32 – 47%	40 – 55%
Range of cost for these improvements (change in vehicle price, USD)	1 500 – 1 800	2 800 – 3 400	4 000 – 5 400	2 500 – 3 400	3 000 – 3 600	4 200 – 5 600

Source: IEA data and analysis, based on results of IEA workshops, review of technical literature, etc.

15

Figure 15.8 highlights the range of potential fuel efficiency benefits that are associated with each of the vehicle configurations shown in Table 15.2. Both gasoline and diesel light-duty vehicles could achieve close to 50% reductions in fuel intensity even without hybridisation, and over 50% with hybridisation. Today's hybrids contain many other technologies, such as light-weight materials and low-rolling-resistance tyres, which could also be applied to non-hybridised vehicles. Therefore, the potential improvements even without hybridisation could approach those for hybridised vehicles as incremental technologies are applied over time. Similarly, gasoline vehicle efficiency could approach that of diesel vehicles over time, as gasoline engines improve and adopt some technologies already present on many diesel vehicles.

Figure 15.8 ▶ Fuel efficiency improvements of different powertrain options

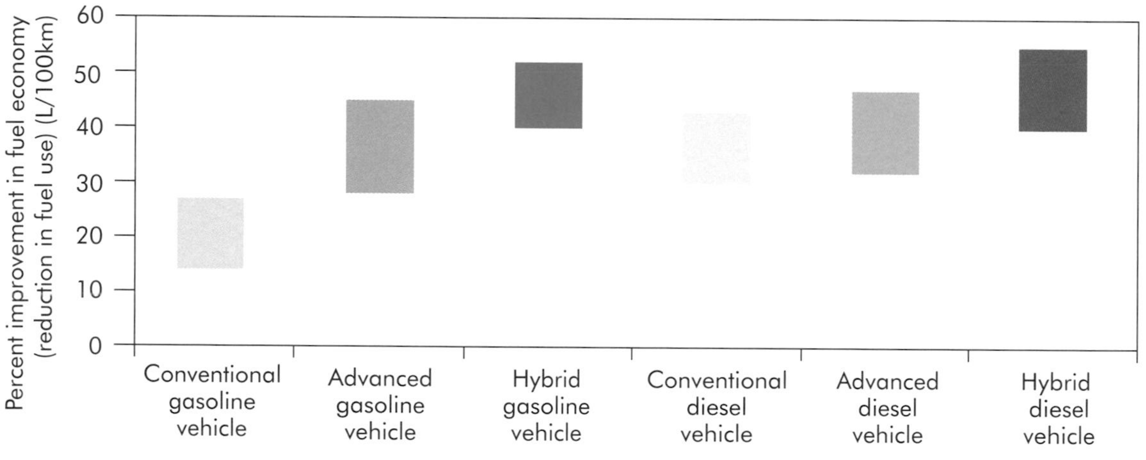

Key point

Advanced gasoline powertrains have the potential to approach the efficiency of diesel powertrains over time; both gasoline and diesel advanced powertrains could approach the efficiency of hybridised systems.

Vehicle hybridisation – involving the addition of an electric motor, a controller and an energy storage system (typically a battery) to the existing engine/fuel system – has proven to be a commercial success, at least in some market segments, despite relatively high costs. The most notable example, the Toyota Prius, has been joined by many other makes and models of hybridised vehicles in the past few years, and most major manufacturers are expected to offer at least one hybrid model (or one model with hybridisation as an option) by 2009 (Passier, *et al.*, 2007).

Hybrid vehicles benefit from a much more efficient use of the internal combustion engine, allowing it to operate steadily at near-optimal loads. This is because the motor/battery system handles some of the peak power requirement, and because engine power can be diverted to recharging the batteries during periods of low load. Hybrids also benefit from innovations such as regenerative braking (which recovers energy during braking and returns this to the batteries, turning the engine off when the car is not moving), and from more efficient components such as continuously variable transmission systems. Some of these components can also be added to vehicles that are not fully hybridised. And like conventional vehicle technologies, hybrid systems can be configured to increase vehicle power rather than (only) improving fuel economy.

Hybrid powertrains, far more than conventional engines, also rely heavily on electronic controls. Full hybrids require a computer to manage the use of the electric motor, the loads on the combustion engine and batteries, engine shutdowns, the use of regenerative braking and to assure proper management and maintenance of the batteries. These vehicles demonstrate that improved electronic design can allow a much better use of the technological potential available, and they are paving the way for the much greater use of hybrid technologies and other complementary fuel saving technologies on non-hybridised, conventional internal combustion engines.

Box 15.2 ▶ A new generation of very small, inexpensive vehicles

A revolution in the types of vehicles available to consumers in developing countries appears likely to begin soon, given recent announcements of plans to offer new models of very small, inexpensive cars in countries such as India and China. Manufacturers are pursuing this strategy with the aim of producing vehicles that would be affordable for most families in rapidly developing areas. Such models could cost less than USD 3 000 and consume as little as four litres per 100 kilometres, around half that of an average US car, and two-thirds that of the average European or Japanese vehicle on sale today (Tata Motors, 2008).

In the ETP Baseline projection, very small cars are assumed to reach a market share of 2% in the OECD countries and 10% in non-OECD countries by 2015, remaining constant thereafter. But given their expected prices, the efficiency benefits that they bring are likely to be counterbalanced by an increase in total car sales, perhaps resulting overall in higher final energy use. The precise impact will depend on how many buyers are first-time motorised vehicle buyers, how many are switching from larger cars, and how many (possibly a high share) are switching from driving motorised two-wheelers. Experience and market research will be needed to obtain a clearer picture of the impacts these vehicles are likely to have on fuel economy and fuel consumption.

Energy storage

Energy storage is critical to hybridisation. Currently, this is provided by batteries. Batteries are being steadily improved, but even the best today – lithium-ion (Li-ion) batteries used in small electronics and beginning to be introduced for larger applications such as vehicles – suffer from high cost and inadequate performance.

Figure 15.9 shows the energy densities (by volume and by weight) of different fuels, adjusted for the fuel efficiency of the engine. The energy density of today's best batteries, and for the foreseeable future, is much lower than that of conventional fuels. As a result, the more a vehicle relies on batteries for energy storage, the more batteries will be used, the heavier the vehicle will be, and the less space will be available for other purposes. This puts practical limits on the benefits that batteries can offer.

Figure 15.9 ▶ Typical energy density of batteries and liquid fuels

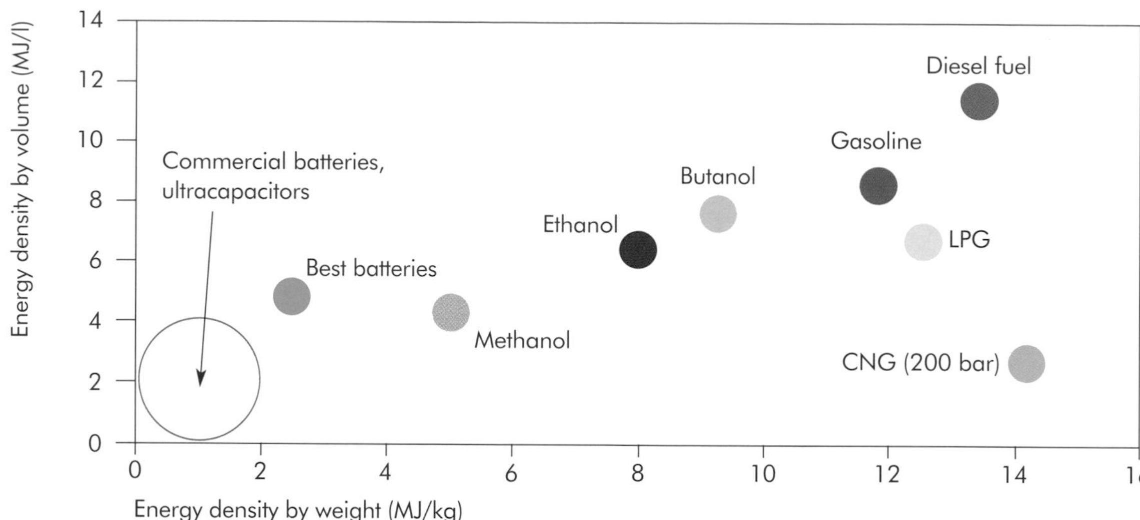

Source: Various, including IEA data on the relationship between volumetric and mass density of batteries and IEA assumptions on the efficiencies of engines (25% to 30% for internal combustion engines) and electric motors (90% to 95%).

Key point

Batteries and ultra-capacitors do not approach the energy density of most liquid fuels.

Batteries are also very expensive per unit of energy they produce. Typical commercial nickel-metal-hydride (NiMH) batteries used on today's hybrids cost around USD 1 000/kWh of storage capacity (ACEEE, 2006). For the Prius this cost amounts to a little more than USD 1 000 per vehicle. Li-ion batteries will offer improved energy and power densities, but their cost per unit of energy appears likely, at least in the very near term, to be as high as today's NiMH batteries. For vehicle electrification to become a viable pathway towards eventually carbon-free vehicle travel, battery costs will need to come down by half to two-thirds, hopefully over the next 5 to 10 years. Batteries must also be able to endure up to 15 years of recharge discharge cycles or else must be replaced during the vehicle's life, perhaps doubling their life-cycle cost impact.

Although still not used commercially in any OEM hybrid vehicle as of early 2008, Li-ion batteries are expected to become the dominant choice within a few years given their technical advantages over NiMH and other battery types. These include much better energy/weight and power/weight ratios, and better cycling (charge/discharge) performance (Passier, *et al.*, 2007). However, Li-ion batteries still suffer from technical challenges, such as durability in vehicle applications. And they must be safe, which has been an issue for Li-ion batteries particularly in vehicle applications, due to their potential for overheating. There is increasing optimism that these technical hurdles will soon be overcome, given current intensive research worldwide and the variety of new formulations being tested. Similar research is also under way on ultracapacitors, which can offer an alternative to, or complement, conventional battery systems.

Box 15.3 ▶ Ultracapacitors: a complement to batteries?

Ultracapacitors represent an alternative to batteries as an energy storage device, and have quite different properties. Ultracapacitors store energy in charged electrodes, rather than in an electrolyte. The rate of energy storage per unit weight or volume is much lower even than for batteries; however the ability of ultracapacitors to quickly deliver this energy – i.e., their power density – can be much higher. Thus ultracapacitors are particularly useful for supplying short bursts of power, such as for vehicle acceleration, where batteries perform poorly. Ultracapacitors are increasingly seen as a potentially important complementary storage device for pure electric vehicles, as well as for fuel cell vehicles, since fuel cell stacks, like batteries, are good at delivering steady amounts of electricity, but not good for peak power boosts.

Recently, ultracapacitors have begun to be used in various test versions of hybrid vehicles, and particularly in plug-in hybrids. Ultracapacitors can be steadily charged by the battery pack and then discharged rapidly when peak power is needed, avoiding using the engine for this purpose. Ultracapacitors can also be recharged effectively using regenerative braking systems, which typically provide electricity at a faster rate than can be fully stored by batteries.

The cost and performance of ultracapacitors have improved dramatically in the past decade. For instance, a decade ago a 2.3-volt ultracapacitor rated at 470 farads cost roughly USD 2 per farad (Miller, 2008). Today, that same ultracapacitor would cost around ten cents per farad, and costs continue to decrease rapidly as ongoing automation replaces hand assembly. But even at these prices they may add several thousand dollars to the price of the vehicle, beyond the cost of the hybrid drivetrain and battery system. Ultracapacitor costs may need to decrease by another factor of 10 to 20, to below one cent per farad, to be affordable in mass-market automotive applications.

Plug-in hybrids

Plug-in hybrid vehicles combine the vehicle efficiency advantages of hybridisation with the opportunity to travel part-time on electricity provided by the grid, rather than through the vehicle's internal recharging system. Plug-in hybrids are a potentially important technology for the reduction of oil use and CO_2 emissions by LDVs, since they offer the opportunity to rely more on the electricity sector, which is less expensive to de-carbonise than other sectors and in the BLUE Map scenario is expected to be fully decarbonised by 2050.

Plug-in hybrids, however, will require significant improvements in energy storage technology, since they will likely need at least 5 and possibly 10 or 20 times the battery capacity of today's non-plug-in hybrids. They will also have to be capable of repeated deep discharges, unlike today's hybrid battery systems, which typically are operated in a near-constant "state-of-charge" mode and are prevented from deep discharge-recharge cycles under any circumstances (Simpson, 2006). If these challenges can be overcome, plug-in hybrids will offer important additional CO_2 reductions, in part because of the very high efficiency of electrical motors, but mainly from the greater share of vehicle travel that will be powered by low-CO_2 grid electricity.

Battery-motor systems are about three times as efficient as even a hybridised combustion engine system. As a result, even with fairly high future electricity prices, the end-use energy cost to the consumer is likely to be significantly lower with plug-in battery operation than with on-board liquid fuel. This may provide an important incentive for consumers to buy and use plug-in hybrids. Actual cost savings will depend on the relative fuel prices for electricity and liquid fuels in any given location, but 50% savings per kilometre are not unlikely.

The fuel savings from operating a plug-in hybrid on grid electricity must, of course, be weighed against the additional cost of purchasing such a vehicle. Table 15.3 provides an indication of the relationship between different levels of battery capacity and their impact on driving range, vehicle cost and the percentage of total driving that might be powered by the battery system rather than the combustion engine.

Table 15.3 ▶ **Plug-in hybrid costs and impacts by driving range**

Plug-in vehicle battery capacity	Vehicle driving range on batteries (km)	Battery storage needed (kWh)	Vehicle battery cost (USD)		Percent of average daily driving on batteries
			Current (USD 1 000/kWh)	Future (USD 300/kWh)	
Low	20 km	5	5 000	1 500	20-40%
Medium	50 km	12.5	12 500	3 750	40-60%
High	80 km	20	20 000	6 000	60-80%

Notes: Calculations assume: a) vehicle efficiency on batteries of 0.16 kWh/km; b) system configured to discharge up to 66% maximum (meaning 50% more battery capacity must be supplied than used in plug-in mode); c) future battery costs eventually drop to USD 300/kWh, less than one-third of current prices; and d) the percentage of daily driving on batteries, at the low end, is based on United States driving profiles (percentages are likely to be higher for drivers in other countries).

As mentioned, estimates of the current or near-term cost for Li-ion batteries are USD 800/kWh to USD 1 000/kWh of capacity. For a medium-range plug-in hybrid (with a range of 50 kilometres, for example), this results in over USD 10 000 in battery costs. This is approximately ten times more expensive than battery costs for current non-plug-in hybrids. Plug-in hybrids may also need a larger motor, adding to their cost. Even without discounting fuel costs, a vehicle driven 200 000 kilometres over its life might save USD 4 000 in fuel costs – not nearly enough to offset such a high battery-purchase cost. However, if battery costs can be reduced to around USD 300/kWh in the future, the resulting battery cost of around USD 3 750 for a 12.5 kWh system would probably be competitive for a vehicle with a 50-kilometre electric range. Cost competitiveness will also depend on future electricity and oil prices.

In the BLUE variant scenarios, a 50-kilometre-range plug-in hybrid is assumed to dominate hybrid sales after 2030, and the percentage of kilometres driven on electricity is assumed to rise over time as recharging times diminish, electric recharging infrastructure spreads and the number of opportunities to recharge the battery during the day increases. The cost of batteries is assumed to start at USD 800/kwh in 2010 and drop with cumulative production either more slowly (in BLUE Map) or more rapidly (in the EV Success case), with a long-term cost of

USD 300/kWh. Our assumptions regarding the share of hybrid vehicles that are pluggable is shown in Table 15.4. Though not modelled here, initial plug-in vehicle offerings might benefit from offering less battery-powered driving range, thereby lowering battery costs and increasing vehicle affordability. Range could then be increased with new models, over time, as battery costs drop.

Table 15.4 ▶ Percentage of hybrid vehicles sold with plug-in capability by ETP scenario, region and year

	OECD countries		Rest of world	
	2030	2050	2030	2050
ACT Map	10%	25%	5%	15%
BLUE Map	33%	67%	20%	50%
BLUE EV Success	50%	90%	30%	75%

Electric vehicles

Electric vehicles benefit from the removal of the entire internal combustion engine system, the drivetrain and fuel tank, giving a savings of up to USD 4 000 per vehicle compared to hybrids. But they require much greater battery capacity than plug-in hybrids and, without a complementary internal combustion engine, they will require a significantly more powerful motor/battery system in order to provide the peak power that drivers expect.

These requirements appear to be major hurdles for the success of pure electric vehicles. For example, if drivers demand 500 kilometres of range (about the minimum for today's vehicles), then even with very efficient battery systems that are capable of repeated deep discharges, the battery capacity will need to be at least 50 kWh, many times more than for a plug-in hybrid with a similar overall range. At current battery prices this would cost up to USD 50 000 per vehicle. Even at a much-reduced future battery cost of USD 300/kWh, this will amount to USD 15 000, which along with the motor controller system (even after subtracting out the savings from eliminating the engine/drivetrain system), probably means a vehicle costing around USD 10 000 more than a comparable hybrid.

One way to reduce this cost would be to provide more recharging opportunities that would be able to sustain electric vehicles with a shorter range. If batteries and charging systems capable of fast recharging times are developed, this will also help. Such batteries are under development and some may be marketed as early as 2008 (Green Car Congress, 2007). If consumers were to accept a range of only 250 kilometres, this would cut battery requirements and costs by half compared to a 500-kilometre-range vehicle. In any case it seems likely that the costs of electric vehicles will need to be reduced to just a few thousand dollars more than a comparable hybrid vehicle in order to have a reasonable chance for commercial success.

Pure electric vehicle prospects would no doubt benefit from the success of plug-in hybrids, in part because plug-ins are likely to help bring down the cost of batteries, motors and control systems. The BLUE Map scenario assumes that after ten years of plug-in hybrid vehicle sales (and on-going RD&D during this time), the costs of batteries are reduced enough to allow initial market deployment of electric vehicles. In The BLUE "EV Success" variant, this occurs in just five years.

Fuel cell vehicles

Fuel cell vehicles represent a very different set of technologies than those discussed so far. The power plant, a fuel-cell stack, is a highly efficient system for converting H_2 into electricity. Vehicles would either store H_2 on board or carry a liquid fuel rich in H_2 (such as ethanol) with an H_2 reformer to take H_2 out of the fuel and feed it into the fuel cell stack.

A wide variety of fuel cell systems and energy storage systems are in development, though at this stage the polymer-electrolyte membrane (PEM) fuel cell system with on-board compressed H_2 storage appears to be the most viable option. Detailed treatments of fuel-cell technologies were provided in *Energy Technology Perspectives 2006* (IEA, 2006) and in *Prospects for Hydrogen and Fuel Cells* (IEA, 2005).

Fuel cell vehicles need to overcome a number of technical hurdles to become viable, and their costs must be brought down significantly. Recent limited production runs of demonstration fuel cell cars have been estimated to cost at least USD 100 000 per vehicle, with fuel cell buses costing upwards of USD 1 million. Moving to large-scale production will help bring some costs down, but some component costs appear likely to remain high. For example, a fuel cell stack/controller system is currently estimated to cost at least USD 500 per kW of power, even in volume production. For a very efficient fuel cell vehicle requiring 75 kW of power, the resulting fuel cell system cost would be USD 37 500. Researchers are looking for ways to bring this cost down to under USD 100 per kW, but whether and when they will achieve this is unclear. A key goal is to cut the use of platinum (used as a catalyst) to a small fraction of its use in previous generations of fuel cells. A good deal of progress has recently been made in this area.

A very efficient fuel cell vehicle is likely to require at least 5 kg of hydrogen stored on board to achieve a range of 500 kilometres. At current costs of about USD 1 000 kg for high pressure (350-bar) cylinder systems, this would cost about USD 5 000 per vehicle. Options to cut costs and reduce storage space include increasing the storage pressure, cooling the H_2, and switching to metal or chemical-based (non-pressurised) storage and other types of systems. None seems likely to achieve technical and commercial success in the near term. Finally, as is true for electric vehicles, driving range could be reduced if drivers would accept it.

In short, the cost of the fuel-cell stack system and the energy storage system must each come down by nearly an order of magnitude for fuel cell vehicles to reach a cost competitive point. A wide range of research programmes are focused on different approaches to achieving such targets, but the ultimate form of success, the level of success (and cost reduction) and the timing of such success are very difficult to predict.

In the BLUE Map scenario, we assume that, through redoubled RD&D efforts over the next ten years, fuel cell vehicles start to be deployed in 2020 at an incremental cost of around USD 10 000 compared to hybrid-electric vehicles. By 2030, as a result of supporting policies, on-going RD&D and cost-reduction from the learning associated with cumulative production, fuel cell vehicles achieve a 5% market (sales) share of LDVs in OECD countries, with incremental costs dropping to about 5 000 per vehicle and continuing to drop thereafter. Market shares in 2050 are assumed to reach 33% in OECD countries and about half that share elsewhere. In the BLUE "FCV Success" variant, earlier and more substantial cost reductions allow initial deployment five years earlier and fuel-cell vehicles reach 10% market share in 2030, at an incremental cost of USD 5 000. Soon after 2030, fuel cell vehicles are nearly cost-competitive with gasoline-hybrid vehicles, and by 2050 they account for nearly all light-duty vehicle sales in OECD countries at a cost similar to hybrid vehicles. In other variants (such as BLUE Conservative), the RD&D-based cost reductions are assumed not to materialise sufficiently to justify the major deployment efforts that would be needed to promote substantial fuel cell vehicle sales.

Modal shift to transit and non-motorised modes

The "modal mix", *i.e.* the share of travel by different travel modes, can have a large impact on energy use. This is true both for passenger and freight travel, and both for urban area and inter-urban area travel.

In any urban area, virtually all travel is accomplished by car, bus, rail, motorised two- or three-wheeled vehicles, bicycles, or walking. These choices have very different characteristics in terms of speed, cost, comfort and energy use. As shown in Figure 15.10, there is a wide range of modal mixes in cities around the world. In Hong Kong (China), for example, over 80% of trips are made either by public transit (*e.g.* bus, tram, train) or by "non-motorised" modes (*e.g.* walking or bicycling). In cities like Houston (United States) only about 5% of trips use these modes; over 90% of trips are by private light-duty vehicles.

Figure 15.10 ▶ Energy consumption for passenger transport versus modal share

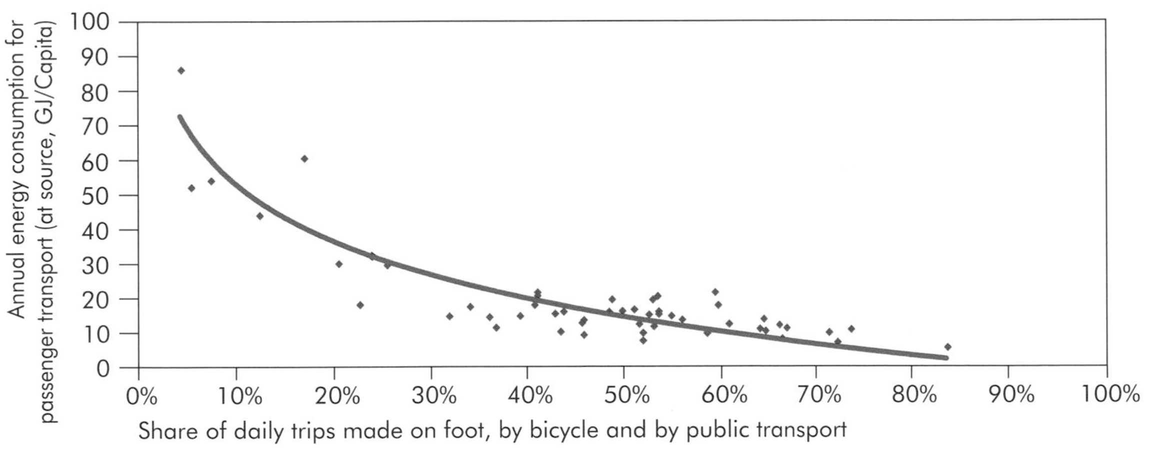

Note: Points represent cities in the SYSTRA data base, from around the world.

Source: UITP, 2006 (Courtesy of SYSTRA).

Key point

Cities with high shares of non-motorised and public transport typically have far lower transport energy use per capita than cities that are more car-dependent.

15

Figure 15.11 ▶ Relationship between GDP per capita and motorised modal share

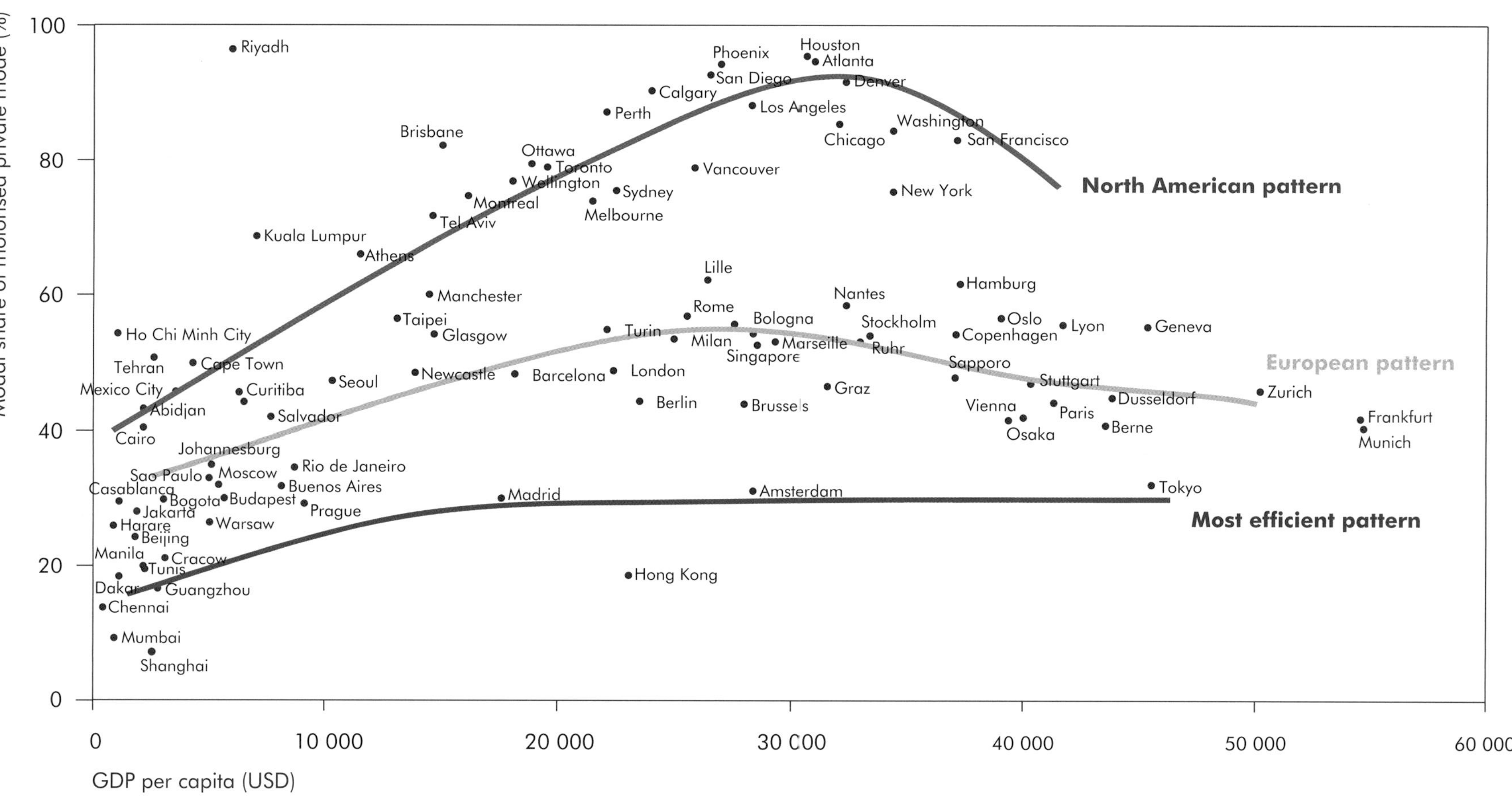

Source: UITP, 2006 (Courtesy of SYSTRA).

Key point

There is a wide range of modal shares for cities of similar incomes with three distinct pathways as incomes rise. If cities in the developing world invest heavily in public and non-motorised transport infrastructure, they may be able to follow more sustainable pathways.

A number of factors influence passenger transport mode shares. Although population and building density are important among these, and are not easy to change, most cities in the developing world have high densities and high shares of efficient modes of transport, and would appear to have an opportunity to maintain and even improve the energy efficiency of their transport systems in the future, if they take strong action. Cities that invest heavily in public transport systems and in maintaining or improving the infrastructure for walking and biking, along with careful spatial planning and other complementary measures, will tend to maintain much higher shares of the most efficient modes than cities that cater more to automobiles (*e.g.* through large investments in road network expansion).

Figure 15.11 plots cities by the proportion of journeys taken in private vehicles (on the vertical axis) and GDP per capita (on the horizontal axis). Most developing cities are in the lower left corner of the figure, with low use of private transport and relatively low per-capita incomes. A key question for these cities is whether they move along a "European" or "North American" pattern of development, as shown in the figure.

Clearly, the dynamics of city growth are complex, and it is not fully clear what circumstances and set of policies are needed to move a city along one pathway or another. But some elements appear critical: strong urban planning, major investments in public transit and non-motorised transport infrastructure, and policies to discourage car use. These clearly go well beyond technology considerations, and so are not covered here in any detail.

Some technologies can however play an important part in achieving a low-energy/ CO_2 transport system in a city. These include:

Bus rapid transit: BRT is an approach to bus systems that mimics a metro system, but uses buses on city streets. The buses typically operate in dedicated lanes, are very large capacity, travel at high average speeds, and can move up to ten times as many people per hour on a lane of traffic than can cars.

Road pricing and congestion charging: these are systems that provide a price or convenience penalty for given categories of private vehicles. The development of improved communications systems has made implementation of electronic toll systems much more practical than it was just a few years ago. London is perhaps the best-known recent example of a city that has implemented an electronic pricing system for vehicles entering the central business district, but similar systems exist in Singapore, Stockholm, Milan and several Norwegian cities. Electronic highway tolls are now prevalent in both North America and Europe.

Public bicycle systems: Paris recently launched the "Velib" system of rental bicycles, available at hundreds of street locations around the city. Within a few weeks, this program doubled the share of bicycle travel in the city (from about 1.5% to 3% of trips). Lyon and Barcelona have similar systems, featuring credit-card-based rentals to ensure system security. Many other cities are now looking at implementing similar programmes.

As an example of the potential impacts of energy efficient transport planning and development on CO_2 emissions, in particular in developing countries, the BLUE scenario (all variants) assumes that in about 1 000 large cities around the world, with a combined population of 500 million people, public and non-motorised transport achieve (and maintain) a share of around 60% of all travel through to 2050. In our Baseline scenario, this share drops to around 30% (with private motorised vehicle share of travel rising to 70%). In the face of rising car (and in many cities 2-wheeler) ownership, the difficulties involved in achieving this different future, and the rigour of the policies needed, are likely to be substantial, but this is not inconsistent with other assumptions in the BLUE scenario.

Based on the relative efficiency of different modes, we estimate that the average transport energy use and CO_2 emissions per year for these cities are close to 40% higher in the Baseline scenario than in the BLUE variant scenarios. Most of the differences between the two scenarios would be likely to occur by 2030 – since by then, without strong policies, many large cities already will have dropped to only a 30% share for transit and non-motorised transport. This estimate also takes into account that in the BLUE variants, LDVs are far more efficient than they are today. In the BLUE scenarios, about 100 Mt per year of CO_2 emissions is saved in 2030, equivalent to about 8% of the developing world's LDV emissions in that year. The annual amount of CO_2 reduction then declines in the years to 2050, as LDVs in the BLUE scenarios become very low-carbon vehicles after 2030.

High speed rail

High speed rail (HSR) is typically defined as steel-wheel-on-rail operation with cruise speeds exceeding 200 km/h. Currently, HSR systems exist in Europe, Japan and other parts of Asia and the east coast of the United States. HSR trips of less than three hours can provide a very attractive alternative to air travel, as the journeys to airports and the process of going through check-in and security screening can make the total travel time longer than HSR. For the BLUE Scenario, HSR becomes an attractive option since: a) it can provide passenger service at lower average energy intensities than air or car travel (per passenger kilometre), and b) the electricity used will be generated primarily by zero-carbon sources after 2030.

Though the energy intensity of HSR varies significantly with operating conditions and passenger load factors, recent experience in Europe and Japan shows the average energy consumption per passenger-kilometre of HSR is generally in the range of one-third to one-fifth that of aeroplane and car energy use per passenger-kilometre (ENN, 2008; Sierra Club, 2001). CO_2 emissions are also dependent on the source of electricity generation. Clearly, with zero-CO_2 generation (such as nuclear or wind power), the total CO_2 emissions of rail systems are near zero (apart from factors such as construction of the trains and track systems themselves, and fossil energy used to heat stations).

A key consideration for HSR construction is the niche it serves. As mentioned, HSR can be competitive with air travel up to at least three hours of HSR travel, or 700 to 800 kilometres. The recent announcement of a new generation of HSR technology (Alstom, 2008) promises even greater speeds and applicable distances. However, HSR is not especially advantageous for journeys of less than 200 kilometres, as conventional rail systems achieve nearly the same overall time performance at much lower cost (SDG, 2004).

Costs of HSR construction vary significantly from country to country, due to differences in land costs, labour costs, financing methods and topography. The costs per kilometre of rail systems can range from around USD 10 million to over USD 100 million (SDG, 2004). The cost of constructing the Channel Tunnel rail link between France and the United Kingdom was four to six times as expensive per kilometre as typical construction costs over flat land.

Many HSR lines are currently proposed and planned around the world. However, their rate of construction is far slower than announced plans would suggest. Europe leads with 2 000 km of high-speed lines in operation, and with another 4 000 km planned for construction by 2020 (ENN, 2008). China is expected to build 3 000 km of high-speed railways within 15 years. Argentina has recently announced plans to build a 700-kilometre line from Buenos Aires to Cordoba, which would be the first high-speed line in Latin America. Many other countries are planning HSR lines, including Brazil, Morocco, Saudi Arabia, Iran, Israel, Turkey, Portugal, Russia, Malaysia (with Singapore), Pakistan, and Vietnam.

For the BLUE scenario, we assume that all currently planned HSR systems are constructed by 2020, and that by 2050, 25% of air travel worldwide under 750 km has shifted to rail. This appears likely to represent about 5% of global air travel at that time. A small share of total car travel is also assumed to have shifted to these HSR systems. Overall we estimate that about 0.5 Gt of CO_2 per year can be saved by 2050, around 3% of Baseline emissions in that year. We assume that countries only build HSR where there are net societal benefits, *i.e.* where any net costs above those paid for by passengers are more than offset by benefits such as reduced congestion on roadways and airports. This suggests a low or negative cost-per-tonne for CO_2. However this scenario is only included in BLUE (and not ACT) to allow for possible high net costs for some projects. In any case, these represent very rough approximations and more research is needed to better determine the overall potential for high-speed rail, its costs and benefits.

Truck and rail freight transport

Surface freight transport is one of the fastest-growing sectors worldwide, and has one of the fastest growth rates in terms of energy use in recent years. In OECD countries, freight energy use has grown faster than passenger transport energy use. Freight transport volumes are generally closely linked to economic growth, and they have grown most strongly in countries such as India and China with high economic growth rates.

As shown in Figure 15.12, since 1990, there has been a slight trend toward lower energy intensities in the stock of trucks in most countries, although with a fairly wide variation in the average for different countries. The average improvement across the OECD between 1990 and 2004 was about 0.7% a year, although since 1999, this rate has been lower, around 0.5%. Differences across countries relate largely to variations in average truck sizes, loads and load factors (tonne-kilometre per vehicle-kilometre).

Figure 15.12 ▶ **Trends in freight truck efficiency in various OECD countries, MJ/tkm**

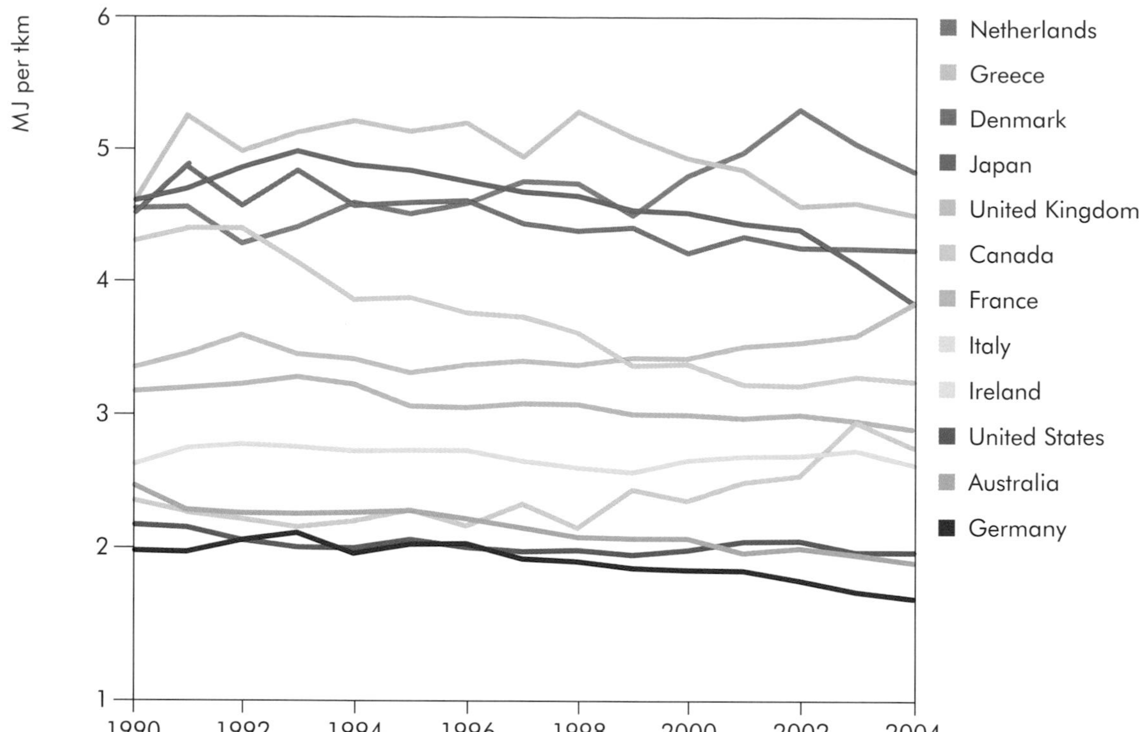

Source: IEA, 2007.

Key point

Freight truck energy efficiency varies considerably by country, reflecting different truck sizes and freight patterns; in most countries, efficiency improvement has been slowing in recent years.

Recent work in countries including the United States suggests that the trend in efficiency improvement has been higher in medium-duty (urban cycle) trucks than in large, long-haul trucks. There may also be a somewhat higher potential for efficiency improvement in urban cycle trucks, given the much better applicability of hybrid systems to these vehicles (Duleep, 2007).

There are four main ways in which energy use and GHG emissions from freight movement could be significantly reduced:

- Improving the **technical efficiency** of goods vehicles, particularly medium and heavy-duty trucks.
- Developing **new propulsion systems and fuels** for medium and heavy trucks. As with LDVs, electric motor and fuel-cell propulsion systems are being developed for many types of heavy duty vehicle, including trucks, buses and trains, and for applications in some types of off-road vehicles such as construction equipment.

- Improving the **operational efficiency** of vehicles and systems, including improving vehicle in-use fuel economy and developing more sophisticated freight logistical systems, for example, via linkages between suppliers and their clients, to significantly increase the efficiency of goods delivery in metropolitan areas.
- **Modal shift**, via increasing investment in rail and water-born transport modes and connected intermodal transfer facilities. This would tend to increase the focus of truck transport on relatively short-distance trips, such as commercial and retail delivery, with more long-distance freight movement handled by more efficient modes.

This section considers each of these four areas in turn.

Trucking technical efficiency

There is a wide variety of truck types, from very small delivery vans to long-haul tractor-trailers that can have a loaded weight of over 30 tonnes (maximum weight limits vary by country). Trucks perform a wide range of different tasks, from urban "stop and go" retail deliveries to long-haul, large-volume movements. Thus while there are a variety of measures for improving efficiency, these may apply very differently to different kinds and sizes of trucks performing different types of services.

For most types of trucking, fuel costs represent a significant share of operating costs. Unlike most cars, goods vehicles are used in commercial applications by operators that aim to minimise costs and therefore maximize efficiency. Trucks are typically designed, and purchased, to meet trucking company requirements for attributes like engine power, hauling capacity, durability and safety at minimum cost. Therefore, the opportunities for improving the efficiency of heavy-duty vehicles, beyond those likely to be adopted autonomously (which therefore appear in the Baseline scenario), are generally thought to be more limited than for personal LDVs.

However, a recent IEA/International Transport Forum workshop (IEA and ITF, 2007) found that many engine and non-engine innovations that have the potential to deliver significant fuel efficiency gains may not yet be fully exploited by truck operators. These include:

- **Downsizing and downweighting** – making trucks smaller, where this would better suit the purpose and making trucks lighter across all size classes. Though loaded weights will tend to be dominated by the goods being moved, significant energy savings are still possible during empty travel and with light loads.
- **Engine/drivetrain** efficiency improvements, such as turbo-charging (with inter-cooling and engine downsizing), advanced higher-compression diesel engines, and increased use of electronic controls.
- **Hybrid drivetrains**, involving adding a motor/battery system to significantly improve urban cycle operation (therefore especially applicable for urban delivery trucks and other short-haul vehicles). Hybrids can improve truck efficiency anywhere from 25% to 45%, depending on the truck's duty cycle (e.g. the relative

percentages of urban and highway driving). Hybrid systems are expensive, but costs are declining and fuel savings for trucks over time can be substantial.

- **Aerodynamic improvements**, especially for long-haul trucks. Cab-top and side fairings are now fairly standard, but benefits could be accrued from better tractor-trailer integration and more aerodynamic trailers (*e.g.* side skirts and rear spoilers).

- **Low-rolling resistance tyres.** Truck tyres have improved over time and nearly all are now second-generation radial tyres. But further reductions in rolling resistance are still possible with available tyre technologies.

- **More efficient auxiliary equipment**, such as cabin heating/cooling systems and lighting. Long-haul trucks in particular use a substantial amount of fuel while stationary, often idling the engine in order to operate auxiliary equipment. The installation and use of specialised auxiliary power units (APUs) for operating auxiliary equipment can save substantial amounts of fuel. Opportunities for connecting to grid electricity at stopping points are increasing.

An important finding of the workshop was that available efficiency technologies (with appropriate measures) appear to offer the potential for long-term reductions in trucking energy intensity of 30% to 40%. This is consistent with efficiency improvements targeted by the United States Department of Energy in its "Twenty-First Century Truck Partnership" (DOE, 2006).

The potential improvements for medium-duty urban cycle trucks may be even greater than for long-haul trucks, given their much better suitability to hybridisation. Improvements in aerodynamics, rolling resistance and accessories will be somewhat less important for medium-duty urban cycle trucks than for long-haul trucks.

The ETP Baseline scenario assumes that recent trends in energy intensity reduction continue until 2020, after which the availability of lower-cost technologies begins to decline. Improvements are expected to occur a little faster for medium-duty than heavy-duty trucks, and also at a faster rate in non-OECD countries, since trucks in these countries are currently at a lower technology level and in-use conditions are often much more severe (and should improve over time). As shown in Figure 15.13, the Baseline scenario shows an overall reduction in energy intensity between 2005 and 2050 of 21% to 32%, depending on truck category and region.

Virtually all potential technology improvements appear likely to pay back their costs in fuel savings over the life of the truck (although truck operators typically demand a much shorter pay-back time than this). In the context of the ACT Map and BLUE Map scenarios, the assumed USD per tonne CO_2 saved is likely to be sufficient to bring forward some of these technologies. In the BLUE Map scenario, we assume all of the technologies described above, including hybridisation (for those truck categories where applicable) are adopted. We therefore assume an average reduction of about 40% (ranging from 35% to 48%) in average truck energy intensity through 2050 (Figure 15.13). In the ACT Map scenario we assume about 75% of the adoption rates and efficiency improvements assumed in the BLUE Map scenario.

Figure 15.13 ▶ Projected change in truck efficiency from technical improvements, 2005-2050 (per cent change in energy use per kilometre)

Source: IEA, 2007.

Key point

Trucks can improve by up to 50% (reduction in energy intensity) through 2050; the greatest improvement potential appears to be in non-OECD countries.

Advanced propulsion systems

As with LDVs, a number of advanced truck propulsion systems are under development, although these are not yet commercially available, with the notable exception of battery/motor systems for use in hybrid medium-duty (e.g. delivery) trucks. These have recently become commercial and models are appearing on the market at an increasing rate. Some pure-electric truck models (and particularly off-road models, such as for construction work, factories, etc.) are commercially available, but these are mostly small niche markets. Hydrogen fuel-cell vehicles are available primarily as demonstration vehicles.

For vehicles used mainly in urban settings, such as delivery trucks and city buses, electric and hydrogen fuel-cell power are both potentially attractive options. Delivery trucks and buses are often centrally refuelled, which helps to overcome fuel infrastructure obstacles. In contrast, long-haul trucks must be able to refuel at reasonable distances, in reasonable amounts of time, which can pose a problem for both electric and fuel-cell systems. Durability also is a key issue for these technologies, particularly fuel cells; whether fuel-cell systems can ever meet the intensive durability requirements of long haul trucks that often travel over 100 000 km/year is an open question.

The BLUE variant scenarios assume that medium-sized trucks and buses operating with battery/electric motor systems or with hydrogen fuel-cell systems follow a similar time line for commercialisation as LDVs, and that component costs drop at a similar rate. For heavy duty short-haul trucks (e.g. urban refuse-hauling trucks), we assume modest penetrations, including plug-in hybrids. For long-haul trucks, we do not assume any penetration of fuel-cell or electric systems even in the BLUE variant scenarios, as these appear likely to occur only when three of the toughest obstacles are overcome (fast refuelling; high durability; and low-cost, high-volume energy storage). This may occur before 2050, but we assume it is more likely that very efficient diesel hybrid propulsion systems will be developed that run partly on biofuels, cutting CO_2 through this combination.

Truck operational efficiency

Operational efficiency in this context refers to the in-use fuel efficiency of trucks. This is a function of how the truck is operated and maintained, and the logistics of how, when and where it is deployed. For example, running fewer but fuller trucks is one logistical improvement that can save energy. Rerouting trucks to shorten delivery distances is another. The basic set of options and technologies includes:

- **On-board diagnostic systems** (real-time fuel-economy computers, data-loggers) to allow both drivers and companies to track efficiency and help ensure that vehicles are optimally driven and maintained.
- **Speed governors and advanced cruise-control systems** can help ensure that vehicles are operated both safely and efficiently.
- **Driver-training programs** and strong vehicle-maintenance systems can result in significant average efficiency improvements.
- **Logistical improvements**, including better truck dispatching and routing systems, load consolidation, and better use of terminals and warehouses. It has been estimated that the use of computerised vehicle routing and scheduling (CVRS) packages can reduce the distance travelled by around 5% to 10% on average (McKinnon, 2007). Changing the location and number of hubs can also have significant impacts, although it is more expensive.

For heavy-duty trucks, driving style is generally acknowledged to have the single greatest influence on vehicle in-use fuel efficiency. Various studies have estimated that regular training in fuel-efficient driving techniques can yield fuel savings of up to 20% per vehicle kilometre, with an average long-term improvement for trained drivers of the order of 5% to 10%. For example, Canada's "Fleet Smart" programme has worked with many fleet operators to achieve these types of impacts over the past decade (NRCAN, 2005).

Overall, we estimate that low-cost changes in vehicle operations and logistics, if applied extensively in each country, could improve average truck in-use efficiency by 5% by 2020, and also cut tonne-kilometres of travel by 5%, for a total energy savings of about 10%. We assume that half of this happens in the Baseline scenario (e.g. due to cost pressures), but that strong policies are needed to achieve the other 5%, which happens in the BLUE Map scenario.

Freight modal switch

Freight movement, like passenger travel, offers a number of ways to improve efficiency through modal switching, mainly from truck to rail, but also, to a limited degree, from truck and air to maritime shipping, and from air to rail.

Rail freight movement in OECD countries is typically one-fifth to one-tenth as energy intensive as truck freight, depending on the type of product being moved. In many countries, rail dominates the movement of raw materials including coal, allowing huge volumes to be moved in long, very efficient train configurations. For lighter products, rail is likely to have a smaller efficiency advantage, though it is still may be significant.

Despite these advantages, rail's share of freight movement has declined steadily in OECD countries over the past 30 years. This is due in part to the time and flexibility advantages offered by trucking, and the development of improved highway systems. But it also reflects capacity constraints in rail systems in many countries. In the European Union there is a major effort underway to expand rail capacity and improve international interoperability, to enable more goods movement by rail, thereby saving energy and cutting the amount of truck traffic on the highways (see, for example EC, 2007).

In the developing world, the situation is often different – extensive rail systems either may not exist or have languished due to underinvestment. As a result, in many countries rail systems are not seen as viable. If this situation could change, based on a new commitment and using new business models, in many countries a new rail infrastructure and services could provide important contributions to both passenger and rail transport, while saving energy.

Rail starts with such a small share of freight movement in most countries that even doubling this share would not have a huge impact on energy use or CO_2 emissions. The BLUE variant scenarios assume that rail capacities are increased enough to reduce truck travel in 2050 by 10%, implying trucking growth worldwide by 2050 of about 160% rather than 170%. In many countries, this would mean construction from scratch of major new rail infrastructure. The true extent of the viability of this option (including the possibility that the potential is actually much larger) requires more detailed country-level and regional analysis than could be performed here. The cost of such a major effort is also unclear, though the benefits would include not only fuel savings but also better safety and less-congested roadways, making the net societal benefits potentially strongly positive.

Aviation

Aviation has been the fastest-growing transport mode in recent years and is likely to continue its rapid growth for many years to come. Aircraft efficiency has been improving steadily over time as airlines respond to high fuel costs, but it is improving at a much slower rate than travel growth. Thus aircraft CO_2 emissions have been rising rapidly. This section covers many of the technologies and fuels that may play an important role in cutting aviation CO_2 in the future. An important caveat is that the discussion here focuses on reductions in CO_2, while in fact there are a number of other aircraft pollutants that may also be important greenhouse gases at high altitudes. These include H_2O, N_2O, NOx and sulphur emissions. The science of how these different emissions affect the climate at high altitude is still developing, and therefore they are not included in the following discussion, but any reductions in CO_2 that result in increases in emissions of other potential greenhouse gases should be treated with caution.

In summary, given past trends and strong incentives in the commercial airline sector to improve efficiency, the Baseline scenario assumes efficiency improvements of about 0.8% per year through to 2050. This yields an overall 30% reduction in energy intensity between 2008 and 2050. In the BLUE variant scenarios, through the additional technologies and measures described below, we increase this annual rate to about 1.2% per year. In the ACT Map scenario an intermediate rate is assumed. In addition to technical improvements, in both scenarios an additional 15% reduction from the Baseline scenario is achieved by 2050 through improved air-traffic systems, load-factor improvements and a degree of modal shift to surface rail. Also, in the BLUE Map scenario, by 2050, 30% of conventional petroleum jet fuel is replaced with Fischer-Tropsch-based biodiesel (biomass-to-liquid, or BtL). The net impacts are shown in Figure 15.14. This also shows the CO_2 reduction in the Baseline scenario relative to a "frozen efficiency" case, *i.e.* if the average aircraft efficiency of 2005 continued unchanged in the future.

Figure 15.14 ▶ ETP aircraft CO_2 emissions projections by scenario

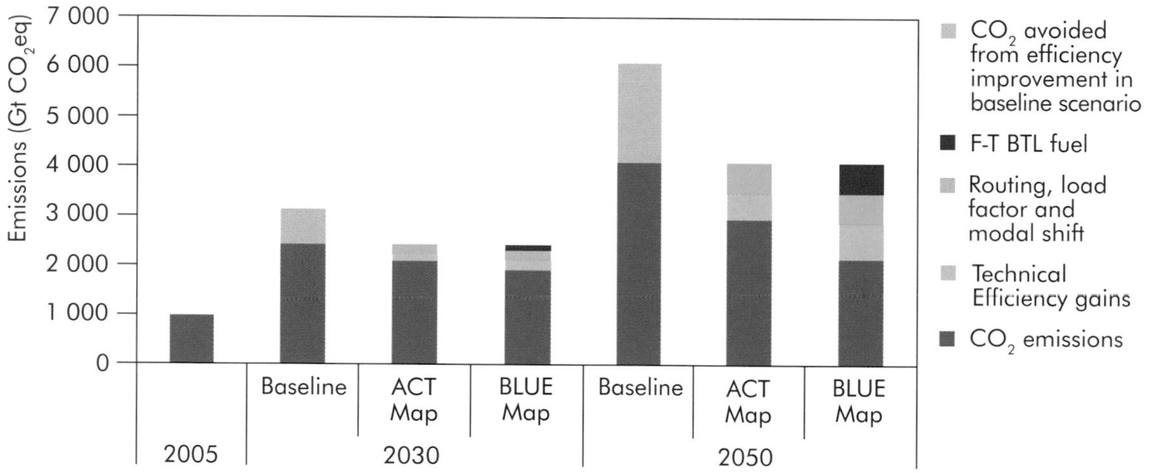

Source: IEA, 2007.

Key point

Substantial aircraft technical efficiency improvements are expected in the Baseline scenario; however additional technical improvements are identified in ACT and BLUE, along with operational improvements and, in BLUE, some use of alternative fuels.

As can be seen, the growth in CO_2 emissions is substantial in the Baseline scenario, increasing four-fold between 2000 and 2050. Without the expected efficiency improvements in the Baseline scenario, this would be an almost six-fold increase. In the BLUE conservative and other BLUE variant scenarios, CO_2 emissions in 2050 are cut by 32% and 42% respectively relative to the Baseline scenario. The difference between the BLUE variants is due to lower biofuels use in the BLUE conservative case. Despite major efficiency improvements and the use of biofuels, CO_2 emissions still double by 2050 in the BLUE Map scenario.

Historical trends and baseline projections

Commercial air travel grew rapidly between 1989 and 1999, averaging a little less than 5% per year in passenger-kilometres (ICAO, 2001). However, the September 11th,

2001 attacks in the United States resulted in a sharp decline in air travel for several years. As a result, international air travel in 2007 only just returned to its previous peak. Its growth rate has also now returned to near historical levels and it appears likely to grow at a similar rate in the future. For example, Boeing projects a global average growth rate to 2026 of about 5% for passenger air traffic and 6% for cargo traffic (Boeing, 2007). This would be the fastest growth rate of any transport mode.

Historically, there have been substantial, fairly steady, improvements in aircraft technical efficiency via improvements in engine efficiency, aerodynamics and weight reduction, along with operational improvements (such as higher "load factors", *i.e.* passengers per flight). In the United States, where the best historical data is available, the combination of technologies and operational improvements has led to a fleet-wide energy intensity reduction of more than 60% between 1971 and 1998, equivalent to an average annual reduction of 3.3%. Efficiency trends for new aircraft in the United States, showing specific aircraft efficiency by date of introduction, are shown in Figure 15.15. This shows that much of the improvement in new aircraft actually occurred before 1980, and that the rate of improvement has been slowing in recent years. However, recent introductions such as the B777 are much more efficient than the fleet average.

Figure 15.15 ▶ Trends in transport aircraft fuel efficiency

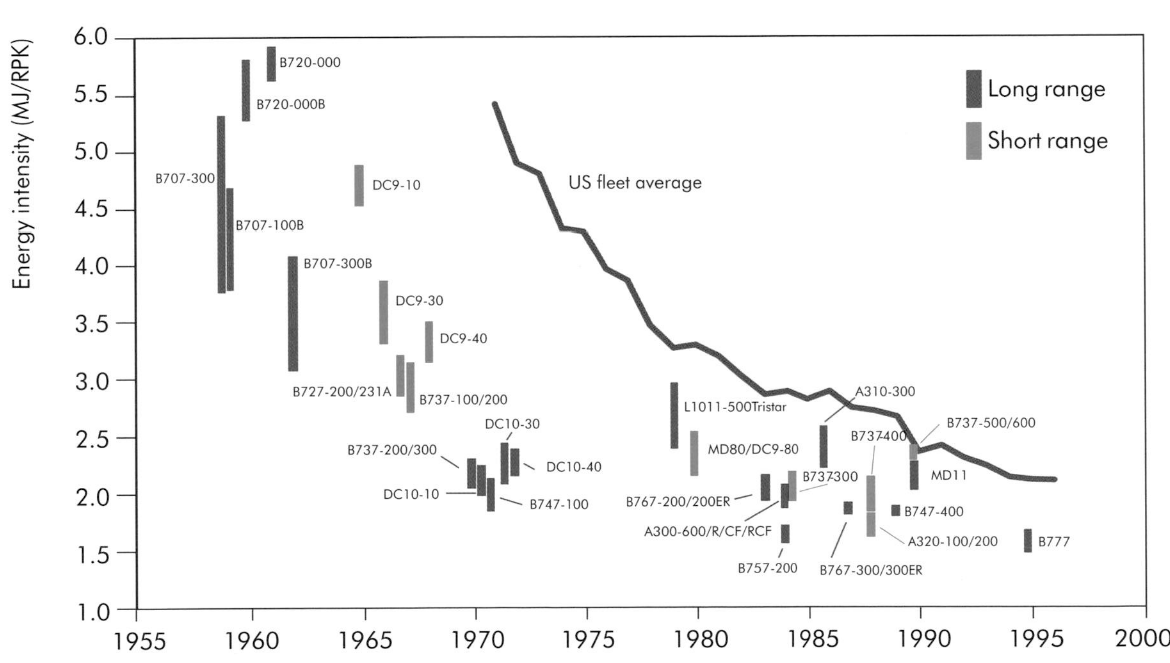

Notes: 1) The bar for each aircraft reflects varying configurations; the line shows estimated fleet average for the United States across all existing aircraft. 2) RPK = revenue passenger kilometre = number of passengers carried x distance flown (in km).

Sources: Lee, *et al.*, 2001 and updates.

Key point

Jet aircraft have evolved dramatically in the past 40 years, and can be expected to continue to improve in energy efficiency in the future; however the rate of improvement is slowing.

Future efficiency improvement rates may be similar to those of recent years, as long as sufficient cost-effective technical improvement options continue to exist. However, there is also a natural tendency for rates of improvement to drop as aircraft move closer to optimal configurations.

Based on estimates of technology availability (discussed below) and taking recent trends into account, the technical potential for efficiency improvement (measured as energy-intensity reduction) in new aircraft appears to be in the range of 25% to 50% by 2050, or about 0.5% to 1.0% per year on average . This is similar to estimates made by Lee, *et al.* (2001), who used the Boeing 777 (introduced in 1995) as a baseline aircraft. However, some of this will already have occurred by 2008 with the introduction of new models such as the Airbus A380 and Boeing 787. Thus an assumption of 0.8% annual improvement is used here.

Given the long lead times required for new technologies to penetrate the entire stock of aircraft, the average efficiency of the stock may lag behind new aircraft efficiency by up to 20 years. On the other hand, since new aircraft sold today are far more efficient than average aircraft and are expected to keep improving, the overall stock of aircraft can also be expected to improve at a steady rate, with an average annual rate that is similar to or slightly faster than the improvement rate of new aircraft.

Increasing operational efficiency and load factors (passenger-kilometres per plane-kilometre) on the existing stock of aircraft continues to offer an important opportunity for efficiency improvement. If the annual historical rate of improvement of 0.2% continues, the worldwide average load factor could nearly reach 0.8 by 2025. This is considered close to an upper bound. The Baseline scenario therefore assumes a 0.2% annual improvement until 2025 (about a 3% overall reduction in energy intensity) and 0% thereafter.

Improving logistical operations and air-traffic controls, such as by reducing delays in landing and allowing aircraft to fly on more optimal routes, may have the potential to reduce the environmental impact per passenger-kilometre by around 10% (IPCC, 1999) This will require changes in certain regulations and harmonisation of air-traffic control technologies and procedures (RCEP, 2007). Since most of this will require new policies and international agreements, by definition we have not included such improvements in the Baseline scenario, though some changes are likely to occur.

The resulting Baseline scenario projections are shown in Table 15.5.

Table 15.5 ▶ **Baseline scenario projections of energy efficiency improvement for newly introduced aircraft**

	Potential annual rate of change	ETP Baseline scenario 2008-2025	ETP Baseline scenario, 2025-2050	ETP Ref case total % change 2008-2050
Technology factors	0.5-1.0%	0.8%	0.7%	25%
Load factor	0.1-0.3%	0.2%	0.0%	3%
Total	0.7-1.2%	1.0%	0.7%	28%

Note: Operational/air traffic improvements are assumed to be negligible in the baseline scenario.

Aviation technologies

Aircraft fuel efficiency improvements largely come from increasing engine efficiencies, lowering weight, and improving lift-to-drag ratios (Karagozian, *et al.*, 2006). Efficiencies in engines, aerodynamics and structure/weight are interdependent.

Propulsion technology potential

Over the past few decades, modifications to gas turbine (jet) engines have increased aircraft fuel efficiency substantially. Engine design has focused on both improving propulsion efficiency and increasing thermal efficiency to reduce fuel consumption. Although an improvement of approximately 30% in fuel consumption is still possible before the theoretical limits are reached, this benefit may be limited to 20% to 25% if engines are to achieve expected future emissions standards for oxides of nitrogen (Karagozian, *et al.*, 2006).

The Boeing 787 is the first large commercial aircraft to incorporate a number of recent technologies. Boeing claims 20% fuel efficiency gains compared to comparable existing aircraft. Eight percent of these gains come from its engines, with the balance from aerodynamic improvements, the increased use of lighter-weight composite materials, and the use of advanced systems (Ogando, 2007; Hawk, 2005).

Potential for improved aerodynamics

The relationship between the lifting force and the drag force of an aircraft is termed the lift-to-drag ratio. The higher this ratio, the less energy is needed to keep the aircraft aloft. Fuel consumption varies roughly inversely with lift-to-drag ratio at cruise speeds. Over the long term, increasing this ratio is potentially the most powerful means of reducing fuel intensity. Lift-to-drag ratios can be increased with wingspan extensions and various modifications to the overall design, including:

Wing modifications: Retrofits of existing commercial aircraft with "winglets" (small additional wings) and wingtip extensions have increased the lift-to-drag ratio by 4% to 7% (Greener by Design, 2005). However, the benefits of this increased lift-to-drag ratio need to be balanced against the additional weight. In the medium-term, winglets and wingtip extensions can provide additional fuel efficiency gains by incorporating new structural materials and active load control systems.

Hybrid laminar flow control: Laminar flow control helps to reduce what is known as pressure drag. An extensive application of hybrid laminar flow control processes to fin, tail-plane and nacelles – as well as to the wings – has shown a potential reduction in fuel consumption of over 15% for medium-range aircraft. More modest applications of this technology, at lower cost, are more typical, with a 2% to 5% improvement in efficiency (Greener by Design, 2005).

Flying wing/blended wind-body configuration: "flying wing" aircraft are a design development in which the entire aeroplane generates lift and is streamlined to minimise drag, in order to produce a high lift-to-drag ratio. The blended wing body is a hybrid of a flying wing and a conventional aeroplane (Figure 15.16). With flying wing concepts, it may be possible to cut the fuel use of new aircraft by 50% compared to the average planes of today. Studies conducted by Boeing show approximately 20% to 25% less fuel consumption compared to advanced, conventional aircraft such as some of the newest plane designs of today (Barr, 2006). The development of flying wing aircraft will require significant technological and operational breakthroughs, and consumer acceptance, but commercialisation by 2025 is possible (Leifsson and Mason, 2004).

Figure 15.16 ▶ Blended wing body: SAX-40 design

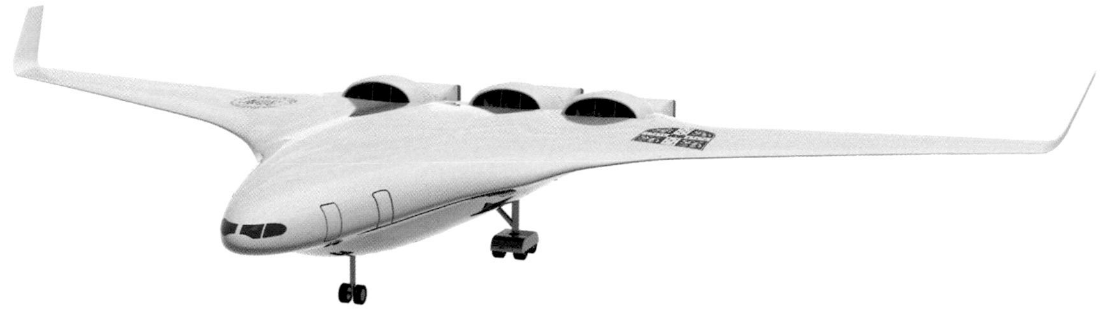

Source: Cambridge-MIT Institute, 2006.

Structure/materials-related technology potential

Light-weighting aircraft by using new materials and composites can also significantly improve fuel efficiency. Much of the current effort of aeroplane manufacturers and component suppliers to reduce fuel consumption and GHG emissions is concentrated in this area.

Carbon-fibre reinforced plastic (CFRP): Carbon-fibre reinforced plastic is stronger and stiffer than metals such as aluminium, titanium or steel, but its relative weight per volume is half that of aluminium and one-fifth of the weight of steel. In addition, CFRP suffers little corrosion and is considerably more fatigue-resistant under ideal manufacturing conditions. One of the key issues for composite materials is to develop ways of assuring such conditions. Full replacement of aluminium by CFRP could provide a 10% weight reduction in medium-range aircraft, and 15% in long-range aircraft (M&C, 2007). CFRP has been increasingly used in aircraft frame construction: the Boeing 787 uses CFRP for 50% of its body (on a weight basis) and this contributes an estimated one-third of its 20% fuel efficiency gains compared to comparable existing aircraft. In the near and medium term, the use of this material in wings, wing boxes and fuselages will increase as the technology matures.

Fibre metal laminate (FML): FML comprises a central layer of fibre sandwiched between one or more thick layers of high-quality aluminium. It is used for about 3% of the recent Airbus A380 fuselage skin, which is the first time it has been used in civil aircraft. FML has also has been developed for aircraft wing applications; it is stronger than CFRP and will allow a further 20% weight reduction compared to CFRP constructions (M&C, 2007). These materials will be increasingly used in the short to medium term.

Light-weighting of engines: The use of light-weight composite materials with high-temperature tolerance in engines not only reduces weight but also allows higher operating temperatures and greater combustion efficiency, both of which lead to reduced fuel consumption. Several promising light-weight, high-temperature composites are under investigation for aviation engine applications (Hoeveler, 2004). However, the benefits of reducing engine weight on fuel consumption, all other things being equal, are relatively small. For example, for a 15 000 km range aircraft, a 10% reduction in engine weight would reduce fuel consumption by a little more than 1%.

Assuming adoption rates that approach a "maximum technology" case, the BLUE Map scenario includes technical efficiency improvements of 10% beyond the Baseline scenario by 2050, *i.e.* a total improvement in fleet average fuel efficiency of 35% from the current average, compared to the 25% improvement envisaged in the Baseline scenario. This does not assume any migration away from current swept-wing aircraft designs to newer designs such as flying wings. If such additional wholesale design changes were undertaken, an additional 10% to 15% improvement might be achievable by 2050.

Operational system improvement potential

Different approaches to the use and deployment of aircraft can also reduce aircraft energy intensity. Examples include:

Continuous descent approach (CDA): The positioning of an aircraft on its final approach influences its fuel consumption as well as noise. Changes in descent angle and various maneuvers can result in higher noise and fuel consumption. In contrast, with modern electronic systems, the CDA concept has become viable, using a smoother descent that reduces changes in engine thrust and therefore saves fuel and reduces noise. Currently, many leading airlines and air-traffic service providers are promoting testing of this procedure. (Greener by Design, 2002).

Improvements in CNS/ATM systems: Improvements in communications, navigation and surveillance (CNS) and air-traffic management (ATM) systems would enable flight paths to be optimised to reduce travel distances, and hence would improve fuel economy. The International Civil Aviation Organization (ICAO) estimates that fuel savings of about 5% could be expected by 2015 in the United States and Europe as a result of specific, planned changes to CNS/ATM systems, although it is uncertain whether the envisioned changes will occur in the given time frame. In the longer term, somewhat greater savings are projected (ICAO, 2004).

Multi-stage long-distance travel: For a given standard of technology there is a travel range that maximises payload fuel efficiency. With today's standard of technology, the most payload/fuel efficient aircraft is one designed for a range of approximately 4 000 km. Studies suggest that a substantial reduction in the fuel used on long-range travel could be achieved by limiting stage lengths to 7 500 km and developing long-range fleets with a mix of aircraft with design ranges of 5 000 km and 7 500 km. However, this would necessitate many more stopovers for long-range travel, which is likely to lengthen travel times and prove unacceptable to many travellers.

The BLUE Map scenario assumes that a 10% reduction in global aircraft energy use can be achieved by 2050 (half by 2025 and the rest after 2025, at a rate of about 0.3% per year) through the optimisation of operational systems.

Aircraft alternative fuels potential

Several requirements need to be satisfied for fuels to be suitable in commercial aviation. Aviation fuels need to deliver a large amount of energy content per unit of mass and volume, in order to minimize fuel carried for a given range, the size of fuel reservoirs, and the drag related to the fuel storage. Aviation fuels also need to be thermally stable, to avoid freezing or gelling at low temperatures and to satisfy other requirements in terms of viscosity, surface tension, ignition properties and compatibility with the materials typically used in aviation.

A number of potential alternative aviation fuels exist. Not all of them, however, would significantly reduce GHG emissions. The most likely alternative fuels for aviation are synthetic jet fuels, since they have similar characteristics to conventional jet fuel. These can be derived from coal, natural gas or biomass. An additional option, in the longer term, is liquid hydrogen, since it delivers a large amount of energy per unit mass (though not per unit volume). Other options, like methane, methanol and ethanol, are characterised by a too-low energy density and energy per unit mass, and are therefore not likely to be used in aviation.

Biodiesel

Biodiesel-like fuels derived from vegetable oils are not generally suitable on their own for commercial aviation applications. Conventional fatty-acid methyl esters freeze at normal aircraft cruising temperatures; they also are not thermally stable at high temperatures in the engine. However, vegetable oils and fatty acid methyl esters (FAME) biodiesel can be hydro-treated, which converts it to a fuel that is much closer in properties to conventional jet fuel and overcomes these problems. Hydrotreating can be carried out at refineries, but it adds an additional cost to the basic cost of producing biofuels.

Fischer-Tropsch (F-T) fuels from fossil feedstocks

Synthetic fuels are high-quality fuels that can be derived from natural gas, coal or biomass. These fuels are typically created via a gasification step, through the formation of a synthesis gas (mainly CO and H_2) and its conversion to liquid hydrocarbon fuels via the Fischer-Tropsch (F-T) process. The F-T process is technically mature, and synthetic jet fuels from coal, natural gas or other hydrocarbon feedstock are chemically similar to conventional kerosene jet fuels – and ideally suited to supplement or replace them. They have high energy density and exhibit excellent low-temperature and thermal stability. They can even provide an efficiency increase compared to conventional jet fuel (Karagozian, *et al.*, 2006). Coal-derived synthetic aviation fuels have already been certified in South Africa, and certification of blends is progressing. Apart from the high cost of production, the main drawback with synthetic fuels produced from fossil fuel is the CO_2 emitted during the manufacturing process. If synthetic fuels are to contribute to GHG emission reductions, CO_2 from the manufacturing process must be captured and stored. Even then, however, the analysis of the full carbon-cycle of these fuels does not show very significant reduction opportunities in comparison with conventional jet fuels.

Given the likely cost reductions for large-scale production of synthetic fuels from natural gas (gas-to-liquid – GTL) and coal (coal-to-liquid – CTL), and the eventual decline in production capacity for conventional oil and oil products such as jet fuel, the Baseline scenario assumes considerable use of synthetic fuel in jet fuel (and in other fuels including diesel and gasoline), reaching 25% of aircraft fuel use by 2050. However, since these are very high-CO_2 fuels, they are assumed to be eliminated in the ACT and BLUE scenarios via efficiency gains and lower demand for fuel.

Fischer-Tropsch (F-T) biomass-to-liquid (BtL) fuels

As discussed in the bioenergy chapter, biomass-to-liquids (BtL) processes using F-T technologies are advancing and are likely to be deployed within the next five to ten years. If so, these fuels may offer an important GHG reduction opportunity for aircraft, since the combustion characteristics of F-T BtL fuels are very similar to those of fossil F-T synthetic jet fuels. In addition, F-T BtL fuels can provide much larger benefits in terms of energy consumption and reductions in GHG emissions on a life-cycle basis than can F-T synthetic jet fuels. According to some analyses focussing on road diesel fuel, GHG savings can exceed 80% on a life-cycle basis (Wang, Wu and Huo, 2007).

While there remain certain technical obstacles, a principal drawback of BtL fuels is their production cost per unit of energy delivered. BtL plants need to be very large to be cost-competitive, but the size of the production facilities conflicts with the sparse nature of the biomass feedstock and the cost of its collection. Since fuel costs are a significant share of total costs in the airline industry, high-cost BtL fuel would not be likely to be adopted without policies that require their use or make them price-competitive with conventional jet fuel.

Liquid hydrogen

Hydrogen is a potential low-CO_2 fuel for aircraft, but its use poses a number of significant challenges. It would most likely be stored on board as a cryogenic liquid (LH_2) to minimise volume. Nonetheless, a number of significant modifications would be required to both engine systems and airframe designs to accommodate liquid cryogenic fuels.

Insulation requirements and pressurization issues make it impossible to store LH_2 in aeroplane wings, as is done with kerosene jet fuels. In addition, though LH_2 has a very high energy density per unit mass (weight), its volumetric energy density is only one-quarter that of current jet fuel. The storage tanks needed for the large volume of cryogenically cooled hydrogen would increase the weight of large commercial aircraft by over 10% (Daggett, *et al.*, 2006). Modifications would also be necessary to the fuel management system and temperature controls.

In sum, use of LH_2 would require a completely different aircraft design, and would pose significant challenges for the engine. It would also require substantial modifications to airport infrastructure. Being gaseous at ambient temperature, H_2 would also be fundamentally different from jet fuel, requiring a completely different fuel distribution infrastructure. Overall, LH_2 is not promising as an alternative fuel for aviation in the near future or the medium term. It could only be viable in the long term if there were significant technological developments, entirely new aircraft designs and substantial infrastructural change.

Overall, BtL fuels appear to offer the best medium-term and, perhaps, long-term potential for technically acceptable, eventually commercial, very low life-cycle CO_2 emission, aircraft fuels. No alternative fuels are assumed to be used in the Baseline scenario. The BLUE conservative scenario assumes that BtL fuel reaches 15% of aircraft fuel use by 2050, while other BLUE variant scenarios assume it reaches a 30% fuel share, with the remainder being conventional petroleum kerosene (jet fuel). In fact, if BtL fuels become commercial and sufficient land is available for feedstock production, their share of aircraft fuel could eventually rise to 100%.

Maritime transport

This section on maritime transport (shipping) represents an initial look at this important mode, and covers selected technology and fuel options. There are other technologies under development in this area, and the IEA will continue to investigate these in the future.

The projections for the Baseline, ACT and BLUE scenarios are shown in Figure 15.17. The ETP Baseline scenario projects energy use and CO_2 emissions from national and international maritime shipping to increase by about 2% per year in the near future, with the rate then declining over time until it is well below 1% per year by 2050. Based on estimates of available technical efficiency and operational improvements provided below, these CO_2 emissions have been cut by about 15% by 2050 in the ACT scenario and by 30% by 2050 in the BLUE scenario. An additional 15% reduction from low GHG biofuels is achieved in the BLUE scenario. The result is that in the BLUE scenario, CO_2 emissions in 2050 are at about the same level as in 2005.

Figure 15.17 ▶ ETP maritime CO_2 emissions projections by scenario

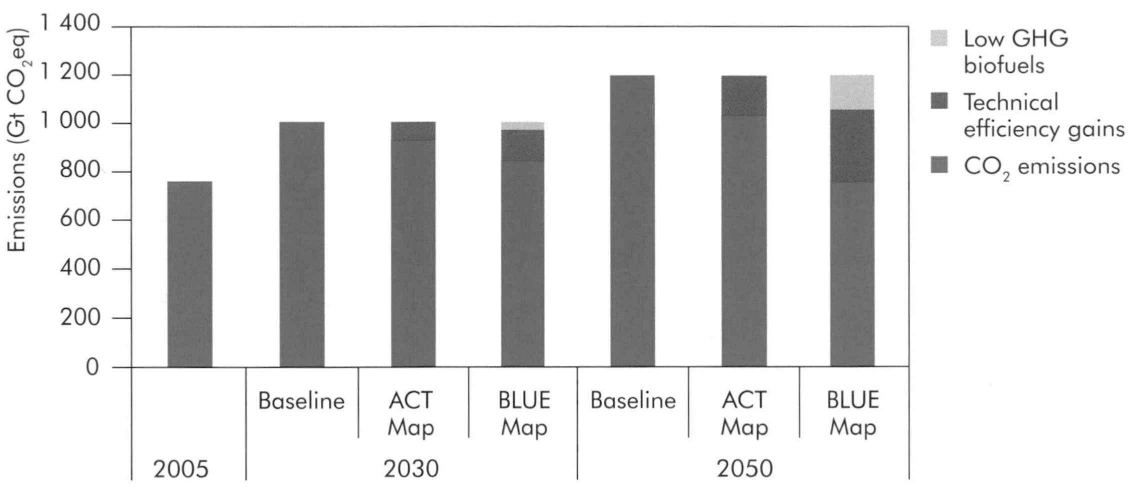

Key point

Maritime energy use is expected to increase by 50% in the Baseline scenario, and remain fairly constant in BLUE Map.

The world shipping fleet consumed approximately nine exajoules (200 Mtoe) of fuel in 2005, about 10% of total transport fuel consumption. Over the past ten years, annual growth in shipping fuel consumption and related CO_2 emissions has averaged about 3%. The energy trends in domestic and international fuel use since 1990 are shown in Figure 15.18.

Figure 15.18 ▶ Energy use in domestic and international shipping, 1990-2005

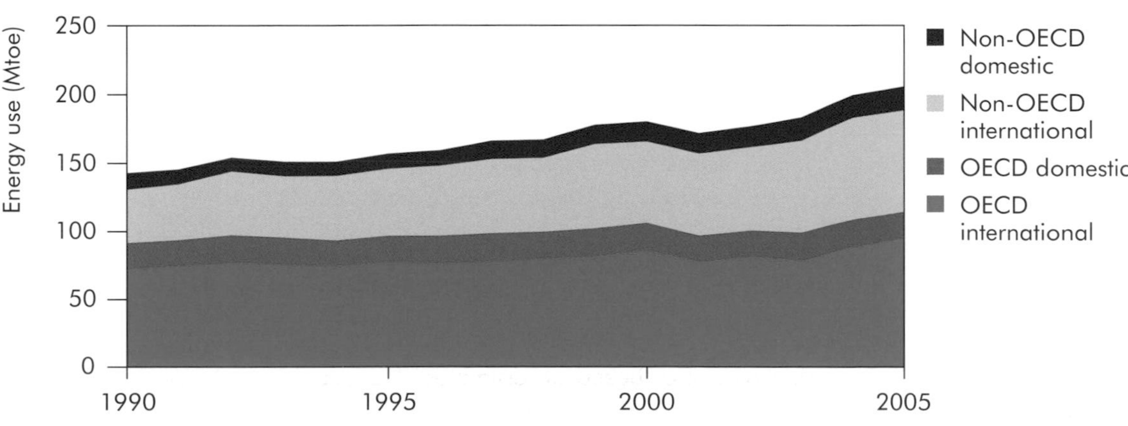

Key point

Compared to domestic shipping, international shipping accounts for most of the energy use, and largest source of growth.

15

International shipping is dominated by three main types of freight movement: dry bulk cargos; container traffic; and crude oil and other hydrocarbons such as liquefied petroleum gas. Of these, container traffic has shown the most rapid growth in recent years, up to 9% per year during the 1990s and early 2000s (Kieran, 2003). The IEA does not have detailed data on freight movement or shipping efficiencies, but data on fuel use indicates a 3% annual increase in recent years, which may be fairly close to the overall growth rate in shipping tonne-kilometres. This suggests a fairly low rate of efficiency improvement (reduction in energy intensity) in shipping. This is an area for further research.

Efficiency technologies

There are several immediately available technologies that can contribute to improving ship energy efficiency and reducing GHG emissions. They include improvements to engine efficiency and hull design (hydrodynamics), as well as operational changes.

The average fuel consumption of ocean-going ships can be reduced up to 30% by optimising propulsion plant configurations. Typically, multi-engine ships operate more efficiently with the minimum number of propulsion units on line. Operating one engine instead of two per shaft at moderate speeds, or with the second shaft trailed at very slow speeds, can reduce fuel consumption by 25% or more (Breslin and Wang, 2004).

Auxiliary electricity demand accounts for a significant share of energy use on ships. Therefore, simple measures such as using fluorescent lights, using motion detectors to turn off lights, and greater use of thermostats to regulate ship-board temperatures can contribute to significant fuel savings on ships.

An emerging technology for use as a secondary propulsion system is the towing sail or kite, which is connected to the ship by a cable and can be adjusted to optimise the use of high-wind resources at sea. The technology has been commercialised for heavy cargo vessels and its sizing and effective loads are expected to rise substantially over the coming decade. Compared to conventional sail propulsion with a mast, towing kite propulsion systems minimise the heeling of ships caused by strong winds and can catch high winds 100 m to 300 m above the deck level. Retrofitting of existing ships is not considered difficult or expensive. With automatic operation and routing optimisation with computerised control, there are claims that this system can reduce fuel consumption in some situations by up to 50% and bring down average fuel costs by 10% to 35% (SkySails, 2006).

Hull design

Ship efficiency can be improved by changing hull designs. Stern flaps and wedges that extend the bottom surface of the hull can be tailored to achieve different goals such as reducing energy consumption, increasing ship speed or a combination of the two. This relatively inexpensive design modification can be used on almost any ship with a major portion of its operation speeds above 15 knots. It can reduce fuel consumption and related CO_2 emissions by 4% to 8% depending on the ship class (Breslin and Wang, 2004).

In addition, using advanced light-weight materials and structures in ship design can reduce hull weight by 25% to 30% and topside weight by 25% to 30%. This can contribute to significant reductions in fuel consumption (Defense Science Board, 2001).

Ship operational improvements

A ship's energy efficiency can be increased simply by slowing down. One shipping company recently cut the speeds of its ocean vessels by about five knots (from 25 knots to 20 knots), with fuel savings of 40% to 50%. More data is needed, but if even a fraction of such savings is possible with modest speed reductions, these may prove to be a cost-effective approach to cutting CO_2 emissions. However, slower speed means a reduction in effective capacity, which may trigger the use of additional ships. But even if a 10% speed reduction triggers 10% more ships, there would be potentially substantial net fuel savings.

Changes in propulsion systems

High-efficiency gas turbine engines

The use of advanced, high-efficiency, inter-cooled recuperative (ICR) gas turbines as the main form of propulsion can reduce fuel consumption by 25% to 30%. Such engines use seawater to cool intake air to increase the efficiency of the compressor, use scavenged waste heat from the exhaust gas to preheat intake air so as to reduce the amount of fuel required, and improve the thermal signature of the ship by reducing stack temperatures (Breslin and Wang, 2004). A number of ships have recently been outfitted with gas turbine engines and many more could be in the future.

Integrated electric drive

Integrated electric drive can reduce fuel consumption and GHG emissions by 15% to 19% (Young, Newel and Little, 2001). Electric ships can operate at or near optimum efficiency and generate power for an integrated distribution system. They are also more efficient.

Shifts to alternative fuels

In the longer term, significant reductions in GHG emissions in the maritime freight industry can be achieved by shifting from the current use of heavy fuel oils (HFO) to new carbon-free fuels. Currently, very fuel-efficient diesel engines using HFO dominate ship propulsion; more than 98% of vessels of over 100 tonnes are diesel-powered. Many of the largest engines, with output exceeding 50 MW, have a thermal efficiency of over 50% through dual-fuel configurations that allow continuous shifting between natural gas (NG) and HFO (Keith, Farrell and Corbett, 2004). This may enable other liquid or gaseous fuels (such as H_2) to be introduced. The shipping sector may be able to avoid some of the obstacles to the introduction of new fuels faced by other sectors. Large ships designed to operate in a limited number of ports world-wide may have lower fuel infrastructure requirements than some other types of vehicles (such as cars or long-haul trucks).

Bio-crude

"Bio-crude", a plant-derived non-refined biofuel, can be made from non-food (e.g. woody) feedstocks via hydrothermal upgrading or other means, and is a ready substitute for conventional fuels in many stationary applications such as boilers, engines and turbines. However, certain characteristics of bio-crude make its use as a transportation fuel difficult. First, bio-crude may be more expensive than heavy fuel oil (depending on crude oil prices, among other things) If higher-grade fuel is needed, upgrading of bio-crude can be achieved by catalytic cracking or hydro-treating – but this will raise the fuel cost further. A second issue is that bio-crude is not as stable as petroleum fuel. Although the chemical composition of bio-crude varies according to feedstock and processing parameters, it can be unstable, which makes it difficult to store and transport. Third, bio-crude is not fully compatible with conventional heavy fuel oil, and it makes a partial introduction in a mixture with conventional fuels difficult without additional fuel upgrading steps (PyNe and IEA Bioenergy, 2007). Nonetheless, bio-crude or derivative products appear to hold potential as low-carbon fuels to at least partly displace current heavy fuel oil in shipping.

Hydrogen and fuel cell

Since many ships currently operate with internal combustion engines or gas turbines that could be retrofitted to handle various gaseous fuels, the shift to hydrogen-fuelled ships might not be too difficult, at least in principle.

However, hydrogen storage and distribution systems remain a challenge. For large ships, the mass of fuel carried rather than its volume is the greatest concern. Liquid hydrogen (LH_2) has high gravimetric energy density, which allows a significant fuel-mass reduction (by a factor of 2.8) compared to current HFO on an identical ship range (Brewer, 1991). It increases useful payload, hence economic returns. While LH_2 can create additional economic gains, it generates substantial new operational requirements from the current HFO system, particularly in terms of required storage and system temperatures and safety systems. On the other hand, H_2 is an extremely clean fuel and has a less-complex fuel-management path than HFO, due to its lower viscosity and low foreign matter content.

Higher efficiencies could be achieved by using H_2 in fuel-cell systems rather than in internal combustion engines or turbine systems. Solid-oxide or molten-carbonate fuel-cell systems could be used, as the high temperatures and long start-up times required for their operation would not be problematic for large ships, However, the upper boundary of current fuel-cell system outputs appears sufficient only to power small commercial vessels. More research is necessary to understand the potential of fuel-cell systems for ship propulsion, because much of the R&D effort so far has concentrated on fuel-cell systems for on-board power generation only. In any case the costs for complete fuel-cell systems for large marine vessels appear likely to be prohibitive in the near term, compared to other options for cutting shipping CO_2 emissions (Keith, Farrell, and Corbett, 2004; Veldhuis, Richardson and Stone, 2007).

In BLUE, international shipping is assumed to adopt biofuels (either a bio-crude, upgraded bio-crude, or BTL diesel, all of which can be produced from non-food biomass feedstocks). Similar to aviation, the biofuel share is assumed to reach 30% of overall fuel use by 2050.

Chapter 16 INDUSTRY

Key Findings

- *Manufacturing industries account for one-third of global energy use. Direct industrial energy and process CO_2 emissions amount to 6.7 gigatonnes (Gt), about 25% of total worldwide emissions, of which 30% comes from the iron and steel industry, 27% from non-metallic minerals (mainly cement) and 16% from chemicals and petrochemicals production. Industrial emissions will double in the Baseline scenario between now and 2050.*

- *The application of the best available technologies worldwide would result in a savings of some 19% to 32% of current CO_2 emissions in this sector. This includes improvements to steam supply systems and motor systems, which offer efficiency potentials of 15% to 30%. Industrial CHP can be cost-competitive, but it is held back by market barriers. CHP can complement new process designs that reduce heat demand per unit of output. A careful case-by-case evaluation is needed.*

- *Direct energy and process CO_2 emissions in the ACT Map scenario in 2050 are 66% above the level of 2005. In the BLUE Map scenario they are 22% below the 2005 level. Fuel and feedstock substitution play an important role, as does CCS in the BLUE Map scenario.*

- *Industrial emissions can be reduced using CO_2 capture and storage, especially in the production of chemicals, iron and steel, cement, and paper and pulp. This option has received limited attention so far, and further RD&D is needed.*

- *Different sub-sectors need different technological developments to maximise their CO_2 saving potential. The energy savings potential of the chemical industry is constrained by the high feedstock intensity of its processes. Alternative feedstocks for the petrochemical industry deserve special attention. Using biomass feedstocks and recycling more plastic waste could reduce life-cycle CO_2 emissions substantially.*

- *More RD&D is needed for solutions such as breakthrough process technologies, and systems approaches such as life-cycle optimisation based on recycling and materials use efficiency.*

Overview

Industry accounted for nearly one-third of the world's primary energy use and approximately 25% of the world's energy and process CO_2 emissions in 2005. This chapter explores the potential to reduce CO_2 emissions in the industrial sector and in particular concentrates on those industrial technologies that hold the promise of large energy and/or CO_2 savings.[1]

16

1. In this analysis: 1) the industrial sector excludes petroleum refineries; 2) unless specified otherwise, energy use figures include petrochemical feedstocks; 3) only CO_2 emissions are covered; 4) energy and CO_2 gains from industrial CHP systems are allocated partly to the industrial sector and partly to the power sector, in accordance with IEA statistical accounting conventions.

Carbon-dioxide emissions in this sector can be reduced in three main ways: through efficiency measures, including waste material recycling and product design changes; through fuel and feedstock substitution (such as the greater use of biomass); and through CO_2 capture and storage (CCS). Neither quality improvements that reduce materials consumption nor improvements in logistics that could reduce freight and trade flow emissions are considered in this analysis. Equally, this discussion does not cover measures to reduce non-CO_2 greenhouse gas emissions, an area in which the chemical and aluminium industries, for example, have made considerable progress in recent years.

Industry is relatively efficient, compared to other sectors. However, improving energy efficiency has an important part to play in reducing industrial emissions. In energy-intensive industries such as chemicals, paper, steel and cement manufacturing, cost-effective efficiency gains in the order of 10% to 20% are already possible using commercially available technologies. The energy intensity of most industrial processes is at least 50% higher than the theoretical minimum determined by the basic laws of thermodynamics. Energy efficiency tends to be lower in regions with low energy prices. Cross-cutting technologies for motor and steam systems would yield efficiency improvements in all industries, with typical energy savings in the range of 15% to 30%. The payback period can be as short as two years, and in the best cases, the financial savings over the operating life of improved systems can run as high as 30% to 50%. In those processes where efficiency is close to the practical maximum, innovations in materials and processes would enable even further gains.

Many relatively new technologies such as smelt reduction, near net-shape casting of steel, new separation membranes, black liquor gasification and advanced cogeneration are currently being developed, demonstrated and adopted in the industrial sector. Some completely new process designs and processing techniques are also on the horizon, although these are unlikely to be commercially available in the next 10 to 15 years. The ACT Map and BLUE Map scenarios assume a high degree of success in the development, commercialisation and implementation of these technologies in all industrial subsectors.

CO_2 capture and storage is an emerging option for industry. This technology is most suited for large sources of off-gases with high CO_2 concentrations such as blast furnaces (iron and steel), cement kilns (non-metallic minerals), ammonia plants (chemicals and petrochemicals), and also black liquor boilers or gasifiers (pulp and paper).

Figure 16.1 shows industrial CO_2 emissions by sector in the Baseline, ACT Map and BLUE Map scenarios. Emissions include process CO_2, largely from cement production (1 Gt in 2005). These direct emissions nearly double by 2050 in the Baseline scenario. However, indirect emissions in power generation more than triple as electricity demand increases faster than total final energy demand. In the ACT Map scenario, direct energy and process emissions in 2050 are 66% above the 2005 level. In the BLUE Map scenario, they are 22% below the 2005 level (Table 16.1). The emission reduction in industry is less than in other sectors, especially in the ACT Map scenario. The reason is that efficiency is already relatively high and options such as CCS are relatively costly.

Iron and steel, non-metallic minerals (notably cement production) and chemicals and petrochemicals constitute the bulk of emissions in all scenarios during the whole period.

Figure 16.1 ▶ Industrial CO_2 emissions by sector in the Baseline, ACT Map and BLUE Map scenarios

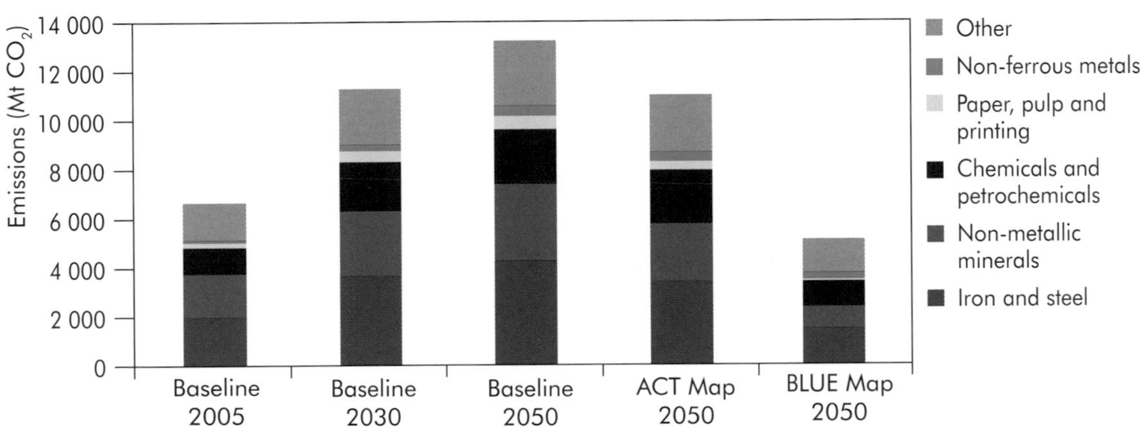

Note: Direct energy and process CO_2 emissions. Iron and steel includes coke ovens and blast furnaces.

Key point

Only in the BLUE Map scenario emissions in 2050 fall below the 2005 level.

Table 16.1 shows emissions by industry sector. In the ACT Map and BLUE Map scenarios, most sub-sectors demonstrate similar reductions in their CO_2 intensities compared to the Baseline scenario. But the economic activity of different sub-sectors grows at different rates in the ETP scenarios between 2005 and 2050, so the emission reductions of individual sectors compared to their 2005 levels differs more markedly.

Industrial energy use and CO_2 emissions profile

Industry accounted for nearly one-third of total global energy use in 2005, including conversion losses from electricity and heat supply.

Total final energy use by industry was 2 763 Mtoe in 2005 (Table 16.2).[2] The approximately 1 000 million tonnes (Mt) of wood and biomass feedstock used by

2. Final energy is the sum of all energy carriers that are used without accounting for upstream energy conversion losses (notably in power generation).

industry, equivalent to 380 Mtoe to 430 Mtoe of biomass, is not accounted for in these figures. The totals in Table 16.2 also exclude energy use for the transportation of raw materials and finished industrial products. Thirteen countries, the G8+5 group, account for two-thirds of industrial final energy use.[3]

Table 16.1 ▶ Industrial CO_2 reductions by sector in the ACT Map and BLUE Map scenarios, 2050

Reference	ACT Map Baseline 2050 (%)	BLUE Map Baseline 2050 (%)	ACT Map 2005 (%)	BLUE Map 2005 (%)
Iron and steel	–20	–65	71	–26
Cement	–22	–68	38	–44
Chemicals and petrochemicals	–2	–53	101	–5
Pulp and paper	–36	–97	83	–91
Nonferrous metals	–9	–24	258	200
Other	–11	–48	54	–10
Total	–16	–61	66	–22

Note: Includes direct energy and process CO_2 emissions. Iron and steel includes coke ovens and blast furnaces. Emissions reductions related to electricity savings are not included.

Most industrial energy use is for raw materials production. This accounts for 68% of total final industrial energy use, with the chemical and petrochemical industry alone accounting for 29% and the iron and steel industry 20%.

Industrial energy intensity (energy use per unit of industrial output, measured in physical tonnage or added value terms) has improved substantially in most sectors over the last three decades across all manufacturing sub-sectors and all regions (Figure 16.2). Increases in levels of activity, however, mean that energy use and CO_2 emissions have increased worldwide. Industrial final energy use increased 65% between 1971 and 2005, an average annual growth of 1.5% (Figure 16.3). But growth rates are not uniform. For example, in the chemical and petrochemical sub-sector, energy and feedstock use has doubled, while energy use for iron and steel production has been relatively flat despite strong growth in global production.

3. The G8+5 includes the G8 nations (Canada, France, Germany, Italy, Japan, Russia, the United Kingdom and the United States), plus the five leading emerging economies (Brazil, China, India, Mexico and South Africa).

Figure 16.2 ▶ The evolution of industrial sub-sector energy intensities, 1990-2004

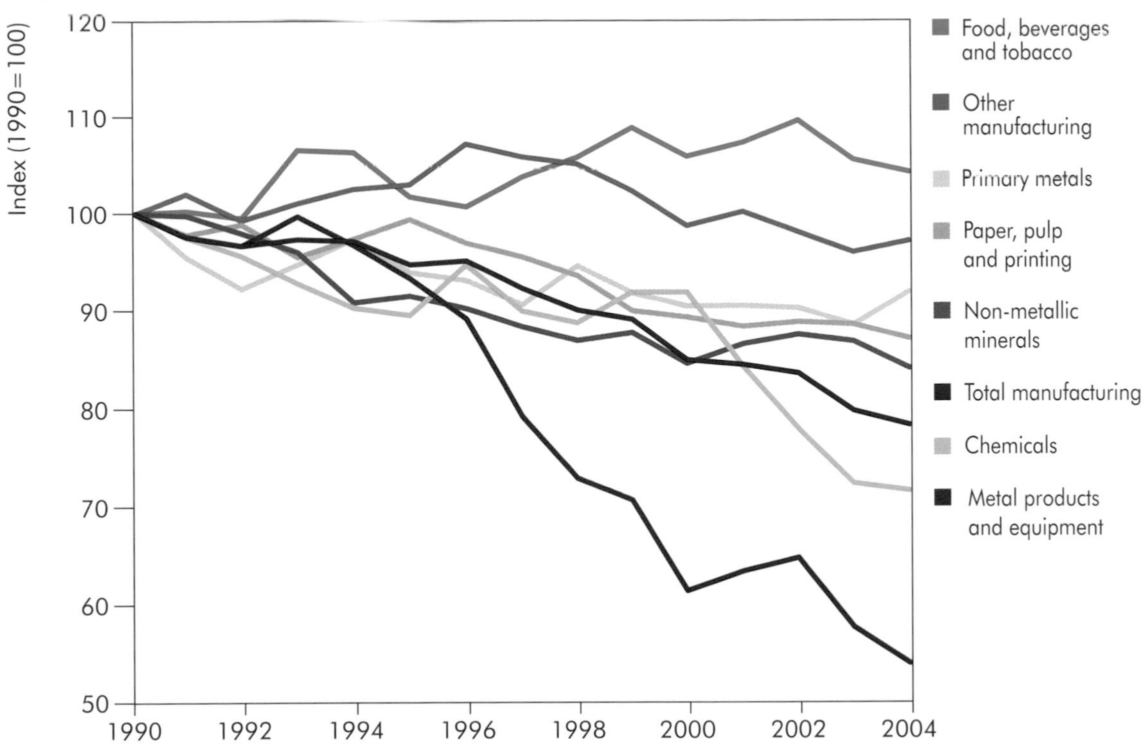

Note: Index based on energy consumption per value added in USD (PPP) 2000.
Source: IEA, 2007a.

Key point

Strong decoupling of energy use and economic activity has been seen in some sectors.

Figure 16.3 ▶ Global industrial energy use, 1971-2005

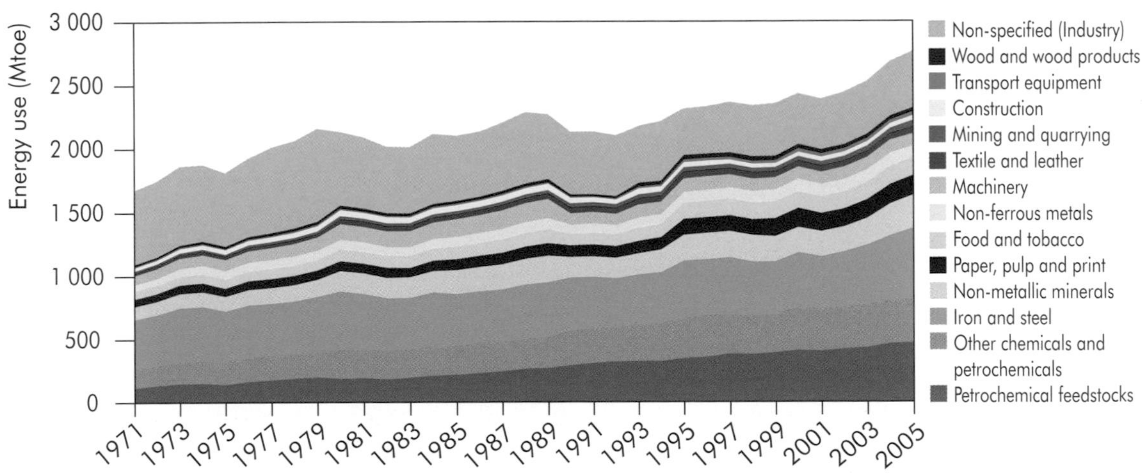

Notes: Iron and steel includes coke ovens and blast furnaces.
The discontinuity around 1990 is caused by developments in Eastern Europe and the Former Soviet Union (FSU) that resulted in a rapid decline of industrial production.
Source: IEA statistics.

Key point

Industrial final energy use increased by 65% between 1971 and 2005, an average annual growth of 1.5%.

Table 16.2 ▶ **Industrial final energy use, world regions and G8+5 countries, 2005 (Mtoe**

	Africa	MidEast	OECD Europe	Transition economies, Europe	Russia	Transition economi Asia
Chemical and petrochemical	11	60	138	20	49	1
of which: petrochemical feedstocks	*8*	*36*	*80*	*12*	*24*	*1*
Iron and steel	10	1	72	35	55	4
Non-metallic minerals	2	0	43	7	14	0
Paper, pulp and print	0	0	37	1	2	0
Food and tobacco	0	0	32	4	8	0
Non-ferrous metals	3	1	15	1	0	1
Machinery	0	0	21	2	6	0
Textile and leather	0	0	10	1	1	0
Mining and quarrying	6	0	4	2	6	1
Construction	2	0	9	2	3	0
Transport equipment	0	0	9	1	4	0
Wood and wood products	0	0	6	1	6	0
Non-specified	56	53	45	12	6	15
Total	**90**	**116**	**440**	**89**	**160**	**24**

	Brazil	Canada	China	France	Germany	India
Chemical and petrochemical	16	19	116	18	31	24
of which: petrochemical feedstocks	*8*	*15*	*42*	*10*	*21*	*19*
Iron and steel	19	6	209	7	15	27
Non-metallic minerals	6	1	109	4	6	11
Paper, pulp and print	8	17	16	3	5	1
Food and tobacco	18	0	20	5	5	8
Non-ferrous metals	5	6	25	1	3	1
Machinery	0	0	29	2	3	1
Textile and leather	1	0	23	2	1	1
Mining and quarrying	3	11	10	0	1	1
Construction	0	1	10	1	1	0
Transport equipment	0	0	8	1	3	0
Wood and wood Products	0	0	3	1	1	0
Non-specified	6	10	19	2	12	56
Total	**82**	**71**	**596**	**49**	**85**	**131**

Note: Iron and steel includes coke ovens and blast furnaces.

Source: IEA statistics.

veloping Asia	OECD Pacific	OECD North America	South & Central America	EU27	OECD	Transition economies	DC	World
192	95	208	35	138	441	70	298	809
102	*65*	*121*	*19*	*80*	*267*	*37*	*165*	*469*
245	67	42	29	71	180	94	286	560
141	16	29	10	44	88	21	154	263
19	13	72	10	35	122	3	30	154
36	9	32	21	31	73	12	58	143
26	11	20	10	12	45	3	39	87
34	13	21	0	21	54	8	34	97
29	4	6	2	9	20	2	31	53
12	4	14	3	4	22	9	21	53
10	5	3	0	7	17	5	13	35
8	2	10	0	9	21	5	8	34
4	1	12	0	7	20	8	4	32
162	21	34	39	36	101	33	310	443
920	**261**	**503**	**160**	**423**	**1 204**	**273**	**1 286**	**2 763**

Italy	Japan	Mexico	Russia	South Africa	United Kingdom	United States	G8+5
11	53	11	49	3	13	177	541
6	*32*	*7*	*24*	*1*	*8*	*98*	*292*
8	45	5	55	7	5	31	439
9	8	2	14	2	3	25	200
3	9	1	2	0	2	55	121
4	4	2	8	0	4	30	106
1	2	0	0	2	1	13	60
5	9	0	6	0	3	21	78
2	0	0	1	0	1	6	39
0	0	2	6	5	0	2	40
0	4	0	3	0	1	2	23
0	0	0	4	0	1	9	28
0	0	0	6	0	0	12	24
3	17	11	6	6	9	13	171
47	**151**	**35**	**160**	**25**	**42**	**397**	**1 871**

16

Regional differences in industry energy use are shown in Figure 16.4. China accounts for about 80% of the growth in industrial production over the past 25 years, and for a similar share in industrial energy demand growth for materials production. Today, China is the largest producer of commodities such as aluminium, ammonia, cement, and iron and steel. The energy efficiency of production in China is, on average, lower than in OECD countries and, being largely coal-based, is also more carbon intensive. That said, the averages hide big differences over the range of plants. New plants tend to be more efficient than old ones, and many new plants are located in developing countries. As a consequence, China has some of the most efficient steel and paper making plants in the world. The most efficient aluminium smelters can be found in Africa, while India has a high share of very efficient cement kilns (IEA, 2007b).

Figure 16.4 ▶ Materials production energy needs, 1981-2005

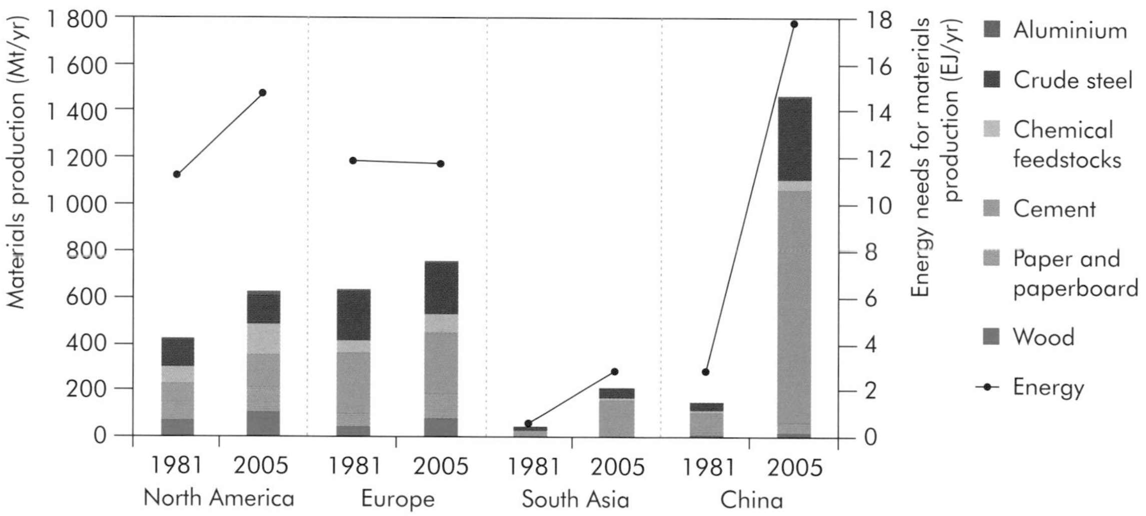

Note: North America includes Canada, Mexico and the United States. Europe includes EU27 excluding the three Baltic States, and including Albania, Bosnia, Croatia, Iceland, the Former Yugoslav Republic of Macedonia, Norway, Serbia, Switzerland and Turkey.

Source: IEA, 2007b.

Key point

China accounts for the bulk of energy demand growth for manufacturing in the past 25 years.

Table 16.3 shows a global breakdown of industrial energy use by fuel and energy carrier. Combustible renewables and waste is largely accounted for by biomass use in the pulp and paper industry.

The discussion in this chapter covers those industrial sectors that produce the most CO_2, *i.e.* iron and steel, non-metallic minerals, chemical and petrochemicals, paper and pulp, and non-ferrous metals. The distribution of CO_2 emissions among sub-sectors is very different from the distribution of energy demand, largely because:

- vast amounts of fossil carbon are stored in petrochemical products;
- some sub-sectors, e.g. cement production, emit large quantities of process CO_2 (unrelated to their energy use);
- fuel mixes differ among industrial sub-sectors.

Table 16.3 ▶ Final energy use by energy carrier and direct CO_2 emissions related to energy use, 2005

	Mtoe/yr	Gt CO_2/yr
Coal and coal products	714	3.10
Natural gas	561	1.28
of which: petrochemical feedstocks	*129*	*0.30*
Oil and oil products	666	1.24
of which: petrochemical feedstocks	*338*	*0.13*
Combustible renewables and waste	180	
Electricity	532	
Heat	110	
Other	0	
Total direct energy emissions	**2 763**	**5.61**
Process emissions (cement and steel)		1.05
Total direct energy and process emissions		**6.66**
Electricity generation emissions		3.19
Total direct and indirect emissions		**9.86**

Note: Iron and steel includes coke ovens and blast furnaces.

Total direct and indirect CO_2 emissions from industry were 9.9 gigatonnes (Gt) in 2005, equivalent to 37% of total global CO_2 emissions (Table 16.3).[4] Iron and steel, non-metallic minerals, and chemicals and petrochemicals were responsible for 72% of direct industrial CO_2 emissions (Figure 16.5 and Table 16.4). These

16

4. This includes coke ovens and blast furnaces that are reported as part of the transformation sector in IEA statistics. It also includes CO_2 emissions from power generation and process emissions.

Table 16.4 ▶ **Industrial direct energy and process CO_2 emissions, world regions and**

	Africa	MidEast	OECD Europe	Transition economies, Europe	Russia	Transition economies, Asia	Developi[ng] Asia
Chemical and petrochemical	23	110	156	36	75	2	290
of which: petro-chemical feedstocks	*20*	*51*	*58*	*24*	*51*	*1*	*95*
Iron and steel	35	5	250	127	124	15	987
of which: process emissions	*1*	*1*	*18*	*5*	*7*	*1*	*47*
Non-metallic minerals	49	44	218	31	45	5	1 063
of which: process emissions	*42*	*43*	*115*	*15*	*20*	*5*	*529*
Paper, pulp and print	0	0	35	1	1	0	52
Food and tobacco	1	0	56	6	4	0	91
Non-ferrous metals	0	2	15	1	0	1	46
Machinery	0	0	29	3	2	0	59
Textile and leather	0	0	17	1	0	0	61
Mining and quarrying	10	1	6	3	7	3	28
Construction	5	0	25	4	3	1	30
Transport equipment	0	0	11	1	2	0	19
Wood and wood products	0	0	3	1	1	0	9
Non-specified	70	132	67	12	3	40	268
Total	**193**	**294**	**890**	**226**	**269**	**68**	**3 003**
of which: process emissions	*43*	*44*	*134*	*20*	*26*	*5*	*576*

	Brazil	Canada	China	France	Germany	India	Italy
Chemical and petrochemical	18	18	183	24	26	39	13
of which: petro-chemical feedstocks	*4*	*13*	*30*	*8*	*12*	*22*	*4*
Iron and steel	47	18	835	26	53	120	26
of which: process emissions	*4*	*1*	*41*	*2*	*4*	*4*	*2*
Non-metallic minerals	25	10	791	18	27	111	40
of which: process emissions	*15*	*7*	*384*	*9*	*12*	*63*	*18*
Paper, pulp and print	4	7	40	4	7	6	5
Food and tobacco	4	0	57	8	8	25	7
Non-ferrous metals	8	3	42	1	3	3	1
Machinery	0	0	55	3	6	2	8
Textile and leather	1	0	46	3	1	5	4
Mining and quarrying	7	20	20	0	1	3	0
Construction	0	4	28	4	2	0	0
Transport equipment	0	0	19	2	3	0	0
Wood and wood products	0	2	9	0	1	0	0
Non-specified	6	21	38	2	3	34	3
Total	**121**	**102**	**2163**	**97**	**142**	**348**	**106**
of which: process emissions	*19*	*8*	*425*	*11*	*16*	*67*	*21*

Note: Iron and steel includes coke ovens and blast furnaces.

-5 countries, 2005 Mt CO_2/yr

OECD Pacific	OECD North America	South & Central America	EU27	OECD	Transition economies	DC	World
94	241	60	157	491	113	482	1086
30	*84*	*25*	*61*	*172*	*76*	*191*	*439*
252	124	74	247	626	266	1 101	1 992
17	*10*	*5*	*17*	*45*	*12*	*54*	*111*
106	146	62	202	471	82	1 218	1 770
60	*69*	*41*	98	*244*	*40*	*656*	*940*
18	75	7	34	128	2	59	189
15	63	8	55	133	10	100	243
15	18	12	13	48	2	59	110
8	27	0	30	64	5	59	129
5	10	3	16	31	1	63	96
8	23	8	7	37	14	47	98
16	10	1	17	51	9	37	96
2	14	0	11	28	3	19	49
0	12	0	4	16	2	9	27
52	72	57	42	191	55	528	775
591	**834**	**292**	**834**	**2 315**	**563**	**3 782**	**6 660**
76	*79*	*46*	*115*	*289*	*52*	*710*	*1 051*

Japan	Mexico	Russia	South Africa	United Kingdom	United States	G8+5
70	14	75	8	13	209	710
	14					
14	*7*	*51*	*6*	*4*	*64*	*240*
178	15	124	25	20	91	1 578
11	*1*	*7*	*1*	*1*	*7*	*87*
56	21	45	12	11	115	1 282
32	*16*	*20*	*6*	*5*	*47*	*634*
13	2	1	0	3	66	157
9	3	4	0	6	60	191
2	0	0	0	1	15	80
7	0	2	0	3	27	112
0	0	0	0	2	10	72
1	3	7	8	1	0	72
12	1	3	1	1	5	60
0	0	2	0	2	14	42
0	0	1	0	0	11	23
42	14	3	10	19	37	234
390	**73**	**269**	**64**	**81**	**659**	**4 614**
43	*17*	*26*	*7*	*6*	*54*	*720*

data exclude upstream CO_2 emissions from the production of electricity (which are allocated to the electricity sector in IEA statistics) and downstream emissions from the incineration of synthetic organic products. The G8+5 countries account for 69% of industrial direct CO_2 emissions (Table 16.4). Therefore, an international sectoral emissions reduction approach for a limited number of countries can have a good coverage.

Figure 16.5 ▶ Industrial direct CO_2 emissions by sector, 2005

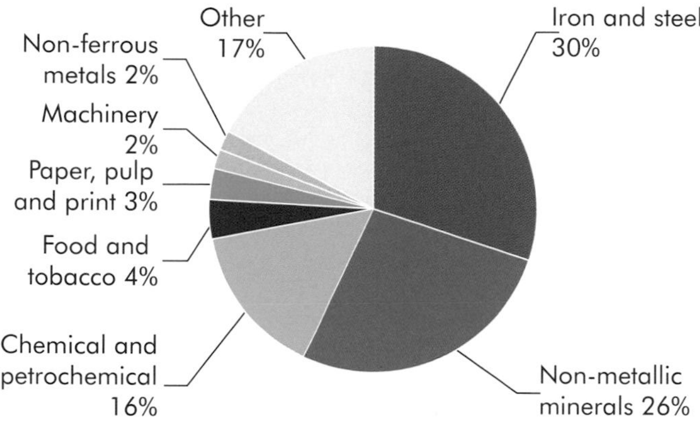

Note: Includes coke ovens, blast furnaces and process CO_2 emissions from cement and steel production. Excludes emissions in power supply; assumes 75% carbon storage for all petrochemical feedstocks.

Key point

Three sectors: iron and steel, non-metallic minerals, and chemicals and petrochemicals account for 72% of direct industrial CO_2 emissions.

Iron and steel

The iron and steel sector is the second-largest industrial consumer of energy and the largest emitter of CO_2. In 2005, it accounted for 20% of world industrial energy use and 30% of energy and process CO_2 emissions.[5] The four largest producers (China, the European Union, Japan and the United States) accounted for 67% of the CO_2 emissions.

Scenarios

Figure 16.6 shows the industrial CO_2 emissions in the Baseline, ACT Map and BLUE Map scenarios. Iron and steel production increases by 134% from 2005 to 2050 in all scenarios. In the Baseline scenario, direct emissions increase by 114%, while energy use increases by 123%. In the ACT Map scenario, direct emissions

5. These figures include energy use and CO_2 emissions from coke ovens and blast furnaces, and also 111 Mt of CO_2 from process emissions, coming from limestone and dolomite use in blast furnaces.

in 2050 are 71% above the 2005 level. In the BLUE Map scenario they are 26% below the 2005 level. Efficiency, fuel and feedstock switching account for 42% of the total emissions reduction from the Baseline in the ACT Map and BLUE Map scenarios. CCS accounts for 33% of total emissions reduction in the BLUE scenario. The remainder (25%) are emissions reductions in power generation.

Figure 16.6 ▶ Iron and steel industry CO_2 emissions in the Baseline, ACT Map and BLUE Map scenarios, 2005-2050

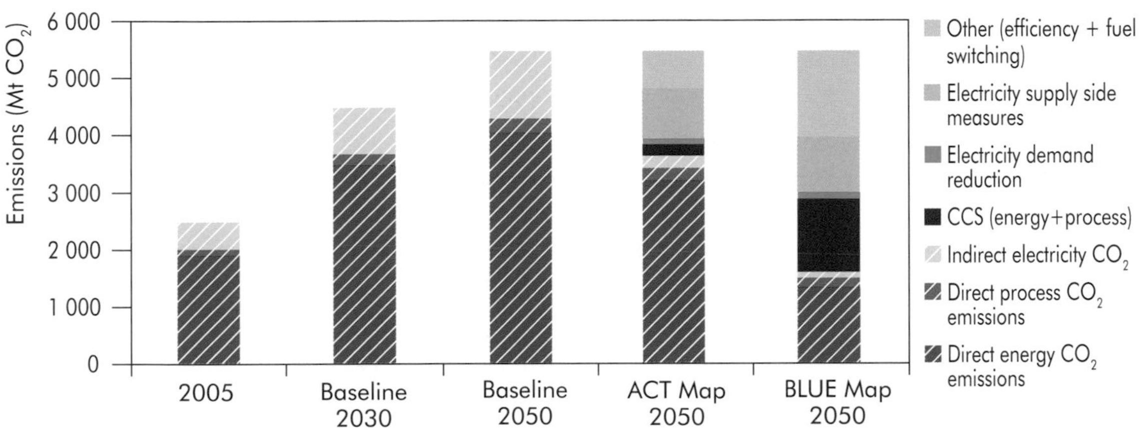

Note: Includes blast furnaces and coke ovens.

Key point

There is potentially an important role for CCS in this sector.

Processing overview

Steel is produced via a dozen or so processing steps, which are carried out in various configurations depending on product mixes, available raw materials, energy supply and investment capital. There are three principal modern processing routes:[6]

- the scrap/electric arc furnace (EAF) method, based on scrap for the iron input;
- the direct reduced iron (DRI)/EAF method, based on iron ore and often scrap for the iron input[7];
- the blast furnace (BF) and basic oxygen furnace (BOF) method, based on 70% to 100% iron ore, with the remainder scrap, for the iron input.

Over the last several decades, EAF production has grown and BOF production has held steady. BOF is still the most widely used process, largely due to local limitations on scrap availability. EAF production is much higher in the United States and Europe, where more scrap is available, than elsewhere. This difference should gradually disappear as other economies mature. DRI/EAF production is widespread

6. A fourth route, the Open Hearth route, has a iron input profile similar to the BOF route, but it is considered outdated technology and is used for only 3% of current production.
7. Direct reduced iron (DRI) can be economically substituted for scrap in places where scrap is in short supply and there are cheap sources of fossil fuels (e.g. stranded gas supplies).

in the Middle East, South America, India and Mexico. Most DRI production is based on cheap, stranded natural gas, except in India, where it is largely coal-based.

The Scrap/EAF route is much less energy-intensive (4 GJ/t to 6 GJ/t) than the BF/BOF route (13 GJ/t to 14 GJ/t).[8] This is because there is no need to reduce iron ore to iron, and it cuts out the need for the ore preparation, coke-making and iron-making steps.[9] Significant energy savings can be made by switching from the BF/BOF to the Scrap/EAF route.

There are considerable differences in the energy efficiency of primary steel production among countries and even between individual plants. These differences can be explained by factors such as economies of scale, the level of waste energy recovery, the quality of iron ore, operations know-how and quality control.

Figure 16.7 compares the CO_2 emissions of the three key processes now in general use. It suggests a potential for emission reductions of 50% to 95%, excluding any reductions that might be achieved through CO_2 capture from blast furnaces. However, the overall potential of EAF is limited by scrap availability. Using gas-based DRI also yields some, more limited, emissions reductions.

Figure 16.7 ▶ CO_2 emissions per tonne of crude steel produced

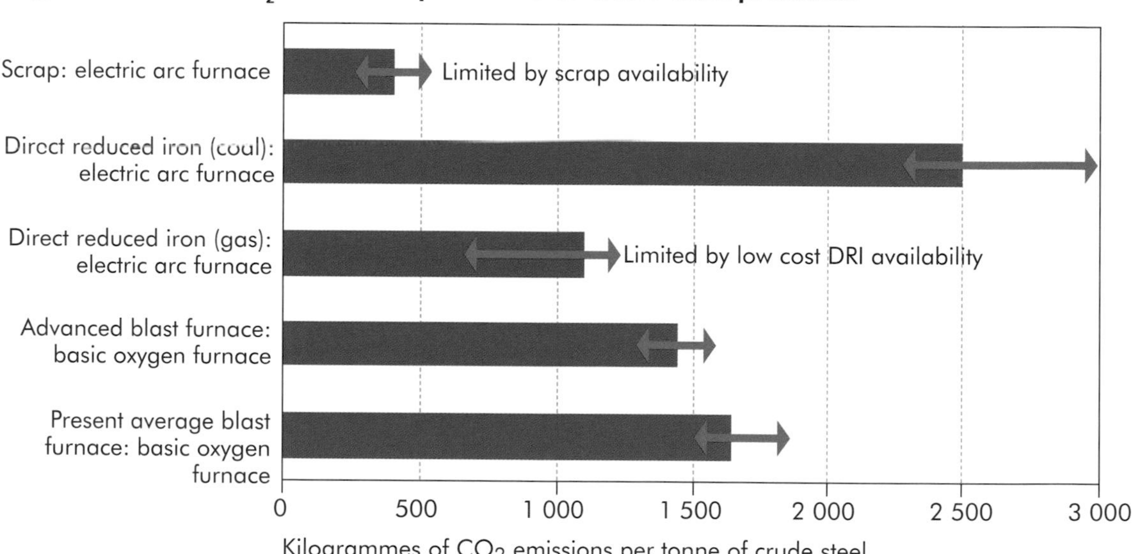

Note: The high and low-end ranges indicate CO_2-free and coal-based electricity, and account for country average differences based on IEA statistics. The range is even wider for plant-based data. The product is crude steel, which excludes rolling and finishing.

Source: IEA, 2007b.

Key point

Crude steel production using scrap yields lower CO_2 emissions than other processes, but is limited by scrap availability.

8. An electric-arc furnace (EAF) uses about 1.6 GJ of electricity per tonne of steel for 100% scrap feedstock and somewhat more with increasing DRI inputs. In actual operation, however, EAF energy use is somewhat higher. To be truly comparable with the BF/BOF process, the electricity should be expressed in primary energy terms. With electricity generation efficiency ranging from 35% to more than 50%, EAF primary energy use is in the range of 4 GJ to 6 GJ per tonne of liquid steel.
9. More scrap can be added in the BOF, which reduces the energy use for this route. However, this implies less scrap recycling in EAFs, so the CO_2 benefit is limited for the iron and steel industry as a whole.

Energy efficiency: BAT

Important emission reductions could be achieved if best available technologies were applied worldwide. Figure 16.8 provides a breakdown of the technological efficiency potentials by country based on current production volume and current technology. The total potential is 340 Mt CO_2. China accounts for nearly half of this potential, due to its high share of total world production. In terms of emission reduction potentials per unit of steel produced, however, a number of other countries have higher potentials. The average global potential is 0.30 t CO_2/t steel produced.

Figure 16.8 ▶ CO_2 emission reduction potentials in 2005, based on best available technology

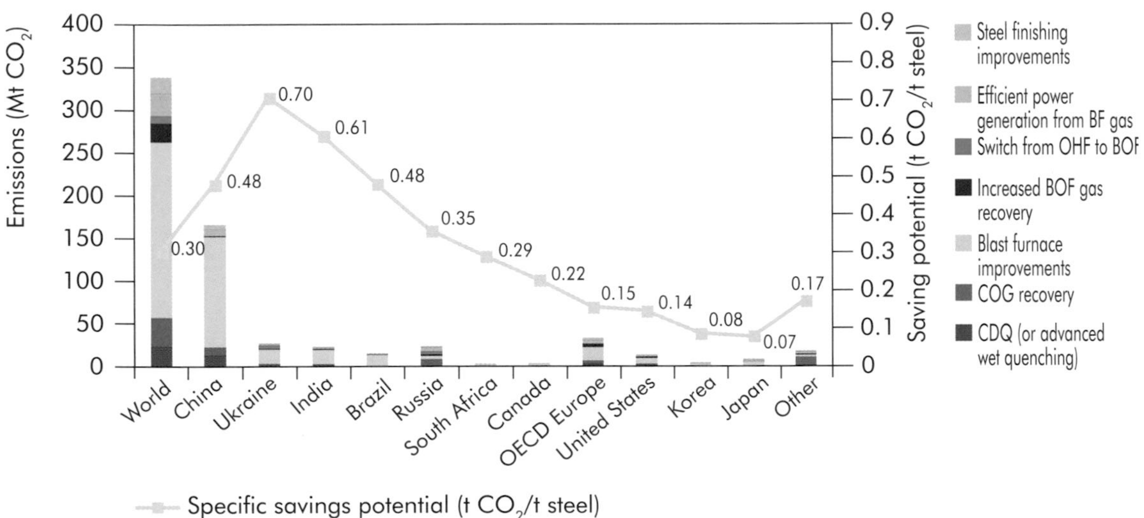

Key point

Blast furnace improvements constitute the single most important efficiency category.

Numerous gas streams from the various steel-making processes contain energy in the form of heat, pressure or combustible content. Recovering and using the energy content of these streams reduces overall energy needs and upstream CO_2 emissions (e.g. in the power sector). The relevant technologies are widely applied in some countries, but virtually non-existent in others. The total potential from the wider application of these technologies is about 100 Mt CO_2 reductions per year worldwide.

16

Energy and materials efficiency: improved and new process technologies

Each processing step adds inefficiency to the overall steel-making process, due to energy and material losses in and between each step. Reducing the number of steps, or the amount of material processed in any step, improves efficiency.

The industry has been trying to develop alternative production processes that minimise the number of coal and ore processing steps. These include:

- injecting pulverised coal as a substitute for coke into the blast furnace;
- new reactor designs that can use coal instead of coke (such as the COREX process);
- still newer reactor designs that can use coal and ore fines (such as FINEX and cyclone converter furnaces).

Coal injection is already a widely applied technology. It is financially attractive because it reduces the need for coke production. It also results in substantial energy savings, as one energy unit of coke is replaced by one energy unit of coal. Trials have shown that coal injection can replace up to half the coke now used in blast furnaces. Assuming that coal and coke have the same energy content, that half of all coke is replaced by injected coal, and that the energy used in coke production is 2 GJ/t to 4 GJ/t coke, the potential for coal savings would amount to 12 Mtoe per year, equivalent to 50 Mt of CO_2.

Process streamlining: smelt reduction and efficient blast furnaces

Small-to-medium-scale iron-making facilities can be made appreciably more efficient through new reactor designs for smelt reduction that substitute a single process for the ore preparation, coke-making and blast furnace iron-making steps of a traditional ore-based facility. In addition, smelt reduction, with its richer CO_2 off-gases, especially when nitrogen free, would be an enabling technology for CCS. The benefits of process streamlining are most pronounced for small-scale and medium-scale plants. Large plants are often more efficient, because of the proportionally lower heat losses of large-scale vessels and economies of scale in recovering energy from heat and off-gas streams. Advanced large-scale blast furnaces are already quite energy efficient. Recent smelt reduction development work has led to the commercially available COREX plant design, which uses coal fines and agglomerated ore. This concept is only marginally economic, but it is the only smelt reduction process in current industrial use, in South Africa, Korea and India. In July 2005, China's Baosteel ordered a new COREX module. The current version of smelt reduction technology is most suitable for medium-scale integrated plants, which are mainly found in developing countries. But these countries lack capital and support infrastructure, and they are often discouraged by the perceived risks involved in new technologies.

More recent smelt reduction designs, such as the FINEX design being developed by POSCO in Korea, aim also to eliminate ore agglomeration.[10] A 1.5 Mt/yr FINEX plant has recently been built at the producer's Pohang Works. HiSmelt, another smelt-reduction design using ore fines, may possibly have a better energy balance

10. Finex uses 700 kg coal/tonne hot metal today, and possibly less than 700 kg/t in the future. A modern blast furnace also uses 700 kg/tonne hot metal for coking, ore preparation and blast furnace.

than FINEX. The first commercial plant of this type is being built in Australia, with other major research projects launched in Japan (a direct iron-ore smelting process), in Europe (a cyclone-converted process) and in the United States.

Next steps include the commercialisation of second-generation smelt reduction processes through demonstration on a near-commercial scale. Today's smelt reduction generates substantial amounts of surplus off-gas, typically about 9 GJ/t of product. Re-using the off-gases of the smelt-reduction plant could lead to significant additional CO_2 reductions.

If blast furnaces were re-designed to use oxygen instead of enriched air (pre-operation nitrogen) and to recycle top gases, it would reduce blast furnace CO_2 emissions by 20% to 25%. Ongoing research is aimed at proving this concept.

Major research projects have been launched in Japan and in Europe (in particular, the Ultra Low CO_2 Steel-making (ULCOS) project). The IISI's CO_2 Breakthrough Programme is a global initiative to explore opportunities and strategies to minimise, eliminate or capture carbon emissions from the steel industry. Both smelt reduction and nitrogen-free blast furnaces would be enabling technologies for CCS. With a significant expansion of smelt reduction and nitrogen-free blast furnaces, as much as 200 Mt CO_2 to 500 Mt CO_2 emissions could be avoided by 2050.

Process streamlining: direct casting

Currently, most steel is continuously cast into slabs, billets or blooms, which have to be reheated when they are later rolled into final shape.[11] Direct casting (*i.e.* near-net-shape casting and thin-strip casting) integrates the casting and hot-rolling of steel into one step, thereby reducing the need to reheat the steel before rolling it. This technology leads to considerable savings of capital and energy. Energy savings may amount to 1 GJ to 3 GJ per tonne of steel. Direct casting may also lead to indirect energy savings because of reduced material yield losses.[12]

The main challenges for the further development of direct casting technology relate to the quality of the product and its usability by steel processors and users. Increased reliability, control and the adaptation of the technology to larger-scale production units will benefit its wider application. To date, productivity problems with direct casting at a large steel-maker have eliminated the expected efficiency gains.

Compared to a current, state-of-the-art casting and rolling facility, the specific energy savings of direct-cast technologies are estimated at about 90%. Estimates for the possible reduction of capital costs range from 30% to 60%. If the use of direct casting can be expanded, upstream emissions could be reduced by up to 100 Mt per year and costs could be reduced at the same time (Table 16.5). Total energy savings will depend on the speed at which strip and near-net-shape casters enter the market.

11. Today, 90% of all steel is cast continuously. The remaining 10% is batch cast into ingots. Continuously cast materials require considerably less reworking and reheating to shape into final products, and have lower materials yield losses (*i.e.*, less material that needs to be remelted and recast).
12. Thin-slab casting gives a 98% yield; thin-strip casting gives a 99% yield.

Table 16.5 ▶ Global technology prospects for direct casting

Direct casting	2008-2015	2015-2030	2030-2050
Technology stage	R&D, Demonstration	Commercial	Commercial
Investment costs (USD/t)	200	150-200	150-200
Energy reduction (%)	80%	90%	90%
CO_2 reduction (Gt/yr)	0-0.01	0-0.03	0-0.1

Note: Investment costs for a traditional continuous caster and hot-rolling mill are about USD 70/t higher than for direct casting.

Increased steel recycling

Steel is the most widely recycled material in the world. Yet the gap between apparent steel consumption and scrap production, accounting for storage, suggests considerable further potential. The absence of detailed statistics makes it impossible to determine the scale of this potential. A better understanding of the global steel materials balance is needed to assess the additional recycling potentials.

Fuel and feedstock substitution

At present, coal and coke are the primary reducing agents used for iron-making – although natural gas for DRI is gaining ground, albeit from a small base, as an alternative.[13] Charcoal-based iron-making is still used in South America, notably in Brazil. The use of charcoal in blast furnaces is currently limited to small furnaces.

Technologies have been developed in Germany and Japan to inject plastic waste into blast furnaces as a substitute for coke and coal. Plastic waste can also be added to the coking oven. This technology is applied commercially at one site in Austria and at two blast furnaces and eight coke ovens in Japan. Experience shows that using plastic waste in the coke oven results in better process stability than using it as a coke or coal substitute. In total, about 0.5 Mt (20 PJ) of plastic waste is used per year by the Japanese iron and steel industry. The option is limited by the availability of clean, chlorine-free plastic waste, and by the competing claims of other uses, such as recycling and incineration. The energy and CO_2 consequences of plastic injection are case-specific. The use of plastics is also limited and is driven as much by the need to recycle plastics and greenhouse gas credits as the motivation to replace coke and coal.

Other energy carriers such as hydrogen and electricity could also be used for iron-making. If they were produced from carbon-free primary energy sources, they could contribute significant CO_2 reductions. But IEA analysis suggests that the cost of such mitigation measures would in most cases exceed USD 50/t CO_2, which would not be competitive with other options in this sector in the ACT Map scenario. Nonetheless, in the BLUE Map scenario, these options could play a role in parts of the world.

13. In the iron-making context, reducing agents are chemicals that help convert iron ore (mostly Fe_2O_3) to iron (mostly Fe).

CO_2 capture and storage (CCS)

Blast furnaces are the largest source of direct CO_2 emissions in the steel-making process, and are prime candidates for CCS. DRI kilns are a less prominent source of emissions, but would also be suitable for CCS.

If blast furnaces were redesigned to use oxygen instead of enriched air and to recycle top gases, their emissions would be sufficiently rich in CO_2 to enable it to be captured with physical absorbents. However, the oxygen-injection blast furnace is not yet proven. Smelt reduction is also an enabling technology for CCS, provided the process uses oxygen.

CCS, used together with oxygen injection, could result in an 85% to 95% reduction in CO_2 emissions. The ULCOS project is undertaking new engineering studies of CO_2 capture and sequestration in iron production. The LKAB experimental blast furnace in Sweden has started testing various CCS configurations for a small-scale blast furnace (with a capacity of only one to two tonnes of iron per hour), with the aim of running a demonstration plant in the period 2015 to 2020. CCS using physical absorbents is likely to be more cost-effective than CCS using chemical absorbents. But blast-furnace gas-reforming and chemical absorption using waste heat is being investigated in Japan, Korea and China.

Current expert estimates suggest that CCS for blast furnaces would cost around USD 40/t CO_2 to USD 50/t CO_2 in capture, transport and storage costs, excluding any furnace productivity changes that could have a significant positive or negative impact on the process economics (Borlée, 2007). The marginal investment costs would be higher for retrofits than for new builds.

DRI production would allow CCS at a relatively low cost, below USD 25/t CO_2. But DRI facilities are concentrated in relatively few countries and are comparatively small scale. As a result, this approach has so far received only limited attention. With the expected rapid growth in DRI production in the Middle East and elsewhere, especially in the BLUE Map scenario, the potential for CO_2 capture could amount to 400 Mt per year by 2050. Overall, CCS in iron and steel production could save around 0.5 Gt to 1.5 Gt of CO_2 per year.

Non-metallic minerals

The non-metallic minerals sector, producing cement, bricks, glass, ceramics and other building materials, is the third-largest industrial consumer of energy and second-largest industrial emitter of CO_2. In 2005, it accounted for 10% of world industrial energy use and 27% of energy and process CO_2 emissions.[14] The four largest producers (China, India, the European Union and the United States) accounted for 75% of these CO_2 emissions.

Global cement production grew from 594 Mt in 1970 to 2 310 Mt in 2005, with the vast majority of the growth occurring in developing countries, especially China.

14. This includes 938 Mt CO_2 of process emissions, coming from the calcination of limestone during clinker production.

In 2005, developed countries produced 563 Mt (24% of world cement production), Transition economies 98 Mt (4% of world output) and developing countries 1 649 Mt (72% of world output).

Scenarios

Figure 16.9 shows the CO_2 emissions attributable to the non-metallic metals industry in the Baseline, ACT Map and BLUE Map scenarios. Cement production increases by 84% from 2005 to 2050 in all scenarios. In the Baseline scenario, direct emissions increase by 76%, while energy use increases by 85%. In the ACT Map scenario, direct emissions in 2050 are 38% above the 2005 level. In the BLUE Map scenario they are 44% below the 2005 level. CCS accounts for 40% of the total reduction of direct emissions in the BLUE Map scenario.

Figure 16.9 ▶ Non-metallic minerals industry CO_2 emissions in the Baseline, ACT Map and BLUE Map scenarios, 2005-2050

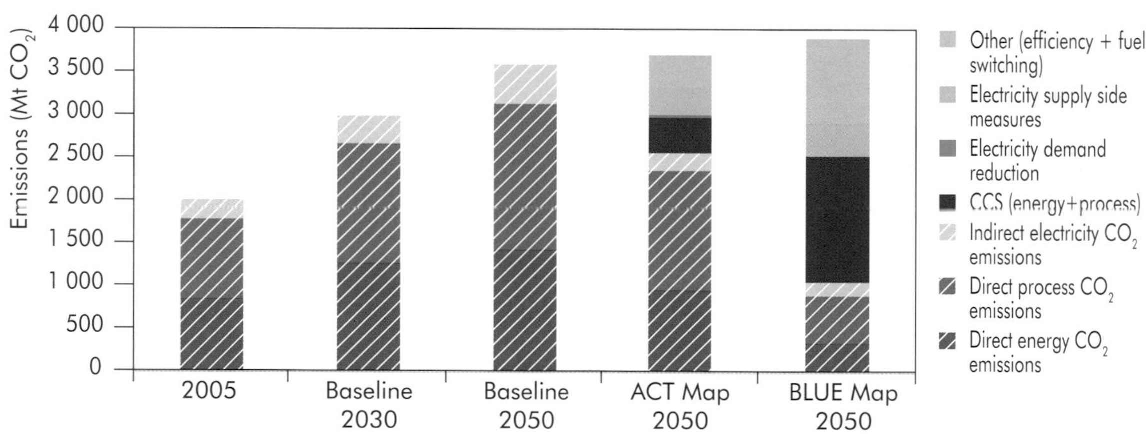

Note: The greater use of alternative fuels, such as wastes and tyres in the ACT Map and BLUE Map scenarios, reduces global emissions by displacing fossil-fuel use at cement facilities, but transfers emissions that would occur at incineration or waste handling facilities to cement plants. The reduced emissions in waste handling are not credited in this graph. Therefore, the total height of the stacked bar rises from Baseline to ACT Map and BLUE Map.

Key point

CCS plays a key role in the BLUE Map scenario.

Processing overview

Cement accounts for 83% of total energy use in the production of non-metallic minerals and 94% of CO_2 emissions. Energy represents 20% to 40% of the total cost of cement production. The production of cement clinker from limestone and chalk by heating limestone to temperatures above 950°C is the main energy consuming process. Portland cement, the most widely used cement type, contains 95% cement clinker. Large amounts of electricity are used grinding the raw materials and finished cement.

The clinker-making process also emits CO_2 as a by-product during the calcination of limestone. These process emissions are unrelated to energy use and account for about 3.5% of CO_2 emissions worldwide and for 57% of the total CO_2 emissions from cement production. Emissions from limestone calcination cannot be reduced through energy-efficiency measures or fuel substitution, but can be diminished through production of blended cement and raw material selection.

Energy efficiency: BAT

The total technical energy efficiency potential in cement-making today equates to a reduction of about 290 Mt CO_2. If clinker substitutes are included, the potential savings rises by about 240 Mt to around 450 Mt CO_2 (Figure 16.10). This shows the importance of fuel and feedstock switching in this sector.

China accounts for more than half of this potential, because of its large production volume and its low energy efficiency. In terms of emission reduction potentials per tonne of cement, a number of countries have potentials similar to China's, and Russia has an even higher potential. The world average potential is 0.18 t CO_2/t cement.

Figure 16.10 ▶ CO_2 emission reduction potentials in 2006, based on best available technology

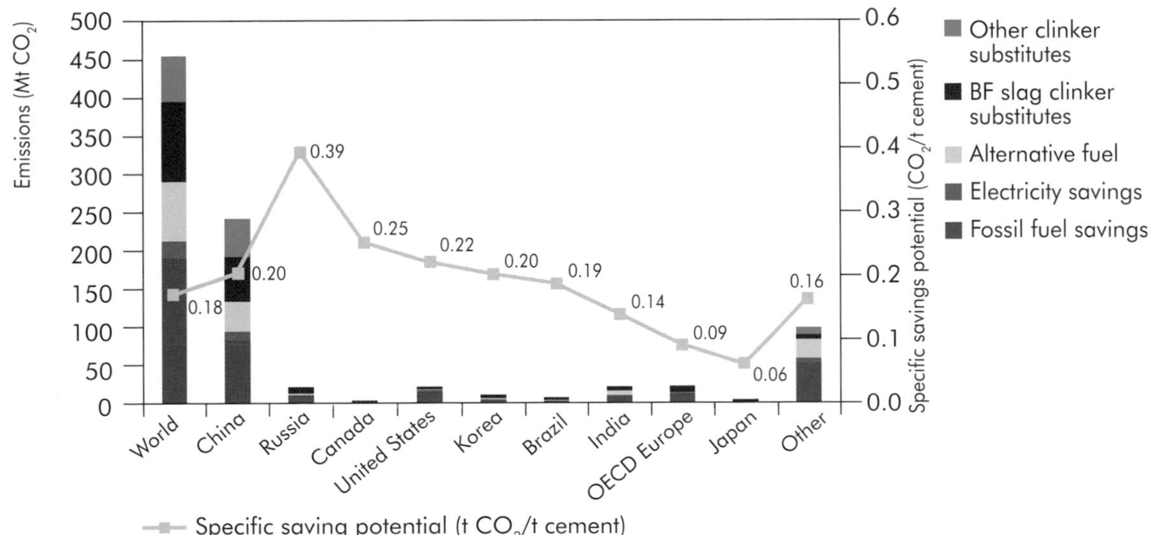

Key point

Worldwide, there is 450 Mt CO_2 savings potential on the basis of existing technology.

16

Heat efficiency and management

Different cement-producing technologies show widely different energy efficiencies (Figure 16.11). In industrial countries, large-scale rotary kilns are used. In developing countries (including China, the largest world producer of cement) markedly less efficient small-scale shaft (vertical) kilns are still widely used. However, the situation in China is changing rapidly due to active government policies to phase out shaft kilns.

The predominant production process for Portland cement clinker is the relatively energy efficient dry process. It is gradually replacing the wet process, which is less efficient because of the additional drying required. The energy efficiency of rotary kilns can be increased significantly by increasing the number of pre-heaters: an increase from 4 to 6 cyclone pre-heaters results in a fuel reduction of about 10%. In the last few decades, pre-calcination technology has also been introduced as an energy-saving measure.

Cement producers are gradually replacing conventional dry kilns with dry kilns incorporating pre-calcining and six-step pre-heaters. This trend is likely to continue with no need for government support. Today's state-of-the-art dry-rotary kilns use approximately 2.9 GJ to 3.0 GJ of energy per tonne of clinker, while a wet kiln uses 5.9 GJ to 6.8 GJ per tonne of clinker.

Figure 16.11 ▶ Energy efficiency of various cement-clinker production technologies

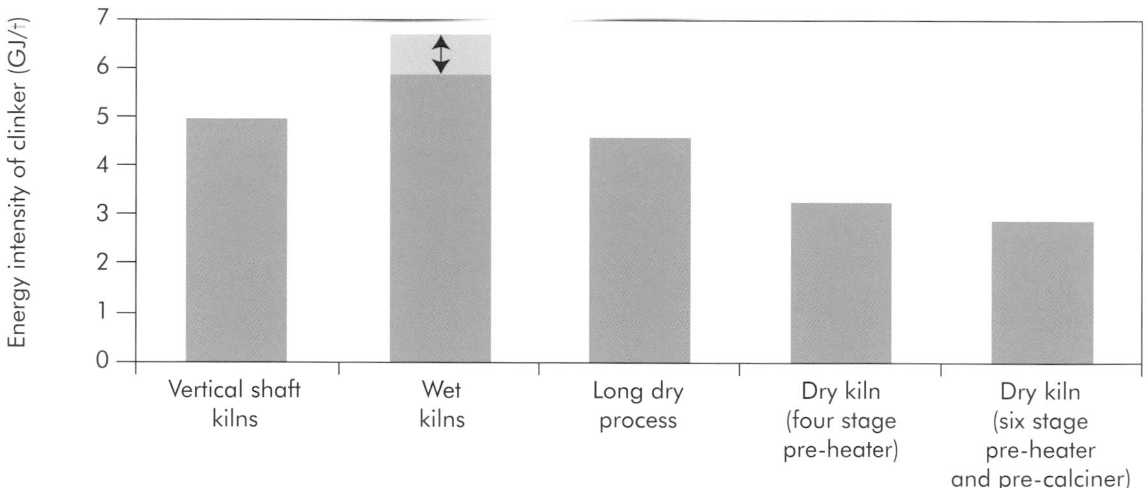

Note: For wet kilns, the arrow represents the range of energy consumption for different wet kiln types.
Source: FLSmidth, 2006.

Key point

Modern dry-process cement kilns use half as much energy as wet process kilns to produce a tonne of cement.

Grinding

Grinding also uses large amounts of electricity. Current state-of-the-art technologies, using roller presses and high-efficiency classifiers, are much more efficient than earlier ones. Yet the energy efficiency of grinding is typically only 5% to 10%, with the remainder converted to heat. Grinding is one key to producing high-strength cements and cements with high fly-ash content, which reduces energy use and CO_2 emissions.

Energy and materials efficiency: new process technologies

Rotary-kiln technology is approaching the limits of its energy efficiency potential. New fluid-bed technologies have been tested, but research has been abandoned. Power generation from low-temperature residual heat has been applied at some kilns which are equipped with preheaters and clinker heat recovery. This requires special power-generation cycles. The potential for power generation for such kilns is about 20 kWh per tonne of clinker, but it is expensive.

Better grinding technologies and additives can lead to products such as high-strength cement which result in a substantial reduction of cement use. High-strength materials are already used in skyscrapers. But they are more costly than conventional cement and their application requires special knowledge.

Fuel and feedstock substitution

Fuel substitution

Another way to reduce emissions is to substitute fossil fuels with waste or biomass. Cement kilns are well suited for waste-combustion because of their high process temperature and because the clinker product and limestone feedstock act as gas-cleaning agents. Used tyres, wood, plastics, chemicals and other types of waste are co-combusted in cement kilns in large quantities. Plants in Belgium, France, Germany, the Netherlands and Switzerland have reached average substitution rates of from 35% to more than 70%. Some individual plants have even achieved 100% substitution using appropriate waste materials. However, very high substitution rates can only be accomplished if a tailored pre-treatment and surveillance system is in place. Municipal solid waste, for example, needs to be pre-treated to obtain homogeneous calorific values and feed characteristics.

The cement industry in the United States burns 53 million used tyres per year, which is 41% of all tyres that are burnt and is equivalent to 0.39 Mt or 15 PJ. About 50 million tyres, or 20% of the total, are still used as landfill. Another potential source of energy is carpets: the equivalent of about 100 PJ per year are dumped in landfills – these could instead be burnt in cement kilns. Although these alternative materials are widely used, their use is still controversial, as cement kilns are not subject to the same tight emission controls as waste-incineration installations.

According to IEA statistics, the cement industry in OECD countries used 1.6 Mtoe of combustible renewables and waste in 2005, half of it industrial waste and half wood waste. Worldwide, the sector consumed 2.7 Mtoe of biomass and 0.8 Mtoe of waste. This equals less than 2% of total fuel use in this sector. From a technical perspective, the use of alternative fuels could be raised to 24 Mtoe to 48 Mtoe, although there would be differences among regions due to the varying availability of such fuels. This would yield CO_2 reductions in the range of 100 Mt to 200 Mt a year.

Clinker substitutes and blended cements

Yet another way to reduce energy and process emissions in cement production is to blend cements with increased proportions of alternative (non-clinker) feedstocks, such as volcanic ash, granulated blast furnace slag from iron production, or fly ash from coal-fired power generation.

The use of such blended cements varies widely from country to country. It is high in continental Europe, but low in the United States and the United Kingdom. In the United States and in China, other clinker substitutes are added directly at the concrete-making stage. Blended cements offer a major opportunity for energy conservation and emission reductions, but their use would in many cases require revisions to construction standards, codes and practices.

In total, the savings potential for blended cements amounts to 300 Mt CO_2 to 450 Mt CO_2 by 2050. The main approaches to this are to use:

- Blast-furnace slag that has been cooled with water, rather than air. About half of all blast-furnace slag is already used for cement-making where the slag is water-cooled and where transport distances and costs are acceptable. If all blast-furnace slag were used, this would yield a CO_2 reduction of approximately 100 Mt CO_2.
- Fly ash from coal-fired power plants. But the carbon content of fly ash can affect the concrete setting time, which determines the quality of the cement. To be used as clinker substitute, high-carbon fly ash must be upgraded. Technologies for this are just emerging. Special grinding methods are also being studied as a way to increase the reaction rate of fly ash, allowing the fly ash content of cement to increase to 70% compared with a maximum of 30% today (Justnes, Elfgren and Ronin, 2005). China and India have the potential to significantly increase the use of fly ash. If the 50% of all fly ash that currently goes to landfill could be used, this would yield a CO_2 reduction of approximately 75 Mt. While the Baseline scenario assumes a rapid expansion of coal-fired power generation and therefore fly ash production, coal-fired power generation decreases in the BLUE Map scenario. This will limit the expansion potential for fly ash in this scenario.
- Steel slag. The CemStar process, which uses a 15% charge of air-cooled steel slag pebbles in the rotary kiln feedstock mix, has been developed and successfully applied in the United States, resulting in a CO_2 reduction of approximately 0.47 t/t steel slag added (Yates, Perkins and Sankaranarayanan, 2004). In China, there are about 30 steel slag cement plants with a combined annual output of 4.8 Mt. However, steel slag quality varies and it is difficult to process, which limits its use. If the total worldwide BOF and EAF steel slag resource of 100 Mt to 200 Mt per year was used this way, the CO_2 reduction potential would be 50 Mt to 100 Mt per year. Further analysis is needed to validate the viability of this option.

Other materials that could be used to a greater extent as clinker substitutes include volcanic ash, ground limestone and broken glass. Such approaches could alleviate clinker substitute availability problems, and possibly pave the way to a 50% reduction of energy use and CO_2 emissions.

In the long term, new cement types may be developed that do not use limestone as a primary resource. These new types are called synthetic pozzolans. The technological feasibility, economics and energy effects of such alternative cements remain speculative.

CO_2 capture and storage (CCS)

The calcination of limestone in cement kilns results in relatively high concentrations of CO_2 in the off gas. This high concentration could allow the use of other absorbents to capture the CO_2. The capture technology might be similar to that for an integrated-gasification, combined-cycle power plant or a pulverised-coal-fired plant capturing CO_2 from the flue gases. Using oxygen instead of air in cement kilns would result in a pure CO_2 off-gas, although process re-design might be needed to avoid excessive equipment wear. The use of CCS in cement kilns would, however, raise production costs by 40% to 90%.

For chemical or physical absorption systems, the cost would be approximately USD 50 to USD 75 per tonne of clinker, or USD 75 to USD 100 per tonne of CO_2 captured. This cost comprises 40% capital cost, 30% cost for the heat, and 30% for transportation and storage. Different process designs using oxyfueling or chemical looping might halve the cost, but these are still in a conceptual stage. More analysis is recommended, especially as the overall saving is potentially significant.

In the ACT Map scenario, only a limited uptake of CCS is assumed. However in the BLUE Map scenario, uptake is substantial and total capture from cement kilns increases to 1.4 Gt CO_2. This high uptake results in substantial additional energy use that offsets some of the energy efficiency gains in the BLUE Map scenario.

Table 16.6 ▶ Global technology prospects for CO_2 capture and storage for cement kilns

CCS	2008-2015	2015-2030	2030-2050
Technology stage	R&D	R&D, Demonstration	Demonstration, Commercial
Costs (USD/t CO_2)	150	100	75
Emission reduction (%)	95	95	95
CO_2 reduction (Gt CO_2/yr)	0	0-0.25	0.4-1.4

Chemicals and petrochemicals

16

The chemicals and petrochemicals sector uses numerous distillation, evaporation, direct heating, refrigeration, electrolytic and biochemical processes to separate and convert materials into final products. It is the largest industrial consumer of energy and the third-largest industrial emitter of CO_2. In 2005, it accounted for 28% of world industrial energy use and 16% of energy and process CO_2 emissions.[15] The industry is highly diverse, with thousands of companies producing tens of thousands of products in quantities varying from a few kilogrammes to thousands of tonnes. Reliable comparative data sets on energy use per unit of product are not available.

A small number of processes stand out in terms of their large energy requirements. The following three activities account for 537 Mtoe of final energy use, which is more than 70% of total energy in the chemical and petrochemical industry:

- high-value chemicals (HVC) from the steam-cracking of naphtha, ethane and other feedstocks to produce olefins (ethylene and propylene) and aromatics (benzene, toluene and xylenes);
- methanol production;
- ammonia production.

The four largest producers of HVC are the United States, the European Union, Japan and China, which together account for 62% of the CO_2 emissions from the manufacture of these products. The four largest producers of ammonia (China, the European Union, India and Russia) account for 72% of energy use in ammonia production.

Scenarios

Figure 16.12 shows the industrial CO_2 emissions in the Baseline, ACT Map and BLUE Map scenarios. From 2005 to 2050, the production of high-value chemicals from liquid feedstocks increases by 109% in the Baseline scenario, 86% in the ACT Map scenario and 57% in the BLUE Map scenario. The decline in the more challenging scenarios stems from increased plastics recycling. Ammonia production increases by 96%, 112% and 137% from 2005 to 2050 in the Baseline, ACT Map and BLUE Map scenarios respectively. The increase in the more challenging scenarios stems from the need for more fertilisers to support the increased use of biofuels. Methanol production increases six-fold from 2005 to 2050 in all scenarios.

In the Baseline scenario, direct emissions from chemicals and petrochemicals production increase by 105%, while energy use increases by 76%. In the ACT Map scenario, direct emissions in 2050 are still double the 2005 level. In the BLUE Map scenario they are 5% below the 2005 level. CCS accounts for more than half of the reductions in direct emissions, or 32% of the total emissions, in the BLUE Map scenario. This is mainly in relation to ammonia production and large CHP units. The role of efficiency and fuel is relatively limited, because of the high feedstock share. It should be noted that important savings due to increased use of CHP have been allocated to the power sector, in line with IEA energy accounting practice. In fact, electricity demand savings have a similar CO_2 reduction effect as the fuel- and feedstock-saving measures. The use of biomass feedstocks results in about 200 Mt to 300 Mt of CO_2 emission

15. Includes energy used as petrochemical feedstocks.

reductions in waste handling that have not been credited to the petrochemical sector in Figure 16.12. Putting proper crediting mechanisms in place will be imperative for this sector.

Figure 16.12 ▶ Chemicals and petrochemicals industry CO_2 emissions in the Baseline, ACT Map and BLUE Map scenarios, 2005-2050

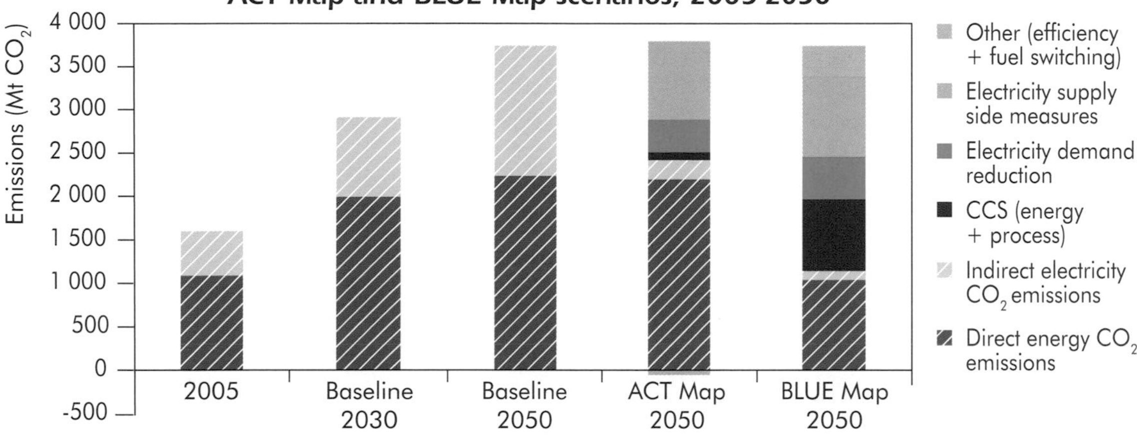

Notes: CO_2 gains from the use of CCS in combined heat and power (CHP) systems are allocated half (for heat) to the chemical and petrochemical sector and half (for electricity) to the power sector, as per IEA statistical accounting conventions.

Key point

A key role for CCS, but there are only limited emissions reductions in the chemicals and petrochemicals sector in the BLUE Map scenario compared to 2005.

Processing overview

Feedstocks

More than half (469 Mtoe/yr) of the total energy consumed in this sector is used in the form of oil, natural gas and coal feedstocks for the production process. Although most of the carbon from the feedstock is locked into final products such as plastics, solvents and methanol, some of this may be released at a later stage – for example, when the product is incinerated. The production and use of chemicals and petrochemicals emits much more fossil CO_2 over the complete life cycle than its share of industrial CO_2 emissions would suggest.

Steam cracking: high value chemicals (HVC)

More than 39% of the chemical and petrochemical industry's final energy use is for the steam cracking of naphtha, ethane and other feedstocks to produce HVCs. Out of a total of 318 Mtoe, only 50 Mtoe is used for energy purposes. Steam-cracking products contain about 268 Mtoe, of which about 36 Mtoe is recycled to the refining industry in the form of by-products for further processing into gasoline and other products.

The energy used in steam cracking depends on the choice of feedstock, the severity of the cracking operation and the furnace design and process technology employed. The choice of feedstock is a key element. To produce one tonne of ethylene requires 1.25 tonnes of ethane, 2.2 tonnes of propane or 3.2 tonnes of naphtha. There is a marked difference in approach in this regard between Asia-Pacific and Western Europe, where naphtha cracking predominates, and North America, the Middle East and Africa, where ethane cracking prevails. This is a consequence of feedstock availability. Ethane crackers tend to be of simpler, less efficient design. North American crackers use on average 32% more energy and European crackers 12% more energy than Asian crackers (Cagnolatti, 2005).

Since the 1970s, steam-cracker design changes have led to a more than 50% decrease in energy consumption. These improvements include gas turbine integration, more extensive process-to-process heat-recovery schemes, integral steam super-heaters, higher-efficiency rotating equipment, multi-stage refrigeration schemes and integrated heat-pump systems (Bowen, 2006).

Methanol

Methanol is used as antifreeze, solvent and fuel. In 2006, global methanol production was 36 Mt, of which 19% was used to make methyl tertiary butyl ether (MTBE), a gasoline additive, 10% was used in the production of acetic acid and 40% in the production of formaldehyde. About 80% of methanol production is natural gas-based, with the remainder being coal-based, predominantly in China. Production is shifting to countries with lower natural-gas costs (the Middle East and Russia). A typical methanol plant uses 30 GJ of natural gas per tonne of methanol, however the latest large-scale auto-thermal reforming plants operate at as low as 28.5 GJ/t (Lurgi, 2006).

Ammonia

Anhydrous ammonia is the source of nearly all the synthetic nitrogen fertilisers produced in the world. Ammonia is produced by combining nitrogen with hydrogen. The nitrogen is obtained from the atmosphere, while the hydrogen is obtained mainly from natural gas – and to a lesser extent from naphtha, coke-oven gas, refinery gases and heavy oil.

Global ammonia production was 145.4 Mt in 2005. Growth is mainly concentrated in West and East Asia, which together account for almost 40% of global production (IFA, 2006). About 77% of world ammonia production is based on natural-gas steam-reforming, 14% on coal gasification, mainly in China, and 9% on the partial oxidation of oil products and heavy hydrocarbon fractions, mainly in India and to a lesser degree in China. A typical heavy-oil based process uses 1.3 times as much energy as a gas-based process; while a coal based process is 1.7 times as energy intensive as gas. A 30% decrease in energy use per tonne of ammonia has been achieved in the last 30 years.

Natural gas costs are 70% to 90% of the production cost of ammonia. Because gas prices play such an important role, the increase in energy efficiency of gas-based ammonia plants has converged with gas price increases. Newer plants have similar efficiencies irrespective of their location.

Energy efficiency: BAT

Steam cracking

Today, typical steam crackers use 18 GJ to 25 GJ per tonne of ethylene cracked for the furnace and product separation. Improvements in cracking could yield large gains in energy efficiency in the long term. Options include higher-temperature furnaces (with materials able to withstand more than 1 100°C), gas-turbine integration (a type of high-temperature combined heat and power unit that generates the process heat for the cracking furnace), advanced distillation columns and combined refrigeration plants. Together, these steps could result in savings of 3 GJ per tonne of ethylene. The total potential for improving energy efficiency from existing technology to the best technology available is about 24 Mtoe.

Ammonia

Data from the International Fertilizer Industry Association (Al-Ansari, 2007) shows that the average energy use for ammonia production in 66 benchmarked plants (not including any in China) is 36.9 GJ per tonne of ammonia produced, ranging from 28 GJ to 53 GJ per tonne of ammonia. The highest capacity plants generally had the best efficiency. Older plants (20+ years old) had energy efficiencies 8% to 10% lower than newer plants. CO_2 emissions ranged from 1.5 Mt CO_2 to 3.1 Mt CO_2 per megatonne of ammonia produced. The average CO_2 emissions were 2.1 Mt CO_2 per megatonne of ammonia, with two-thirds process-related and one-third from fuel combustion.

Compared to the BAT of 28 GJ per tonne, this survey demonstrates an energy-saving potential of almost 48 Mtoe per year if all production was based on natural gas feedstocks. This would represent a reduction in energy consumption by 25% and reduce greenhouse gas emissions by 75 Mt CO_2.

The Integrated Pollution Prevention and Control Directive of 2006 refers to 26 techniques and technologies that aim at improved energy efficiency, emission reductions and waste management, including improvements such as the use of gas-heated reformers (GHR) that offer smaller surface areas and less heat loss. Palladium membrane units for hydrogen separation can provide 2 GJ of savings per tonne. CO_2 removal technologies, product ammonia separation and developments in ammonia synthesis can also reduce energy consumption (Rafiqul, *et al.*, 2005).

In most ammonia plants, CO_2 is separated from hydrogen at an early stage, generally using solvent absorption. Energy savings can be achieved by using new solvents, with a potential of up to 1.4 GJ per tonne of ammonia produced. Much of the CO_2 separated is used to produce urea, a popular type of nitrogen fertiliser.

Energy and materials efficiency: new process technologies

Steam cracking

The integration of gas turbines with cracking heaters reduces the specific energy for ethylene production by about 10% to 20% of the overall energy requirements. The hot off-gas from the gas turbine is used as combustion air for the furnace. Eleven plants designed by Lummus and based on the integration concept are operating successfully.

Biomass feedstock

Use of biomass feedstocks instead of petroleum feedstocks holds the greatest potential for reducing energy use in the petrochemicals industry. There are four principal ways to produce polymers and other organic chemicals from biomass:

- Direct use of several naturally occurring polymers, usually with some thermal treatment, chemical derivatisation or blending.
- Thermochemical conversions of biomass (*e.g.*, the Fischer Tropsch process and the methanol-to-olefins process, MTO) via pyrolysis or gasification, followed by synthesis and further processing. Rapid expansion of MTO in the near future will allow the use of low-cost coal and stranded gas feedstocks.
- "Green Biotechnology", which produces biopolymers (or their precursors) in genetically modified field crops such as potatoes or miscanthus.
- "White Biotechnology" (also referred to as industrial biotechnology), which makes use of fermentation processes (for most bulk products) next to enzymatic conversions (mainly for specialty and fine chemicals).

Bio-based chemicals offer substantial potential to save energy and greenhouse gas emissions, in some cases (e.g. the production of cellulose fibre as an alternative to synthetic fibre) by as much as 60%.

Large savings can also be achieved from the use of White Biotechnology – such as the production from bio-ethanol of ethylene, which can be used in polyethylene and in a wide range of chemical derivatives.[16] It has been estimated that non-renewable energy use and life-cycle greenhouse gas emissions can be reduced by more than one-third compared to petrochemical ethylene, if ethylene is produced from bioethanol made from maize in a moderate climate and using current technology. Using the same feedstock and more advanced fermentation and separation technologies, the savings can be increased to 50%. If fermentable sugar from sugar cane is used instead of maize, ethylene production is a net producer of energy instead of a consumer (even using current technology). This is a consequence of the high yields of tropical sugar cane cultivation and the large amounts of waste biomass produced, which can be used to generate power and hence replace fossil-fuel based electricity.

Other processing options include the thermochemical conversion of biomass and the "high-thermal upgrading" (HTU) naphtha-steam cracking process. Carbon credits, as long as they encompass carbon savings beyond the factory gate (for example in waste incineration), could provide a real incentive where biomass feedstocks are used. Higher oil prices will also favour biomass feedstocks. The development of ethanol as a transportation fuel could also enable the use of

16. Econcern is involved in rebuilding the Methanor plant in Delfzijl to produce bio-methanol using the glycerine wastes from bio-diesel production. Also, both Dow and BASF use these wastes to produce certain specialty chemicals.

bioethanol as a feedstock. Two full-scale ethanol-to-ethylene plants of 300 kt and 350 kt are planned to come on-stream in Brazil in 2009 and 2011.

Technically, much of the total demand for organic chemicals and polymers could be produced from bio-based feedstocks. Diffusion will primarily depend on the relative price levels of bio-based and petrochemical feedstocks, technological progress, government support and synergies with biofuel production. The largest benefits in terms of energy savings and greenhouse gas abatement could be achieved by combining bio-based chemicals with a combined strategy of reuse, recycling and energy recovery.

Biopolymers

The production of biopolymers received much attention in the 1990s, but a number of materials failed commercially, mainly because of their high production costs compared to polymers from oil feedstocks. Work has continued on some bioplastics since then. Opinions vary regarding their prospects. In the most optimistic case, with a significant market share, the emission-reduction potential would be several hundred Mt CO_2. However, the cost effectiveness of these technologies remains uncertain, and industry experts are sceptical regarding the growth prospects. Also, the main gain is during the waste-handling stage: *i.e.* beyond the factory gate and therefore mostly outside current crediting systems.

Table 16.7 ▶ Global technology outlook for biomass feedstocks and biopolymers

	2008-2015	2015-2030	2030-2050
Technology stage	R&D, Demonstration	Demonstration	Demonstration, Commercial
Investment costs (USD/t)	5 000-15 000	2 000-10 000	1 000-5 000
Life-cycle CO_2 reductions	50%	70%	80%
CO_2 reduction (Gt/yr)	0-0.05	0.05-0.1	0.1-0.3

Plastic waste recycling and energy recovery

Three key recovery options exist for plastics: mechanical recycling, feedstock recycling, and energy recovery. Only 20% to 30% of plastic waste can be mechanically recycled. The remainder can be used for energy recovery. Assuming an energy content of 30 GJ to 40 GJ per tonne of waste, the primary energy saving potential is estimated to be 48 Mtoe to 96 Mtoe per year.

Today, only 10 Mt of plastic waste is recycled. This is less than 10% of the overall waste generated, although significantly higher percentages are recycled in the United States, Japan and Europe than in other countries. About 30 Mt of plastic waste is incinerated. Energy recovery is approximately 500 Mtoe to 17.9 Mtoe (primary energy equivalent). This is equal to about 3% of the energy used in production.

Membranes

One of the most energy-intensive operations in the chemical industry is separation. Separation technologies, such as distillation, fractionation and extraction, use up to 40% of all the energy consumed in the chemical industry and can account for more than 50% of plant operating costs.

Membranes can replace energy-intensive separation processes in the chemicals industry, and also in the food processing, paper, petroleum refining and metals industries. Current production based on membranes is small, however, and no suitable membranes exist at present for many processes. New membranes with different qualities are being developed for the separation of specific gas mixtures, although more research is needed to improve their performance. The cost of a new membrane system is often higher than that of currently used separation technologies. The annual operating costs of membranes are often also higher than those of other separators, mainly because membranes foul easily and need to be replaced.

Membrane technologies now in the R&D phase have the potential to achieve substantial cost reductions. Depending on the application and the separation efficiency of the membrane, these may be between 20% and 60%.

Membranes for important energy consuming separations in the chemical industry may need a few decades for development and deployment (Table 16.8). The development of membrane reactors (combining chemical conversions and separation in a single reactor) is an area that still needs considerable research.

Table 16.8 ▶ Global technology prospects for membranes

Membranes	2003-2015	2015-2030	2030-2050
Technology stage	R&D, Demonstration	Demonstration, Commercial	Commercial
Internal rate of return	8%	10%	15%
Energy savings (%)	15%	17%	20%
CO_2 reduction (Gt/yr)	0-0.03	0.1	0.2

CO_2 capture and storage (CCS)

CCS is not readily applicable to most chemical production processes, except in ammonia plants (see above) and in large-scale CHP units. A few other processes generate high-concentration CO_2 flows where CCS would be applicable, but the volumes are small.

Process intensification

Process intensification or plant miniaturisation which often comprises a set of often radically innovative principles in process and equipment design is estimated to increase energy efficiency in the petrochemical sector by 5% in the next 10 – 20 years and 20% over the next 30 – 40 years (SenterNovem, 2007). The main barrier for its development is large scale demonstration.

Pulp and paper

The pulp and paper sector is the fourth-largest industrial consumer of energy and emitter of CO_2. In 2005, it accounted for 6% of world industrial energy use and 3% of energy and process CO_2 emissions. The four largest paper producers (the European Union, the United States, China and Japan) accounted for 80% of the CO_2 emissions.

The pulp and paper industry also produces energy as a by-product, and already generates about 50% of its own energy needs from biomass residues. This means that the CO_2 intensity of the industry is relatively low, and the CO_2 reduction potentials are correspondingly limited. But greater efficiency would nonetheless free up scarce bioenergy resources that could be used to replace fossil fuels elsewhere.

Scenarios

Figure 16.13 shows the industrial CO_2 emissions in the Baseline, ACT Map and BLUE Map scenarios. Primary and recycled paper production increases by 164% from 2005 to 2050 in all scenarios. Direct emissions increase by 184%, while energy use increases by 143%, in the Baseline scenario by 2050. The indirect emissions in power generation increase even more quickly, as electricity demand increases faster than total final energy demand. In the ACT Map scenario, direct emissions in 2050 are 83% above the 2005 level. In the BLUE Map scenario they are 91% below the 2005 level. Efficiency, fuel and feedstock switching account for 40% of the reduction from the Baseline of direct emissions in the BLUE Map scenario. CCS accounts for 9% of the total emissions reduction in this scenario. The remainder (46%) are the result of emission reduction efforts in power generation.

Processing overview

Energy use in the pulp and paper industry is divided among a number of different pulp production processes and paper production. The need for large amounts of steam makes combined heat and power (CHP) an attractive technology. Most modern paper mills have their own CHP units. Chemical pulp mills produce large amounts of black liquor, which is used to generate electricity, but with relatively low conversion efficiencies. New technologies that promise higher conversion efficiency could have important energy benefits, particularly in terms of electricity production and possibly biofuels.

Figure 16.13 ▶ Pulp and paper industry CO_2 emissions in the Baseline, ACT Map and BLUE Map scenarios, 2005-2050

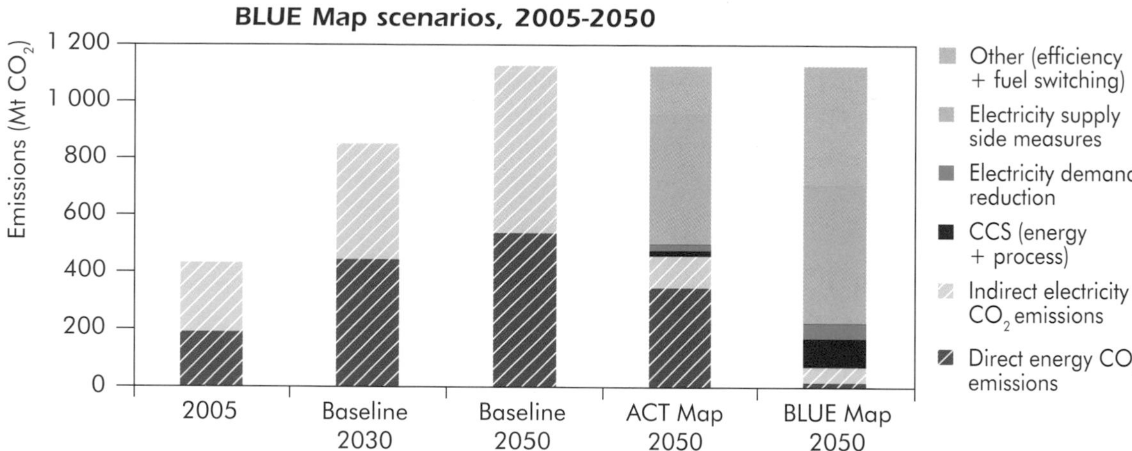

Note: CO_2 gains from the use of CCS with combined heat and power (CHP) systems are allocated half (for heat) to the pulp and paper sector and half (for electricity) to the power sector, as per IEA statistical accounting conventions.

Key point

Widespread use of CCS can result in a nearly-carbon-neutral pulp and paper sector.

In theory, pulp and paper could be produced without CO_2 emissions. To do so, all waste paper would need to be used for energy recovery. But from the viewpoint of the energy and resource system as a whole, it would make more sense to recycle as much paper as possible and to use the wood surplus to produce biofuels or electricity.

There remains significant scope to improve the energy efficiency of processes, for example, in mechanical pulping. Large investments have been made in Canada and Scandinavia to improve energy efficiency in pulping, but these savings have been primarily offset by a shift towards higher-quality pulp, which has a higher specific energy consumption per tonne.

Much of the past improvement in energy efficiency has resulted from increased heat recovery where the recovered steam is used to dry the pulp and paper. More than 90% of the electricity used in mechanical pulping is transformed to heat. The main source of further energy efficiency gains is heat recovery. Integrated mechanical, chemical, recycled pulp and paper mills provide the best solution for improving efficiency and minimising CO_2 emissions, because pulp drying can be avoided and the excess energy from the chemical pulp mill can be used efficiently in the paper-making. The energy efficiency of integrated pulp and paper mills is 10% to 50% better, depending on the grade of paper produced, than stand-alone mills.

Almost half of all paper is produced from waste paper. Recycling plants tend to be smaller and more dispersed than primary paper production facilities, and their energy needs for paper making are higher. But the energy that would have gone into pulp-making is saved. This saving far exceeds the additional energy they use. In many developed countries, more paper is recycled than produced.

Energy efficiency: BAT

The European Commission (EC) has produced a widely recognised BAT reference document on paper and pulp, the key findings of which are reproduced in Table 16.9.

Table 16.9 ▶ Best available technology (BAT)

	Heat GJ/t	Electricity GJ/t
Mechanical pulping		7.5
Chemical pulping	12.25	2.08
Waste paper pulp	0.20	0.50
De-inked waste paper pulp	1.00	2.00
Coated papers	5.25	2.34
Folding boxboard	5.13	2.88
Household and sanitary paper	5.13	3.60
Newsprint	3.78	2.16
Printing and writing paper	5.25	1.80
Wrapping and packaging paper and board	4.32	1.80
Paper and paperboard not elsewhere specified	4.88	2.88

Sources: EC, 2001; Finnish Forestry Industries Federation, 2002.

IEA analysis shows that the energy intensity of *heat* use compared to BAT across the key countries varies from a remaining improvement potential of 35% for Canada to 43% better than BAT for Japan.[17] For *electricity*, this remaining improvement potential varied from 32% for the United Kingdom to 3% better than BAT for Germany.

Canada and the United States are among the countries with the most energy-intensive pulp and paper industries in the world. The average technical age of their pulp and paper mills is perhaps the oldest. Both are rich in wood resources. The United States is the largest chemical pulp producer and Canada is the largest mechanical pulp producer.

17. The fact that the EEI of Japan, Sweden and Finland fall well above BAT indicates either that the BAT savings are exaggerated or that there are issues of data consistency and comparability across countries. Different reporting methodologies, system boundaries, problems related to CHP accounting, high recovered paper use rates and a high level of integrated mills (in the case of Japan) could explain the unexpectedly high energy efficiency index of these countries.

Figure 16.14 ▶ Energy efficiency potentials, based on best available technology

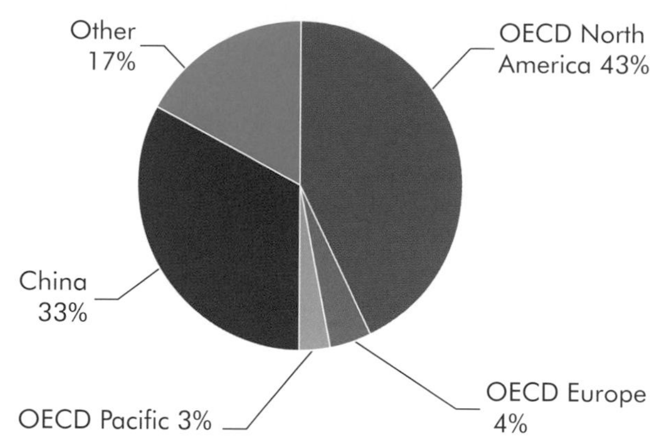

Key point

The highest potential improvement from the use of BAT exists in North America.

Energy and materials efficiency: new process technologies

Current pulp and paper facilities in many OECD countries are nearing the end of their operating lives and will need to be replaced over the next 10 to 15 years. This presents an excellent opportunity for new technology deployment to have an impact on energy savings in the medium term. The most promising energy savings technologies in the industry are likely to come from black-liquor gasification and bio-refinery concepts, advanced paper drying technologies, and increased paper recycling.

Black-liquor gasification and bio-refinery concepts

The paper industry produces black liquor as a by-product – this is normally burned in a recovery boiler. Given the high water content of black liquor, the efficiency of existing recovery boilers is limited. Electricity production is also limited, because the recovery boilers produce steam at low pressures for safety reasons.

Gasification offers opportunities to increase the efficiency of black liquor recovery by conversion to syngas, which can be used in gas-turbine power generation. Teams from the United States, Sweden and Finland are collaborating in the development of the technology. The internal rate of return of an investment in such power generation has been estimated at 16% to 17%, if the electricity can be sold at USD 0.04/kWh. Further research is needed to increase the reliability of the gasifier. The use of a gasifier with a gas turbine has not yet been demonstrated, and the total capital costs of a black liquor gasification-combined cycle system are estimated to be 60% to 90% higher than those for a standard boiler system. In addition to the energy efficiency benefit, gasification makes it possible to enhance pulping by modifying conventional pulping liquors.

Alternatively, the syngas can be used as a feedstock to produce chemicals: in effect turning the paper mill into a bio-refinery. In Europe, policies aimed at increasing the share of biofuels in transportation have sparked interest in using black liquor gasifiers to produce dimethyl ether (DME) as a replacement for diesel fuel.

Black liquor production is projected to grow to 79 Mtoe by 2025. Based on the performance of a typical kraft plant in the south-eastern United States, a pulp plant will be able to produce and sell in the order of 220 kWh to 335 kWh of excess electricity per tonne of pulp. If the overall electric efficiency was raised by 10%, and the steam efficiency remained the same, 79 Mtoe of black liquor per year would yield an additional 8 Mtoe of electricity annually. The savings in terms of primary energy would be in the range of 12 Mtoe to 19 Mtoe, depending on whether a gas- or coal-fired power plant was displaced. The CO_2-savings potential is in the range of 30 Mt to 75 Mt per year (Table 16.10).

Table 16.10 ▶ Global technology prospects for black liquor gasification

Black liquor gasification	2003-2015	2015-2030	2030-2050
Technology stage	R&D, Demonstration	Demonstration, Commercial	Commercial
Investment costs (USD/t)	300-400	300-350	300
Energy reduction (%)	10-15%	10-20%	15-23%
CO_2 reduction (Gt/yr)	0-0.01	0.01-0.03	0.1-0.2

Advanced paper drying technologies

In paper production, energy is needed to dry process fibres. Technical potentials to reduce energy use in the paper industry by 30% or more have been identified in various countries, with cost-effective potentials of at least 15% to 20%.

New process designs focus on more efficient water-removal techniques – for example, by combining new forming technologies with increased pressing and thermal drying. In the long term, the need to use water can be re-evaluated, and other ways of managing the fibre orientation process for optimal paper quality, such as through the use of super-critical CO_2 and nanotechnology, may be possible.

Paper drying consumes about 25% to 30% of the total energy used in the pulp and paper industry. Assuming that energy efficiency improvements of 20% to 30% are possible in this production stage, overall energy savings are estimated at 17 Mtoe.

Table 16.11 ▶ Global technology prospects for energy-efficient drying technologies

Efficient drying	2003-2015	2015-2030	2030-2050
Technology stage	R&D	Demonstration, Commercial	Commercial
Investment costs (USD/t)	800-1 100	700-1 000	600-700
Energy reduction (%)	20-30%	20-30%	20-30%
CO_2 reduction (Gt/yr)	0-0.01	0.01-0.02	0.02-0.05

Increased paper recycling

Paper recycling is another important potential contributor to energy savings. Paper recycling rates are already high in many countries, varying between 30% in the Russian Federation to 64% in China. But increased recycling of paper is feasible. The recovery rate in most non-OECD countries is 15% to 30% lower than in OECD countries, although the rate at which waste paper is actually recycled in developing countries is higher than the recovery rate suggests as large amounts of waste paper are imported from OECD countries. Between 10 GJ and 20 GJ can be saved per tonne of paper recycled, depending on the type of pulp and the efficiency of the pulp production it replaces. The net effect on CO_2 emissions is less clear, as some pulp mills use biomass, while recycling mills may use fossil fuels. However, biomass that is not used for paper production could potentially be used for dedicated power generation, with potentially higher power production rates than municipal solid waste (MSW) incineration would generate.

CO_2 capture and storage (CCS)

The production of chemical pulp generates large amounts of CO_2 from biomass when black liquor is combusted for energy and the recovery of chemicals.

Hektor and Berntsson (2007a) have analysed the use of chemical absorption technology for black liquor boilers and conclude that capture and storage would be economic at a CO_2 price of USD 30 to USD 50 per tonne of CO_2. These costs apply to modern pulp mills that generate sufficient surplus heat for the capture process. The same authors (2007b) conclude that, for integrated pulp and paper mills, integration with natural-gas, combined-cycle (NGCC) power generation coupled with CCS and maximised production of biofuels for use elsewhere would be the most economic configuration.

The total black liquor production worldwide is around 72 Mtoe, which gives a CCS potential of around 300 Mt of CO_2 per year. The BLUE Map scenario assumes 200 Mt of CCS in 2050.

Non-ferrous metals

The non-ferrous metals sector produces aluminium, copper and a number of other materials such as zinc, lead and cadmium. It is the fifth largest industrial consumer of energy and emitter of CO_2. In 2005, it accounted for 3% of world industrial energy use and 2% of energy and process CO_2 emissions.

The main primary producers of aluminium are located in China, North America, Latin America, Western Europe, Russia and Australia. The aluminium industry is the single largest industrial consumer of electricity in Australia, accounting for about 13% of total final electricity consumption. The industry is of similar importance in other countries with low-cost electricity, such as Norway, Iceland, Canada, Russia and the Middle East. In recent years, several new smelters have been built in Africa. New smelter projects are being developed in the Middle East on the basis of access to lower-cost electricity.

Most growth in recent years has been in China, a trend expected to continue in the immediate future. China's production is expected to double between 2005 and 2008, from 7 Mt to 14 Mt. The rapid growth is driven by low investment cost for smelters, about a third of those in Western countries, offset by higher energy costs. Chinese consumption was around 13 kg per capita in 2007, compared with 20 kg to 35 kg per capita in OECD countries. Only about 10% of China's aluminium ends up in products for export (ENAM, 2007).

Scenarios

Figure 16.15 shows the industrial CO_2 emissions in the Baseline, ACT Map and BLUE Map scenarios. In the Baseline scenario, direct emissions of non-ferrous metals production nearly quadruple, while energy use increases by 277%. In the ACT Map scenario, direct emissions in 2050 are 3.5 times the 2005 level. In the BLUE Map scenario they are three times the 2005 level. Direct emissions are halved in BLUE Map (200 Mt reduction). Efficiency, fuel and feedstock switching account for more than half of the reduction from the baseline of direct emissions in the ACT Map and BLUE Map scenarios. However, direct emissions are dwarfed by indirect emissions in power generation, and an important part of the strategy for this sector is to locate smelters on remote sites with ample CO_2-free electricity potential, for example from hydropower.

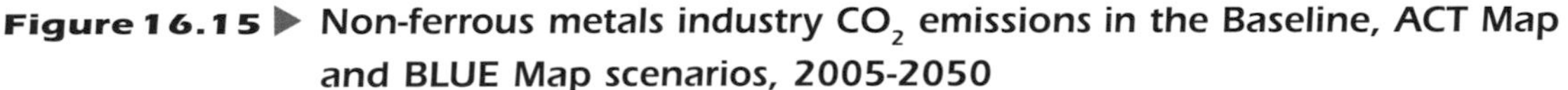

Figure 16.15 ▶ Non-ferrous metals industry CO_2 emissions in the Baseline, ACT Map and BLUE Map scenarios, 2005-2050

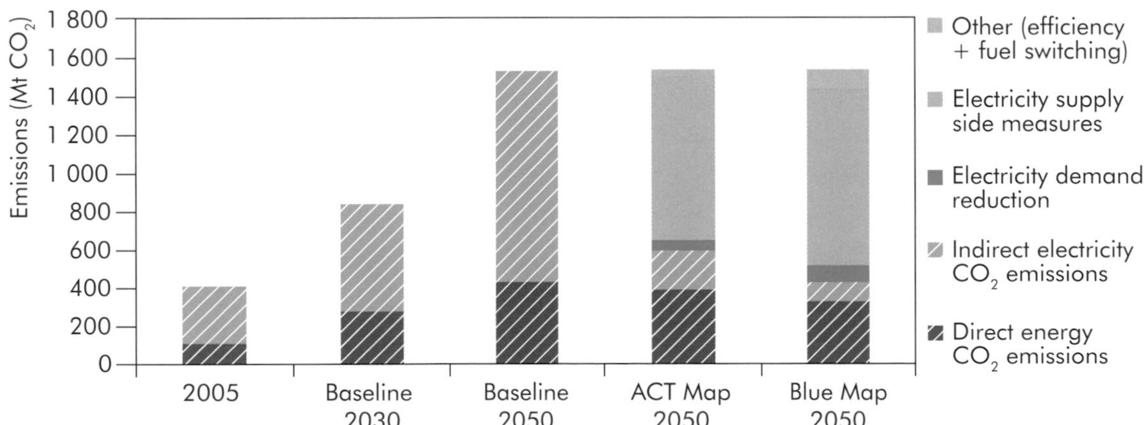

Key point

Electricity use and its emissions are the key issues for the non-ferrous metals industry.

Processing overview

Aluminium production can be split into primary aluminium production and recycling. Primary production is about 20 times as energy intensive as recycling and represents the bulk of energy consumption. With world alumina production at 60 Mt, total energy use was 16 Mtoe in 2005.

Energy efficiency: BAT

Primary aluminium is produced in three distinct steps: bauxite (ore) mining, alumina refining and aluminium smelting. Most of the energy consumed in alumina refineries is in the form of steam. The calcining (drying) of the alumina also requires large amounts of high temperature heat. Because of their high demand for steam, modern plants use CHP systems. The average energy consumption of Australian refineries is 11.8 GJ per tonne of alumina produced. The global average was 12.0 GJ/t in 2006, with a regional range from 11.2 GJ/t to 14.5 GJ/t (Table 16.12).[18] This could be reduced to around 9.5 GJ/t through better heat integration and improved CHP systems. The production of 1 kg of aluminium requires about 2 kg of alumina.

Table 16.12 ▶ Regional average energy use of metallurgical alumina production, 2006

	GJ/t Alumina
Africa and South Asia	14.5
North America	11.9
Latin America	11.2
East Asia and Oceania	11.8
Europe	13.1
Weighted average	12.0

Source: World Aluminium, 2007a.

The main energy use in aluminium production is for the electrochemical conversion of alumina into aluminium in the Hall-Héroult process. The difference in efficiency between the best and worst plants is approximately 20%. This can be attributed to different cell types and to the size of the smelters, which is generally related to the age of the plant. Modern prebake Hall-Héroult smelters use about 50 GJ to 55 GJ of electricity per tonne of product. Older configurations (Søderbergs) may use up

18. These figures do not include the energy consumption figures for Chinese alumina production, where the energy intensive process required for alumina production from the domestic bauxite (which accounts for over half of their production) is more than double the International Aluminium Institute (IAI) reported level.

to 60 GJ per tonne of aluminium. The theoretical minimum energy use is about 20 GJ per tonne. About 18 GJ of pitch and petroleum coke (petcoke) is needed per tonne of aluminium for the production of the anodes. Another 7.4 Gt of energy is consumed per tonne of aluminium for other uses in the smelters. Multiplied by the aluminium production volume, this represents another 19 Mtoe of industrial energy use.

Table 16.13 ▶ Regional average electricity use for primary aluminium production, 2006

	kWh/t aluminium
Africa	14 622
North America	15 452
Latin America	15 030
Asia	15 103
Europe	15 387
Oceania	14 854
Weighted average	15 194

Source: World Aluminium, 2007b.

The industry plans to retrofit or replace existing smelters in order to reduce electricity consumption to 14 500 kWh per tonne (52.2 GJ per tonne) in the short term, and then to 14 000 kWh to 13 500 kWh per tonne as new smelters are built and older ones are retired. New world-class plants achieve 13 000 kWh per tonne. Technologies under development such as drained cells (drained cathodes) and inert anodes offer the promise of further smelter efficiencies.

Energy and materials efficiency: new process technologies

Inert anodes

The development of inert anodes could end CO_2 emissions stemming from the use of carbon anodes, and also eliminate emissions of perfluorocarbons (a category of powerful greenhouse gases) from the electrolysis process. Electricity consumption could also be reduced by some 10% to 20% compared to today's advanced smelters. The technology is, however, suited only for new smelters, because the cell design has to be changed fundamentally. The ultimate technical feasibility of inert anodes is not yet proven, despite 25 years of research. More fundamental research on materials will be needed and anode wear-rates of less than five millimetres per year will have to be attained.

Figure 16.16 ▶ CO_2 reduction potentials, based on best available technology

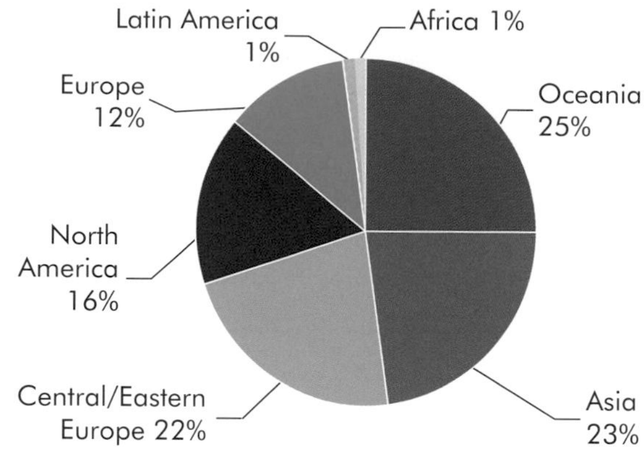

Key point

A relatively small potential remains for CO_2 reduction based on energy efficiency.

Table 16.14 ▶ Global technology prospects for inert anodes and bipolar cell design in primary aluminium production

Inert anodes	2003-2015	2015-2030	2030-2050
Technology stage	R&D	Demonstration	Commercial
Investment costs (USD/t)	N/A	Cost savings	Cost savings
Energy reduction (%)	N/A	5-15%	10-20%
CO_2 reduction (Gt/yr)	N/A	0-0.05	0.05-0.2

General equipment and recycling

Steam supply

A large share of industrial energy use is in the form of low-temperature heat, for which steam is usually the preferred energy carrier. The efficiency of steam boilers can be as high as 85%, but average efficiency is lower – due mainly to low load factors and poor maintenance. Average boiler efficiency in China is about 65%, but the boiler is often only one part of a steam supply system. Steam and heat losses from pipes and ducts are important as well. There are no detailed statistics regarding overall system efficiencies.

The main efficiency options are to replace the steam boiler with a CHP system or a heat pump. Calculating the actual efficiency gains, however, is very site-specific. An efficient steam supply system can result in higher efficiencies, but even greater emissions savings may be achievable by reductions in steam demand. In the last few decades, for example, the chemical industry has successfully developed new catalysts and process routes that significantly reduce steam use.

The figures in Table 16.15 indicate the savings potentials for steam systems only and do not include any possible measures related to reducing steam demand.

Table 16.15 ▶ Steam system efficiency measures

	Typical savings (%)	Typical investment (USD/GJ steam)	Use in OECD countries (%)	Use in non-OECD countries (%)
Steam traps	5%	1	50%	25%
Insulation pipelines	5%	1	75%	25%
Feedwater economisers	5%	10	75%	50%
Reduced excess air	2%	5	100%	50%
Heat transfer	1-2%	–	75%	50%
Return condensate	10%	10	75%	50%
Improved blowdown	2-5%	20	25%	10%
Vapour recompression	0-20%	30	10%	0%
Flash condensate	0-10%	10	50%	25%
Vent condenser	1-5%	40	25%	10%
Minimise short cycling	0-5%	20	75%	50%
Insulate valves and fittings	1-3%	5	50%	25%

Sources: United States Department of Energy, 2002; IEA estimates.

Much of this potential has already been achieved in OECD countries, but inadequate attention to routine maintenance of some measures, such as steam traps, valves and heat-transfer surfaces significantly reduces the benefit derived from these measures. In many developing countries, the losses from steam supply systems remain substantial. Insulation is often non-existent in Russia, for example. In China, many small-scale boilers operate with considerable excess air and incomplete combustion of coal. Poor coal quality is the main cause for the low efficiency of Chinese boilers.

Electric motor-drive systems

Motor-driven equipment such as compressors, pumps or fans account for 60% of the electricity consumed in the industrial sector and for more than 30% of all electricity use.

Improved motors could save significant amounts of energy on a continual basis. Optimisation of motor systems can typically result in 20% to 25% efficiency gains. It is estimated that up to 7% of global electricity demand could be saved if the energy efficiency of motors and their related drive systems were to be cost-optimised.

In Europe alone, studies suggest that the implementation of energy efficiency options for motors could result in 29% savings. The total investment cost of such a programme would be USD 500 million, while the annual saving would amount to USD 10 billion (Keulenaer, *et al.*, 2004).

The performance of motor systems can be improved by optimising them to meet end-use requirements. Since the power consumption of the drive varies based on the cube of the motor rotation speed, small changes in motor speed can yield large energy savings. In the absence of electronic variable speed controls, the bulk of the energy used on motors in many industries is simply converted into waste heat.

The electricity demand of industrial motor systems can be reduced by:

- Using high-efficiency motors.
- Proper sizing of the motor to the load requirements. Many motors are oversized and, therefore, run at suboptimal load factors. This significantly reduces efficiency and power use.
- Using adjustable speed drives (ASDs) to match speed and torque to the load requirements. The savings potential here depends critically on the load. Systems operating at around full load would be worse off by about 3% if they used ASD electronics. The savings potential, therefore, needs to be assessed for each individual motor system. In general, savings of 10% to 20% can be achieved, but savings up to 60% are possible for specific systems if ASD is applied instead of throttling.
- Replacing inefficient throttling devices and/or simplifying (or even avoiding) wasteful mechanical transmissions.
- Optimising systems, including the motor-driven equipment (fans, pumps, compressors, traction and conveyance systems), distribution (pipes, ducts, and flow control devices such as valves, regulators and dampers) and end-use equipment (including tools, presses, heat exchangers and mixers) to deliver the required energy service most efficiently.

- Proper maintenance and repair. For example, poor rewinding can damage motors and lower their efficiency significantly, and dirty heat-exchange surfaces or filters can reduce system efficiency.
- Maintaining acceptable levels of power quality.

High-efficiency motors use better quality materials, are made more precisely, and are about 85% to 95% more efficient than many motors in current use, depending on size. Although the cost of an efficient motor may be 20% more than standard motors, motor losses decrease by 20% to 30%. In most applications, the pay-back time is less than three years. Using new motors instead of rewinding used ones is another efficiency option, as rewinds cause an overall efficiency reduction of 1.5%. The replacement of standard efficiency motors with high-efficiency models is likely to capture only about 10% of the energy saving potential. The remainder will come from a combination of proper motor sizing, appropriate use of adjustable speed drives, and other measures listed above. More than 90% of all industrial motors in the European Union operate at or below standard efficiency, while more than 70% of all motors in the United States and Canada are high- or premium-efficiency motors (Brunner and Niederberger, 2006).

Compressors, pumps and fans consume more than half the energy used for industrial motor applications. Pumps are very important in the chemical industry, where they use 37% to 76% of motor power, but compressor consumption varies widely in the same industry, from 3% to 55%. Pump systems, compressor systems and fans are often coupled with too-powerful motors, especially for small and medium power uses. As a consequence, the systems operate most of the time at only a fraction of their optimal load. This results in significant efficiency losses. In industrial pumps, energy efficiency can vary between 40% and 90%, depending on the design and the application.

Although motor system components are widely-traded commodity goods, there are large variations in the market penetration of high-efficiency motors and motor-system components around the globe. Countries, such as Canada and the United States, that have implemented energy performance standards at relatively high efficiency levels have market shares for high-efficiency motors of over 70%. The market share in countries without them, such as European countries, is below 10% or 15%, despite voluntary programmes such as the Motor Challenge Programme.

The prevalence of energy efficient motors has substantially increased, but the potential increase in motor *system* efficiency remains largely unrealised due to the lack of national standards and policies to encourage companies to integrate energy efficiency into their management practices. The United States programme has been partially successful in building awareness through voluntary approaches such as training, case studies, publications and technical assistance, but these are time-intensive, plant-by-plant efforts that fall far short of the total savings potential (McKane, 2005). Given the savings potential in terms of total electricity use, a much more comprehensive approach is warranted and needed.

The total energy savings potential for upgrades in motors and motor systems has been estimated to be from 15% to 25% and it could be higher when emerging technologies are included. The total energy savings will depend on the market penetration of new motors, controls and system improvements. In turn, this rate will depend on the success of government programmes to support their adoption and of technology transfer programmes. Depending on the application, some measures can be applied as retrofits to existing motors and motor systems, while others can only be applied to new motors. Most systems can be adapted in some way to improve energy efficiency.

Table 16.16 ▶ Cost estimates for emerging motor technologies

Technology	Current capital costs	Capital costs by 2025	Operating & management costs	Payback by 2025	Notes
New motors					
Super-conductor	Higher than existing motors	Lower than existing motors	Lower than existing motors	Up to one year	If wire costs decrease, the payback period will be short to none. At present only for large motors.
Permanent magnet	Roughly equal	Roughly equal	Lower	One to three years	
Copper rotor	Higher	Potentially lower	Lower	Up to one year	If die casting costs decrease, payback periods will be short to none.
Written pole	60% higher	30% higher	Lower		
Switched reluctance (SR)	50% higher	25% higher	Unclear		Controls are more complex, but SRs are more efficient. The choice will be driven by reliability.
System and end-use improvements					
Optimisation by experts	None	None	Higher initially, then lower	Up to one year	Cost of expertise outweighed by energy-efficiency savings.
Optimisation tools	None	None	Higher initially, then lower	Up to one year	Cost of time spent on tools outweighed by energy-efficiency savings.
Training programmes	None	None	Higher initially, then lower	About one year	Cost of employee time (in training) outweighed by energy-efficiency savings.
Premium lubricants	50-150% higher	50-150% higher	Lower	About one year	Premium lubricants last three to four times as long.
Controls					
Advanced adjustable-speed drives (ASDs)	Higher	Higher	Significantly lower	One to four years	Initial capital costs are comparable to those for conventional ASDs. Advanced ASDs that provide sag control pay for themselves once they prevent a single shutdown.

Source: Worrell, Price and Galitsky, 2004.

Table 16.17 ▶ Global technology prospects for motor systems

Motor systems	2003-2015	2015-2030	2030-2050
Technology stage	R&D, Demonstration, Commercial	Demonstration, Commercial	Commercial
Internal rate of return	20-40%	30-50%	60%
Energy reduction (%)	under 20%	10-20%	15-20%
CO_2 reduction (Gt/yr)	0-0.05	0.1-0.3	1.0-1.4

Chapter 17 BUILDINGS AND APPLIANCES

Key Findings

- *In the Baseline scenario, final energy demand is projected to increase by 80% between 2005 and 2050, while CO_2 emissions (including upstream emissions from electricity at the 2005 emission factor) are projected to increase by 129% from 8.8 Gt CO_2 to 20.1 Gt CO_2. This is driven by a doubling of the residential building area between 2005 and 2050 and a tripling of the services building area, higher ownership rates for existing energy consuming devices and new types of energy services, and the only modest improvement in energy efficiency in the Baseline scenario.*
- *However, the ACT Map and BLUE Map scenarios show the vital role the buildings sector can play in achieving low-cost CO_2 reductions. In the ACT Map scenario, CO_2 emissions are reduced by 35% below the Baseline scenario level in 2050 to 13.2 Gt CO_2 (using the 2005 CO_2 emissions factor for electricity generation). In the BLUE Map scenario, CO_2 emissions are reduced by 43% below the Baseline scenario level in 2050 to 11.5 Gt CO_2.*
- *These figures, however, mask an even more dramatic change. In the BLUE Map scenario electricity generation is largely decarbonised in 2050. Accounting for upstream electricity sector emissions using the BLUE Map electricity emissions factor in 2050 means that CO_2 emissions from buildings are 85% lower than the baseline level in 2050. This results in buildings sector CO_2 emissions in 2050 being 65% lower than their level in 2005.*
- *Buildings consumed 2 914 Mtoe of energy in 2005. The residential and service sectors accounted for 2 569 Mtoe of this, with the residential sector accounting for two-thirds and the service sector one-third of this energy use. About 25% of the energy consumed was electricity, making buildings the largest electricity consumer.*
- *Globally, space and water heating are estimated to dominate final energy use, accounting for around two-thirds of final energy use. Cooking accounts for around 10% to 13%, while lighting, cooling and other appliances account for the balance. However, the associated upstream emissions from electricity production make the end-uses dominated by electricity consumption more important from a CO_2 abatement perspective.*
- *In the ACT Map scenario, energy consumption in the buildings sector in 2050 is 32% (1 684 Mtoe) below the Baseline scenario level. In the BLUE Map scenario, energy consumption in 2050 is 41% (2 143 Mtoe) lower than in the Baseline scenario. Fossil fuel use is reduced significantly, while the use of solar and modern biofuels increases significantly in both the ACT Map and BLUE Map scenarios. In the residential and service sectors, more than half of the savings occur in space and water heating.*
- *In the ACT Map scenario, direct CO_2 emissions from coal, oil and gas are reduced by 6% below their 2005 level, to 3.2 Gt CO_2 in 2050. In the BLUE Map scenario,*

direct emissions are 45% below their 2005 levels. The additional savings in the BLUE Map scenario require a significantly higher marginal abatement cost than the ACT Map scenario.

- *In the BLUE Map scenario, the reduction of direct emissions to significantly below 2005 levels requires all new buildings in cold climates to meet passive house standards (or their equivalent) from 2015. Given the slow turnover of the housing stock, a combination of retrofit and early replacement of building shells to passive house standards will be required (200 million dwellings in OECD countries) that doesn't occur in the Baseline scenario. It also requires very significant fuel switching in the buildings sector. Electrification, modern bioenergy and solar technologies will have to replace technologies based on oil, coal, gas and traditional biomass in cooking, space heating and water heating. Achieving the additional savings of the BLUE Map scenario means applying these measures and technologies to market segments where the marginal abatement cost is high.*
- *The scenario results show that emissions can be reduced significantly by applying best available technologies to the building envelope and in heating, ventilation and air conditioning (HVAC), lighting, appliances and cooking.*
- *Key technologies in reducing emissions from space and water heating in existing buildings are heat pumps and solar heating. While, energy-efficient new buildings can reduce heating demand by as much as a factor of ten compared to the average new buildings constructed today. The additional cost is comparatively small. Passive buildings have very low heat losses through a combination of compact design, their orientation towards sunlight, very good insulation, high air tightness, the avoidance of thermal bridges and heat recovery in the ventilation system.*
- *While the ACT Map scenario results can be achieved with technologies that are widely available today and that are economic based on life-cycle cost, the outcomes envisaged in the BLUE Map scenario will require emerging and more expensive technologies. Some of these will only be economic at relatively high levels of CO_2 reduction incentive, at least when they are initially deployed.*
- *Policies will be needed to help promote, demonstrate and rapidly deploy new and tighter standards, if the techniques and technologies needed for passive buildings are to be widely deployed before significant new building stock is built. Policies also have to ensure that the construction techniques and technologies applied in new houses enter the market in the refurbishment of existing buildings. The policy challenges in the ACT Map scenario are significant. In the BLUE Map scenario they are very demanding indeed. Achieving the outcomes envisaged in the BLUE Map scenario will require unprecedented efforts and co-ordination by policy makers, investors, developers, technology developers, manufacturers, equipment installers and consumers. The BLUE Map scenario also requires new construction and installation skills in the buildings sector.*

Overview

Residential, service sector and public buildings encompass a wide array of technologies in the building envelope and its insulation, space heating and cooling systems, water heating systems, lighting, appliances and consumer products, and business equipment. Other technologies also play an important role, for example, intelligent lighting helps to reduce and manage energy loads. Energy consumption in buildings is highly influenced by local climates and cultures, and even more so by individual users.

Unlike consumer goods, buildings can last for decades, even centuries. More than half of the existing building stock will still be standing in 2050. Buildings are much more frequently renewed than replaced. A considerable portion of many buildings is changed in timeframes much shorter than the lifetime of the building. Lighting systems and numerous appliances as well as heating, ventilation and air conditioning (HVAC) systems are often changed after 15 to 20 years. Even facades and windows need renovation. Office equipment is often changed after 3 to 5 years, while household appliances are often changed over a period of 5 to 15 years. Consumables such as light bulbs are changed in much shorter timeframes. Choosing the best available technology at the time of renovation or purchase is important in reducing energy demand in buildings at least cost.

Building emissions are growing rapidly, due to the rapid expansion both of building areas and of the ownership of energy-consuming equipment. Policies to improve energy efficiency in new and existing buildings need to be designed to ensure that new structures are built to the highest standards of efficiency relevant to the policy goal set. Policies should foster new technologies both in buildings themselves and in the energy-using equipment inside of them.

A wide range of technologies are already available that can significantly reduce CO_2 emissions in new and existing buildings. Many of these technologies are already economic, based on total life-cycle costs. But non-economic barriers can significantly slow their penetration in the absence of well-designed government policies.

Several recently developed technologies (e.g. high-performance windows, vacuum-insulated panels, high-performance reversible heat pumps) when combined with integrated passive solar design, can achieve 80% reductions in building energy consumption and GHG emissions. A number of other technologies are under development (e.g. integrated intelligent building control systems) which, with further research, development and demonstration, could have an increasingly large impact over the next two decades. The large-scale adoption of many of these technologies will be dependent on rapid commercial demonstration and deployment. This will need to include the training of professionals in an integrated approach to the design and use of combinations of technologies.

Low building stock turnover: the need for energy efficiency refurbishment

The long lifespan of building shells has a significant impact on the speed at which policies and technological improvements can have an impact on energy consumption. But energy consumption in buildings is in part determined by appliances, fittings and heating and cooling systems that have very different, and generally much shorter, economic lifetimes (see Figure 17.1).

Figure 17.1 ▶ Economic lifetimes of energy equipment and infrastructure

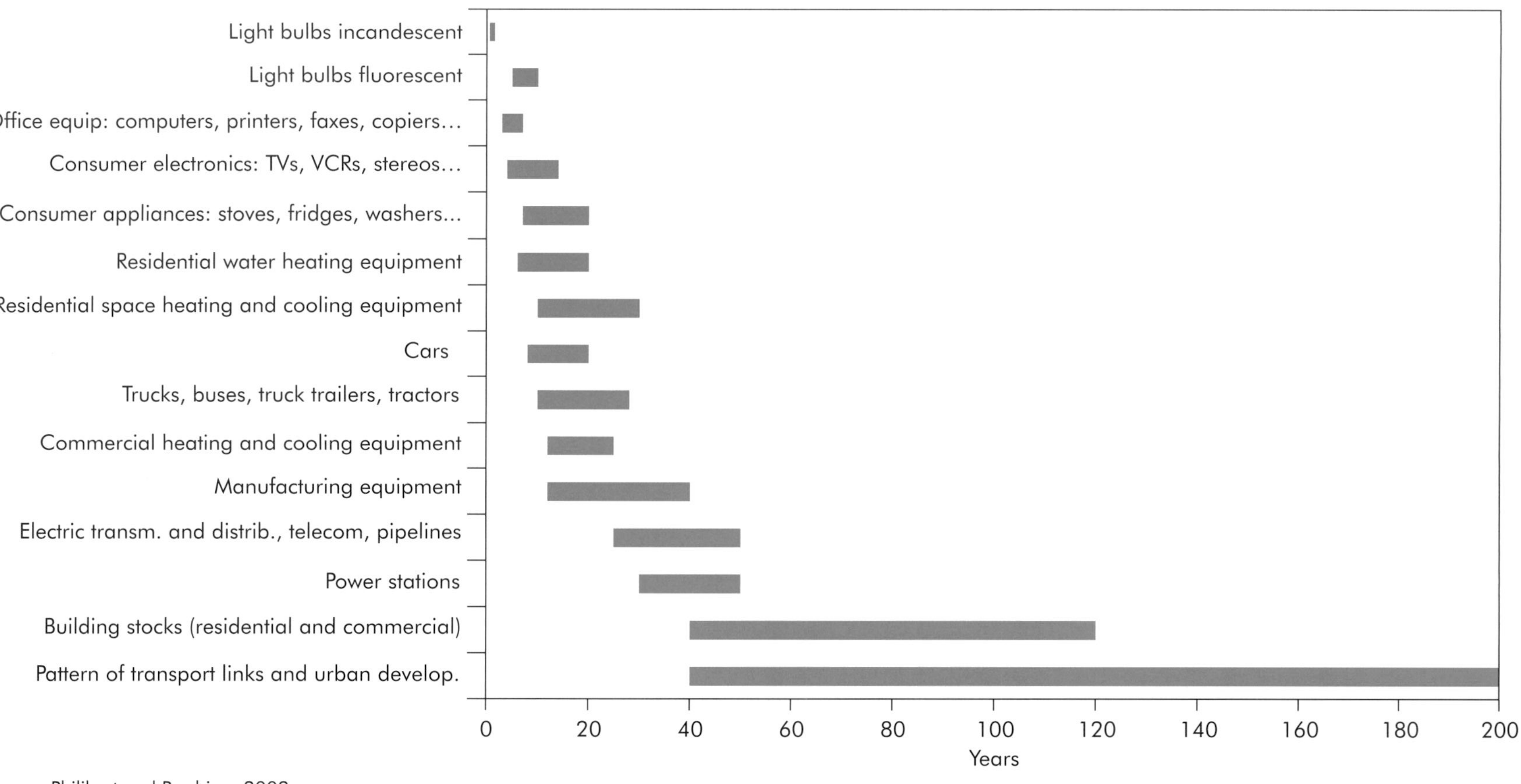

Source: Philibert and Pershing, 2002.

Key point

The building stock is very long-lived, early policy action is imperative to achieving low-cost change.

The age of a building has a significant impact on its heating requirements. Data from Germany suggest that energy consumption per square metre for pre-1970s homes can be between 55% and 130% higher than for more modern buildings. In OECD countries, a significant share of the building stock was built before 1970 and is only retired very slowly (Table 17.1 and Figure 17.2). Developing countries tend to have higher building stock turnover rates, with average lifespans often in the range of only 25 to 30 years.

Table 17.1 ▶ **Dwelling stock and retirement rates in selected EU countries, 1980-2002/03**

	Total stock (000)					Retirements (000)					
	1980	1990	1995	2000	2002/03	1980	1990	1995	2000	2003	average
Czech Republic	3 495	3 706	n.a.	3 828	n.a.	16	n.a.	n.a.	2	1.8	0.26%
Denmark	2 162	2 375	2 437	2 509	2 561	8	n.a.	n.a.	n.a.	n.a.	0.37%
France	24 717	26 976	28 221	n.a.	2 945	n.a.	22	22	18	21	0.29%
Germany	25 406	26 327	35 266	37 630	38 158	n.a.	n.a.	21.5	n.a.	n.a.	0.06%
Hungary	3 542	3 853	3 989	4 077	4 134	16.4	7.4	6.4	6.1	4.7	0.22%
Netherlands	4 849	5 892	6 283	6 651	6 764	14.9	11.6	13.7	13.5	17.8	0.24%
Poland	9 794	11 022	11 491	11 485	12 030	26.2	7.5	10	6.2	4.9	0.10%
Spain	14 580	17 220	n.a.	n.a.	14 184	116.6	10.1	8.9	15	15.5	0.32%
Sweden	3 680	4 045	4 234	4 294	4 351	2.1	1	2.5	4.6	1.5	0.06%
United Kingdom	21 517	23 383	24 341	25 283	25 617	45	15.1	n.a.	n.a.	n.a.	0.14%

Source: Norris and Shiels, 2004.

The very low retirement rate of the residential building stock in OECD countries is a significant constraint on reducing heating and cooling demand, particularly in more ambitious CO_2 reduction scenarios. Service sector buildings are generally less constrained in this respect, as they are subject to much earlier retirement or significant refurbishment. Some 200 million residential dwellings in OECD countries will have to be refurbished to new energy standards to achieve the savings in the BLUE Map scenario.

Figure 17.2 ▶ **Age distribution of the housing stock in selected countries**

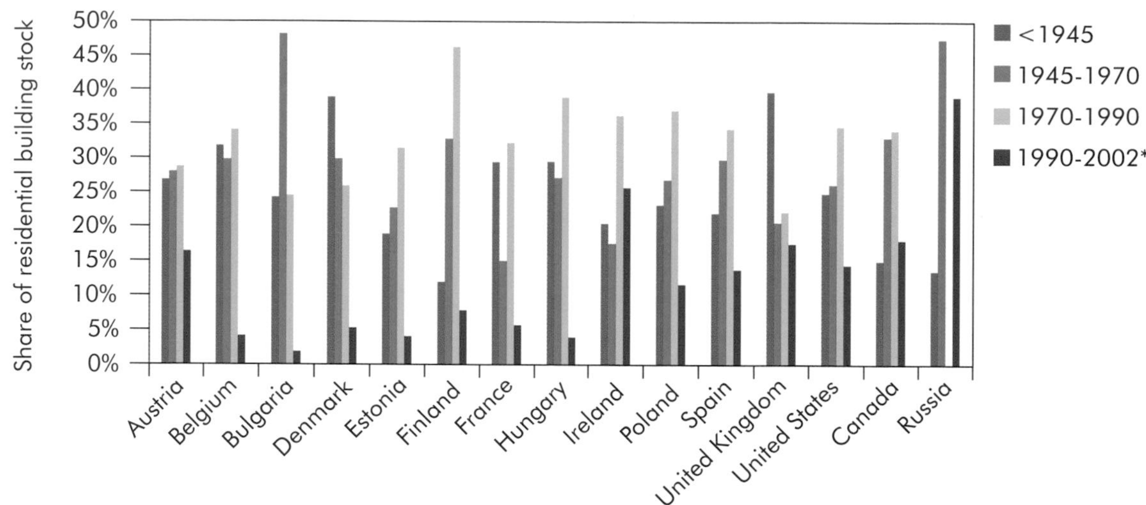

* Final year varies by country.

Note: Some data sources are for slightly different periods.

Sources: Norris and Shiels, 2004; Natural Resources Canada, 2007; Energy Information Administration, 2007; UNECE, 2004.

Key point

More than half of the building stock in many OECD countries was built before 1970.

Status and trends in the global buildings sector

Energy use in buildings currently accounts for 38% of global total final energy consumption.[1] Of this, 45% is consumed in OECD countries, 10% in countries in transition, and around 46% in developing countries.

Different regions have different energy use patterns, as shown in Figure 17.3. In OECD countries, natural gas and oil products dominate energy consumption, primarily due to the importance of space heating. In transition economies, district heating plays an important role that, together with gas, accounts for two-thirds of total building energy use. In developing countries, traditional biomass for heating and cooking accounts for 56% of total energy consumption. Electricity only accounts for 15% and reflects low electrification rates in many developing countries.

Although data on end-use energy consumption is sketchy outside OECD countries, space and hot water heating are estimated to account for around two-thirds of global energy consumption, and cooking for 10% to 13%. The remaining electricity use is for lighting, cooling and other appliances and electrical equipment. However, there are significant variations among countries: for example, it is estimated that

1. In this chapter, the buildings sector includes the projections for the agriculture, fishing and "other non-specified" sectors in the IEA statistics. In 2005 they accounted for 345 Mtoe, or 13% of the buildings sector total.

space and water heating in China accounts for around three-quarters of all energy consumed in the buildings sector (Lawrence Berkeley National Laboratory and IEA analysis); while these uses might account for as little as a quarter in Mexico (Sheinbaum, Martinez and Rodriguez, 1996; and IEA analysis).

Figure 17.3 ▶ Final energy consumption in the service and residential sectors by region, 2005

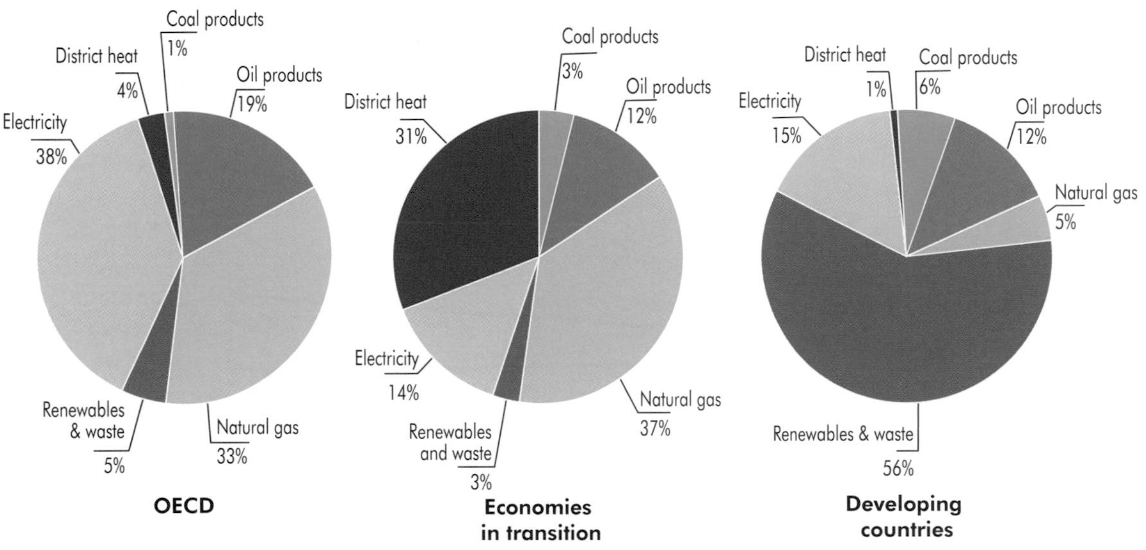

Key point

Natural gas and oil account for around half of residential and services energy consumption in the OECD, while district heat is important in transition economies. Renewables and waste dominate in developing countries.

Demand drivers in the scenario analysis

Energy demand in the residential sector is driven by population, geography, income and cultural factors. These factors have an impact on the number and size of households, the heating or cooling load, the number and types of appliances owned and their patterns of use. Demand in households in different countries and even within countries can differ enormously. For example, the average household in China is estimated to have had 6.7 lights in 2003, as compared to 40 lights in the average Swedish household. Similar factors influence demand in the service sector.

Global population is projected to grow from around 6.5 billion in 2005 to 9.2 billion in 2050. The growth in household numbers is driven by population growth, but also by a continuing trend towards fewer people per household. The global number of households is projected to grow by 63% between 2005 and 2050 – some 50% faster than population growth. The recent trend towards larger household floor area is likely to continue, although this will be muted in many mature economies. Service sector floor area growth also continues to be rapid, with a projected increase of 195% between 2005 and 2050. In 2050, the global average service sector floor area per capita will be around today's per capita level in France, Japan and the United Kingdom. After rising initially, the global average floor area in the service sector per unit of GDP will decline slightly by 2050, as floor area growth begins to slow in the sector.

Figure 17.4 ▶ Population, households and service sector floor area projections, 2005-2050

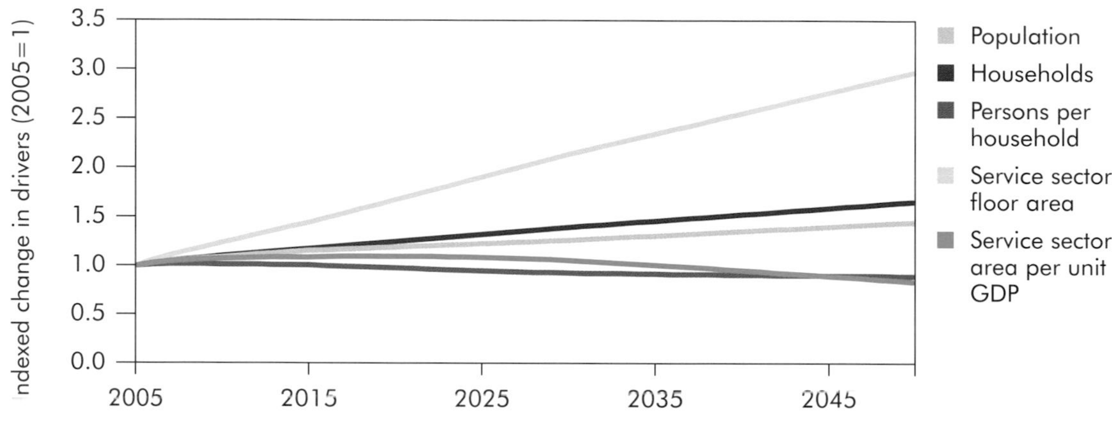

Key point

Growth in service sector floor area is very rapid, while the growth in the numbers of households exceeds population growth.

There are some problems concerning the data in many OECD countries, while robust data for developing countries is often unavailable. This can be addressed to some extent by using indices, but the absence of intensities to compare across regions and countries introduces another element of uncertainty in projecting out to 2050. Improved data, for drivers and energy consumption by end-use, would help to reduce uncertainties surrounding the projections.

Global results of the Baseline scenario

Energy demand in the buildings sector increases from around 2 914 Mtoe in 2005 to 5 257 Mtoe in 2050 in the Baseline scenario, or 1.3% per year (Figure 17.5). The residential sector accounts for around 60% of this growth and the service sector for around 30%. The remainder is attributable to agriculture, fishing and the "other non-specified" sector.

Figure 17.5 ▶ Energy demand in the buildings sector in the Baseline scenario, 2005-2050

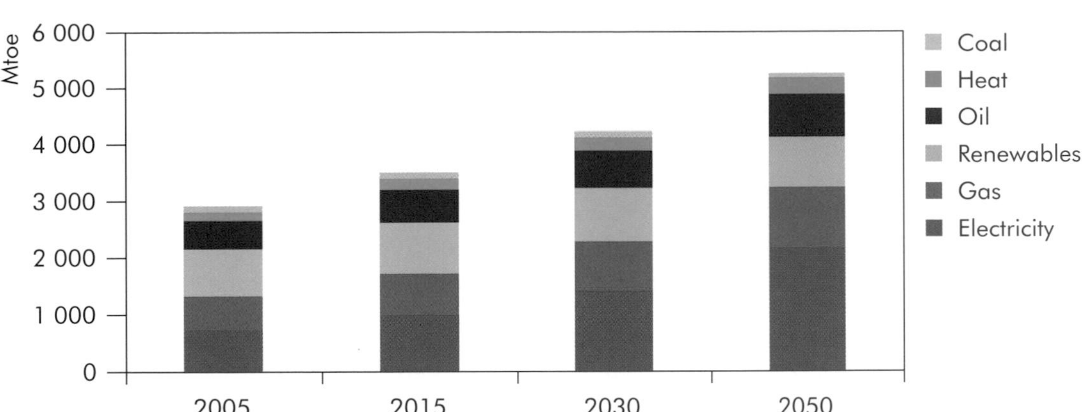

Key point

Buildings sector energy consumption grows by around 80% in the Baseline scenario.

Non-biomass renewables grow the most rapidly, at 5.9% per year between 2005 and 2050. However, they still only represent 2% of the sector's energy consumption in 2050. In contrast, the demand for biomass declines slightly, as the impact of the improved efficiency of its use and the switch to modern commercial fuels continues in developing countries. Electricity demand grows at 2.4% per year, becoming the largest energy source in the buildings sector by 2015 and accounting for 41% of the sector's energy consumption in 2050. Heat consumption increases at 1.5% per year, gas consumption at 1.3% per year and oil consumption at 1% per year. Coal consumption declines at 1% per year.

Electricity demand in the residential sector is projected to continue to grow rapidly, at 2.7% per year on average, increasing its share from 19% to 36% between 2005 and 2050. Non-biomass renewables, predominantly solar, grow rapidly from a low base between 2005 and 2030, but more slowly thereafter.

Energy demand in the service sector is projected to double between 2005 and 2050 growing at around 1.7% per year. As in the residential sector, growth is higher in the early part of the projection period, with growth of 2.2% per year between 2005 and 2015, falling to 1.6% per year between 2030 and 2050. Other renewables, predominantly solar, are projected to grow the most rapidly, at 8.8% per year, between 2005 and 2050, albeit from a low base. In the Baseline scenario, the demand for purchased heat grows at 2.5% per year, slightly faster than the demand for biomass, which expands at 2.1% per year. The demand for electricity grows at 2.1% per year and remains the single most important fuel in the service sector. The consumption of gas and oil in the service sector grows at 1.5% and 0.9% per year respectively between 2005 and 2050, while coal demand declines at 1.2% per year.

The Baseline scenario results by sector and region

CO_2 emissions from the building sector increase by 129% between 2005 and 2050.[2] The rapid growth in electric end-uses means that the CO_2 emissions attributable to electricity consumption in the buildings sector grow by 180%. In the residential sector, energy demand is projected to grow by around 1.2% per year (Figure 17.6) in the Baseline scenario. Growth is more rapid in the early part of the projection period, with a growth of 1.7% per year between 2005 and 2015, falling to 0.9% per year between 2030 and 2050 as household growth slows and demand for heating, cooling and appliances saturates to some extent.

In the service sector, energy demand is projected to grow by around 1.7% per year in the Baseline scenario. Service sector energy consumption is projected to remain dominated by consumption in the OECD countries. In the service sector, the OECD countries account for around half of the growth in energy consumption between 2005 and 2050. This is despite the more rapid projected energy consumption growth in developing countries, as the importance of the service sector grows over this period. Service sector energy consumption grows at 3.2% per year in Latin America, 3.1% per year in the Middle East, 2.7% per year in Africa, 2.6% per year in developing Asia and 2.3% per year in the transition economies. In the OECD countries it ranges from 1.9% to 0.8% per year.

Figure 17.6 ▶ Global residential and service sector energy demand in the Baseline scenario, 2005-2050

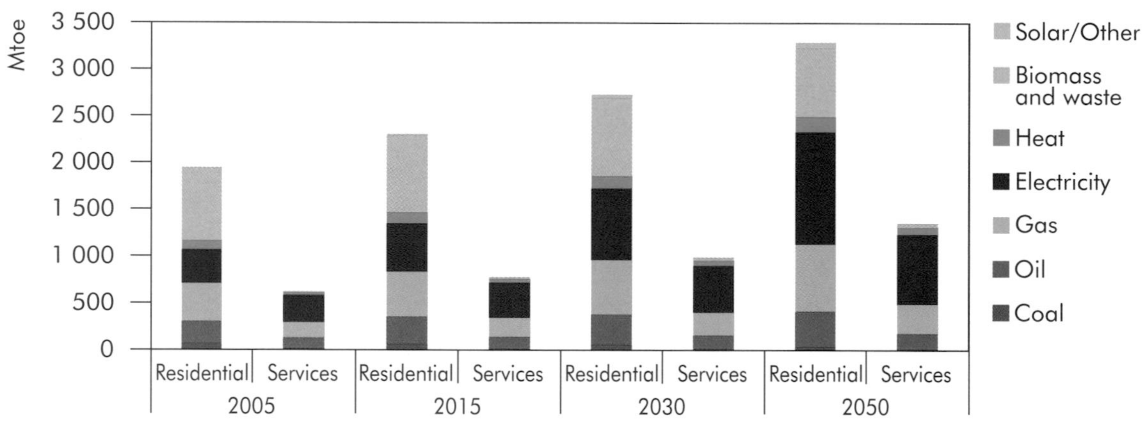

Key point

Service sector energy demand growth, at 1.7% per year, is faster than the 1.2% growth in the residential sector.

2. These calculations use the 2005 electricity-sector CO_2 emissions factor to allocate upstream power generation CO_2 emissions to the electricity consumed in the residential and services sectors. Any reduction or increase in the CO_2 intensity of power generation is then attributable to the power generation sector.

OECD countries

Between 1990 and 2004, total final energy use in the residential sector (corrected for yearly climate variations) rose by 14%.[3] Although space heating is by far the dominant use in the residential sector, and grew by 5% from 1990 to 2004, its share of total energy use decreased from 59% to 54% in that period (Figure 17.7). This reflects a significant reduction in the per-capita energy requirement for space heating, driven by a combination of higher efficiencies of space-heating equipment and improved thermal performance of new and existing dwellings.

Figure 17.7 ▶ Household energy use by end-use in 15 IEA countries, 2004

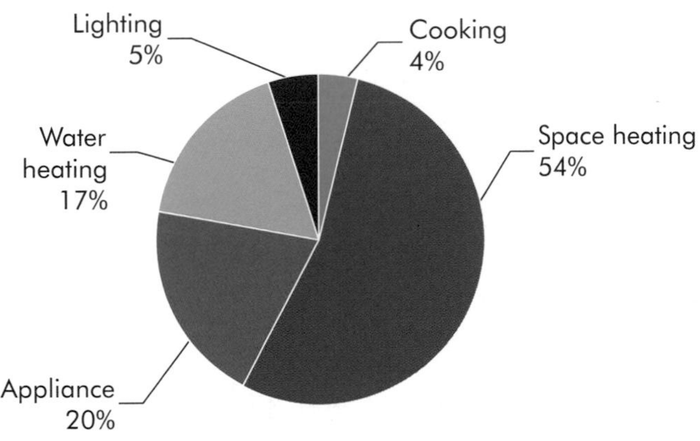

Key point

Space and water heating dominate energy consumption in households in IEA countries.

The most rapidly growing household demand for energy is for appliances, with consumption increasing by around half between 1990 and 2004/05, largely attributable to a rapid increase in the use of a wide range of small electrical appliances and, in some cases, air conditioning. Policies such as minimum energy performance standards have had some impact in curbing the increase in energy consumption of large appliances, which now represent only 50% (and falling) of total appliance energy consumption. However, total appliance energy consumption is growing in importance. In the late 1990s, appliances overtook water heating as the second-highest energy-consuming category. The remaining end-uses – lighting and cooking – each account for around 4% to 5% of final energy use.

Between 1990 and 2004, the economic activity of the service sector, as measured by value-added output, showed a 45% increase.[4] During the same period, total

3. The household sector includes those activities related to private dwellings. It covers all energy-using activities in apartments and houses, including space and water heating, cooking, lighting and the use of appliances.
4. The service sector includes activities related to trade, finance, real estate, public administration, health, education and commercial services.

final energy use increased by 26%, representing a 14% decline in energy intensity per unit of output. The overall demand trend has been driven by strong growth in electricity use, which increased by 50% between 1990 and 2004.

Service sector floor area is expected to grow, driven by economic growth, at around 1.4% per year between 2005 and 2050. This is around a doubling of floor space between now and 2050. Space heating and lighting and other electric uses dominate energy consumption, between them accounting for around four-fifths of the total energy consumption, which is evenly split between them. Water heating accounts for around 13% and cooling and ventilation 9%.

Figure 17.8 ▶ OECD buildings sector energy consumption by end-use in the Baseline scenario, 2005-2050

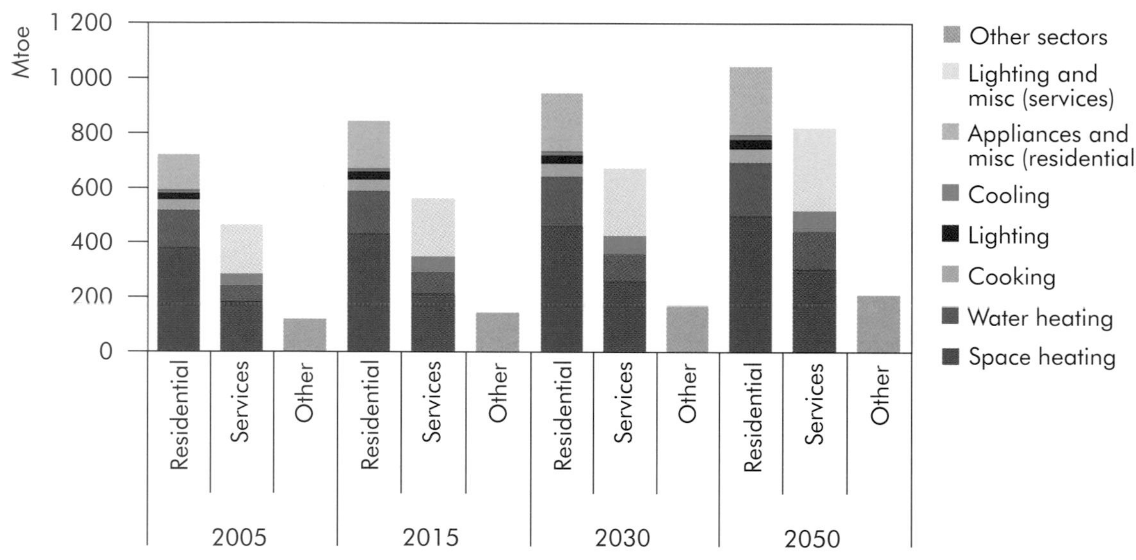

Key point

Service sector demand growth is more rapid than in the residential sector.

In the Baseline scenario, energy consumption in the buildings sector grows by 1% per year in the OECD countries between 2005 and 2050. This is slower than the growth in floor areas in both the service and residential sectors, implying a continuing improvement in the intensity of energy consumption in the sector due to a mixture of structural and efficiency effects.

Solar and other renewables grow the most rapidly, at 4.5% per year, but from a low base. However, they reach only 2% of the sector's consumption in 2050. The next fastest growing fuels are bioenergy and electricity. Electricity increases its share from 38% in 2005 to 45% in 2050. Bioenergy goes from 4% to 5%. Heat demand grows at 1.2% per year, gas at 0.8% per year and oil products at 0.2% per year; coal use declines at 2.3% per year.

Non-OECD countries

Non-OECD countries account for around 55% of buildings sector energy consumption. This share is set to grow as developing countries' populations and economic growth outpaces that of the OECD countries. China, India and the transition economies will together account for about one-third of the world population in 2050 and for the majority of space heating demand outside OECD countries. This growth has very significant implications for the projected energy demand in the scenario analysis.

Figure 17.9 ▶ Non-OECD buildings sector energy consumption by fuel in the Baseline scenario, 2005-2050

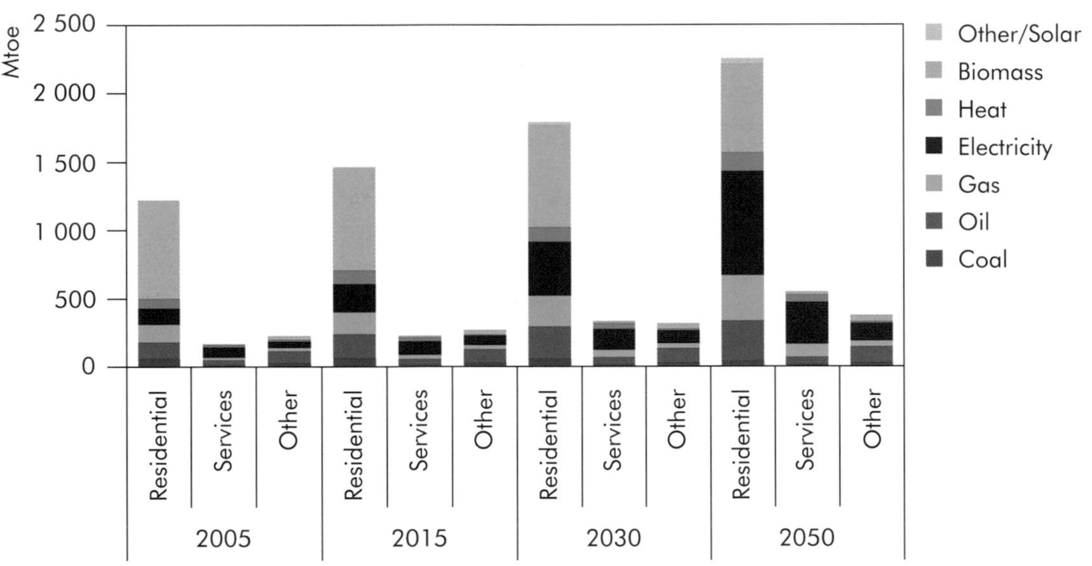

Key point

Service sector energy demand growth is rapid, while in the residential sector biomass declines in importance.

The energy consumption of non-OECD countries in the buildings sector is projected to grow by 98% between 2005 and 2050. Residential sector energy demand is projected to grow by 84% and demand in the service sector will increase even more rapidly – by 227% between 2005 and 2050, albeit from a low base. Solar and other non-biomass renewables are projected to grow the fastest, but similarly from a low reported base. Electricity is expected to grow the next fastest at 4.2% and 3.3% respectively for the residential and commercial sectors. Coal consumption is expected to decline in each sector.

China and India

Rising household incomes and an urban construction boom in China have pushed up energy use in buildings (in line with housing floor area per person), while in India, rising incomes and growing numbers of households are also pushing up demand. In China, rising incomes and the increased urbanisation of a middle class have also spurred the beginnings of a substantial switch from solid fuels (biomass and coal). In India, however, the shift is away from traditional biomass, wastes and animal dung to commercial fuels such as kerosene, LPG and electricity.

The Baseline scenario assumes China will add an average 530 million square metres of new urban residential floor space per year to 2050, while the proportion of the population living in cities grows from 40% to 60% by 2030 and to 73% by 2050. Average household size, which dropped from 4.5 people in 1985 to 3.5 people in 2005, is projected to continue to diminish, to 2.9 people in 2050. Residential floor area in India is projected to be 3.2 times as high in 2050 as in 2005, as the number of people per household continues to decrease and floor area per capita increases with income growth.

China has building energy-efficiency standards. However, compliance with building standards in new buildings is generally low: around 60% in the northern region, 20% in the central region and 8% in the southern region.

Rapid income growth and declining appliance prices have caused ownership of large appliances to soar in recent years in India and China, especially in urban China, although some appliances are experiencing slower growth as they reach saturation levels. Appliance efficiency improvements are expected to offset part of the impact of rising appliance ownership on residential electricity demand.

Figure 17.10 ▶ China and India buildings sector energy consumption by fuel in the Baseline scenario, 2005-2050

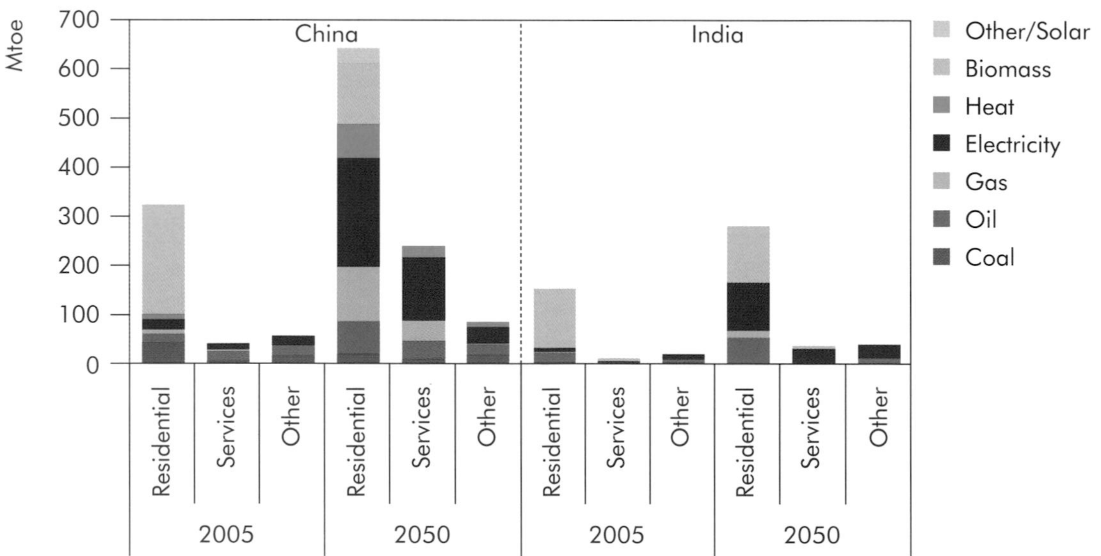

Key point

China and India experience rapid growth in energy demand in the buildings sector and reduce their reliance on biomass.

The service sector's share of the economy, together with its share of total energy consumption, is projected to continue to increase between now and 2050 in both China and India. This will be driven by an almost five-fold increase in the service-sector floor area in China, and an even larger increase in India.

In the Baseline scenario, final energy demand in India for buildings grows by 93% between 2005 and 2050. Residential demand grows more slowly than service sector demand, largely as a result of switching from traditional biomass, which is used very inefficiently, to modern fuels. The number of Indians relying on biomass for cooking and heating drops from 668 million in 2005 to around 300 million in 2050, while the share of the population with access to electricity rises from 62% to 99%.

In China, energy consumption in the buildings sector grows by 129% between 2005 and 2050. Biomass demand declines at 1.3% per year and coal demand at 0.6% per year. Gas growth is 6.1% per year, while electricity grows at 4.5%, heat at 5.0%, solar and other renewables at 6%, and oil products at 1.6%. The service sector increases its share of the buildings sector energy consumption to around 25% by 2050, as its growth of 4% per year outstrips that of the residential sector (Figure 17.10).

Transition economies

The transition economies account for around 10% of total buildings sector energy use. Russia's ageing population, which is likely to decline by 2050, means there is almost no growth in the number of households between now and 2050, although the floor area of households is expected to increase as incomes rise. Russia is experiencing something of a construction boom.[5] The average size of new apartments being constructed, at 83 m^2, is some 63% larger than the stock average.

The transition economies have significant heating needs. Space heating is estimated to account for around 60% of service sector energy use and slightly more than two-thirds of residential sector energy consumption. Although many Russian apartment blocks are not as inefficient as is widely believed, significant inefficiencies mean that residential energy consumption could still be substantially reduced (UNECE, 2004).

In the service sector, floor area is projected to grow by 2.7% per year as economic activity expands. In the Baseline scenario, the energy consumption of the buildings sector in the transition economies grows at 1% per year between 2005 and 2050. Residential sector energy consumption grows at 0.5% per year, and service-sector consumption at 2.3% per year. Energy consumption in the other sub-sectors also continues to grow at around the sector average.[6]

5. There is the possibility of a shortage in cement products in Russia in the coming years, at least on a regional basis (International Cement Forum, Moscow, 2007).

6. These projections should be treated with caution, due to the high share of "other non-specified", which makes it difficult to identify plausible drivers other than past growth patterns.

Figure 17.11 ▶ Transition economies buildings sector energy consumption by fuel in the Baseline scenario, 2005-2050

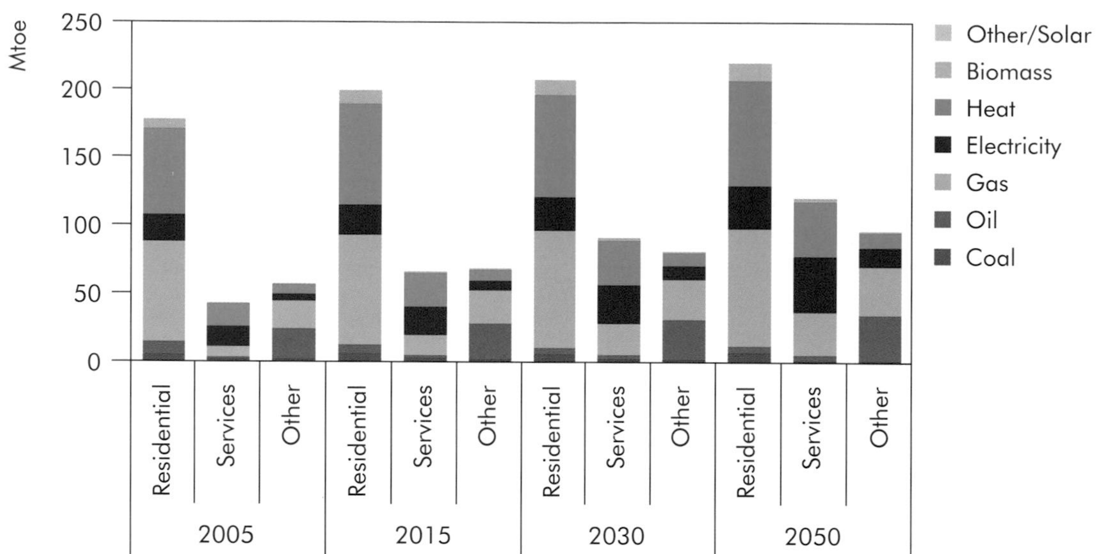

Key point

Residential energy demand growth is modest compared to the service sector due to a declining population and saturation in per household energy demand.

The ACT Map and BLUE Map scenarios

In the ACT Map scenario, energy consumption in the buildings sector is between 17% (Africa) and 37% (OECD North America) lower than in the Baseline scenario in 2050, with the largest absolute reduction (495 Mtoe) occurring in developing Asia. In the BLUE Map scenario, these reductions range from 27% to 49%, with the largest absolute saving (620 Mtoe) also occurring in developing Asia (Figure 17.12). Regional differences between the ACT Map and BLUE Map scenarios are driven by various factors, including the relative difficulty of decarbonising the electricity generation sector in different regions.

In the ACT Map scenario, CO_2 emissions from the buildings sector are cut to 35% below the Baseline scenario level in 2050, although this is still 50% higher than 2005 levels (Figure 17.13). In the BLUE Map scenario, CO_2 emissions are cut by 43% compared to the Baseline scenario. These figures are based on the 2005 electricity sector CO_2 emissions factor and don't take account of the de-carbonisation of the electricity sector. However, the near complete decarbonisation of the electricity system in the BLUE Map scenario means that electrification, particularly for space and water heating, as well as for cooking, becomes a significant abatement option.

On the basis of the BLUE Map electricity CO_2 emissions factor in 2050, emissions attributable to the buildings sector would be reduced to 85% below the Baseline scenario level in 2050.

Figure 17.12 ▶ Buildings sector energy consumption by region and scenario, 2050

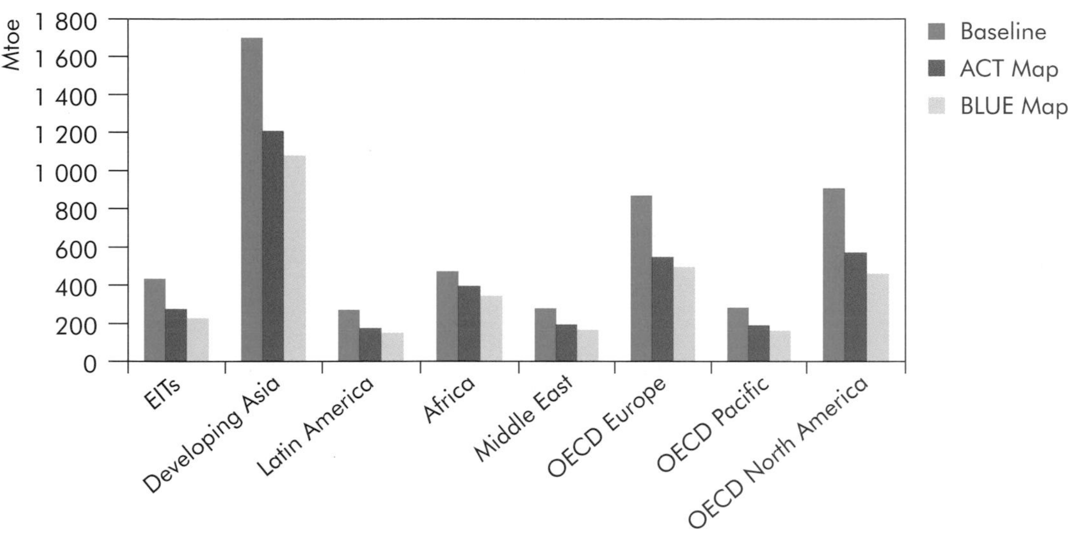

Key point

Developing Asia dominates total consumption in 2050, with OECD countries accounting for most of the rest.

Figure 17.13 ▶ Buildings sector CO_2 emissions by scenario, 2005-2050

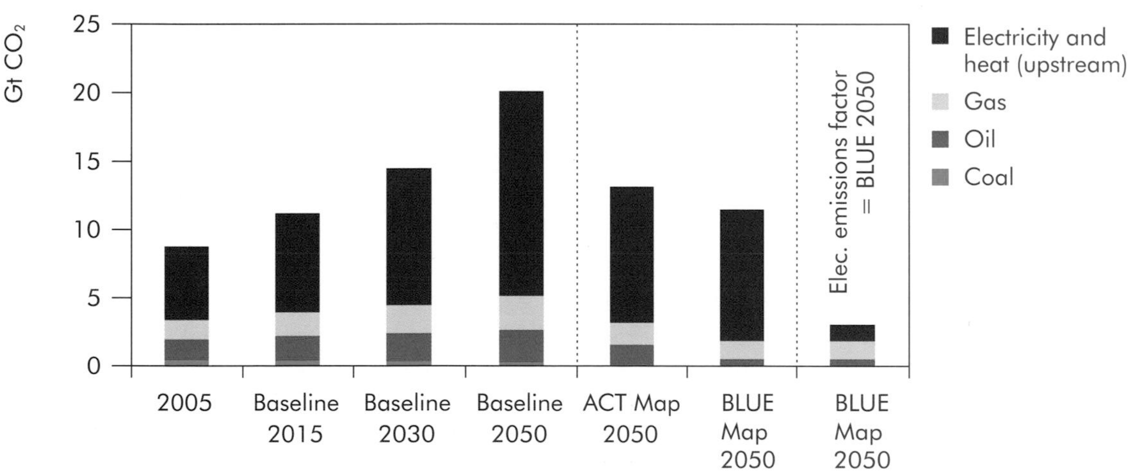

Key point

Taking into account the decarbonisation of the electricity sector, the buildings sector is largely decarbonised in the BLUE Map scenario by 2050.

In the ACT Map scenario, energy demand in the buildings sector is around one-third lower than in the Baseline scenario in 2050. In the BLUE Map scenario this increases to a 41% reduction below the baseline in 2050 (Figure 17.14). In the ACT Map scenario the consumption of individual fuels reduces by between 31% and 41%, except for non-biomass renewables, which increase by 144% over their baseline level in 2050. In the BLUE Map scenario, the demand by fuel drops by between 35% and 65% depending on the fuel, except for non-biomass renewables, which increase by 285% above their 2050 baseline level.

Figure 17.14 ▶ Buildings sector energy demand by scenario, 2005-2050

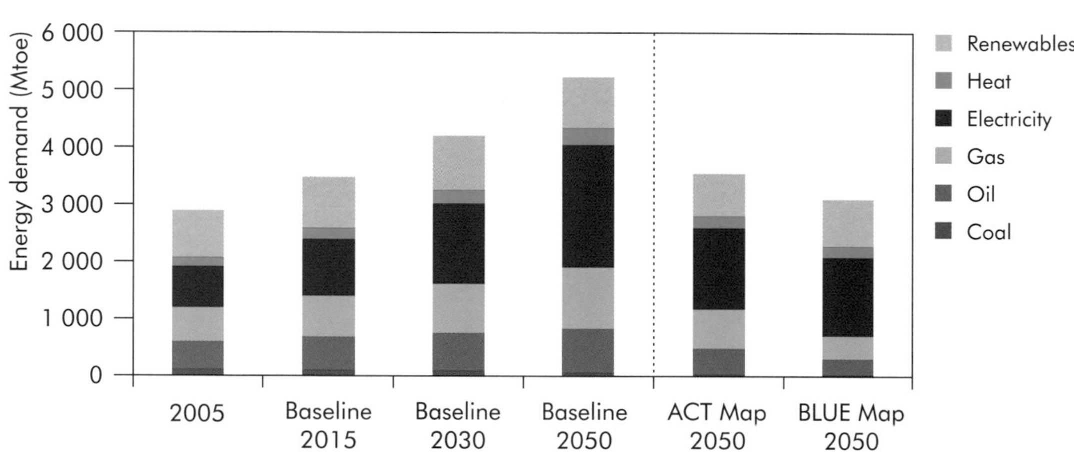

Key point

Energy demand is reduced by around one-third below the Baseline level in 2050 in the ACT Map scenario and by 41% in the BLUE Map scenario.

In the ACT Map scenario, residential energy demand reduces by 31% relative to the Baseline level in 2050 (as shown in Table 17.2). Demand for all fuel sources declines, except for non-biomass renewables, which increase by 128% as a result of additional deployment policies. In the BLUE Map scenario, energy demand in the residential sector reduces by 38%. Demand for all fuels declines even more significantly, except for non-biomass renewables, which grow even more strongly, by 270%.

In the service sector, energy demand reduces by 41% compared to the Baseline level in 2050 in the ACT Map scenario and by half in the BLUE Map scenario. Significant reductions in fossil-fuel use occur in the ACT Map and BLUE Map scenarios as a result of fuel switching and energy efficiency.

In the BLUE Map scenario, space heating accounts for 41% of the total savings of 1 267 Mtoe in the residential sector, primarily in the OECD countries and China. This assumes the rapid tightening of building standards by 2015 to passive house levels of heating demand of around 15 kWh/m^2 to 20 kWh/m^2 per year. This is supplemented by improvements in heating systems and the use of gas condensing boilers wherever gas is used (space or water heating). Water heating accounts for

20% of the savings, as system efficiency is improved through the use of solar water heating, gas condensing boilers and heat pumps. Solar water heating provides between 16% and 45% of hot water needs depending on the region by 2050. Heat pumps supply between 10% and just over half of space heating needs in 2050 depending on the country. Increased deployment of heat pumps helps stimulate improved efficiency (coefficients of performance) and lower costs as a result of increased learning-by-doing.

Table 17.2 ▶ Reduction below the Baseline scenario in 2050 by scenario

	Residential		Services	
	ACT Map	BLUE Map	ACT Map	BLUE Map
Coal	–58%	–90%	–56%	–68%
Oil	–46%	–74%	–61%	–82%
Gas	–31%	–61%	–48%	–75%
Electricity	–30%	–27%	–39%	–45%
Heat	–37%	–45%	–31%	–17%
Biomass	–34%	–42%	–28%	–27%
Other/Solar	128%	270%	328%	538%
Total	**–31%**	**–38%**	**–41%**	**–50%**

Figure 17.15 ▶ Residential and service sector energy demand by scenario, 2050

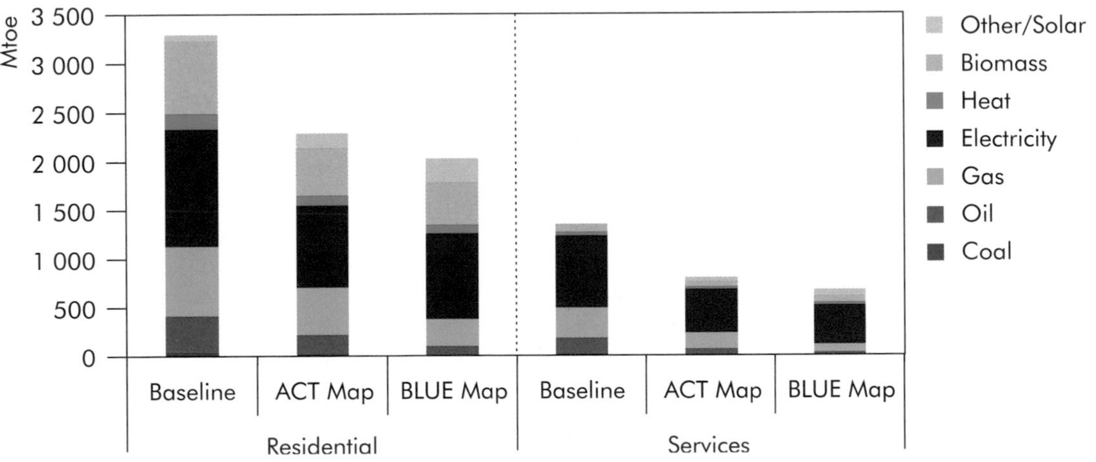

17

Key point

Fossil fuel use in the BLUE Map scenario is 23% of the Baseline level in 2050 in the service sector and 34% of the Baseline level in the residential sector.

Solar hot water heating is a particularly economic CO_2 abatement option in many developing and OECD countries with limited frost, good sunshine hours and intensity. In this case, direct systems without secondary loop and control can be used. In colder climates, solar hot-water heating becomes much more expensive.

Figure 17.16 ▶ Residential and service sector savings below Baseline in the BLUE Map scenario by end-use, 2050

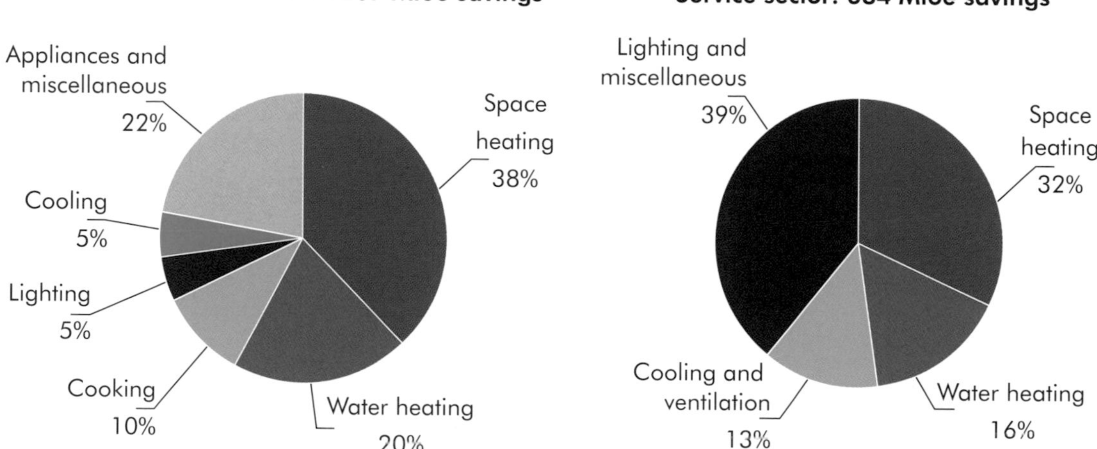

Key point

Space and water heating account for around half of the energy savings below the Baseline level in 2050 in the residential and service sectors.

In the ACT Map scenario, appliances are shifted to least life-cycle cost levels, whereas in the BLUE Map scenario these are shifted towards best available technology. Reductions in energy demand for lighting and appliances account for around a third of the total savings in the BLUE Map scenario, as a result of improvements in their efficiency. Lighting efficiency is improved by around two-thirds to three-quarters in the BLUE scenario, reducing energy consumption to around half the Baseline level.

Energy consumption in the service sector is reduced by 684 Mtoe below the Baseline scenario in BLUE in 2050, accounting for just less than one-third of the reduction in the buildings sector. Reductions in space heating, lighting and miscellaneous end-uses dominate these savings, accounting for around 71% of the total. As in the residential sector, savings stem from a tightening of building envelope standards from 2015 onwards for all new construction, as well as tightening the standards for major refurbishments. More rapid building-stock replenishment in the commercial sector allows these measures to have a faster affect than in the residential sector.

Key technologies and measures to reduce CO_2 emissions in the buildings sector

The energy efficiency of buildings can be improved in many different ways. Some of the most significant, particularly in terms of their contribution to the large reductions in CO_2 emissions envisaged in the ACT Map and BLUE Map scenarios, are considered in more detail below.

The building shell, hot water heating and system issues

Envelope

The effectiveness of the building envelope depends on the insulation levels and thermal properties of walls, ceiling, and ground or basement floor. Improvements can reduce heating requirements by a factor of two to four compared to standard practice. This can be achieved at a cost of only a few percent of the total cost of residential buildings, and at little or no net incremental cost in service-sector buildings (Demirbilek, *et al.*, 2000; Hamada, *et al.*, 2003; Hastings, 2004). In countries that have mild winters but still require heating (including developing countries), modest amounts of insulation can readily reduce heating requirements by a factor of two or more, as well as substantially reducing indoor summer temperatures (Taylor, *et al.*, 2000; Florides, *et al.*, 2002; Safarzadeh and Bahadori, 2005).

In many cases, improvements to building envelopes can achieve net cost savings for the owner, even in the short term. But typically investments are needed early, while savings are achieved over a period of years. This creates a need for financing. Retrofitting high-rise residential buildings with energy-efficiency improvements when they are refurbished can yield energy savings of up to 80% and negative life-cycle costs. The economics of retrofitting detached or terraced houses is usually poorer: in the United Kingdom, for example, a range of measures for retrofitting ceiling and cavity walls with insulation have been estimated to cost anywhere from USD 1 310/t CO_2 saved where insulation is already thick to a net negative cost of as much as USD –444/t CO_2 saved where this is not the case (Shorrock, *et al.*, 2005).

The difference in costs between renovation and reconstruction/demolition is often not large, however, the latter generally gives better opportunities to improve energy efficiency and the value of the site/building. However, reconstruction usually engenders higher CO_2 emissions from the construction work and these will not be recovered rapidly from the lower energy consumption during occupation without the building being built to a high energy efficiency standard. An example for Switzerland shows that reconstruction that meets a heating demand standard of 220 MJ/m^2/year (~60 kWh/m^2/year) would not cover the additional energy demand from reconstruction until after a 30 year period, when looking at the primary energy requirement. However, if the standard met was 120 MJ/m^2/year (~33 kWh m^2/year) this would occur after around 20 years (Econcept, 2002). In the United Kingdom, new build to a low-carbon home standard would be expected to have lower life-cycle energy consumption, including embodied energy in the construction, between 7 to 15 years after construction. For the comparison between refurbishment and new build, new build would have lower lifecycle energy consumption between around 11 and 24 years after the build (Palmer, *et al.*, 2006).

A range of retrofit options for building insulation in Canada show abatement costs ranging between USD –368/t CO_2 saved to 203/t CO_2 saved. For new houses, moving to a more energy efficient design standard (the Canadian R-2000 standard) rather than the minimum standard can save significant amounts of energy at a abatement costs in the range of USD –36/t CO_2 saved to USD 228/t CO_2 depending on circumstances (Seeline Group, 2005 and IEA analysis). In the United States, the average abatement cost for building shell measures (tightening of new building standards and retrofits) is estimated to be around USD –42/t CO_2 abated (McKinsey, 2007a). In Germany, renovation to a low-energy standard is expected to have negative abatement costs, while renovation to passive house standards is currently estimated to be very expensive, with an abatement cost of at least USD 800/t CO_2 (McKinsey, 2007b). Retrofitting wall insulation in the new European Union countries is estimated to have negative abatement costs of between USD –4 to USD –162/t CO_2, while for roof insulation the range was USD –63 to USD –149/t CO_2. Insulating floors/cellar ceilings was generally less economic with abatement costs ranging from USD –81 to USD 160/t CO_2 (Ecofys, 2005).

Windows

The thermal performance of windows has improved greatly through the use of multiple glazing layers, low-conductivity gases (argon in particular) between glazing layers, low-emissivity coatings on one or more glazing surfaces, and the use of very low conductivity framing materials such as extruded fibreglass. Windows are available with heat losses of only 25% to 35% of standard non-coated double-glazed (or 15% to 20% of single-glazed) windows. It is important that glazing with low-conductivity gases is well maintained, as a loss of filling can result in performance deterioration of up to 60%.

Glazings that reflect or absorb a large fraction of the incident solar radiation while maximising the transmission of visible sunlight can reduce solar heat gain by up to 75%, thus reducing the need for cooling.

The cost of glazing and windows, even with these technological improvements, has remained constant or even dropped in real terms (Jakob and Madlener, 2004).

The costs of replacing single glazing with more efficient glazing can be very low when windows need replacing (anywhere from around USD –57 to USD –490/t CO_2 saved), but can otherwise be an expensive option (Shorrock, 2005 and Ecofys, 2005).

Hot water

The efficiency of hot-water systems can be improved in several ways, from installing hot-water cylinder insulation to installing condensing boilers or heat pumps. Solar hot-water heating systems, depending on the location, could provide as much as 60% to 70% of domestic hot-water needs, and perhaps up to 50% of the hot-water needs of service-sector buildings (up to 250°C). Solar hot-water heating systems can cost USD 1 to USD 2 per watt of capacity, with the cost of energy supplied varying depending on the location and sunshine hours per year. The United States R&D goal is to halve the cost of energy produced by a solar hot-water system that delivers 2 500 kWh per year to USD 0.04/kWh, *i.e.* substantially below the electricity tariff of residential customers.

Switching from an inefficient boiler to a condensing gas boiler is generally very economic and has negative abatement costs, while hot-water cylinder insulation is also strongly economic – a negative abatement cost in the United Kingdom of USD –250 to USD –545/t CO_2 saved (Shorrock, 2005). A range of hot-water insulation and water saving devices showed negative costs of USD –209 to USD –360/t CO_2 saved in Canada (Seeline Group, 2005). In the United States, the average abatement cost of options for hot water is estimated to be around USD –8/t CO_2 abated (McKinsey, 2007a).

Systems integration

Buildings are complex systems. All of their components contribute to overall energy demand. These components need to be considered together, as an integrated package. The interaction between them is often only partially understood at the design stage. Researchers, designers and architects are trying to find ways to more systematically optimise the integration of the individual components to reduce energy consumption. Building-energy simulations can model internal environmental conditions as a result of changes in the use of the building. A growing number of tools are available.

An example of effective technology integration are "zero-energy" buildings. Zero-energy buildings consume energy, but their energy demand is balanced, on average, by the energy they produce. Another concept is zero-carbon buildings, where the net CO_2 emissions from the building are zero over a year. Minimising the cost of these buildings requires an integrated systems approach. The challenge is significant in service sector buildings where complex designs, operational parameters and user behaviour combine in ways that are not always foreseeable.

Demand-side management

Demand-side management (DSM) tools can play an important role in reducing CO_2 emissions from peak electricity generation where supply-side options are expensive. DSM influences the amount or pattern of energy use – for example, by reducing demand during peak periods when energy-supply systems are constrained. Peak-demand management does not necessarily decrease total energy consumption. But it can reduce the need for investments in networks and/or power plants, particularly peak-load plant. Better DSM will depend heavily on the development and deployment of smart grids, smart appliances and advanced metering. DSM plays an important role in the BLUE Map scenario both by helping to minimise the cost of de-carbonising peak electricity generation and by potentially requiring less back-up for intermittent renewables.

Cooling systems: air conditioning

Technology status

Air conditioning systems cool, ventilate, humidify and de-humidify buildings. The efficiency of the air conditioners available on the market varies substantially. The least-efficient portable air conditioner currently available has an energy efficiency ratio of less than 1.5 W/W (watts cooling output per watts power input), compared to the most efficient split-room air conditioners, which can achieve more than 6.5 W/W. There is room to improve even on this – for example, through using variable-speed drive compressors, improving heat transfer at the heat exchangers, optimising the refrigerant, utilising more efficient compressors, and optimising controls.

New standards in effect in 2006 in the United States call for an improvement of 30% over the previous standard introduced in 1992. Japan's Top Runner has set far higher performance requirements than those in place in other OECD countries. Most air conditioners are driven by heat pumps. The efficiency of this technology has improved significantly in recent years. For example, the coefficient of performance (COP) of heat-pump air conditioners increased from around 4.3 in 1997 to around 6.6 in 2006, while some COPs reach 9.0.

Developments are underway to use solar power for cooling purposes. Evaporative coolers also work well in hot, dry climates. These units cool the outdoor air by evaporation and blow it inside the building. Evaporative coolers cost about half as much to install as central air conditioners and use about a quarter as much energy.

In climates that are both hot and cold (seasonally or at different times of the day), reversible heat pumps can provide both heating and cooling needs. The efficiency of these systems depends both on the COP of the unit, and on the building and the integration of the system into it. Recovery of ventilated hot or cold air can also help improve efficiency.

Costs and potential for cost reductions

Well-designed passive solar homes can minimise or eliminate the need for air conditioning. Good "non-passive" building design should, in any case, be able to significantly reduce the need for air conditioning in many climatic conditions.

But where air conditioning is deemed necessary, more efficient cooling systems offer the potential for significant energy savings at low cost. More efficient systems, although initially more expensive, can have lower life-cycle costs. However, there is a wide range in terms of costs, from a negative cost of energy saved in the case of replacement systems up to USD 0.03/kWh. Programmable thermostat controls can save energy and money. Shifting to an energy-star rated air conditioning unit can result in negative abatement costs (Seeline Group, 2005).

A number of options in the United States for the residential sector exhibit strong negative abatement costs, such as advanced unitary compressors for central air-conditioning units at an abatement cost of USD –95/t CO_2 saved, and Cromer cycles for humid climates at a negative abatement cost of USD –80/t CO_2 saved (Sachs, 2004). For the service sector, an advanced roof-top air conditioner unit could save over 4 000 kWh per year at a negative cost of USD –72/t CO_2 saved. In the European Union, shifting to least life-cycle costs would reduce the electricity consumption of split air conditioners by 38% at a negative abatement cost of between USD –117 and USD –600/t CO_2 saved (Riviere, 2008)

In India today, room air conditioner electricity consumption could be cut by around 10% to 11% (for USD –14 to USD –65/t CO_2 saved) to around 30% (for USD 120 to USD 170/t CO_2 saved). This latter cost range could fall to between USD 50 and USD 100/t CO_2 by 2030 (McNeil, *et al.*, 2005 and IEA analysis). Split system heat pump type air conditioning systems could potentially reduce China's air conditioner electricity consumption by 27% at a cost of USD –20/t CO_2 saved (Fridley, *et al.*, 2001 and IEA analysis). In the service sector, higher-efficiency refrigeration units can often achieve significant savings at negative costs (McKinsey, 2007b).

Barriers

Cooling technologies are generally mature, but they are continually being improved. There are many air conditioning products on the market, but users often lack an understanding of the most appropriate technology for a specific use. Some more efficient systems are initially expensive, even though they may be cheaper on a lifetime basis. The installation of more advanced systems can be difficult too, adding to costs. There has been a lack of good comparative information to help the consumer. Improvements in control systems have the potential to achieve additional savings by ensuring that coolers only run when necessary.

The number of air conditioners in use is growing rapidly. Consumers need to understand the benefits of more energy-efficient appliances. Air conditioning can be a major energy consumer, often increasing the running costs of a building by up to 50%. Air conditioning is also the major driver of peak power loads in many OECD countries and the variable demand peaks it creates are very expensive for utilities to serve. Technology development and deployment will depend in part on ensuring that such pricing consequences are passed on to consumers.

The tightening of energy efficiency standards for new buildings and major refurbishments would help encourage the introduction of more-efficient cooling technologies, although care needs to be taken to ensure tighter thermal envelopes don't raise cooling needs. New building codes could ensure, for example, that more efficient air conditioners were installed. If such steps were taken, they should be supported by the training and certification of more installers to ensure that this does not become a bottleneck. The development of better cooling and ventilation controls, accompanied by measures to promote their deployment, could also have a significant impact.

Appliances

Technology status

The continuing demand for new large and small appliances, often with new functionality, is resulting in rapidly increasing electricity consumption in both the residential and service sectors. While traditional large appliances are still responsible for most household electricity use, electronic home entertainment and information and communications equipment now accounts for more than 20% of residential electricity consumed in most countries. This rapid technology penetration offers opportunities to roll-out more efficient appliances, but this effect to date has been overwhelmed by the increased uptake of new devices.

In general, most established household appliances, for example residential refrigerators, have become more efficient in their use of energy in recent years. However, in these and many other appliances, the impact of efficiency gains has been diminished by an increase in the size of products and the increasing range of products. This is most clearly seen in home entertainment appliances, where a rapid switch from CRT televisions to more efficient LCD screens in recent years has not resulted in energy savings, because the switch has been accompanied by an expansion in average screen sizes and an increase in viewing hours and the number of televisions per household.

Potentials and costs

In developed countries, energy efficiency policies for major appliances have achieved efficiency gains of 10% to 60% in most major economies in recent years. This has been achieved at the same time as real consumer prices have fallen by 10% to 45% (IEA, 2007a). This has been due to a combination of factors including the availability of low-cost electronic control technologies, improved materials and reduced manufacturing costs. Experience and economies of scale have also contributed.

Despite recent gains, most regional and national studies conclude that the technical potential exists for 30% to 60% of further energy efficiency improvements in appliances (Wuppertal, 2005; ECI, 2007; Sachs, 2004). Estimates of the cost-effective potential suggest that at least 25% savings can be achieved. International studies have also demonstrated that the potential savings from appliances in developing and transitional countries are greater than in developed countries, because of their ability to leap-frog to more efficient technologies. (IEA, 2006c; WEC, 2006; WEC, 2007).

Several countries have undertaken studies of design options. In a recent detailed review under the European Commission eco-design directive, the savings potential has been identified for a range of appliances. The least life-cycle cost savings are available at zero cost. Moving to best available technologies (BAT) would initially be very expensive, but with deployment and cost reductions associated with the growing penetration of the BATs, this could be significantly reduced and even come to a negative cost (Table 17.3).

Table 17.3 ▶ Comparison of BAT for cold appliances and energy efficiency options in the European Union and China and India, with energy savings and CO_2 abatement costs

	BAT/improvement characteristics		CO_2 abatement cost	
	Incremental cost today (USD)	**Energy savings** kWh per year	**Before deployment** USD t/CO_2	**After deployment**
European Union				
Upright freezer	394	110	465 to 1 356	–151 to 461
Chest freezer	400	148	198 to 905	–339 to 223
Average for freezers	397	129	349 to 1 097	–259 to 324
Fridge-freezers	367	139	171 to 871	–364 to 190
India				
Refrigerator: direct cool	32	180		–38
Refrigerator: frost free	54	440		–46
China				
Refrigerators	96	261		–28

Note: EU analysis excludes France, due to high share of nuclear.
Sources: Presutto, *et al.*, 2008; McNeil, *et al.*, 2005; Fridley, *et al.*, 2001 and IEA analysis.

Barriers

The bulk of this savings potential could be achieved without major technological development (McKinsey, 2007c). The primary concern is to create sufficient market pull to encourage widespread deployment of the best existing technologies. Despite the achievements to date, which have been largely policy led, further deployment of energy efficient appliances continues to face many barriers. In most developed countries, low energy costs and rising affluence mean that the overall running cost of appliances is a small proportion of household incomes. And it is an expenditure that remains largely hidden.

While energy labels have become widespread for major appliances, there is very little available public information on the running costs and savings potential of smaller appliances. In addition, labels do not usually specify the highest efficiency potential for each type of appliance. As a result, few consumers have the ability to make informed decisions about relative life-cycle costs. Such information could provide a market pull for new, more efficient appliances. For example, consumers are largely unaware of the consumption of current TV technologies; and there is little market incentive for the commercialisation of LCD televisions with back-light modulation or organic LEDs, technologies that could reduce consumption by approximately 50%.

The lack of appropriate protocols for appliances connected to digital networks is a major barrier to energy efficiency, since without them, connected devices may not utilise automatically low-power modes when not in use. This will become increasingly important, yet also harder to rectify, as more appliances are connected into networks.

National and regional energy efficiency programmes can do much to remedy the situation. However, many countries, especially developing countries, have limited capacity to design and implement appropriate policies and measures. The resources to do so have generally been undersupplied, even in more developed economies (IEA, 2007b). National and regional policy development needs to be underpinned by a thorough knowledge of end-use energy consumption and trends. This requires the regular collection and analysis of bottom-up data for a range of appliances and equipment. This will improve both the appropriate targeting of policies and the evaluation of individual measures once implemented.

To tap into the potential for low-cost energy and greenhouse gas savings, policies are required that provide an incentive at all stages of the supply chain to bring energy efficient technologies to market. A broad range of policy measures are available, including regulatory and voluntary approaches, fiscal measures and procurement policies. Many have been tried successfully by some countries. These need to be replicated in more countries and regions, and applied to a wider range of appliances, particularly those in the area of home entertainment and information and communications technologies.

Policies need to be developed for small electronic appliances which will remain relevant despite the rapid evolution of products. For example, the IEA has proposed that a generic approach to standby power requirements should be applied to the majority of appliances so that precise product definitions become unnecessary. In general, policies need to ensure that manufacturers design all their devices with the ability to move automatically to the lowest power needed for their required functionality. This will minimise the time that appliances that no-one is using continue to consume unnecessary power.

For example, the power level required to stay connected to digital networks should be minimised. In addition, for networks to support energy-efficiency objectives, the network and all connected devices must be able to communicate power-management commands in a common language. This requires that some basic energy efficiency principles are enshrined in the technical standards and protocols used by such devices.

Lighting

The life-cycle costs of new, efficient lighting systems are often the same as or lower than existing systems. Many new lighting solutions are so cost-effective that it makes sense to prematurely retire old inefficient lighting systems and retrofit the efficient ones. Voluntary market transformation programmes, such as the European

Greenlights programme, have provided numerous case studies where retrofitted lighting systems have had very short payback periods, and have shown internal rates of return on investment of over 20%.

Lighting entails greenhouse gas emissions of 1 900 Mt of CO_2 per year, equivalent to 70% of the emissions from the world's light passenger vehicles. The demand for artificial light is far from being saturated. While an average North American consumes 101 megalumen-hours each year, the average inhabitant of India uses only three megalumen-hours (IEA, 2006a).

Lighting use is currently very inefficient. Light is routinely supplied to spaces where no one is present. This could readily be reduced by the use of time-scheduled switching, occupancy sensors and daylight-responsive dimming technologies, all of which are mature and fully proven techniques with high savings returns. Over-lighting also occurs, even though people are insensitive to light levels beyond certain thresholds. There are vast differences in the efficiency of competing lighting sources and in the way lighting systems are designed to deliver light to where it is needed. And poor architecture has created a need for lighting that should not be necessary: uninspired and thoughtless building design has created dark boxes where the largest, cleanest and highest-quality source of light – daylight – often cannot reach. Each of these areas holds major potential to reduce lighting energy needs without compromising lighting service, and the technologies to do so are widely available today.

A number of already fully commercialised technologies could significantly reduce lighting demand. They include incandescent, fluorescent and high-intensity discharge lamps; the ballasts and transformers that drive them; the luminaires in which they are housed; and the controls that operate them. Day-lighting and daylight sensors are also important alternatives. A market shift from inefficient incandescent lamps to compact fluorescent lamps (CFLs) would cut world lighting electricity demand by 18%. If end-users were to install only efficient lamps, ballasts and controls, global lighting electricity demand in 2030 would be almost unchanged from 2005, and could actually be lower between 2010 and 2030 (IEA, 2006a). This could be achieved at a global average negative cost of USD –161 per tonne of CO_2 saved, but it would require strong policy action.

In the service sector, the use of high-efficiency ballasts, slimmer fluorescent tubes with efficient phosphors, and high-quality luminaires produces savings that are just as impressive. For street and industrial lighting, there are great savings to be had from discontinuing the use of inefficient mercury vapour lamps and low-efficiency ballasts, in favour of higher-efficiency alternatives.

Solid-state lighting is emerging as a promising efficient lighting technology for the near future. Over the last 25 years it has undergone sustained and significant improvements in efficiency that hold the prospect of it outperforming today's mainstream lighting technologies in a growing number of applications. If current progress is maintained, solid-state lighting may soon make inroads into general lighting. Solar-powered solid-state lighting already offers a robust, low-energy and economic solution to the needs of households reliant on fuel-based lighting.

Technology status

The efficiency of different lamp types is illustrated in Figure 17.17. Not all forms of lighting can substitute for all others. But large gains could be achieved, for example, from substituting lower-efficiency versions of a given lamp and ballast technology for higher-efficacy equivalents from within the same technology. This can produce significant gains for linear fluorescent lamps, for example.

Figure 17.17 ▶ System efficacy of light sources for general lighting

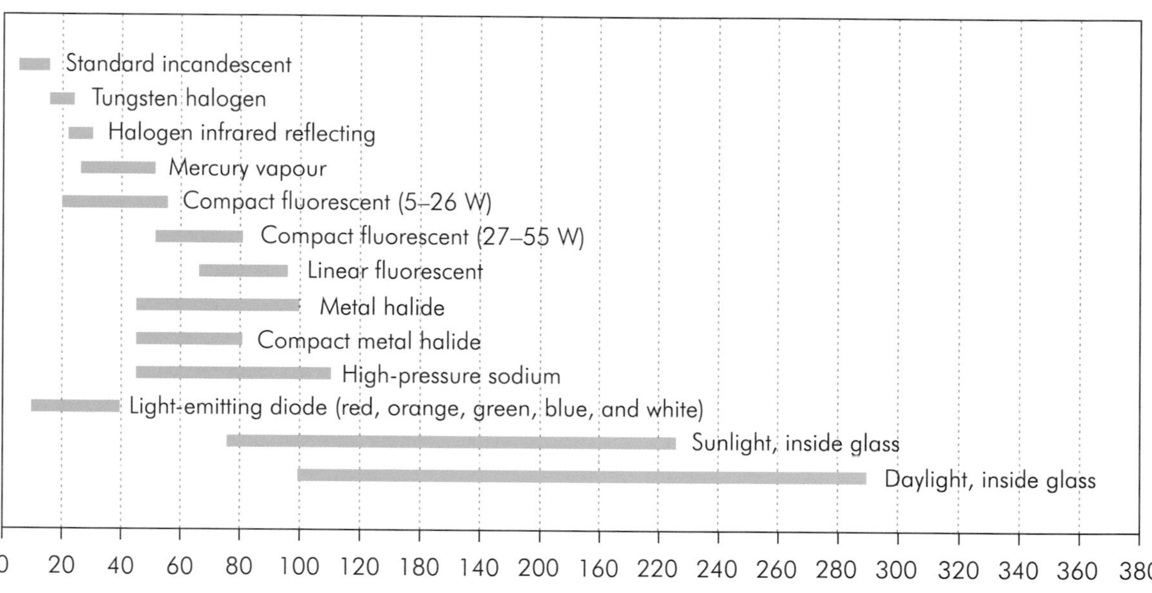

Key point

Energy-efficient lighting technologies are many times more efficient than standard incandescent lights.

The evolution of lamp efficiency over time is shown in Figure 17.18. Lighting technologies such as incandescent, tungsten halogen and high-pressure mercury are considered mature technologies with little room for increased luminous efficiency, whereas semiconductor (e.g. LED) and metal halide lamps are considered to offer high potential for further technical improvements. In the near term, however, the greatest gains from lamp changes are to be had from substituting new high quality CFLs for inefficient standard incandescent lamps, from phasing out mercury vapour lamps, and from using higher efficiency ballasts and linear fluorescent lamps.

Heat pumps

Heat pumps include a wide range of products that transform low temperature heat from sources such as air, water, soil or bedrock into higher temperature heat that can be used for heating. Heat pumps can also be reversed and function as space-coolers. Most heat pumps operate on a vapour-compression cycle and are driven by an electric motor. Some heat pumps use the absorption principle, with gas or waste heat as the driving energy. This means that heat rather than mechanical energy is supplied to drive the cycle. Absorption heat pumps for space air conditioning can be gas-fired, while industrial installations are usually driven by high-pressure steam or waste heat. Heat pumps are most suitable for use in cooling, space heating, hot water, and industrial heat. This section focuses on their heating applications.

Figure 17.18 ▶ Evolution of luminous efficacy of major light sources used for general lighting

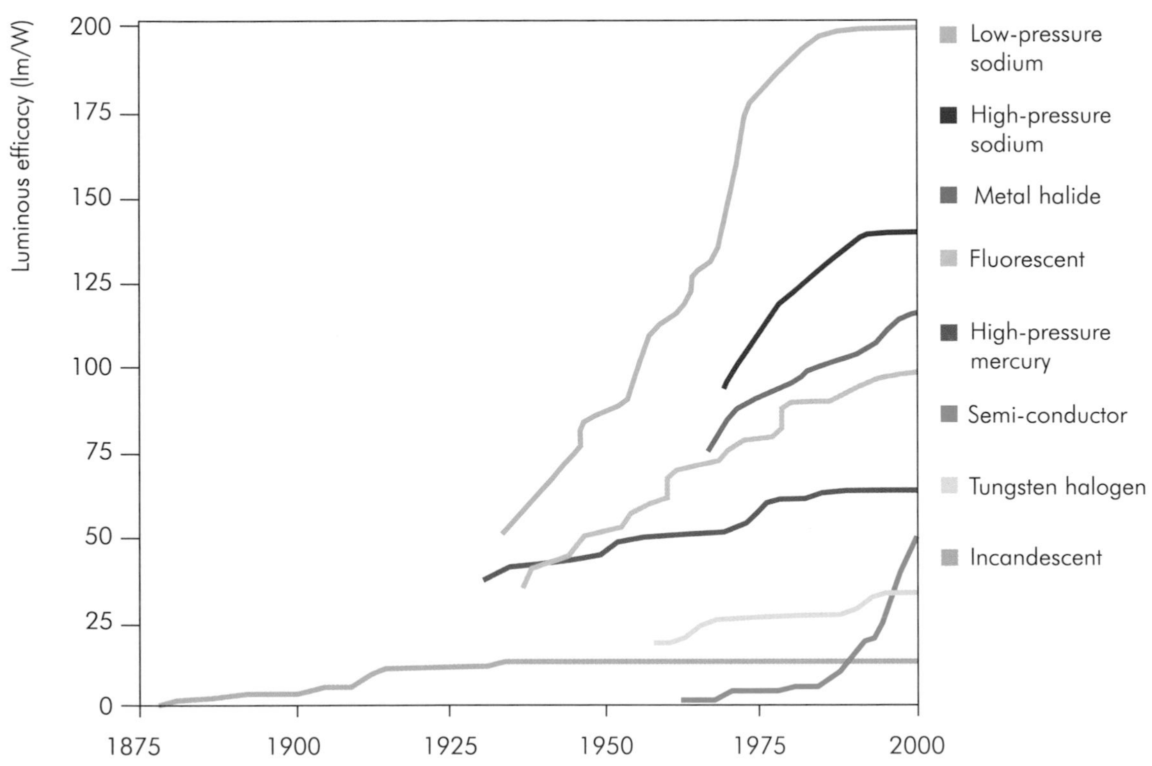

Key point

There has been significant improvement in the luminous efficacy of energy efficient lighting technologies, although many are now mature technologies.

Technology description/status

Electric heat pumps typically use about 20% to 50% of the electricity used by electric resistance heaters for space and water heating. They can reduce primary energy consumption for heating by as much as 50% compared to fossil-fuel-fired boilers. Ground-source heat pumps are more efficient than air-sourced systems in cold conditions, but have higher initial capital costs. According to the United States

Environmental Protection Agency, ground-source heat pumps can reduce energy consumption up to 44% compared to an air-source heat pump. However, significant improvements in air-to-air heat pumps have been made in recent years and they can now operate down to temperatures of -20°C. They are less efficient than ground-source heat pumps, but avoid the substantial capital costs involved in the ground loops.

Heat pumps have been gaining market share in some OECD countries. For example, in Sweden, about 48% of all electrically heated homes have heat pumps. There are many reversible heating/cooling systems that are particularly attractive, where heating loads are moderate and there is a significant summer cooling load. Heating-only heat pumps have a significant market share in a number of countries, notably Sweden, Switzerland, the United States, Germany, France, Austria and Canada.

Heat pumps can also be used for hot-water production. Their efficiency has improved considerably in recent years. The performance coefficient of the ECO Cute heat pump hot-water system increased from around 3.5 in 2001 to around 4.9 in 2006. The ECO Cute heat pump for residential hot water provision is highly efficient, but currently has a capital cost around two to two-and-a-half times more expensive than conventional options. This is declining over time. Such pumps could in time present a significant CO_2 abatement opportunity.

Costs and potential for cost reductions

Heat pumps are considerably more expensive than boilers, although running costs are much lower. While a typical condensing gas boiler may cost USD 1 500, a heat pump will cost about USD 5 000. The gas boiler would use about 50 GJ gas per year, while the heat pump would use 15 GJ electricity per year. Replacing a gas boiler with a heat pump would result in a reduction in CO_2 emissions of 2.8 tonnes per year (provided the electricity was CO_2-free) at a lifetime cost of around USD 160/t CO_2 saved. In the United Kingdom, ground-source heat pumps currently have a CO_2 abatement cost of around USD 100 to USD 200/t CO_2 saved for existing residential dwellings, although this rises to between USD 380 to USD 900/t CO_2 saved for buildings meeting the recent 2000 building codes. In the service sector, the CO_2 abatement cost of heat pumps for space heating is around USD 200/t CO_2 saved. In Canada, heat pumps for space heating might yield CO_2 savings at a cost of between USD 143 to 432/t CO_2 saved, although, in some regions and cases the abatement costs would be negative with current energy prices (Seeline Group, 2005 and Hanova, *et al.*, 2007). In the United States, abatement costs for heat pump hot water systems that replace electric resistance systems would be high, at around USD 400/t CO_2 saved, even after extensive deployment (Sachs, 2004 and IEA analysis). For large service sector buildings, ground source heat pump systems are likely to be economic and have negative abatement costs where they provide, space and water heating, as well as cooling in summer (Sachs, 2004).

Heat pumps represent expensive CO_2 abatement options for space or water heating in developing countries. For example, in China, the average gas hot-water heater has a tank storage size of eight to ten litres and a capital cost of around USD 100. The equivalent of the Japanese ECO Cute heat pumps have much greater capacities and capital costs that would be as much as USD 5 000 in China. However, high-efficiency reversible heat pumps for cooling and space heating are potentially an important abatement option in China and other developing countries or regions with moderate heating loads and significant cooling loads over summer.

Barriers

Ground-source heat pumps still face some technical barriers, even though many technologies are available on the market. There is a lack of confidence in the technology, which has resulted in a low deployment rate. This is often a result of inadequate information about the costs and benefits and because of the absence of a well established supply and service industry. Uncertainty over the relationship between actual average efficiency and published coefficients of performance (COPs) also have an impact.

Solar thermal heating

The annual growth in global installed capacity of solar thermal systems for water heating increased significantly each year from 1999 to 2005 (Figure 17.19) (REN 21, 2006). Accounting for retirements, over 15 GW_{th} of net new capacity was added in 2006, increasing total installed capacity by 16%. China had the greatest increase in solar hot-water capacity in 2005 – with Europe, India and several other countries also experiencing accelerated growth.

Figure 17.19 ▶ Annual incremental capacity of plate and evacuated tube solar collectors installed by region, 1999-2005

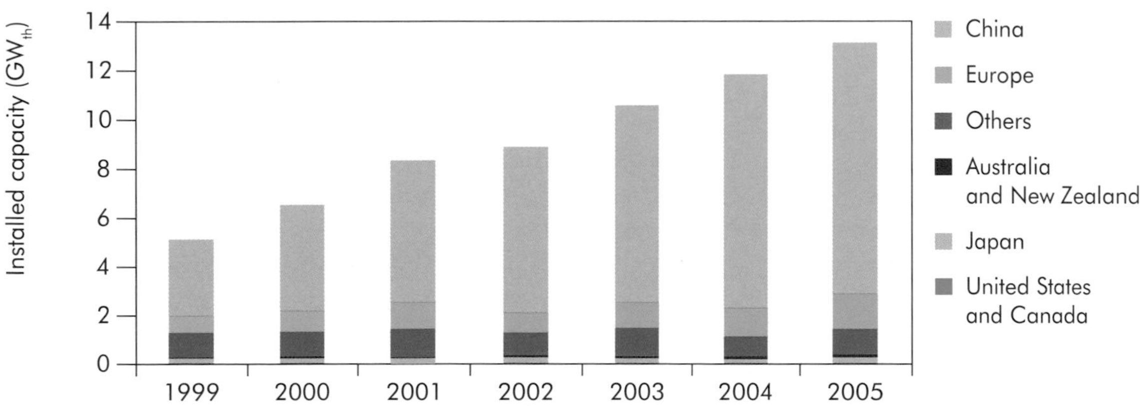

Source: SHC, 2007.

Key point

Annual installed capacity has been growing rapidly in China, which now dominates the total.

China has experienced fairly consistent growth in solar thermal water heating and is by far the largest market, with around 60% of total global capacity installed (Figure 17.20) (Philibert, 2006; REN 21, 2006). In Turkey, solar thermal collectors to provide domestic hot water are popular, mainly because they are the cheapest option – due to relatively high commercial energy prices for conventional heating sources and high solar insolation.

Figure 17.20 ▶ Total capacity of glazed flat plate and evacuated tube water collectors in December, 2005

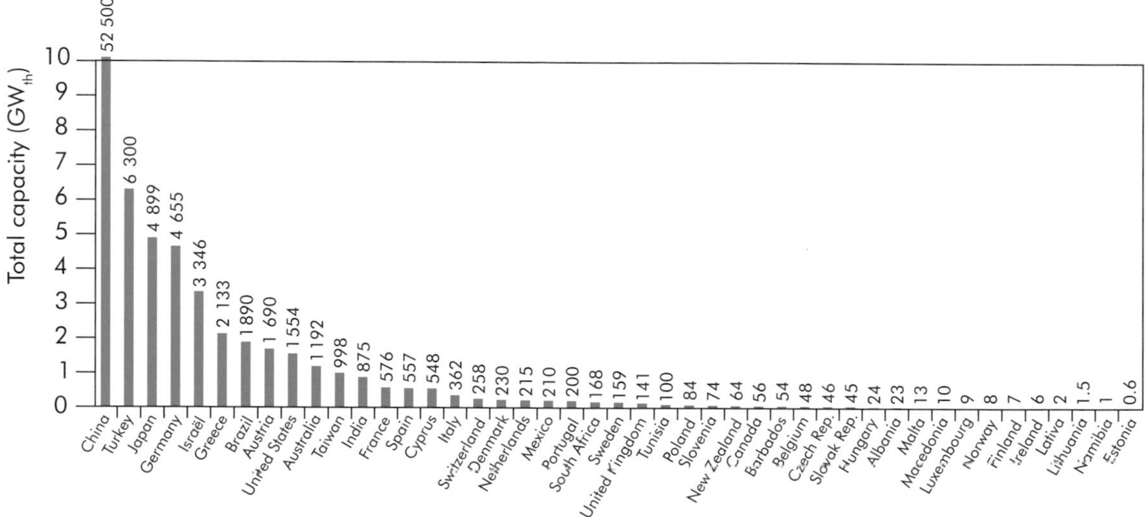

Note: China's capacity is not shown in full on the chart due to scaling factors.
Source: SHC, 2007.

Key point

China dominates total installed capacity, with more than eight times more capacity than the country with next largest installed capacity.

Technology description/status

There are two types of solar thermal heating system: passive and active. Passive systems use windows directed mainly towards sun, whereas active systems are relatively complicated (with collectors, heat storage and controls) and most commonly require a back-up system. In active heating systems, water or another heat transfer fluid is circulated through a duct and heated by solar radiation on the collector panel. The amount of heat energy captured per square metre of collector surface area varies with design and location, but typically can range from 300 kWh/m^2/yr to 800 kWh/m^2/yr. Some designs use a heat transfer fluid that when warmed flows to a storage tank or a heat pump, where the heat is then transferred to water that can then be used as hot water or for space heating.

Solar thermal technologies are relatively mature and have been shown to be reliable and cost-competitive in appropriate circumstances. Solar water heaters have already reached a significant market share in some countries. Solar thermal heat is also used for crop drying, heating of buildings, and higher-grade industrial heat purposes (Rantil, 2006). Barriers to deployment in some situations include planning constraints, high up-front capital costs and a shortage of skilled trades people.

The full potential of solar thermal systems has not been reached in most IEA countries due to relatively high capital costs and relatively long (five to ten years or more) payback periods, compared with conventional water heating systems. However, in other countries such as China, simple, cheap systems (e.g. without freeze protection) are manufactured that have reached the mass market and can compete, especially where conventional hot water systems are expensive or energy supply options are limited.

Under optimal conditions, it has been estimated that the use of conventional energy inputs of gas or electricity for water heating in latitudes below 40° could be cut by around 50% in applications that require temperatures up to 250°C, and perhaps by as much as 60% to 70% for domestic water heating energy with temperatures up to around 60°C. At this level, the coefficient of performance (COP) of solar water heaters is comparable to that of heat pumps. However, actual savings are partly dependent on the users' behaviour and the timing of the hot water demand.

Promising new designs include "combi-systems" that combine water and space heating. This extends the operation period and, thus, improves profitability. Active solar space and water heating systems usually need a back-up system that uses electricity, bioenergy or fossil fuels. These back-ups add to overall system costs (IEA, 2006b). New technology integrates a solar-assisted heating system with a heat pump resulting in ultra-high efficiencies of 125% to 145% compared to a condensing boiler at around 107% (Daniëls and Farla, 2006).

Solar hot-water heating has strongly negative or modest abatement costs where good insolation levels occur and cheap evacuated tube systems are available and appropriate. For instance, in Zimbabwe, solar hot-water heating can yield discounted cost savings of USD 1 000 over 15 years (Batidzirai, 2008). Solar hot-water heating is estimated to have an abatement cost of around USD 30/t CO_2 in South Africa. In Hong Kong, solar hot-water systems that replace gas-fired systems could save CO_2 at a negative cost of around USD –850/t CO_2 (Li and Yang, 2008). In contrast, in cold climates requiring freeze protection, abatement costs can be high, for example, in the United Kingdom, the abatement cost could be over USD 1 000/t CO_2 (Shorrock, *et al.*, 2005).

Barriers

Solar water heaters are a mature technology and are readily available in many countries. Where support policies are in place to encourage uptake by building owners, especially if the payback period is longer than five years, they are making good progress into the market. Barriers include the high cost of systems for cold-climate countries, which have to include freeze protection, and the lack of low-cost heat storage and back-up systems that can match solar heat supply to demand loads. However, even in developing countries, simple systems manufactured locally with a cost of only USD 400 represent a significant barrier to their uptake at present.

Solar thermal systems are already widely used in countries such as Cyprus, China, Germany, Austria, Turkey and Israel – primarily for hot-water supply, but also for heating swimming pools and residential space heating. Elsewhere, without government incentives, they remain at the early market stage. Unglazed, glazed and evacuated tube water collectors have solar thermal market shares of 15%, 40% and 45% respectively following recent growth in the latter (SHC, 2007).

Policy and RD&D needs

Solar heating and cooling technologies are already close to competitiveness, with the potential for a reasonably quick return on investment in appropriate circumstances. Solar water-heating technologies are reliable, but their capital costs can make them appear more expensive to the potential purchaser compared to conventional water heating systems, even when they are competitive on the basis of life-cycle costs. During the last decade, capital cost reductions of around 20% have been observed for each doubling of installed capacity of solar water heaters. Combi-systems in particular have profited from this cost reduction and consequently increased their market share. More RD&D investment can help to drive these costs down further. Priority areas for attention are discussed below.

Materials and components

Effective optical coatings on surfaces and anti-reflective, self-cleaning glazing materials need to be developed. To prolong service intervals and lifetime, the ability of materials and components to withstand high temperatures needs to be improved: innovative plastic materials together with better insolation materials could reduce costs and increase efficiency. New flat-plate collectors that can be more easily integrated into building facades and roofs need to be designed. Further market potential is seen in photovoltaic-thermal combined collectors that can deliver warm water as well as generate electricity.

Advanced systems

Small-scale water heating applications in single-family houses dominate the solar thermal market. To broaden the market for solar heating systems, the range of applications needs to be enlarged to include hotels, schools and other commercial buildings. Current solar heating systems often have a back-up system. This means that users can profit directly only from fuel savings compared to a conventional system. Stand-alone systems without back-up could be used in combination with high-efficiency storage applications and well-insulated buildings to improve their competitiveness.

Larger-scale systems, with capacities of several hundred kilowatts for solar-assisted district heating schemes or for industrial applications with capacities in the megawatt scale, need further development, possibly based on concentrating solar heating (CSH) technologies. CSH technology is at the early development stage, with several promising collector designs close to demonstration, but with industrial applications needing to be identified. Collector and component designs need to be optimized for medium temperature use and to meet the requirements of industrial applications. Testing procedures for the durability of the materials and components also need to be developed.

Building design integration

Architectural design will play a major role in the broader market penetration of solar heating and cooling options. The components need to become standardised elements of modern buildings, rather than being retrofitted. Good building design will avoid such issues as glare.

Standards, regulations and test procedures

Some solar heating installations have not performed as well as promised by the manufacturer (Philibert, 2006). New standards, regulations and testing procedures, coupled with appropriate labelling could accelerate market uptake by building up consumer trust in products. This is especially important for new solar technologies such as evacuated tubes and combi-systems: many manufacturers are entering the market and it is difficult for consumers to identify quality products. Standard testing procedures on such details as collector panel resistance to hailstones could also enhance international trade of these technologies.

Passive houses and zero-energy buildings

Technology description/status

The efficiency of individual parts of a building and the components of its HVAC systems play an important role in the efficiency of its energy use. But the design and the way these individual parts interact is also important. There is increasing interest in buildings that have extremely low energy consumption and CO_2 emission profiles such as passive houses, zero-energy buildings and zero-carbon buildings. Often these are developed as integrated designs, where particular attention is paid to efficiency through all phases of the design and construction of the building. Indeed, this is necessary if the additional investment cost of these buildings is to be affordable.

In Europe, the passive house standard is potentially the next step in building codes, after low-energy buildings. The passive house design should achieve a level of 15 kWh/m^2 per annum for heating and cooling, compared to low-energy standards of around 60 kWh/m^2 to 80 kWh/m^2 for heating only. Standards that meet this level, taking into account local conditions and construction techniques, will need to be developed in all cold-climate countries in the BLUE Map scenario.

The construction of passive houses has moved beyond the demonstration phase in certain regions of central Europe, particularly in Germany and Austria, but they only constitute a small percentage of new builds. The technology is beginning to spread to other countries – mainly in Europe. Zero-energy or zero-carbon buildings will also need to be developed, although their deployment maybe modest until cost reductions in the individual components occur. However, the potential is large and many houses in the BLUE Map scenario will meet either zero-energy or zero-carbon status, particularly given that the majority of the 1 200 GW of solar PV capacity deployed in this scenario will be mounted on buildings.

Costs and potential for cost reductions

The potential for energy savings through passive buildings will depend on the overall demand for new buildings. These vary substantially in different IEA countries and in developing countries. Often these demands even vary for different types of buildings or for different regions or states within an individual country. The cost of zero-energy or zero-carbon buildings will depend heavily on developments in solar PV, but these improve significantly with the large-scale deployment of solar PV in the BLUE Map scenario.

The typical additional investment cost for passive houses is in the range 6% to 8%, but can be more. Over a 30-year economic life before refurbishment, the typical costs for a new passive building will, in most regions with significant heating loads, be lower than the costs for a traditionally designed building. However, the pay-back period can be very long for passive houses, around 30 years in Belgium for example (Audenaert, 2008). Refurbishment to passive house standard is also still an expensive option, requiring an abatement cost of perhaps USD 800/t CO_2 in Germany at present (McKinsey, 2007b). However, these costs are expected to come down over time as industry gains experience in these types of refurbishments.

Where options such as local heat, cooling or electricity production (for example, using solar collectors, photovoltaic systems, local small windmills or biofuels) can be tapped in parallel, passive buildings can become zero-energy or zero-carbon buildings. Experience in Germany has shown that typical existing multi-family houses can save as much as 90% of the costs for heating if in the course of renovation they adopt passive house technologies.

In India, interest in "green buildings" (modelled on the LEED rating system) is growing and typical additional investment costs are 8% to 10% more than what a basic building would cost. Payback periods are in the range of 5 to 7 years (Srinvas, 2006).

Barriers

There are many barriers to the construction of passive, zero-energy and zero-carbon buildings. As with many energy-efficient technologies, initial costs are high and building owners may perceive that the long-term benefits are uncertain if the additional investment is not reflected in re-sale values. Little information is available to decision makers about the benefits and potential of passive, zero-energy and zero-carbon buildings.

Some aspects of passive buildings need specially designed products or particular construction or installation skills that are not economically justifiable in small runs or for businesses building only a small number of passive houses.

Policy and RD&D needs

There is still a need to develop the concept for passive buildings – to ensure that this fits with all types of building, that it fits with heating and cooling needs, and that it will apply in all regions.

There is also a need to develop an ultra-passive building standard for buildings with a heating demand of 7 kWh/m^2 per year, or less. This needs to ensure that, beyond ultra-efficient heating and cooling, such buildings have energy-efficient systems for water heating and their internal loads from equipment and installations are kept very low.

Solutions for passive buildings that will ensure proper integration with renewable energy sources are needed so that passive buildings can be developed further into real zero-energy or zero-carbon buildings. In particular, there is a need to develop intelligent solutions to supply such buildings with their very small but essential energy needs for ventilation, heating, cooling and hot water.

Projects need to be put in place that can demonstrate this technology, particularly in office buildings, schools and other non-residential buildings. Schools, public offices and other service-sector buildings offer opportunities to promote the relevant technologies, because they are used by the public and can raise awareness of the potential of passive buildings more widely.

Bioenergy technologies

Biomass and waste currently provide 10% of global primary energy supply. More than 80% of this is used for heating or cooking. While biomass is the only affordable fuel for the poor in large parts of the world, it is a major source of environmental pollution and health problems. Concerns over CO_2 emissions are largely secondary in this context.

In developing countries, especially in rural areas, 2.5 billion people rely on biomass, such as fuelwood, charcoal, agricultural waste and animal dung, to meet their energy needs for cooking. In many countries, these resources account for over 90% of household energy consumption.

Without strong new policies to expand access to cleaner fuels and technologies, the number of people in developing countries relying on traditional biomass as their main fuel for cooking will continue to increase as the global population increases. According to WEO projections, in the developing world the share of the population relying on biomass will decline from 52% to 42% by 2050 (WEO, 2005). That is still, however, one-third of the world's population.

Improved cooking methods and a switch to modern biofuels are an important step in improving the efficiency of bioenergy use and shifting the use onto a more sustainable footing.

Biofuels for buildings

There are a range of fuels that can substitute for, or supplement the use of, biomass in the household energy mix. Liquefied petroleum gas (LPG) is already quite well established in some countries, but neither LPG nor kerosene will contribute to CO_2 emissions reduction when replacing traditional biomass. Ethanol gel and dimethyl ether (DME) from bioenergy sources are potentially very important and will contribute around 50 Mtoe in the ACT Map scenario and almost 150 Mtoe in the BLUE Map scenario. Biogas has considerable potential in many rural communities, though the capital costs are significantly higher than those of liquid fuels.

DME has the potential to be an important substitute for traditional biomass. Unlike methanol, DME is non-toxic. It can be produced from a wide range of feedstocks including coal, natural gas and biomass. Current DME production takes place in two-steps. First methanol is produced from syngas, which is then catalytically dehydrated into DME. However, new production processes are under development where DME is produced directly from syngas in a single step. Various process designs have been proposed for the co-production of methanol and DME, and for the cogeneration of DME and electricity.

DME can be used as a fuel for power generation turbines and diesel engines, or as a replacement for LPG in households. Current global DME production amounts to 0.15 Mt per year. Its main current use is as an aerosol propellant for hairspray. Two coal-based DME plants are in operation in China, with a total capacity of 40 kt a year. A rapid expansion of Chinese DME production is planned, to more than 1 Mt a year (0.03 EJ/yr) in 2009 (Fleisch, 2004), and further gas-based projects are planned in the Middle East. Biomass DME is an important option in the BLUE Map scenario, with around 150 Mtoe of biomass-derived DME being consumed by 2050, with virtually all of this being consumed in developing countries.

Costs and potential for cost reductions

Investment costs for a conventional DME production process amount to USD 11/GJ to USD 20/GJ per year (Sakhalin Energy, 2004). The capital investment costs for bio-DME production are estimated to be between USD 450 and 1050 per tonne of biomass input, with conversion efficiencies between 45 and 65% (Londo, *et al.*, 2008). Production costs could be in the order of USD 11.6 to 14.5/GJ in Sweden, but lower than this in developing countries (Atrax Energy, 2002 and IEA analysis).

Small-scale heating plants

In developed countries, biomass heating systems are achieving higher efficiencies and lower emissions through the use of homogenous dry fuel, such as sawdust pellets or wood chips, and by operating the plant continuously to meet constant heat loads. Smaller and smaller units will in future be equipped with flue gas cleaning, and particle separation and catalysts, especially in densely populated areas, where they will be necessary to achieve air quality standards.

In most small-scale power plants, steam boilers based on fluidised bed technology are used with high power-to-heat ratios of 0.3 to 0.35 with a full load, and less at partial load. Smaller CHP plants (<5 MW) using solid biomass are typically grate-fired with main steam pressures of 50 bar to 60 bar. These have lower power-to-heat ratios, typically around 0.2. In plants smaller than 1 MW, the steam is often produced in a grate boiler and the electricity generated from a steam engine. Investment costs for these systems are low (about USD 615/kW_{th}). The development of small-scale (1 MW to 5 MW) plants with lower investment costs and better heat-to-power ratios is a promising area for further work. These can make an important contribution to the energy consumption of the service sector – and in some cases the residential sector, where collective heating and hot water heating is feasible.

Some boiler designs enable several types of biomass to be used as fuel. Typical minimum sizes of small-scale combustion technologies are shown in Table 17.4.

Table 17.4 ▶ Biomass combustion technology by scale of heat output

Combustion technology	Minimum output (MW)	Typical output (MW)
Mechanical grate	1	2-30
Fluidised bed	2	10
Circulating fluidised bed	7	20
Gasification	0.5	2-10

Source: Jalovaara, *et al.*, 2003.

Several straw-fired district heating plants have been constructed since 1980. District heating plants have maximum boiler temperature of 120°C and the maximum pressure is 6 bar. Overall plant efficiencies are typically about 85%, with a power-to-heat ratio of 0.25 (NetBioCof, 2007). Energy straw costs delivered to the heating plant are about USD 68/t, or about USD 17/MWh.

At the farm scale, there are two classes of boilers, batch-fired and automatically fed. Batch-fired boilers are always installed in combination with a storage tank that can absorb the heat energy from one firing (one to four bales). In this way, the energy content of the straw is used more efficiently, since the boiler can operate at full load. Automatic boilers are fed by a conveyor that is loaded with straw bales approximately once a day. The conveyor feeds bales into the boiler automatically at a rate linked to the varying heat demand.

Recent technological advances in the design of these boilers has achieved higher efficiencies and reduced local air emissions. Batch-fired boiler efficiency has increased from 35% to 40% in 1980 to 77% to 82% today, due to better control of the air supply.

Domestic heating systems

Woody biomass can easily be used for heating in houses and in the service sector. Lightweight fireplaces and stoves provide the heat quickly and with high outputs. In heat-retaining fireplaces, the heat is stored in a retaining structure from which it is released evenly into the room over a longer period of time, at an efficiency of about 80% to 85%.

With good planning and sensible use, fireplaces and furnaces can provide 10% to 100% of the heat requirements of a house. In well-designed and maintained stoves, the wood will burn cleanly. Poorly designed or maintained systems, or the use of wet biomass, will release significant amounts of particles and other impurities into the atmosphere, however. The quality of the firewood or pellets used will also affect the stove's emissions

Pellets

Pellet stoves can be semi-automated and use fans for combustion air and hot air circulation, for which they need access to an electricity supply. The combustion equipment is designed for a homogenous and dry fuel, with a high energy value and low ash content in stable conditions. Pellet combustion equipment is, therefore, often unsuitable for the combustion of wood chips, for example, which can have a moisture content of up to 50% if freshly processed. Compressed pellets therefore need to be fabricated using dry sawdust or straw, or similar, with <15% moisture content.

Pellet burners and boiler efficiencies can be about 80%, although if the pellet burner is installed into an old boiler, the efficiency drops to around 65%. The usual maintenance required takes about 10-15 minutes every one to two weeks. Pellet production costs in Austria and Sweden have been investigated (Thek & Obernberger, 2004). Costs ranged between USD 10.0/GJ and USD 12.9/GJ for feedstock that is wet and USD 5.0/GJ and USD 7.8/GJ for dry feedstock. Over half of the cost of pellets is attributable to raw material and drying costs (Figure 17.21).

Figure 17.21 ▶ Pellet production cost breakdown

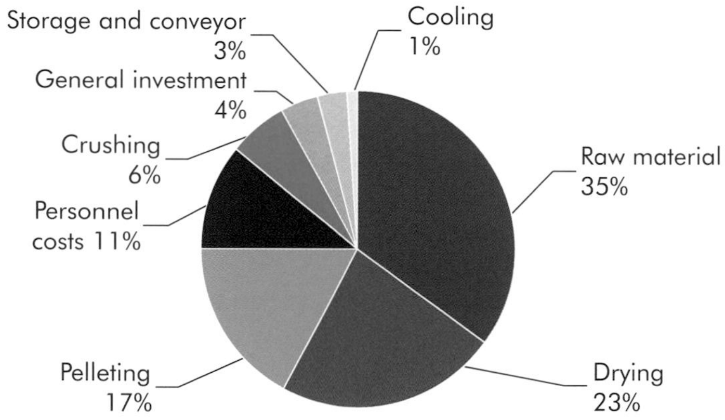

Source: Thek & Obernberger, 2004.

Key point

Pellet production costs mainly depend on the cost of the raw biomass material and the amount of drying needed to bring it down to around 15% moisture content suitable for pelleting.

Annex A IEA ENERGY TECHNOLOGY COLLABORATION PROGRAMME

IEA global energy research

IEA Implementing Agreements (IAs) provide the framework to advance the most efficient use of energy possible. Partnering with industry and non-member countries, the IEA Energy Technology Collaboration network is a cost-effective, global network.

Many Implementing Agreements include participants from non-member countries. The Energy Technology Data Exchange allows access to their extensive database of scientific information to more than 60 non-IEA countries. The Climate Technology Initiative engages with non-member countries to share best practice, to build capacity, and to facilitate technology transfer and financing.

Improving energy efficiency, whether in the buildings and commercial services, electricity, industry or transport sectors, is crucial for our environment and for energy security. Thirteen Implementing Agreements currently research various aspects of these end-use sectors. One recently created Agreement will analyse issues related to electricity transmission and distribution.

Fossil fuels are at the core of energy demand in the transport and electricity generation sectors and will be for many more years. The work of six IAs focuses on finding ways to make the most of existing resources, while at the same time getting the most from every barrel of oil or tonne of coal more cost-efficiently and more energy-efficiently.

Fusion power has great potential for power generation, though research in this area is costly. Nine IAs co-ordinate national and regional fusion programmes and share experimental results to accelerate development.

Renewable energy technologies provide clean, flexible, stand-alone or grid-connected electricity sources, but they need the correct policy environment and public-private partnerships to facilitate deployment and to further reduce costs. Ten Implementing Agreements research renewable energy technologies. The focus of one new Implementing Agreement is on examing barriers and solutions to renewable technology deployment.

By combining efforts, Implementing Agreement participants save time and resources. Implementing Agreements largely respond to the goals of IEA countries: energy security, environmental protection and economic growth. The work of the Implementing Agreements covers the full range of R&D portfolios, working in all aspects of energy – supply, transformation and demand.

Figure A.1 ▶ **Global energy technology network**

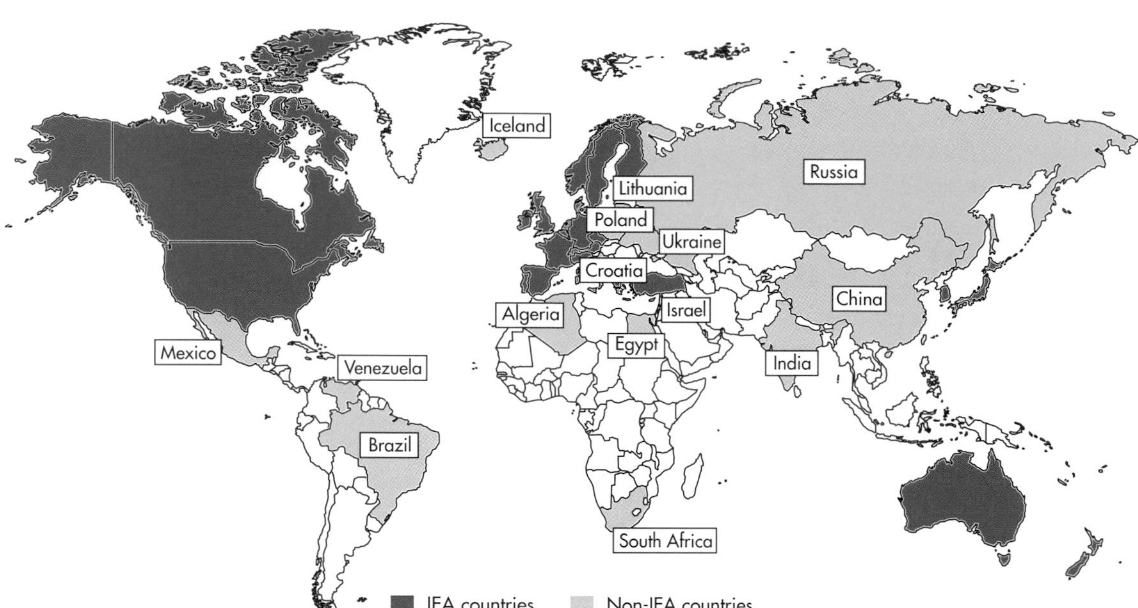

The boundaries and names shown and the designations used on maps included in this publication do not imply official endorsement or acceptance by the IEA.

Table A.1 ▶ **Activity portfolios***

		Basic Science	R&D[1]	Demonstration[2]	Deployment[3]	Information Exchange
Cross-cutting	Climate Technology Initiative				•	•
	Energy Technology Data Exchange					•
	Energy Technology Systems Analysis		•			•
End-use *Buildings*	Buildings and Community Systems		•	•		•
	District Heating and Cooling		•	•		•
	Energy Storage		•	•		•
	Heat Pumping Technologies		•	•		•
Electricity	Electricity Networks		•	•		•
	Demand-Side Management		•	•		•
	High-Temperature Superconductivity	•	•	•		•
Industry	Emissions Reduction in Combustion	•	•	•		•
	Industrial Energy-Related Technology Systems		•	•		•

* Shading and bullet indicates primary focus, which does not exclude significant activities in other areas.
1. Including modelling and technology assessment.
2. Including research, advice and support of demonstration of the particular technology.
3. Including market introduction and technology transfer.

Table A.1 ▶ **Activity portfolios*** (continued)

		Basic Science	R&D[1]	Demonstration[2]	Deployment[3]	Information Exchange
Transport	Advanced Fuel Cells	•	•	•	•	•
	Advanced Materials for Transportation	•	•	•		•
	Advanced Motor Fuels	•	•	•		•
	Hybrid and Electric Vehicles	•	•	•	•	•
Fossil fuels	Clean Coal Centre		•	•	•	•
	Clean Coal Sciences	•	•			•
	Enhanced Oil Recovery	•	•			•
	Fluidized Bed Conversion	•	•	•		•
	Greenhouse Gas R&D Programme	•	•	•	•	•
	Multiphase Flow Sciences	•	•		•	•
Fusion	Environmental, Safety and Economic Aspects	•	•		•	•
	Fusion Materials	•	•			•
	Large Tokamaks	•	•			•
	Nuclear Technology of Fusion Reactors	•	•			•
	Plasma Wall Interaction TEXTOR	•	•			•
	Reversed Field Pinches	•	•			•
	Spherical Tori	•	•			•
	Stellarator Concept	•	•			•
	Tokamaks Poloidal Field Divertors	•	•			•
Renewables	Bioenergy	•	•	•		•
	Deployment				•	•
	Geothermal	•	•	•		•
	Hydrogen	•	•	•		•
	Hydropower		•	•		•
	Ocean Energy Systems		•	•		•
	Photovoltaic Power Systems		•	•	•	•
	Solar Heating and Cooling	•	•	•		•
	SolarPACES	•	•	•	•	•
	Wind Energy Systems		•	•		•

* Shading and bullet indicates primary focus, which does not exclude significant activities in other areas.
1. Including modelling and technology assessment.
2. Including research, advice and support of demonstration of the particular technology.
3. Including market introduction and technology transfer.

Table A.2 ▶ **Energy sectors***

		Supply	Transformation[1]	Demand[2]
Cross-cutting	Climate Technology Initiative	•	•	•
	Energy Technology Data Exchange	•	•	•
	Energy Technology Systems Analysis	•	•	•
End-use *Buildings*	Buildings and Community Systems		•	•
	District Heating and Cooling		•	•
	Energy Storage		•	•
	Heat Pumping Technologies		•	•
Electricity	Demand-Side Management		•	•
	Electricity Networks		•	•
	High-Temperature Superconductivity		•	•
Industry	Emissions Reduction in Combustion		•	•
	Industrial Energy-Related Technology Systems		•	•
Transport	Advanced Fuel Cells		•	•
	Advanced Materials for Transportation		•	•
	Advanced Motor Fuels		•	•
	Hybrid and Electric Vehicles		•	•
Fossil fuels	Clean Coal Centre	•	•	
	Clean Coal Sciences	•	•	
	Enhanced Oil Recovery	•	•	
	Fluidized Bed Conversion		•	
	Greenhouse Gas R&D Programme		•	
	Multiphase Flow Sciences	•	•	
Fusion	Environmental, Safety and Economic Aspects	•	•	
	Fusion Materials	•	•	
	Large Tokamaks	•	•	
	Nuclear Technology of Fusion Reactors	•	•	
	Plasma Wall Interaction TEXTOR	•	•	
	Reversed Field Pinches	•	•	
	Spherical Tori	•	•	
	Stellarator Concept	•	•	
	Tokamaks Poloidal Field Divertors	•	•	

* Shading and bullet indicates primary focus, which does not exclude significant activities in other areas.
1. Including electricity generation and distribution, industrial processes.
2. Including energy consumption and optimisation.

Table A.2 ▶ **Energy sectors*** (continued)

		Supply	Transformation[1]	Demand[2]
Renewables	Bioenergy	•	•	•
	Deployment	•		
	Geothermal	•	•	•
	Hydrogen	•	•	•
	Hydropower	•	•	•
	Ocean Energy Systems	•	•	
	Photovoltaic Power Systems	•	•	•
	Solar Heating and Cooling	•	•	•
	SolarPACES	•	•	•
	Wind Energy Systems	•	•	•

* Shading and bullet indicates primary focus, which does not exclude significant activities in other areas.
1. Including electricity generation and distribution, industrial processes.
2. Including energy consumption and optimisation.

Implementing Agreements

To access all links to Implementing Agreement websites, see www.iea.org/techagr.

Cross-cutting activities

Climate Technology Initiative (CTI)	www.climatetech.net
Energy Technology Data Exchange (ETDE)	www.etde.org
Energy Technology Systems Analysis Programme (ETSAP)	www.etsap.org

End-use

Buildings

Buildings and Community Systems	www.ecbcs.org
District Heating and Cooling	www.iea-dhc.org
Energy Storage	www.iea-eces.org
Heat Pumping Technologies	www.heatpumpcentre.org

Electricity

Demand-Side Management	http://dsm.iea.org
Electricity Networks, Analysis and R&D	www.iea-enard.org
High Temperature Superconductivity	www.iea.org/tech/scond/scond.htm

Industry

Emissions Reduction in Combustion	www.ieacombustion.com
Industrial Energy-Related Technology Systems	www.iea-iets.org

Transport

Advanced Fuel Cells	www.ieafuelcell.com
Advanced Materials for Transportation	www.iea-ia-amt.org
Advanced Motor Fuels	www.iea-amf.vtt.fi
Hybrid and Electric Vehicles	www.ieahev.org

Fossil Fuels

Clean Coal Centre	www.iea-coal.org.uk
Clean Coal Sciences	http://iea-ccs.fossil.energy.gov
Enhanced Oil Recovery	www.iea.org/eor
Fluidised Bed Conversion	www.iea.org/tech/fbc/index.html
Greenhouse Gas R&D Programme	www.ieagreen.org.uk
Multiphase Flow Sciences	www.etsu.com/ieampf

Fusion

Environmental, Safety, Economic Aspects of Fusion	www.iea.org/techagr
Fusion Materials	www.frascati.enea.it/ifmif
Large Tokamaks	www-jt60.naka.jaea.go.jp
Nuclear Technology of Fusion Reactors	www.iea.org/techagr
Plasma Wall Interaction in TEXTOR	www.fz-juelich.de/ief/ief-4/en
Reversed Field Pinches	www.iea.org/techagr
Spherical Tori	www.iea.org/techagr
Stellerator Concept	www.iea.org/techagr
Tokamaks with Poloidal Field Divertors	www.aug.ipp.mpg.de/iea-ia

Renewable Energies and hydrogen

Bioenergy	www.ieabioenergy.com
Deployment	www.iea-retd.org
Geothermal	www.iea-gia.org
Hydrogen	www.ieahia.org
Hydropower	www.ieahydro.org
Ocean Energy Systems	www.iea-oceans.org
Photovoltaic Power Systems	www.iea-pvps.org
Solar Heating and Cooling	www.iea-shc.org

SolarPACES	www.solarpaces.org
Wind Energy Systems	www.ieawind.org

For more information

- The free brochure ***Frequently Asked Questions*** provides a brief overview of the energy technology collaboration programme.

English	www.iea.org/Textbase/Papers/2005/impag_faq.pdf
Spanish	www.iea.org/Textbase/papers/2005/impag_faqespagnol.pdf
Portuguese	www.iea.org/textbase/papers/2007/impag_faq_port.pdf
Chinese	www.iea.org/Textbase/papers/2005/impag_faqchinois.pdf
Russian	www.iea.org/Textbase/papers/2005/impag_faqrusse.pdf

- For highlights of the recent activities of the Implementing Agreements, see the free publication, ***Energy Technologies at the Cutting Edge***.
  www.iea.org/Textbase/nppdf/free/2005/IAH2005mep_Full_Final_WEB.pdf

- To learn more about the IEA Committee on Energy Research and Technology (CERT), its working parties and expert groups, consult the IEA website.
  www.iea.org/about/stancert.htm

- More about the strategy of the CERT can be found in the ***CERT Strategic Plan 2007-2011.***
  www.iea.org/cert/cert/CERT_Strategic_Plan.pdf

- The free downloadable publication, ***Mobilising Energy Technology*** describes activities and achievements of the CERT Working Parties and Expert Groups.
  www.iea.org/Textbase/publications/free_new_Desc.asp?PUBS_ID=1514

- To review the rules and regulations under which Implementing Agreements operate, see the free brochure, ***IEA Framework***.
  www.iea.org/Textbase/techno/Framework_text.pdf

- To receive regular updates on the activities of the IEA international energy technology network, including its Implementing Agreement activities, subscribe to the free newsletter, ***IEA OPEN Energy Technology Bulletin***.
  http://mailing.iea.org

Annex B FRAMEWORK ASSUMPTIONS

This Annex provides the framework assumptions used in the development of *Energy Technology Perspectives 2008*.

Demographic assumptions

The world's population is now 6.5 billion. Between now and 2050 world population will surge by more than 37% – from 6.5 billion to 9.2 billion, with Asia and Africa leading the way (UN, 2007a). The G8+5 population will drop from 56% of the world's population today to 48% in 2050 (Table B.1).

Table B.1 ▶ **Population projections, 2005-2050**

	2005 (million)	2015 (million)	2030 (million)	2050 (million)
Canada	32 268	35 191	38 880	42 754
France	60 496	63 746	66 269	68 270
Germany	82 689	81 825	79 090	74 088
Italy	58 093	59 001	57 385	54 610
Japan	128 085	126 607	117 794	102 511
Russia	143 202	136 479	124 121	107 832
United Kingdom	59 668	62 787	65 895	68 717
United States	298 313	329 010	364 427	405 415
Brazil	186 405	210 048	233 884	254 085
China	1 315 844	1 388 600	1 438 394	1 408 846
India	1 103 371	1 302 535	1 489 653	1 658 270
Mexico	107 029	115 756	1 269 211	132 278
South Africa	47432	50 260	52 958	55 590
Total	3 622 795	3 961 844	4 254 963	4 430 267
World	**6 464 750**	**7 295 135**	**8 246 665**	**9 191 287**
Share of G8+5	56%	54%	52%	48%

Source: United Nations, 2007a.

Today, slightly more than half of the world's population lives in urban areas, the majority in developing countries. The percentage of urban dwellers has increased by 10% in the last 25 years. The percentage of urban dwellers is projected to increase to 60% in 2030 (United Nations, 2005). We extrapolate that 70% of the population will be living in cities by 2050.

Between 2000 and 2030, Asia's urban population will increase from 1.36 billion to 2.64 billion, Africa's from 294 million to 742 million, and Latin America and the Caribbean from 394 million to 609 million. As a result of these shifts, developing countries will have 80% of the world's urban population in 2030. By then, Africa and Asia will include almost seven out of every ten urban inhabitants in the world (UNFPA, 2007).

Today, the global median age is 28 years. Over the next four decades the world's median age will likely increase by ten years, to 38 years. The proportion of population 60 years or over is projected to rise from 11% in 2007 to 22% in 2050 (UN, 2007b). This aging will have important consequences for the energy consumption, as the lifestyle and needs of older people differ from those of young people.

Macroeconomic assumptions

Global GDP is projected to grow four-fold between 2005 and 2050 to a level of USD 227 trillion per year (Table B.2). In European countries and in Japan it nearly doubles. In North America it grows to two and a half times its current level. The main growth will be in transition economies and in developing countries (Figure B.1). GDP in China and India will grow nearly ten-fold. Chinese GDP will be 70% higher than that of the United States. India will be close to the Organisation of Economic Co-Operation and Development (OECD) Europe in GDP terms. The global share of the G8+5 countries is projected to increase slightly overall from 69% today to 73% in 2050.

Figure B.1 ▶ **World GDP by region in 2005 and 2050 (purchasing power parity based)**

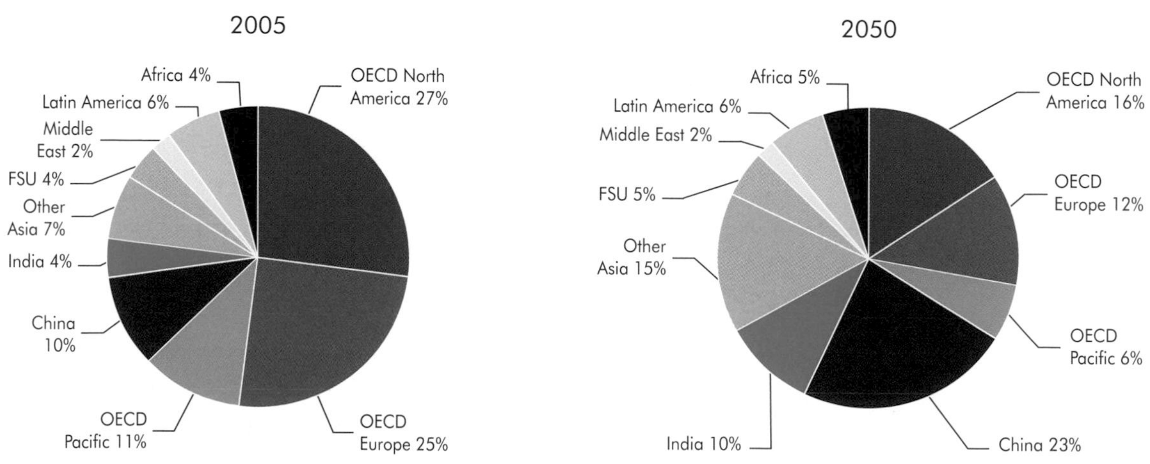

Sources: World Bank, 2007; IEA, 2007.

Table B.2 ▶ **GDP projections, 2005-2050 (purchasing power parity based)**

	GDP growth			GDP index (2005=100)		
	2005-2015 (%/yr)	2015-2030 (%/yr)	2030-2050 (%/yr)	2015	2030	2050
OECD	2.5	1.9	1.4	131	174	230
North America	2.6	2.2	1.6	133	184	252
United States	*2.6*	*2.2*	*1.5*	*133*	*184*	*248*
Europe	2.4	1.8	0.7	130	170	195
European Union	*2.3*	*1.8*	*0.7*	*128*	*168*	*193*
Pacific	2.2	1.6	1.6	127	161	221
Japan	*1.7*	*1.3*	*1.3*	*120*	*146*	*189*
Transition economies	4.7	2.9	3.4	166	254	497
Russia	*4.3*	*2.8*	*3.4*	*159*	*240*	*469*
Developing countries	6.1	4.4	3.5	192	366	728
Developing Asia	6.9	4.8	3.6	208	421	854
China	*7.7*	*4.9*	*3.8*	*226*	*463*	*977*
India	*7.2*	*5.8*	*3.6*	*215*	*501*	*1015*
Middle East	4.9	3.4	2.9	169	279	495
Africa	4.5	3.6	3.6	162	276	560
Latin America	3.8	2.8	2.8	151	228	396
Brazil	*3.5*	*2.8*	*2.8*	*146*	*221*	*384*
World	**4.2**	**3.3**	**2.6**	**157**	**256**	**428**

Sources: Hawksworth, 2006; IEA 2006, 2007.

Figure B.2 shows per capita GDP in 2005 and 2050. While some convergence takes place, GDP in most developing countries remains significantly below the level of OECD countries. Global average per-capita GDP grows by 187% to USD 24 400.

Figure B.2 ▶ **Per captita GDP in 2005 and 2050 (purchasing power parity based)**

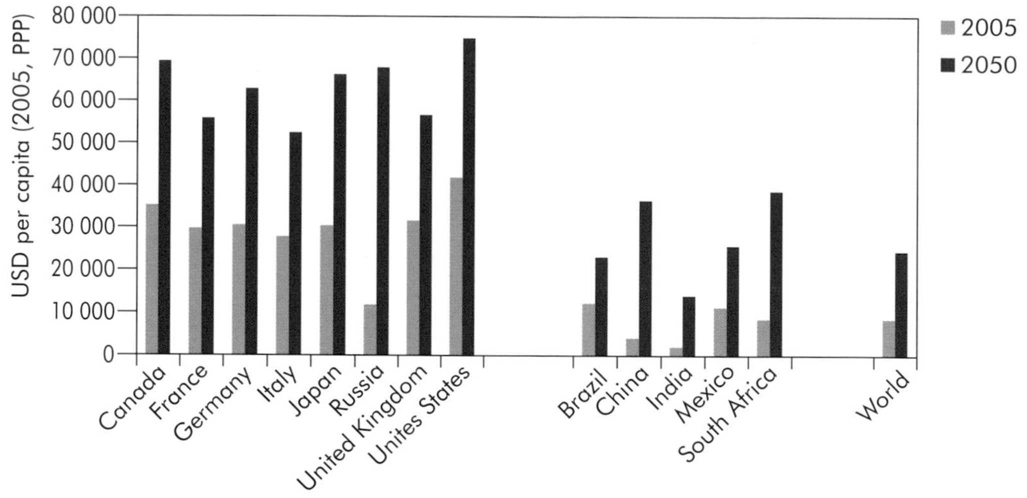

Sources: IEA, 2007; World Bank, 2007.

International energy prices

Energy price projections are calibrated to the *World Energy Outlook 2007* (IEA, 2007) assumptions. Figure B.3 shows the marginal oil supply cost curve for the world.

Figure B.3 ▶ **Oil supply curve**

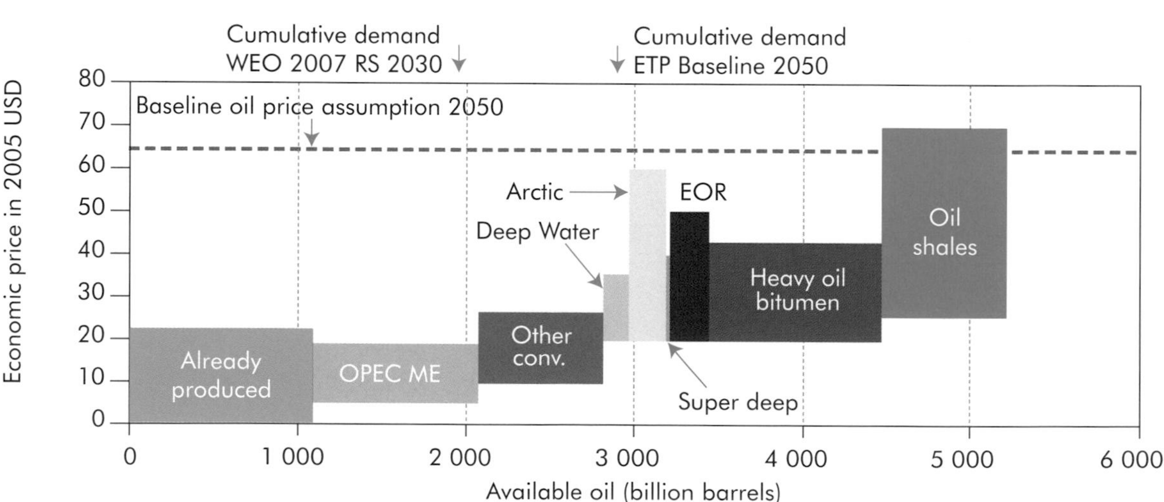

Source: IEA, 2005.

This curve conveys two important messages:

(a) The world is not running out of oil. Even in 2050, we will have used only about half of the earth's conventional and non-conventional oil resources.

(b) Even by 2050, marginal oil production costs are in the range of USD 30/bbl to USD 60/bbl.

Unconventional oil resources are largely located outside OPEC (Organisation of the Petroleum Exporting Countries). Their production costs will act as a long-terme ceiling on the cost of oil supplies. It is also notable that above USD 60/bbl, alternatives such as biofuels, coal-to-liquids and gas-to-liquids become cost-effective. On these assumptions, the oil price has been capped at USD 65/bbl for the period 2030 to 2050. This is the OECD import price for a basket of oil qualities. Certain high quality oil types such as North Sea Brent or Western Texas Intermediate may trade at a higher price than the average (Table B.3). As demand is reduced in the ACT and BLUE scenarios, prices are lower. However, the precise price reduction will depend on many factors.

Despite the recent oil price hike to USD 100/bbl, fossil fuel resources and reserves are still plentiful. Although the development of unconventional resources is very capital intensive, new resources such as oil sands, arctic resources and oceanic gas hydrates could be developed. It seems unlikely that a restriction on the physical resource availability of fossil fuels will be a major driver to reduce consumption in the period between now and 2050.

Overall, the trend to heavier fossil fuels (more coal, heavy oil) and energy-intensive tertiary production technologies results in higher CO_2 emissions for the same amount of fossil energy delivered. This is compounded by the impact of the replacement of gas-fired generation by a switch to low-cost coal.

Countries with large indigenous resources of fossil fuels will be tempted to use them. These are also countries where supply costs are lowest. Two responses could be envisaged: these countries may lower the price of fossil fuels in response to global CO_2 policies, or they may use their resources themselves. Especially for Russia and the Middle East, both of these responses must be considered.

Table B.3 ▶ **Oil, gas and coal price projections for the Baseline scenario (USD 2006)**

Real terms	Unit	2006	2030	2050
IEA crude oil imports	Barrel	62	62	65
Natural gas				
United States imports	MBtu	7.22	7.88	8.00
European imports	MBtu	7.31	7.33	7.50
Japanese imports	MBtu	7.01	7.84	8.00
OECD steam coal imports	tonne	63	61	61

Sources: IEA, 2007; this study.

B

Methodology

This analysis is based on a combination of four approaches:

- **Global perspective:** the Baseline scenario for 2005 to 2030 is based on the World Energy Model results, as used for the IEA's *World Energy Outlook 2007*. This scenario has been further elaborated to include the period 2030 to 2050. The IEA *Energy Technology Perspectives* model of global energy supply and demand has been used to analyse the ACT and BLUE scenarios for the period 2005 to 2050.

- **Country perspective:** MARKAL and TIMES models for individual countries have been used to assess the potential for emissions reduction, in co-operation with the Energy Technology Systems Analysis Programme.

- **Sector perspective:** the IEA secretariat has developed sector models with country- and region-level detail for industry, the residential and service sectors, and the transport sector. These spreadsheet models are detailed simulation tools that serve as repositories for information from experts and different models. They also serve as a communication tool between the modelling groups.

- **Technology perspective:** the present and future characteristics of technology options and their potentials have been assessed based on expert information from the IEA Implementing Agreements and other sources. A global marginal abatement cost curve for 2050 has been developed.

The primary tool used for the analysis of the ACT and BLUE scenarios is the IEA *Energy Technology Perspectives* model (ETP). This global 15-region model permits the analysis of fuel and technology choices throughout the energy system, from energy extraction through fuel conversion and electricity generation to end-use. The model's detailed representation of technology options includes about 1 000 individual technologies.

The ETP model belongs to the MARKAL family of bottom-up modelling tools (Fishbone and Abilock, 1981). MARKAL has been developed over the past 30 years by the Energy Technology Systems Analysis Programme (ETSAP), one of the IEA Implementing Agreements (ETSAP, 2003). The ETP-MARKAL model uses cost-optimisation to identify least cost mixes of energy technologies and fuels to meet energy service demand, given constraints like the availability of natural resources.

The focus of the study is on the G8+5 countries. This level of detail is not available from the ETP model, so additional country level analyses were undertaken. Some regions in the ETP model are large, and cover a range of areas with vastly different energy-resource availability and energy demands. In such cases, the use of regionalised country models can add value. For this analysis, the IEA secretariat co-operated with its ETSAP Implementing Agreement and some of the key modelling groups that participate in this agreement. The insights from their models, which are based on the same approach as the ETP model, were used to refine the analysis.

The following institutes and their MARKAL/TIMES modelling groups were involved in the ETP 2008 analysis:

- Canada: Natural Resources Canada (NRCAN)
- China: Tsinghua University, Energy Research Institute (ERI)
- France: Ecole Nationale Supérieure des Mines de Paris, (ENSMP), Sofia-Antipolis
- Germany: Institut für Energiewirtschaft und Rationelle Energieanwendung (IER), Stuttgart
- European Union: NEEDS model project team
- Italy: National Agency for New Technologies, Energy and the Environment (ENEA)
- Japan: Japanese Institute of Energy Economics (JIEE)
- United Kingdom: AEA Technology plc
- United States: Brookhaven National Laboratories
- South Africa: University of Cape Town.

There are no such models for Brazil, Mexico and Russia. It is recommended that such tools be developed in the coming years.

For this study, the ETP model has been supplemented with detailed demand-side models for all major end-uses in the industry, buildings and transport sectors. These models were developed to assess the effects of policies that do not primarily act on price. These demand-side models explicitly take capital-stock turnover into account, and have been used to model the impact of new technologies as they penetrate the market over time.

Investment modelling limitations

The investment analysis presented is, inevitably, a partial assessment of the investment needs for energy consuming equipment and, to a lesser extent, of the needs in the upstream energy sector. In the industrial, residential and commercial sectors, only major energy consuming equipment and devices have been covered, as sufficient data does not exist to accurately project the quantity and price of a wide range of small energy-consuming devices – from telephone chargers in homes to coffee machines in business and industry.

There is a question of what boundary to place on investment costs. For example, for cars, the model uses consumer prices, because energy efficiency improvements apply to a wide range of the car's components; including engines, drive-trains, appliances, structural weight, aerodynamics and tyres. For building improvements in the residential and service sectors, however, the model only counts the marginal increase in costs for more energy efficient homes, because a breakdown of the costs of energy efficiency compared to the fabric or structure of a building would be arbitrary, while including the total construction cost would result in buildings taking up a disproportionate share of investment needs, when their primary role is shelter.

As a result of these issues, and the generally more widely available information on the marginal cost of energy efficiency options, the relative increase or decrease in investment needs in the ACT and BLUE scenarios compared to the Baseline scenario should be treated with greater confidence than the absolute level of investment in the baseline.

The investment needs for the exploration, production and transport of coal, oil and gas have also not been calculated in this study. However, *World Energy Outlook 2007* estimated these to be USD 10.3 trillion by 2030. These costs are non-linear with relation to energy demand growth, and so are difficult to estimate out to 2050 given the wide range of uncertainties surrounding decline rates and capital costs. However, adding upstream investments in coal, oil and gas to the investment needs presented in this analysis for the period to 2030 increases the Baseline scenario total for both the demand and the supply-side (including upstream) to USD 117.5 trillion. This figure is directly comparable with the supply-side-only investment figure in *World Energy Outlook 2007* of USD 21.9 trillion to 2030 (USD 10.3 trillion of which is upstream investment in the exploration, production and transportation of coal, oil and gas). So in the period to 2030, including demand-side investment needs increases to total investment needs to almost 5.4 times more than the supply-side only investments.

Marginal abatement curve limitations

Marginal abatement cost curves are powerful tools for analysis and presentation purposes. However, a number of methodological problems exist that may affect the use of marginal abatement curves for decision making and long-term energy policy making:

- There is no unique baseline reference technology, but the choice of the reference affects the emission reduction potential and the cost.
- Options interact. For example, with regard to the allocation of scarce resources such as biomass, or the CO_2 impacts of electrification (which depend on the carbon intensity of electricity).
- The abatement curve does not really represent marginal cost/marginal CO_2 effects, because oil and gas prices are static, while they change in the ACT and BLUE scenarios.
- There is no single "true" cost figure for options that affect long-life capital stock, there is only a cost range.
- The more refined the analysis is in terms of regional detail, technology and demand characterisation; the wider the cost range will be and the more nuanced the estimate of emission reduction potentials will be. This is especially important for renewables and the viability of CO_2 storage.

- Costs are not always clear. For example, with regard to energy efficiency, some economists argue that options with negative costs do not exist, while engineering analysis suggests otherwise. The costs of a modal shift in transportation are very difficult to estimate. Also, a shift to smaller cars reduces cost, but consumer welfare is also reduced significantly, which is not included in an analysis of the financial consequences.
- In certain cases, important fringe benefits exist (for example, in the case of urban transportation) which may affect cost estimates significantly.
- 2050 technology projections are very uncertain, therefore only wide cost ranges can be given for certain options.

Annex C TECHNOLOGY DEVELOPMENT NEEDS

Table 4.1 of Chapter 4 (Research, Development and Demonstration) identifies a range of technology needs. Priority needs to be given to those technologies which, as well as offering potentially significant CO_2 emission reductions, seem most likely to respond to efforts to achieve technology breakthroughs and cost reductions. This annex identifies development needs and objectives for a range of technologies that will need to be brought forward to deliver the goals implicit in the ACT Map and BLUE Map scenarios.[1]

The annex is divided into four parts: power generation and supply, industry, buildings and appliances, and transport.

The first set of tables in each section shows the targets for *new* technologies that would need to be met through RD&D to achieve the goals implicit in the ACT Map and BLUE Map scenarios. The second set of tables in each section outlines technology targets for *existing* key technologies. Some cost targets are covered in the relevant technology chapters elsewhere in this document and in Chapter 3 (Technology Roadmaps). The third set of tables qualitatively describes the RD&D breakthroughs required to achieve the targets.

As indicated in Chapter 4, technology breakthrough is not necessarily dependent on large-step, revolutionary innovations. It can also be dependent on a series of smaller, incremental, evolutionary innovations. The technology development needs illustrated here only describe significant R&DD breakthroughs in earlier phases of the innovation cycle. All of these technologies would also benefit from further continuous innovation in the later phases of the cycle – that is, after deployment and commercialisation. Some of those continuous innovation needs are described in individual technology chapters.

1. The technologies addressed in this annex are those that are considered critical to achieving the goals in 2050 presented in the ACT Map and BLUE Map scenarios. There are other technologies (such as nuclear fusion technology) that may be essential to achieve significant CO_2 emission reductions after 2050. This annex does not deal with those longer-term technologies.

Power generation and supply

Table C.1 ▶ RD&D targets for **new** technologies in power generation

Sector	Technologies	Technical target: Current	ACT Map (Year)	BLUE Map (Year)
Renewable	**Geothermal**			
	Enhanced geothermal system (EGS)	A few pilot projects; problems with deep drilling cost & fracturing	Solve technical problems 50-100 GW (2050)	Solve technical problems 100-200 GW (2050)
	Ocean energy			
	New tidal	Demos/integrated systems	New systems with higher potential & low environmental impact (2030)	
	Wave	Pilot/demo	100 working demos for various technologies (2030)	
	Solar photovoltaic			
	Thin film	6-10% efficiency	15-18% efficiency (2050)	20-25% efficiency (2030)
	3rd generation ultra high efficiency cells	N/A	Technologies understood, demonstration plants in niche market applications (2050)	Fully developed and deployed with above 40% efficiency (2025)
	3rd generation ultra low cost cells			Fully developed and deployed with 10-15% efficiencies (2025)
	Offshore wind			
	Deepwater	N/A	Demo (2010)	
	Biomass			
	Black liquor Integrated gasification combined cycle (IGCC) + CO_2 capture and storage (CCS)	Pilot plant without CCS demo 2020	30 GW by 2050 Demo 2015	50 GW by 2030
Fossil	**CCS coal**			
	CCS advanced steam cycle with flue-gas separation	12% point efficiency loss (2010)	8% point efficiency loss (2020-2030)	8% point efficiency loss (2015-2020)
	CCS advanced steam cycle with oxyfueling	10% point efficiency loss (2010)	8% point efficiency loss (2020-2030)	8% point efficiency loss (2015-2020)

Table C.1 ▶ **RD&D targets for new technologies in power generation** (continued)

Sector	Technologies	Technical target		
		Current	ACT Map (Year)	BLUE Map (Year)
Fossil	CCS IGCC	7 - 9% point efficiency loss (2010)	5 - 6% point efficiency loss (2020-2030)	5 - 6% point efficiency loss (2015-2020)
	CCS Gas CCS Chemical absorption flue-gas separation	8% point efficiency loss (2010)	7% point efficiency loss (2020-2030)	7% point efficiency loss (2015-2020)
	CCS Combined cycle with oxyfueling	11% point efficiency loss (2010)	8% point efficiency loss (2020-2030)	8% point efficiency loss (2015-2020)
	Ultra supercritical steam cycle (USCSC) (coal) High temperature (700-800C steam)	45% efficiency	50-55% efficiency (2030)	50-55% efficiency (2020)
Nuclear	**Nuclear Generation III+**	Pilot	Demonstration (2015)	
	Nuclear Generation IV	N/A	Demonstration (2030)	

Note: Year in parentheses represents the first year of deployment for new technologies.

Table C.2 ▶ **Technical targets for existing technologies in power generation**

Sector	Technologies	Technical target		
		Current	2030 ACT Map/BLUE Map	2050 ACT Map/BLUE Map
Renewable	**Biomass IGCC**	Demos	Cost reduction for small-scale systems, efficiency increase, slagging problems solved	
	Concentrating Solar Power	Demos; optimal systems configuration not yet fully established	Mass production	Mass production (2025); combination with direct current (DC) long range transmission
	Geothermal Hydrothermal	Higher success rate drilling; better prediction of "sweet spots"	Deeper wells for higher temperatures (3-5 km)	
	Hydro Large	Work on reservoir management	Acceptable environmental impact; solve water management problems	

C

Table C.2 ▶ **Technical targets for existing technologies in power generation** (continued)

Sector	Technologies	Technical target		
		Current	2030 ACT Map/BLUE Map	2050 ACT Map/BLUE Map
	Small	Small-scale turbines	Cost effective technologies	
Renewable	**Solar Photovoltaic**			
	c-Si	12-15% efficiency	ACT Map: above 20% by 2015/ BLUE Map: around 25% by 2015	Replaced by other PV technologies
	Wind			
	Onshore wind	Larger turbines; better wind forecasting; operate over wider wind speed range	Mature	
	Offshore wind	Demos near shore; corrosion problems	Mass production; low cost systems for deep water	
Fossil	**Coal IGCC**	38-44% LHV without CCS	46-49% efficiency without CCS and 36-42% efficiency with CCS	51-54% efficiency without CCS and 45-48% efficiency with CCS
	Combined cycle (natural gas)	60%	65% integration with fuel cells	65% integration with fuel cells
	Fuel cells Solid oxide fuel cell (SOFC) Molten-carbonate fuel cell (MCFC)	< 45% efficiency	>50-58% efficiency; integration with gas turbines	

Table C.3 ▶ **RD&D breakthroughs required for technologies in power supply**

Sector	Technologies	RD&D breakthroughs	Stage
Renewable	**Biomass**	*Biomass supply:* Biomass resource identification; supply productivity increase, e.g. through genetically modified organism (GMO); increase in energy crop production (whole supply chain system analysis, focusing on lignocellulosic feedstock, including lignocellulosic content of classical energy crops; plant breeding (including GMO); and land use change analysis)	Basic science
		Increase of forest and agricultural residue usage (optimisation of production chains and logistics to local conditions; production of agrofibre and fibre-containing waste and energy for paper mills; development of recycling technologies; and integration with existing forest products and biofuel facilities)	Applied R&D

Table C.3 ▶ RD&D breakthroughs required for technologies in power supply (continued)

Sector	Technologies	RD&D breakthroughs	Stage
Renewable	**Biomass**	*Biomass IGCC:* Reliable, continuous-feed and automated gasification of biomass on a small scale; fuel and gas clean up; and demonstration of oxygen- and air-blown plant	Deployment/ commercialisation
	Concentrating solar power	Development of new technologies at system level and relevant scale (towers using pressurised air with solar hybrid-gas turbines; towers with air receivers to significantly increase working temperatures and conversion rates; power and desalination plants; heat storage as an alternative to back-up with fossil fuels; and solar-assisted or solar-only production of hydrogen or other energy carriers or materials for general purposes)	Basic science
		Component improvements and scaling-up of first-generation technologies; development of direct-steam generation for trough plants	Applied R&D
	Geothermal	Enhance the productivity of geothermal reservoirs; EGS development to use more marginal areas and more complex geothermal systems, including hot low-permeability rock; deep well drilling; improve economics of geothermal energy through the production of super-critical hydrous fluids (T=450-600°C) within drillable depths (~ 5 km) to increase well power outputs by a factor of ten; tapping the heat from active volcanoes; and economies of scale in plant manufacturing by improving conventional approaches or producing smaller modular units	Basic science
		System integration and optimisation	Applied R&D
	Ocean energy	*Wave and tidal technologies:* Wave behaviour and hydrodynamics of wave absorption; structure and hull design methods; mooring; power take-off systems; and deployment methods *Tidal stream current systems:* Basic research on water stream flow patterns and cavitations; and applied science on supporting structure design, turbines, foundations and deployment methods *Turbines and rotors:* Materials to resist marine environments and control systems for turbine speed and rotor pitch *Salinity gradient systems:* Development of functioning and efficient membranes	Basic science/ applied R&D
	Offshore wind	Foundations and subsurface structures (floating platforms for deep water); offshore wind resource data gathering and verification with higher resolution; and understanding of ecological and other environmental impacts	Basic science

Table C.3 ▶ **RD&D breakthroughs required for technologies in power supply** (continued)

Sector	Technologies	RD&D breakthroughs	Stage
Renewable	**Offshore wind**	Developing robust, low-maintenance offshore turbines with increased reliability and availability; grid R&D (wind meteorology and its impact on power fluctuations and wind forecasting; development of high voltage cable systems; grid code and offshore security standards; control and communications systems of large offshore wind farms); and transport and logistics	Applied R&D
	Onshore wind	Turbine efficiency improvement; turbine scale-up; more efficient turbine siting; and storage technologies	Applied R&D demonstration/ deployment/ commercialisation
	Solar photovoltaic (PV)	*Module technologies:* Research on materials/structure/recycling for thin film; comprehensive understanding of the underlying chemistry, physics and materials properties for new PV concepts for third-generation PV (stability and efficiency improvement of organically sensitised cells/inorganically sensitised cells/ other nano-structured devices with potential for very low cost, polymer and molecular solar cells; development of stable, high quality transparent conductor and encapsulant materials; and novel conversion concepts for super high efficiency and full spectrum utilisation)	Basic science
		Module technologies (higher efficiency and lower material intensity for C-Si module and thin film); balance of system; building integration; optimisation of systems aspects (storage, grid optimisation, etc.); and advanced manufacturing (new processes and equipment for high yield, low-cost, large-area manufacturing; and adaptation of other technology manufacturing methods)	Applied R&D
Fossil	**CCS**	*CO_2 capture:* Reduction of CO_2 capture cost and selection of the most cost effective option within a limit of USD 0.02 to USD 0.03 for additional production cost of electricity; testing of the different technological routes and validation of the most efficient technologies for capture and storage; development of new capture concepts such as membranes, solid absorbers and new thermal processes; and a minimum of 20 full-scale CCS projects demonstration to accelerate technology testing and the learning curve *Storage:* Sufficient proof of a high degree of CO_2 retention for deep saline aquifers, depleted oil and gas reservoirs and non-useable mine coal seams; and monitoring and measurement systems to validate the storage retention in various geological formations and develop criteria to select and rank appropriate sites *For all gasification CCS technologies (including biomass):* Development of low cost oxygen supply technology; and development of system technology to use oxygen, including oxygen-blown, high pressure gasifier turbines	Applied R&D/ demonstration

Table C.3 ▶ **RD&D breakthroughs required for technologies in power supply** (continued)

Sector	Technologies	RD&D breakthroughs	Stage
Fossil	**CCS**	Storage (modelling to forecast the long-term fate of stored CO_2)	Basic science/ applied R&D/ demonstration
	Coal IGCC	Ion transport membranes for oxygen separation; coal pre-drying technologies for lignite using waste heat; efficient coal feeding technology at high pressure; IGCC-CCS integration (hydrogen turbines, physical absorption, etc.); new higher efficiency turbines; IGCC demos for different coal types (lignite, high-ash coal, etc.); IGCC integration of larger fuel cells for coal-fuel gas; and polygeneration test plants to reduce costs	Demonstration/ deployment/ commercialisation
	Combined cycle (natural gas)	Natural gas turbine design and additional efficiency improvements; turbines with higher firing temperatures and the use of reheat with measures to reduce NOx formation; catalytic combustors; and aerodynamic efficiencies of components to reduce the number of compressor and turbine stages and to improve turbine-stator and blade cooling mechanisms	Applied R&D
	Fuel cells	New designs and materials for greater mechanical and chemical stability and higher temperatures; advanced interconnectors and sealants; *in-situ* monitoring techniques; low cost ceramic processing and manufacturing; compact and high performance gas-to-gas heat exchangers; advanced fuel processing and appropriate gas cleaning technology; and alternative electrolytes for lower operating temperatures	Applied R&D/ demonstration
	USCSC (coal)	Nickel based super-alloys for larger components and higher temperatures; fabrication (including welding) of high temperature alloy tubes; develop methods for more rapid testing of such materials; and metallurgical and control problems	Basic science/ applied R&D
Nuclear	**Nuclear generation IV**	Development of the system (sodium-cooled fast reactors; gas or lead-cooled fast reactors; high temperature reactors; supercritical water reactors; molten salt reactors; and accelerator driven sub-critical systems) and the associated fuel cycles (e.g. Partitioning and Transmutation [P&T] and actinide recycling); materials to enhance safety, solutions to the nuclear waste problem, nuclear fuels and fuel-cycle processes; and development of internationally approved safety standards and designs	Basic science/ applied R&D
Electricity system	**Storage**	Large-scale storage; and storage of electricity as hydrogen	Applied R&D
		Small-scale storage, e.g. compressed air and electricity storage; battery technologies; flywheels; and magnetic storage in superconducting coils	Basic science

Table C.3 ▶ **RD&D breakthroughs required for technologies in power supply** (continued)

Sector	Technologies	RD&D breakthroughs	Stage
Electricity system	**T&D system**	Alternatives for pylons, e.g. underground transmission	Basic science
		Development of DC transmission system	Applied R&D
		Development of superconductors for loss-free transmission (development and up-scaling of coated conductor; and chemical deposition of superconductor layers)	Demonstration

Industry

Table C.4 ▶ **RD&D targets for new technologies in industry**

Technologies	Technical target		
	Current	ACT Map (year)	BLUE Map (year)
CCS			
Blast furnaces (iron/steel)	Pilot plant tests started in October 2007	195 Mt CCS (2050)	1 240 Mt CCS (2050)
Cement kilns (cement)	95% CO_2 reduction	400 Mt CCS (2050) (energy + process)	1 380 Mt CCS (2050) (energy + process)
Feedstock substitution (chemicals/ petrochemicals) Biopolymer	First demos polylactic acid	N/A	
Monomer (ethylene, olefins, propylene, aromatics from bio-ethanol, bio-methanol and biomass)	First demos for ethanol-to-ethylene, methanol-to-olefins	26 Mtoe biomass feedstocks by 2050	81 Mtoe biomass feedstocks by 2050
Plastics recycling/ energy recovery (chemicals/ petrochemicals)	Back-to-polymer proven; back-to-monomer and back-to-feedstock not widely applied; energy recovery electric efficiency <25%	Better collection/separation technologies; reduced cost for processing	
Process innovation in basic materials production processes			
Direct casting (iron/steel)	5% of world production	15% world production in 2050 (solve materials quality problems by 2035)	25% world production in 2050 (solve materials quality problems by 2025)

Table C.4 ▶ RD&D targets for **new** technologies in industry (continued)

Technologies	Technical target		
	Current	ACT Map (year)	BLUE Map (year)
Smelt reduction (iron/steel)	1.5 Mt/yr; FINEX demonstration plant started in 2007	195 Mt/yr (2050)	414 Mt/yr (2050); develop smelt reduction + CCS
Membranes (chemicals/petrochemicals)	Occasional application	Develop new membranes and systems that allow generic application for gas and liquid separation	
Black liquor gasification (chemical pulp making)	A few unsuccessful demos in the 80s and 90s	Better process control	High efficiency, safe operation and integration with CCS; gradual transition to bio-refineries
Inert anode (aluminum)	N/A	5-10% energy reduction (2030)	5-10% energy reduction (2020)

Note: Year in parentheses represents the first year of deployment for new technologies.

Table C.5 ▶ Technical targets for **existing** technologies in industry

Technologies	Technical target		
	Current	2030 ACT Map/BLUE Map	2050 ACT Map/BLUE Map
Fuel substitution in basic materials production processes (various industries)	N/A	50-100 Mtoe biomass; 16-49 Mtoe other renewables	200 Mtoe biomass; 94 Mtoe other renewables

Table C.6 ▶ RD&D breakthroughs required for key technologies in industry

Technologies	RD&D breakthroughs	Stage
Bio-refineries	*Pulp and paper:* Black liquor to methanol pilot plants	Demonstration
	Biomass for various industries: Lower-cost biomass collection system for large-scale plants	Applied R&D
CCS	*CCS overall:* Reduce capture cost and improve overall system efficiencies; and storage integrity and monitoring	Basic science/ applied R&D
	CCS for blast furnace (iron/steel): Development of new blast furnace with oxygen and high temperature CO_2 mixture	

Table C.6 ▶ **RD&D breakthroughs required for key technologies in industry** (continued)

Technologies	RD&D breakthroughs	Stage
CCS	*CCS for cement kilns (cement):* Use of physical absorption systems (Selexol or other absorbents); use of oxygen instead of air; and process redesign to accommodate potentially higher process temperatures	
	CCS for black-liquor (paper): Integration with IGCC + CCS and maximised production of biofuels for other use	
Feedstock substitution	*Cement:* Clinker substitute (reduction of carbon contents by upgrading of high carbon fly ash through froth flotation, triboelectrostatic separation, or carbon burn-out in a fluidised bed; special grinding to increase the pozzolanic reaction rate of fly ash; and use of steel slag)	Applied R&D
	Chemical and petrochemical: Biopolymer: e.g. polyactic acid; polytrimethylene terephthalate fibres; polyhydroxyalkanoates; monomers from biomass and more advanced fermentation and separation technology: e.g. butanol; and naphtha products from biomass FT process	Applied R&D
Fuel substitution	Electric heating technologies; and development of suitable heating and drying technologies	Applied R&D
	Heat pump: Higher temperature application; larger system; and higher coefficient of performance (COP)	
Plastics recycling/ energy recovery	Chemicals and petrochemicals: Better low cost separation technologies; and dedicated high efficiency energy recovery technologies	Applied R&D
Process innovation in basic materials production processes	*Aluminium:* Development of inert anodes; fundamental materials research; bipolar cell design; and anode wear rate of less than 5 mm per year	Basic science
	Cement: Development of high performance cement using admixture	Basic science
	Chemicals and petrochemicals: Increased natural nitrogen fixation (new nitrogen fertiliser formation and understanding of steps that lead from recognition signals exchanged between the plant and bacteria to the differentiation and operation of root nodules; the genes responsible in rhizobia and legumes; the structural chemical bases of rhizobia/legume communication; and the signal transduction pathways responsible for the induction of the symbiosis-specific genes involved in nodule development and nitrogen fixation); and use of membranes (performance improvement for various membranes for specific gases; liquid and gas membranes for liquid-liquid extraction and cryogenic air separation; and development of membrane reactors)	Basic science/ applied R&D

Table C.6 ▶ **RD&D breakthroughs required for key technologies in industry** (continued)

Technologies	RD&D breakthroughs	Stage
Process innovation in basic materials production processes	*Iron/steel:* Smelt reduction (reduction of surplus gas); and direct casting – i.e. near-net-shape casting and thin-slip casting (increased reliability, control and the adaptation of the technology to larger-scale production units; product quality improvement; and usability improvement by steel processors and users)	Demonstration/ deployment/ commercialisation
	Pulp and paper: Black liquor gasification: increase reliability of gasifier	Applied R&D
	Gasifier with a gas turbine	Demonstration

Building and appliances

N.B. There is no table for RD&D targets for *new* technologies for this sector.

Table C.7 ▶ **RD&D targets for existing technologies in buildings and appliances**

Technologies	Technical target (index)		
	Current	2030 ACT Map/BLUE Map	2050 ACT Map/BLUE Map
Electric appliances	1	1.15-1.5	1.25-2
Heating and cooling technologies			
Heat pump	1	1.4/1.6	1.8/2
Air conditioning efficiency	1	1.3/1.5	1.4/1.7
Lighting systems			
Light Emitting Diodes (LED)	1	4/7	6/10

Note: Index is for efficiency improvement.

Table C.8 ▶ **RD&D breakthroughs required for key technologies in buildings and appliances**

Technologies	RD&D breakthroughs	Stage
Heating and cooling technologies	Reasonable-cost, high temperature heat pump systems (new and retrofit applications); and system integration and optimisation with geothermal heat pumps	Applied R&D
Lighting systems	Improvement of semiconductor; and modification and optimisation of known light emitting substances for LED	Applied R&D
	New materials for LED ; and stability of organic LED	Basic science

Transport[2]

N.B. There is no table for RD&D targets for *new* technologies for this sector.

Table C.9 ▶ **RD&D targets for existing technologies in transport**

Sector	Technologies	Technical target		
		Current	ACT Map (Year)	BLUE Map (Year)
Vehicles	Hydrogen fuel cell vehicles (stacks)	5-10 years of life	15 years of life (2030)	15 years of life (2020)
	Plug-in hybrid/ electric vehicles	Ni-MH battery	Viable Li-Ion battery (2030)	Viable Li-Ion battery (2020)

Note: Year in parentheses represents the first year of deployment for new technologies.

Table C.10 ▶ **RD&D breakthroughs required for technologies in transport**

Sector	Technologies	RD&D breakthroughs	Stage
Vehicles	Hydrogen fuel cell vehicles	Material investigation for solid storage; cost reduction and improvements in durability and reliability of hydrogen on-board gaseous and liquid storage; cost reduction for fuel cell system; and durability improvement of fuel cell stack and balance of system components (system controller, electronics, motor, and various synergistic fuel economy improvements, etc.)	Basic science/ applied R&D/ demonstration
	Plug-in hybrid/ electric vehicles	Energy storage capacity and longer life for deep discharge (further development of Li-ion batteries, e.g. Li-polymer, Li-sulphur, etc; ultra-capacitors and flywheels; systems that combine storage technologies, such as batteries with ultra-capacitors); and optimisation of materials characteristics and components for batteries	Basic science/ applied R&D/ demonstration
Fuels	Advanced biodiesel (BtL with FT process)	Feedstock handling; gasification/treatment; co-firing of biomass and fossil fuels; syngas production/treatment; and better understanding of cost trade-offs between plant scale and feedstock transport logistics	Applied R&D/ demonstration
	Ethanol (cellulosic)	Feedstock research; enzyme research (cost and efficiency); system efficiency; better data on feedstock availability and cost by region; land use change analysis; and co-products and bio-refinery opportunities	Basic science/ applied R&D/ demonstration
	Hydrogen	Development of hydrogen production, distribution and storage systems	Applied R&D

2. This section only discusses road transport related technologies and does not address technology development needs in other transportation sectors such as aviation, rail and marine transport sectors.

Annex D COMPREHENSIVE LIST OF KEY NEW ENERGY TECHNOLOGIES

Although only 17 roadmaps have been elaborated, many more technologies play an important role in the ACT and BLUE scenarios. These are listed in this annex. This list also includes some technologies that may play important roles after 2050, such as nuclear fusion technologies. Even this list is not exhaustive.

Power supply

Biomass

- Biomass co-combustion in coal-fired power plants (10% to 20%)
- Biomass/waste gasification

CO_2 capture and storage (CCS): coal

- Chemical looping
- Oxyfueling (burner and boiler design)
- Post-combustion capture (new chemical absorption systems)
- Pre-combustion capture

CCS: gas

- Chemical looping
- Oxyfueling
- Post-combustion capture

Coal

- Advanced pressurised fluidised bed combustion (PFBC)
- Integrated gasification combined cycle (IGCC)
  - Gasifiers
  - Hydrogen gas turbines
  - Systems integration
- Integrated gasification fuel cell combined cycle (IGFC)
  - Integration large-scale gasifiers and fuel cells
- Drying (enabling technology)
- Mine methane electricity generation
- Ultra supercritical steam cycles (USCSC)
- Underground gasification

Combined heat and power (CHP)

- Fuel cell CHP
  - Proton exchange membrane fuel cell (PEMFC) for micro-systems
  - Solid oxide fuel cell (SOFC) and molten-carbonate fuel cell (MCFC) for large systems
- Micro CHP units (under 20 kW)

  - Micro-turbine
  - Organic Rankine cycle
  - Stirling engines

Concentrating solar power (CSP)

- Dish system
- Heat storage system
- Tower/central system
- Trough system

Distributed generation

Efficient large-scale oxygen separation, e.g. based on membranes (enabling technology)

Fuel cells

- Solid oxide fuell cell (SOFC)
- Molten-carbonate fuel cell (MCFC)
- Proton exchange membrane fuel cell (PEMFC)

Gas

- High efficiency gas turbines
- High temperature gas turbines
- Hybrid power generation with fuel cells
- Low cost bottoming cycles

Geothermal

- Enhanced geothermal system (hot dry rock – permeability, earthquakes)
- Low temperature resources via binary plant technology
- Organic Rankine cycles/Kalina cycles

High performance power electronics

- High efficiency inverter

Hydro

- Large hydro system
- Reduced environmental footprint
- Small hydro system
  - Very low head hydro turbines
- Water management systems (enabling technology)

Landfill methane electricity generation

Large-scale electricity storage

- Compressed air energy storage systems (CAES)
- Pumped hydro storage

Nuclear fusion

- New materials and components for fusion reactors
  - Breeder blanket and shield technologies (tritium handling and processing, radiation shielding)
  - First wall
  - High flux, high energy neutron source
- Reversed Field Pinches (RFPs)
- Spherical Torus
- Stellarator concept
- Tokamak concept
  - Thermonuclear Reactors
  - Poloidal Field Divertors

Nuclear generation III+

- Advanced fission reactors
- Advanced fuel cycles
- New fuel forms and materials

Nuclear generation IV

- Closed proliferation – resistant fuel cycles
- Disposal of radioactive wastes
  - Accelerator-driven sub-critical systems dedicated to transmutation of nuclear waste
  - Disposal at intermediate depth enough for general underground use
  - Geological disposal
  - Shallow land disposal
- Fast reactor cycle
  - Fast reactors (e.g. gas/lead-cooled)
  - Fuel cycle
- Gas core reactors (Uranium conversion facility [U-C-F], Uranium Hexafluoride [UF6], Plasma Vortex)
- High temperature reactors
- Molten-salt-cooled graphite-matrix fuel advance high-temperature reactors (AHTR)
- Molten-salt reactors
- Smooth shift from light water reactor cycle to fast reactor cycle
  - High decontamination process prior to conversion of reprocessed uranium
- Supercritical water reactors

Ocean energy

- Ocean thermal energy conversion (OTEC)
  - Ocean temperature gradient
- Osmotic
  - Salinity gradient
- Tidal/marine current
  - New tidal generator for current system
- Wave
  - Nearshore wave
  - Offshore wave
  - Shoreline wave

Offshore wind: near-shore and deepwater/floating

- Foundations and subsurface structures
- Offshore turbines
- Offshore wind resources and data
- Transport and logistics

Onshore wind

- 5 MW+ turbines
- Micro-wind power generation
- Wind turbines producing compressed air for storage/supply levelling

Photovoltaics (PV): solar (2nd + 3rd generation)

- Compound crystalline solar cell
- Crystalline-silicon solar
- Dye-sensitised solar cell
- Thin-film Copper-Indium-Diselenide (CIS)-based solar cell
- Thin-film solar cell

Small-scale electricity storage

- Battery technologies
- Compressed air and electricity storage
- Flywheels
- Magnetic storage in superconducting coils

Smart grids (power system control)

- High efficiency power transmission/transformation
  - Direct current (DC) transmission systems (enabling technology)
  - Energy efficient/conservation transformer
  - Flexible alternating current (AC) transmission systems (enabling technology)
  - Low cost and high efficiency underground electricity transmission (enabling technology)
  - New types of conductors (enabling technology)
    - Gas-insulated lines (GIL)
    - High current composite conductors
    - High temperature superconducting (HTS) wires
    - Superconductors
  - System layout for reduced loss
- Information systems for management of production and demand units
  - Dynamic thermal power rating techniques
  - Integration of large amounts of intermittent renewable through dedicated information communication technology (ICT) platforms
  - Wide area monitoring systems (WAMS)
- Power system stabilisation
  - Suppressing influence of PV and wind systems on grid

Industry

Aluminium process

- Inert anodes for aluminium smelters

Bioplastics

Biorefineries

- Use of biomass residue (*e.g.* black liquor in pulp and paper process)

CCS

- Ammonia plants
- Black liquor boilers (pulp and paper process)
- Black liquor gasifiers (pulp and paper process)
- CO_2 capture nitrogen-free blast furnace (iron and steel process)
- CO_2 capture + smelt reduction (iron and steel process)
- Oxyfueling cement kilns (cement process)
- Post-combustion capture cement kilns (cement process)

Cement process

- Blast furnace slag granulation for cement making
- Clinker substitute (slag, natural pozzolans, synthetic pozzolans)
- Higher performance cement with admixture
- Kiln waste heat use for power generation

Chemicals/petrochemicals process

- Feedstock substitutions
  - Biopolymer (*e.g.* polyactic acid; polytrimethylene terephthalate fibres; and polyhydroxyalkanoates)
  - Monomer (ethylene, olefins, propylene, aromatics from bio-ethanol, bio-methanol and biomass)
    - Ethanol-to-ethylene (dehydration)
    - Methanol-to-olefins (enabling technology)
  - Naphtha products from biomass through Fisher-Tropsch (FT) process
- Fertiliser
  - Air nitrogen-fixation in crop plants
  - Low cost substitutes for urea fertiliser
  - Nitrogen fertilisers with reduced loss and better uptake
- Membranes
- Plastic recycling/energy recovery

CHP

- Biomass-based CHP

Energy efficient air separation

Energy efficient grinding technologies

Energy efficient motor systems

Energy efficient steam systems

Fuel efficiency improvements

Gas turbine : cracking furnace integration

Increased recycling (steel, aluminium, plastics, paper)

- New waste separation technologies
- New collection systems
- Product design methods and rules that facilitate recycling

Industrial heat pumps

- High temperature heat pump
- Mechanical vapour recompression

Iron and steel process

- Coke dry quenching/advanced wet quenching
- Coke-oven sensible waste heat use for coke oven gas-reforming to hydrogen and hydrogen use for iron-ore reduction
- Direct casting
- Near-net-shape casting
- Nitrogen-free blast furnace
- Smelt reduction

Materials efficiency of use

New materials to reduce materials production needs (in tonnes)

New waste heat recovery technology (blast furnace slag, steel slag)

Process integration improvement

Process intensification

Product redesign

Pulp and paper processes

- Black liquor gasifiers
- Energy efficient paper drying technologies

Buildings/Appliances

Bioenergy heating and cooling

Building energy management system (BEMS) or intelligent building system

- Automated sensors and controls
- Energy conserving information equipment
- Home energy management system (HEMS)
- Load balancing
- Reduced stand-by losses
- Smart control and user interfaces
    - Advanced blind and lighting controller using wireless sensors
    - Control of thermally activated buildings
    - Use of weather and occupancy forecasts for optimal building control

Building shell insulation

- Advanced airtight housing/building
- Advanced vacuum insulation products (2nd generation)

- Coloured-glass solar façade system for heating and cooling
- Electro-chromic glazing
- High performance insulating rockwool reinforced aerogel matrix
- Sun shading
- Switchable glazing
- Thermally activated ceiling panel with phase-change materials (PCM)
- Thermal storage
- Vacuum insulation

CHP
- Fuel-cell-based CHP
- Small-scale biomass-based CHP (*e.g.* Stirling engines, micro-turbines)

District heating and cooling systems
- Geothermal (direct, low and medium temperature applications)
- New techniques to minimise heat transfer losses

Efficient appliances

Efficient lighting
- Compact fluorescent light bulb (CFL)
- Fluorescent
- Light emitting diode (LED)
- Organic electroluminescence (EL) light emitting device

Efficient office equipment

Heat/cold recovery
- Mechanical ventilation with heat recovery
- Waste water heat recovery

Heat/cold storage

Heat pumping technologies
- Air-source heat pumps
- Geothermal heat pumps (indirect, very low temperature geothermal applications)
- Water source heat pumps

Liquid biofuels for cooking/heating

Passive solar heating/cooling

PV building integration

Solar heating and cooling
- Advanced materials-based solar thermal system
- Open absorption system for cooling and air conditioning
- Solar-based long-term sodium hydroxide heat storage
- Solar thermal absorption cooling
- Superior collectors based on advanced polymeric materials, vacuum insulation and sophisticated heat storage media, combined with intelligent heat management controls

Ultra-efficient heating, ventilation, air conditioning residential (HVACR)

Transport

Efficient and clean internal combustion engines (ICEs)

- Clean diesel ICEs
- Efficient gasoline ICEs
- Hydrogen in ICEs

Electric power storage for electric/hybrid/plug-in hybrid vehicles

- Capacitor
- Lithium-ion battery
- Low-cost high-density batteries
- Nickel-hydrogen battery

Electric vehicles

Energy efficient auxiliary equipment

Fuel efficient tyres

High performance aircraft

- Efficient aircraft frame (aerodynamics)
  - Flying wing
  - Hybrid laminar flow control
  - Wing modification
- Enhanced engine cycles
- Lightweight materials

Hybrid vehicles and plug-in hybrids

Hydrogen airplanes

Hydrogen fuel cell vehicles

- Hydrogen onboard storage
  - Hydrogen storage materials (inorganic, alloy, carbonaceous and organic)
- Low-cost and high-durability fuel cells
- Renewable-hydrogen-powered fuel cell vehicles
- Solid-state storage (hydrides)

Intelligent transport system (ITS) or better traffic management/information systems

New materials for light-weighting (enabling technology)

High performance ships

- Efficient hull design (hydrodynamics)
- Enhanced engine cycles
  - High efficiency gas turbines
  - Integrated electric drive
- Lightweight materials
- Secondary propulsion
  - Auxiliary sails/kites for ships

Trains
- Energy conserving trains
- High speed trains
- Hybrid diesel trains

Cross-cutting

CCS: CO_2 pipeline transportation systems

CCS: oxygen separation

CCS: storage
- Geologic sequestration
  - Depleted oil and gas fields
    - Closure of old well leaks
  - Injection to oil reservoirs for enhanced oil recovery (EOR)
  - Storage in deep, un-mineable coal seams
  - Use of large saline formation
- Terrestrial sequestration
  - Biological sequestration

Fuels

1st generation biofuels
- Bioethanol (cane ethanol with higher conversion efficiency and system integration)
- Biodiesel

2nd generation biofuels
- Advanced biodiesel
- Biobutanol
- Biomethanol
- Ligno-cellulosic ethanol

3rd generation biofuels
- Hydrogen produced from biomass

Biocrude for marine freight shipping

Biomass resources supply
- Energy crops
- Harvest, storage and transport of biomass residues (agricultural, wood, trees and forest, animal wastes, pulp and paper residues)
- Plant breeding
- Supply productivity increase, e.g. through genetically modified organism (GMO)

Coal upgrading
- Coal de-ashing
- Upgrading low rank coal

FT biomass-to-liquid (BtL) fuels for aircraft

Hydrogen production

- Advanced (high efficiency and low cost) electrolysis
  - Low temperature electrolysers
  - High pressure electrolysers
  - High temperature electrolysers
  - High pressure and high temperature electrolysers
  - Proton exchange membrane (PEM) electrolysers
  - Sulphur-iodine cycle hydrogen production from nuclear
- Biochemical fermentation
  - Anaerobic environment (dark fermentation)
  - Phototrophic environment (photo-driven fermentation)
- Co-production from coal/biomass
- Gasification
- Photo-catalysts
- Renewable cycles
  - Wind-, solar- and geothermal-powered electrolysis
  - Direct conversion of water via sunlight
  - High temperature conversion of water using CSP
  - Biomass gasification applications

Hydrogen infrastructure

- Chemical hydrogen storage
- Compressed and liquid hydrogen transport and storage
- Geological storage (large- and medium-scale above-ground and underground, e.g. depleted gas field, aquifers, caverns or buried tanks, stationary storage)
- Hydrogen gas refueling stations
- Hydrogen pipelines

Utilisation of heavy oil/heavy crude oil

- CCS for unconventional crude processing plants
- Synthesised diesel fuel from asphalt
- Upgrading/utilisation of oil extract/bitumen from oil sands

Annex E DEFINITIONS, ABBREVIATIONS, ACRONYMS AND UNITS

This annex provides information on definitions, abbreviations, acronyms and units used throughout this publication.

Fuel and process definitions[1]

Adsorption
Adsorption occurs in coal seams when methane accumulates on the surface of a solid or a liquid adsorbent, forming a molecular or atomic film (the adsorbate). The process is different from absorption, in which a substance diffuses into a liquid or solid to form a solution.

API gravity
Specific gravity measured in degrees on the American Petroleum Institute scale. The higher the number, the lower the density. Twenty-five degrees API equals 0.904 kg/m^3. Forty-two degrees API equals 0.815 kg/m^3.

Aquifer
An underground water reservoir. If the water contains large quantities of minerals, it is a saline aquifer.

Associated gas
Natural gas found in an oil reservoir, either separate from or in solution with the oil.

Biomass
Biological material that can be used as fuel or for industrial production. Includes solid biomass such as wood and plant and animal products, gases and liquids derived from biomass, industrial waste and municipal waste.

Black liquor
A by-product from chemical pulping processes which consists of lignin residue combined with water and the chemicals used for the extraction of the lignin.

Brown coal
Sub-bituminous coal and lignite. Sub-bituminous coal is defined as non-agglomerating coals with a gross calorific value between 4 165 kcal/kg and 5 700 kcal/kg. Lignite is defined as non-agglomerating coal with a gross calorific value less than 4 165 kcal/kg.

1. More detailed information can be obtained by consulting the annual IEA publications *Energy Balances of OECD Countries, Energy Balances of Non-OECD Countries, Coal Information, Oil Information, Gas Information* and *Electricity Information.*

Clean coal technologies (CCT)
Technologies designed to enhance the efficiency and the environmental acceptability of coal extraction, preparation and use.

Coal
Unless stated otherwise, coal includes all coal: both coal primary products (including hard coal and lignite, or as it is sometimes called "brown coal") and derived fuels (including patent fuel, coke oven coke, gas coke, coke oven gas and blast furnace gas). Peat is also included in this category.

Coking coal
Hard coal of a quality that allows the production of coke suitable to support a blast furnace charge.

Coke oven coke
The solid product obtained from the carbonisation of coal, principally coking coal, at high temperature. Semi-coke, the solid product obtained from the carbonisation of coal at low temperatures, is also included, along with coke and semi-coke.

Electricity production
The total amount of electricity generated by a power plant. It includes own-use electricity and transmission and distribution losses.

Energy intensity
A measure of total primary energy use per unit of gross domestic product.

Enhanced coal-bed methane recovery (ECBM)
A technology for the recovery of methane (natural gas) through CO_2 injection into un-economic coal seams. The technology has been applied in a demonstration project in the United States and is being tested elsewhere.

Enhanced gas recovery (EGR)
A speculative technology in which CO_2 is injected into a gas reservoir in order to increase the pressure in the reservoir, so more gas can be extracted.

Enhanced oil recovery (EOR)
Also known as tertiary oil recovery, it follows primary recovery (oil produced by the natural pressure in the reservoir) and secondary recovery (using water injection). Various EOR technologies exist, such as steam injection, hydrocarbon injection, underground combustion and CO_2 flooding.

Enteric fermentation
Enteric fermentation refers to the fermentation that takes place in the digestive systems of ruminant animals (cows, sheep and other livestock), and that results in methane emissions.

Fischer-Tropsch (FT) synthesis
Catalytic production process for the production of synthetic fuels. Natural gas, coal and biomass feedstocks can be used.

Fuel cell
A device that can be used to convert hydrogen or natural gas into electricity. Various types exist that can be operated at temperatures ranging from 80°C to 1 000°C. Their efficiency ranges from 40% to 60%. For the time being, their application is

limited to niche markets and demonstration projects due to their high cost and the immature status of the technology, but their use is growing fast.

Gas
Includes natural gas (both associated and non-associated, but excludes natural gas liquids) and gas-works gas.

Gas to liquids (GTL)
The production of synthetic crude from natural gas using a Fischer-Tropsch process.

Hard coal
Coal of gross calorific value greater than 5 700 kcal/kg on an ash-free but moist basis and with a mean random reflectance of vitrinite of at least 0.6. Hard coal is further disaggregated into coking coal and steam coal.

Heat
In IEA energy statistics, heat refers to heat produced for sale only. Most heat included in this category comes from the combustion of fuels, although some small amounts are produced from geothermal sources, electrically powered heat pumps and boilers.

Heavy petroleum products
Heavy petroleum products including heavy fuel oil.

Hydro
The energy content of the electricity produced in hydropower plants assuming 100% efficiency.

Integrated gasification combined-cycle (IGCC)
A technology in which a solid or liquid fuel (coal, heavy oil or biomass) is gasified, followed by use for electricity generation in a combined-cycle power plant. It is widely considered a promising electricity generation technology, due to its potential to achieve high efficiencies and low emissions.

Interstitial spaces
Interstitial spaces occur in coal mines, and are voids between the constituent fragments of imperfectly compacted coal and surrounding geology, including rocks, sands, gravels, sandstones, conglomerates or tuffs.

Liquefied natural gas (LNG)
Natural gas that has been liquefied by reducing its temperature to –162°C at atmospheric pressure. In this way, the space requirements for storage and transport are reduced by a factor of over 600.

Light petroleum products
Light petroleum products include liquefied petroleum gas, naphtha and gasoline.

Middle distillates
Middle distillates include jet fuel, diesel and heating oil.

Non-conventional oil
Includes oil shale, oil sands based extra heavy oil and bitumen, derivatives such as synthetic crude products, and liquids derived from natural gas (GTL).

Nuclear
Nuclear refers to the primary heat equivalent of the electricity produced by a nuclear plant with an assumed average thermal efficiency of 33%.

Oil
Oil includes crude oil, natural gas liquids, refinery feedstocks and additives, other hydrocarbons and other petroleum products (such as refinery gas, ethane, liquefied petroleum gas, aviation gasoline, motor gasoline, jet fuel, kerosene, gas/diesel oil, heavy fuel oil, naphtha, white spirit, lubricants, paraffin waxes and petroleum coke).

Other petroleum products
Other petroleum products include refinery gas, ethane, liquefied petroleum gas, aviation gasoline, motor gasoline, jet fuel, kerosene, gas/diesel oil, heavy fuel oil, naphtha, white spirit, lubricants, paraffin waxes and petroleum coke.

Other renewables
Includes geothermal, solar, wind, tide and wave energy for electricity generation. The direct use of geothermal and solar heat is also included in this category.

Other transformation, own use and losses
The use of energy by transformation industries including the energy losses in converting primary energy into a form that can be used in the final consuming sectors. It includes energy use and loss by gas works, petroleum refineries, coal and gas transformation and liquefaction. It also includes energy used in coal mines, in oil and gas extraction and in electricity and heat production. Transfers and statistical differences are also included in this category.

Power generation
Fuel use in electricity plants, heat plants and combined heat and power (CHP) plants. Both public plants and small plants that produce fuel for their own use (autoproducers) are included.

Renewables
Energy resources, where energy is derived from natural processes that are replenished constantly. They include geothermal, solar, wind, tide, wave, hydropower, biomass, and biofuels.

Purchasing power parity (PPP)
The rate of currency conversion that equalises the purchasing power of different currencies. It makes allowance for the differences in price levels and spending patterns between different countries.

Steam coal
All other hard coal that is not classified as coking coal. Also included are recovered slurries, middlings and other low-grade coal products not further classified by type. Coal of this quality is also commonly known as thermal coal.

Synthetic fuels
Synthetic fuel or synfuel is any liquid fuel obtained from coal or from natural gas. The best known process is the Fischer-Tropsch synthesis. An intermediate step in the production of synthetic fuel is often syngas, a mixture of carbon monoxide and

hydrogen produced from coal which is sometimes directly used as an industrial fuel.

Technology transfer
The term "technology transfer" has two definitions. The first definition is the process of converting scientific findings from research laboratories into useful products by the private sector. The second definition is used more in economic development literature and involves cross-border transmission of technology from one country to another.

Traditional biomass
Refers mainly to non-commercial biomass use.

Total final consumption
The sum of consumption by the different end use-sectors. TFC is broken down into energy demand in the following sectors: industry, transport, other (includes agriculture, residential, commercial and public services) and non-energy uses. Industry includes manufacturing, construction and mining industries. In final consumption, petrochemical feedstocks appear under industry use. Other non-energy uses are shown under non-energy use.

Total primary energy supply
Total primary energy supply is equivalent to total primary energy demand. This represents inland demand only and, except for world energy demand, excludes international marine bunkers.

Regional definitions

Africa
Algeria, Angola, Benin, Botswana, Burkina Faso, Burundi, Cameroon, Cape Verde, Central African Republic, Chad, Comoros, Congo, Democratic Republic of Congo, Côte d'Ivoire, Djibouti, Egypt, Equatorial Guinea, Eritrea, Ethiopia, Gabon, Gambia, Ghana, Guinea, Guinea-Bissau, Kenya, Lesotho, Liberia, Libya, Madagascar, Malawi, Mali, Mauritania, Mauritius, Morocco, Mozambique, Namibia, Niger, Nigeria, Réunion, Rwanda, São Tomé and Principe, Senegal, Seychelles, Sierra Leone, Somalia, South Africa, Sudan, Swaziland, United Republic of Tanzania, Togo, Tunisia, Uganda, Zambia, and Zimbabwe.

Central and South America
Antigua and Barbuda, Argentina, Bahamas, Barbados, Belize, Bermuda, Bolivia, Brazil, Chile, Colombia, Costa Rica, Cuba, Dominica, Dominican Republic, Ecuador, El Salvador, French Guiana, Grenada, Guadeloupe, Guatemala, Guyana, Haiti, Honduras, Jamaica, Martinique, Netherlands Antilles, Nicaragua, Panama, Paraguay, Peru, St. Kitts-Nevis-Anguilla, Saint Lucia, St. Vincent-Grenadines and Suriname, Trinidad and Tobago, Uruguay and Venezuela.

China
China refers to the People's Republic of China.

Developing countries

China, India and other developing Asia, Central and South America, Africa and the Middle East.

Former Soviet Union (FSU)

Armenia, Azerbaijan, Belarus, Estonia, Georgia, Kazakhstan, Kyrgyzstan, Latvia, Lithuania, Moldova, Russia, Tajikistan, Turkmenistan, Ukraine and Uzbekistan.

Group of Eight (G8)

Canada, France, Germany, Italy, Japan, Russia, the United Kingdom and the United States.

G8+5 countries

The G8 nations (Canada, France, Germany, Italy, Japan, Russia, the United Kingdom and the United States), plus the five leading emerging economies – Brazil, China, India, Mexico and South Africa.

IEA member countries

Australia, Austria, Belgium, Canada, Czech Republic, Denmark, Finland, France, Germany, Greece, Hungary, Ireland, Italy, Japan, Republic of Korea, Luxembourg, Netherlands, New Zealand, Norway, Portugal, Slovak Republic, Spain, Sweden, Switzerland, Turkey, United Kingdom and United States.

Middle East

Bahrain, Iran, Iraq, Israel, Jordan, Kuwait, Lebanon, Oman, Qatar, Saudi Arabia, Syria, the United Arab Emirates and Yemen. For oil and gas production it includes the neutral zone between Saudi Arabia and Iraq.

OECD member countries

Australia, Austria, Belgium, Canada, Czech Republic, Denmark, Finland, France, Germany, Greece, Hungary, Iceland, Ireland, Italy, Japan, Republic of Korea, Luxembourg, Mexico, Netherlands, New Zealand, Norway, Poland, Portugal, Slovak Republic, Spain, Sweden, Switzerland, Turkey, United Kingdom and United States.

Organisation of Petroleum Exporting Countries (OPEC)

Algeria, Angola, Ecuador, Indonesia, Iran, Iraq, Kuwait, Libya, Nigeria, Qatar, Saudi Arabia, United Arab Emirates and Venezuela.

Other developing Asia

Afghanistan, Bangladesh, Bhutan, Brunei, Chinese Taipei, Fiji, French Polynesia, Indonesia, Kiribati, Democratic People's Republic of Korea, Malaysia, Maldives, Mongolia, Myanmar, Nepal, New Caledonia, Pakistan, Papua New Guinea, the Philippines, Samoa, Singapore, Solomon Islands, Sri Lanka, Thailand, Vietnam and Vanuatu.

Transition economies

Albania, Armenia, Azerbaijan, Belarus, Bosnia-Herzegovina, Bulgaria, Croatia, Estonia, the Federal Republic of Yugoslavia, the former Yugoslav Republic of Macedonia, Georgia, Kazakhstan, Kyrgyzstan, Latvia, Lithuania, Moldova, Romania, Russia, Slovenia, Tajikistan, Turkmenistan, Ukraine and Uzbekistan.

Western Europe

Austria, Belgium, the Czech Republic, Denmark, Finland, France, Germany, Greece, Hungary, Iceland, Ireland, Italy, Luxembourg, the Netherlands, Norway, Portugal, Spain, Sweden, Switzerland, Turkey and the United Kingdom.

Abbreviations and acronyms

AC	Alternating current
AFC	Alkaline fuel cell
AFR	Africa
API	American Petroleum Institute
APU	Auxiliary power unit
ASU	Air separation unit
ATR	Auto thermal reforming
AUS	Australia
BF	Blast furnace
BFB	Bubbling fluidised beds
BEMS	Building energy management system
BFB	Bubbling fluidised beds
BIGCC	Biomass integrated gasification with combined cycle
BKB	Brown coal briquettes
BOF	Basic oxygen furnace
BOP	Balance of plant
BtL	Biomass to liquids
CA	Chemical absorption
$CaCO_3$	Calcium carbonate
CAES	Compressed air energy storage systems
CAN	Canada
CaO	Calcium oxide
CAT	Carbon abatement technologies
CBM	Coal-bed methane
CC	Combined cycle
CCC	Clean coal centre
CCS	CO_2 capture and storage
CDM	Clean development mechanism
CDU	Crude distillation unit
CEFV	Clean energy financing vehicle
CENS	CO_2 for EOR in the North Sea
CERT	Committee on Energy Research and Technology
CESF	Clean energy support fund
CFB	Circulating fluidised beds

CFL	Compact fluorescent light-bulb
CH_4	Methane
CHI	China
CHOPS	Cold heavy oil production with sand
CHP	Combined heat and power
CIS	Copper-Indium-Diselenide
CMM	Coal mine methane
CNG	Compressed natural gas
CO	Carbon monoxide
CO_2	Carbon dioxide
CO_2 eq	Carbon dioxide equivalent
COP	Coefficient of performance
CRUST	CO_2 re-use through underground storage
CSA	Central and South America
CSLF	Carbon Sequestration Leadership Forum
CSP	Concentrating solar power
CSS	Cyclic steam stimulation
CTL	Coal-to-liquids
CUCBM	China United Coal-Bed Methane Corporation
CUTE	Clean Urban Transport for Europe
DC	Direct current
DI&M	Direct inspection and maintenance
DICI	Direct injection, compression ignition
DISI	Direct injection spark ignition
DME	Dimethyl ether
DMFC	Direct methanol fuel cell
DOE	Department of Energy, United States
DRI	Direct reduced iron
DTI	Department of Trade and Industry, United Kingdom
EAF	Electric arc furnace
EC	European Commission
ECBM	Enhanced coal-bed methane recovery
ECE	Economic Commission for Europe (UN)
EDI	Energy development index
EEU	Eastern Europe
EGR	Enhanced gas recovery
EGS	Enhanced geothermal systems
EIA	Environmental impact assessment
EL	Electroluminescence
ELAT®	Solid polymer electrolyte electrode
ENSAD	Energy Related Severe Accident Database

EOH	Ethanol
EOR	Enhanced oil recovery
EPA	Environmental Protection Agency, United States
EPR	European pressurised water reactor
ETP	*Energy Technology Perspectives*
ETSAP	Energy Technology Systems Analysis Programme
EU	European Union
EUR	Euro
EV	Electric vehicle
FBC	Fluidised bed combustion
FC	Fuel cell
FCB	Fuel cell bus
FCC	Fluid catalytic cracker
FCV	Fuel cell vehicle
FDI	Foreign direct investment
FGD	Flue gas desulphurisation
FSU	Former Soviet Union
FT	Fischer-Tropsch
GDE	Gas diffusion electrode
GDL	Gas diffusion layer
GDP	Gross domestic product
GEF	Global Environment Fund
GHG	Greenhouse gas
GIF	Generation IV International Forum
GIL	Gas insulated lines
GIS	Geographical information system
GNEP	Global Nuclear Energy Partnership
GMO	Genetically modified organism
GTL	Gas-to-liquids
GWP	Global warming potential
H_2	Hydrogen
HEMS	Home energy management system
HFC	Hydrogen fuel cell
HHV	Higher heating value
HLW	High level waste
HMFC	Hydrogen-membrane fuel cell
HRSG	Heat recovery steam generator
HSA	Hydrogen storage alloy
HTGR	High temperature gas cooled reactor
HTS	High temperature superconducting
HV	High voltage

HVACR	Heating, ventilation, air conditioning residential
HVC	High value chemicals
IAEA	International Atomic Energy Agency
IBAD	Ion beam assisted deposition
ICE	Internal combustion engine
ICT	Information communication technology
IEA	International Energy Agency
IET	International emissions trading
IGCC	Integrated gasification combined-cycle
IGFC	Integrated gasification fuel cell combined-cycle
IMF	International Monetary Fund
IND	India
INPRO	Innovative nuclear reactors and fuel cycles
IPCC	Intergovernmental Panel on Climate Change
IPHE	International Partnership for a Hydrogen Economy
IPP	Independent power producer
ITER	International Thermonuclear Experimental Reactor
ITS	Intelligent transport system
JI	Joint implementation
JPN	Japan
LC	Ligno cellulose
LDV	Light-duty vehicle
LED	Light emitting diode
LFG	Landfill gas
LH_2	Liquid hydrogen
LHV	Lower heating value
LNG	Liquefied natural gas
LPG	Liquefied petroleum gas
LTF	Low temperature flash
LULUCF	Land use, land use change and forestry
MCFC	Molten carbonate fuel cell
ME	Major economies
MEA	Middle East
MEA	Mono ethanol amine
MeOH	Methanol
MEX	Mexico
$MgCl_2$	Magnesium chloride
MgO	Magnesium oxide
MIT	Massachusetts Institute of Technology
MOF	Metal organic framework
MOST	Ministry of Science and Technology, China

MSC	Multiple service contract
MSW	Municipal solid waste
MTBE	Methyl tertiary butyl ether
MTO	Methanol-to-olefins
NaOH	Sodium hydroxide
NDRC	National Development and Reform Commission, China
NEA	Nuclear Energy Agency
NEDO	New Energy and Industrial Technology Development Organisation
NEI	Nuclear Energy Institute
NGCC	Natural gas combined-cycle
NGL	Natural gas liquid
NGO	Non-governmental organisation
NO_x	Nitrogen oxides
NPT	Nuclear Non-Proliferation Treaty
NRCAN	Natural Resources Canada
NSG	Nuclear Suppliers Group
O&M	Operating and maintenance
ODA	Other developing Asia
OECD	Organisation for Economic Co-operation and Development
OPEC	Organisation of Petroleum Exporting Countries
ORMOSILs	Organically modified silicates
OSPAR	Oslo Convention and Paris Convention for the Protection of the Marine Environment of the North-East Atlantic
OTEC	Ocean thermal energy conversion
OxF	Oxy-fueling
PA	Physical absorption
PAFC	Phosphoric acid fuel cell
PCC	Pulverised coal combustion
PCM	Phase change materials
PCSD	Pressure cyclic steam drive
PEC	Photo electrochemical cell
PEM	Proton exchange membrane
PEMFC	Proton exchange membrane fuel cell, *or* polymer electrolyte membrane fuel cell
PFBC	Pressurised fluidised bed combustion
PISI	Port injection spark ignition
PM-10	Particulate matter less than ten microns in diameter
POX	Partial oxidation
PPA	Power purchase agreement
PPP	Purchasing power parity
PSA	Pressure swing absorption
Pt	Platinum

P&T	Partitioning and Transmutation
PV	Photovoltaics
PWR	Pressurised water reactor
R&D	Research and development
RD&D	Research, development and Demonstration
RDD&D	Research, development, demonstration and deployment
RET	Renewable energy technologies
RFPs	Reversed field pinches
RPS	Renewables portfolio standards
SACS	Saline aquifer CO_2 storage
SAGD	Steam assisted gravity drainage
SC	Supercritical
SCR	Selective catalytic reduction
SCSC	Supercritical steam cycle
SECA	Solid state energy conversion alliance
S-I cycle	Sulphur-Iodine cycle
SKO	South Korea
SMES	Superconducting magnetic energy storage
SMR	Steam methane reforming
SMR	Small- and medium-sized reactor
SO_2	Sulphur dioxide
SOEC	Solid oxide electrolyser cell
SOFC	Solid oxide fuel cell
SUV	Sports utility vehicle
T&D	Transmission and distribution
TFC	Total final consumption
TPES	Total primary energy supply
U-C-F	Uranium conversion facility
UF6	Uranium Hexafluoride
UNCLOS	United Nations Convention for the Law of the Sea
UNDP	United Nations Development Programme
UNEP	United National Environment Programme
UNFCCC	United Nations Framework Convention on Climate Change
UNFPA	United Nations Population Fund
USC	Ultra supercritical
USCSC	Ultra supercritical steam cycle
USD	United States dollars
VHTR	Very high temperature reactor
WAMS	Wide-area monitoring systems
WBCSD	World Business Council for Sustainable Development
WEM	World Energy Model

WEO	*World Energy Outlook*
WEU	Western Europe
WHO	World Health Organisation
WNA	World nuclear reactors
WTO	World Trade Organisation

Units

A	ampere
atm	atmosphere (unit of pressure)
bar	a unit of pressure nearly identical to an atmosphere unit. 1 bar = 0.9869 atm (normal atmospheric pressure is defined as atmosphere)
bbl	barrel
bcm	billion cubic metres
boe	barrels of oil equivalent. 1 BOE = 159 litres
°C	degrees Celsius
EJ	exajoule = 10^{18} joules
GJ	gigajoule = 10^{9} joules
Gt	gigatonne = 10^{9} tonnes (1 tonne x 10^{9})
Gtpa	gigatonne per annum
GW	gigawatt = 10^{9} watts
GWh	Gigawatt hour
ha	hectare
hr	hour
kt	kilotonnes
kW	kilowatt = 10^{3} watts
kW_{el}	kilowatt electric capacity
kWh	kilowatt hour
kW_{th}	kilowatt thermal capacity
l	litre
lge	litre gasoline equivalent
m^2	square metre
m^3	cubic metre
mb	million barrels
mbd	million barrels per day
Mbtu	million British thermal units
MDG	Millennium Development Goals
Mha	million hectares
MJ	megajoule = 10^{6} joules
mm	millimetre

mpg	miles per gallon
Mt	megatonne = 10^6 tonnes
Mtce	million tonne of coal equivalent
Mtoe	million tonnes of oil Equivalent
Mtpa	million tonnes per annum
MW	megawatt = 10^6 watts
MWe	megawatt electrical
MWh	megawatt-hour
Nm^3	normal cubic metre (at 0 degrees Celsius and at a pressure of 1.013 bar)
Pa	Pascal
PJ	petajoule = 10^{15} joules
Ppbv	parts per billion by volume
ppm	parts per million
t	tonne = metric ton = 1 000 kilogrammes
t/h	tonnes per hour
toe	tonne of oil equivalent
TW	terawatt = 10^{12} watts
TWh	terawatt-hour
V	Volt
W	watt
Wp	watt-peak
μm	micrometer

Annex F REFERENCES

CHAPTER 1

FCO (Foreign and Commonwealth Office) (2005), "Climate Change, Clean Energy and Sustainable Development", FCO, UK, *http://www.g8.gov.uk/Files/kfile/PostG8_Gleneagles_Communique.pdf.*

Federal Press Office (Germany) (2007), *Growth and Responsibility in the World Economy*, Summit Declaration, G8 Summit, Heiligendamm, Germany, 6-8 June 2007, Federal Press Office, Germany, *http://www.whitehouse.gov/g8/2007/g8agenda.pdf.*

IEA (International Energy Agency) (2006), *Energy Technology Perspectives 2006: Scenarios and Strategies to 2050*, OECD/IEA, Paris.

IEA (2007), "Communiqué: Meeting of the Governing Board at Ministerial Level", OECD/IEA, Paris, *http://www.iea.org/Textbase/press/pressdetail.asp?PRESS_REL_ID=225.*

IEA (2007), *World Energy Outlook 2007*, OECD/IEA, Paris.

IPCC (Intergovernmental Panel on Climate Change) (2007), *Climate Change 2007: Mitigation of Climate Change: Contribution of Working Group III to the Fourth Assessment Report of the Intergovernmental Panel on Climate Change* [B. Metz, *et al.* (eds.)], Cambridge University Press, Cambridge, UK and New York.

Nordhaus, W.D. (2007), "The Stern Review on the Economics of Climate Change", *Journal of Economic Literature,* Vol. 45, No. 3, September.

Stern, N. (2007), *The Economics of Climate Change: The Stern Review*, Cambridge University Press.

CHAPTER 2

IEA (International Energy Agency) (2004), "Oil Crises and Climate Challenges: 30 Years of Energy Use in IEA Countries", OECD/IEA, Paris.

IEA (2006), *Energy Technology Perspectives 2006: Scenarios and Strategies to 2050*, OECD/IEA, Paris.

IEA (2007a), *World Energy Outlook 2007*, OECD/IEA, Paris.

IEA (2007b), *Energy Use in the New Millennium: Trends in IEA Countries*, OECD/IEA, Paris.

IEA (2007c), *Tracking Industrial Energy Efficiency and CO_2 Emissions*, OECD/IEA, Paris.

IPCC (Intergovernmental Panel on Climate Change) (2007), *Climate Change 2007: Mitigation of Climate Change,* Contribution of Working Group III to the Fourth Assessment Report of the Intergovernmental Panel on Climate Change [B. Metz, *et al.* (eds.)], Cambridge University Press, Cambridge, UK and New York.

Lin, J., *et al.* (2006), *Achieving China's Target for Energy Intensity Reduction in 2010: An Exploration of recent Trends and possible Future Scenarios*, Lawrence Berkeley National Laboratories, University of California, Berkeley, CA.

OECD (Organisation for Economic Co-Operation and Development) (2008), "Environmental Outlook 2050", OECD, Paris.

CHAPTER 4

Alic, J., D. Mowery and E. Rubin (2003), *US Technology and Innovation Policies: Lessons for Climate Change.* The Pew center on Global Climate Change. Washington DC.

Anderson, D. (2006), *Costs and Finance of Bating Carbon Emissions in the Energy Sector.* London: Imperial College London.

Bozeman, B. (2000), "Technology Transfer and Public Policy: A Review of Research and Theory", *Research Policy*, Vol. 29, pp. 627-655.

Davis, G. and B. Owens (2003), "Optimizing the Level of Renewable Electric R&D Expenditures Using Real Options Analysis", *Energy Policy,* Vol. 31, No. 15, pp. 1589-1608.

DIUS (Department for Innovation, Universities and Skills, United Kingdom) and BERR (Department for Business, Enterprise and Regulatory Reform, United Kingdom) (1997 to 2007), *R&D Scoreboards*, United Kingdom. Available at *www.innovation.gov.uk/rd_scoreboard/?p=46.*

Dooley, J. (1998), "Unintended Consequences: Energy R&D in a Deregulated Market", *Energy Policy,* Vol. 26. No. 7, pp. 547-555.

Edmonds, J., *et al.* (2007), *Global Energy Technology Strategy Addressing Climate Change: Phase 2 – Findings from an International Public–Private Sponsored Research Program,* Global Energy Technology Strategy Program (GTSP).

Financial Times. (2008), "US Cash threatens Europe's Clean Tech Advantage," January 22, 2008, p. 17.

Foxon, T. (2003), *Inducing Innovation for a Low-Carbon Future: Drivers, Barriers and Policies,* The Carbon Trust, Imperial College Centre for Energy Policy and Technology, London.

Grabowski, H. and J. Vernon (1990), "A New Look at the Returns and Risks to Pharmaceutical R&D", *Management Science,* Vol. 36, No. 7, pp. 804-821.

Griliches, Z. (1992), "The Search for R&D Spillovers", *Scandinavian Journal of Economics*, Vol. 94, pp. 29-47.

Grubb, M. (2004), "Technology Innovation and Climate Change Policy: An Overview of Issues and Options", *Keio Economic Studies,* Vol. 41, No. 2, pp. 103-132.

Harhoff, D. (1999), "Citation Frequency and the Value of Patented Inventions", *Review of Economics and Statistics*, Vol. 81, No. 3, pp. 511-515.

IEA (International Energy Agency) (2007a), *Government Energy Technology R&D Budgets*, 2007 edition, OECD/IEA, Paris, *www.iea.org/Textbase/stats/index.asp.*

IEA (2007b), *Reviewing R&D Policies: Guidance for IEA Review Teams*, OECD/IEA, Paris.

IEA (2007c), "Trends in RD&D Priorities and Funding", paper presented at the International Workshop of the IEA Expert Group on R&D Priority Setting and Evaluation, 3-5 September 2007, Utrecht.

IEA (2007d), *Energy Technologies at the Cutting Edge*, IEA, Paris.

IEA (2008), *IEA Energy Technology Agreements,* OECD/IEA, Paris. Available at *www.iea.org/Textbase/techno/ia.asp*, accessed 12 February 2008.

Johannsson, T. and, J. Goldemberg (2002), *Energy for Sustainable Development: a Policy Agenda,* United Nations Development Programme (UNDP), New York.

Jones, C. and J. Williams (1997), "Measuring the Social Return to R&D", Finance and Economics Discussion Series, 1997-12, Federal Reserve Board, Washington DC.

Kogut, B. (1988), "Joint Ventures: Theoretical and Empirical Perspectives", *Strategic Management Journal*, Vol. 9, No. 4, pp. 319-332.

Luiten, E. and K. Blok (2004), "Stimulating R&D of Industrial Energy-Efficient Technology. Policy Lessons – Impulse Technology", *Energy Policy*, Vol. 32, pp. 1087-1108.

Luiten, E., K. Blok and H. van Lente (2006), "Slow Technologies and Government Intervention: Energy Efficiency in Industrial Process Technologies", *Technovation*, Vol. 26, No. 9, pp. 1029-1044.

Mansfield, E. (1977), *The Production and Application of New Industrial Technology*, W. W. Norton, New York.

Margolis, R. and D. Kammen (1999). "Evidence of Under-investment in Energy R&D in the United States and the Impact of Federal Policy", *Energy Policy* , Vol. 27, pp. 575-584.

Murphy, L. and P. Edwards (2003), *Bridging the Valley of Death: Transitioning from Public to Private Sector Financing*, National Renewable Energy Laboratory, Golden, CO.

Nadiri, I. (1993), *Innovations and Technological Spillovers,* National Bureau of Economic Research, Cambridge, MA.

Nemet, G. and D. Kammen (2007), "U.S. Energy Research and Development: Declining Investment, Increasing Need, and the Feasibility of Expansion", *Energy Policy*, Vol. 35, No.1, pp. 746-755.

Neuhoff, K. (2005), "Large Scale Deployment of Renewables for Electricity Generation", *Oxford Review of Economic Policy*, Vol. 21, No 1, pp. 88-107, Oxford University Press. Oxford.

Norberg-Bohm, V. (2002), "Pushing and Pulling Technology into the Marketplace: The Role of Government in Technology Innovation in the Power Sector", in Norberg-Bohm (ed.), *The Role of Government in Energy Technology Innovation: Insights for Government Policy in the Energy Sector*, Energy Technology Innovation Project, Belfer Center for Science and International Affairs, John F. Kennedy School of Government, Harvard University.

NSB (National Science Board) (1998), *Industry Trends in Research Support and Links to Public Research,* USGPO, Washington DC.

OECD (Organisation of Economic Co-Operation and Development) (2007a), "Research and Development Statistics–Government Budget Appropriations or Outlays for R&D (GBAORD) by Socio-Economic Objective", Source OECD Science and Technology Statistics, OECD, Paris, *www.oecd.org*.

OECD (2007b), "Technology and Innovation Policies in OECD Countries: Perspectives for Energy Technology R&D" Presentation by Dirk Pilat, Head, Science and Technology Policy Division, OECD, at IEA Workshop on Using Long-Term Scenarios for R&D Priority Setting", Paris, 15-16 February 2007, *www.iea.org/Textbase/work/workshopdetail.asp?WS_ID=294*.

PCAST (President's Committee of Advisors on Science and Technology) (1997), *Report to the President on Federal Energy Research and Development for the Challenge of the Twenty-First Century*, Office of the President, Washington DC.

PCAST (1999), *Powerful Partnerships: the Federal Role in International Co-Operation on Energy Innovation*, Office of the President, Washington DC.

Sagar, A. and J.P. Holdren (2002), "Assessing the Global Energy Innovation System: Some Key Issues", *Energy Policy*, Vol. 30, pp. 465-469.

Sakakibara, M. (2000), *Formation of R&D Consortia: Industry and Company Effects.* Los Angels: Anderson Graduate School of Management, UCLA.

Scherer, F. (1999), *New Perspectives on Economic Growth and Technological Innovation*, Brookings Institution Press, Washington D.C.

Schock, R., *et al.* (1999), "How Much is Energy Research & Development Worth as Insurance?" *Annual Review of Energy and Environment*, Vol. 24, pp. 487-512.

Solow, R. (1957), "Technical Change and the Aggregate Production Function", *Review of Economics and Statistics*, Vol. 39, pp. 312-320.

Stern, N., *et al.* (2006), "The Stern Review on the Economics of Climate Change", UK Treasury, January 2007, Cambridge University Press, Cambridge, United Kingdom, *www.hm-treasury.gov.uk/independent_reviews/stern_review_economics_climate_change/stern_review_report.cfm.*

Stiglitz, J. and S. Wallsten (1999), "Public–Private Technology Partnership: Promises and Pitfalls", *American Behavioural Scientist*, Vol. 43, No. 1, pp. 52-77.

CHAPTER 5

BCG (Boston Consulting Group) (1968), "Perspectives on Experience", BCG, Boston, Massachusetts.

Coulomb, L. and K. Neuhoff (2006), "Learning Curves and Changing Product Attributes: the Case of Wind Turbines", University of Cambridge, United Kingdom.

DeCicco, J. (2000), "Hybrid Vehicles in Perspective: Opportunities, Obstacles and Outlook", paper presented at Intertech Conference, Hybrid Vehicles 2000, Ontario, Canada.

Durstewitz, M. and M. Hoppe-Kilpper (1999), Wind Energy Experience Curve for the German "250 MW Wind-Program". IEA International Workshop on Experience Curves for Policy Making – The Case of Energy Technologies, Stuttgart, Germany.

ECN (Energy Research Centre of the Netherlands) (2004), "Learning from the Sun: Final Report of the Photex Project", ECN, Netherlands.

ECN (2005), "Technical and Economic Characterization of Elected Energy Technologies – EU SAPIENTIA Project", ECN, Netherlands.

Ellis, M., *et al.* (2007), "Do Energy Efficient Appliances Cost more?", Paper presented at the European Council for an Energy Efficient Economy (ECEEE) 2007 Summer Study.

Gallagher, K.S. (2006), "Limits to Leapfrogging in Energy Technologies? Evidence from the Chinese Automobile Industry", *Energy Policy,* Vol. 34, pp. 383-394.

Gielen, D., *et al.* (2004), "Technology Learning in the ETP Model", paper presented at the Sixth IAEE European Conference on Modelling in Energy Economics and Policy, Zurich, Switzerland, 2-3 September 2004.

Gillingham, K., R.G. Newell and K. Palmer (2006), "Energy Efficiency Policies: A Retrospective Examination", *Annual Review of Environment and Resources,* Vol. 31, pp. 161-192.

Harmon, C. (2000), "Experience Curves of Photovoltaic Technology", IR-00-014. IIASA, Laxenburg, Austria.

Hinnells, M. (2005), "The Cost of a 60% Cut in CO_2 Emissions from Homes: What do Experience Curves tell us?", paper presented at the Fifth British Institute of Energy Economics (BIEE) Academic Conference, Oxford, September 2005.

Hoffmann, W. (2006), "PV Solar Electricity Industry: Market Growth and Perspective", *Solar Energy Materials and Solar Cells,* Vol. 90.

IEA (International Energy Agency) (2000), "Experience Curves for Energy Technology Policy", OECD/IEA, Paris.

IEA (2003a), *World Energy Outlook 2003*, OECD/IEA, Paris.

IEA (2003b), "Creating Markets for Energy Technologies", OECD/IEA, Paris.

IEA (2006a), *World Energy Outlook 2006*, OECD/IEA, Paris.

IEA (2006b), "Lights Labours Lost: Policies for Energy-Efficient Lighting", OECD/IEA, Paris.

IEA (2006c), *Energy Technology Perspectives*, OECD/IEA, Paris.

IEA (2007), "Tackling Investment Challenges in Power Generation", OECD/IEA, Paris.

Isles, L. (2006), "Offshore Wind Farm Development: Cost Reduction Potential", PhD Thesis, International Institute for Industrial Environmental Economics (IIIEE) at Lund University, Lund, Sweden.

Jaffe, A., R. Newell and R. Stavins (1999), "Energy-Efficient Technologies and Climate Change Policies: Issues and Evidence", *Resources for the Future Climate Issue Brief No. 19*, Resources for the Future, Washington, DC.

Jakob, M. and R. Madlener (2003), "Exploring Experience Curves for the Building Envelope; an Investigation for Switzerland for the Period 1975-2020", paper presented at the International Workshop on Experience Curves: A Tool for Energy Policy Analysis and Design, IEA, Paris, France, 22-24 January.

Junginger, M. (2005), "Learning in Renewable Energy Technology Development", PhD Thesis, Utrecht University, Netherlands.

Kouvaritakis, *et al.* (2000), "Modeling Energy Technology Dynamics Methodology for adaptive Expectations Models with Learning by Doing and Learning by Searching", *International Journal of Global Energy Issues* 14 (2000) (1-4), pp.104–115.

Laitner, S. and A. Sanstad (2004), "Learning-by-Doing on Both the Demand and Supply Sides: Implications for Electric Utility Investments in a Heuristic Model", *International Journal of Energy Technology and Policy*, Vol. 2.

Lako, P. (2002), "Learning and Diffusion for Wind and Solar Power Technologies", paper presented within the Very Long Term Energy Environment Modelling (VLEEM) Project, Energy Research Centre of the Netherlands, April 2002.

Masani, A. and P. Frankl (2002), "Forecasting the Diffusion of Photovoltaic Systems in Southern Europe: A Learning Curve Approach", *Technological Forecasting & Social Change,* Vol. 70, pp. 39-65.

McDonald, A. and L. Schrattenholzer (2001), "Learning Rates for Energy Technologies", *Energy Policy*, Vol. 29, International Institute for Applied Systems Analysis (IIASA), Laxenburg, Austria.

Neij, L., *et al.* (2003), "Final Report of EXTOOL – Experience Curves: A Tool for Energy Policy Programmes Assessment", Lund, Sweden.

Nemet, G.F. (2006), "Beyond the Learning Curve: Factors Influencing Cost Reductions in Photovoltaics", *Energy Policy*, Vol. 34, 3218-3323.

New Energy Finance (2007), "Venture Capitalist Warned against Over-Exuberance", Press Release, 14 May, London.

Newell, R.G. (2000), "Balancing Policies for Energy Efficiency and Climate Change", *Resources*, Summer 2000, Vol. 140, pp. 14-17.

Nilsson, H. (2006), "Financial Incentives for Dispersed Investment in Sustainable Energy", available at Leonardo Energy, *http://www.leonardo-energy.org/drupal/node/986.*

Poponi, D. (2003), "Analysis of Diffusion Paths for PV Technology based on Experience Curves", *Solar Energy*, Vol. 74, pp. 331-340.

Riahi, K., *et al.* (2004), "Technological Learning for Carbon Capture and Sequestration Technologies", *Energy Economics*, Vol. 26, No. 4, pp. 539-564.

Rosenquist, *et al.* (2004), "Energy Efficiency Standards for Residential and Commercial Equipment: Additional Opportunities", Lawrence Berkeley National Laboratory (LBNL) paper, available at *http://repositories.cdlib.org/lbnl/LBNL-56207.*

Rubin, E., *et al.* (2006), *Estimating Future Costs of* CO_2 *Capture Systems using Historical Experience Curves, Proceedings from International Conference on GHG*, Carnegie Mellon, IEA/GHG/IA, Norway.

Sagar, A. and K.S. Gallagher (2004), "Energy Technology Demonstration and Deployment", in *Ending the Energy Stalemate: A Bipartisan Strategy to Meet America's Energy Challenges*, National Commission on Energy Policy, Washington, DC.

Sagar, A. and B. van der Zwaan (2006), "Technological Innovation in the Energy Sector: R&D, Deployment and Learning-by-Doing", *Energy Policy*, No. 34, Harvard and ECN.

Sims R., *et al.* (2007), "Renewable Heating and Cooling Paper", IEA REW/RETD, forthcoming.

Uyterlinde, M., *et al.* (2007), "Implications of Technological Learning on the Prospects for Renewable Energy Technologies in Europe", *Energy Policy*, Vol. 35, pp. 4072 – 4087.

Watanabe, C. (1995), "Identification of the Role of Renewable Energy", International Institute for Applied Systems Analysis (IIASA), Laxenburg, Austria.

Wene, C.-O. (2007a), "Technology Learning Systems as Non-Trivial Machines", *Kybernetes*, Vol. 36, No. 3/4, pp. 348-363.

Wene, C.-O. (2007b), "A Cybernetic Perspective on Technology Learning", in T. Foxon, J. Köhler, and C. Oughton, (eds.), *Innovations for a Low Carbon Economy: Economic, Institutional and Management Approaches*, Edward Elgar, London (forthcoming).

Williams, R.H. (2002), "Facilitating Widespread Deployment of Wind and Photovoltaic Technologies", *Energy Foundation, 2001 Annual Report*, pp. 19-30, The Energy Foundation, San Francisco.

Zwaan, B. van der and A. Rabl (2004), "The Learning Potential of Photovoltaics: Implications for Energy Policy", *Energy Policy*, Vol. 32, pp. 1545-1554.

CHAPTER 6

IEA (International Energy Agency) (2006), *World Energy Outlook 2006*, OECD/IEA, Paris.

IEA (2007a), *World Energy Outlook 2007*, OECD/IEA, Paris.

IEA (2007b), "Financing Energy Efficient Homes", OECD/IEA, Paris.

IMF (International Monetary Fund) (2007), *World Economic Outlook: Globalization and Inequality*, IMF, Washington, DC.

UNEP (United Nations Environment Programme) and New Energy Finance (2007), *Global Trends in Sustainable Energy Investment 2007*, UNEP, Paris.

Upton, S. (2007), *Getting to the Bottom of the Well: A Proposal to Reveal the Scale, Pattern and Impacts of Subsidies to Fossil Fuels*, International Institute for Sustainable Development, Winnipeg, Manitoba, Canada.

World Bank (2006), *The World Bank Annual Report 2006*, Washington DC.

CHAPTER 7

Alakangas, E. and M. Flyktman (2001), "Biomass CHP Technologies", *VTT Energy Reports*, Vol. 5.

Armor, A.F. (1996), "Fossil Power Plant Residual Life Optimization in the USA", *Modern Power Systems*, Vol. 16, No. 1, pp. 41, 43-45.

BERR (Department for Business, Enterprise & Regulatory Reform, UK) (2007), "Analysis of Carbon Capture and Storage Cost-Supply Curves for the UK", BERR, UK, *www.berr.gov.uk/files/file36782.pdf.*

Bradshaw, J. and T. Dance (2004), "Mapping Geological Storage Prospectivity of CO_2 for the World's Sedimentary Basins and Regional Source to Sink Matching", in M. Wilson (ed.), *Greenhouse Gas Control Technologies: Proceedings of the 7th International Conference on Greenhouse Gas Technologies, 5-9 September, 2004, Vancouver, Canada*. Greenhouse Gas Technologies Cooperative Research Centre (CO2CRC), Elsevier Science, Amsterdam, Netherlands.

CDM (Clean Development Mechanism) Methodological Panel (2006), "Draft Recommendation on CO_2 Capture and Storage as CDM Project Activities Based on the Review of Cases, NM0167, NM0168 and SSC_038", CDM, Bonn.

Coninck de, H., *et al.* (2006), *Acceptability of CO_2 Capture and Storage: A Review of Legal, Regulatory, Economic and Social Aspects of CO_2 Capture and Storage*, ECN, Netherlands.

DEFRA (Department of Food, Environment and Agriculture, UK) (2000), *The CHPQA Standard*, Issue 1, DEFRA, London, *www.chpqa.com/guidance_notes/documents/Standard_-_FINAL_VERSION.pdf.*

IEA (International Energy Agency) (2004), "*Prospects for CO_2 Capture and Storage, Energy Technology Analysis*", OECD/IEA, Paris.

IEA (2005), "Prospects for Hydrogen and Fuel Cells", OECD/IEA, Paris.

IEA (2006), *Energy Technology Perspectives: Scenarios and Strategies to 2050*, OECD/IEA, Paris.

IEA (2007a), "Electricity Information 2007", OECD/IEA, Paris.

IEA (2007b), "Fossil-Fuel-Fired Power Generation", OECD/IEA, Paris.

IEA (2007c), *World Energy Outlook 2007*, OECD/IEA, Paris.

IEA (2007d), "IEA Energy Technology Essentials, Fuel Cells", Fact Sheet, OECD/IEA, Paris, *www.iea.org/textbase/techno/essentials6.pdf.*

IEA (2007e), *Legal Aspects of Storing $CO_{2:}$ Update and Recommendations*, *Source OECD Energy*, Vol. 2007, No. 11, June, pp. i-144.

IEA (2007f), *Tracking Industrial Energy Efficiency and CO_2: Emissions*, OECD/IEA, Paris.

IEA (2007g), "Near-Term Opportunities for Carbon Dioxide Capture and Storage" - 2007- *Summary Report of the Global Assessments Workshop*, OECD/IEA, Paris 2007, *http://www.iea.org/Textbase/publications/free_new_Desc.asp?PUBS_ID=1979.*

IEA (2008a), "CO_2 Abatement Potential of the Modernisation of Coal-Fired Power Plants", OECD/IEA, Paris, forthcoming.

IEA (2008b), "CO_2 Abatement Potential of New Technology Developments in Coal-Fired Power Plants", OECD/IEA, Paris, forthcoming.

IEA (2008c), "CO_2 Capture and Storage: A Key Carbon Abatement Option", OECD/IEA, Paris, May 2008.

IEA CCC (IEA Clean Coal Centre) (2007), "Research and Development Needs for Clean Coal Deployment", OECD/IEA, Paris.

IEA CSLF (Carbon Sequestration Leadership Forum) (2007), "Near-Term Opportunities for Carbon Dioxide Capture and Storage", summary report of the International Workshop on Global Assessments for Near-Term Opportunities for Carbon Dioxide Capture and Storage, San Francisco and Olso, CCS, June 21-22, 2007.

F

IEA GHG (IEA Greenhouse Gas R&D Programme) (2004), "Overview of Monitoring Requirements for Geological Storage Projects", Report No PH4/29, November.

IEA GHG (2007a), "Expert Workshop on Financing Carbon Capture and Storage: Barriers and Solutions", IEA GHG, July, *www.iea-coal.org.uk/publishor/system/component_view.asp?LogDocId=81771&PhyDocId=6420.*

IEA GHG (2007b), "CO_2 Capture Ready Plants", Technical Study, Report No. 4, London.

IPCC (Intergovernmental Panel on Climate Change) (2005), "Carbon Dioxide Capture and Storage: Special Report of the Intergovernmental Panel on Climate Change", Cambridge University Press, Cambridge, UK and New York.

IPCC (2007), "Fourth Assessment Report – Climate Change 2007: Synthesis Report", IPCC, *www.ipcc.ch.*

Loyd, S. (2007), "New Thermal Power Plant Technologies: Technology Choices for New Projects – CCGT, IGCC, Supercritical Coal, Oxyfuel Combustion, CFB, etc.", paper presented at the Coaltrans Conference, 2nd Clean Coal & Carbon Capture: Securing the Future, London, September 2007.

Mandil, C. (2007), "The Role of CCS in Climate Change Mitigation", keynote speech delivered at the IEA/CSLF Early Opportunities Workshop, Global Assessment, June 21-22, 2007, Oslo.

MIT (Massachusetts Institute of Technology) (2007), "The Future of Coal: An Interdisciplinary MIT Study", MIT, Cambridge, Mass.

Maurstad, O. (2005), *An Overview of Coal based Integrated Gasification Combined Cycle:(IGCC) Technology*, Sept 2005, MIT, Cambridge, Mass, *http://sequestration.mit.edu/pdf/LFEE_2005-002_WP.pdf.*

NGU (Norsk Geologiske Undersøkelse) (2006), "Best Practice for the Storage of CO_2 in Saline Aquifers – Observations and Guidelines from the SACS and CO_2 STORE Projects", November, *www.ngu.no/FileArchive/91/CO2STORE_BPM_final_small.pdf.*

Paterson, I.R. and J.D. Wilson (2002), "Use of Damage Monitoring Systems for Component Life Optimisation in Power Plant", *International Journal of Pressure Vessels and Piping*, Vol. 79, No. 8, pp. 541-547.

Philibert, C., J. Ellis and J. Podkanski (2007), "Carbon Capture and Storage in the CDM, OECD/IEA Project for the Annex I Expert Group on the UNFCCC", www. *iea.org/textbase/papers/2007/CCS_in_CDM.pdf.*

PTRC (Petroleum Technology Research Centre) (2004), "IEA GHG Weyburn CO_2 Monitoring and Storage Project Summary Report 2000-2004", Wilson M., M. Moonea, and D. Reiner (eds.), GHGT7 Conference, 5-9 September 2004, Vancouver, Canada.

Remme, U. and K. Bennaceur (2007), "CCS Latest Dataset", presented at the IEA Workshop on Energy Technology Perspectives – Towards Country Level Granularity, June 2007, Paris.

SPE (Society of Petroleum Engineers) (2002), "Practical Aspects of CO_2 Flooding", *SPE Monograph* 22, P.M. Jarrell, *et al.* (eds.), Richardson, Texas.

WEC (World Energy Council) (2008), Private Communication from Mrs Elena Nekhaev, February.

Wright, I. (2006), "CO_2 Geological Storage – Lessons Learnt from In Salah (Algeria)", paper presented at the EU-OPEC CCS Conference, Riyadh, September 21, 2006.

Zakkour, P., *et al.* (2005), "Developing Monitoring, Reporting and Verification Guidelines for CO_2 Capture and Storage under the EU ETS", DTI R277. Environmental Resources Management (ERM) and Det Norske Veritas (DNV).

ZEP (The European Technology Platform for Zero Emission Fossil Fuel Power Plants) (2006), "Strategic Research Agenda", *www.zero-emissionplatform.eu/website/library.*

CHAPTER 8

CEA (Commissariat à l'Energie Atomique) (2002), "Radiotoxicity of Spent Fuel", Clefs CEA, No. 46, *www.cea.fr/var/cea/storage/static/gb/library/Clefs46/pagesg/clefs46_16.html.*

CEA (2005), "Partitioning and Transmutation of Long-Lived Radionuclides", CEA, France.

DGEMP (Direction Générale de l'Énergie et des Matières Premières, France [General Directorate for Energy and Raw Materials]) (2004), "Summary of the DGEMP Study of Reference Costs for Power Generation", DGEMP, France, *www.industrie.gouv.fr/energie/electric/cdr-anglais.pdf.*

DTI (Department of Trade and Industry, UK) (2007), "The Future of Nuclear Power", May 2007, DTI, UK.

GTZ (Deutsche Gesellschaft für Technische Zusammenarbeit GmbH) (2001), "Ministerial Declaration" in *Water: A Key to Sustainable Development*, report of the International Conference on Freshwater, Bonn, 3-7 December 2001, pp. 20-22.

IAEA (International Atomic Energy Agency) (1997), "Nuclear Desalination of Sea Water", TECDOC 1444, IAEA, Vienna.

IAEA (2000), "Status of non-electric Nuclear Heat Applications: Technology and Safety", TECDOC 1184, IAEA, Vienna.

IAEA (2005), "Innovative Small and Medium Sized Reactors: Design Features, Safety, Approaches and R&D Trends", TECDOC 1451, IAEA, Vienna.

IAEA (2006), "Nuclear Power Reactors in the World," Reference Data Series No. 2, IAEA, Vienna.

IAEA (2007), "Status of Small Reactor Designs Without On-Site Refuelling", TECDOC 1536, IAEA, Vienna.

IAEA (2008), Power Reactor Information System Database, IAEA, Vienna, *www.iaea.org/programmes/a2/.*

IEA (International Energy Agency) (2006), *World Energy Outlook 2006*, OECD/IEA, Paris.

IPCC (Intergovernmental Panel on Climate Change) (2007), "Climate Change 2007: Mitigation of Climate Change", Contribution of Working Group III to the Fourth Assessment Report of the Intergovernmental Panel on Climate Change [B. Metz, *et al.* (eds.)], Cambridge University Press, Cambridge, UK and New York.

Keystone Center (2007), "Nuclear Power Joint Fact Finding", the Keystone Center, Keystone, Colorado.

MIT (Massachusetts Institute of Technology) (2003), "The Future of Nuclear Power", July, MIT.

NEA (Nuclear Energy Agency) (1982), "Convention on Third Party Liability in the Field of Nuclear Energy of 29th July 1960, as amended by the Additional Protocol of 28th January 1964 and by the Protocol of 16th November 1982", OECD/NEA, Paris, *www.nea.fr/html/law/nlparis_conv.html and www.nea.fr/html/law/nlbrussels.html.*

NEA (2000), "Nuclear Education and Training: Cause for Concern?", OECD/NEA, Paris.

NEA (2004a), "Nuclear Competence Building", OECD/NEA, Paris, *www.oecdbookshop.org/oecd/display.asp?sf1=identifiers&lang=EN&st1=92-64-10850-5.*

NEA (2004b), "Nuclear Energy: the Hydrogen Economy", *NEA News*, Vol. 22, No. 2, *www.nea.fr/html/science/hydro/iem3/H2-3rdmtg-agenda.pdf.*

NEA (2005a), "Uranium 2005: Resources, Production and Demand", Report No. 6098, OECD/NEA, Paris.

NEA (2005b), "Projected Costs of Generating Electricity", 2005 Update, OECD/NEA

NEA (2006), "French R&D on the Partitioning and Transmutation of Long-lived Radionuclides", OECD Papers, Vol. 6, No. 7, November, pp. 1-87, OECD/NEA, Paris.

NEA (2007), "Risks and Benefits of Nuclear Energy", OECD/NEA, Paris.

NEI (Nuclear Energy Institute) (2007), "Manufacturing Capacity Assessment for New U.S. Nuclear Plants", NEI, Washington, DC.

NEI, (2008a), "Licence Renewals", NEI, Washington, DC, *www.nei.org/filefolder/US_Nuclear_License_Renewal_Filings.xls.*

NEI (2008b), "Power Uprates", NEI, Washington, DC, *www.nei.org/filefolder/US_Nuclear_Power_Uprates_by_Plant.xls.*

NEI (2008c), "Climate Change Initiatives", NEI, Washington, DC, *www.nei.org/keyissues/protectingtheenvironment/climatechangeinitiatives/.*

Nuclear Industries Association, UK (2006), *The Capability to Deliver a New Nuclear Build Programme*, Nuclear Industries Association, London, *www.niauk.org/position-papers.html.*

Oak Ridge Institute for Science and Education (2007), "Nuclear Engineering Enrolments and Degrees Survey, 2006 Data".

Royal Academy of Engineering, UK (2004), "The Cost of Generating Electricity", Royal Academy of Engineering, London.

Stricker, L. and J. Leclerq (2004), "An Ocean Apart", Nuclear Engineering International, December, pp. 20-26.

Sustainable Development Commission, UK (2006),"The Economics of Nuclear Power", *www.sd-commission.org.uk/index.php.*

Tarjanne, R. and K. Luostarinen (2003), "Competitiveness Comparison of the Electricity Production Alternatives", Research Report, Lappeenranta University of Technology, Finland.

United Kingdom Environmental Audit Committee (2006), "Keeping the Lights on; Nuclear, Renewables and Climate Change".

University of Chicago (2004), "The Economic Future of Nuclear Power", US Department of Energy, Washington, DC.

WNA (World Nuclear Association) (2005), "The New Economics of Nuclear Power". WNA (2006-07), "World Nuclear Power Reactors 2006-07", *www.world-nuclear.org/info/reactors.html.*

WNA (2007), "Waste Management in the Nuclear Fuel Cycle", April, WNA website, *www.world-nuclear.org/info/inf04.html.* WNA (2008), website, WNA Reactor Database.

CHAPTER 9

Alakangas, E. and M. Flyktman (2001), "Biomass CHP Technologies", *VTT Energy Reports,* July.

Asikainen, A., *et al.* (2007), "Cost of Forest Biomass Supply and Harvesting Technology Markets in EU 27", in M. Savolainen (ed.), *Bioenergy 2007*, proceedings of the Third International Bioenergy Conference and Exhibition, Jyväskylä, Finland, 3-6 September, Finnish Bioenergy Association, Jyväskylä, Finland, pp. 345-352.

Briggs, M. (2004), "Widescale Biodiesel Production from Algae", *www.unh.edu/p2/biodiesel/article_alge.html*

EUBionet 2 (2006), *ET – Bioenergy Final Report, www.eubionet.com/ACFiles/Download.asp?recID=4773.*

European Bio-CHP (2006), "CHP Plants Key Figures", *www.dk-teknik.dk/cms/site.asp?p=1042*

FAOSTAT (Food and Agriculture Organization Corporate Statistical Database) (2007), on-line database, United Nations Food and Agriculture Organisation (FAO), *http://faostat.fao.org/*.

Fargione, J., *et al.* (2008), "Land Clearing and the Biofuel Carbon Debt", *Science,* Vol. 319, No. 5867, pp. 1 235-38, *www.sciencexpress.org.*

Haberl, H., K.H. Erb and F. Krausmann (2007), *Human Appropriation of Net Primary Production,* Internet Encyclopaedia of Ecological Economics, The International Society for Ecological Economics, *www. ecoeco.org/pdf/2007_march_hanpp.pdf, accessed 19 March, 2008.*

Helynen, S., *et al.* (2002), *The Possibilities of Bioenergy in Reducing Greenhouse Gases,* (In Finnish), VTT Research Notes 2145, Technical Research Centre of Finland, *www.vtt.fi/inf/pdf/tiedotteet/2002/T2145.pdf.*

Hoogwijk, M.A., *et al.* (2003), "Exploration of the Ranges of the Global Potential of Biomass for Energy", *Biomass and Bioenergy*, Vol. 25, pp. 119-133.

IEA (International Energy Agency) (2006), *Energy Technology Perspectives 2006*, OECD/IEA, Paris, *www.iea.org*.

IEA (2007a), "Renewables for Heating and Cooling: Untapped Potential", OECD/ IEA, Paris.

IEA (2007b), *World Energy Outlook 2007*, OECD/IEA, Paris.

IEA (2007c), *Bioenergy Project Development and Biomass Supply: Good Practice Guidelines*, OECD/IEA, Paris.

IEA Bioenergy (2007), *Potential Contribution of Bioenergy to the Worlds Future Energy Demand,* OECD/IEA Bioenergy, Paris, *www.ieabioenergy.com.*

IPCC (2007), "Climate Change 2007: Mitigation", Contribution of Working Group III to the Fourth Assessment Report of the Intergovernmental Panel on Climate Change, Cambridge University Press, Cambridge, UK.

Junginger, M., *et al.* (2005), "Technological Learning and Cost Reductions in Wood Fuel Supply Chains in Sweden", *Biomass and Bioenergy*, Vol. 29, pp. 399-418.

Lindh, T., *et al.* (2007), "The Development of Reed Canary Grass Fuel Chain", in M. Savolainen (ed.), *Bioenergy 2007*, proceedings of the Third International Bioenergy Conference and Exhibition, Jyväskylä, Finland, 3-6 September, Finnish Bioenergy Association, Jyväskylä, Finland.

Parikka, M. (2004), "Global Biomass Fuel Resources", *Biomass and Bioenergy*, Vol. 27, pp. 613-620.

Read, P. (2005), "Addressing the Policy Implications of Potential Abrupt Climate Change: a Leading Role for Bio-Energy", Special Issue of Mitigation and Adaptation Strategies for Global Change, July, *www.accstrategy.org/simiti.htm.*

Savolainen, I., S. Tuhkanen and A. Lehtilä (eds.) (2001), "Technology and Mitigation of Greenhouse Gas Emissions: Background Study for the Finnish Climate Change Action Plan", (In Finnish) Ministry of Trade and Industry Publications, Finland.

Searchinger, T., *et al.* (2008), "Use of US. Croplands for Biofuels Increases Greenhouse Gases Through Emissions from Land Use Change", *Science*, Vol. 319. No. 5867, pp. 1238-1240, *www.sciencemag.org/cgi/content/full/319/5867/1238.*

VTT (Technical Research Centre of Finland) (2007), *Bioenergy Technology Review, Internal Report for IEA*, VTT Technical Research Institute of Finland, Edita Prima, Helsinki, September.

CHAPTER 10

Auer, H., *et al.* (eds.) (2007), *Action Plan: Guiding a Least Cost Grid Integration of RES-Electricity in an Extended Europe,* Energy Economics Group at Vienna University of Technology and GreenNET-Europe, Vienna, *www.greennet-europe.org.*

BTM Consult ApS (2007), *International Wind Energy Development: World Market Update 2006*, BTM Consult ApS, Denmark, *www.btm.dk.*

BTM Consult ApS (2008), *International Wind Energy Development: World Market Update 2007*, BTM Consult ApS, Denmark, *www.btm.dk.*

Danish Energy Authority (2005), *Offshore Wind Power: Danish Experience and Solutions*, Danish Energy Authority, Copenhagen, *www.ens.dk/graphics/Publikationer/Havvindmoeller.*

DEWI (Deutsches Windenergie-Institut GmbH [German Wind Energy Institute]) (2006), DEWI website, *www.dewi.de.*

DTI (Department of Trade and Industry) (2007), "Study of the Costs of Offshore Wind Generation", United Kingdom, *www.berr.gov.uk/files/file38125.pdf*

Estanqueiro, A., R. Castro, P. Flores, J. Ricardo, M. Pinto, R. Rodrugues and J. Lopes (2008), "How to Prepare a Power System for 15% Wind Energy Penetration: the Portuguese Case Study", *Wind Energy*, Vol. 11, No. 1, pp. 75-84.

Global Wind Energy Council (2008), Global Wind Energy Council website, *www.gwec.net.*

IEA Wind (2007a), "IEA Wind Energy Annual Report 2006", Executive Committee for the Implementing Agreement for Co-operation in the Research, Development and Deployment of Wind Energy Systems of the International Energy Agency, July 2007, *www.ieawind.org.*

IEA Wind (2007b), *Design and Operation of Power Systems with Large Amounts of Wind Power: State-of-the-Art Report*, IEA Wind Implementing Agreement, *www. ieawind.org/Annex XXV.*

Jensen, P.H., P.E. Morthorst, S. Skriver and M. Rasmussen (2002), *Økonomi for Vindmøller i Danmark – Etablerings-, Drifts- og Vedligeholdelsesomkostninger for Udvalgte Generationer* (in Danish), Risø National Laboratory for Sustainable Energy, Technical University of Denmark, Roskilde.

Lemming, J.K., P.E. Morthorst and N. E. Clausen (2007), *Offshore Wind Power: Experiences, Potential and Key Issues for Deployment*, Report to the International Energy Agency, Risø National Laboratory, Technical University of Denmark, Roskilde.

Lemming, J.K., P.E. Morthorst and N.E. Clausen, *et al.* (2008), *Contribution to Wind Power Chapter: Energy Technology Perspectives 2008*, Report to the International Energy Agency, Risø National Laboratory, Technical University of Denmark, Roskilde.

Succar, S. and R. Williams (2008), *Compressed Air Energy Storage: Theory, Operation and Applications*, Princeton Environmental Institute Report, Princeton University, New Jersey.

CHAPTER 11

DLR (German Aerospace Center) (2006), *Trans-CSP - Trans-Mediterranean Interconnection for Concentrating Solar Power*, Institute of Technical Thermodynamics, Stuttgart, Germany.

DLR (2007), *Aqua-CSP - Concentrating Solar Power for Seawater Desalination,* Institute of Technical Thermodynamics, Stuttgart, Germany.

DOE (US Department of Energy) (2002), *Feasibility of 1 000 Megawatts of Solar Power in the Southwest by 2006*, Report to Congress, August, Washington DC.

EPIA (European Photovoltaic Industry Association) and Greenpeace (2007), *Solar Generation IV – 2007: Solar Electricity for over One Billion People and Two Million Jobs by 2020*, EPIA and Greenpeace, Brussels and Amsterdam, September.

EUPVPLATF (European Photovoltaic Technology Platform) (2007), *Strategic Agenda, EU PV Technology Platform*, Brussels, 2007, *www.eupvplatform.org*.

Ferrière, A. (2005), "Les Centrales Solaires Thermodynamiques: l'Etat de l'Art et les Perspectives Mondiales", paper presented at the Meeting, les Énergies Renouvelables: l'Alternative sans Crise, ENSAM Institute of Corsica, Bastia, France.

Frankl P., E. Menichetti and M. Raugei (2008), *Technical Data, Costs and Life Cycle Inventories of PV Applications*. NEEDS (New Energy Externalities Developments for Sustainability), report prepared for the European Commission, to be published.

Goetzberger, A. (2002), "Applied Solar Energy", Fraunhofer Institute for Solar Energy Systems (FhG/ISE).

Grätzel, M. (2000), "Perspectives for Dye-Sensitized Nanocrystalline Solar Cells" *Progress in Photovoltaics: Research and Applications,* Vol. 8, No.1, pp. 171-185.

Hoffmann, W. (2004a), "PV Solar Electricity Industry: Market Growth and Perspectives", paper presented at the 14th International Photovoltaic Science and Engineering Conference, Bangkok, January 2004.

Hoffmann, W. (2004b), "A Vision for PV Technology Up to 2030 and Beyond: An Industry View", Brussels, September 2004.

IEA (International Energy Agency) (2005), "Renewables Information 2005", OECD/IEA, Paris.

IEA PVPS (International Energy Acency Photovoltaic Power Systems Programme) (2007), *Trends in Photovoltaic Applications: Survey Report of selected IEA Countries between 1992 and 2006*, Report IEA-PVPS T1-16.

Mills, D. (2004), "Advances in Solar Thermal Electricity Technology", *Solar Energy*, Vol. 76, pp. 19-31.

National Petroleum Council (2007), *Facing the Hard Truths about Energy*, Presentation to the IEA, 24 September, Paris.

Neij, L.(2007), "Cost Development of Energy Technologies – an Analysis Based on Experience Curves". NEEDS (New Energy Externalities Developments for Sustainability), report prepared for the European Commission, www. *needsproject.org*.

NEDO (New Energy and Industrial Technology Development Organization) (2004), *Overview of PV Roadmap Toward 2030*, NEDO, Kawasaki, Japan.

Pharabod, F. and C. Philibert (1991), *LUZ Solar Power Plants: Success in California and Worldwide Prospects*, DLR (German Aerospace Center) and IEA-SSPS (SolarPACES), Köln, Germany.

Philibert, C. (2004), "International Energy Technology Collaboration and Climate Change Mitigation Case Study: Concentrating Solar Power Technologies", Information Paper, OECD/IEA, Paris.

Philibert, C. (2006), "Barriers to Technology Diffusion: The Case of Solar Thermal Technologies", Information Paper, OECD/IEA, Paris.

PHOTON (2007), *Photon International*, No. 10, p. 98, October.

Pitz-Paal, R., J. Dersch and B. Millow (eds.) (2005), *ECOSTAR: European Concentrated Solar Thermal Road-Mapping*, Roadmap Document, Deutsche Forschungsanstalt für Luft- und Raumfahrt e.V. (DLR), Köln, Germany.

PVNET (Photovoltaic Network for the Development of a Roadmap for PV) (2004), *PVNET Roadmap for European Research and Development for Photovoltaics*, EC Project, Final Report.

PV-TRAC (Photovoltaic Technology Research Advisory Council) (2005), *A Vision for Photovoltaic Technology*, PV-TRAC, European Commission, Brussels.

Sargent & Lundy LLC Consulting Group (2003), *Assessment of Parabolic Trough and Power Tower Solar Technology Cost and Performance Forecasts*, Department of Energy and National Renewable Energy Laboratory, Chicago, Illinois.

Steinfeld, A. and R. Palumbo, (2001), "Solar Thermochemical Process Technology", in R.A. Meyers (ed.), *Encyclopedia of Physical Science and Technology*, Academic Press, Vol. 15, pp. 237-256.

Steinfeld, A. (2005), "Solar Thermochemical Production of Hydrogen: A Review", *Solar Energy,* Vol. 78, Issue 5, pp. 603-615.

CHAPTER 12

Augustine, C., J.W. Tester and B. Anderson (2006), *A Comparison of Geothermal with Oil and Gas Well Drilling Costs*, Proceedings of the 31st Workshop on Geothermal Reservoir Engineering, Stanford University, California, 30 January to 1 February, SGP-TR-179.

Bhuyan, G.S. and A. Brito-Melo (2007), *The Strategy for the Next Five Years: the International Energy Agency's Ocean Energy Systems (IEA-OES) Implementing Agreement*, proceedings of the 7th European Wave and Tidal Energy Conference, Porto, Portugal.

Bjarnason, B. (2007), "IGA International Geothermal Association", Presentation IHA World Congress, May, Antalya, Turkey.

Boud, R. and T. Thorpe (2002), "Financing of Wave Energy Projects", in WaveNet, *Results from the Work of the European Thematic Network on Wave Energy*, WaveNet, UK, *www.wave-energy.net/Library/introLib.htm*.

Bromley, C.J. and M.A. Mongillo (2008), "Geothermal Energy from Fractured Reservoirs: Dealing with Induced Seismicity", *IEA Open Energy Technology Bulletin*, No. 48, February, *www.iea.org*.

Carbon Trust (2006), *Future Marine Energy: Results of the Marine Energy Challenge: Cost Competitiveness and Growth of Wave and Tidal Stream Energy,* Carbon Trust, UK, *www.carbontrust.co.uk*.

EPRI (Electric Power Research Institute) (2005), "Oregon Offshore Wave Power Demonstration Project", EPRI, Palo Alto, CA.

Heidinger, P., J. Dornstädter and A. Fabritius (2006), "HDR Economic Modelling: HDRec Software", *Geothermics*, Vol. 35, pp. 683-710.

IEA (International Energy Agency) (2005), *Renewable Energy: RD&D Priorities,* IEA/ OECD, Paris.

IEA OES (IEA Ocean Energy Systems Implementing Agreement) (2006), *Review and Analysis of Ocean Energy Systems Developments and Supporting Policies,* AEA Energy & Environment, UK.

Kaltschmitt, M. and S. Frick (2007), *Economic Assessment of Geothermal Energy Generation*, paper presented at the Engine Mid-Term Conference, Potsdam, January 11th 2007, *http://conferences-engine.brgm.fr/getFile.py/access?contribId=30&sessionId=2&resId=0&materialId=slides&confId=4.*

Khan, J., *et al.* (2008), Ocean Wave and Tidal Current Conversion Technologies and their Interaction with Electrical Networks, proceedings of the IEEE Power Engineering Society (IEEE PES) General Meeting, 24-28 June, Tampa, Florida.

Scanlon, A. (2007), *Hydropower's Greenhouse Footprint*, International Hydropower Association, Sutton, UK.

Schwab, A. (2007), "Pumped Storage: Innovation and Demand", paper presented at the International Hydropower Association (IHA) World Congress on Advancing Sustainable Hydropower, May 29-31 2007, Antalya, Turkey.

Taylor, R. (2007), *Hydropower Potentials*, International Hydropower Association.

Weilepp, J. (2007), "Wave Power: Wells Turbine Technology", paper presented at the IHA World Congress on Advancing Sustainable Hydropower, May 29-31 2007, Antalya, Turkey.

CHAPTER 13

DLR (German Aerospace Centre) (2006), "Trans-Mediterranean Interconnection for Concentrating Solar Power", DLR and the Federal Ministry for the Environment, Nature Conservation and Nuclear Safety, Germany, *www.trec-uk.org.uk/reports.htm.*

ICF Consulting (2003), *Overview of the Potential for Undergrounding the Electricity Networks, in Europe*, Report for the European Commission, ICF, London, *http://ec.europa.eu/energy/electricity/publications/doc/underground_cables_ICF_feb_03.pdf.*

NEDO (New Energy and Industrial Technology Development Organization) (2006), "Energy and Environment Technologies", NEDO, Japan, *www.nedo.go.jp/kankobutsu/pamphlets/kouhou/2006gaiyo_e/93_142.pdf.*

Rudervall, R., *et al.* (2000), "High Voltage Direct Current (HVDC) Transmission Systems", Technology Review Paper, Energy Week 2000, Washington, DC, March 7–8, 2000, *www.worldbank.org/html/fpd/em/transmission/technology_abb.pdf.*

Shepard, S. and S. van der Linden (2001), "Compressed Air Energy Storage Adapts Proven Technology to Address Market Opportunities", *Power Engineering*, April.

Suresh, P.R. and S. Elachola (2000), "Distribution Loss of Electricity and Influence of Energy Flows: a Case Study of a Major Section in Kerala", *Kerala Research Programme on Local Level Development*. Centre for Development Studies, Discussion Paper No. 23, September.

Thijssen, G. (2002), "Electricity Storage and Renewables", Electricity Storage Association (ESA), Morgan Hill, CA and Transmission & Distribution Counselling (KEMA), Arnhem, Netherlands, *www.electricitystorage.org/pubs/2002/Lisbon_May_2002_KEMA.pdf.*

Vattenfall (2007), *Global Mapping of Greenhouse Gas Abatement Opportunities up to 2050: Power Sector Deep-Dive*, Vattenfall, Stockholm, *www.vattenfall.com.*

CHAPTER 14

Chesnaye de la, F.C. and J.P. Weyant (eds.) (2006), "Multigas Mitigation and Climate Policy", *The Energy Journal*, Special Issue, December.

EIA (Energy Information Administration, US) (2004), *International Energy Annual 2002*. EIA, Washington, DC.

Fisher, B.S., *et al.* (2007), "Issues Related to Mitigation in the Long Term Context", in IPCC, *Climate Change 2007: Mitigation of Climate Change: Contribution of Working Group III to the Fourth Assessment Report of the Intergovernmental Panel on Climate Change* [B. Metz, *et al.* (eds.)], Cambridge University Press, Cambridge, UK and New York.

IEA (International Energy Agency) (2006), "Optimising Russian Natural Gas: Reform and Climate Policy", *SourceOECD Energy*, Vol. 2006, No. 13, July, pp. i-204.

IPCC (Intergovernmental Panel on Climate Change) (2001), "Summary for Policy Makers: A Report of Working Group I of the Intergovernmental Panel on Climate Change", in IPCC, *Climate Change 2001: Synthesis Report – Contribution of Working Groups I, II, and III to the Third Assessment Report of the Intergovernmental Panel on Climate Change* [R.T. Watson, *et al.* (eds.)], Cambridge University Press, UK and New York.

UNEP (United Nations Environment Programme) (2002), "Climate Change 2002, Technical Summary".

US EPA (United States Environmental Protection Agency) (2003), "International Analysis of Methane and Nitrous Oxide Abatement Opportunities: Report to Energy Modeling Forum", Working Group 21, U.S. EPA, Washington, DC, *http://www.epa.gov/climatechange/economics/pdfs/methodologych4.pdf.*

US EPA (2006), *Global Mitigation of Non-CO_2 Greenhouse Gases 1990-2020 (EPA Report 430-R-06-003)*, U.S. EPA, Washington, DC, *http://www.epa.gov/nonco2/econ-inv/downloads/GlobalAnthroEmissionsReport.pdf.*

CHAPTER 15

ACEEE (American Council for an Energy Efficient Economy) (2006), "Plug-In Hybrids: An Environmental and Economic Performance Outlook", ACEEE, *http://aceee.org/pubs/t061.htm.*

Alstom (2008), "Alstom Unveils the AGV", Alstom, Levallois-Perret, France, *www.alstom.com/pr_corp_v2/2008/corp/48523.EN.php?languageId=EN&dir=/pr_corp_v2/2008/corp/&idRubriqueCourante=23132.*

Barr, L. (2006), "Lab Tests Flying-Wing Aircraft for Fuel Efficiency", *Air Force Print News Today,* June 13th, *www.afmc.af.mil/news/story_print.asp?id=123021722.*

Boeing (2007), "Current Market Outlook: 2007", Boeing Market Analysis Division, US, *www.boeing.com/commercial/cmo/.*

Breslin, D.A. and Y. Wang (2004), "Climate Change, National Security, and Naval Ship Design", *Naval Engineering Journal*, Vol. 116, pp. 27-40.

Brewer, G.D. (1991), *Hydrogen Aircraft Technology*, CRC Press, Boca Raton, FL.

Cambridge-MIT Institute (2006), *Silent Aircraft Initiative*, *http://silentaircraft.org/.*

CAN-Europe (Climate Action Network Europe) (2003), "Climate Technology Sheet No. 9: Hydrogen Production", *www.climnet.org/CTAP/techsheets/CTAP09_H2Production.pdf.*

Daggett, D., *et al.* (2006), "Alternative Fuels and Their Potential Impact on Aviation", NASA, Hanover, MD, *http://gltrs.grc.nasa.gov/reports/2006/TM-2006-214365.pdf.*

Defense Science Board (2001), *More Capable War Fighting through Reduced Fuel Burden*, Task Force on Improving Fuel Efficiency of Weapons Platforms, Defense Science Board, Washington, DC.

DOE (US Department of Energy) (2006), "Twenty First Century Truck Partnership: Roadmap and Technical White Papers", DOE, US, *www1.eere.energy.gov/vehiclesandfuels/pdfs/program/21ctp_roadmap_2007.pdf.*

Duleep, K.G. (2007), *Fuel Economy of Heavy-duty Trucks in the USA*, presented at IEA Workshop on Fuel Efficiency Policies for Heavy Duty Vehicles, June 2007, *http://www.iea.org/Textbase/work/2007/vehicle/Duleep.pdf.*

EC (European Commission) (2007), "Rail Transport and Interoperability", *http://ec.europa.eu/transport/rail/interoperability/tsi_revised_en.htm.*

ECMT/IEA (European Conference of Ministers of Transport/International Energy Agency) (2005), *Making Cars More Fuel Efficient: Technology for Real Improvements on the Road*, OECD/IEA, Paris.

ENN (Environmental News Network) (2008), "High Speed Rail Advances Globally, Crawls in the US", *Green Energy News*, February 11, Vol. 12, No. 47, *www.green-energy-news.com/arch/nrgs2008/20080012.html.*

Green Car Congress (2007), "Toshiba Launches New Li-Ion Battery Business: Plans to Enter Hybrid and Electric Vehicle Market", Green Car Congress, December 11th, *www.greencarcongress.com/2007/12/toshiba-launche.html.*

Greener by Design (2002), *Air-Travel – Greener by Design: Improving Operations, The Technology Challenge, Market-based Options*, Greener by Design, Royal Aeronautical Society, London.

Greener by Design (2005), *Air Travel – Greener by Design: Mitigating the Environmental Impact of Aviation: Opportunities and Priorities*, Greener by Design, Royal Aeronautical Society, London.

Hawk, J. (2005), "The Boeing 787 Dreamliner: More Than an Airplane", presentation to AIAA/AAAF, Aircraft Noise and Emissions Reduction Symposium, American Institute of Aeronautics and Astronautics and Association Aéronautique et Astronautique de France, *www.aiaa.org/events/aners/Presentations/ANERS-Hawk.pdf.*

Hoeveler, P. (2004), "Future Technologies for Civil Aero Engines", *Flug Review*, Vol. 1/2004, Bonn, Germany, *www.flug-revue.rotor.com/FRHeft/FRHeft04/FRH0401/FR0401d.htm.*

F

ICAO (International Civil Aviation Organization) (2001), "ICAO News Release", June 13, Montreal, Canada, *http://www.icao.int/cgi/goto_m.pl?icao/en/new_arch_2001.htm.*

ICAO (2004), "Operational Opportunities to Minimize Fuel Use and Reduce Emissions", ICAO Circular 303-AN/176, ICAO, February, Montréal, Quebec.

IEA (International Energy Agency) (2005), *Prospects for Hydrogen and Fuel Cells*, Energy Technology Analysis, OECD/IEA, Paris.

IEA (2006), *Energy Technology Perspectives 2006: Scenarios and Strategies to 2050*, OECD/IEA, Paris.

IEA (2007), *Energy Use in the New Millenium: Trends in IEA Countries*, OECD/IEA, Paris

IEA and ITF (International Transport Forum) (2007), "Fuel Efficiency for HDVs – Standards and other Policy Instruments: Towards a Plan of Action", summary and proceedings of the IEA/ITF workshop on Standards and Other Policy Instruments on Fuel Efficiency for HDVs, Paris, 21-22 June 2007, OECD/IEA, Paris, *www.iea.org/textbase/work/2007/vehicle/Workshop_Summary.pdf.*

IPCC (Intergovernmental Panel on Climate Change) (1999), *Aviation and the Global Atmosphere*, Cambridge University Press, Cambridge, UK and New York.

Karagozian, A., *et al.* (2006), *Report on Technology Option for Improved Air Vehicle Fuel Efficiency: Executive Summary and Annotated Brief*, United States Air Force Scientific Advisory Board, Washington DC.

Keith, D.W., A. Farrell and J.J. Corbett (2004), "True Zero-Emission Vehicles: Hydrogen Fuelled Ships with Carbon Management", Department of Engineering, Carnegie Mellon University, *http://lib.kier.re.kr/balpyo/ghgt5/Papers/E8%202.pdf.*

Kieran, P. (2003), "World Trends in Shipping and Port Reform", Port Reform Seminary, South Africa, *www.dpe.gov.za/res/PeterKieranWorldTrendsinShippingandPortReform.pdf.*

Lee, J.J., *et al.* (2001), "Historical and Future Trends in Aircraft Performance, Cost, and Emissions", *Annual Review of Energy and Environment*, Vol. 26, pp. 167-200.

Leifsson, L.T. and W.H. Mason (2004), "The Blended Wing Body Aircraft", Virginia Polytechnic Institute and State University, Blacksburg, VA, *www.aoe.vt.edu/research/groups/bwb/papers/TheBWBAircraft.pdf.*

Lovins, A., *et al.* (2004), *Winning the Oil Endgame*, Rocky Mountain Institute, Colorado.

M&C (2007), "New Delft Material Concept for Aircraft Wings Could Save Billions", *TUDelft* website, Delft University of Technology, 24 September, *www.tudelft.nl/live/pagina.jsp?id=a7e23c9d-a6b2-4dbb-8ea5-c7601acbbd1e&lang=en.*

McKinnon, A. (2007), *CO_2 Emissions from Freight Transport in the UK*, Report prepared for the Climate Change Working Group of the Commission for Integrated Transport, United Kingdom.

Miller, J.M. (2008), "Ultracapacitors Challenge the Battery", *Worldandl.com*, Issue 6, *www.worldandi.com/subscribers/feature_detail.asp?num=23938*.

NRCAN (Natural Resources Canada) (2005), "Fleetsmart On the Road", *FleetSmart Newsletter*, Vol. 1/2005, *http://oee.nrcan.gc.ca/transportation/business/newsletter?attr=16*.

Ogando, J. (2007), "Boeing's 'More Electric' 787 Dreamliner Spurs Engine Evolution", *Design News*, June 4, accessed 28 November, 2007, *www.designnews.com/article/CA6441575.html*.

Passier, G., *et al.* (2007), *Status Overview of Hybrid and Electric Vehicle Technology: Final Report Phase III, Annex VII: Hybrid Vehicles*, IEA Hybrid and Electric Implementing Agreement, OECD/IEA, Paris, *www.ieahev.org/pdfs/annex_7/annex7_hev_final_rpt_110108.pdf*.

PyNe (Biomass Pyrolysis Network) and IEA Bioenergy (2007), "Bio-Oil: Pyrolysis Liquid", *www.pyne.co.uk/*.

RCEP (Royal Commission on Environmental Pollution) (2007), "The Environmental Effects of Civil Aircraft in Flight: Special Report", RCEP, London.

SDG (Steer Davies Gleave) (2004), "High-Speed Rail: International Comparisons", *www.cfit.gov.uk/docs/2004/hsr/research/index.htm*.

Sierra Club (2001), "High-Speed Rail As a Solution to Airport Congestion", Sierra Club, *http://lomaprieta.sierraclub.org/HighSpeedRail.html*.

Simpson, A. (2006), "Cost-Benefit Analysis of Plug-In Hybrid Electric Vehicle Technology", Paper presented at the 22nd International Battery, Hybrid and Fuel Cell Electric Vehicle Symposium and Exhibition (EVS-22), Yokohama, Japan, October 23-28, 2006, Conference Paper NREL/CP-540-40485, *www.nrel.gov/vehiclesandfuels/vsa/pdfs/40485.pdf*.

SkySails (2006), "SkySails – Turn Wind Into Profit: Technology Information", Hamburg, Germany, *http://skysails.info/index.php?id=6&L=1*.

Tata Motors (2008), "Tata Motors Unveils the People's Car", *www.tatamotors.com/our_world/press_releases.php?ID=340&action=Pull*.

UITP (International Association of Public Transport) (2006), *Mobility in Cities Database*, Courtesy of SYSTRA, *http://uitp.org/publications/Mobility-in-Cities-Database.cfm*.

Velduis, I.J.S., R.N. Richardson and H.B.J. Stone, (2007), "Hydrogen Fuel in a Marine Environment", *International Journal of Hydrogen Energy*, Vol. 32, No. 13.

Wang, M., M. Wu and H. Huo (2007), "Life-Cycle Energy and Greenhouse Gas Results of Fischer-Tropsch Diesel Produced from Natural Gas, Coal, and Biomass", Paper presented at the SAE Government/Industry Meeting, Washington, DC, May 14-16, 2007, *www.clf.org/uploadedFiles/CLF/Programs/Clean_Energy_&_Climate_Change/Climate_Protection/Regional_Greenhouse_Gas_Initiative/Exhibit%20A.pdf*.

Young, S., J. Newel and G. Little (2001), "Beyond Electric Ship", *Naval Engineering Journal*, Vol. 113, No. 4.

CHAPTER 16

Al Ansari, F. and G. Williams (2007), *IFA Benchmarking of Global Energy Efficiency in Ammonia Production*, Paper presented at the IFA-IEA Workshop on Energy Efficiency and CO_2 Reduction Prospects in Ammonia Production, March 13th, Ho Chi Minh City.

Berntsson, T., *et al.* (2007), *Swedish Pulp Mill Biorefineries: A Vision of Future Possibilities*, Chalmers University of Technology, Sweden.

Borlée, J. (2007), "Low CO_2 Steels: ULCOS Project", paper presented at the IEA workshop, Deploying Demand Side Energy Technologies, 8-9 October, OECD/IEA, Paris.

Bowen, C.P. (2006), *Development Trends for Ethylene Crackers: Existing Technologies and RD&D*, paper presented at the IEA/CEFIC Workshop, Feedstock Substitutes: Energy Efficient Technology and CO_2 Reduction for Petrochemical Products, 12-13 December, OECD/IEA, Paris.

Brunner, C. and A. Niederberger (2006), "Motor System Model: A Tool to Support, Efficient Industrial Motor System Policies and Programs", A+B International, Zürich, Switzerland.

Cagnolatti, A.A. (2005), *Global Ethylene Plant Performance Comparisons,* paper presented at the 2005 AIChE Spring National Meeting, 17th Annual Ethylene Producers Conference, 11-14 April, Atlanta, GA.

DOE (United States Department of Energy) (2002), *Steam System Opportunity Assessment for the Pulp and Paper: Chemical Manufacturing, and Petroleum Refining Industries*, National Renewable Energy Laboratory, DOE, Washington, D.C.

EC (European Commission) (2001), *Best Available Techniques in the Non-Ferrous Metals Industry,* IPPC (Integrated Pollution Prevention and Control), EC, Brussels.

ENAM Research (2007), Aluminium Sector China Visit, December 13.

Finnish Forest Industries Federation (2002), *Possibilities of Reducing CO_2 Emissions in the Finnish Forest Industry*, Finnish Forest Industries Federation, Helsinki.

FLSmidth (2006), *Cement Plant Pyro-Technology*, paper presented at the IEA-WBCSD workshop, Energy Efficiency and CO_2 Emission Reduction Potentials and Policies in the Cement Industry, 4-5 September, OECD/IEA, Paris.

Hektor, E. and T. Berntsson (2007a), "Future CO_2 Removal from Pulp Mills: Process Integration Consequences", *Energy Conversion and Management*, Vol. 48, No. 11, pp. 3025-3033.

Hektor, E. and T. Berntsson (2007b), "Reduction of Greenhouse Gases in Integrated Pulp and Paper Mills: Possibilities for CO_2 Capture and Storage", Chalmers University of Technology, Sweden.

IEA (International Energy Agency) (2007a), *Energy Use in the New Millennium: Trends in IEA Countries*, OECD/IEA, Paris.

IEA (2007b), *Tracking Industrial Energy Efficiency and CO_2 Emissions*, OECD/IEA, Paris.

IFA (International Fertilizer Industry Association) (2006), *Energy Efficiency in Ammonia Production,* Executive Summary for Policy Makers, *www.fertilizer.org*.

Justnes, H., L. Elfgren and V. Ronin (2005), "Mechanism for Performance of Energetically Modified Cement Versus Corresponding Blended Cement", *Cement and Concrete Research*, Vol 35, No. 2, pp. 315-323.

Keulenaer H. de, *et al.* (2004), *Energy Efficient Motor Driven Systems,* European Copper. Institute, Brussels.

Lurgi (2006), "Lurgi MegaMethanol", Lurgi, Frankfurt, Germany, *www.lurgi.com/website/fileadmin/pdfs/brochures/Br_MegaMethanol.pdf.*

McKane, A. (2005), *Industrial Standards Framework Overview,* paper presented at the UNIDO/DIP Experts Group Meeting, Phattaya City, Thailand.

Rafiqul, I., *et al.* (2005), "Energy Efficiency Improvements in Ammonia Production: Perspectives and Uncertainties", *Energy*, Vol. 30, No. 13, pp. 2487-2504.

Sobolev, K., and T.R. Naik (2005), *Performance as a Factor for Sustainability of the Cement Industry*, paper presented at the Third CANMET/ACI International Symposium, Sustainable Development of Cement and Concrete, 5-7 October, Toronto, Canada.

World Aluminium (2007a), "Energy Used in Metallurgical Alumina Production", International Aluminium Institute, London, *www.world-aluminium.org*.

World Aluminium (2007b), "Electrical Power Used in Primary Aluminium Production", International Aluminium Institute, London.

Worrell, E., L. Price and C. Galitsky (2004), "Emerging Energy-Efficient Technologies in Industry: Technology Characterizations for Energy Modeling", Lawrence Berkeley National Laboratory, Report No. LBNL-54828, Berkeley, CA.

Yates, J.R., D. Perkins and R. Sankaranarayanan (2004), "Cemstar Process and Technology for Lowering Greenhouse Gases and Other Emissions While Increasing Cement Production", Hatch, Canada, *http://hatch.ca/Environment_Community/Sustainable_Development/Projects/Copy%20of%20CemStar-Process-final4-30-03.pdf.*

CHAPTER 17

Atrax Energy (2002), *Bio-DME Project: Phase 1*, Atrax Energy, Report to Swedish National Energy Administration.

Audenaert, A., *et al.* (2008), Economic Analysis of Passive Houses and Low-energy Houses Compared with Standard Houses, *Energy Policy*, Vol 36, pp. 47-55.

Batidzirai, B., *et al.* (2008), Potential of Solar Water Heating in Zimbabwe, *Renewable and Sustainable Energy Reviews*, Elseveir B.V., article in press.

Econcept (2002), *Neubauen statt Sanieren? Schlussbericht*, Econcept, Zurich.

Daniëls B.W. and J.C.M. Farla (2006), *Optiedocument Energie en Emissies* (Options for Energy and Emissions), Energy Research Centre of the Netherlands (ECN), Petten, The Netherlands.

Demirbilek, F.N., *et al.* (2000), "Energy Conscious Dwelling Design for Ankara", *Building and Environment*, Vol. 35, No. 1, January, pp. 33-40.

EC (European Commission) (2008), "Energy Efficiency" website of reports commissioned by the European Commission, *http://ec.europa.eu/energy/demand/legislation/eco_design_en.htm.*

Ecofys (2005), *Cost-effective Climate Protection in the Building Stock of New EU Member States, Ecofys*, Cologne.

EIA (Energy Information Administration) (2007), *Residential Energy Consumption Survey*, EIA, Washington, DC, *www.eia.doe.gov/emeu/.*

Fleisch, T. (2004), "DME Opportunities and Challenges", paper presented at the First International DME Conference, Paris, 12-14 October.

Florides, G.A., *et al.* (2002), "Measures Used to Lower Building Energy Consumption and Their Cost Effectiveness", *Applied Energy*, Vol. 73, No. 3, pp. 299-328.

Fridley, D., *et al.* (2001), *Technical and Economic Analysis of Energy Efficiency of Chinese Room Air Conditioners*, Lawrence Berkeley National Laboratory (LBNL), Berkeley, CA; China National Institute of Standardization (CNIS), Beijing, China; and Beijing Energy Efficiency Center (BECon), Beijing, China.

Hamada, Y., *et al.* (2003), Development of a Database of Low Energy Homes around the World and Analyses of their Trends, *Renewable Energy*, Vol. 28, pp.321-328.

Hanova, J., *et al.* (2007), *Ground Source Heat Pump Systems in Canada: Economics and GHG Potential*, Resources for the Future, Washington, DC.

Hastings, S.R. (2004), "Breaking the 'Heating Barrier: Learning from the First Houses Without Conventional Heating", *Energy and Buildings*, Vol. 36, No. 4, pp. 373-380.

IEA (International Energy Agency) (2005), *World Energy Outlook 2005*, OECD/IEA, Paris.

IEA (2006a), *Light's Labour's Lost: Policies for Energy-Efficient Lighting*, OECD/IEA, Paris.

IEA (2006b), *Renewables Information 2006*, OECD/IEA, Paris.

IEA (2006c), *World Energy Outlook 2006*, OECD/IEA, Paris.

IEA (2007a), *Experience with Energy Efficiency Regulations for Electrical Equipment*, OECD/IEA, Paris.

IEA (2007b), *Scaling Up Energy Efficiency: Bridging the Action Gap*, OECD/IEA, Paris.

Jakob, M. and R. Madlener (2004), "Riding Down the Experience Curve for Energy-Efficient Building Envelopes: the Swiss Case for 1970-2020", *International Journal Energy Technology and Policy*, Vol. 2, Nos. 1-2.

Jalovaara, J., J. Aho, E. Hietamäki and H. Hyytiä. (2003), "Best available Techniques in small 5-50 MW Combustion Plants in Finland" (In Finnish), *The Finnish Environment 649*, Environmental Protection. 126 p.

Li, H. and H. Yang, (2008), Potential Application of Solar Thermal Systems for Hot Water Production in Hong Kong, *Applied Energy*, Article in Press.

Londo, H., *et al.* (2008), *Biofuiels Cost Developments in the EU27+ until 2030*, Refuel WP4 final report, ECN, Petten.

McKinsey (2007a), *Reducing U.S. Greenhouse Gas Emissions: How Much at What Cost?*, McKinsey & Company, New York.

McKinsey (2007b), *Costs and Potentials of Greenhouse Gas Abatement in Germany*, McKinsey & Company, New York.

McKinsey (2007c), "A cost curve for greenhouse gas reduction", *The McKinsey Quarterly*, February.

McNeil, M., *et al.* (2005), *Potential Benefits from Improved Energy Efficiency of Key Electrical Products: The Case of India*, LBNL, Berkeley, CA.

NetBioCof. (2007), "New and advanced Concepts in Renewable Energy Technology Biomass", *First-State-Of-The-Art Report, http://www.netbiocof.net/*.

Norris, M. and P. Shiels (2004), *Regular National Report on Housing Developments in European Countries*, Department of the Environment, Heritage and Local Government; Dublin.

NRCAN (National Resources Canada) (2007), Residential End-Use Model Database, NRCAN, Ottawa, June, *www.nrcan.ca*.

Palmer, J., *et al.* (2006), *Reducing the Environmental Impact of Housing*, Environmental Change Institute, Oxford.

Philibert, C. (2006), *Barriers to Technology Diffusion: The Case for Solar Thermal Technologies*, OECD/IEA, Paris.

Philibert, C. and J. Pershing (2002), *Beyond Kyoto – Energy Dynamics and Climate Stabilisation*, OECD/IEA, Paris.

Presutto, M., *et al.* (2008), *Task 7: Scenario, Policy, Impact and Sensitivity Analysis*, DGTREN, Lot 13: Domestic Refrigerators & Freezers, TREN/D1/40-2005, Brussels.

Rantil, M. (2006), "Concentrating Solar Heat: Kilowatts or Megawatts?", paper presented at the Renewable Heating and Cooling, from RD&D to Deployment, Technology and Policy Seminar, 5 April, Paris.

REN 21 (Renewable Energy Policy Network for the 21st Century) (2006), *Global Status Report 2006, www.ren21.net.*

Riviere, P., *et al.* (2008), Preparatory Study on the Environmental Performance of Residential Room Conditioning Appliances (airco and ventilation), DGTREN, Contract TREN/D1/40-2005/LOT10/S07.56606.

Sachs, H., *et al.* (2004), *Emerging Energy-Savings Technologies and Practices for the Buildings Sector*, ACEEE, Washington, DC.

Safarzadeh, H. and M.N. Bahadori (2005), "Passive Cooling Effects of Courtyards", *Building and Environment,* Vol. 40, No. 1, pp. 89-104.

Sakhalin Energy (2004), "Sakhalin II Project: LNG or DME – The Facts", *www.sakhalinenergy.com/.*

Seeline Group (2005), *Technology Assessment Study and TRC Analysis*, Seeline Group, Ontario Power Authority.

SHC (IEA Solar Heating and Cooling Programme) (2007), *Solar Heat Worldwide: Markets and Contribution to the Energy Supply 2005*, IEA Solar Heating and Cooling Programme, AEE, Institut für Nachhaltige Technologien, Austria.

Sheinbaum, C., M. Martinez and L. Rodriguez (1996), "Trends and Prospects in Mexican Residential Energy Use", *Energy*, Vol. 21, No. 6, pp 493-504.

Shorrock, L., *et al.* (2005), *"Reducing Carbon Emissions from the UK Housing Stock"*, Building Research Establishment, Watford, UK.

Srinvas, S. (2006), *Green Buildings in India: Lessons Learnt*, Indian Green Building Council, Hyderabad.

Taylor, P.B., *et al.* (2000), "The Effect of Ceiling Insulation on Indoor Comfort", *Building and Environment,* Vol. 35, No. 4, pp. 339-346.

Thek, G. and I. Obernberger (2004), "Wood Pellet Production Costs under Austrian and in Comparison to Swedish Framework Conditions." *Biomass and Bioenergy* 27, 671-693.

UNECE (United Nations Economic Commission for Europe) (2004), *Country Profiles on the Housing Sector – Russia*, UN, Geneva.

WEC (World Energy Council) (2006), *Energy Efficiencies: Pipe-Dream or Reality?*, WEC, London.

WEC (2007), *Deciding the Future: Energy Policy Scenarios to 2050*, WEC, London.

Wuppertal Institute (2005), *Target 2020: Policies and Measures to Reduce Greenhouse Gas Emissions in the EU*, A report on behalf of WWF European Policy Office, Wuppertal Institute, Germany.

ANNEX B

ETSAP (Energy Technology Systems Analysis Programme) (2003), *Documentation for the MARKAL Family of Models*, ETSAP, *www.etsap.org/MrklDoc-I_StdMARKAL.pdf*.

Fishbone, L.G. and H. Abilock (1981), "MARKAL: A Linear-Programming Model for Energy Systems Analysis: Technical Description of the BNL Version", *International Journal of Energy Research*, Vol. 5, No. 4, pp. 353-375.

Hawksworth, J. (2006), *The World in 2050*, PriceWaterhouseCoopers, UK.

IEA (International Energy Agency) (2005), *Resources to Reserves,* OECD/IEA, Paris.

IEA (2006), *Energy Technology Perspectives 2006: Scenarios and Strategies to 2050*, OECD/IEA, Paris.

IEA (2007), *World Energy Outlook 2007*, OECD/IEA, Paris.

UN (United Nations) (2005), *World Urbanization Prospects: The 2005 Revision Population Database*, UN Department of Economics and Social Affairs, *http://esa.un.org/unup/index.asp?panel=1.*

UN (2007a), "World Population Prospects: The 2006 Revision", UN Department of Economics and Social Affairs, *www.un.org/esa/population/publications/wpp2006/wpp2006.htm.*

UN (2007b), *World Population Ageing 2007*, UN Department of Economics and Social Affairs, New York.

UNFPA (United Nations Population Fund) (2007), *State of World Population 2007: Unleashing the Potential of Urban Growth*, UNFPA, New York, *www.unfpa.org/swp.*

World Bank (2007), "2005 International Comparison Program: Preliminary results", 17 December, World Bank, Washington DC.

IEA PUBLICATIONS, 9, rue de la Fédération, 75739 PARIS CEDEX 15
PRINTED IN FRANCE BY STEDI MEDIA
(61 2008 021 P1) ISBN : 92-64-04142-4 - 2008